# WASHINGTON
## DISCOVERY GUIDE

**A remarkably useful handbook
for motorists, RVers and other explorers**

*By Don W. Martin & Betty Woo Martin*

*Pine Cone Press* • Columbia, California

## BOOKS BY DON AND BETTY MARTIN

*NEVADA IN YOUR FUTURE* ● 1994
*WASHINGTON DISCOVERY GUIDE* ● 1994
*THE ULTIMATE WINE BOOK* ● 1993
*NORTHERN CALIFORNIA DISCOVERY GUIDE* ● 1993
*OREGON DISCOVERY GUIDE* ● 1993
*THE BEST OF NEVADA* ● 1992
*THE BEST OF THE WINE COUNTRY* ● First printing 1991; second printing 1994
*INSIDE SAN FRANCISCO* ● 1991
*COMING TO ARIZONA* ● First printing 1991; second printing 1993
*THE BEST OF ARIZONA* ● 1990; revised 1993
*SAN FRANCISCO'S ULTIMATE DINING GUIDE* ● 1988
*THE BEST OF THE GOLD COUNTRY* ● First printing 1987; second printing, 1990; revised 1992
*THE BEST OF SAN FRANCISCO* ● 1986; revised 1990, 1994

**Copyright © 1994 by Don W. Martin and Betty Woo Martin**
All rights reserved. No written material, maps or illustrations from this book may be reproduced in any form, other than brief passages in book reviews, without written permission from the authors. Printed in the United States of America.
**Library of Congress Cataloging-in-Publication Data**
Martin, Don and Betty—
Washington Discovery Guide
Includes index.
1. Washington state—description and travel
2. Washington state—history

**ISBN: 0-942053-16-8**
Library of Congress catalog card number 93-93647

Illustrations ● **Bob Shockley,** Mariposa, Calif.
Cartography ● **Vicky Biernacki, Dave Bonnot & Keith Farley,**
Columbine Type and Design, Sonora, Calif.

**THE COVER** ● *Burroughs Mountain, reached by a short hike from the Sunrise area of Mount Rainier National Park, offers an awesome vista of Rainier's glistening glaciers. The silvery ribbon of the White River is far below. Look carefully and you'll see a ground squirrel pestering the hiker (the author's son Dan) for a handout.* — **Don W. Martin**

*Sculpted by centuries of wind and rain, 700-foot-high Steamboat Rock is an imposing presence along State Highway 155 south of Grand Coulee Dam.*

— **Betty Woo Martin**

I shall be telling this with a sigh
Somewhere ages and ages hence:
Two roads diverged in a wood, and I—
I took the one less traveled by,
And that made all the difference.
— **Robert Frost,** *Road Not Taken* **(1916)**

This book is dedicated to our brother and brother-in-law Arnold K. Martin, a good-old-boy Oregonian who, for much of his life, called Washington his home.

4

# CONTENTS

## MAPS

# INTRODUCTION

**THIS BOOK WAS WRITTEN FOR YOU**, whether you're among the millions of annual visitors to Washington State or the nearly five million residents looking for backyard discoveries.

If you're a visitor—or if you're contemplating a visit—the book will help you make sense of this large, scenic and fascinating state. If you're a resident, you've probably compiled a long list of places you intend to explore "when you get around to it." This book is designed to get you going.

Further, this is a *Discovery Guide*, which separates the fun and the fascinating from the ordinary and the obvious. It was written for travelers with a sense of adventure, not for tourists who merely collect locations.

Washington is the second most populated state in the West, after California. We would hardly expect you to cover it in one monumental exploration, as we did during our research. As a visitor from the outside, you can use our guide as a sampler to select a specific region, since we've picked the best that Washington has to offer. Each chapter will fit comfortably into a one or two week vacation. As a resident, you can keep the book handy for future reference, pulling it from shelf or glove compartment whenever you want to spend a long weekend or a vacation in your state.

If you *did* follow our tracks through Washington, you would discover one of America's the most fascinating and multi-faceted states. You would scuff curious toes at seaweed and seashells on remote beaches. You would follow moss-lined trails into thick evergreen forests, and explore the endless reaches of a high prairie. You certainly would follow the course of the Columbia, that great river of the west. You'd walk the history-rich streets of Seattle, one of America's grand cities, and enjoy its rich stew of international delights. You might then take a ferryboat across the Puget Sound to that amazing Olympic Peninsula and survey—less than an hour apart—some of Washington's wettest and driest regions.

I was born in next-door Oregon, and I've never been very far from the Evergreen State, at least in spirit. We natives of the Pacific Northwest—that tree-covered square that comprises Washington and Oregon—have always had a special affinity for our neighboring state. I've lived in Washington briefly, visited there countless times as a travel writer, and watched its fortunes rise and fall through the decades.

This is the third in our series of Discovery Guides. We began with my home state of Oregon, then focused on Northern California where Betty and I now reside. Washington is a logical next choice. Like the others, this book is both comprehensive and selective, covering all of the Evergreen State's more interesting regions. We skip lightly over communities with limited tourist appeal (sorry about that, Marysville), while focusing on areas that visitors want to visit. After we spent many months in a detailed review of my former neighboring state, we've uncovered the delightfully obscure and we've updated the obvious, to create a book that is indeed a Discovery Guide.

We've sorted through the wonders of this amazing slice of the beautiful Pacific Northwest, and saved the very best just for you.

**Don W. Martin**
On the road in Washington

# THE WAY THINGS WORK

When most folks go on vacation, they either drive their family sedan or RV, or they fly to a city and rent a car. We have thus written this book for the way you travel, steering you along major highways and minor byways to the state's most appealing places.

The **Washington Discovery Guide** takes you mile by mile, with attendant maps, from one corner of the state to the other. Along the way, we suggest interesting stops, and detours to little discoveries that other guidebooks may have missed. In towns with visitor appeal, we review the attractions and activities, and we suggest places to eat and sleep. We guide you carefully through the larger communities, with detailed driving routes to their most interesting attractions and areas.

## ATTRACTIONS

Don't rely too much on hours listed for attractions and museums in this book, since many places change them more often than a deadbeat changes his address. Times shown are as current as we could ascertain by checking brochures, asking folks and simply copying them down when we visited. Often, hours are shorter during the off-season. If you're going out of your way to visit an attraction, call to ensure that it's open. Prices change, too, inevitably upward, so use those shown only as guidelines.

☺ *Special places:* Our little smiling faces mark Washington's special places—the best visitor lures in each area. These range from major attractions and excellent museums that belong on your "must see" list, to undiscovered jewels. Several restaurants and lodgings earn grins in addition to their regular ratings because of their particular charm, exceptional facilities or food, great views or other distinctive features.

## DINING

Our intent is to provide a selective dining sampler. We focus on restaurants in or near visitor attractions, so we won't send you to a neighborhood shopping center in search of recently thawed salmon. We *do* recommend tucked away diners that have become legend for their food and atmosphere. Restaurants suffer a high attrition rate, so don't be crushed if one that we recommend has become a laundromat by the time you get there.

Choices are based more on overviews of food, service and ambiance, not on the proper doneness of a specific halibut fillet. Further, we try to offer the typical regional dining experience, from a Native American salmon bake to a lumberjack breakfast. Of course, one has to be careful when recommending restaurants. People's tastes differ. Also, the chef might have a bad night, or your waitress might be recovering from one. Thus, your dining experience may be quite different from ours.

Restaurants are graded with one to four wedges, for food quality, service and ambiance.

Δ **Adequate**—A clean cafè with basic but edible grub.

ΔΔ **Good**—A well-run establishment that offers good food and service.

ΔΔΔ **Very good**—Substantially above average; excellent fare, served with a smile in a fine dining atmosphere.

ΔΔΔΔ **Excellent**—We've found culinary heaven, with great seafood and a good white wine list!

Price ranges are based on the tab for an average dinner, including soup or salad (but not wine or dessert). Obviously, cafés serving only breakfast and/or lunch are priced accordingly.

**$**—Average dinner for one is $9 or less

**$$**—$10 to $14

**$$$**—$15 to $24

**$$$$**—$25 and beyond

**Ø**—**Smoke free dining:** Most restaurants have non-smoking sections these days; they're required in many cities. Our symbol indicates a place that has a separate smoke-free dining room.

## LODGING

Our sleeping selections are somewhat arbitrary, since the book can't list them all. Nor does it attempt to; the idea is to recommend facilities near points of interest as you drive through Washington. We suggest clean, well-run accommodations in all price ranges. In choosing pillow places, we often rely on the judgment of the American Automobile Association because we respect its high standards. We also include some budget lodgings that may fall short of Triple A ideals, but still offer a clean room at a fair price. Of course, one can't anticipate changes in management or the maid's day off, but hopefully your surprises will be good ones.

Bed & breakfast inns and mountain hideaways are part of the Washington vacation experience, and we've made a point of seeking these out. To earn a spot in our book, a facility must be a full scale bed & breakfast inn, offering three or more guest rooms or cottages. Folks who rent out the spare bedroom while Marcella is away at college, and those who offer single-unit vacation home rentals, aren't included. (In some areas where B&Bs are scarce, we have listed two-unit facilities.) For a statewide B&B directory, contact Washington State Bed & Breakfast Guild, 2442 NW Market Street, #355, Seattle, WA 98107; (206) 548-6224.

We use little Monopoly © style symbols to rate the selected lodgings:

⌂ **Adequate**—Clean and basic; don't expect anything fancy.

⌂⌂ **Good**—A well run place with comfortable beds and most essentials.

⌂⌂⌂ **Very good**—Substantially above average, often with facilities such as a pool, spa or restaurant.

⌂⌂⌂⌂ **Excellent**—An exceptional lodging with beautifully appointed rooms and extensive amenities.

**Ø**—**Non-Smoking rooms** are available, or the entire facility is smoke free (common with bed & breakfast inns). Incidentally, most B&Bs do not allow pets. Inquire when you make reservations so your poor pooch doesn't have to spend the night sulking in the back seat of your car.

Our price ranges are based on figures provided by the establishments. They are subject to change—almost always upward. Price codes below reflect the range for a standard room during high season. Call ahead to confirm current prices and availability. It has been our experience that the lower end rooms are the first to go.

**$**—a double room for $35 or less

**$$**—$36 to $49

**$$$**—$50 to $74

**$$$$**—$75 to $99

**$$$$$**—$100 and beyond

It's always wise to make advance reservations, particularly during weekends and local celebrations (listed at the end of most community write-ups). If you don't like the place and you'll be in the area for more than a day, you can shop around after the first night and—hopefully—change lodgings.

## CAMPING

Washington offers an abundance of camping facilities, especially in its national parks and forests, and state parks. It is thus a *nirvana* for RVers and happy tenters. Most communities, of course, have a goodly number of RV parks, and you'll find RV camps within driving distance of larger cities such as Seattle. Listed prices indicate a campsite for two people per night. Some outfits charge more for extra bodies; others do not.

As the second most populous state in the West, Washington generates its own camping crowds, so make reservations as early as possible, particularly on summer weekends. For details, see **Getting camped** in Chapter one.

## A BIT ABOUT THE AUTHORS

The husband and wife writing team of Don and Betty Martin has authored more than a dozen guidebooks. Don, who provides most of the adjectives, has been a journalist since he was 17. He was a Marine correspondent in the Orient, then he worked on the editorial side of several California newspapers. Later, he served as associate editor of the California State Automobile Association's travel magazine. A member of the Society of American Travel Writers, he now devotes his time to writing, photography, travel and—for some curious reason—collecting squirrel and chipmunk artifacts.

Betty, who does much of the research, photography and editing, offers the curious credentials of a doctorate in pharmacy and a California real estate broker's license. A California native, she's also a freelance travel writer and photographer who has sold material to assorted newspapers and magazines.

A third and most essential member of the team is *Ickybod*, a green 1979 Volkswagen camper, the Martins' home on the road. Without *Ick*, they might have been tempted to solicit free lodging and meals, and this guidebook wouldn't be quite so honest.

## A FEW WORDS OF THANKS

In a sense, guidebooks are written by committee. The authors only provide the research, the adjectives and the editing, while hundreds of other sources furnish facts and background information. Among our primary helpers were **Mary Baker** of the Washington State Tourism Development Division; **Timothy R. Manns**, chief of interpretation and visitor services, North Cascades National Park; **Jim Fletcher**, information supervisor, Washington State Ferries; **Barry Anderson**, manager of the Seattle/King County News Bureau; **Celese Brune**, interpretive naturalist, Mount St. Helens National Volcanic Monument; **Maurie Sprague**, information specialist for Olympic National Park; and **Loren E. Lane**, resource education specialist for Mount Rainier National Park.

Helpful contributions also came from dozens of folks at city and county chambers of commerce and visitors bureaus, and offices of the U.S. Forest Service, National Park Service and Bureau of Land Management.

## CLOSING INTRODUCTORY THOUGHTS:
### *Keeping up with the changes*

Nobody's perfect, but we try. This guidebook contains thousands of facts and a few are probably wrong. If you catch an error, let us know.

Information contained herein was current at the time of publication, but of course things change. Drop us a note if you find that an historic museum has become an auto repair shop or the other way around; or if a restaurant, motel or attraction has opened or closed. Further, we'd like to know if you discover a great undiscovered attraction, café or hideaway resort. And we certainly want to learn if you have a bad experience at one of the places we've recommended.

All who provide useful information will earn a free copy of a Pine Cone Press publication. (See listing in the back of this book.)

Address your comments to:

> *Pine Cone Press*
> P.O. Box 1494
> Columbia, CA 95310

# TRAVEL TIPS

Whether you travel by car, RV or commercial transit, these tips will help make any trip more enjoyable and economical.

**Reservations** ● Whenever possible, make advance room reservations. Otherwise, you'll pay the "rack rate," the highest rate that a hotel or motel charges. Also, with a reservation, you won't be shut out if there's a convention or major local celebration.

**Car rentals** ● The same is true of rental cars; you'll often get a better rate by reserving your wheels ahead. **Important note:** Car rental firms may try to sell you "insurance" (actually collision damage waiver) to cover the vehicle. However, you may already have this protection through your own auto insurance company. Check before you go and take your policy or insurance card as proof of coverage.

**Trip insurance** ● If you're flying, trip insurance may be a good investment, covering lost luggage, accidents and missed flights (essential if you have a no-refund super saver). Most travel agencies can arrange this coverage.

**Medical needs** ● Always take spare prescription glasses and contacts. Take the prescriptions for your lenses and any drugs you may be taking. Don't forget sun protection, such as a wide brimmed hat and sun block, since you may be spending more time outdoors.

**Cameras and film** ● If you haven't used your camera recently, test it by shooting a roll of film before you go. Test and replace weak camera and flash batteries. If you're flying, hand carry your camera and film through the security check.

## *Final checklist*

There's more to trip departure than putting out the cat. Check off these essentials before you go:

___ Stop newspaper and other deliveries; put a hold on your mail.

___ Lock off or unplug your automatic garage door opener.

___ Arrange for indoor plant watering, landscaping and pet care.

___ Make sure your phone answering machine is turned on; most of these devices allow you to pick up messages remotely.

___ Don't invite burglars by telling the world via answering machine or voice mail that you're gone. Put several lights on timers and make sure newspapers and mail don't accumulate outside.

___ If you're going on a long trip, arrange for future mortgage and other payments to avoid late charges.

___ Take perishable food from the refrigerator and lower the fridge and water heater temperatures to save energy.

___ Double check the clothes you've packed (extra shoes, matching belts); make sure your shaving and cosmetic kits are complete.

___ Take more than one type of credit card, so you won't be caught short if one is lost or stolen.

___ Get travelers checks and/or take your bank debit card.

___ Have your car serviced, including a check of all belts, tires and fluid levels. For long desert stretches, take extra water and oil.

___ Turn out the lights, turn off the heat and put out the cat.

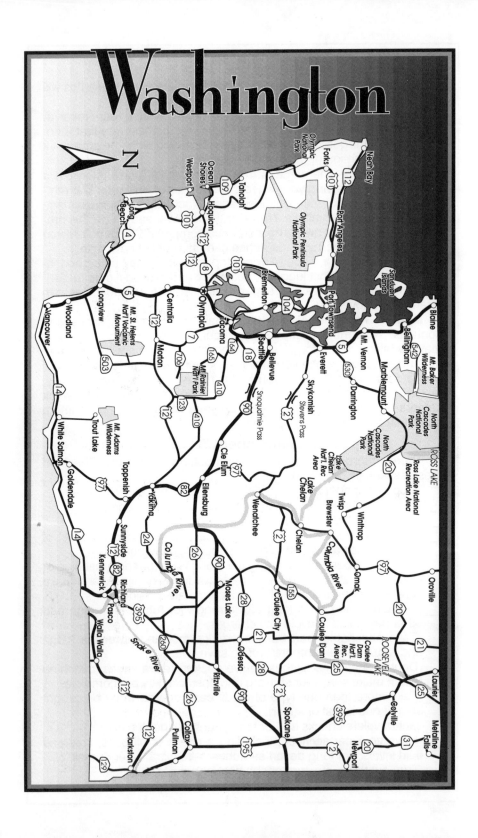

Chapter one

# WASHINGTON
### Getting to know you

**THE KEY TO SOLVING** a jigsaw puzzle is to start with a corner piece and work from there. We prefer the upper left hand corner, which gives prospective to the overall structure and provides a growing point of reference as you build.

Washington is a key corner piece to the American puzzle map, geographically at least. In many ways, it is a topographical and sociological key as well. If we were coming from abroad for our first exploration of the United States, we might be tempted to start here. In a manageable package, one can find an American sampler: a thriving city with diverse cultural and dining lures, verdant mountain reaches, wilderness seacoasts, a fabulous network of inland waterways sprinkled with get-away islands, one of America's great river systems, a swatch of the Wild West, and even a bit of the wine country.

The Evergreen State is a copious cultural stew as well. It is seasoned with large Asian, Bavarian and Scandinavian communities, and one of the most accomplished Native American cultures in the country. Canada just to the north adds its own special flavors. Neighboring Victoria is so richly British that the Strait of Juan de Fuca separating it from the mainland might as well be the English Channel.

Despite its cornerstone location, Washington suffered an identity crisis during its formative years. It was lumped in with Oregon and Idaho as the

"Oregon Country" until the region was formalized as the Oregon Territory in 1848. The area north of the Columbia River was referred to as "northern Oregon" until it became Washington Territory five years later. Still, most migrants followed the Oregon Trail into the lower region, so Washington was slow a-growing. It didn't achieve statehood until 1889, thirty years after Oregon.

It has made up for lost time in the century-plus since its admission to the Union. Although a third smaller than Oregon, Washington has almost twice the population—nearly five million compared with 2.8 million. Most of it is stuffed into the busy Puget Sound area. Spreading outward from Seattle, it contains well over half the state's total population. Like Oregon, Washington has a thinly-populated eastern half, which is primarily a high and dry prairie created by the rainshadow of the Cascades. Unlike Oregon, it has one significant eastern town—Spokane, with a regional population approaching 200,000. Incidentally, Washington is the smallest state west of Iowa, unless you count Hawaii.

## GETTING THERE & ABOUT

Two major highways converge in America's northwest corner, providing a handy funnel for motorists and RV travelers. Interstate 5 crosses the Columbia River into Vancouver, after its long haul from California across Oregon. It then passes through Olympia and Seattle before continuing on to Canada. Incidentally, major border crossings such as Blaine on Interstate 5 become very congested on Friday and Sunday evenings as citizens from both nations swarm back and forth. In summers, you can anticipate delays of several hours or more. (Border delays are discussed as part of Seattle and Vancouver radio and TV traffic reports.) It's best to plan your crossing in either direction on weekdays or late at night.

Interstate 90 crosses the state from east to west, nudging Spokane and ending in Seattle. An alternate favored by many is I-84, which follows Oregon's scenically acclaimed Columbia River Gorge. It terminates in Portland. A quick right hand turn carries travelers up I-5 or I-205 (the Portland bypass) into Washington. A state highway follows the Washington shore of the Columbia gorge. It's also scenically appealing, even without the famous waterfalls of the Oregon side.

Interstate 82, branching off I-84 in northeastern Oregon, cuts diagonally across Washington, southeast to northwest, linking up with I-90 in Ellensburg. For those heading west on I-84, it's a more direct route to Seattle than the Columbia River gorge, but not nearly as stimulating. It travels through the state's major farm belt.

Journeying south to north, U.S. 101 enters the state at Astoria and heads up the Pacific Coast into the Olympic Peninsula. It then wraps back south to trace the outline of the peninsula, and ends in Olympia. Washington's coast, shorter than Oregon's, is cut by deep bays, so the highway is forced inland for much of the way. However, smaller roads offer exploration of this wilderness coastline, which is every bit as stunning as that of the lower state.

Inland, the main north-south artery is U.S. Highway 97, arriving from north central Oregon and passing through the central Washington farm belt to Yakima (*YAK-i-ma*). It picks up the curving northern tail of the Columbia River and then its Okanogan tributary, and follows this stream to Canada.

West to east, several highways cross the craggy beauty of the Cascade

Range. For a scenic spiral rivaling Oregon's Mount Hood Loop Highway, head eastward on Highway 12 to Mount Rainier National Park, swing north on State Route 123 to State 410, and follow it west to Tacoma. Farther north, U.S. Highway 2 departs Everett bound for the Cascades, and then wanders east across the state to Spokane. Washington's most imposing mountain route is State Highway 20, which heads east from Anacortes and snakes through North Cascades National Park. It then wanders along the state's mostly-wooded northland.

**FLYING** ● Seattle is an important national and international stop, served by most major American and several foreign carriers. The airport, **Sea-Tac,** is midway between Seattle and Tacoma. For an update on flight schedules, departure, arrivals and airport parking, call (800) 544-1965 or (206) 431-4444.

Other towns with commercial air service are **Bellingham, Port Angeles, Yakima, Spokane, Wenatchee, Moses Lake, Walla Walla, Pullman** and the Tri-Cities of **Richland-Pasco-Kennewick**.

**TRAINING** ● Amtrak's **Coast Starlight** runs between San Francisco and Seattle, with connections from various Oregon and California points. The station is at Third Avenue South and South King Street. The **Pioneer** links Seattle to eastern America, via Salt Lake City, and the **Empire Builder** takes the northern route through Montana to Chicago. The **Mount Rainier** has frequent service between Seattle, Tacoma, Olympia and Portland. For schedules and information, call (800) USA-RAIL. The local Seattle number is (206) 464-1930.

**BUSING** ● **Greyhound** operates a relatively frequent schedule with reasonably modern (and always smoke-free) buses along I-5 and eastward along I-90. Elsewhere in the state, bus service thins out considerably. Greyhound's information/reservations number is (800) 531-5332 or (206) 624-3456. Assorted independent operators serve the rest of Washington on a more or less irregular basis. Some have taken over abandoned Greyhound routes.

If you'd like to get lost in the Sixties and still be assured of getting where you're going, the **Green Tortoise** runs a funky but clean and generally regular bus service along I-5 between San Francisco and Seattle. The last time we checked, it offered San Francisco departures at 8 p.m. on Mondays and Fridays.

**FERRYING** ● The grandest way to explore this water-rimmed land is aboard the Washington State Ferries that fan out over Puget Sound. The ferry system is simple and comprehensive, covering dozens of shoreside and island communities of western Washington. You simply drive aboard, park your vehicle, adjourn to passenger decks and watch the scenery slide past. Some boats have light meal service; all have vending machines.

For specifics and schedules, call (800) 84-FERRY (within Washington only) or (206) 464-6400. In Canada, get information by calling (604) 381-1551 or (604) 656-1531. Incidentally, Canadian currency is accepted, at the prevailing exchange rate. To obtain a ferry schedule, call any of the above numbers or write: Marine Transport Division, Washington State Ferries, 801 Alaskan Way, Seattle, WA 98104-1487. Headquarters is on Coleman Dock at Pier 52. For more on the ferries, see the box in Chapter 5 on page 185.

In addition to the state-operated system, several private firms run ferry service. Other outfits offer whale-watching and seal-watching trips, charter fishing and sightseeing service. We list these within write-ups of the communities they serve.

Several ferries sail to British Columbia's Vancouver Island and Victoria. Washington State ferries land at Sidney north of Victoria, sailing from Anacortes via the San Juan Islands. Among the private ferry operations:

The *MV Coho* sails from Port Angeles to Victoria; call (206) 457-4491 in Port Angeles or (206) 622-2222. The *Victoria Clipper* offers daily summer service from Seattle's pier 63 to Victoria, along with service from Port Townsend and Port Angeles; phone (800) 888-2535 or (206) 448- 5000. You'll find more details under Seattle in Chapter 4 and Port Townsend and Port Angeles in Chapter 6.

Both state and private ferries can be mobbed on summer weekends. If you must catch one on a Friday evening, Saturday morning or Sunday evening, arrive at least two hours before departure time, get in line and settle down with a good book. (Reservations aren't accepted on state ferries except for runs between the San Juan Islands and Vancouver Island. Most private operators accept reservations.) Also, try to avoid ferries during the morning and evening commute hours on weekdays throughout the year.

Alaska state ferries sail from a terminal in Bellingham up the famous **Inside Passage.** Although passengers can hop on and off these sea-going ferries at will, advance reservations are absolutely essential for vehicles and staterooms in summer. Several cruise ships also ply the Inside Passage, and some depart from Seattle, although we prefer the Alaska state ferries. One can stop en route to explore the towns of southeast Alaska, then catch a later ferry to continue the trip. For details, contact the Alaska Marine Highway, P.O. Box R, Juneau, AK 99801; (800) 642-0066.

**GUIDED TOURS** ● Washington and Oregon often are marketed as a package by tour companies. You can find several conducted tours that include pieces of both; check with a travel agent for specifics. Two companies offering Northwest outings are **Tauk Tours,** 11 Wilton Rd., Westport, CT 06880, (203) 226-6911; and **Maupintour,** 1515 Saint Andrews Drive, Lawrence, KS 66046; (800) 255-6162.

**Elderhostel,** which specializes in learning vacations for seniors and often uses college dorms and classrooms, offers several Washington programs. If you're 60 or older and you love to learn while traveling, contact Elderhostel at 75 Federal Street, Boston, MA 02110-1941; (617) 426-8056.

## Fishing, clamming and hunting

For some odd bureaucratic reason, Washington has separate agencies for hunting and fishing. The Department of Wildlife handles hunting and freshwater fishing, while salmon fishing, shellfish digging and saltwater sportfishing come under the Washington State Department of Fisheries. (Addresses of both are listed at the end of this chapter.)

Naturally, fishing is outstanding in this water-oriented state. Charter boats ply waters of the Puget Sound, while inland streams and rivers offer salmon and trout. Many mountain lakes are stocked with bass and trout, as are reservoirs on the Columbia, Snake and other rivers.

Shellfish abound in the state's cool coastal waters and Puget Sound. Dungeness crabs and razor clams are a particular delicacy. The State Department of Fisheries tells you all about mollusk digging in its *Salmon, Shell-*

*"Good grief, what is that thing?" Ugly but tasty, geoduck clams are plentiful in Washington's Puget Sound mudflats.*
— © **Bob & Ira Spring**

*fish, Bottomfish, Sport Fishing Guide.* Be sure to check for closed seasons, when the so-called "red tide" (a plankton) makes some shellfish toxic. Call the "Red Tide Hotline" at (800) 562-5632 for current information.

A fishing license is required for anyone 14 and older; it's $17 a year for residents and $48 for non-residents. Three-day permits are $9 for residents and $17 for visitors. Residents 70 and over can get a one-year license for $3; it's not available for visitors. Combined hunting/fishing license is $29; it's also not available for visitors. No license is required for shellfish, except for razor clams anywhere in the state, and Hood Canal shrimp.

## Winter sports

Washington has 20 downhill ski resorts, nearly a dozen cross-country ski areas with groomed trails, and many snowplay areas. Most winter sports activities are in the Cascades, although three downhill areas are along the state's eastern edge—in the Selkirks near Spokane and Colville, and the Blue Mountains east of Walla Walla.

Four ski areas near Snoqualmie Pass are within an hour's drive of Seattle, and some rental agencies offer cars equipped with traction devices and ski racks. Take your pick of ski conditions—deeper snowfalls, wetter snow and warmer weather west of the Cascades, or drier snow and colder weather east of the Cascades and in eastern Washington.

For details on winter sports, contact the Washington State Ski Industries Association, (206) 623-3777. Washington State Parks and Recreation Commission, (206) 586-0185, has cross-country ski brochures and snowmobile trail guides. For more on snowmobiling, check out the Washington State Snowmobile Association, 55 W. Washington Street, #191, Yakima, WA 98903; (509) 452-1506.

# TOURING: WHEN TO COME

Tourism is an important part of Washington's economy, although popular areas don't get as swamped with camera-clutchers as California. However, most tourist areas are busy between Memorial Day and Labor Day.

Make summer lodging and camping reservations early, particularly for areas within easy reach of Seattle. Like Portland and San Francisco, it's large enough to generate big weekend get-away crowds; nearby visitor lures fill up quickly. On sunny weekends, they can become mob scenes. We recall an August visit to Mount St. Helens on a dazzling summer Sunday when even the visitor center parking lots were filled to capacity.

## Rain today, probably followed by tomorrow

If you're not familiar with Northwest weather (pay attention, Californians), you must factor the climate into your travel plans. Most of western America's storms are brewed in the Gulf of Alaska. Summer high pressure ridges generally keep them north of California, but they slip into British Columbia and western Washington with regularity. These aren't nasty storms, but merely low clouds and drizzle that often obscure all those dazzling snowcapped peaks. A typical summer cycle offers a couple of days of overcast, followed by a few sunny ones. Even on a sunny day, clouds can slip in at a moment's notice.

The weather east of the Cascades is more predictable, with clear warm days and temperatures that often climb into the low 100s.

Best of all, you'll love Washington in the fall, when the weather is most stable and the crowds are gone. You can enjoy balmy, wind-free days and crisp, cool nights. Late August through late September offers the best odds for western Washington sunshine. Fall is relatively brief this far north; by October, winter weather patterns begin to develop. Also, there's no absolute guarantee of autumn sunshine. That cloud cover seething over the Gulf of Alaska can move south any time of the year.

Snow is rarely a problem in the state, since it stays mostly to the higher elevations. Seattle gets a few dustings a year, and rare snowstorms can make things nasty, since traffic in this hilly city tends to slide into Puget Sound. Washington's main highways are rarely closed by winter storms, although those breaching the Cascades are often shut down temporarily by snow. Always check before heading into the mountains in winter.

Taking both climate and crowds into account, here's a quick preview of when to go where:

**SPRING** ● Parks all over the state are a-dazzle with rhododendron and azalea blooms in springtime. It's also a good time to explore central and eastern Washington. Browse through farmers markets for fresh produce or hit roadside stands in the Richland-Pasco-Kennewick Tri-Cities area, and the Puyallup Valley east of Tacoma. Check out the immense Grand Coulee Dam project, walk the prim and prosperous streets of Spokane, or catch a jetboat ride up Hells Canyon of the Snake River out of Clarkston.

In western Washington, the gray whales head north to Alaska in spring, and you can watch them pass the coastline from March through May. Outfits in Westport and Grayland offer whale-watching cruises. For indoor activities, catch a Seattle Mariners' game at the rain-proof Kingdome. Another nice thing about spring in Washington—the days are *long* this far north.

**SUMMER** • Sure they're crowded, but summer is the best time to visit Mount Rainier, North Cascades and Olympic national parks and the popular Mount St. Helens National Volcanic Monument. These mountain parks appeal to campers and hikers, and many of the trails aren't clear of snow until midsummer. Also, most of the parks' guided ranger hikes and other activities are scheduled between Memorial Day and Labor Day weekend. Of course, summer is a good time to explore the entire state if you don't mind being part of the crowd. All activities and attractions are functioning then.

**FALL** • This also is a good time for the mountain parks, before snow closes the high country trails. The weather's usually clear and you can see all those dazzling peaks. Autumn is a great time to explore the San Juan Islands, and perhaps sign up for a kayaking expedition. Again, the weather is more predictable then. When you're sitting in a kayak surrounded by all that water, you don't want rain drizzling down your neck.

**WINTER** • Seattle! Well of course it's a great city any time of the year, brimming with cultural and culinary lures. However, if you're limited to a winter vacation, this metropolitan center is your best bet, since there's no off-season for its many activities. With the summer crowds gone, you won't have to worry about reservations or waiting lines. Rainfall? It's mostly a light drizzle. Seattle's annual precipitation is 32 to 35 inches, about the same as San Francisco and less than New York. Snowfall is rare. When it does drip, come in out of the rain to enjoy a play or concert, tour a museum, dine on salmon, or catch a Sonics or Seahawks game. (Tickets generally are available for Sonics games, and for the Seahawks when they're in a slump.)

If you like coastal storm watching, head for the Pacific Coast for an uncrowded, cozy winter vacation. Beach side resorts and bed & breakfast inns have lots of vacancies then, and a crackling fireplace can be very sensual with a storm brooding outside your window.

More nice winter moments: Seattle, Tacoma, Cathlamet, Bellingham and other waterside communities feature lighted boat parades during the holidays. Leavenworth, the mountain town with a Bavarian theme, stages a Christmas time tree-lighting ceremony.

## What to wear

Come dressed in layers to best deal with the state's temperate but temperamental climate. Inland Washington can get downright hot in summer, while chilly sea breezes keep the Puget Sound and coastal areas cool in July. Expect occasional summer thunder showers in the Cascades and light rain the Puget Sound area. Eastern Washington offers warm, dry summers and crisp, cold winters.

## What to bring

It's not a dry state, so you don't need to bring your own booze. Liquor is readily available by the drink in saloons and restaurants. However, you may find hard liquor prices higher here than in states such as California and Nevada, since it is price-fixed and sold only in state stores. And they're closed on Sundays. However, mixed drinks are available in bars and restaurants, if you feel the need to wet your whiskers on the Sabbath. Wine and beer are sold in supermarkets and mini-marts.

It's illegal to bring alcohol into the state, although there are no border checks. So if you're tempted to pick up some cheap gin or scotch in California or Nevada before heading north, don't tell anyone we suggested it. (And don't wait until you get to Oregon; that's a price-fixed state, too.)

If you plan to explore Washington's eastern reaches, facilities are few and scattered in some regions, so take the usual out-back precautions. Carry extra engine oil, coolant, an emergency radiator sealant, spare belts, radiator hoses and tools to install these things. Take plenty of water and a survival kit in case of a mishap or breakdown. The kit should include first aid essentials, non-perishable foods, a can-opener, a powerful flashlight, small shovel, matches, aluminum foil (for signaling) and a space blanket so you can snooze in the shade of your car. It's not unusual for the mercury to hit 110 in eastern Washington.

## Don't get bugged

Mosquitoes love the damp, cool climate of the Pacific Northwest and they're particularly active in spring. Although abatement programs keep them at bay in urban areas, they thrive in the countryside, so keep repellent handy. This is particularly essential for back-country hiking, since you can't retreat to a car or building when the small beasties zero in on you.

Should you wonder, the latest theory about mosquitoes is that they're attracted by body heat. They have lousy vision and limited smelling ability, but they can sense a warm body moving through the brush. During mosquito season, generally from early spring through mid-summer, wear long pants and sleeves outdoors. They keep you from radiating much body heat and they offer smaller skin targets for these nasty little beaks.

# GETTING CAMPED

Among the many things that Washington and Oregon have in common are outstanding state park systems. We've toured throughout America and Canada and have never found a better selection of nicely located and well-maintained state-run campgrounds.

A two-page state park brochure lists alphabetically the 80 parks with camping facilities, and the 37 without, and it's available at most visitor centers and tourist bureaus. Or contact: Washington State Parks and Recreation Commission, Public Affairs Office, 7150 Cleanwater Lane (P.O. Box 42650), Olympia, WA 98504-2650; (206) 753-2027. In summer, you can call toll free (800) 562-0990 weekdays from 9 to 5. The office also has brochures on many of the individual parks.

State park camping prices are $5 to $7 for primitive sites, $10 for standard sites and $14 for utility sites. Primitive sites are generally for tent camping only, including hiker/biker camps; some have only pit potties. Standard sites have picnic and barbecue facilities, nearby water, usually flush potties and sometimes showers; they'll accommodate tents or RVs. Some sites, however, may be too small for large rigs. Utility sites have water, electric and sometimes sewer hookups; most have showers nearby. There are no day use or boat launching fees at state parks. Extra vehicles are $4, although RV tow-alongs are exempt from this. At some heavily impacted state park campgrounds, a $1 surcharge is added to the regular camping fee.

Twelve state parks offer advanced reservations from Memorial Day weekend through Labor Day weekend, as well as space-available sites. Applications must be made by mail, directly to the parks involved. They may be postmarked as early as January 1 for that calendar year, and they must be mailed at least two weeks in advance. For details, get application forms and a copy of the brochure, *How to Make a Reservation at a Washington State Park.* They're available at most state parks, or you can call any of these park numbers: (206) 753-2027 or (206) 753-7143 in Olympia; (206) 755-9231 in Burlington; (206) 931-3907 in Auburn; (509) 662-0420 in Wenatchee or (509) 545-2315 in Pasco. Forms also may be available at border welcome centers and at various visitor centers around the state.

Parks on the reservation system are Belfair, Birch Bay, Fort Canby, Fort Flagler, Grayland Beach, Ike Kinswa, Lake Chelan, Lincoln Rock, Moran, Pearrygin Lake, Steamboat Rock and Twin Harbors.

Because of lack of demand and/or budget constraints, many state parks close from October through March. Some keep their picnic and other facilities open but close their campgrounds. Others remain open with limited services, and may shut down flush potties and other running water to avoid freeze-ups.

**National park** campgrounds in Washington all operate on a first-come, first-served basis. Since the state isn't as inundated with visitors as California, it's not too difficult to find sites in summer. The ritual is simple: show up fairly early in the morning, and you generally can catch a vacating campsite. Don't wait until the posted check-out time (usually 1 to 3 p.m.), because others will have scooped up the vacancies by then. Mount Rainier and Olympic are very busy on summer weekends, particularly when the sun is out. North Cascades, farther afield, is not so crowded and many U.S. Forest Service campgrounds are nearby. Mount St. Helens Volcanic National Monument has no camping, although a good number of forest service sites are just outside its boundaries.

The **U.S. Forest Service** has dozens of campgrounds in Washington and a few take reservations, up to 120 days in advance. For information, call (800) 283-CAMP. As in most states, Washington's forest service campgrounds generally do not have hookups, and many have chemical toilets. However, the price is right—from $10 down to nothing, and many rival state park campgrounds in the beauty of their settings.

Forest Service "Camp Stamps" save about 15 percent of campsite costs. They're also convenient, since you don't have to worry about having the right currency to poke into those little slots. You can purchase any amount in denominations of $1, $2, $3, $5 and $10. Send a check or money order to: Camp Stamps, U.S. Forest Service, P.O. Box 96090, Washington, DC 20090-6090.

Obviously, summer is the busy season for all campgrounds. The busiest areas are in western Washington, particularly in the Cascades near Seattle, the Pacific Coast, the Olympic Peninsula, and in San Juan Islands. In our extensive travels, during which we lived in Ickybod, our elderly semi-reliable VW camper, we generally had little trouble getting campsites by arriving at our chosen campground early in the day in the more popular areas. Toughest tickets are on Friday and Saturday nights, particularly at national parks and state parks in the areas mentioned above. Mount Rainier National Park is a mob scene on sunny summer weekends.

Most of Washington's **safety roadside rests** allow weary travelers to snooze for up to eight hours. They must be in self-contained RVs or trailers—or they can stretch out in the seats of their cars, for that matter. Pitching tents isn't allowed. Rolling out sleeping bags on the grass is frowned upon, although we've seen people do it. If you're tempted, stay clear of the pet areas.

## HANDICAPPED TRAVELERS

People with mobility problems can get permits to use handicapped parking spaces by applying at any Department of Motor Vehicles office. Proof of impairment must be provided. These permits aren't limited to the driver; they can be used if any occupant of the car is physically impaired. Incidentally, there is a stiff fine if able-bodied persons park their vehicles in handicapped spaces.

**Washington State ferries** offer reduced rates for handicapped travelers, if they have identification establishing their disabilities. (Residents and long-term visitors may want to apply for a *Washington State Ferries Persons with Disabilities Travel Permit* or a *Transit Regional Reduced Fare Permit.*) Most, but not all, ferry terminals are equipped to handle foot passengers with mobility problems. Obviously, vehicle passengers can get aboard, although some ferries don't have elevator access to passenger decks. Call Washington State Ferries at (800) 84-FERRY (within the state only) or (206) 464-6400 for details. For the hearing impaired, TDD relay service is available through (800) 833-6388 or (206) 587-5500.

**Golden Access Passes,** available free to handicapped persons at national park and U.S. Forest Service offices, provide half-price camping at national forest campgrounds, and free admission to all national parks and monuments.

Among agencies that handicapped travelers will find useful are: **Travel Information Center,** 12th Street and Tabor Rd., Philadelphia, PA 19141, (215) 329-5715; **Society for the Advancement of Travel for the Handicapped,** 26 Court Street, Brooklyn, NY 11242; (718) 858-5483; **American Foundation for the Blind,** 15 W. 16th Street, New York, NY 10011; (800) 323-5463; and **Mobility International USA,** P.O. Box 3551, Eugene, OR 97403. Two federal government pamphlets, *Access Travel* and *Access to the National Parks,* are available by writing: **U.S. Government Printing Office,** Washington, DC 20402.

An extremely helpful publication is *Access to the World—A Travel Guide for the Handicapped* by Louise Weiss. Available at many bookstores, it's published by Holt, Rinehart & Winston of New York.

## SENIOR TRAVELERS

Anyone 62 or older can obtain a free **Golden Age Pass** that provides half-price camping in U.S. Forest Service campgrounds and free admission to all national parks and monuments (similar to the Golden Access Pass for the handicapped).

Nearly every attraction and museum in Washington and the rest of the country now offers senior discounts. They're also available on most public transit systems, and many restaurants and hotels offer reduced rates as well. Seniors 65 and older receive a 50 percent passenger discount on the Washington State ferries (but not for the vehicles they're driving).

A fine organization that serves the interests of seniors is the **American**

**Association of Retired Persons,** 1919 K Street Northwest, Washington, DC 22049; (202) 872-4700. For a nominal annual fee, AARP members receive information on travel and tour discounts and other stuff of interest to retired folk. **Elderhostel** is a useful travel-oriented organization for 60-plus seniors; contact the organization at 75 Federal Street, Boston, MA 02110-1941; (617) 426-8056. (See "Touring" above.)

# THE LAY OF THE LAND

Washington is a land defined by water, from its Pacific shores through the Puget Sound to the Columbia River. Its northern border is the ruler-straight 49th parallel that separates America from Canada. Another straight line cleaves it from Idaho, except for a short squiggle formed by the Snake River below Clarkston. From there, most of this jigsaw puzzle piece has rough edges. The western boundary is the shoreline of the Pacific. The Puget Sound has left an ungainly notch in the northwestern corner. The Columbia River forms Washington's interlocking border with Oregon, except for a straight line running east from Kennewick.

Basically, the state has two climatic regions, sawed in half by the Cascade Range. Western Washington, the soggiest and most interesting part, is primarily a water wonderland, wrapped into the Puget Sound. This great inland sea reaches more than halfway down the state, extending from the Canadian border south to Olympia. Thousands of islands and tree-thatched shorelines beg exploring. The San Juan Islands near the north end are particularly intriguing. The Olympic Peninsula, isolated from the mainland by Puget Sound's intrusion, is equally fascinating. It's a richly varied region of rain forests, wilderness coastline and the perpetually snowcapped Olympic Mountains.

Moving inland, you encounter the tumbled, handsomely rugged wall of the Cascade Range, which rivals the Olympic Peninsula as Washington's favorite playground. It's home to Mount Rainier National Park, North Cascades National Park and the headline-grabbing Mount St. Helens National Volcanic Monument. The Cascade Range is around 25 million years old, although most of its volcanoes date back a mere million. St. Helens, of course, did her latest volcanic dance in 1980.

Tucked into the middle of western Washington, Seattle is the state's urban and cultural core. On a good day (best odds are in September and October) you can look both ways to the snowy heights of its cradling Olympic and Cascade mountains.

East over the Cascade crest, the traveler tumbles down to a high prairie, which stretches relatively undisturbed, almost to the Idaho border. It's the most arid part of the state, since the Cascades grab most of those rain squalls sweeping down from Alaska. However, the area around Wenatchee and Yakima is hardly burned brown. This is the state's agricultural belt; Washington's response to Oregon's Willamette Valley and California's Central Valley. Continuing east, you pass through vast wheat fields of the rolling Palouse Country.

Two other mountain ranges rumple eastern Washington's overwise gently rolling terrain. The Rockies, rambling northward from Idaho into British Columbia, nip the state's northeastern tip, above Spokane. They're called the Selkirk Mountains here. To the southeast, Oregon's mighty Wallowas follow the curving course of Hells Canyon of the Snake River into Washington.

# THINGS WASHINGTON

The state's climate, profusion of waterways and natural abundance have created several distinctive foods and crafts. As a visitor, you'll want to check these out.

**Salmon** ● You probably know that salmon are born in freshwater streams, then they journey to the ocean and live in saltwater for most of their adult life. Each year, they return to their precise spot of birth to lay eggs, fertilize them, and then perish. Major runs are in the spring and fall. Washington has an abundance of salmon and there are two ways to see them: at hatcheries in fish ladders, rearing tanks and viewing rooms; and on your plate at dinner. Several large hatcheries offer fine salmon-viewing facilities. The best is the Cowlitz Salmon Hatchery between I-5 and Mossyrock, off State Highway 12. Not surprisingly, many Washington restaurants feature salmon.

**Oysters** ● If you're an oyster fan, head for Willapa Bay on the southwestern Washington coast. It's one of the world's major oyster producing areas and several "oyster farmers" sell them fresh and smoked. Local stores stock them as well. Equally famous are the small Olympia oysters of the southern Puget Sound.

**It's the berries** ● Blackberries abound in western Washington, ripening from August through early September. Look for vines along roadsides and enjoy an *al fresco* lunch, or pick some for dessert or cereal topping if you're RVing. Blackberries often find their way into specialty foods, and some restaurants feature blackberry pies. Huckleberries are common in the mountains, particularly in Gifford Pinchot National Forest surrounding Mount St. Helens. The forest service even issues a brochure, describing the finer points of huckleberry picking and listing some recipes. What's a Gifford Pinchot? He was the founder of the U.S. Forest Service.

On the domestic side, blueberries and Loganberries are popular, and they're often are sold at roadside stands, mostly in western Washington.

**Aplets and Cotlets** ● These are curiously tasty candy squares made with gelatin, walnut and apple juice (Aplets) or puréed apricots (Cotlets). Similar to the *locum* candy of Armenia and Turkey, they're produced by Liberty Orchards in the tiny town of Cashmere, and distributed over much of the country. Tours are conducted through the facility, which is just off Highway 2 between Leavenworth and Wenatchee; see Chapter 7 under "The Skykomish Corridor."

**Historic murals** ● Many communities, particularly in western Washington, have decorated their downtown areas with murals, generally depicting local history. Among the major "mural centers" are Toppenish, off I-84 in south central Washington, with several large historical murals; Anacortes, gateway to the San Juan Islands, with more than 40 small murals gracing its old brick and masonry; Centralia off I-5 south of Olympia; Sumner, east of Tacoma; and the small communities around Willapa Bay in Southwestern Washington. Most chambers of commerce in these communities offer mural walk maps.

**Washington specialties** ● Several stores called Made in Washington feature specialty foods, seafoods, wines, recipe books, clothing, handicrafts and artwork produced in the state. You'll find a large one at Pike's Market at Post Alley and Pine in Seattle (206-467-0788); four others are in the Puget

Sound area. For their locations, and to receive a catalog of Washington products, call (800) 645-3474. To obtain a farmer-to-consumer **Farmers Market Guide**, see the end of this chapter.

*Antiques* ● Collectibles and antiques certainly aren't unique to Washington. However, several towns abound with antique shops. Among places to load up on memorabilia are downtown Vancouver and Kalama, Centralia Square and Duffy's Mall in Centralia, Tacoma's Antique Row along Broadway, Pacific Run Antique Mall in Tacoma/Parkland, Pioneer Square area in Seattle, Star Center in Snohomish, downtown Issaquah, Everett Publick Market in Everett, downtown Anacortes, Yesterday's Village in Yakima, and Showplace Antique Mall in Ellensburg.

*The Chinook Look* ● Several Native American tribes of the Puget Sound area—Chinooks among them—are noted for their fine carvings on wooden panels and totems. These distinctive designs find their way into clothing fashions, architectural shapes, business logos and of course, souvenirs. Some of the better crafts and gift shops sell wooden items carved by tribal members. Check tags carefully to make sure your souvenir didn't originate in Taiwan. A good example of the stylized Chinook look is the helmet design of the National Football League's Seattle Seahawks.

*Washington wines* ● "To understand the story of Washington wine you've got to learn how great the story is. It's a miracle!" So wrote Leon Adams, the noted California-based wine historian. Local wines have gained world note in recent years, winning medals from San Francisco to Paris. Whites are the state's best, including Chardonnay, Sauvignon Blanc, Semillon, Chenin Blanc and Gewürztraminer. Among the better reds are Cabernet Sauvignon, Merlot and Pinot Noir. Washington has three federally-recognized appelations: the large Columbia Valley of east central Washington, and the smaller Yakima Valley to the west and Walla Walla Valley to the east. Many wineries offer tours and tasting, which we discuss in more detail, particularly in Chapter 8.

For a touring guide to the Evergreen State's wine country, send $2 to: Washington Wine Commission, P.O. Box 61217, Seattle, WA 98121; (206) 728-2252.

*Washington Huskies* ● Although Seattle has several major league teams, Washingtonians save most of their sporting spirit for the football Huskies of the University of Washington. Their recent ascent to the national championship turned Huskies admiration into near worship. Stadium seats are the toughest ticket item in the state. Fans have been passing them down through families for generations.

# IN THE BEGINNING

Western Washington's soggy climate was more of a boon than a bane for its earliest residents. Native Americans, blessed with an abundance of fish, game and wild fruit, could shed nomadic tendencies and settle down in one place. Also, if the Bering land bridge theory is true, the Northwest was one of the first areas settled by these travelers from Asia. They had many stable generations to develop one of the most advanced native cultures in the Americas.

Early dwellers built remarkably sophisticated board long-houses, carved elaborate canoes and cruised throughout the Puget Sound and its many islands. They thrived on salmon, whales, deer, elk and berries and made medical potions from the ample plant life. Wild game provided plenty of skins for clothing, essential in this damp climate. Elaborately painted totems and carved panels are legendary among these clans.

East of the Cascades, Native Americans followed migratory patterns of bison and elk, living a nomadic existence more typical of the western plains Indians. However, the Columbia and Snake rivers did offer an abundance of salmon, so life wasn't all that tough. It also provided transit westward. Evidence from mound excavations indicates that tribal groups from eastern and western Washington met periodically at The Dalles—the rapids of the Columbia River—for rendezvous and swap meets.

When outsiders came to Washington, the coastal dwellers were quite willing to gather furs for them in exchange for weapons and other trade goods. Otter and beaver trapping was the first major commercial activity in the future state. However, the earliest visitors were more interested in getting *through* this area than to it. They sought the Northwest Passage as a short cut from the western to the eastern hemisphere.

### Did Juan sail into the sound?

Juan de Fuca, a Greek navigator sailing for Spain, claimed to have discovered some sort of passageway as early as 1592. However, there is no strong evidence that he found his way into Washington waters. Nearly two centuries passed before other visits by outsiders were recorded. Juan Pèrez, sailing up from Mexico in 1774 under the flag of Spain, apparently was the first to set foot on local soil. Bruno Heceta and Juan Francisco de la Bodega y Quadra came the following year. History's first encounter between whites and coastal Indians wasn't too pleasant. Quadra sent a boatload of men ashore to gather fuel and water, and they were killed by hostile residents.

The world outside paid little attention to this area until 1778, when Captain James Cook put in at Nootka Sound on Vancouver Island for ship repair. Obviously a better statesman than Quadra, he gathered a huge cargo of furs from the locals and sold them in Canton. Word about the Northwest's abundance spread quickly. England hurried to establish a fur trading industry, which would be dominated for decades by the legendary Hudson's Bay Company. Ten years after Cook's visit, Captain John Meares found the narrow passage between Vancouver Island and the mainland. He sailed into the island-studded Puget Sound and named the strait in honor of Juan de Fuca.

As interest in the Northwest grew, three countries became involved in a pushing match for domination. Russia sent fur-trapping expeditions south from Alaska. In 1792, America's Captain Robert Gray discovered the mouth of a great river and named it for his ship—*Columbia Rediviva,* which means "Columbus lives again." That same year, England's Captain George Vancouver explored the great sound to the north and named it in honor of one of his chief navigators, Peter Puget. Both Gray and Vancouver laid claim to the area for their respective governments. Although the Russians withdrew, troubled by problems at home, England and the United States continued pressing for sovereignty of the area.

In 1803, President Thomas Jefferson purchased the entire Mississippi-Missouri watershed for three cents an acre from cash-strapped Napoleon Bonaparte of France. Wondering what one got for three cents, he launched captains Meriwether Lewis and William Clark up the Missouri. Actually, he was more interested in finding a land and water route to the Pacific "for purposes of commerce." In other words, President Jefferson was eager to establish an American toe-hold in the rapidly developing Northwest.

Lewis and Clark worked upstream to the headwaters of the Missouri River, crossed the continental divide and picked up the source of the Clearwater. This led them to the Snake and ultimately the Columbia. The Corps of Discovery arrived at the mouth of the Pacific on November 15, 1805 and set up camp on the north side, intending to remain and explore until spring.

The future Washington State might have had the honor of hosting the group's winter camp, but as usual, the weather didn't cooperate. It was so wet and windy that the small band crossed to the Oregon side. They found a more sheltered spot on a small tributary the local Indians called the Netul River. (It's now the Lewis and Clark River, and their camp, Fort Clatsop, is a national historic site.)

After this remarkable expedition, American settlement of the Northwest began in earnest. In 1810, John Jacob Astor sent men and money west to establish the Pacific Fur Company, to compete against the Hudson's Bay Company. This precipitated an extended war of words—and an occasional musket shot—between America and Great Britain over control of the area. The British, backed up by gunboats, convinced Astor's group to abandon Astoria during the War of 1812. However, England never occupied the place and the Americans returned a few years later.

In 1818, the two nations drew up a loose joint occupancy agreement. It was renewed in 1827, subject to termination on a 12-month notice by either party. Meanwhile, the Hudson's Bay Company, assuming that the Columbia River would become the border between the two countries, moved its headquarters to Vancouver in 1824. It flourished as a regional trading center for decades, and the center of civilized society from Hawaii to Utah.

The trickle of American settlers into the Northwest turned into a flood after the Oregon Trail was blazed in 1842. Between 1840 and 1869, 250,000 to 300,000 pioneers followed this dusty path. One in ten perished en route, mostly from disease, thirst and hunger. Native Americans were responsible only for a few hundred pioneer deaths, while tens of thousands of them died at the hands of the whites.

### North along the Cowlitz

Although most early settlers went south from the Columbia, a few followed the Cowlitz Trail north along the tributary of that name. This took them along the present route of Interstate 5, ending at lower Tumwater Falls near Olympia. Thus, Washington's earliest communities were in this region. If you count its trading post status, Vancouver is the oldest Washington settlement, although Tumwater was the first civil community (1845), followed by Olympia (1850), Steilacoom (1851), Port Townsend and Seattle (both 1852). Steilacoom was the first to be incorporated, although it's now little more than a charming historical nub on the southwest Puget shoreline.

There was no regional government in the early 1840s, since the area was still under loose joint occupancy with England, so the Americans banded together to draw up their own laws. They set up a jury and property rights system, leading to the establishment of a civil authority in 1843. Not surprisingly, this provisional government began pressing for a formal division of land between the United States and England. It came with the establishment of the 49th parallel in 1846, and Vancouver suddenly found itself in American territory. The Treaty of 1846 did guarantee property rights of all British settlements, but the Hudson's Bay Company sold its rights for

$650,000. The otters and beavers were practically trapped out by this time, so the firm had little to gain by keeping its American inholdings.

This vast block of the American northwest, loosely referred to as Oregon Country, was formalized as the 400,000-square-mile Oregon Territory in 1848. Most settlement continued to go south, and the "northern Oregonians" above the Columbia River felt they were being poorly represented. Citizens groups convened at Cowlitz Landing (near present-day Toledo) in 1851 and Monticello (near Longview) in 1852, demanding their own regional government. The *Olympia Columbian* proclaimed on October 16, 1852:

*Citizens of northern Oregon! It behooves you to bestir yourselves, and proclaim your independence of the territorial authority exerted over you by the Willamette Valley.*

After receiving dispatches from the two conventions, Congress agreed in 1853 to establish a separate entity. Locals wanted to call it Columbia Territory. However, Representative Richard H. Stanton of Kentucky argued that the name would be confused with the District of Columbia. He suggested that it be changed to Washington Territory. (To this day of course, Washington State and Washington, D.C., are *still* being confused.)

The original territory included northern Idaho. When Oregon achieved statehood in 1859, the rest of Idaho and a piece of Wyoming that had been part of the Oregon territory were added to Washington. Idaho won territorial status in 1863 and Washington took its present shape. However, it wasn't granted statehood until 1889. The territory was predominantly Republican and the Democratic-controlled Congress used a variety of excuses to keep it out of the Union. "Too thinly populated," they said. "Too far away. Besides, the border with Canada hasn't been settled yet."

### Where's the border?

The latter point was somewhat valid. Although the border had been drawn along the 49th parallel, and then south around Vancouver Island, the sovereignty of the San Juan Islands was left in limbo. This led to one of the strangest wars in history, in which the only casualty was a pig. In 1859, an American settler shot a British oinker that was rooting in his potato patch. The irate British wanted him tried under their laws, but the American settlers refused to sanction it. Troops from both countries became engaged in a standoff that lasted until 1872, when Germany's Kaiser Wilhelm I, serving as an arbitrator, awarded the islands to the United States. (Details in the "Pig War" box on page 196.)

Despite Congressional reluctance to grant it statehood, Washington grew quickly in the latter half of the 19th century. Fewer than a thousand Americans lived north of the Columbia in 1850, then the number jumped to 75,000 in thirty years. The completion of the Northern Pacific and Great Northern railways in the 1880s brought new hoards. When statehood finally was achieved in 1889, Washington had more than 350,000 residents.

Growth continued into the next century. Spokane became the gateway to silver, gold and lead strikes in neighboring Idaho in the 1880s. The famous Klondike gold rush of 1897-1900 drew swarms of goldseekers through Seattle and up the Inside Passage to Alaska, along with a couple of good publicists—novelist Jack London and poet Robert Service. After the turn of the century, the Alaska-Yukon-Pacific Exposition was held on the future campus of the University of Washington. Nearly four million visitors attended, and America learned more about this prosperous corner of their nation.

The Great Depression had a powerful impact on Washington, and two familiar slang expressions emerged from those hard times. "Hooverville," a term for drifter camps, was first used to describe a packing crate shantytown near the Seattle waterfront. "Skid Row" is a distortion of the term "skid road," a wooden chute used to slide logs from lumber camps to mills. The first was built along Seattle's present-day Yesler Way in the 1850s. During hard times, out-of-work loggers congregated along these roads. The term eventually was applied to any area where the down-and-out gathered.

Washington was a major beneficiary of President Franklin D. Roosevelt's New Deal programs, with the construction of the Grand Coulee, Bonneville and other dams on the Columbia. After the Pearl Harbor attack, the state's cheap, abundant hydroelectric power became a magnet for the war industry. The resulting munitions industry gave Washington a quick economic boost. During the 1930s, the Boeing Airplane Company had developed America's first successful bomber, the B-17, and it quickly became the aerial weapon of choice during the war. Wartime shipbuilder Henry J. Kaiser installed a huge shipyard on the Columbia River in Vancouver, specializing in "baby flattops"—cargo ships with carrier decks. One of the nation's first atomic plants was built at Hanford, in central Washington.

These and other industries employed tens of thousands of workers during the war. Many stayed on to spur a post-war boom. Boeing continued its success by getting into the commercial jet market, which it still dominates. Seattle celebrated its prosperity with its financially successful 1962 World's Fair. It brought nearly ten million visitors and the city's most prominent landmark—the Space Needle. Spokane followed suite a decade later with Expo '74, the first world exposition to focus on the environment. Appropriately, it resulted in the cleanup of the polluted Spokane River and rehabilitation of a dilapidated industrial area. It is today a park and cultural center.

Of course, states heavily dependent on a few specialized industries are subject to economic roller coaster rides. The end of the war ended Vancouver's shipbuilding days, and it took that community decades to recover. Seattle's economy tends to rise and fall with aircraft orders. A billboard posted during an extremely bad downturn made coast-to-coast headlines:

*Will the last person to leave Seattle please turn out the lights?*

Lumbering is another industry subject to economic dementia. Washington, Oregon and Idaho supply 60 percent of the nation's timber, and the northern spotted owl has extinguished the lights on many lumber camps.

However, descendants of the seafarers, trappers, miners, lumberjacks and sodbusters who came to the great Northwest are made of tough stuff. They will weather these rough economic rides. Some say Washington is surviving too well. The Seattle-Olympic Interstate 5 corridor is growing so rapidly that it's beginning to resemble southern California's Santa Ana Freeway with pine trees.

Obviously, hard times will never extinguish the Evergreen State's lights.

## JUST THE FACTS

**Size** ● 66,709 square miles of land area, plus inland waterways for a total of 68,192; twentieth state in size. Measurements at the extremes are 341 miles by 238 miles.

**Population** ● 4,866,700 (1990 census). Largest city by far is Seattle with 516,300, and 2,559,200 in its greater metropolitan area. The next ten are Spokane (177,200), Tacoma (176,700), Everett (70,000), Yakima (54,900), Bellingham (52,200), Vancouver (46,500), Renton (41,700), Bremerton (38,100), Redmond (35,800) and Olympia (33,900).

**Elevations** ● Highest point is Mount Rainier at 14,411 feet; lowest is the interior of Ebey Island in Puget Sound, five feet below sea level.

**Admitted to the Union** ● November 11, 1889; became a territory March 2, 1853. State capital is Olympia.

**Time zone** ● Pacific.

**Area codes** ● (206) west of the Cascades and (509) to the east.

**Traffic laws** ● Same speed laws as most other states—55 on highways unless otherwise posted and 65 on most freeways outside urban areas (60 for trucks and trailers). If five or more vehicles are behind you on a two-lane road, you're required to use the next turnout to let them pass. Washington State Police use radar, but they aren't fanatics. Some do employ unmarked cars, usually white. Safety belts must be worn by occupants of all private vehicles; helmets are required for motorcyclists. Radar detectors are legal.

**Taxes** ● Statewide sales tax is 6.5 percent, with cities and counties permitted to add another half percent. Some special districts may tack on tax, too. Seattle collects a 7 percent lodging tax and the rest of King County 2.8 percent. Some other areas have lodging taxes, up to 2 percent.

**Alcoholic beverages** ● Hard liquor is sold only in state-operated stores, with high prices and rather arbitrary hours (never on Sunday). Wine and beer are available at various retail outlets. Drinking hours in licensed establishments are 6 a.m. to 2 a.m., and the legal sipping age is 21. Personal importation of any alcohol is prohibited, although there are no border checks.

**Pooches and kitties** ● Visitors' pets much be licensed in their home state and dogs more than four months old must have proof of a recent rabies vaccination.

**Official things** ● **Nickname**—Evergreen State; also the Chinook State for its most popular salmon; **state motto**—"Al-ki," which means bye and bye in Chinook (the Native American language, not fish talk); **state song**—"Washington My Home," penned by one Helen Davis of South Bend; **state flower**—coast rhododendron; **state tree**—western hemlock; **state bird**—willow goldfinch; **state quadruped**—Roosevelt elk; **state fish**—steelhead; **state rock**—petrified wood; **official colors**—green and gold.

## To learn more

**State welcome centers**—These are set up at points of entry to load up visitors with information on the state. They're located across the Oregon-Washington border in Vancouver, off I-5 at exit 1-D; the Custer Rest Area, seven miles south of the Canadian border on I-5; Sea-Tac International Airport at baggage claim level #9; Oroville, four miles south of the Canadian border on U.S. 97; Spokane River Rest Area, westbound I-90 at exit 299; Megler Rest Area, half a mile from the Astoria Bridge on Highway 401 in Ilwaco; Maryhill State Park, just over the Columbia River from Oregon on U.S. 97; and at Umatilla, off Interstate 82, half a mile from the border. Some info centers are open the year around; others from Memorial Day through Labor Day weekend.

**General travel information**—Travel Development Division, General Administration Building, Olympia, WA 98504; (206) 586-2088.

**Seattle area tourism**—Seattle-King County Convention and Visitors

Bureau, 800 Convention Place, Seattle, WA 98504; (206) 461-5800.

**Weather/highway conditions**—Call the National Weather Service at (206) 526-6087. For snow and mountain pass conditions, dial (900) 407-PASS nationally or (206) 434-PASS in Washington, October 1 through April 15.

**Commercial transportation**—A brochure covering airline, bus and shuttle services, *Passenger Transportation Options in Washington*, is available from the State Department of Transportation, (206) 705-7921.

**State park camping**—State Parks and Recreation Commission, P.O. Box 42650, Olympia, WA 98504-2650; (800) 562-0990 or (206) 753-2027.

**Other state camping and picnicking areas**—State Department of Natural Resources, c/o Photo and Map Sales, P.O. Box 47031, Olympia, WA 98504; (206) 902-1234.

**National park and forest information**—U.S. National Park and Forest Service office, 915 Second Avenue, Room 422, Seattle, WA 98174; (206) 553-1070.

**Ferry systems**—Washington State Ferries, Pier 52, Coleman Dock, Seattle, WA 98104-1487; (800) 84-FERRY (within Washington only) or (206) 464-6400.

**Hunting and freshwater fishing**—Department of Wildlife, 800 Capitol Way North, Olympia, WA 98504; (206) 753-5700.

**Salmon, shellfish and saltwater sportfishing**—Washington State Department of Fisheries, P.O. Box 43141, Olympia, WA 98504-3141; (206) 586-1425.

**Canada border crossing information**—U.S. Customs Service, (206) 442-4676.

**Bed & breakfast inn directory**—Washington State Bed & Breakfast Guild, 2442 NW Market Street, #355, Seattle, WA 98107; (206) 548-6224.

**Biking and bike trails**—State Department of Transportation, Transportation Building, Olympia, WA 98504, (206) 705-7277; also Cascade Bicycle Club, (206) 522-BIKE.

**Fairs and festivals**—Washington State Fair Association, P.O. Box AB, Moses Lake, WA 98837; (509) 765-6080.

**Farmers markets**—Washington State Farmers Market Association, 11910 C Meridian E., Suite 29, Puyallup, WA 98373.

**Hiking**—Washington State Trails Directory, (206) 586-2102.

**Hostels**—Washington State American Youth Hostels, 419 Queen Anne Avenue N., #101, Seattle, WA 98109; (206) 281-7306.

**Hotel/motel directory**—Washington Hotel/Motel Association, 3605 132nd Avenue, SE, Suite 320 (One Newport Building), Bellevue, WA 98006; (206) 957-4587.

**Wine tasting**—Washington Wine Commission, P.O. Box 61217, Seattle, WA 98121; (206) 728-2252; free brochure or a tasting guide for $2.

# PHOTO TIPS: PRETTY AS A PICTURE?

As we travel, we've watched scores of people take hundreds of photos and shoot thousands of feet of videotape. We can tell by their set-ups that most of the shots will be poor and they'll be disappointed when they get back home. By following a few simple steps, you can greatly improve your images. These pointers won't make you a pro, but they'll bring better results the next time you point and shoot.

## *Still cameras*

Most of these suggestions work with the simplest fixed focus cameras, even the disposables, in addition to more complex ones.

**1. Get the light right.** In photography, light is everything. Avoid shooting objects that are hit by direct sunlight; it washes them out. Try to catch light coming from an angle to accentuate shadows, giving depth and detail to your subject. Photo light is best from sunup to mid-morning and from mid-afternoon to sunset.

**2. Frame your photos.** Before you shoot, compose the image in the viewfinder. Eliminate distracting objects such as signs or utility poles by changing your position. Or, line up your shot so the offending sign is behind a bush. When shooting people, make sure a utility pole or tree isn't sprouting from a subject's head.

**3. Create depth, not clutter.** If you're shooting scenery, give dimension to the photo with something in the background (craggy mountains), the middleground (someone in the meadow) and the foreground (a tree limb to frame the photo). On the other hand, if you're focusing on a specific object such as wildlife or an intriguing rock formation, keep the photo simple; don't clutter it.

**3. Take pictures, not portraits.** Endless shots of Auntie Maude standing in front of the scenery and squinting into your lens are pretty boring. Everyone already knows what she looks like, so let professionals at home shoot the family portraits.

**4. Put life in your lens.** On the other hand, people *do* add life to scenic photos. Instead of posing them in front of the scenery, let them interact with it. The kids can add life to beach scenes by feeding the gulls or building sand castles. Ask your mate to stroll from the historic building or perch carefully on the canyon rim. Maybe Aunt Maude can extend a tentative finger toward the prickly cactus. Also, have people wear bright clothes to add splashes of color to the photo.

## *Video cameras*

**1. Follow the above principles** for lighting, framing and posing. You may want to create your own titles by shooting identifying signs.

**2. Plan ahead.** Think of what you're going to shoot before you pull the trigger. Be a good director and plot each sequence.

**3. Hold her steady.** You're shooting *moving* pictures, which means that the subjects should be moving, not the video camera. Keep it steady and let people walk in and out of the picture. Limit your panning; give viewers a chance to focus on the scenery.

**4. Don't doom your zoom.** A zoom lens is a tool, not a toy. Keep your zooming to a minimum, or you'll make your audience seasick.

## Chapter two

# SOUTHWEST WASHINGTON
### From Vancouver to volcanoes to the big river

---

**WE BEGIN** where Washington began, in the most versatile corner of this versatile state. The southwest is a microcosm of the rest of Washington, offering a menu of thick woodlands, imposing peaks, sandy seacoasts and history-rich towns.

Many visitors catch their first glimpse of the Evergreen State here, coming from the south through Portland on Interstate 5 and crossing the Columbia River to Vancouver. Others arrive from the east on I-84 and swing north, having experienced Oregon's side of the splendid Columbia River Gorge.

They see, greatly modified, what the earliest explorers saw. This is a land marked by water, trees, mountains and buttermilk skies—the archetypical Pacific Northwest landscape. The Columbia River, wider than a mile, flows serenely past, carrying two million gallons of water per second toward the Pacific. Where mankind has not built, evergreens sprout. On a clear day, the volcanic peaks of the Cascade Range show their snowy crowns. On most days, of course, the peaks hide their heads in the clouds.

In this region, Washington's roots go deeper than those of its well-watered trees. Boston navigator Captain Robert Gray sparked America's interest in the Pacific Northwest when he discovered the mouth of the Columbia. He sailed across its dangerous sand bars in 1792. Lewis and Clark ended their epic journey in this corner in 1805, and would have wintered on the Washington side had it not been for soggy weather.

The British built the first major settlement at Vancouver in 1824. They

# TRIP PLANNER

**WHEN TO GO** ● Fall offers the most predictable weather in Washington's soggy southwest corner, although some attractions and museums reduce their hours then. Summer offers a mix of overcast skies and sunshine, and the most crowds in the more popular areas. Most things are reachable in winter in the southwest, except the heights of Mount St. Helens and Mount Rainier.

**WHAT TO SEE** ● Vancouver's Officer's Row and Fort Vancouver National Historic Site; Mount St. Helens National Volcanic Monument and Mount Rainier National Park; Northwest Trek wildlife park near Eatonville; Cowlitz Salmon Hatchery near Mossyrock; historic Oysterville; Fort Canby State Park; Cowlitz County Historical Museum in Kelso; the Columbia River Gorge; Bonneville and The Dalles dams on the Columbia River; Maryhill Museum and Stonehenge in Sam Hill Country.

**WHAT TO DO** ● Have a margarita over the river at Who-Song and Larry's in Vancouver; climb to the crater rim and hike the Ape Canyon trail in Mount St. Helens Volcanic National Monument; hike the trail to Burroughs Mountain from Sunrise and the Skyline Trail from Paradise in Mount Rainier National Park; go fly a kite on Long Beach; pig out on seafood and chips at Ship Inn, Astoria (wrong state, great fish and chips); climb Beacon Rock; and spend an elegant weekend at Skamania Lodge in the Columbia River Gorge; study the heavens through the Goldendale Observatory's public telescopes.

## Useful contacts

**Battle Ground Chamber of Commerce,** 1012 E. Main St., Battle Ground, WA 98604; (206) 687-1510.

**Goldendale Chamber of Commerce,** P.O. Box 524 (126 W. Main St.), Goldendale, WA 98620; (800) 648-5462 or (509) 773-3400.

**Kelso Chamber of Commerce,** 105 Minor, Kelso, WA 98626; 577-8058.

**Lewis River Valley Coalition,** P.O. Box 503, Cougar, WA 98616; (206) 263-6030.

**Long Beach Peninsula Visitors Bureau,** P.O. Box 562, Long Beach, WA 98631; (800) 451-2542 or (206) 642-2400.

**Longview Chamber of Commerce,** 1563 Olympia Way, Longview, WA 98632; (206) 423-8400.

**Mount Adams Chamber of Commerce,** P.O. Box 449, White Salmon, WA 98672; (509) 493-3630.

**Vancouver/Clark County Visitors & Convention Bureau,** 404 E. Fifteenth St., Suite 11, Vancouver, WA 98663; (800) 377-7084 or (206) 693-1313.

**Woodland Chamber of Commerce,** P.O. Box 1012 (1225 Lewis River Rd.), Woodland, WA 98674; (206) 225-9552.

## Southwestern Washington radio stations

KMUZ, 94.7-FM, Portland—easy listening
KISN, 97.1-FM, Vancouver—oldies
KWFF, 99.5-FM, Portland—country
KXXO, 96.1 FM, Olympia—top forty; light rock
KUKN, 94.5 FM, Kelso-Longview—country
KMNT, 102.9-FM, Centralia-Chehalis—country
KTLU, 88.5 and 90.3-FM, Tacoma-Seattle—National Public Radio.
KKEE, 94.3-FM, Astoria—rock
KAST, 92.9-FM, Long Beach—soft rock
KUPL, 98.5-FM and 1330-AM, Olympia—country
KAST, 1370-AM, Long Beach—news and talk
KVAS, 1230-AM, Astoria—country
KGY, 1240-AM, Olympia—top 40 and news

shared occupancy of this region with early American pioneers, who swung north from the Oregon Trail. This corner became part of the Oregon Territory when the British-American boundary was settled at the 49th parallel. It was here—near present-day Toledo and Longview—that American residents met and petitioned Congress to grant them their own territory. Not surprisingly, all of the state's earliest communities are in the southwest, beginning with Tumwater, settled 1845 at the end of the Cowlitz Trail. The Cowlitz River, flowing west out of the Cascades and then south to the Columbia, had shaped an inviting valley for the newcomers.

One can imagine their relief on arrival, after surviving the 2,000-mile crossing to Oregon, and then the final bushwhack north through heavy timber. Your Washington entry will be considerably less strenuous, but probably not as exhilarating. Coming from the south or the east, you have two easy freeway choices for access. Both I-5 and I-205 will hurry you through the growing suburbs of Portland, Oregon's largest city. Try to avoid it at rush hour. (Should you want to linger, our *Oregon Discovery Guide* will point you in some interesting directions.)

We prefer the I-5 approach, since we enjoy snaking over the webwork of bridges and overpasses along Portland's handsome waterfront. Also, the trip across the Interstate Bridge into Washington takes you to an ideal starting point—a welcome center operated jointly by Washington and the Vancouver/Clark County Visitors Bureau.

# Vancouver

**Population: 46,500**                                      **Elevation: 42 feet**

Communities claiming to be the oldest in Washington, such as Tumwater (first settlement) and Steilacoom (first incorporated town) tend to overlook Vancouver. Perhaps, in a fit of provincialism, they disqualify it because it was a *British* colony, and a fur-trading post at that. Hardly the sort of place where one puts down the plow and raises up children.

Technicalities aside, Vancouver was the first settlement in Washington, started in 1824 by the Hudson's Bay Company. Further, it wasn't just a wilderness outpost. It was built as headquarters for the company's Pacific Department, re-located from Fort George near the mouth of the Columbia, in present-day British Columbia. The move was intended to head off America's growing presence in the area. During two brief decades of glory, it ruled over five trading stations and 23 forts. It was the centerpiece of an empire extending from Oregon north to British Columbia and east through Idaho. Its trade routes reached west to the Sandwich Islands and beyond to the mystic Orient.

Fort Vancouver's chief factor, Dr. John McLoughlin, was easily the most powerful man in this corner of the world. However, as more gringos arrived on the Oregon Trail, he realized that American domination of the area was inevitable. He defied company orders by providing shelter, seed, farm tools and encouragement to the newcomers. Forced out of the company in 1845 for his pro-American sympathies, he moved across the river to present-day Oregon City, where he'd already purchased land. Indeed, this Quebec-born physician is described by historians as the "father of Oregon." A few years after the international border was set in 1846, the Hudson's Bay Company sold its trading post to the Americans. The original fort fell to ruin and was destroyed by fire in 1866.

Vancouver would see more glory days, however. The U.S. Army had established a barracks above the original British fort in 1849. By the end of that century, it had become the social and cultural center of the Pacific Northwest. Fine Victorian mansions were built along Officers' Row, occupied both by military commanders and leading merchants of the fast-growing city of Vancouver. The town thrived as a busy port for river traffic headed for gold and silver mines in eastern Washington and Idaho, and as a provisioning center for this growing region.

The Depression sent Vancouver into a slump during the first half of this century. It rebounded when Henry J. Kaiser leased land from pioneer families and built a huge World War II shipyard. Today, it is a thriving suburb of Portland. Like Dr. McLaughlin, many its citizens may identify more with Oregon than with Washington. It does, however, offer its own employment base, centered around paper pulp and aluminum production.

## Driving Vancouver

As you cross the Columbia River, Vancouver appears as a neat and bustling but ordinary riverfront town. However, its historic fort area and well-preserved old downtown give it special appeal. Also, with a plenitude of motels and restaurants, it's a good place to pause and plan your tourist attack on Washington State.

Shortly after you clear the Interstate Bridge on I-5, take exit 1-D and follow signs eastward to the **Washington Information Center.** It's open daily from 8 to 6 Memorial Day through Labor Day, and 8:30 to 4:30 the rest of the year.

From here, continue through the parking lot, turn right onto Fourth Plain Boulevard, go east a few blocks to a stoplight, and turn right again onto Fort Vancouver Way. Across the street is **Vancouver Central Park,** an inviting place with emerald green lawns rimmed by thick woodlands. Continue down Fort Vancouver Way a few blocks, past **Clark College,** and you enter a traffic circle at the **U.S. Army Barracks Vancouver.**

☺ Dance around the traffic circle to your left onto Evergreen Boulevard, and you're on **Officers' Row,** lined with grand old shade trees and splendidly restored 19th century mansions. Most are occupied by professional offices and condos, although two are open to the public. We describe the 1850 **Grant House** folk art center and cafè (1101 Officers' Row) and the 1866 **Marshall House** museum exhibits (1301 Officers' Row) under "Attractions" below.

☺ The **Fort Vancouver Visitor Center** is a couple of blocks beyond the Marshall House. From there, you can follow a landscaped lane—by foot or by vehicle—down to **Fort Vancouver National Historic Site**, just above the riverfront on East Fifth Street. Exhibits in the visitor center cover the fort's role as a trading post and later U.S. Army post, while the historic site is a partial reconstruction of the original trading post. A third attraction, **Pearson Air Museum,** is nearby, a focal point of the oldest continually operating airfield in America.

If you or your parents were involved in the frenetic American war industry during World War II, you may enjoy visiting the site of the **Kaiser Vancouver Shipyard**. (Perhaps you were a Rosie riveter.) Several exhibits at a riverfront park and viewing platform recall those days when Vancouver was a wartime boomtown.

To get there, continue east from the air museum on Fifth Street more than a mile to Grand Boulevard, turn right and follow it down to State Route 14, the Lewis and Clark Highway. Turn right again to double back a couple of miles toward town. Watch on your left for a sign at a traffic light, indicating a **riverfront viewing tower** and boat launch. At the sign, turn left into an industrial park and quickly left again to parallel your course back along Highway 14. After two miles of industrial park, which occupies the site of the former shipyard, turn right at a landscaped park. The road takes you down to the Kaiser exhibit and viewing platform.

When you've finished reading about baby flattops, Mr. Kaiser and the American defense industry, you can climb the three-story platform for nice views of the mighty Columbia. Wide and smooth enough to be a lake, it's busy with barges, freighters and pleasure craft. Across the way, air traffic rumbles skyward from **Portland International Airport**

Find your way back to Highway 14 and follow it west into Vancouver. As you approach its juncture with I-5, exit onto Washington Street, which carries you into the **historic downtown area.** It's a pleasant blend of restored 19th and early 20th century buildings, mixed in with new architecture. Although a few empty storefronts mark typical urban business flight, the area is tidy and interesting, if you like old brick and masonry. It's laid out in a compact grid with Daniels, Columbia, Washington, Main and Broadway running south to north, and Sixth through Thirteenth going west to east. What should be Tenth Street is Evergreen Boulevard, and a turn eastward will take you back to Officers' Row. En route, you'll pass the monumental **Providence Academy** at 400 East Evergreen. Built in 1873 of 300,000 locally-made bricks, it now houses small shops.

Among downtown attractions are the **Clark County Museum** at Main and Sixth, and several appealing old brick and stone churches. One houses the **Columbia Art Center** at Daniels and Evergreen. Check out the **Covington House** at 4201 Main, an 1848 log cabin. **Esther Short Park,** at Columbia and West Eighth, is Washington's oldest public square, set aside in 1853. Worthy of a look are the park's 1867 **Slocum House,** now used as a community theater, plus an imposing woodcarving of a Native American, and a bronze monument to pioneer women.

Also worth a pause is the **Victorian Marketplace** at Evergreen and Columbia, a small courtyard shopping mall with few boutiques. **McFarland's Deli and Eatery** here is a good place to catch lunch (listed below under "Where to dine").

In case you didn't load up on brochures at the welcome center, stop by the **Vancouver/Clark County Convention and Visitors Bureau** at 15th and E streets, housed in a modern brick office complex; it's open weekdays 9 to 5. The parking lot is in back, between 15th and 16th streets. The bureau's *Vancouver USA Heritage Tours* brochure will help steer you through the historic downtown area and Officers' Row. You can get stuff from a brochure rack in the hall when the office is closed.

A nice way to end a day here is with a riverfront dinner or cocktails at one of two Columbia-view cafès, **Who-Song and Larry's Restaurant and Cantina** or the **Charthouse.** Both have decks over the water. We particularly like the cantina's ambiance and the chips 'n' salsa that arrive free with a drink order. To reach the restaurants, follow Columbia Street toward the river until it swings eastward under I-5 freeway as Columbia Way.

**Old Apple Tree Park** out this way contains the Northwest's oldest apple tree. It was planted at the behest of Dr. McLoughlin in 1826 and it still bears fruit.

## ATTRACTIONS
### In order of appearance

☺ *Officers' Row* • *Evergreen Street, between Fort Vancouver Way and East Reserve Street. Grant House at 1101 Officers' Row; museum (206) 696-9699; café (206) 699-1213. Tuesday-Saturday 10 to 4 and Sunday noon to 5; museum admission $2, kids and seniors $1. See "Where to dine" below for meal hours. Marshall House at 1301 Officers' Row; (206) 693-3103. Weekdays 9 to 5 and weekends 11 to 6 (may close for special events); donations appreciated.*

Two former commanding officers' homes are among the 21 restored mansions along the row. The area was falling to ruin and threatened with demolition when the City of Vancouver bought the crumbling buildings from the Army for $1 each. It then floated a $10 million bond issue to restore them. The project was completed in 1987 and rents from tenants are paying off the bonds.

The two public buildings are named for famous former military tenants. Ulysses S. Grant was stationed here as a brevet captain shortly after the Grant House was built in 1850. It's now a folk art museum with changing exhibits, and a restaurant (listed below). The Marshall House is named for General George C. Marshall, originator of the Marshall Plan that helped re-build post-war Europe. He was district commander here from 1936 until 1938. This beautifully restored Queen Anne Victorian is an exhibit center operated by the City of Vancouver, with period furnishings, displays concerning Marshall's illustrious career and a 20-minute slide show about Fort Vancouver and Officers' Row.

☺ *Fort Vancouver National Historic Site* • *Visitor center on East Evergreen Boulevard; daily 9 to 5; free. Historic site a quarter mile below on East Fifth Street; daily, summer 9 to 5 and winter 9 to 4; $2 per person, $4 for family groups, free for seniors; (206) 696-7655.* ⊡ A fine museum at the visitor center traces Fort Vancouver's history from its beaver pelt days to the U.S. Army era. A 15-minute video is shown on request. One learns that 60,000 pelts a year were "harvested" in the Northwest until the beavers were nearly annihilated toward the middle of the last century. The Hudson's Bay Company motto was *Pro pelle cutem,* Latin for "a skin for a skin." This must have been rather disconcerting for the poor animals.

The nearby fort is a faithful reconstruction of the original stockade, which was built not to protect the British traders from Indians, but to fend off a possible American attack. Visitors enter the grassy compound through an extensive 1825-style garden. They can poke through several squared-log buildings, including a blacksmith shop, dispensary and kitchen. In the more formal white clapboard McLoughlin house, you learn that the British lived rather graciously in this wilderness outpost, enjoying seven course dinners on Blue Willow china and sterling tea service. Within the fort's spiked log stockade, you can almost imagine life here more than a century ago—if you can tune out the jet noise from Portland International across the river. A three-story bastion offers slotted views through gun ports of the Columbia and surrounding countryside. Living history demonstrations and tours are given periodically at the fort.

☺ **Pearson Air Museum** ● *Pearson Airpark, 1105 E. Fifth St.; (206) 694-7026. Wednesday-Sunday noon to 5. Adults $2, kids $1.* ⊔ Opened in 1905 and now part of the U.S. Army Vancouver Barracks, Pearson Airpark is the oldest operating airport in America. A hanger houses a fine collection of vintage aircraft, mostly tail-draggers from the 1920s and 1930s. Kids can get their wings at a gift shop while mom and pop study historic photos and flight regalia. A monument nearby marks the completion of the first non-stop polar flight from the former Soviet Union to the United States, in 1937. They were headed for Oakland, California, but ran short of fuel.

**Clark County Historical Museum** ● *1511 Main St.; (206) 695-4681. Tuesday-Sunday 1 to 5; donations appreciated.* ⊔ Clark County's yesterdays are preserved in mockups of a typical country store, doctor's office and print shop. A railroad exhibit in the museum basement focuses on the Portland-Seattle Railway that boosted early settlement, and the construction of rails through the Columbia River Gorge. While not professional, the museum is pleasingly done, without a lot of pioneer clutter.

**Covington House** ● *4208 Main St.; (206) 696-8171. Open June through August, Tuesdays and Thursdays 10 to 4; free.* ⊔ Erected in 1848 as the first school in Washington, this simple log cabin has a few pioneer exhibits. It was built by Richard and Anne Covington near the fort and moved downtown in the 1920s.

## ACTIVITIES

**Farmers market** ● Held at Fifth and Broadway, Saturdays 9 to 3, from May through October; (206) 737-8298.

**Heritage tours** ● Walks through Officers' Row and historic Vancouver are conducted by the Heritage Trust of Clark County; (206) 699-2359.

**Railway excursion** ● Lewis and Clark Railway offers 2.5-hour excursions from Battle Ground, northeast of Vancouver, along the scenic Lewis River to Moulton Falls. Regular rides are $10 for adults and $5 for kids; meal trips and holiday runs also are scheduled. Contact: Lewis and Clark Railway, 1000 E. Main St., Battle Ground, WA 98604; (206) 687-2626.

**Scenic flights** ● Vancouver Aviation, 101-A E. Reserve St., Vancouver, WA 98661; (206) 695-3821. The firm offers Mount St. Helens and Portland scenic flights, plus dinner flights with a hop over Portland to Hillsboro.

## ANNUAL EVENTS

**Rose Show** at Vancouver Mall, mid-June; (206) 896-1765.

**Fort Vancouver Days** city-wide celebration, late June through early July; (206) 693-1313.

**Town Plaza Antique Show,** mid-July at 5400 E. Mill Plain Blvd.; (206) 694-8691.

**Fort Vancouver Brigade Encampment,** late July, with period costumes and exhibits; (206) 696-7655.

**Clark County Fair** early August in nearby Ridgefield; (206) 573-1921.

**Northwest Antique Airplane Fly-in,** late August at Evergreen Airport, 13800 E. Mill Plain Blvd.; (206) 892-5028.

## WHERE TO DINE

**The Chart House** ● △△ **$$$**

⊔ *101 E. Columbia Way; (206) 693-9211. American, mostly seafood; full bar service. Lunch weekdays 11:15 to 2, dinner nightly 5 to 10. Major credit cards.* ☐ Franchise seafood and prime rib place with pleasingly simple nautical dècor and river-view dining, indoors or out.

☺ **Grant House Café** ● ΔΔ **$$** Ø

☐ *1101 Officers' Row; (206) 699-1213. American; wine and beer. Lunch Tuesday-Saturday 11 to 3, Sunday brunch 10 to 2, closed Monday. MC/VISA, AMEX.* ☐ Disarmingly charming little cafè in the historic Grant House, all done up in Victorian furnishings, with bentwood chairs and pink nappery. Menu features Northwest and other American specialties, ranging from Northwest forest salad to old fashioned chicken & dumplings.

☺ **The Hidden House** ● ΔΔΔ **$$$** Ø

☐ *100 W. Thirteenth St. (at Main); (206) 696-2847. American-continental; full bar service. Lunch weekdays from 11, dinner Tuesday-Sunday from 5, closed Monday. MC/VISA, AMEX.* ☐ Hardly hidden, this stylish 1885 red brick mansion is Vancouver's most elegant restaurant. It's named for the pioneer Hidden family that made its money in bricks and other local industries. The dining room is a study in Victorian opulence, with stained glass, polished woods and print wallpaper. The fare, not original but nicely done, ranges from scampi and mahi mahi to chicken piccata and vegetarian lasagna.

**McFarland's Deli and Eatery** ● △ **$**

☐ *Victorian Marketplace at Evergreen and Columbia; (206) 694-5107. Weekdays 6 a.m. to 5:30 p.m., Saturdays 9 to 3.* ☐ Nice little cafè serving light breakfast and lunch fare; adjacent Java House offers coffees and pastries. Dining tables in an attractive courtyard.

☺ **Who-Song and Larry's Restaurant and Cantina** ● ΔΔ **$$**

☐ *111 E. Columbia Way; (206) 695-1198. Mexican-American; full bar service. Monday-Thursday 11:30 to 10, Friday-Saturday 11:30 to 11 and Sunday 10 to 10 (brunch 10 to 2). MC/VISA, AMEX.* ☐ An exceptionally appealing place in spite of—or perhaps because of—its brightly contrived Mexican gimmickry. This member of the El Torito chain perches over the river, serving great margaritas with chips 'n' salsa. The joint jumps and the menu is typical Gringo-Mexican, ranging from the requisite fajitas to a rather good shrimp pico pico with salsa and lemon rice. Indoor and outdoor dining.

## WHERE TO SLEEP

**Best Western Ferryman's Inn** ● ⌒⌒⌒ **$$$** Ø

☐ *7901 NE Sixth Ave. (I-5 exit 4), Vancouver, WA 98665; (206) 574-2151. Couples $54 to $54, singles $49. Major credit cards.* ☐ Nicely-furnished 133-unit motel with TV movies, radios, room phones, rental VCRs; indoor pool, spa, exercise room.

**Comfort Inn** ● ⌒⌒ **$$$** Ø

☐ *13207 NE 20th Ave. (at 134th Street), Vancouver, WA 98686; (800) 221-2222 or (206) 574-6000. Couples $45 to $59, singles $40 to $53. Major credit cards.* ☐ Fifty-eight attractively furnished rooms with TV movies, phones, refrigerators and microwaves; continental breakfast; exercise room; laundry facilities.

**Nendel's Suites** ● ⌒⌒⌒ **$$** Ø

☐ *7001 NE Highway 99 (I-5 exit 4 east), Vancouver, WA 98665; (800) 547-0106 or (206) 696-0516. Couples $44.75 to $54.50, singles $40.25 to*

*$42.50. Major credit cards.* ❑ All-suite hotel with kitchens; 72 units with TV movies, phones, rental VCRs; coin laundry, pool and spa.

### Red Lion Inn at the Quay ● ⌂⌂⌂ $$$$ Ø

❑ *100 Columbia St. (at the waterfront), Vancouver, WA 98660; (206) 694-8341. Couples $88 to $110, singles $73 to $105. Major credit cards.* ❑ Attractive 160-unit lodge with river-view or courtyard-view rooms; TV movies, phones; pool, boat dock. **Restaurant** serves 6 a.m. to 10 p.m.; American; dinners $10 to $16; full bar service.

### Salmon Creek Motel ● ⌂ $$ Ø

❑ *11901 NE Highway 99 (exit 36 northbound), Vancouver, WA 98686; (206) 573-0751. Major credit cards.* ❑ Couples and efficiency units $42 to $50, singles $38 to $45. MC/VISA. Eighteen units with TV movies, room phones; some two-bedroom family units and efficiencies (no utensils).

### Value Motel ● ⌂ $

❑ *708 NE 78th St. (at Highway 99), Vancouver, WA 98686; (206) 574-2345. Couples $22 to $40, singles $20 to $30, kitchenettes from $40, or $200 weekly. MC/VISA.* ❑ Simple, clean new motel with TV and phones, coin laundry. Near downtown.

## WHERE TO CAMP
### Vancouver and north toward Mount St. Helens

**Battle Ground Lake State Park** ● *18002 NE 249th St., Battle Ground, WA 98604; (206) 687-4621. RV and tent sites, $10. No reservations or credit cards.* ❑ Nineteen miles northeast of Vancouver, then three miles east on State Highway 503. Shaded, nicely-spaced sites with tables and fire pits, flush and pit potties. Nature trails, lake with marina, boat launch and swimming.

**Big Fir Campground & RV Park** ● *5515 NE 259th St., Ridgefield, WA 98642; (800) 532-4397 or (206) 887-8970. RV and tent sites, $14.50 to $16. Reservations accepted; Major credit cards.* ❑ Thirteen miles north of Vancouver on I-5, then four miles east from Ridgefield exit 14. Tree-shaded sites with showers, picnic tables, barbecues; mini-mart, fishing, horseshoes, volleyball and board games.

**Columbia Riverfront RV Park** ● *1881 Dike Rd., Woodland, WA 98674; (800) 845-9842 or (206) 225-8051. RV sites only, $15.50 to $17.50. Reservations accepted; MC/VISA.* ❑ I-5 exit 22 above Woodland, then west on Dike Access Road. Showers, swimming pool, cable TV and phone hookups, coin laundry, fishing, picnic and recreation area.

**Jantzen Beach RV Park** ● *1503 N. Hayden Island Dr., Portland, OR 97217; (800) 443-7248 or (503) 289-7626. RV sites from $20. Reservations accepted; MC/VISA.* ❑ Full hookups, some shaded sites and pull-throughs; showers, laundry, pool, rec room and playground. Although it's in Oregon, it's within minutes of Vancouver. Take exit 308 off I-5 north of Portland onto Hayden Island in the Columbia River and go west.

**Lewis River RV Park** ● *3125 Lewis River Rd., Woodland, WA 98674; (206) 225-9556. RV and tent sites, $12.50 to $13.75. Reservations accepted; MC/VISA.* ❑ State Highway 503 exit from I-5 at Woodland, then five miles east; on the Lewis River. Some shaded sites and pull-throughs. Showers, swimming pool, boat dock and boat rentals, mini-mart, coin laundry, horseshoes, fishing, rec field, hiking trails; golfing nearby.

**99 RV Park** ● *1913 Leichner Rd., Vancouver, WA 98686; (206) 573-0351. RV sites only, $11. Reservations accepted.* ⛺ Five miles north on I-5; take 134th Street (exit 7) a block east to Highway 99, then south a third of a mile and right on Leichner Road. Showers; coin laundry, beauty shop, RV service; near shops and restaurants.

**Paradise Point State Park** ● *At La Center, south of Woodland; (206) 263-2350. RV and tent sites, $10. No reservations or credit cards.* ⛺ Nineteen miles north of Vancouver on I-5; take La Center exit 16 east, then immediately north on a frontage road and follow it a mile. Shaded spots, tables and fire pits; flush and pit potties. Lake with boat launch, swimming areas; nature trails.

# VANCOUVER TO ST. HELENS

Vancouver properly calls itself the gateway to Mount St. Helens National Volcanic Monument. Indeed, its citizens felt the tremors, saw the smoke and breathed the ash when the restless volcano threw a tantrum in 1980. The crater is just over 40 miles northeast, as the cinders fly. Another 40 miles beyond is Mount Rainier National Park, so the pair offers a handy tour package for visitors.

Mount St. Helens is America's only natural preserve that arrived as a media event, with screaming banner headlines and vivid video coverage on the six o'clock news. It thus holds special intrigue in this day of mini-cams and instant information. Although Mount Rainier National Park is one of our most magnificent monuments with its

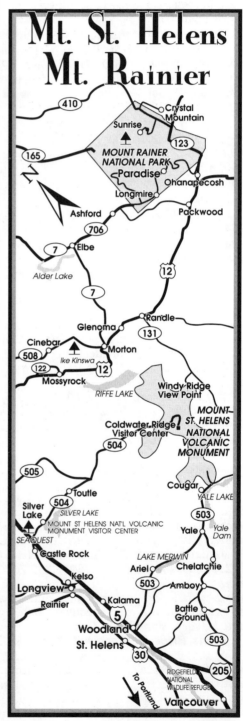

arctic heights and glistening glaciers, St. Helens gets most of the attention in this area. It's rimmed by visitor centers, both official and contrived. One of the best—an official one at Silver Lake—is many miles from the park. It's reached by turning east from I-5 north of Vancouver onto State Highway 504 at Castle Rock. Many citizens take this quick drive, study the center's exhibits, watch the videos, talk with desk-bound rangers and never approach the mountain.

Several airports in the region offer scenic flights. Mount St. Helens ash figurines are southwest Washington's gimmick souvenir of choice. (In several days' exploration of these two parks, we never encountered souvenirs made from Rainier glacier silt.)

There are two logical approaches to Mount St. Helens from Vancouver—through Battle Ground and Amboy via state highways 502 and 503, or up to Woodland on I-5 and then east. We prefer the latter route, since it takes you through the appealing Lewis River Valley, and alongside two reservoirs.

But first, a few notes on the Battle Ground-Amboy approach: Despite its intriguing name, **Battle Ground** is but a rural backwash of Vancouver with little to lure visitors. The name comes from an incident in 1855 when a group of Indians imprisoned at Fort Vancouver escaped, and their leader was accidentally killed in this area. The pursuing soldiers humanely let the fugitives bury their chief, and there was no battle. Still, the name was attached to a farming hamlet established there in 1902. Battle Ground's main items of interest are its old train depot and the **Lewis and Clark Railroad,** whose excursions we've listed above.

An administrative office of Mount St. Helens National Volcanic Monument is four miles northeast of **Amboy** on Highway 503. Hours are 7:30 to 5 weekdays. Although monument exhibits are limited, you can pick up a brochure and copy of *Volcano Review,* a seasonal information guide.

If you choose our preferred route and head north from Vancouver on I-5, you'll pass through rolling pasturelands and farmlands that once were forests. The Columbia River, flowing north before its final westward run to the Pacific, parallels the freeway, although it remains hidden until you approach **Woodland.** Just short of that small town, you pass tiny **La Center** and the exit to **Paradise Point State Park** (listed above).

Woodland was a quiet farming and lumbering town and a freeway fueling stop until it became a Mount St. Helens gateway. Several service stations, small motels and family cafés now cluster around the interchange. The town's local claim to fame is **Hulga Klager Lilac Gardens,** an extensive floral display rimming a Victorian estate. Hulga hybridized award-winning lilacs, and she planted and tended thousands of other blooming plants until her death at age 95, in 1960. To see the extensive gardens, now open to the public, drive west through old downtown Woodland and go left onto South Pekin Road. Signs point the way. The gardens are open daily 10 to 4; $1 donation. House tours are conducted in summer; call (206) 225-8996.

# Mount St. Helens National Volcanic Monument

The statistics will—forgive the pun—blow you away. Like a giant maiden with a troubled stomach, this mountain had been grumbling and fussing for several weeks in the spring of 1980. Scientists eager to study an awaking volcano hurried to plant seismometers and take her pulse. As she grew more restless, residents and visitors were advised to leave.

On the morning of May 18, an hour and a half before a caravan of Spirit Lake area residents was to return and remove their belongings, the mountain exploded. An earthquake had triggered a landslide, which literally took the cap off a giant north-facing pressure dome. Millions of cubic yards of rock and ash roared down the mountain and filled Spirit Lake, raising its level by 180 feet. Ash plumes soared several miles in the air and then fell to earth, blanketing several nearby communities. Hot ash and mud flows, fed by melted snowfields, rushed down riverbeds, gouging new valleys. Four billion board feet of lumber was destroyed. Trees were plastered against the mountains for miles around. They fell with the contours of the hot shock waves, and lay like hastily combed thick hair. Fifty-seven people died in one of North America's worst natural disasters, some as far as 25 miles away. A 240-square mile area was devastated, 220 homes were destroyed and dozens of miles of road and rails were ripped up.

When the smoke and ash cleared, the once beautiful and nearly symmetrical cone was gone, replaced by an ugly gash on the north side. Gorgeous Spirit Lake, home to the stubborn and now-legendary Harry Truman, was a muddy mire of ash and floating logs. (See box.) The mountain was 1,312 feet lower; a pristine wilderness of lush evergreens and waterways was a no-man's land, like a giant set for a World War I movie.

Officials of Gifford Pinchot National Forest, which surrounds St. Helens, wanted to set aside much of the blast area as a natural preserve. It would allow scientists to watch and study as the area recovered, undisturbed by man. Mount St. Helens National Volcanic Monument was created in 1982.

The area's rapid recovery is perhaps its most intriguing feature. We've been there several times since the eruption, and each time we are amazed at the speed with which plant and animal life has been reestablished. Within a year of the blast, bright purple fireweed poked timidly through thick layers of ash. Now, baby evergreen forests are peppering the slopes like free-form Christmas tree farms. Returning to Mount St. Helens is like visiting an outdoor museum that offers changing exhibits.

## The essentials

**Visitor facilities:** Mount St. Helens Visitor Center is at Silver Lake, five miles east of I-5 on State Route 504. Mailing address: 3029 Spirit Lake Highway, Castle Rock, WA 98668-8944. Call (206) 274-2103 or (206) 274-2100 for 24-hour recorded information. It's open year-around (except Christmas, Thanksgiving and New Year's Day), April-September from 9 to 6 and October-March 9 to 5. The new multi-million dollar Coldwater Ridge Visitor Center is 46 miles farther up the road, inside the monument; (206) 274-2131. It's open summer 9 to 6 and winter 9 to 5. Smaller visitor facilities are at at 42218 NE Yale Bridge Road in Amboy, open weekdays 7:30 to 5; Pine Creek Information Center 18 miles east of Cougar, open daily 9 to 6; and Woods Creek Information Center south of Randle, open daily 9 to 5.

At any one of these centers, pick up a copy of the *Volcano Review*, which tells you what's happening where in the monument.

**Hiking and climbing:** Many miles of trails now wind through the blast zone and around the flanks of the peak. Anyone who ventures off the trails in "recovery study areas" faces a minimum $100 fine. Free climbing permits for a hike up to the south rim are available in advanced by contacting monument headquarters. Forty unreserved permits are issued each day

# THE MAN WHO DIED OF STUBBORNNESS

*If it's gonna take me, let it come and get me. If it takes my goddamn mountain, let it take Truman with it.*

Who can guess what Harry Truman's last thoughts were when his beloved mountain came down on top of him. No one will ever know what he was doing at that moment, for he and his Mount St. Helens Lodge are buried beneath several hundred feet of volcanic debris.

Moonshiner, mechanic, prospector and then lodge owner, Harry had lived beside Spirit Lake for 54 years. He wasn't about to let the threat of a volcanic eruption dislodge him. In one of his last interviews—with journalist Mary Ann Gervais, who slipped past roadblocks to reach the lodge—Truman admitted to being "scared pinkless." But he refused to leave.

*What would I do? I'd die down there, being away from this place. If the mountain wants to take me down that hill feet first, let her try. I'm not goin'. I'd worry myself sick about my place—I'd die sure in hell.*

So the profane, gently cranky 83-year-old man sipped his Shenley's and Coke, tended to his 15 cats and waited out the mountain. Others in the Spirit Lake area obeyed orders to evacuate in the weeks before the eruption, but not Harry. "Young man," he told a *London Daily Mail* reporter, "it would take an act of God and three acts of Congress to shift old Truman from here." The world and the press watched and waited—and quoted Harry Truman. When that act of God came at 8:32 a.m., March 18, 1980, he was still there.

Harry was born in 1896 in a rude West Virginia cabin. His father was a lumber camp foreman, his mother the camp cook. The family moved to Chehalis in 1907 and Harry grew up tramping Mount St. Helens' foothills. He joined the Army during World War I, served in France as an aviation mechanic and learned to fly. Back home after the war, he sold moonshine during Prohibition, tinkered with those new horseless carriages and ran an auto repair shop.

## Harry comes to the mountain

In 1928, he bought half interest in a dilapidated lodge at Spirit Lake. A few months later, the vociferous Harry had a falling out with his partner and he finished buying him out. He never left his mountain, except to go "down there" occasionally to visit family and friends, and to pick up supplies and lumber to expand his holdings. He built a thriving fishing lodge, with a restaurant, guest rooms and rental boats. Some say he financed the lodge's expansion after finding gold coins that had been buried on the mountain by members of a stranded pack train.

He became a legend in his time, even before his stubborn bout with the threatening volcano made headlines. Cantankerous yet friendly, he would judge prospective guests by the look of their face or their clothes. He would as likely send someone packing as to offer his warm mountain hospitality. He accidentally shooed Chief Justice William O. Douglas off his property, thinking him to be some "pussy footin' government man." After learning of his mistake, he chased down after him, and the two became lifelong friends. When Douglas died, Harry blamed it on his friend's penchant for young wives:

*Those young girls killed him, you know. I told him if he didn't quit that messin' around, it would kill him.*

Harry owned an immaculate pink 1957 Cadillac convertible, which he kept on the mountain, refusing to drive it down to safety. After St. Helens began to grumble, he told reporters he had a hidden mine, where he would sit with his Cadillac and his whiskey to wait out the eruption.

For more than half a century, Mount St. Helens had been Harry's home, his livelihood and his podium. Now, it is his monument.

and may be requested the day before your climb at Jack's Store, five miles south of Cougar on Highway 503. (See box on page 47)

**Food and lodging:** Most of Mount St. Helens' facilities are outside the monument, or on its edges, to minimize disturbance of the recovering mountain. There are no overnight accommodations inside, although several of campgrounds rim the monument, and neighboring towns such as **Cougar** and **Randle** offer motels and small resorts. The Cascade Peaks Restaurant and gift shop operates near Windy Ridge, on the monument's eastern side, open in summer from 8 a.m. to 8 p.m. The new Coldwater Ridge Visitor Center has a cafeteria with outdoor decks, serving from 9 to 5.

**When to go:** The weather's most reliable in August and September; the absolute best time to visit is during a narrow window from early to late September, when skies are often blue and crowds are thin. Expect flocks of folks in summer, of course, and on most sunny spring-summer-fall weekends. Like other Cascade peaks, St. Helens often generates its own weather, brewing clouds that cloak the peak and the crater. Thus, even that late summer window offers no guarantee of sunshine.

**Winter activities:** The Silver Lake and Coldwater Ridge visitor facilities remain open in winter, although Coldwater Ridge may be temporarily closed by snow. There are cross-country skiing and snowmobile areas on the south slope; snow-park permits are available from stores in the Cougar area. Windy Ridge facilities are closed by winter snow, usually October into May.

**RV Advisory:** Access roads and paved roads within the monument are easily negotiable by an RV or trailer, although many stretches are rather winding. The spiraling climb up to Coldwater Ridge is well engineered with passing lanes, and RV parking is available at the visitor center. The only route we would not advise for a large RV or trailer is Forest Road 26 north from Meta Lake on the eastern side of the monument. Although it's paved, much of it is one-lane with small passing pockets.

## Commercial activities outside the monument

**Scenic flights:** These outfits offer overflights from surrounding airports: Vancouver Aviation, 101-A E. Reserve St., Vancouver, WA 98661, (206) 695-3821; Conquest Helicopters, Toutle, WA 98649; (206) 274-6789; Blue Bird Helicopters, 107 Cougar Crest Dr., Cougar, WA 98616, (206) 238-5326; and Spanaflight, Pierce County Airport, 167th and Meridian East, Puyallup, WA 98373; (206) 848-2020.

**Guided tour:** For van tours of the mountain "led by eyewitness survivors," contact Mount St. Helens Adventure Tours, Castle Rock, WA 98611; (206) 274-6542.

**Volcano film:** *The Eruption of Mount St. Helens* film is shown hourly (summer/winter hours vary) at the wide-screen CineDome Theater, 1239 Mount St. Helens Way NE, Castle Rock, WA 98611; (206) 274-8000.

## Driving the monument

Our route will take you east from Woodland to Cougar on State Highway 503, then you'll approach Mount St. Helens from the south. Although the gaping crater faces north, the southern exposure is our favorite. It offers some fine hiking, and it's never crowded. From there, we'll loop around the east side, drive up to Windy Ridge for a peek into that awesome cavity, then continue on to Mount Rainier.

First, however, drive north from Woodland on I-5 to visit the two fine

# THE RIM HIKE: BECAUSE IT'S THERE?

"Are you sure we're having fun?" I called out to my son Dan, who was far ahead of me in the scramble over the broken lava flow.

"Ask me when we get to the top," he panted back.

The climb to Mount St. Helens' rim from the south side of the monument provides a rare opportunity to perch on the edge of a crater and stare into the steaming depths of an active volcano. However, it is a privilege not easily attained. The round-trip is nine miles and the elevation gain is nearly a mile— 4,500 feet. There is no water on the trail, and no shade on the upper half.

The hike begins innocently enough—a pleasant two-mile uphill stroll along the old Ptarmigan Trail through a lush, shaded forest. The last two and a half miles, however, will try the souls of hardened hikers. First, you must scramble carefully among the scattered lava boulders of the centuries-old Monitor lava flow, pulling yourself up through chunks the size of freight trucks. An erratic line of posts stuck into lava cracks helps guide you. Even with the posts, hikers have picked several routes along this lava ridge, and each seems a bit tougher than the other. Once you've cleared the ridge, convinced that it was one of the tougher climbs you've tackled recently, you step onto the fresh cinder scatter of the 1980 eruption. The scramble turns into an exhausting slog.

## A Wagnerian scene

Your final wearying trudge to the crater's edge yields quick reward: a view like nothing you have seen before. The jagged knife-edge rim drops almost vertically, hundreds of feet to the crater below. The ominous lava dome, which seems only a distant bulge from other vista points, is a massive, broken mound. Strata from earlier eruptions is clearly visible on the crater walls. Steam puffs from fissures and mini-landslides grumble down the steep rim. They blend their dust with the steam from the fumarols, creating a kind of Wagnerian smog that hangs over the vast cavity. Nothing is alive up here except hikers and an occasional passing insect. Far below, a sightseeing helicopter circles within the crater, looking like a tiny dragonfly in the mist.

You pull your gaze from the crater and look around. Ruined Spirit Lake is just beyond the gaping mouth of the north-facing crater. If you've had the good fortune to pick a sunny day, you see glossy, glacier-draped Mount Rainier before you, the great bulk of Mount Adams to your right, the slender feminine cone of Mount Hood to the south. On an exceptionally clear day, Mount Jefferson and others of Oregon's section of the Cascades may appear.

## An unstable rim

The crater rim climb is permitted the year around, but it requires a long slog through snow with proper equipment from late fall through late spring. In summer, requirements are simpler: tough shoes, lots of water, sun protection and a good dose of stamina. You'll also need a permit from mid-May through October.

For peak periods, particularly summer weekends, it's best to get your permit in advance, by mail: Mount St. Helens Volcanic National Monument, 42218 NE Yale Bridge Rd., Amboy, WA 98601. For information, call (209) 247-5800. One hundred climbers a day are permitted up the Monitor Ridge trail; 60 by advance permit and 40 on a first come, first served basis. These are issued the day before at Jack's Store in the hamlet of Yale, on State Highway 503, five miles west of Cougar. All climbers, whether with mail permits or day-before permits, must sign in and out at a register outside the store.

We had no problem getting a day-before permit on a mid-September weekday, but it's best to write in advance if you're planning a hike any day between mid-June and Labor Day Weekend.

visitor centers which can't be reached from heart of the monument. If you're hurrying toward Seattle and not following our convoluted route, this is a *must* stop. North of Woodland, I-5 brushes the edge of the Columbia River, passing the hamlet of Kalama and the larger communities of Kelso and Longview. We visit them in the Columbia corridor section of this chapter.

☺ At Castle Rock exit 49, drive about five miles east to the **Mount St. Helens Visitor Center** at Silver Lake. It's housed in a modern glass and wooden structure with high vaulted ceilings. You're more than 40 miles from the monument, and Mount St. Helens' ruined crater is only vaguely visible from here. However, fine graphics and other exhibits give you a vivid sequential picture of events leading up to and following the blast. You can walk through a model of the mountain's innards, catch movies and slide shows and test your volcano knowledge with a computer.

Opposite the visitor center, **Seaquest State Park** offers shaded and nicely spaced campsites, for $14 with hookups and $10 without. From here, a winding, well-engineered road and a couple of graceful new bridges take you up the Toutle River Valley to a new state-of-the-art interpretive facility. En route, a couple of unofficial visitor centers offer the chance to buy a Mount St. Helens ash ashtray or other useful mementos.

As you spiral upward, you'll enter the blast zone and begin to see the awesome power of the 1980 eruption. Many of the blown-down trees here have been salvaged, since they're outside the monument. Within the monument, everything has been left where it fell. The highway is high on the north flank of the **Toutle River Valley,** which was scoured and widened by a mudflow following the eruption. Far below, the stream meanders along the basin floor, like a river in a glacial-carved valley. It's difficult to imagine that this valley floor was shaped in minutes instead of centuries.

☺ **Coldwater Ridge Visitor Center,** a modernistic structure completed in 1993, offers fine views of the crater and lava dome. Again, excellent displays, films and videos tell you more than you ever wanted to know about volcanoes in general and this one in particular. Busy with leading-edge electronic displays, it's perhaps the most high-tech interpretive center in any national park or monument. Intriguing "touch video" exhibits let you and the kids repopulate the mountain with proper plant life and critters. Visitors have a clear sideways view of the yawning crater seven miles away. It still steams ominously, as if sleeping fitfully. You can buy a St. Helens burger or volcano burger at a cafeteria, carry it out to a patio deck and dine with a million-dollar view. A road leads down to former Coldwater Creek, now Coldwater Lake, created when a debris avalanche dammed the stream. Facilities include a boat launch, picnic area and interpretive trail.

Expect both visitor centers to be crowded in summer. On weekends when the sky is clear and the mountain is out, thousands rush here from the heavily-populated Puget Sound area. We had problems finding parking places on a sunny August Sunday.

From Coldwater Ridge, retrace your route back to Woodland, then head east on Highway 503. If you're a fisherperson and/or you've got a boat in tow, the Lewis River Valley recreation area offers ample opportunities. Stop by the **visitor information center** of the Woodland Chamber of Commerce at 1225 Lewis River Road (Highway 503). For advance information, contact the chamber or the Lewis River Valley Coalition, listed in our Trip Planner at the beginning of this chapter.

The highway passes wooded foothills and woodsy homes as it climbs gently uphill, matching the lazy curves of the Lewis River. At several river access areas, you can wet a line or your entire body. **Lewis River Salmon Hatchery** is about five miles east of Woodland and a mile off the highway. Here, you can learn about the rearing of Chinook, sockeye, coho and chums. It's open during daylight hours.

At the tiny hamlet of **Ariel,** the river becomes a lake behind **Merwin Dam.** You can launch your boat or pause at a tree-shaded picnic area here, provided by Pacific Power and Light Company. The town consists of an appealingly shabby general store cantilevered over a valley that's carpeted with a Christmas tree farm. **Lelooska Gallery** in Ariel displays a nice selection of contemporary and old style Western and Native American art, crafts and jewelry. Beyond Ariel, the highway offers pleasing views of Lake Merwin as it meanders higher into the Cascades. At **Yale,** a second dam creates **Yale Lake,** with more boating facilities, swimming bays and picnic areas.

You soon enter the woodsy village of **Cougar,** gateway to the southern part of Mount St. Helens National Volcanic Monument. Although you catch occasional glimpses of the gray, snow-patched peak, you see no hint of destruction here, for Cougar is huddled on the mountain's sheltered side. Offering food and lodging, it's a good place to pause and plan your St. Helens visit.

Haven't yet picked up you souvenir St. Helens ceramic ash squirrel? **Cougar Ceramics Factory Outlet** offers all sorts of "ashware," including a before-and-after lift-off volcano model. **Blue Bird Helicopters** (listed above) operates out of Cougar, and its landing pad has a rather interesting assortment of sky cranes and other choppers.

## WHERE TO DINE

### The Landing • ∆ $$

❑ *Highway 504; (206) 238-5299. American; full bar service. Daily 6 a.m. to 9 p.m. MC/VISA.* ❑ Simple family cafè with a rural interior and menu to match: steak, deep-fried shrimp, fried chicken, chicken fried steak and such.

### Wildwood Inn • ∆∆ $$

❑ *Highway 504; (206) 238-5222. American; full bar service. Monday-Thursday 7 a.m. to midnight, Friday 7 to 2 a.m., Saturday-Sunday 8 to midnight. MC/VISA.* ❑ Attractive alpine style restaurant with knotty pine interior and logging artifacts from Lewis Valley's early days. Typical American menu, plus a good selection of micro-brews.

## WHERE TO SLEEP

### Lone Fir Resort • ∆∆ $$ Ø

❑ *16806 Lewis River Rd., Cougar, WA 98616; (206) 238-5210. Couples and family units $38 to $40, kitchen units $50 to $85.* ❑ Well maintained units in wooded setting; coin laundry, pool; mini-mart and service station. Mount St. Helens helicopter flights. RV park listed below.

## WHERE TO CAMP

### Ariel to Cougar and beyond

**Bigfoot RV Park** • *16730 Lewis River Rd., Cougar, WA 98603; (206) 238-5224. RV and tent sites from $12. Reservations accepted.* ❑ Rustic but clean park with sites scattered among the trees in Cougar; fire pits, showers, lawn areas.

***Cougar Camp*** • *c/o Pacific Power and Light, Cougar, WA 98603. Tent sites only, $8. No reservations or credit cards.* ☐ Small lakeside campground just above Cougar, with picnic tables, barbecue pits and boat launch.

***Lone Fir Resort*** • *16806 Lewis River Rd., Cougar, WA 98616; (206) 238-5210. RV and tent sites, $8 to $14. MC/VISA, DISC.* ☐ Nicely maintained campground with grassy sites, showers, barbecues, cable TV; pool, coin laundry, horseshoes.

***Swift Camp Recreation Area*** • *Highway 503 at Swift Reservoir; operated by Pacific Power and Light. RV and tent sites, $8. No hookups; no reservations or credit cards.* ☐ A few miles east of Cougar, half mile west of the Pine Creek Visitor Information Center (see below). Nicely wooded sites near the reservoir; tables and barbecues; flush potties, no showers. Picnic area, kiddie play area, boat launch.

***Volcano View Campground*** • *438 Yale Bridge Rd., Ariel, WA 98603; (206) 4329. RV and tent sites, $7 to $11.50. No credit cards.* ☐ On State Route 503 toward Amboy, a mile south of Lewis River Road Junction, between Ariel and Cougar. Some sites with St. Helens view. Showers, water and electric hookups; rec room and rec field, spa, coin laundry, mini-mart.

## Mount St. Helens South

About seven miles beyond Cougar, watch on your left for Forest Road 83, which leads to an uncrowded interpretive area in the path of a mudflow. Ape Cave, one of the West's longest lava tubes, is up this way, along with the **Climbers' bivouac,** the trailhead for the climb to the rim. (See "Hiking and climbing" above.)

A couple of miles up the road, Forest Road 8303 branches to the left, taking you to **Ape Cave.** The visitor center is open 9 to 5 and the cave is open 9 to 9. If you get there before 4 p.m., you can rent a lantern. Otherwise, plan to have at least two light sources and a warm jacket, because it's black and chilly in there. Guided lantern walks are conducted at 12:30, 1:30 and 2:30 during summer. You have a choice of two routes in the tube. The upper passage, 1.25 miles, is filled with rockfall and takes a bit of scrambling. The lower passage, less than a mile, is an easy stroll. This is a surprisingly large tube, shaped like a subway tunnel. Northern Californians will note its similarity to Bay Area Rapid Transit's transbay tube, complete with chubby twin lava "rails" in some areas. The cave is wet and a few stubby "lavacicles" have formed on the ceiling. No apes here; it was named for the St. Helens Apes, a local hiking club whose members conducted tours here in the 1950s.

Back on Forest Road 83, you follow a gentle serpentine course through evergreens, catching brief glimpses of Mount St. Helen's blown-away summit. Then a roadside sign signals your approach to the ashflow: "You are entering a scoured landscape, where life arises in the wake of a mudflow."

The green trees vanish as you enter the "Lahar"—an Indonesian word for mudflow. St. Helens fills the horizon like a wounded giant. Interpretive trails take you through the mudflow, where a wide river of hot ash and snowmelt, the consistency of wet cement, flashed past. Some brutalized trees still stand on the edge, their bark stripped away. Two excellent hiking trails begin here, one leading downward, the other up.

*Often overlooked is Mount St. Helens' south side at Lahar, where a hot ash flow scoured the landscape. Trails lead upward from here.* — **Betty Woo Martin**

☺ **Lava Canyon Trail** takes you downhill through the narrow basaltic Muddy River gorge that was uncovered when the mudflow stripped away sheltering foliage. The river is misnamed here. It's a crystalline stream that dances dramatically down through this steep chasm, marking its course with several foaming waterfalls. The trail comes in three stages: an easy half mile of asphalt, a steeper one-mile stretch deep into this rock-walled gorge, and a scary 2.5-mile cliff-hanger notched into the canyon's high shoulders. The lower portion is recommended only for experienced hikers with no vertigo problems. Don't try it in your Florsheims.

☺ **Ape Canyon Trail** is our favorite outing in the monument. Following the edge of the mudflow, it ducks in and out of thick forest as it climbs five miles up the devastated flanks of the mountain. It's a pleasing if steep stroll in summer, trimmed with Indian paintbrush, blue lupine and the white saucers of cow parsnip. In late August, ripening salmonberries will tempt you to pause. After a three-mile stretch through thick forest, you emerge high on the flanks of St. Helens. The peak seems close enough to reach out and touch; the narrow slot of Ape Canyon falls away to your right. On a good day, you can see the snowy cones of mounts Rainier, Hood and Adams. You can pick up the June Lake Trail here, and hike a short distance west into another mudflow area. Scattered boulders and naked trees speak of that violent day in May. If you can make shuttle arrangements, continue north on the Ape Canyon Trail, which merges with the Loowit Trail and takes you to Windy Ridge.

# Mount St. Helens East

From Lahar, return to the main highway and continue your loop southeast around the mountain. You shortly encounter the **Pine Creek Information Center,** open daily 9 to 6. It offers a well-done 20-minute movie about the past, present and re-vegetating future of St. Helens, a good selection of books and maps, and helpful rangers.

From here, it's 43 miles to Windy Ridge. The road winds leisurely through a mature forest, then at **Clearwater Viewpoint** on your left, you get a good view of the crater and the blast zone around it. Just around the next bend, the imposing mass of Mount Rainier looms, beckoning you to visit it next. A left turn onto Forest Road 99 takes you on a 17-mile spiral through the devastation area to Windy Ridge. You're in the main blast zone here. Even though nature is rapidly healing this giant wound, you can see and sense the incredible power of an exploding volcano: the scatter of fallen trees combed around the contours of hills and valleys, and the ashen complexion of the landscape.

*RV advisory:* The route is kinky and steep in places, but paved and negotiable, even by larger rigs. Several turnouts allow you to pull over and let others pass.

Interpretive sites along this route tell you about that fateful day in the spring of 1980:

**Miner's car:** This rusting hulk once was a Pontiac that was blown across the road. A marker tells you that the owners, a mining couple with a nearby cabin, were among the eruption's fatalities.

☺ **Meta Lake:** You can walk a short interpretive trail from the miner's car or drive to the Meta Lake turnout. Although this area lay in the path of the blast, it's rejuvenating quickly, with snow-protected silver fir and mountain hemlocks as much as 20 feet high. The lake, in a sheltered basin, is beginning to look pretty again.

☺ **Independence Pass Viewpoint:** Many people bypass this vista, because a steep quarter-mile hike is required. It's worth the effort! The trail takes you through a splintered and blown-away forest to a high crest for an excellent view of Spirit Lake and the lava dome.

**Donnybrook Viewpoint** offers another view of Spirit Lake with several interpretive signs about that once-beautiful pond. No, we don't know why it isn't called Spirit Lake Viewpoint. **Smith Creek Viewpoint** provides a good gander down at the log-strewn, muddy delta of Smith Creek. It was turned briefly into a roaring stream by the eruption.

☺ **Windy Ridge,** which almost always is, provides the closest approach to the crater by vehicle. The silently steaming maw is about four miles away. For a good day's workout, hike the 165 steps up a sloping ladderway to an ash-covered mound for a good view of the mountain and Spirit Lake.

The only permanent facilities here are a wind shelter where ranger talks are given, and restrooms. This is the trailhead for a network of paths toward the crater and around the crest.

☺ The **Truman Trail** is the most popular hike out of here. It follows an old access road around the lip of a foreground hill, then takes you across several mud flows directly below the crater. You'll get a good view of that bulging lava dome. Since this pumice plain was "ground zero" of the blast zone, re-vegetation has been slow. Most of the topsoil is somewhere between here and Canada. Moonscape comes too easily as a descriptive term; it's more like a dry, thinly vegetated desert.

From the Truman Trail, you can merge with the Loowit Trail to join the rather extensive network that circles the mountain. There is no access to the crater rim from this side.

# ST. HELENS TO RAINIER

You have two choices for your northward trek to Mount Rainier. Near Meta Lake, you can fork left and follow forestry road 26, or continue east on road 99 to road 25. The latter route follows Iron Creek Valley, and eventually deposits you in Randle, the monument's northern gateway.

*RV advisory:* As we mentioned above, narrow, twisting Route 26 is not recommended for motorhomes, and particularly not for trailer rigs. Small RVs can make it.

Although Route 26 is single-lane with turnouts most of the way, it's quite interesting. It takes you through a slender valley that's thick with blown-over timber, and eventually into a forest that was out of reach of the blast. At **Ryan Lake interpretive site,** graphics discuss this transition zone from dead to living trees. When you reach the surviving forest area, watch a for sign to the left, directing you to **Quartz Creek Big Trees,** a stand of ancient Douglas fir.

Highway 26 eventually merges with route 25, headed for **Randle.** As you approach this small town, you pass yet another Mount St. Helens and Gifford Pinchot National Forest visitor center, open 9 to 4. Randle itself, at the juncture of the forestry road and U.S. Highway 12, lacks the woodsy charm of Cougar. This small town in the Cispus agricultural valley offers a store or two and a motel or two. Although beyond the blast zone, Randle felt the fury of the St. Helens eruption. It was pelted with cinders and layered with seven inches of ash.

If you've not yet gotten your St. Helens ashware souvenir, **Sweetbriar Hollow** on Highway 12 (497-3535) offers the usual selection.

National forest campgrounds abound between Mount St. Helens and Randle, and there's an RV park in town. From here, our route takes you about ten miles northeast on Highway 12 to **Packwood.** It's a bit larger and more attractive than Randle, with a woodsy alpine look to many of its buildings. The town offers a few more motels and restaurants, although services are somewhat scant for a gateway to a major national park. It's most appealing attraction is the vision of glistening Mount Rainier peeking between foreground peaks.

About nine miles north of Packwood on U.S. 12, a left turn onto State Highway 123 takes you into the southeastern corner of Mount Rainier National Park, although the entrance station is a bit farther along. As you drive this route, you won't see much of Mount Rainier, for hides behind foothills for most of the way. However, it will put in many dramatic appearances after you enter the park and  start heading toward the visitor areas of Sunrise and Paradise.

## WHERE TO DINE IN RANDLE /PACKWOOD

**Big Bottom Bar & Grill** • ΔΔ **$$**

❐ *Highway 12, Randle; (206) 497-9982. American; full bar service. Daily 10 a.m. to 1 a.m. MC/VISA.* ❐ This appealing, woodsy place is mostly a bar with a small café in back, offering comfortable Naugahyde booths. Try the wing stingers (chicken wings with cayenne pepper), or the more tepid chicken, pork ribs, steak, ham steak or fried gizzards.

**Club Café** • Δ **$**

❐ *Highway 12, Packwood; (206) 494-5977. American; wine and beer. Daily 6 a.m. to 10 p.m. MC/VISA.* ❐ Semi-scruffy but neat place serving large, inexpensive portions of chicken fried steak, ribs and other simple American fare.

**Peters Inn** • ΔΔ **$$**

❐ *13051 Highway 12, Packwood; (206) 494-4000. American; Full bar service. Daily 5 a.m. to 9 p.m. MC/VISA.* ❐ Rustically attractive mountain café specializing in veal, seafood, ribs and steaks, including rural reliables such as chicken fried steak and liver and onions. Large salad bar. Home-made desserts earn local raves.

## WHERE TO SLEEP

**Cowlitz River Lodge** • ⌂⌂⌂ **$$$** Ø

❐ *13069 Highway 12 (P.O. Box 488), Packwood, WA 98361; (206) 494-4444. Couples and singles $50 to $60. Major credit cards.* ❐ Very attractive woodsy-modern inn with 32 rooms; TV movies and phones; spa; free continental breakfast.

**Randle Motel** • ⌂ **$$**

❐ *9780 Highway 12, Randle, WA 98377; (206) 497-5346. Couples from $35. MC/VISA.* ❐ This small motel offers basic rooms for basic rates, plus inexpensive RV parking.

## WHERE TO CAMP

**Maple Grove RV Park** • *175 Cispus Rd. (P.O. Box 205), Randle, WA 98377; (206) 497-2741. RV and tent sites, $9 to $15. Reservations accepted.* ❐ Showers; coin laundry, mini-mart, rec room, swimming and fishing in the Cowlitz River. Restaurant, lounge and par three golf adjacent.

**La Wis Wis Campground** • *Highway 12 near Highway 123, north of Packwood, just outside Mount Rainier National Park. RV and tent sites, $8 to $10. No reservations or credit cards.* ❐ Attractive U.S. Forest Service campground within a short drive of the park. Well-spaced, shaded sites with barbecues and picnic tables; flush potties. This is a handy overflow campground when all Rainier National Park spaces are taken—although it, too, can fill up on summer weekends.

# MOUNT RAINIER NATIONAL PARK

Until Mount St. Helens got all that media attention, massive Mount Rainier—with its garlands of perpetual glaciers—was the king of Washington's peaks. Old timers still refer to it simply as "The Mountain." Its a commanding presence in the Puget Sound area, a picture postcard backdrop for Olympia, Tacoma and Seattle. It's often obscured by clouds, and when they depart, residents look eastward, smile and say: "The mountain's out!"

It was called *Tahoma* by Native Americans, who refused to climb it, since it was home to spirits. The mount's modern name came from an obscure source. It was sighted by George Vancouver in 1792 and named for a friend, Rear Admiral Peter Regnier. It has since been misspelled.

The mountain itself is hardly obscure. Washington's tallest peak at 14,411 feet, Rainier is a magnificent, dominant presence visible from much of the state. It's the most glaciated American peak outside of Alaska, with 25 glaciers glistening from its rugged blue-gray flanks. In total mass and extent of its base, it is the largest mountain in the country. It's covered with more snow and ice than all the other Cascade volcanoes combined. It is, indeed, America's great pyramid. In *Mount Rainier: The Story Behind the Scenery*, naturalist author Ray "Skip" Snow writes:

*The splendor of altitude, the serenity of tall timber, the haunting presence of an explosive time gone by and yet to come are the vivid and abiding impressions given by Mount Rainier.*

One of several volcanic crowns punctuating the Cascade Range, Rainier was built up over the past million years by successive lava flows. At its peak—pun not intended—it towered about 16,000. Then 5,800 years ago, with no TV cameras to record the event, the crown suddenly collapsed into a steaming avalanche that buried a 125-square-mile area under a 100-foot-deep sea of mud. Communities of Puyallup, Kent and others between the mountain and Puget Sound sit atop that mudflow.

The mountain sleeps today, but fitfully. About 14 minor eruptions were noted by early settlers during the last century. In 1963, a large rock slide—perhaps sparked by a steam eruption—rattled from Little Tahoma Peak down onto Emmons Glacier.

First to climb the mountain were Hazard Stevens, America's youngest Civil War general, and local miner Philomon Beecher Van Trump. Guided to Mazama Ridge by a local Indian, they continued on their own and reached the summit on August 17, 1870. Naturalist John Muir followed in 1888, in the company of photographer Arthur C. Warner. Their glowing accounts and photos soon earned national fame for the mountain. Encouraged by Muir, and by railroad companies who wanted to haul tourists, President William McKinley designated Rainier as the nation's fifth national park on March 2, 1899.

## The essentials

**Visitor facilities:** Park services are focused in four areas: Sunrise on the mountain's northeastern slope, Paradise on the southern flank, Longmire to the southwest, and Ohanapecosh in the southeast corner. Sunrise and Paradise, on high mountain ridges, are good starting points for hiking, and both offer visitor centers and restaurants. In-park lodgings are at Paradise and at Longmire, the historic visitor area that dates back to the last century. Ohanapecosh, adjacent to a campground, has a small interpretive center. Visitor centers are open daily from 9 to 6 in summer, with shorter hours the rest of the year.

Entrance fee is $5 per car. You can get an annual pass for $15, or a Golden Eagle pass for $25 that's good for all national parks and monuments during a calendar year. Golden Age and Golden Access passes, for seniors and handicapped, provide free entry. Entrance gates are at Stevens Canyon in the southeast corner (Ohanapecosh is within the park but outside that gate); White River, which leads to Sunshine; and Nisqually, west of Longmire and just east of the town of Ashford. Of the communities near the park, Ashford offers the most visitor accommodations, followed by Packwood.

For park information: Superintendent, Mount Rainier National Park, Ashford, WA 98304; (206) 569-2211. Set your car radio to 1610-AM for 24-hour recorded information.

**Activities:** Mount Rainier is primarily a hiking and sightseeing park. If your schedule permits, wait for a clear day when the mountain is "out" and the views are fabulous. Even on overcast days, however, you can admire the park's close-up features. The route between the Stevens Canyon and Nisqually entrances has several turn-outs that feature roadside exhibits, canyon vistas or short hikes. On clear days, the views of Rainier from this road are ever-changing and awesome. The park offers the usual array of ranger programs and hikes, plus slide programs and films at the visitor centers. For specifics, pick up a free copy of the *Tahoma* newsletter at entrance stations or visitor centers.

About four thousand people a year achieve Mount Rainier's summit, although the climb takes special equipment, skill, training and endurance. Inquire at a park visitor center about proper preparation. The most popular starting point is Paradise; the Guide House here is the park's official climbing center.

**Food and lodging:** For in-park lodging information, contact Mount Rainier Guest Services, P.O. Box 108, Ashford, WA 98304; (206) 569-2275. Overnight facilities are at the grand old 126-unit Paradise Inn and the recently renovated 25-room National Park Inn at Longmire. Paradise Inn is open from late spring through early fall, while Longmire offers accommodations the year around. Make reservations *early*, particularly for the summer season. If you're planning a summer weekend visit, a year in advance isn't too soon. Lodging rates range from $55 to $84 per couple. (Rooms at the National Park Inn are all non-smoking.)

Restaurants are located at Longmire, Paradise and Sunrise, and a small general store at Longmire offers grocery items. Sunrise has an informal and inexpensive cafeteria, open from 9 a.m. to 6 p.m. Meals at Paradise and the National Park Inn range from $7 to $20, and both have full bar service. The Paradise Inn dining room is open from 7 to 9 a.m., noon to 2 and 5:30 to 8:30 p.m., with a 11 to 2:30 Sunday brunch. National Park Inn restaurant hours are 7 a.m. to 8 p.m. Both have non-smoking areas.

There's are no service stations in the park, so plan accordingly. (We didn't, and had to backtrack from Ohanapecosh to Packwood for a fill-up.)

**Camping:** Several campgrounds are inside the park and all are on a first-come, first-served basis. They fill up quickly in summer, particularly on weekends. The trick is to get there early in the morning, wait for someone to vacate, then stake your claim. RV and tent sites, wooded and reasonably well-spaced, are $6 to $8 per night, with picnic tables, barbecues and flush potties; no showers or hookups. Our preferred stops are Ohanapecosh (or the U.S. Forest Service's La Wis Wis just outside the park), and White River, on the road to Sunrise.

**When to go:** Like Mount St. Helens, Mount Rainier offers the best weather from August through September. October can be nice, although an early rain or snowfall can chill your visit. If the weather's a question, head for Sunrise, since it's on the eastern side of the mountain and more likely to be sunny. With its awesome mountain vistas and easy hiking access to the high country, it's our favorite part of the park. On busy summer weekends, Sunrise will be a *little* less crowded than Paradise or Longmire.

**Winter activities:** Facilities at Longmire remain open the year around, and it becomes a ski touring center during winter, offering rental equipment, although there are no groomed trails. Although Paradise Lodge closes in winter, the road is kept open. It's a popular cross-country skiing, tubing and sledding area. Of course, winter storms may close it temporarily. The road to Sunrise isn't kept open in winter.

*RV Advisory:* While some park roads are steep and winding, all are paved and negotiable by larger rigs. The climb to Sunrise is the park's most challenging, but it's well engineered. Just don't look over the edge if that sort of thing bothers you.

## Driving the park

If you've elected to follow our St. Helens-to-Rainier route, you'll enter the park boundary near **Ohanapecosh**, above Packwood. You haven't passed through an entrance station yet, so stop at the visitor center adjacent to the campground for orientation. Get a copy of *Tahoma* to find out what's going on. (Two connecting state highways, 123 and 410, pass through the park over Cayuse Pass without going through a park entry gate.)

Ohanapecosh is the park's back door. Most folks approach from the west on State highways 7 and 706, a busy corridor between the Puget Sound area and Ashford. Then they hit their first visitor facilities at historic Longmire. However, we prefer roads less traveled, and we'll pass through the Longmire area on the way out. If you're camping or RVing, the odds of finding a campsite are better at Ohanapecosh or nearby La Wis Wis than in the park's more popular areas.

Highway 123 north of Ohanapecosh takes you on a gently twisting climb toward **Cayuse Pass,** with frequent glimpses of the great mountain off to the left. After topping the pass, a three-mile downhill spiral delivers you to the Sunrise junction. Turn left and you'll soon pass through the White River entrance station. The sweeping climb toward Sunrise is visually spectacular. You'll be pressed to keep your eyes on the road; they'll flit between views of colossal Rainier and the lower sawtooth ridges of the Cascades. At **Sunrise Point,** the road hair-pins around a parking area. It's an inviting place to pause and admire the scenic alpine surrounds, which gallop off in all directions. Interpretive signs explain the geology of the area.

☺ **Sunrise** is a few miles beyond, clinging to a high ridge at 6,400 feet. Its grand old peaked-roofed visitor center, ranger station and cafeteria occupy one of the Northwest's most spectacular settings. Here, Rainier is a commanding presence, dominating the scene with its wrinkled skin of blue-ice glaciers. The serrated Cascades fill the opposite horizon and the glacier-fed White River sparkles far below in a wooded, V-shaped valley.

You may want to head for the ranger station or visitor center to learn what activities are scheduled. They're open Sunday-Friday 9 to 6 and Saturday 9 to 7. If you've brought your hiking shoes, ask for a map of the Sunrise trail system. The large shingle-sided visitor center, once a hikers' shelter, contains several interpretive exhibits. The cafeteria serves light fare and an adjacent store offers fixin's for a hiking lunch and a few gift items. The only overnight accommodation here is a walk-in campground a mile away.

*Hikers enjoy an alpine panorama from one of Mount Rainier's most imposing vista points—the Burroughs Mountain ridge above Sunrise.* — **Don W. Martin**

☺ The **Burroughs Mountain trail** is our favorite hike from Sunrise. It's a medium-tough workout, about 7.5 miles round trip, with an elevation gain of a thousand feet. The trek takes you on a dramatic transition from thick green forest decorated with lupine, through a flower-adorned meadow to a high tundra cloaked with multi-colored lichen. Rainier fills your horizon as you hike. It seems close enough to touch, yet it dances out of reach as you approach. Follow signs to First Burroughs, where you enter the tundra, then continue across a razorback ridge to Second Burroughs. It's a rock-strewn shelf directly opposite the peak and separated from it by the vast gulf of the White River Valley.

You could spend hours here, watching the light change on the mountain's crags and glaciers, perhaps following the progress of wispy clouds that briefly beard its face. During our last visit, a herd of mountain goats grazed in the valley far below. On your return, you can fork to the right and follow the Sunrise Rim Trail, high up on the edge of White River Valley. However, you'll drop into a deep bowl at the walk-in campground, and then have to trudge uphill to reach Sunrise.

## SIDE TRIP: THE TWIN PASS LOOP

After you've done Sunrise, you can retrace your route over Cayuse Pass, and then head into the main part of the park by turning west through Stevens Canyon gate. First, however, you may want to take a scenic detour to the east. It carries you over Chinook Pass on Highway 410, out of the park and down through the American River Canyon, and then west over White

Pass on U.S. Highway 12, and right back into the park.

*RV advisory:* You need to love mountain driving to take this detour, since it involves plenty of up-and-down spiraling. The highways are well engineered, however. We think the supplemental scenery is worth this dizzying ride.

The route over **Chinook Pass** is a cliff-hugger, carved out of tilted bedrock. The highway frequently curves back onto itself, like a cat chasing its tail. Just beyond the pass, a turnout offers impressive views of the classic glacier-carved American River valley. A sign advises that this twisting highway was built in 1932 to link the Yakima Valley to Puget Sound. It was named in honor of Stephen T. Mather, first director of the National Park Service.

As you continue downward, you'll soon notice the rainshadow effect of the Cascades. In contrast to the soggy, often overcast western side, the east slope is generally bright and sunny, with annual rainfall under 15 inches. The underbrush disappears and the trees begin to thin out as you drop down from the mountains. Just above **Cliffdell**, the American River merges into the Naches and the terrain begins to level. Cliffdell itself consists of a particularly appealing alpine resort.

☺ *Whistlin' Jack Lodge* ● ⌂⌂⌂ *$$$$*

☐ *20800 State Highway 410, Naches, WA 98937; (800) 827-2299 or (509) 658-2433. Motel units from $79, cottages with kitchenettes from $120, with hot tubs from $130. MC/VISA.* ☐ Exceptionally attractive place, done up in knotty pine and heavy beams. Some rooms with fireplaces and hot tubs. A full-sized elk greets visitors in the lobby; a gift shop, restaurant and bar are adjacent. Rustic early American **Dining room** serves breakfast, lunch and dinner, entrées from $10 to mid-teens. Menu items include Cajun style ribs, liver and onions, steaks and fresh fish.

Whistlin' Jack is worth a pause, even if you aren't hungry or sleepy. Check out the bar with its cozy booths and fieldstone fireplace, or relax on the outdoor patio over the river. The complex also has a deli and grocery. Hay rides and trail rides are scheduled in summer. In winter, you can rent cross-country ski gear and snowmobiles.

Below Cliffdell, the forest surrenders to beige grasslands and rumpled hills marked by rocky outcroppings and caprock cliffs. Near the scattered hamlet of **Nile Valley,** too small to be on most maps, make a hard right turn onto westbound U.S. Highway 12. You enter the 94,718-acre **Oak Creek Game Range,** a mix of prairie grass and woodlands. Watch for deer, chukker, partridge and grouse; it's a major elk range in winter.

Following the cascading course of the Tieton River, you begin climbing a glacial valley toward White Pass, soon returning to evergreen forests. The route is more gentle and less twisting than Chinook Pass. At the large earthfill **Tieton Dam,** you pop into a tunnel and emerge beside **Rimrock Lake.** It's popular with boaters, swimmers and fisherpersons.

**White Pass** offers a couple of inns and restaurants, and it draws skiers from November through May. It offers four double chairs, a rope tow and poma, with 1,500-feet of vertical drop over a dozen trails. The ski area also has groomed cross-country trails. Facilities include ski rentals and school, cafeteria and bar. For details: White Pass Company, P.O. Box 354, Yakima, WA 98907; (509) 453-8731; snow phone is (509) 672-3100. In summer or winter, White Pass offers a good place to grab a bite or spend the night:

### The Village Inn ● ⌂⌂ $$$

☐ *P.O. Box 3039, White Pass, WA 98937; (206) 672-3131. Rooms $68 to $100 (four to six people), suites $80 to $135, efficiencies $48 to $85. MC/VISA.* ☐ Condo units with kitchens and private baths; some fireplaces. Heated pool; ski facilities adjacent. **Summit House Restaurant** serves daily 11 to 9; Alpine-style dining room with American menu (beef, chicken, seafood and some Italian); full bar service; fireplace and outdoor deck.

Dropping down the west side from White Pass, you'll catch nice vistas of the snow-patched Cascades—dominated, of course, by Rainier. A few miles below the pass, stay alert for a turnout on your left, just beyond a runaway truck ramp. It's marked by a small "scenic viewpoint" sign.

☺ **The Palisades** is a collection of basaltic columns forming the sheer face of a 486-foot canyon. Shaped by rapid cooling of a lava flow, these bas relief columns were exposed by erosive forces of the Clear Fork River. This is a great spot for a picnic or a scenic pause, offering views of the sheer canyon wall, thickly wooded Backbone Ridge beyond and the handsome profile of Mount Rainier beyond that.

## Back into the park

A few miles below the Palisades, you'll complete your loop. Turn north onto State Highway 123, pass the entrance to Ohanapecosh, and then turn left onto Stevens Canyon Road and pass through the Stevens Canyon gate. Just beyond the gate, pause at the **Grove of the Patriarchs** to stroll through a glade of Douglas firs, five hundred to a thousand years old, that rival California's redwoods in size. Beyond here, Stevens Canyon Road rambles over **Backbone Ridge** and then along **Stevens Ridge,** offering changing views of Rainier as you head west toward Paradise and Longmire.

☺ **Box Canyon** is a required stop—a narrow slot of a mossy walled ravine. A half-mile walk takes you along the edge of this rocky cleft, which is up to 180 feet deep and only a few feet wide. Beyond Box Canyon, the road scales the wall of Stevens Ridge, offering dizzying views down to **Stevens Canyon.**

☺ A few miles further, a road junction points you uphill to **Paradise.** Like Sunrise, it's a visitor enclave nested high in Rainier's flanks, with imposing views of the peak. Take time to study exhibits along the spiraling walkway of the new **Henry M. Jackson Memorial Visitors Center,** built in honor of the state's noted conservationist and U.S. senator. This modernistic circular structure is open from 9 a.m. to 7 p.m., offering excellent interpretive displays, films, slide shows and a gift and nature shop.

Even if you aren't overnighting at Paradise, take time for a stroll through the grand old lobby of **Paradise Inn.** This shingle-sided building is the park's most impressive structure, with log trusses, unusual log buttresses and two massive cut-stone fireplaces. The dècor is "Western rustic," accented with Native American rugs and blankets. The dining room serves breakfast, lunch and dinner with breaks in between, plus Sunday brunch from 11 to 2. A snack bar serves continuously from 9 to 5. Complimentary tea is offered on the balcony between 3 and 5 daily. A large gift shop is open from 8 to 9.

Like Sunrise, Paradise has an extensive trail system, and it's the primary staging point for assaults on the peak. The Guide House offers advise, climbing maps and equipment rentals. If you really want to get high, Rainier Mountaineering has a three-day program featuring a one-day seminar followed by a two-day summit climb. Call (206) 569-2227 for information.

☺ **Skyline Trail** is the best hike out of Paradise, a somewhat tough 4.5 miles with more than 2,000 feet elevation gain. This loop trail takes you over Mazama Ridge, past Sluiskin Falls and to **Panorama Point** for simply awesome views of the mountain above and the tree-clad valleys below. You then hike along the scraggy edge of **Nisqually Glacier;** take the **Glacier Vista** spur to the right for the closest approach. The trail then leads you along the edge of Nisqually's moraine and back to Paradise. From Sluiskin Falls, a half-mile fork to the right will take you to **Paradise Glacier,** once famous for its ice caves. These blue-ceiling grottoes are no more, however. Like most glaciers on the mountain, Paradise is melting and the caves have been dissolving. The ceiling of the largest collapsed in 1990.

Paradise is often overcast, so you can only hope this side of the mountain is in a sunny mood for your visit. It occupies a south-facing ridge, where moist Pacific breezes collide with warmer inland air. In winter, this creates massive snowfalls, averaging more than 630 inches. In fact, the area holds the world's record of 1,122 inches (nearly a hundred feet!), set in the winter of 1971-72.

From Paradise, continue east about nine miles toward Longmire. A series of turnouts offer glimpses and graphics of the park's flora and fauna. at **Narada Falls** just below the Paradise junction, a short trail takes you to this 200-foot cataract's foaming base. **Christine Falls,** not clearly marked but worth seeing, is just down the highway. It drops through a narrow slot of a canyon.

☺ For a serious workout and awesome cataract vistas, take the 1.6-mile hike along the **Comet Falls Trail,** a quarter of a mile below Christine Falls. The steep route, with a 1,400-foot elevation gain, takes you along the rocky ravine of Van Trump Creek, past several small cataracts. Then, you cross a wooden bridge and stand below one of Washington's most impressive waterfalls. **Comet Falls** indeed resembles a comet. Its glistening head crests a sheer basaltic cliff, and its tail plunges more than 300 feet, like a silvery, unraveling rope.

Back on the highway, you soon reach **Longmire.** It has been the park's main concession center since 1857, when James Longmire hacked a trail to the mountain's lower flanks from the Puget Sound. He later guided visitors into the upper slopes, although he didn't make it to Rainier's crest until 1883. In that same year, he established Longmire's Medical Springs; the Longmire Springs Hotel followed in 1890.

This area, occupying a wooded glen, is more interesting for its history than its appearance. From here, the mountain is a distant crown above thickly wooded foothills. The recently-rennovated **National Park Inn,** dating from 1917, is the third hotel built on this spot, a descendant of Jim Longmire's original. It offers comfortable rooms (all non-smoking) and a cozy little restaurant that serves breakfast, lunch and dinner. The **Longmire Museum,** occupying an ancient shingle-sided structure nearby, has exhibits on the natural and human history of the park. A general store has a good selection of staples; it's open from 8 to 8. Longmire's most interesting structure is the **Administration Building,** constructed from 1928 to 1930 from massive river stones. It now houses park offices and a hiker information center. From Longmire, a nine-mile drive west along the Nisqually River Valley takes you out of the park and into Ashford.

# Ashford-Elbe area

Ashford is an ordinary little community, close to being drab, although it offers a fair selection of lodgings and restaurants. Worth a look is the **Ashford Country Store,** with a false front and plank floors. Now a mini-mart (with video rentals, of course), it still functions as an old style general store with hardware items and other country essentials.

Another seven miles down State Highway 706 is Elbe, a pleasantly funky little town that's comprised mostly of elements of the **Mount Rainier Railroad.** A steam train carries passengers on a 14-mile run to Mineral Lake. Other pieces of rolling stock, no longer rolling, are used for a restaurant, lounge and an unusual motel (see below).

Even if you aren't planning to hop aboard the dinner train or excursion train, it's fun to poke around the old cars, watch the steamers chuff in and out of the yard, and perhaps have a drink or dinner at the dining car restaurant. Pause for a peek into the Little White Church just across the tracks from the railyard.

## ASHFORD-ELBE ATTRACTIONS

☺ **Steam train ride** • *Mount Rainier Scenic Railroad, P.O. Box 921, Elbe, WA 98330; (206) 569-2588. Operates Memorial Day through September, weekends in the shoulder season and daily mid-June through Labor Day. Scenic train rides $6.95 for adults, $5.95 for seniors, $4.95 for teens and $3.95 for kids. Cascadian Dinner Train runs weekends (Saturday or Sunday) April through November, serving a five-course prime rib dinner for $55 per person. MC/VISA, DISC.* ☐ Steam-drawn excursion coaches rumble along ancient rails on the hour and a half run to Mineral Lake, with views of Mount Rainier en route. On the dinner train, a tuxedo-clad waitstaff serves patrons in a handsome old 1920s dining car.

**The Little White Church** • *Elbe Evangelical Lutherische Kirche, Elbe. Services March through November, the third Sunday of each month at 2:30 p.m.* ☐ This tiny white-steeple Lutheran Church is a real charmer. Built in 1893, it seats only 46 people and was listed in Ripley's Believe It or Not as the smallest church in America.

## WHERE TO DINE

☺ **Alexander's Inn** • ∆∆∆ $$$ Ø
☐ *37515 State Highway 706, Ashford; (206) 569-2323. American with a Northwest focus; wine and beer. Daily 7 a.m. to 8:30 p.m. in summer; shorter hours the rest of the year. MC/VISA.* ☐ Very attractive early American dining room installed in a shingle-sided 1892 inn. Settle into a knotty pine booth, listen to soft background music and try entrèes such as pork tenderloin, fresh halibut in sweet red bell pepper sauce, veal scaloppine with apples in caramelized sauce and applejack, or trout from the restaurant's own pond.

☺ **Copper Creek** • ∆∆ $$
☐ *35707 Highway 706, Ashford; (206) 569-2326. American; wine and beer. Daily 7 a.m. to 9 p.m. in summer, 8 a.m. to 7 p.m. Thursday-Sunday in fall and spring, closed January-February. MC/VISA.* ☐ Appealingly rustic country-style dining room featuring sugar-cured ham, steaks, local trout and fried chicken, served with warm home-made bread. Fresh berry pies sitting at the hostess desk will lure you into the rural Americana dining room.

### Mount Rainier Dining Company ● ▵▵ $$
◻ *Highway 706, Elbe; (206) 569-2505. American; full bar service. Week-days 8 a.m. to 9 p.m., weekends 6 to 9. MC/VISA, DISC.* ◻ Fused-together railroad cars comprise this simply attired but cute restaurant, decorated with model trains on a plate-rail shelf. Enter through a caboose and select steak, liver and onions, mulligan stew or spaghetti from the busy menu.

## WHERE TO SLEEP

### Alexander's Inn ● ⌂⌂⌂ $$$$ Ø
◻ *37515 E. State Highway 706, Ashford, WA 98304; (800) 654-7615 or (206) 569-2300. Couples $75 to $89 with bath, $49 to $75 without; suites $75 to $125; also adjacent "Forest House" that sleeps up to eight, from $175. MC/VISA.* ◻ Fourteen rooms stylishly done in early American and European furnishings, with stained glass windows and print wallpaper. Hot tub overlooking trout pond; free continental breakfast. Smoke-free facility.

### Gateway Inn ● ⌂⌂ $$$
◻ *38820 E. State Highway 706, Ashford, WA 98304; (206) 569-2506. Couples $50 to $60, singles $30 to $35. MC/VISA, AMEX.* ◻ Clean, rustic rooms in log cabins just outside park entrance. TV in rooms; some two-room units with fireplaces. Cozy little **Gateway Inn Restaurant** serves American fare 7 a.m. to 10 p.m.; dinners $10 to $25; full bar service. The complex, just outside the park gate, also includes a mini-mart, small gift shop and campground (listed below).

### Hobo Inn ● ⌂ $$$$
◻ *P.O. Box 921 (State Highway 706), Elbe, WA 98330; (206) 569-2500. Couples and singles $70 to $85. MC/VISA, DISC.* Eight rather snug guest rooms built into vintage railroad cabooses. Some furnished with vintage washstands, conductor's desks and other original equipment; spa tubs in some units.

### Nisqually Lodge ● ⌂⌂⌂ $$$$ Ø
◻ *31609 E. Highway 706, Ashford, WA 98304. Couples and singles $67 to $77. Rates include continental breakfast. Major credit cards.* ◻ Very attractive woodsy-style inn, between Ashford and the park gate. Twenty-four rooms with TV, phones; spa.

## WHERE TO CAMP

### Big Creek Campground ● *Forestry Road 52, Ashford, WA 98304; (206) 494-5515. RV and tent sites, $8. No reservations or credit cards.* ◻ U.S. Forest Service campground; wooded, well-spaced sites with barbecues and picnic tables; flush potties; no showers. Go west about five miles from the park on Highway 706, then south two miles on Forestry Road 52.

### Gateway Inn RV Park ● *38820 E. State Highway 706, Ashford, WA 98304; (206) 569-2506. RV sites; water and electric $12, full hookups $15. Reservations accepted; MC/VISA, AMEX.* ◻ Small RV park adjacent to motel and restaurant; showers

# Side trip: Eatonville and Northwest Trek

As we mentioned earlier, Highway 7 is a major corridor between the national park and Puget Sound cities. We aren't taking this route since we'll head next for the southwest Washington coast. However, a brief detour is in order, to explore a couple of worthy attractions.

From Elbe, head northwest on Highway 7 past **Alder Lake,** which offers fishing, boating and swimming. Just beyond tiny **La Grande,** take State Highway 161 north toward Eatonville. (It's marked by a brown Northwest Trek Wildlife Park sign.) You'll catch views of Rainier as you prowl through this wooded and brushy countryside.

**Eatonville** is a pleasant little town with a mix of old wooden false front, brickfront and modern buildings. From the downtown area, follow a sign to the right to the **Visitor Information Center** of the chamber of commerce, open weekdays 9 to 5. It's in Malcom's Milltown Center at 220 Center Street East. From there, an historic walking tour map will steer you past most of the town's old buildings. Eatonville was established as a lumbering community in 1889 by T.C. Van Eaton; his descendants still live in the area.

From Eatonville, continue north about two miles on Highway 161, then turn left at a sign indicating the Pioneer Farm Museum. After a quarter of a mile, go right down Ohop Valley Road for a mile and a half.

*Pioneer Farm Museum* ● *7716 Ohop Valley Rd., Eatonville; (206) 832-6300. Daily 11 to 5 from Father's Day weekend through Labor Day; weekends only in fall and spring; closed in winter. Pioneer Farm Tour or Native American Seasons Tour, $4 each; both for $7; less for kids.* ☐ Billed as a "hands-on 1887 homestead," the outdoor museum offers an interesting scatter of old log and whipsaw board buildings. During the farm tour, folks can try their skills at milking cows, churning

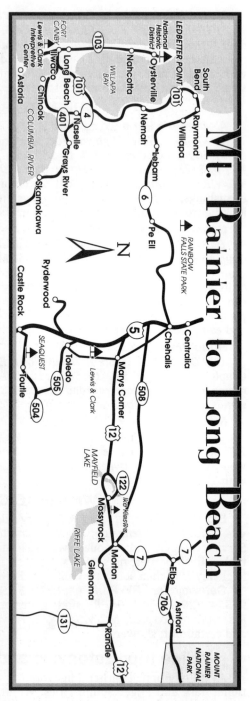

butter and other bucolic chores. The Native American tour, given weekends only, takes visitors through a "tribal gathering place" where hunting and fishing skills and food preparation are demonstrated. An old cabin houses a museum, general store and rural-theme curio and souvenir shop.

Return to Highway 161 from the farm museum and drive another three miles to one of the West's finest wildlife parks:

☺ **Northwest Trek** ● *11610 Trek Drive East, Eatonville; (800) 832-TREK or (206) 832-6117. Park opens daily at 9:30; tram tours hourly 10 to 4 weekdays and 10 to 5 weekends. Adults $7.50, seniors $6.50, youths $5, tots $2 (prices include tram ride). MC/VISA.* ❑ Operated by the Metropolitan Park District of Tacoma, this nicely-maintained wildlife park exhibits the flora and fauna of the American and Canadian Northwest. A tram follows a winding asphalt road through woodlands and meadows, where herds of elk, deer, caribou, bison and mountain goats roam. They've become remarkably indifferent to the tram, so you'll be very close to them. Before or after the tram ride, you can stroll past a state-of-the-art bear exhibit, peer into the eyes of a handsome silver-mane wolf (and hear his cry over a phone) and visit with other critters in open air enclosures. Nature-oriented gifts are sold at a curio shop, and you can grab a bite at a snack bar. One of the appealing features of this fine park is that it's all non-smoking, except for the picnic area.

## MOUNT RAINIER TO THE PACIFIC

Retrace your route through Eatonville, then continue south on Highway 7, past Elbe to Morton. En route, you'll pass a series of privately-owned recycling forests. Whether or not you support clear-cutting, you'll be interested in the gradual progression from recently cut swatches to sections that were planted two decades ago and are beginning to look like forests again. Signs along the way tell you when this section was cut and that one was thinned. Here indeed, forestry becomes agriculture, although the crop is much slower than wheat or corn.

**Morton,** no surprise, is a lumbering town. Since it's surrounded by privately-held forests not subject to spotted owl rationing, it's a rather busy community. Although it offers no tourist lures, it does have a couple of motels and restaurants, in case you need to take a break from the road.

In Morton, you pick up Highway 12 and head west through more forest, mostly uncut. After topping a rise, you begin a long downward slide alongside **Riffe Lake,** backed up behind Mossyrock Dam. It offers the typical reservoir lures of fishing, boating and swimming. Approaching the hamlet of **Mossyrock,** you have a couple of camping opportunities. To reach the first, turn left and drive through the town of Mossyrock and follow signs to Mossyrock Dam. For the second, turn right at the Mossyrock junction and follow State Highway 122 about four miles:

*Mossyrock Park* ● *202 Ajlune Rd., Mossyrock, WA 98564; 983-3900. RV and tent sites; water and electric $11, no hookups $8, tent sites $5. No credit cards.* ❑ Campsites in crowded clusters separated by green areas; neat and well-maintained. Coin laundry and showers; swimming, fishing, boat launching and other lake activities.

*Ike Kinswa State Park* ● *873 Harmony Road, Silver Creek, WA 98585-9706; (206) 983-3402. RV and tent sites; hookups $15, no hookups $11. Reservations available in summer by requesting a form from the park. No credit cards.* ❑ Well-spaced, wooded sites on Mayfield Lake, some near the water.

Picnic tables, barbecues, showers; picnic and swimming areas; snack bar.

Downtown Mossyrock, about a mile off the highway, is worth a brief peek. The small business district consists of a handful of old false front stores. En route, notice the string of 1930s style matched brick high school, junior high and grade schools.

Pressing west on Highway 12, you'll emerge from cultivated woodlands and roll through a green countryside of pasturelands and farms. At **Salkum,** about eight miles from Mossyrock, turn left onto Fuller Road for an interesting detour to an excellent salmon hatchery and then to one of the Northwest's oldest missions.

☺ After a few miles, Fuller Road T-bones into Spencer Road; turn left and follow it a couple of miles to **Cowlitz Salmon Hatchery.** We have a short attention span for most hatcheries, although this one is particularly well set up for visitors. Little yellow fish prints take you into an interpretive center, where a gallery provides views down into the spawning room. From there, follow the prints to a fish ladder where—during spring and fall runs—you can watch weary, travel-battered salmon working their way back into the hatchery.

Retrace your route on Spencer Road; six miles takes you to a turnoff to **Cowlitz Trout Hatchery,** interesting, but not as well set up for visitors. The road to the hatchery is easy to miss; a small white sign on the right shoulder of Spencer Road tells you to turn left. If you pass Blue Creek Bait and Tackle Shop, you've overshot. Continuing west on Spencer Road from the trout place, you come upon one of Washington's earliest settlements.

☺ **St. Francis Xavier Mission** is a tidy looking complex with a handsome brick church and carefully-tended cemetery shaded by mature evergreens. It marks the site of the first British mission in the Northwest, founded by Catholic missionaries from Quebec in 1838. Step inside the vestibule, where graphics tell you about the mission's history. The sanctuary is attractively simple, with stained glass windows and an odd rounded ceiling.

Continue past the mission to a stop sign and turn right (north) onto the Jackson Highway, which will take you back to U.S. Highway 12. En route you pass **Lewis and Clark State Park** with campsites for $10, a playfield, equestrian area, old growth forest exhibit and hiking trails. Beyond the park and just short of Highway 12 is **Jackson House Historic Site,** on your left. The rude log cabin here was built in 1848 by John R. Jackson, one of the area's first settlers. The cabin is sparsely furnished, unattended and generally locked, so your visit may be limited to a glimpse through the windows. A monument out front discusses Jackson's role as a sheriff, assessor and territorial representative. Just north of here are the twin cities of Chehalis and Centralia. Although not tourist centers, they offer a few attractions worthy of pause. The logical approach is to take Highway 12 west to Interstate 5 and then go north to Chehalis. A simpler if slower approach is to stay on Jackson Highway, which eventually enters the town's side door.

# Chehalis

**Population: 6,500**                                      **Elevation: 196 feet**

A farming, lumbering and commercial center, Chehalis dates from 1873, when a group of settlers platted a town and snatched the Lewis County seat from Claquato (now extinct). It began life as Saundersville, then became Chehalis six years later, named for local Indians. The town today is best described as pleasantly nondescript, although the downtown area offers some interesting old brick and masonry.

If you stay with Jackson Highway, you'll pass through a long and uninteresting commercial fringe. The highway becomes Market Street, which takes you downtown. Although the area is somewhat active, a few empty storefronts suggest the usual flight of businesses to the suburbs. Note the red brick, wedge-shaped **St. Helens Inn** as you enter the business district. It appeared to be between tenants when we last passed. On the outer edge of downtown, as Market merges with a couple of other streets, look to your left for the 1912 brick railroad station, now housing the town's yesterdays:

☺ *Lewis County Historical Society Museum* • *599 NW Front Street; (206) 748-0831. Tuesday-Saturday 9 to 5, Sunday 1 to 5, closed Mondays. Adults $2, seniors $1.50 and kids $1.* ☐ This nicely-done museum offers the usual exhibits regarding pioneer life, lumbering and such. Among the more interesting displays are a blacksmith shop, restored Model-A sports roadster, 18th century kitchen and parlor groupings. The best attraction is the depot, which is listed on the National Register of Historic Landmarks.

From the depot, follow National Avenue northward for about three blocks, then turn left at the I-5 sign onto Chamber of Commerce Way. It's aptly named, since it shortly delivers you to the **Twin Cities Chamber of Commerce** visitors center, open Monday-Friday 9 to 5. Beyond the chamber, hop onto the freeway, drive a short distance north and then take exit 81 onto Mellen Street and the other twin.

## Centralia

**Population: 12,100**                                    **Elevation: 188 feet**

Centralia is a larger and equally ordinary rendition of Chehalis, although it has a more interesting beginning. Pioneer James C. Cochran of Missouri came west with his slave George Washington, freed him and adopted him as his son. Cochran homestead a large chunk of land in 1850. He later sold a slice of it to Washington, who platted a town and began selling lots. Within a decade, Centerville was a thriving commercial area, with Washington as its driving force. It was the only community in the state founded by a black. The town name later was fancied up as Centralia.

Although smaller Chehalis has the county seat and museum, Centralia has its own appeal—a collection of murals on its well-preserved downtown buildings. To reach them, keep following "Highway 507" and "City center" signs from the freeway through several twists and turns. You'll eventually wind up on one-way South Tower Avenue, the main drag. The first mural decorates the appealing old Fox Theater at Tower and East Locust. Others are scattered about downtown, and a map available from the Twin Cities chamber will help you find them.

If you're an antiquer, you'll want to park, and then walk and shop in downtown Centralia. Several antique stores are in this area, and you can find 80 dealers under one roof at **Centralia Square,** 201 S. Pearl St.; (206) 736-6406. Those who prefer more contemporary shopping will find a surprisingly large collection of **factory outlet stores** at Freeway exit 82.

Another Centralia attraction, off-beat but interesting, is the state's first and largest coal-fired generating plant. Two-hour tours of the **Centralia Steam Plant** can be arranged by calling (206) 736-9901 weekdays between 8 and 4:30. They're given Tuesdays and Thursdays only. Even if you aren't here on a tour day, this huge complex is worth an exterior look. To reach it, follow Tower Avenue through town, turn left from Tower onto Sixth Street, then right onto Pearl Street. Green steam plant signs will keep you on track as you cross the Skookumchuck River. After a mile or so, turn left at the "Shafer Park/Centralia Steam Plant" sign onto Big Hanaford Road. The park is off to the right, and you continue another four miles to the plant. To see the open-pit coal mine that feeds the facility, continue two miles past the plant. At a Y-intersection, turn left onto Toro Road and go another two miles, up to Gate 16 for an overview of the mines, with the steam plant in the background.

Retrace your route along Pearl Street, which returns you to downtown's one-way grid. Turn right onto West Main Street opposite a park and head west. It swerves to the right to become Harrison Street, which takes you to the exit 82 interchange and all those factory outlet stores. From here, take Borst Avenue west to the 1852 **Fort Borst Park.** It features a reconstruction of the blockhouse that once protected Centralia. The large park also offers a small lake, arboretum, rhododendron garden and the usual picnic areas and kiddie playground. Those 14 and under can angle for trout in the lake. Nearby is the 1860 **Joseph Borst Home,** which can be toured weekdays by appointment; call (206) 736-7687.

Return to the freeway, go briefly south toward Chehalis and head west out State Highway 6. Before you go too far, pause for a brief visit to the 1858 **Claquato Church,** about two miles out of town on your right. The white clapboard structure with an unusual octagonal bell tower is the oldest surviving Protestant Church in the state.

## ACTIVITY

**Steam train rides** ● Chehalis-Centralia Railroad, 1945 S. Market St., Chehalis; (206) 748-9593. Twelve-mile round trips between Chehalis and Centralia on cars pulled by an old logging locomotive; also longer trips to Ruth. Summer weekends only; adults $6.50 and kids $4.50; Ruth trip, adults $10.50 and kids $8.50. Dinner excursions also offered.

## WHERE TO DINE IN CHEHALIS/CENTRALIA

### Azteca Restaurant ● △△ $$

□ 118 N. Tower Avenue (near Main); Centralia; (206) 736-0973. Mexican; wine and beer. Monday-Thursday 11 to 9:30, Friday-Saturday 11 to 10:30, Sunday noon to 9. MC/VISA. □ Typical Mexican fare served in a very appealing setting. The cute little café with carved wooden booths and Latin artifacts is housed in a handsome old brick building.

### ☺ Country Cousin Restaurant ● △△ $$

□ 1054 Harrison Street, Centralia; (206) 736-2200. American; full bar service. Daily 5:30 a.m. to midnight. Major credit cards. □ Clever, gimmick-ridden farm style restaurant with entrées such as breaded veal cutlets, chicken fried steak and po'k chops. A cow moos as you enter the door, farm implements hang from walls and rough-hewn posts hold up the ceiling.

### ☺ Mary McCrank's Restaurant ● △△ $$ ∅

□ 2923 Jackson Highway, Chehalis; (206) 748-3662. American; wine and beer. Tuesday-Saturday 11:30 to 2:30 and 5 to 8:30, Sunday noon to 8. MC/VISA. □ Charming old dinner house in business since 1935, offering reasonably-priced home-cooked grub. The menu features such rural fare as chicken livers and onions, pork chops, and chicken and dumplings. Several down-home dining offer views of landscaped grounds and a creek; some are smoke free.

### Rumors Bar & Grill ● ∆ $

☐ 575 N. Main Street, Chehalis; (206) 748-3967. American; full bar service. Monday-Saturday 6 a.m. to 3 p.m. and Sunday 7 to 3. MC/VISA. ☐ Handy lunch stop for museum visitors, with an assortment of soups, salads and French dip; also breakfast fare. Try the Rumorburger with eggs, bacon, ham and cheese.

## WHERE TO SLEEP

### Cascade Non-Smokers' Motel ● ⌂⌂ $$ Ø

☐ 550 SW Parkland Dr. (two blocks from I-5), Chehalis, WA 98532; (206) 748-8608. Couples and singles $35.74 to $39.89. MC/VISA. ☐ A 29-unit smoke-free motel with TV movies and room phones; on 12 acres with an adjacent park and playground. Next-door **Kit Carson Restaurant** serves American fare 6 a.m. to 11:30 p.m.; full bar service.

### ☺ Ferryman's Inn ● ⌂⌂⌂ $$ Ø

☐ 1003 Eckerson Rd. (I-5 exit 82), Centralia, WA 98531; (206) 330-2094. Couples $46 to $52, singles $40 to $43, kitchenettes and suites $40 to $52. Major credit cards. ☐ Very well-maintained, affordably-priced motel; 84 rooms with TV movies and phones; pool, spa, coin laundry, exercise room; free continental breakfast.

### Pony Soldier Motor inn ● ⌂⌂ $$ Ø

☐ 112 Interstate Ave. (at 13th), Chehalis, WA 98532; (800) 634-7669 or (206) 748-0101. Couples $46 to $50, singles $42 to $46, suites $60. Major credit cards. ☐ Sixty-nine nicely done rooms with TV movies and phones, some refrigerators and microwaves; pool and spa; free continental breakfast.

## CHEHALIS TO THE COAST

State Highway 6 wanders westward through a pleasing mix of pasturelands and conifers. Blackberry vines invite you to pause and pick, tiny towns whisk past and white clapboard houses loll under yard-tree canopies. Sixteen miles out of Chehalis, you encounter **Rainbow Falls State Park.** The falls are little more than a riffle in a passing creek, although the park is an appealing retreat, with creekside trails and campsites tucked beneath evergreens (flush potties and showers; $10).

**Pel Ell** offers gas pumps, a couple of family cafès, a state liquor store and that's about it. **Francis** is marked on the map, although it consists only of a New England style Catholic church and a couple of houses. **Lebam** is a bit larger, with a tavern and cafè, grocery store and a kiosk with a map of Pacific County. Aptly named, the county is Washington's southwest cornerstone, an area rich in beaches, oyster farms and aquatic history. **Menlo** comes and goes in the wink of a church steeple and an old general store.

You're in the **Willapa Valley,** whose rain-soaked streams drain into large Willapa Bay. The inlet is formed by skinny, low-lying Long Beach Peninsula, which is home to some of the state's earliest settlements and some of its most popular ocean playgrounds. As you press closer to the bay, the landscape becomes increasingly lush. You're entering one of the soggiest corners of the state, a place where fenceposts sprout and moss covers nearly everything that isn't moving. Look carefully as you drive and you'll see an occasional abandoned house enshrouded with vines and creepers, like jungle-clad Mayan ruins.

Embracing Willapa Bay, Pacific County is hands down the oyster capital of the world. The muddy bottom of the almost-landlocked bay offers ideal habitat for the slippery critters. Native Americans harvested them wild for centuries before the first intruders arrived. William Clark of Lewis and Clark fame ventured into this corner from Fort Klatsop in 1805, and carved his name on a sapling near present-day Long Beach. His journals don't mention whether he had oysters for lunch.

The oyster industry was started by crewmen from the schooner *Robert Bruce,* which ran aground and burned in 1851. The men salvaged what they could, built cabins south of present-day South Bend and hired local Indians to harvest the oysters. Three years later, Astoria residents I.A. Clark (no relation to William Clark) and R.H. Espy learned about Willapa Bay's oyster bounty from an Indian friend, Nahcati. In 1854, the pair rafted across the Columbia, got themselves a canoe and began paddling northward through a dense fog. Guided by Nahcati beating a stick against a hollow tree, they put ashore on Long Beach Peninsula. They immediately began laying out a village, appropriately named Oysterville. Other oyster centers soon followed on both sides of the bay. Many still survive, marked by ivory piles of shells around weathered shucking sheds.

Today, of course, the oysters come from commercial beds. Native mollusks were greatly depleted by heavy harvesting in the last century, then the survivors were wiped out by a series of winter freezes in the 1880s. They were replaced by the hardier *ostrea giga* or triploid oyster from Japan. Generating $20 million a year, oysters comprise the area's largest industry. Incidentally, being a commercial oyster is no fun. The critters are neutered to keep their little minds off sex. With no mating cycle, they stay tender and firm the year around.

There is no public oyster-digging in Willapa Bay, since all tidal flats are privately owned. Visitors can buy them fresh from oyster farms and markets, and one will be hard-pressed to find a café or bar that doesn't offer oyster shooters.

I've never been able to shoot a raw oyster and I just barely like them fried. Oysters aside (preferably), this is one of Washington's most inviting corners. Although seaside commercialism has muted much of Long Beach's charm, other communities are rustically appealing. The region offers a pleasing mix of sandy beaches and sheltered coves. And if a local here tells you to go fly a kite, it's an invitation, not an insult. Long Beach is the state's most popular kite center and host to one of the world's largest kite festivals.

The area starts turning on its charm when you reach U.S. Highway 101 at a delightfully scruffy old town at the head of the Willapa River estuary.

# Raymond

**Population: about 1,000**                    **Elevation: sea level**

☺ Founded as a lumber shipping port at the turn of the century, Raymond hasn't changed much since then. To explore its compact little business district, head first for the **visitor information center,** just off Highway 101 at Durea and Fifth streets. It's open Tuesday 10 to 8, Thursday

10 to 5 and Saturday 10 to 3. After picking up a brochure or two, including a guide to historic buildings, follow Fifth Street alongside a three-block-long city park. It's something of an outdoor museum, with a collection of antique wagons, farming and lumbering equipment and several nicely-done wooden carvings.

Opposite the outdoor equipment collection is **Dennis Company Trading Center** at Fifth and Blake; it's marked by an imposing 85-foot mural of an old-timey logging scene. Built in 1912 by Stewart Lake Dennis, it's still a busy hardware and mercantile, with a few historic exhibits among the merchandise. Hours are Monday-Saturday 7:30 to 5:30 and Sunday 10 to 3.

If you follow State Highway 105 north along the northern edge of Willapa Bay, you'll pass through the stretched-out beach town of **Grayland** and wind up in **Westport.** It's an exceptionally cute town clinging to the very tip of a sandspit forming the bent elbow of **Grays Harbor.** Since this large natural harbor is the southern anchor of the Olympic Peninsula, Westport is covered in Chapter six.

# South Bend

**Population: 1,600**                                       **Elevation: 11 feet**

After your Raymond prowl, head south on U.S. 101 toward another old time charmer. South Bend calls itself the oyster capital of the world, and piles of shells around a processing plant at the north edge of town lend credence to this claim. Established late in the last century, South Bend managed to shuck the Pacific County seat from Oysterville in 1893. It gets its name from its site on a bend of the Willapa River estuary. Its brief business district of false front stores stand along Highway 101.

☺ Check out the curious Monticello-style **Pacific County Courthouse** by turning left onto Memorial Drive (at the blue Sea Quest Motel sign), then drive two blocks uphill. Branded as a "gilded palace of reckless extravagance" when it was built in 1911, this Greek revival structure with its steel and stained glass dome is worth a peek. Back on the highway, you'll see the town's store-front exhibit center on your left:

*Pacific County Museum* • *1008 W. Robert Bush Dr. (Highway 101); (206) 875-5224. Monday-Saturday 11 to 4 and Sunday noon to 4; donations appreciated.* ☐ This simple, uncluttered archive focuses on the history of the local oyster industry, lumbering and shipping. Its gift shop has a good selection of books, and it also serves as a visitor information center for this corner of Washington.

Just beyond is the town's small **waterfront and marina** with a fishing fleet and visitor information kiosk. If you'd like to sample the local product (smoked or slithery), pause at the curious combination of a Shell service station and **Willapa Oyster Company** Seafood Market, across from the waterfront on Highway 101 at Central Avenue. It offers fresh, canned and smoked oysters and other local seafoods. Hours are Monday-Saturday 7 a.m. to 9 p.m. and Sunday 8 to 8; (206) 875-5894.

Beyond South Bend, the estuary widens into Willapa Bay with its oyster-rich mudflats rimmed by forests. Twelve miles from town, turn right for a short drive to **Bay Center,** a nautically rustic little town occupying a peninsula. Its oyster sheds on weathered pilings and turn-of-the-century homes are more suggestive of maritime New England than coastal Washington.

## WHERE TO DINE
### South Bend to Bay Center
**Boondocks Restaurant** • ΔΔ **$$**

◻ *1015 W. Robert Bush Dr. (Highway 101), South Bend; (206) 875-5155. American, mostly seafood; full bar service. Daily 8 to 9, closed Mondays from November to March. MC/VISA.* ◻ Attractive restaurant perched over the waterfront with bay views from the dining room and coffee shop. Oysters are a specialty, of course, along with several other seafood dishes. The dining room is an appealing mix of nautical and early American, with scalloped curtains and maple chairs.

**Blue Heron Inn** • Δ **$$**

◻ *Bay Center; (206) 875-9990. American, mostly seafood; wine and beer. Daily 7 a.m. to 10 p.m.* ◻ Small Naugahyde nautical café that's more attractive inside than out. A specialty is all-you-can-eat oysters for $11.95; also snapper, steak and oyster combination.

## WHERE TO SLEEP
**Maunu's Mountcastle Motel** • △ **$$**

◻ *524 Third St., Raymond, WA 98577; (800) 400-5571 (in the 206 area code only) or (206) 942-5571. Couples $40 to $45, singles $36 to $40, kitchenettes $5 extra. Major credit cards.* ◻ A 28-unit motel with TV, room phones; some room refrigerators.

**Marings Courthouse Hill Bed & Breakfast** • △△△ **$$$** Ø

◻ *602 W. Second St. (near Cedar), South Bend, WA 98586; (206) 875-6519. Couples $50 to $65, singles $45 to $50. Two units with private baths; full breakfast. MC/VISA.* ◻ This Victorian style B&B features a mix of antique and traditional furnishings, with room phones and TV. It began life in 1892 as a church and became a private residence. It's a block east of the courthouse, offering views of the Willapa River.

**H & H Motel & Café** • △ **$$** Ø

◻ *E. Water Street at Highway 101, South Bend, WA 98586; (206) 875-5442 or (206) 875-5523. Couples $39 to $42, singles $32. MC/VISA.* ◻ Sixteen-unit motel with TV. **H & H Café** serves American fare, mostly seafood; 5 a.m. to 10 p.m.; dinners $8 to $12; full bar service.

## WHERE TO CAMP
**Bay Center KOA** • *P.O. Box 315 (three miles off U.S. 101 on Bay Center Dike Road), Bay Center, WA 98427; (206) 875-6344. RV and tent sites; full hookups $20, water and electric $17.50, no hookups $15. Reservations accepted; MC/VISA.* ◻ Sixty spaces in a wooded setting with a trail to the beach. Showers, picnic tables, barbecues, TV hookups; coin laundry, minimart, rec hall; beachcombing and clam digging.

**Bruceport County Park** • *Highway 101, five miles south of South Bend; (206) 875-5261. RV and tent sites; full hookups $12, water and electric $10.50, no hookups $8.50. Reservations accepted.* ◻ Wooded campground with some bay-view sites; barbecues and picnic tables and showers, a few grocery items, kids play area, caged bird exhibit. Cluttered but well-maintained county campground operated by concessionaires.

**Gypsy Trailer Park** • *524 Central St., South Bend, WA 98577; (206) 875-5165. RV sites only, $10. Reservations accepted.* ◻ Mobile home park with 10 RV spaces; full hookups and cable TV; showers, coin laundry. Four blocks off the highway.

## The Long Beach Peninsula

Continuing south from Bay Center, Highway 101 swings inland through a thick woodland, where trees vastly outnumber residents. In the non-town of **Nemah,** you can follow a road 2.5 miles through a virtual rain forest to **Nemah Salmon Hatchery,** open weekdays 8 to 4:30. It's not terribly interesting, although the drive through the moss-draped forest is appealing. Back on U.S. 101, you'll shortly approach its junction with State Highway 4. Turn west, staying with 101, for a 13-mile drive along the bottom of Willapa Bay. This area is so lush that even the bay shore is green, although that's scum, of course.

☺ **Willapa National Wildlife Refuge** occupies much of this lower bayshore, plus Long Island within the bay and Leadbetter Point at the peninsula's northern tip. Established in 1937, it's home to water birds, black-tailed deer and elk herds. Several turnouts along the highway between Nemah and the Long Beach Peninsula invite you to fetch your binoculars and indulge in a bit of wildlife spotting. For details on the reserve, contact: Willapa National Wildlife Refuge, Ilwaco, WA 98624; (206) 484-3482.

Isolated Long Island, with hiking trails winding through thick old-growth forest, is the best place to see birds, deer, elk and even an occasional bear. However, it's a bit of a chore to get there, since there are no scheduled trips. If you have a boat in tow or an inflatable tucked into the trunk, you can simply paddle out, walk the brushy trails and camp in one of several primitive campsites. There's a launch ramp at refuge headquarters, on Highway 101 between Nemah and Ilwaco, and another at Nahcotta, halfway up Long Beach Peninsula. The rest of you will have to seek out a boat rental. Try one of the charter companies in Ilwaco (listed below, under "Activities.") They normally do only fishing charters, but they may have boats to rent.

## Long Beach

**Population: 1,200**                    **Elevation: sea level**

Pressing westward on Highway 101 across the bottom of Willapa Bay, you'll hit a stop sign at **Seaview,** a suburb of Long Beach. A **Visitor Information Center**, open daily 9 to 5 in summer (shorter hours in the off-season), is immediately to your right. Since you're now pointed north, we suggest that you first explore the skinny Long Beach Peninsula, and then go south to Ilwaco and Fort Canby State Historic Park. They're on the peninsula's lower tip, near the mouth of the Columbia River.

Long Beach got its start in 1880, when one Henry Harrison Tinker bought an acre of land from a settler and platted the town of Tinkerville. He started with a beachside tent city, then he followed with cottages and a resort hotel. Eventually, the town shed its inelegant name in favor of Long Beach. Next-door Seaview took shape in 1881 when area resident Jonathan L. Stout homestead land just below Tinker's holdings. He, too, built beach-front accommodations, highlighted by the large Seaview Hotel and ballroom, completed in 1886. Folks from all over the Northwest came by stagecoach, river steamer and eventually via the Ilwaco Navigation Company's Clamshell Railroad, to lie in the uncertain summer sun of Long Beach and Seaview.

Today's Long Beach is two things at once—twenty-eight uninterrupted miles of Pacific strand, and a community that has capitalized on that situation. Long Beach the beach is one of Washington's most popular surfside playgrounds. Tourist promoters say it's the longest continuous beach in the world. Long Beach the town, predictably, is total tourist immersion—a slender stretch of motels, T-shirt shops, carny rides, go-carts, bumper cars, moped and bike rentals, shooting galleries, video game parlors and kite shops.

You'll be struck by the contrast between the busy, touristy west side of Willapa Bay and the uncrowded, thickly wooded countryside and quaint old towns on the eastern shore. Obviously, Long Beach is long on tourist gimmicks and short on esthetics. This isn't a criticism; just a comment. It's a clean and pleasant community offering an abundance of family fun. Further, it's located a block inland from the beach, so the strand itself is practically free of commercialism.

Out there, life is certainly a beach. You can fly a kite, surf fish, bundle up beside sheltering driftwood, dig for shellfish, jog, stroll and even drive your car on the strand—with proper precaution. Despite all that sand and water, swimming is unsafe. Facing the open sea, with no sheltering harbor, Long Beach invites wicked riptides, undercurrents and rogue waves. Quicksand pits called "crab holes" can draw unexpected waders in over their heads. Further, the water is icy cold, even in summer.

### A beach boulevard: don't be a stick-in-the mud

If you drive on the beach, it's best to go where others have gone immediately before you, to avoid getting stuck. The firmest sand is above the high tide line and below the sand dune line. You'll find firm footing along most of this corridor, although you can encounter unexpected soft spots. Vehicles are forbidden near the surf and on any dunes. If you *do* get stuck, dig some of the loose sand away from your drive wheels, tuck mats or boards under them, then drive out slowly and steadily. Beach speed limit is 25 mph and of course, all foot traffic has the right-of-way. Some sections of the beach, including all clam beds, are closed to traffic, and some sections are only open seasonally, so check for signs before you enter the strand. In addition to these restrictions, all general laws governing auto licensing and equipment apply to vehicles driving on a beach.

## Driving the Long Beach peninsula

Heading north through Long Beach on Pacific Avenue (State Highway 103), you'll find good coastal access—either for your feet or your vehicle— at Tenth Street. It's opposite Nendel's Edgewater Inn. A boardwalk spans half a mile of inshore dunes here, linking Tenth to Bolstad Street. Graphics along the walk discuss the history and wildlife of the area. For a sand-free picnic, you can spread your fare on one of the boardwalk tables.

☺ If possible, come during the **Washington State International Kite Festival,** which is focused on the beach near the boardwalk in mid-August. Hundreds of multicolored flyers slice through the sky above the surf, performing amazing aerobatics. Particularly impressive is the competition formation flying, when teams sail their kites with the skill and tight precision of the Blue Angels.

Long Beach Peninsula is home to Washington's largest cranberry bogs— although they're small compared with those near Bandon, Oregon, which is home to most of the nation's little red berries. You can sample cranberry specialty foods at the **Cranberry House,** 200 S. Pacific Way; (206) 642-8585. If you'd prefer to sample assorted Northwest wines and cheeses, pause at **The Wine Shop,** 609 Pacific Way at Seventh Street Southwest. Just beyond, at Fifth Street, is **Marsh's Free Museum,** which is more of an oversized gift and shell shop. It does offer a goodly collection of pioneer artifacts, peek-a-boo machines and old coin music boxes; (206) 642-2188.

To learn about kites, step into the small **World Kite Museum** at Third Street just off Pacific Way, where assorted American and international kites are on display. Folks there also conduct periodic kite-making classes. It's open 11 to 5 Friday through Monday in summer, then weekends only from September through May; adults $1, kids and seniors 50 cents, family groups $3; (206) 642-4020.

The drive north along this flat, low-lying peninsula isn't terribly interesting, since the highway and most other roads are in from the ocean and the bay. If you're traveling in a camping rig, you'll find an abundance of commercial RV parks along here.

The thick string of tourist commercialism thins out as you proceed northward. At several points along the way, including **Loomis State Park,** you can get down to the beach. After about ten uneventful miles, you'll hit a stop sign near the suburb of **Ocean Park.** Turn right and follow a road to the most interesting hamlet on the peninsula.

## Oysterville

**Population: approximately 250**                                    **Elevation: 10 feet**

☺ Oysterville is a small collection of weathered buildings—including a few Victorians—that make up Oysterville National Historic District. This quiet gathering of old homes, some tucked behind tidy picket fences, is a wonderful departure from the intensive tourism of Long Beach. Many of the old commercial structures have been converted to private homes; some are marked with signs indicating their age and former use. The town was born in 1854 and a year later, it became the seat of Pacific County. It held that post "until the South Bend raiders came on Sunday morning, February 5, 1893, and carried away the records."

☺ Definitely worth a pause is the 1892 **Oysterville Church,** a small New England-style chapel on your left as you enter town. It's a real charmer, with an elaborate red and white witch's hat bell tower, kerosene lamps, a pot bellied stove, wooden pews and a still-functioning pump organ. Call 665-4268 to find out when it's open. Try to come on a Sunday in July or August, when music vespers are held at 3 p.m. Near the church is the bell-towered **Oysterville School,** built in 1908 and active until 1957. It's now a community center.

From the historic district, follow Weather Beach Road toward the bay to **Oysterville Sea Farm,** where you can buy fresh and smoked oysters and clams. Hours of this rustically nautical shack are 11 to 5, daily from June to October, then weekends and holidays the rest of the year; (206) 665-6585. Head back through Oysterville and you'll rejoin Highway 103 near **Oysterville Store.** It's mostly a mini-mart and souvenir shop, although it retains the wooden floors and pot-bellied stove of an old general store. It's open daily 9 to 5:30; (206) 665-4766.

Pressing north from Oysterville, you'll pass under a canopy of ancient evergreens, and then run out of road at **Leadbetter Beach State Park.**

Within the park, the thick forest yields to grassy dunes and marshes. Leadbetter is essentially a nature preserve, with no camping or picnicking facilities, but lots of trails winding among the grasslands to the mudflat beaches. You can fetch a trail map from a brochure rack at a parking area. Part of Willapa National Wildlife Refuge, this is a fine place for birdwatching and for plucking wild blackberries and tame strawberries and huckleberries.

As you retrace your route from Leadbetter Beach, continue straight ahead onto Sandridge Road, toward tiny **Nahcotta** instead of following Highway 103 around to the right. This charming hamlet offers a mix of old false front and a few modern stores and homes. You can catch a snack at **Nahcotta Natural Foods Store and Café,** on the main street. If you feel the need for more oysters, pause at **Jolly Roger Oysters** at Nahcotta's weathered waterfront (left down 273rd Street). The oyster fleet at anchor, with the bay behind and thick woods of Long Island and the mainland beyond, provides a tranquil scene.

From Nahcotta, the drive south along the bayside is uneventful, lacking both forests and commercialism. Small farms, rural homes and occasional cranberry bogs separate the road from the bay mudflats. More bogs are inland, particularly off Cranberry Road, north of an **Ocean Spray** cranberry processing facility. In late fall, when the bogs are flooded to facilitate harvesting, the millions of berries floating on the surface form fascinating patchworks of red. The rest of the year, they're merely square sections of vines and mud, like leafy rice paddies. Although Ocean Spray doesn't offer tours, you can visit the Washington State University **Cranberry Research Unit** on Pioneer Road, just north of Long Beach. It's open weekdays 9:30 to 4; (206) 642-2031. During the Ilwaco Cranberry Festival each October, guided tours are conducted to harvest areas; call (800) 451-2542 or (206) 642-2400 for details.

Beyond the bogs, you'll blend back onto the highway; continue south to Ilwaco and Fort Canby State Park at the peninsula's southern reach.

## Ilwaco

**Population: 800**                                        **Elevation: sea level**

Considerably more charming than Long Beach, Ilwaco is tucked among headlands in the hilly southern section of the peninsula. Downtown offers a mix of old false front and modern buildings, without the souvenir shop mentality of its neighbors to the north. At a stop light downtown, continue straight ahead to the weathered old working waterfront, offering a couple of seafood markets and cafés. It's also home port for most of the charter fishing companies in the area. You can stroll along the waterfront to watch fishing boats and processing houses at work. For fresh or smoked fish, check out **Jesse's Ilwaco Fish Company.**

Return to the downtown area and turn right a block short of the traffic light onto Lake Street for a visit to the local house of memories:

*Ilwaco Heritage Museum* ● *115 SE Lake St.; 642-3446. Monday-Saturday 10 to 5 and Sunday 10 to 4; hours vary seasonally. Adults $1.25, seniors $1 and kids 50 cents.* ▢ Although an amateur effort, this small museum avoids the clutter of many archives, offering displays on Native Americans, early settlers, oystering and lumbering. It also has a fair selection of books on local and Northwest history.

From the museum, return to the stop light (Spruce Street) and follow signs west on State Highway 100 toward one of the best reasons for spending time in this area:

☺ **Fort Canby State Park** • *State Route 100; (206) 642-3078. Interpretive Center and Lewis and Clark exhibit open daily 10 to 5; donations appreciated. Campground; details listed below. North Head and Cape Disappointment lighthouses closed to public; may be viewed from the outside.* ☐ Occupying one of the most historic sites on the West Coast, Fort Canby State Park offers an historic mix, ranging from Lewis and Clark's trek to lighthouses to ruins of an old fortification.

Cape Disappointment, just upstream from the treacherous Columbia River sandbars, was fortified in 1864. In 1875, the fort was named in honor of General Edward Canby, killed in the Modoc Indian wars in the Lava Beds area of northeastern California. Only a few vine-clad ruins of the fort remain today. The park's main lures are two lighthouses—one on the Pacific and one on the Columbia, an excellent Lewis and Clark exhibit, and hiking trails through thick rain forest.

As you approach the wooded hills surrounding the fort, look for a sign directing you to the North Head Lighthouse parking area, on your right. A gently inclined gravel path leads to this off-white candlestick of a tower. More impressive than the lighthouse are the views up and down the coast from this small peninsula. Continue into the main part of the park, following directions to the visitor center. En route, you'll pass the few surviving remnants of Fort Canby. Although Lewis and Clark's Corps of Discovery wintered on the Oregon side of the Columbia, they first put ashore here at Cape Disappointment. The new interpretive center honors that brief visit with an excellent exhibit concerning their epic trek westward.

From the visitor center parking area, you can take a rather steep three-quarter-mile trail to the black-and-white-striped Cape Disappointment Light. If you'd like to save some shoe-leather, drive down to the U.S. Coast Guard facility on the Columbia shore, then walk a shorter trail to the lighthouse. From there, you can follow another trail down to Waikiki Beach, a sheltered cove bearing absolutely no resemblance to its namesake. It was named in honor of a Hawaiian crewman, among the hundreds of sailors who drowned through the years when ships foundered at the mouth of the Columbia.

Heading back through Ilwaco, a right turn onto Spruce Street takes you onto southbound Highway 101 toward Astoria. You'll pass through **Chinook,** a properly rustic little old fishing village. Turn right down Portland Street for a look at its small port, offering a single seafood market and a few fishing boats. It occupies the site where Captain Robert Gray put ashore after breaching the Columbia sandbars in his *Columbia Rediviva,* and the site of a Lewis and Clark encampment. Two miles beyond are the well-tended remnants of another early military facility:

☺ **Fort Columbia State Park** • *Highway 101; (206) 777-8221 or (206) 642-3078, Interpretive center and museum open Wednesday-Sunday 9 to 5 in summer; by appointment only the rest of the year; both free. Park open all year, 8 a.m. to dusk.* ☐ This Army garrison was established in 1896 to protect local settlers, and it remained active until the end of World War II. The 600-acre campus is terraced into a steep slope above the Columbia. Several original structures survive, including bunkers and lookouts, gun batteries and a dozen wood-frame buildings. Exhibits in the Fort Columbia Museum focus on late 19th to early 20th century military life. You can follow a network of trails about the grounds and pause for a picnic with river views.

Just beyond the fort, Highway 101 enters a tunnel, then emerges to offer a sudden view of the four-mile-long Astoria Bridge. The town of Astoria, carefully arranged on the hilly Oregon shore, is certainly worth a side trip. It's one of the oldest communities in the West, with an impressive collection of historic buildings and an outstanding maritime museum. You can learn about it and other points south in our *Oregon Discovery Guide.* ⧠ If you like seafood and chips, it's worth the trip across the bridge for a feast at the **Ship Inn,** which we list below despite its being in the wrong state.

From the Astoria Bridge, choose either side of the great river to begin your final episode in this southwestern Chapter, the Columbia Corridor.

## ACTIVITIES ON THE LONG BEACH PENINSULA

*Fishing charters* • Beacon Charters & RV Park, P.O. Box 74 (at the port), Ilwaco, WA 98624, (206) 642-2138; Chetlo Charters, Port of Chinook, WA 98614, (206) 777-8360; Ilwaco Charter Service, P.O. Box 323 (at the port), Ilwaco, WA 98264, (206) 642-3232; Pacific Salmon Charters, P.O. Box 519, Ilwaco, WA 98264, (800) 831-2965 or (206) 642-3466; Tidewind Charters, P.O. Box 206, Ilwaco, WA 98264, (206) 642-2111.

*Horseback riding* • Double D Horse Ranch, 10th St. SW, Long Beach (near Nendel's), (206) 642-2576; featuring beach rides.

*Kites and kite flying* • Long Beach Kites, 104 N. Pacific Avenue, Long Beach, (206) 642-2202; and Stormin' Norman's Kites, 205 S. Pacific Avenue, Long Beach, (206) 642-3482.

*Surrey rides* • Cherokee Stables, Long Beach, (206) 642-4099.

## ANNUAL EVENTS

For information on these and other events, call the Long Beach Peninsula Visitors Bureau at (800) 451-2542 or (206) 642-2400.

**World's Longest Beach Run,** mid-June in Long Beach.

**Northwest Regional Stunt Kite Competition,** late June in Long Beach.

**Washington State International Kite Festival**, mid-August in Long Beach.

**Jazz & Oyster Festival**, mid-August in Oysterville.

**Ilwaco Cranberry Festival,** mid-October in Ilwaco.

**Long Beach Peninsula Water Festival,** late October, at various places on the peninsula.

## WHERE TO DINE

☺ *The Ark Restaurant and Bakery* • ∆∆∆∆ **$$$**

⧠ *On the Nahcotta dock, Nahcotta; (206) 665-4133. Northwest cuisine, mostly seafood; full bar service. Dinner Tuesday-Sunday (Wednesday-Sunday in the off-season), plus Sunday brunch. MC/VISA, AMEX.* ⧠ This local legend, rustically stylish and perched over the Nahcotta oyster fleet, has earned considerable culinary raves. The chef-owners have written three cookbooks, drawn from their changing menu. In can range from fresh local fish done in interesting spices and sauces to medallions of veal.

☺ *Dog Salmon Café* • ∆∆ **$$**

⧠ *Highway 103 near Tenth, Long Beach; (206) 642-2400. American, mostly seafood; full bar service. Daily 8 a.m. to 9:30 p.m. in summer; shorter hours the rest of the year. Major credit cards.* ☐ This properly rustic place in a weathered building is both a visual and a culinary treat. The look is Northwest Native American, with artwork and carvings on grasscloth walls. Start your gastronomical trip with a choice of seafood cocktails, then follow with seafood linguine or fettuccini, broiled halibut in lemon butter, Cajun shrimp or local littleneck clams. Chicken stir fry and a chop or two occupy the meat side of the menu. A cocktail lounge/sports bar is adjacent.

### 1st Place Seafood and Oyster Bar • Δ $

☐ *First Place Shopping Center, Highway 103 a block north of Tenth, Long Beach. American, mostly seafood; wine and beer. Daily 7 a.m. to 7 p.m.* ☐ This oyster bar and espresso cafè is a good lunch stop, featuring oyster shooters, steamer clams and other light seafood entrèes; dining tables indoors or out. Its seafood market counter offers a selection of fresh and smoked oysters and seafood.

### Kopa Wecoma Restaurant • ΔΔ $$ Ø

☐ *Highway 103 near Tenth, Long Beach; (206) 642-4224. Northwest cuisine, mostly seafood; no alcohol. Daily noon to 9. No credit cards.* ☐ Curiously attractive restaurant in a cottage, with plush blue booths, wood paneling and simulated Tiffany lamps. The menu focuses on local oysters and other seafood, including deep-fried shrimp and fillet of cod. If you must have meat, you can get a steak and oyster entrèe. The restaurant is smoke-free. Kopa Wecoma, incidentally, means "by the sea" in Chinook.

### Lightship Restaurant • ΔΔ $$$

☐ *409 W. Tenth (in Nendel's Edgewater Inn), Long Beach; (206) 642-5252. American; full bar service. Daily 8 a.m. to 10 p.m. Major credit cards.* ☐ It's the only area restaurant with an ocean view; the interior look is unimaginative nautical modern. Fresh local seafood can be excellent however. The menu also lists teriyaki chicken, grilled pork chops, pepper steak and other American fare. The adjacent Columbia Bar also offers ocean views.

### ☺ Ship Inn • ΔΔ $$

☐ *One Second Street at Marine Drive, Astoria, Ore.; (503) 325-0033. American, mostly seafood; full bar service. Daily 11:30 to 9:30. MC/VISA, DISC.* ☐ This is one of the best places on the Northwest coast to pig out on seafood and chips—halibut, prawns, oysters, scallops or a combination thereof. The servings are huge and inexpensive. The menu also features English specialties such as Cornish pasties and pork sausages. The dècor is basic nautical, with picture-window views across the waterfront to the Columbia River and Astoria Bridge. To reach Ship Inn, cross over the bridge, turn east onto Marine Drive (U.S. Highway 30), drive a few blocks to Second Street and turn left.

### ☺ The Shoalwater • ΔΔΔΔ $$$ Ø

☐ *Highway 103 at 45th in the Shelburne Inn, Seaview; (206) 642-4142. Northwestern cuisine, mostly seafood; full bar service. Daily noon to 9, plus Sunday brunch in summer from 11 to 2. Major credit cards.* ☐ Outstanding seafood served in a pleasing, smoke-free Victorian setting. The best catch is fresh local fare creatively prepared. Try the salmon with a cranberry-blueberry mustard sauce, or Dungeness crab cakes with red pepper mayonnaise. With an excellent wine list and wickedly delicious in-house desserts, this is one of Washington's better restaurants.

# WHERE TO SLEEP

**Arcadia Court** ● △ **$**

▢ *P.O. Box 426 (North Fourth & Boulevard), Long Beach, WA 98631; (206) 642-2613. Couples $37 to $39, singles $35 to $37, kitchenettes $49 to $79. Major credit cards.* ▢ Eight-unit motel in the dunes near the beach, with room TV; barbecues and picnic tables.

**Boardwalk Cottages** ● △ **$$$** ∅

▢ *800 S. Ocean Beach Blvd., Long Beach, WA 98631; (206) 642-2305. Couples $60 to $90, singles $60 to $70, kitchenettes $60 to $95. MC/VISA, DISC.* ▢ A 10-unit cottage complex with TV; all smoke-free. Near the beach.

**Heidi's Inn** ● △△ **$$** ∅

▢ *P.O. Box 776 (Highway 101 at city center, near boat basin), Ilwaco, WA 98624; (800) 576-1032 or (206) 642-2387. Couples $42 to $49, singles $37 to $42, kitchenettes $110 to $150 (off-season only). MC/VISA.* ▢ A 24-unit motel with TV, phones and room refrigerators; indoor spa, hospitality room.

**Lighthouse Motel** ● △ **$$$**

▢ *Route 1, Box 527 (2.5 miles north), Long Beach, WA 98631. Couples and housekeeping units from $44.50. MC/VISA.* ▢ An eight-unit motel with TV; some one and two bedroom cabins with decks and full kitchens. Some ocean-front units.

**Nendel's Edgewater Inn** ● △△△ **$$$** ∅

▢ *P.O. Box 793 (Tenth Street, off Pacific Avenue), Long Beach, WA 98631; (800) 562-0106 or (206) 642-2311. Couples and singles $55 to $78, suites $68 to $92. Major credit cards.* ▢ Attractive 84-unit inn just off the beach, with ocean view rooms; TV and phones; some refrigerators and microwaves. Some ocean-front units. **Lightship** restaurant listed above.

**Our Place at the Beach** ● △△ **$$$**

▢ *South Ocean Boulevard at S. 14th (P.O. Box 266), Long Beach, WA 98631; (800) 538-5107 or (206) 642-3793. Couples $50 to $55, singles $45, kitchenettes from $70, suites from $45. Major credit cards.* ▢ A 25-unit lodge near the beach with TV, room phones, refrigerators in all units; spa, sauna, steam room and weight room.

**Pacific View Motel** ● △△ **$$$** ∅

▢ *203 Bolstad (P.O. Box 302), Long Beach, WA 98631; (206) 642-2415. Couples and singles 50 to $70. MC/VISA.* ▢ Ten cabins facing the ocean, all with full kitchens and one or two bedrooms. TV in rooms.

☺ **Sou'Wester Lodge** ● △△ **$$** ∅

▢ *Beach Access Road (38th Place; P.O. Box 102), Seaview, WA 98644; (206) 642-2542. Couples and kitchenettes $31 to $99, singles from $28; some rates include breakfast. MC/VISA, DISC.* ▢ A rustic 20-unit resort with lodge rooms and beach cabins, on three acres facing the dunes and shaded by Douglas firs. TV and room movies available on request. Cultural activities scheduled during "fireside evenings," including seminars, art exhibits, plays and chamber music.

☺ **Sunset View Resort** ● △△△ **$$$**

▢ *P.O. Box 399, Ocean Park, WA 98640; (800) 272-9199 or (206) 665-4494. Motel units for two to four people $50 to $60, ocean-view units with* kitchens and fireplaces $70 to $90, suites with kitchens and fireplaces $80 to $130. Major credit cards. ⌷ Very appealing resort tucked into seven acres of trees, nine miles north of Long Beach. Fifty-four units with TV and phones; sauna and hot tubs. Barbecues, horseshoes, volleyball and a variety of other recreational facilities.

### Super Eight Motel ● ⌂⌂ $$$ Ø
⌷ P.O. Box 220 (Pacific Avenue at Fifth Street South), Long Beach, WA 98631; (800) 800-8000 or (206) 642-8988. Couples $66 to $88, singles $61 to $83, suites $96. Major credit cards. ⌷ Well-kept 51-unit hotel with TV movies, phones; free light breakfast.

### Fort Columbia Youth Hostel ● ⌂ $
⌷ Fort Columbia State Park, P.O. Box 224, Chinook, WA 98614-0224; (206) 777-8755. Hostel members $8.50, non-members $11.50, under 18 with parents $4.25, couples' private room surcharge $6. MC/VISA. ⌷ Typical hostel facilities in an intriguing facility—the converted former Fort Columbia hospital. Biking and hiking trails and other park facilities (listed above).

## Bed & breakfast inns

### Boreas Bed & Breakfast ● ⌂⌂⌂ Ø
⌷ P.O. Box 1344 (607 N. Beach Blvd.), Long Beach, WA 98631; (206) 642-8069. Couples $65 to $95, singles $55 to $85. Four units, two private and two share baths; full breakfast. MC/VISA. ⌷ Renovated 1920s beach house sitting in the dunes, furnished with an eclectic mix of American antique and contemporary. Fireplace in seaview living room; spa; path through the dunes to the beach; loaner bicycles.

### Gumm's Bed & Breakfast Inn ● ⌂⌂⌂ $$$ Ø
⌷ P.O. Box 447 (3310 Hwy. 101 at 33rd Ave.), Seaview, WA 98644; (206) 642-8887. Couples $65 to $75, singles $60 to $70. Four rooms with two private and two share baths; full breakfast. MC/VISA. ⌷ Nicely restored 1911 Northwest craftsman building that once served as the Long Beach Peninsula hospital. Individually decorated rooms with TV; stone fireplace in large living room; sun porch and hot tub.

### The Inn at Ilwaco ● ⌂⌂⌂ $$$ Ø
⌷ 120 NE Williams St. (at Spruce), Ilwaco, WA 98624; (206) 642-8686. Couples and singles $55 to $80. Some private and some shared baths; full breakfast. MC/VISA. ⌷ A cozy nine-unit inn housed in a refurbished 1928 church. Guest rooms are tucked upstairs, with slanted ceilings and dormer windows; they're furnished in early American style. The church's former sanctuary is now a performing arts center, offering a variety of plays and concerts.

### Kola House Bed & Breakfast ● ⌂⌂⌂ $$$ Ø
⌷ P.O. Box 646 (211 Pearl St.), Ilwaco, WA 98624; (206) 642-2819. Couples $65 to $75, singles $60 to $70. Five rooms with TVs and private baths; full breakfast. MC/VISA. ⌷ Nautical-style Victorian built in 1919, with a mix of modern and American antique furnishings. Two rooms with Columbia River view; one with fireplace. Hot tub, sauna and pool table in basement.

### Moby Dick Hotel & Oyster Farm ● ⌂⌂⌂ $$$$ Ø
⌷ Bay Avenue & Sandridge, Nahcotta, WA 98637; (206) 665-4543. Couples $65 to $85, singles $55 to $75. Ten rooms, one private and nine share

*baths; full breakfast. MC/VISA.* ☐ Unusual inn housed in a World War II Coast Guard structure, originally built in 1929. Rooms and public areas are done in the style of the 1930s; some units have bay views.

☺ **Poulsbo Bed & Breakfast** ● ⌂⌂⌂ $$$ Ø

☐ *P.O. Box 428 (3911 N Place), Seaview, WA 98644; (206) 642-4393. Couples and singles $65. Five rooms with shared baths; full Danish-style breakfast. No credit cards.* ☐ An 1887 cottage furnished in Victorian antiques with a Danish porcelains and a nautical theme. Attractive grounds with a pond, waterfall and croquet lawn. Danish breakfasts with aebleskivers, homemade breads, meats, cheeses and fruit.

☺ **Scandinavian Gardens Inn** ● ⌂⌂⌂ $$$$ Ø

☐ *Route 1, Box 36 (1610 California), Long Beach, WA 98631; (206) 642-8877. Couples $65 to $110, singles $55 to $100. Five units, all with private baths; full breakfast. MC/VISA.* ☐ Scandinavian inn occupying a ranch-style building, with decorative touches such as *rosemaling* artwork and hand-woven wall hangings. Rooms done in cheery colors, with a mix of antique and contemporary furnishings. Imported Scandinavian queen beds; cedar-lined sauna

## WHERE TO CAMP

**Andersen's on the Ocean** ● *Highway 103 at 138th (Route 1, Box 480), Long Beach, WA 98631; (800) 645-6795 or (206) 642-2231. RV and tent sites, $12 to $14. Reservations accepted; MC/VISA.* ☐ Sites near the beach; showers, cable TV; coin laundry, fishing, clamming and fish-cleaning station; playground.

**Cove RV and Trailer Park** ● *411 Second Ave. SW, Ilwaco, WA 98624; (206) 642-3689 or (206) 642-4317. RV and tent sites, $15 with full hook-ups. Reservations accepted; MC/VISA.* ☐ Showers, cable TV, picnic tables; coin laundry, fish and clam cleaning station; short walk to fishing, boating and the center of town.

**Fort Canby State Park** ● *P.O. Box 488, Ilwaco, WA 98624-0488; (206) 642-3078. RV and tent sites, $10. Reservations accepted in summer by requesting a form from the park; no credit cards.* ☐ Picnic tables and barbecues, flush potties; mini-mart, boat launching, fishing, trails; other state park activities listed above.

**Ilwaco KOA** ● *P.O. Box 549 (two miles south on U.S. 101), Ilwaco, WA 98624; (206) 642-3292. RV and tent sites, $15 to $19. Reservations accepted; MC/VISA.* ☐ Showers; coin laundry, mini-mart, Columbia River fishing access, rec room and playground.

**Oceanic City Center RV Park** ● *Fifth and Pacific, Long Beach, WA 98631; (206) 642-3836 or 642-2472. RV sites only, $9 to $13. Reservations accepted; MC/VISA.* ☐ Small park near downtown Long Beach; showers, cable TV; clam and fish cleaning facilities.

**Sou'Wester Lodge & Trailer Park** ● *38 Place Beach Access Rd. (P.O. Box 102), Seaview, WA 98664; (206) 642-2542. RV and tent sites, $14.50 to $18.75. Reservations accepted; MC/VISA.* ☐ Sites on the beach; showers, TV hookups; picnic area, coin laundry, fish and clam cleaning station. South of highways 101 and 103.

# THE COLUMBIA CORRIDOR

By every measure, the Columbia is northwestern America's Old Man River. Of all the streams on the continent, only the Mississippi, St. Lawrence and Mackenzie have a greater water volume. The Columbia is the largest river flowing into the Pacific. It begins in Columbia Lake in the foothills of British Columbia's Rockies, 2,700 feet above sea level. After meandering south through Canada and eastern Washington, it heads west to form the Washington-Oregon border, reaching the sea 1,264 miles from its source.

Gathering tributaries and strength as it flows, it drains 250,000 square miles in seven states, carrying 180 million acre feet of water into the Pacific each year, at an average rate of two million gallons per second. It's nearly five miles wide at the mouth, and early sailors failed to chart it as a river, thinking it to be an inlet. Today, the lower Columbia is more of a chain of lakes than a river, since it's one of the most harnessed (environmentalists would say harassed) streams in the world. With more than a dozen dams, it generates 80 percent of the Northwest's hydroelectric power and 40 percent of the entire nation's hydroelectric output.

As you follow its final stages through southwestern Washington, it will indeed resemble a long lake. Our trek along the Columbia Corridor takes you from the Astoria Bridge to the U.S. Highway 97 junction in central Washington, a distance of nearly 200 miles. On this entire stretch, even as it carves the famous Columbia Gorge through the Cascade Range, the river drops an average of only six inches per mile. Pacific tides affect its water level more than 100 miles upstream.

## Astoria to Vancouver

If you were tempted to slip across the river to visit historic Astoria, as we suggested earlier, you might want to begin your exploration of the Columbia Corridor by following U.S. 30 east on the Oregon side. It's a more direct route, since Washington's State Highway 401 arches 12 miles northward before joining east-bound State Route 4. From there, Highway 4 travels away from the river until it reaches Cathlamet, offering little of interest.

Eastbound from Astoria, Highway 30 skims the river's edge for about ten miles. This is the Columbia's widest section, with the opposite shore more than five miles away. As you squint through the mist at the distant shoreline, it's easy to understand how the stream was mistaken for an inlet. The highway then swings inland until it reaches the townlet of **Westport,** where you can catch the charming old **Puget Island Ferry** to Cathlamet on the Washington side. It's one of the few surviving Columbia ferries, with a capacity of about a dozen vehicles. The boat chugs back and forth every 45 minutes or so, from 5:45 a.m. until around 10 p.m. The fare is $2 for a car and driver, plus 50 cents for passengers.

The ferry crossing is brief, since it lands on Puget Island in midstream. After a short drive through lush woods and dairy country, you'll cross a bridge over the river's north channel to **Cathlamet,** an appealing little town of Victorian homes and false front stores. Note the **fire hall and city hall**, sharing a white clapboard Victorian. From there, signs will direct you to the town's archive:

*Wahkiakum County Historical Museum* ● *65 River Street; (206) 795-3954. Open Tuesday-Sunday May through October and Thursday-Sunday the*

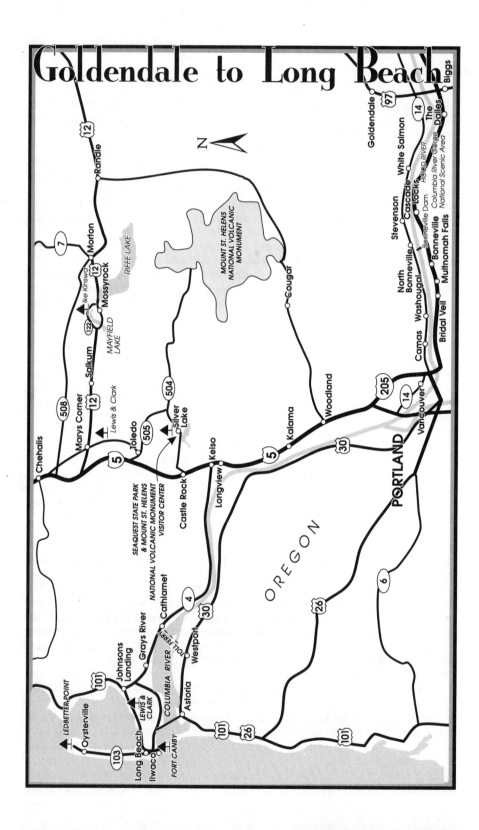

*rest of the year, 1 to 4 p.m. Free; donations appreciated.* ☐ This small cottage museum offers a busy, undisciplined clutter of pioneer artifacts. Its most predominant feature is outside—a 70-ton steam locomotive that hauled logs for the Crown Zellerbach Corporation in the 1920s. A park, picnic tables and trail to the waterfront are adjacent.

From the museum, return to the main drag (Butler Street) and head north toward Highway 4. Note the old Greek-Federalist **Wahkiakum County Courthouse** as you leave town. Should you wonder, Cathlamet was named for a local Indian tribe. It was settled back in 1846 by James Birnie of the Hudson's Bay Company, and known initially as Birnie's Retreat. It has chugged along since then as a small lumbering and dairying center.

The 25-mile run from Cathlamet to Longview offers almost constant exposure to the wide Columbia, with occasional turnouts where you can pause to watch tugboats in the mist and other river traffic. It's a pleasant drive, thickly wooded and thinly populated. A few miles beyond Cathlamet, a sign sends you three miles inland to the **Abernathy Salmon Culture Technology Center,** a high-blown title for a fish hatchery. It's open from 8 to 4:30. With the usual rearing tanks but no visitor center, it's of interest only to serious hatchery aficionados.

The ancient lumbering town of **Stella,** about 15 miles from Cathlamet, offers the small **Stella Historical Society Museum.** The structure, an 1871 clapboard, is more interesting than the small gathering of pioneer artifacts inside. It's open weekends only from 11 to 4. A couple of buildings on stilts over the water comprise the rest of the town; it has no services.

# Longview-Kelso

**Longview: 31,500; Kelso 11,800          Elevation: 13 and 26 feet**

These sturdy blue-collar communities offer little of tourist appeal, although they're handy stopovers and provisioning centers. Both have active visitor bureaus that will ply you with Southwest Washington information. Kelso, like so many other communities hereabouts, begs to be known as a gateway to Mount St. Helens.

The area's roots reach back a considerable distance, since this was the site of the 1852 Monticello Convention, during which settlers petitioned Congress to separate Washington from the Oregon territory. The town of Kelso came later, founded in 1884 by Peter Crawford and named for his hometown in Scotland. (The two Kelsos are now sister cities.) Longview came along later still, established in 1923 as a planned industrial community. Wide streets and sweeping (if sometimes confusing) boulevards around a central park give evidence to its calculated geography. Both communities are tucked around the merger of the Columbia and Cowlitz rivers.

A drive through these twin cities will guide you past a few points of interest. Stay alert, however, since Longview was laid out—not in a grid—but in a radius from its central park and civic center.

As you approach, Route 4 becomes Ocean Beach Highway. Blue signs will steer you to the Visitor Information Center, beginning with a half-right turn onto Nichols Boulevard (State Highway 432). You'll pass an appealing area of elegant homes, along the edge of **Lake Sacajawea Park.** After a mile or so, turn left onto Washington Way, which takes you toward the hub of a civic center. If you blend onto the loop drive around the park-like center and make a couple of left turns, you'll soon see Olympic Way; do a half-right for a short distance to the **Longview Chamber of Commerce** at 1563 Olympia. It's open weekdays 9 to 5.

Within the parklands surrounding the civic center is one of America's more harmlessly silly attractions—**Nutty Narrows Bridge** at Olympia Way near 18th. It's a squirrel crossing, complete with suspension spans, over the busy street. Local developer Amos J. Peters had it built in 1963 to provide safe passage for the critters. A huge squirrel statue shaped from a tree trunk, which looks somewhat squirrel-chewed, stands adjacent, along with an old steam logging train. Nearby is the **Monticello Convention Monument,** with plaques describing Washington's separation from the Oregon Territory.

From the city center, take Olympia Way northwest, about five blocks back to Ocean Beach Highway (Route 4), and make a hard right. After a few more blocks, some quick maneuvers will get you into old downtown Kelso and an excellent museum. As the highway approaches the Cowlitz River, take a half-left (at a double left turn lane) onto Washington Way, then an immediate half right onto West Main Street. You'll cross the river on an old steel girder bridge and the route becomes Kelso's Allen Street. If you're on a newer bridge, you've messed up. Continue across the river and take the first available right, which will drop you south to Allen. The museum you seek is about four blocks from the river, on Allen between Fourth and Fifth:

☺ *Cowlitz County Historical Museum* ● *405 Allen St.; (206) 577-3119. Tuesday-Saturday 9 to 5 and Sunday 1 to 5. Free; suggested donation $1 for adults, $2 for family groups and 50 cents for kids.* ⊡ This is one of the finest small museums in the Northwest. The professionally-done archive traces the region's development from Native Americans to the Hudson's Bay Company to lumbering, fishing and shipping. Among its excellent exhibits are a full-scale loggers' bunkhouse, a general store, and a dugout canoe and other Indian artifacts. Blown-up old time photos cover the walls; particularly impressive is a photo-mural of loggers taking a lunch break in the woods.

Downtown Kelso is busy with old storefronts, with some Victorian homes around the edges. A thick walking-tour brochure available at the museum will guide you past many of them. Having finished with downtown, continue east on Allen Street, cross under the freeway and turn left onto Minor Road for a pause at the **Tourist and Volcano Information Center.** Operated by the Kelso Chamber of Commerce, it's a nicely done little St. Helens visitor center with assorted photos, models and cut-aways of the big bang. The center is open daily 8 to 6 from May through October, and Wednesday-Sunday from 9 to 5 the rest of the year.

Continue your Columbia Corridor run by hopping onto I-5 and heading south toward Vancouver. Like most freeways, it offers swift travel, but little of interest. There is very little settlement along here, despite the population densities of Longview-Kelso above and Vancouver-Portland below.

As you approach **Kalama** about 18 miles from Kelso, you'll note the massive containment building of the **Trojan Nuclear Power Plant** to your right. Although it seems close enough to hit with a rock, it's across the Columbia River in Oregon. Technical problems shut it down in 1992, and it may or may not be ominously chuffing steam vapors when you pass.

Tiny Kalama is worth a visit, with an old fashioned brick-front main street east of the freeway and a busy new river port to the west. It offers a collection of antique shops and a few motels and cafès. **Pyramid Ales,** on the frontage road across the freeway, is one of the state's larger micro-breweries, open weekdays 10 to 4; (206) 673-2121. Tours and tastings are arranged whenever a few people gather. The hearty ales and beers are excellent, although the Pyramid Sphinx Stout is stout enough to drop your socks.

From the brewery, you can go right to a small boat basin, or left to a riverside park with picnic tables and a playground. Just beyond is **Lewis J. Rasmussen RV Park** with gravel sites, showers; $12 with water and electric, and $7 without. It's operated by Cowlitz County; (206) 673-2626.

Continue south from the RV park on the westside frontage road and you'll eventually blend back onto I-5. There's little of interest to interrupt you for the rest of the run to Vancouver. Stay with the freeway through that city until the last Washington exit (1-A); it takes you east on Highway 14 along the Columbia.

# THE COLUMBIA RIVER GORGE

Neighboring Oregon gets most of the Columbia Gorge glory, since the acclaimed waterfalls and the cliff-clinging Columbia Gorge Scenic Highway are on that side. A point of historical trivia: That famous highway was built by a Seattle resident, railroad heir Samuel Hill. He also created the Maryhill Museum and a replica of Stonehenge on the Washington side of the Columbia, which we will encounter at the end of this chapter.

We won't play favorites between the two states, so we'll suggest that the Washington side of the gorge—less the waterfalls—is equally scenic. Certainly a loop trip would be in order and if you're tempted, our *Oregon Discovery Guide* deals with the south side in suitable detail.

Most folks are properly awe-struck when they first see the gorge. How on earth did the Columbia managed to carve such a wide, steep-walled chasm through a mountain range? A series of prehistoric cataclysms called the Missoula Floods created this mighty channel. Geologists speculate that the Columbia has been flowing for at least 26 million years. When the Cascades began their slow rise about six million years ago, the river managed to weave a V-shaped canyon through the uplifts. Then, within the last 100,000 years, ice age glaciers alternately dammed upstream flows and then broke loose. These Missoula Floods sent great walls of water downstream, scouring away the mountains to leave the thousand-foot-high basaltic cliffs that remain today.

The gorge forms a natural wind tunnel, which draws multi-colored mini-fleets of windsurfers. On most days, you'll see flocks of triangular sails weaving in and about the river barge traffic. East of the Vancouver-Portland population mass, both sides of the gorge are thinly populated. The only towns of any size, Mount Hood and The Dalles, are on the Oregon side. Both are important windsurfing areas.

*RV advisory:* Highway 14 through the gorge is well engineered and easily handled by larger RVs and trailer rigs. You will encounter some steep climbs, twists and turns. There are occasional campgrounds and RV parks along the route; see "Where to camp in the gorge" below.

Columbia Gorge begins about 20 miles from Vancouver, after State Highway 14 passes through Washougal, just beyond Camas. The route is a freeway between Vancouver and Camas, often elevated above the flat landscape

*The Columbia River Gorge panorama from atop 848-foot Beacon Rock is one of the most imposing vistas in the state.* — **Betty Woo Martin**

to offer river views. Fifteen miles from Vancouver, you can take the **Camas-Washougal** business loop. However, there's little of interest to see and lots of stop lights to slow your progress. Camas is built around the huge James River Corporation Pulp Mill, whose commanding presence is visible from Route 14.

Beyond Washougal, you'll see the shoreline rise as the gorge begins cutting through the Cascades. You pass a brown "Columbia River Gorge National Scenic Area" sign and immediately begin climbing Washington's side of the chasm. Squint across the river and you'll see the tiny gray dot of Oregon's Crown Point observation house. During the early part of your climb, much of your view of the gorge will be shielded by trees. It suddenly emerges as a spectacular panorama after you start downhill from a highway pass. A long turnout invites you to pause and study the sheer basaltic cliffs that embrace the mile-wide river.

**Skamania** is a tiny town cradled in the Cascade slopes, offering a general store, deli, café and gas pumps. For the next fifty miles, the gorge is a near-constant companion as the highway tips down near water's edge, then climbs low passes for aerial views. A few miles beyond Skamania, you'll encounter one of the world's most imposing monoliths and yes, it can be climbed.

☺ **Beacon Rock State Park** ● *Highway 14, east of Skamania; (509) 427-8265. No day use fee; campsites $10 (see below).* ◻ The world's second largest monolith (after the Rock of Gibraltar), Beacon Rock is an ancient volcanic plug jutting 848 feet above the Columbia shoreline. Lewis and

Clark gave the promontory its name. Oregon Trail travelers, ferrying through the gorge, watched eagerly for this bold knob, for it marked the end of rapids and smooth sailing to trail's end at Oregon City.

A state park campground and picnic areas are across the highway. However, the best reason to stop at the rock is to climb it. Despite its vertical rise, this isn't a technical climb, but a one-mile grunt up a series of switchbacks and stair steps. Railings will temper your fear of falling. This is about as impressive a short hike as you'll ever take, with regal views of the gorge from the top. The climb was made possible by Henry J. Biddle, who bought the rock in 1915 and spent the next two years carving and hammering a trail to the top. His heirs gave it to the state in 1935.

A few miles beyond Beacon Rock is **North Bonneville,** a settlement occupied mostly by workers from Bonneville Dam, which is just upriver. A bit beyond the town, turn right and follow signs under the red and white high tension towers toward **Fort Cascades Historic Site.** A kiosk focuses on the Lewis and Clark Trail, the Oregon Trail water route and the old town and fort that once occupied this site.

When settlers first began crossing the Oregon Trail in the 1840s, they had to build rafts at the Dalles and brave the Columbia River rapids, since the gorge walls were too sheer for a land trail. (All the rapids have since been drowned by dams, incidentally.) The town of Cascades was established here in 1850, at the end of upriver navigation. Here, pioneers could reassemble their wagons and trek off into Washington, or catch downriver steamboats. Indians attacked the settlement in 1856 and an Army unit led by Lieutenant Phil Sheridan (of later Civil War fame) came to quell the uprising. The troops stayed to build Fort Cascades, which functioned until 1861. A mile and a half loop trail takes you to the site of the town and fort, although nothing remains but signs. It is a nice walk along the river, however, made more pleasant in August by an abundance of blackberries.

If you drive east along the Dam Access Road from the fort site (paralleling Highway 14), you'll encounter part of the large Bonneville Dam project:

☺ **Second Powerhouse** • *Daily 9 to 5. Self-guided tours; free.* ☐ Most Bonneville Dam visitor facilities are on the Oregon side, although this newer element sits on Washington's shore. Completed in 1983, the Second Powerhouse more than doubles Bonneville's output, to a million-plus kilowatts. Price tag was $662 million, compared with the main dam's modest $83 million in the 1930s. That inflationary jump included relocating the town of North Bonneville two miles downstream—lock, stock and public park. Visitors can stroll past rows of humming generators, then down into one of the turbine pits to watch the 62-inch spinning shaft. From the turbine room, an escalator takes visitors to a fish viewing room with displays concerning fish migratory habits and the now-outlawed fish wheels that once snatched millions of salmon from the Columbia.

To visit the main element of this hydroelectric enterprise, continue north to the steel-girder **Bridge of the Gods**, cross the Columbia to the town of **Cascade Locks** and drive west on Interstate 84. (Bridge of the Gods, incidentally, was named in honor of a supposed natural bridge across the Columbia, which likely existed only in Indian legend.)

☺ **Bonneville Dam, Lock and Fish Hatchery** • *Cascade Locks, OR 97014-0150; (503) 374-8820. Visitor center open daily 9 to 8 in summer and 9 to 5 the rest of the year.* ☐ Completed in 1937, Bonneville has been around for so long that it has acquired national historic landmark status. It's actually three separate dams, set in a staggered line across two midstream islands. The main visitor facility and fish hatchery are on Bradford Island, reached by a bridge from the southern shore.

Like many of President Franklin D. Roosevelt's New Deal projects, the facility was crafted carefully, with Art Deco touches and with tourism in mind. For instance, the hatchery on the western end of the island more resembles a park than a fish nursery. Landscaped paths take you past special viewing ponds, where you can see the usual trout and steelhead, plus smaller versions of the giant Columbia sturgeon, which can attain lengths of 18 feet.

The dam's visitor center, at the island's eastern end, is spread over four floors, and self-guiding tours begin at parking lot level. Here, a nicely-done museum focuses on the history of the Columbia. You can then elevate to a rooftop viewing area or descend to a theater level to see movies and slides about the dam. Next stop is the fish viewing room, where assorted salmon and trout swim lazily past. Best viewing seasons are fall and spring.

Incidentally, being a salmon is no piece of cake. For every 8,000 born in upstream hatcheries, only five make it back for a final spawning fling. And then they die. As if their lives weren't tough enough, a small gift shop at the hatchery sells smoked and canned salmon, salmon jerky and salmon leather.

Back on Highway 14, you can pause for brochures at a **Washington State Information Center** just beyond the Bridge of the Gods. Then continue on to the only town of substance on the gorge's Washington side.

# Stevenson

**Population: 1,100**                     **Elevation: about 100 feet**

Terraced above the river, this somewhat handsome old town is the seat of Skamania County. It offers a small selection of motels, cafès and campgrounds and it's a serious windsurfing center.

☺ Assuming the thing stays on schedule, the impressive new 15,000-square-foot **Columbia Gorge Interpretive Center** will stand alongside the highway just west of Stevenson. Opening was set for 1994. It is to house exhibits on the geology, flora, fauna and human history of the Columbia, its gorge and surrounding Cascade Range. The **Skamania County Historical Society Museum** is to share this new space.

If things aren't on schedule, you'll find the historical museum where we left it, on the eastern side of town, in the cut-stone Skamania County Courthouse annex. To get there, turn left up Columbia Street, then left again onto Vancouver Avenue. Exhibits include typical pioneer artifacts, plus the world's largest rosary collection, with 4,000 sets of those Catholic love-beads. Hours are noon to 5 Monday-Saturday and 1 to 6 Sunday.

The **Chamber of Commerce Visitors Center** is on the left downtown, opposite Leavens Street. It's open Monday-Friday 8 to 5, Saturday 9 to 5 and Sunday 10 to 5; shorter hours in the off-season. When it's closed, you can pick up brochures from a rack outside.

## ACTIVITIES

*Backpacking* ● Cascade Mountain Backpackers, (509) 427-8548 or (509) 427-4187.

*Carriage rides* ● Columbia Gorge Carriage Company, (509) 427-8526.

*Gorge tours* ● Columbia Gorge Tours, (800) 885-4416, (509) 427-7800.

**Horseback and hay wagon rides** • Columbia Gorge Outfitters, Skamania Lodge, (509) 427-2549.

**River rafting** • Renegade River Rafting, (209) 427-7238.

**Scenic cruises** • Sternwheeler *Columbia Gorge* departs from Cascade Locks on two-hour Columbia River cruises, with food and beverage service, (503) 374-8427 or (503) 223-3928. *The Whatever* cruise boat offers eight-hour and longer voyages on the Columbia; P.O. Box 3, North Bonneville, WA 98639, (509) 427-4347.

**Scenic flights** • The Dalles Municipal Airport, Dallesport, WA 98617, (509) 767-2359; or Air Columbia, (800) 886-4416 or (509) 427-7800.

## WHERE TO DINE

**Betty's Silver Grill** • ∆ $

◻ *Second Street (Highway 14) at Leavens; (509) 427-5399. American; no alcohol. Daily 8 to 8.* ◻ Basic café serving typical steaks, chops and pastas, most entrées under $10. The lemon pepper fish was rather palatable.

**Big River Grill** • ∆∆ $$ Ø

◻ *Second Street at Leavens; (509) 427-4888. Northwest pub grub; wine and beer. Tuesday-Sunday 11:30 to 10, closed Monday. MC/VISA.* ◻ Very appealing, smoke-free brewpub serving an assortment of micro-brews with appropriate fare, such as spicy meats, sausages, chicken wings and such. Old style interior with wooden booths, warm wood paneling and drop lamps dropping from high ceilings.

## WHERE TO SLEEP

**River View Motor Inn** • ⌂⌂ $$ Ø

◻ *Frank Johns Road, Stevenson, WA 98648; (509) 427-5628. Couples $35 to $47, singles $30 to $37. Major credit cards.* ◻ A 21-unit motel with TV movies, room phones, some refrigerators; efficiency units.

☺ **Skamania Lodge** • ⌂⌂⌂⌂ $$$$ Ø

◻ *P.O. Box 189, Stevenson, WA 98648; (800) 221-7117 or (509) 427-7700. Couples and singles $85 to $145. Major credit cards.* ◻ Exceptionally attractive resort in the woods above Stevenson, with a river view. Room phones, TV movies, some refrigerators. The lodge interior is particularly striking, with carved woods, beam ceiling, cut stone fireplace and Northwest Indian décor. Its full resort amenities include an indoor pool, fitness center, spa, massage room, 18-hole golf course, tennis, bike rentals and horseback riding. Smoke-free **Dining Room** serves contemporary Northwest fare; 7 a.m. to 10 p.m.; dinners $18 to $26; full bar service.

## WHERE TO CAMP IN THE GORGE

**Beacon Rock RV Park** • c/o Skamania, WA; (509) 427-8473. RV and tent sites; $10 to $14. Reservations accepted. ◻ Private RV park near Beacon Rock State Park. Full hookups, TV; showers, recreation room, coin laundry.

**Beacon Rock State Park** • Highway 14, east of Skamania; (509) 427-8265. RV and tent sites; $10. No reservations or credit cards. ◻ Well-spaced, shaded sites with picnic tables and barbecues; showers, hiking, picnic area.

**Lewis & Clark Campground & RV Park** • Evergreen Drive (off milepost 27 near North Bonneville), c/o Stevenson, WA 98648; (509) 427-5559 or 427-5982. RV and tent sites; $10 to $13. Reservations accepted. ◻ Showers; some pull-throughs; coin laundry, rec room and rec field.

## Mount Adams Country

Beyond Stevenson, the highway drops down to the river's edge, ducking through several small tunnels as it hugs the base of those sheer basaltic cliffs. After nearly 30 miles of splendid river scenery, you enter remote, thinly populated Klikitat County. An **Information Center** is on the left, at the far end of a Bridge Mart convenience store, just beyond the turnoff to the Hood River Bridge. The gorge walls have lowered here to reveal the near-perfect cone of **Mount Hood,** dominating the Oregon horizon. The bulkier **Mount Adams** commands the skyline to the north.

Beyond the visitor center, you'll nudge the hamlets of **Bingen** and—just up a steep hill from the highway—**White Salmon.** They're both a bit scruffy, offering little of visitor value. You might pause for a sip at the **Mont Elise Winery Sales Room** on the highway in Bingen at 315 W. Steuben Street. It's open daily noon to 5; (509) 493-3001. A slice of Washington's wine country, which we explore in Chapter 8, is south of here. The **Gorge Heritage Museum,** just beyond the White Salmon turnoff, is housed in an old steepled church, offering a few pioneer artifacts and Columbia Gorge history exhibits; it's open 12:30 to 4:30 weekends only.

Highway 141 heads north from Bingen, toward the **Mount Adams Wilderness,** with its hiking trails, alpine lakes and primitive campsites. At 12,276 feet, Adams is Washington's second highest peak, cradled between Gifford Pinchot National Forest and the huge Yakima Indian Reservation. It receives few visitors, since only rough dirt roads reach its foothills; only backpackers can reach its heights.

If you're limited to a family sedan or RV, you can still explore the lower reaches of "Mount Adams Country" in the summer and early fall, before snow buries the upland roads. Head north on Highway 141 along the White Salmon River for 25 miles to **Trout Lake.** You're on the drier eastern slope of the Cascades here, passing through prairie and ranchlands. You then climb into pines in Mount Adams' flanks. From Trout Lake, bumpy four-wheel-drive roads lead higher up the mountain. To stay on pavement, head east on Glenwood Road, along the foothills toward the pioneer community of **Glenwood** in the lower tip of the Yakima Indian Reservation. From here, Glenwood-Goldendale Road takes you past **Outlet Falls** of the Klikitat River Gorge. It then curves south and links with State Route 142, which returns to the Columbia River at **Lyle.**

If you head west from Trout Lake, you'll pass an **ice cave** after 10 miles; it can be reached from Ice Cave Forest Campground. A few miles beyond is **Big Lava Bed Geologic Area,** a lava flow and worn-down bowl of an ancient crater. You'll hit gravel and dirt en route to and beyond the lava flow, although it can be handled by the family bus. The road curves west, blends back onto asphalt and returns you to Highway 14 at Carson. A map showing these and other Klikitat County loop tours is available at the information center, or contact the Mount Adams Chamber of Commerce; see the Trip Planner at the start of this chapter.

## Back to the Columbia

Back on east-bound Highway 14, the hills become lower and drier as you approach the eastern side of the Columbia Gorge. Although smaller, the cliffs are still impressive—sheer-walled basaltic bluffs and columns with beige crewcut prairies on their terraced tops.

☺ For a particularly nice view of the eastern gorge, pause at the **Chamberlain Lake Rest Stop,** several miles east of Bingen. Well-tended grassy picnic slopes high above the river offer vistas of those dark, terraced cliffs. Mount Hood adds a snowy accent beyond.

The road continues hugging the river and its shrinking gorge as it approaches the hamlet of **Dallesport.** Just beyond, a bridge crosses the Columbia to The Dalles, a particularly historic community where the Oregon Trail entered the river. You may be tempted to cross over to explore the town and another major dam that reaches between the two states:

☺ *The Dalles Lock and Dam ● P.O. Box 564, The Dalles, OR 97058; (503) 296-1181. Tours available weekdays 9 to 4, April through September. Visitor center open daily 9 to 5 the rest of the year.* ☐ This is a dam tour with a couple of twists. You reach the structure by riding a converted work train, which departs every half hour from a visitor center in Seufert Park. A guide regales you with statistics as you travel. This is the world's fourth largest hydroelectric dam, capable of lighting 18 million 100-watt light bulbs with the 22 generators in its half-mile-long turbine room. Once on the other side, you can wander about on your own, or stay with your chatty tour guide.

The visitor center is a fine little museum concerning the Native American and new American history of the Columbia. Photos recall the days when Indians used dip-nets to catch spawning salmon struggling up Celilo Falls above the dam. The falls were drowned during the filling of Lake Celilo behind The Dalles Dam in 1957.

If you'd like a close-up view of a boat lifter and dropper in action, pause at **The Dalles Lock,** back on the Washington side. A small park here is open daily from 9 to 5. Visitors can stare right down into the giant rectangle of water to watch its slow-motion filling or draining, and then marvel at the opening of the massive gates. Plan on 20 minutes.

## What the Sam Hill?

Beyond The Dalles Dam, after passing through tiny **Wishram** and **Wishram Heights,** you'll encounter two imposing structures built by the railroad heir who created Oregon's Columbia Gorge Highway. Samuel Hill, son-in-law of Great Northern Railway president James J. Hill, was a Quaker pacifist, attorney and engineer. He once owned 7,000 acres of Klikitat County's tawny rolling grasslands, and the region is still referred to as "Sam Hill Country."

In 1907, he laid out a 34-acre town center on the slopes above the Columbia, with a church, hotel, offices, garages and shops. He hoped to create a utopian Quaker farm community. His venture failed; the town was abandoned and most of the buildings eventually burned. However, Sam left two legacies. He built a replica of England's Stonehenge at the town site, and he donated his river-view mansion four miles west for an art museum. It's remarkable for its beauty, its fine collection and its remote location. The nearest town is Goldendale, not exactly a bastion of culture.

You first encounter **Maryhill,** Sam's castle-turned-art museum. A few miles east, just past the U.S. Highway 97 junction, is **Stonehenge,** his imposing monument to the county's fallen World War I heroes.

☺ *Maryhill Museum of Art ● 35 Maryhill Museum Dr., Goldendale, WA 98620; (509) 773-3733. Open daily March 15 to November 15, 9 to 5. Adults $4, seniors $3.50, kids 6 to 16, $1.50.* ☐ Sam Hill commissioned his mansion in 1914, then when his town failed, he decided to turn it into a museum. It was dedicated by Queen Marie of Rumania in 1926, but not opened to the public until 1940. *Time Magazine* called it the "loneliest museum in the world." However, it out-draws the major art centers of Seattle and Portland. Its excellent collection includes 19th century French decorative arts, Rodin sculptures and working figures, Queen Marie memorabilia and Native American artifacts.

☺ **Stonehenge** ● *Grounds open daily 7 a.m. to 10 p.m.; free.* ◻ This replica is in much better shape than the original, built in 1350 B.C. on the Salisbury Plain of England. Commissioned by Hill as America's first World War I monument, it honors Klikitat County's 13 men who died in that conflict. This circle of massive stone columns was started on July 4, 1918, and completed in 1929. A pacifist, Hill thought the original Stonehenge was built as a temple of human sacrifice. (More likely, it was a primeval observatory.) He decided to replicate it on the site of his utopian town to honor those sacrificed in the war. If you feel the need for a Stonehenge U.S.A. T-shirt, the Sam Hill Country Grocery is adjacent.

Just north of Stonehenge, on Highway 97, is **Goldendale,** a farm community of about 3,300. It offers two attractions—one just beyond downtown on the main street and the other atop a nearby hill. Signs from Highway 97 will direct you there.

**Klickitat County Historical Museum** ● *127 W. Broadway; (509) 773-4426 or (509) 773-4791. Daily 9 to 5 May through September, by appointment the rest of the year.* ◻ Occupying a handsome Queen Anne Victorian, the museum contains attractively furnished rooms and a few pioneer artifacts. If you're there when it's closed, the stately building is worth a look.

☺ **Goldendale Observatory State Park** ● *Off Columbus Avenue; (509) 773-3141. Summer hours are Sunday-Thursday 1 to 5 and 7 to 11, then Friday-Saturday 1 to 5 and 7 to 1 a.m. Off-season hours are: Wednesday-Sunday 1 to 5 and 7 to 11 during April; and Saturday 1 to 5 and 7 to 9, then Sunday 1 to 5 the rest of the year.* ◻ This hilltop park, a short drive north of downtown, offers imposing views of the surrounding countryside including—on a clear day—mounts Hood, St. Helens, Adams, Rainier and Adams. However, the view is more interesting at night. Visitors can take turns at a 24.5-inch telescope and other eyepieces to study the planets and stars. The main 'scope is one of the largest in America available for public viewing. Four serious amateur astronomers from Vancouver built the Goldendale Observatory in 1973, then their non-profit group turned it over to the state in 1980.

Not surprisingly, Goldendale Observatory was a popular gathering place for viewing the 1979 total eclipse and the 1985-86 visit of Halley's Comet.

## Chapter three

# *PUGET SOUND SOUTH*

## Capitol campus to Tacoma and the Kitsap

*THE COMMERCIAL HEARTLAND* of Washington is concentrated around a vast inland waterway once thought to be the fabled Northwest Passage. Its thousands of islands and the large Kitsap Peninsula provided a natural growth area in those days when most people and goods traveled by water.

Today, the sound is home to more than half the state's population. Water is no barrier for these land-bound residents, since the Washington State Ferry system serves this complex of islands and channels.

The existence of this vast waterway was first suggested by Greek navigator Juan de Fuca in 1592. It's doubtful, however, that he actually found the sound. In 1788, when British Captain John Meares did locate its narrow opening, he named the strait in de Fuca's honor. Captain George Vancouver followed Meares into this great inland sea in 1792. One of his top navigators, Peter Puget, continued southward to Point Defiance and the Narrows, opposite present day Tacoma. The sound was named in his honor.

For today's navigators, Puget Sound offers a wonderland of wooded islands, major cities and rustically nautical towns. Of course, the constant comingling of water and land brews the area's soggy weather. However, beach-combing, seafood-dining, island-hopping and city-searching do not require sunshine.

We established earlier that the Cowlitz River flowing into the Columbia provided a tempting pathway for Oregon Trail pioneers who chose to head

# TRIP PLANNER

**WHEN TO GO** • The Puget Sound region is an all-year area. It rarely snows here and drizzly weather doesn't prevent sightseeing or museum-hopping. The Capitol Campus buildings in Olympia and museums in Olympia and Tacoma are open the year around. Given a choice, we'd come in late summer or fall when the sun is the most cooperative.

**WHAT TO SEE** • The Legislative Building (capitol), Temple of Justice and Capitol Conservatory on the Capitol Campus, plus the Washington State Capital Museum in Olympia; Fort Lewis Military Museum; Tribal Cultural Center in Steilacoom; Washington State Historical Society Museum and Point Defiance Park with its zoo, aquarium, Fort Nisqually and other attractions in Tacoma; Meeker Mansion in Puyallup; Ryan House Museum in Sumner and Foothills Historical Museum in Buckley.

**WHAT TO DO** • Take the Olympia Brewery tour in Tumwater; hike the one-mile boardwalk at Olympia's Percival Landing and stroll the paths of Capitol Lake Park; load up on oysters at the legendary Olympic Oyster House; step into cavernous Union Station, stroll or bike the Ruston Way waterfront parklands and take a Commencement Bay harbor tour in Tacoma; ride the ferry to Vashon Island and motor across its bucolic landscape.

## Useful contacts

**Greater Olympia Visitors and Convention Bureau**, 316 Schmidt Place, Tumwater, WA 98502; mailing address: P.O. Box 7249, Olympia, WA 98501; (206) 357-3370.

**Gig Harbor-Peninsula Chamber of Commerce,** 3125 Judson St., Gig Harbor, WA 98499; (206) 851-6865.

**Olympia/Thurston County Chamber of Commerce**, 1000 Plum St. Olympia, WA 98501; (206) 357-3362.

**Puyallup Area Chamber of Commerce,** 322 Second St. SW, Puyallup, WA 98371; (800) 634-2334 or (206) 845-6755.

**Tacoma-Pierce County Visitor & Convention Bureau,** 906 Broadway, Tacoma, WA 98402; (206) 627-2836.

## Southern Puget Sound radio stations

Most Seattle stations come in loud and clear (see Chapter four) plus these locals:

KXXO, 96.1 FM, Olympia—top forty; light rock
KKEE, 94.3-FM, Astoria, Ore.—rock
KUPL, 98.5-FM and 1330-AM, Olympia—country
KCLU, 90.3-FM, Tacoma-Seattle—National Public Radio.
KPBS, 88.5-FM, Tacoma-Seattle—National Public Radio
KGY, 1240-AM, Olympia—top 40 and news

north. Leaving the river as it swung eastward, they pressed on to the inviting waters of Puget Sound, where they established the state's first community at Tumwater in 1845. Olympia, Steilacoom, Port Townsend and Seattle soon followed—all on the lower reaches of the sound.

We shall reach in the same direction in this chapter, traveling as those first pioneers did, northward from the Columbia. We already explored most of what's interesting along the busy I-5 corridor, up to and including Centralia. There is nothing of visitor intrigue between there and Puget Sound.

# Tumwater/Olympia
**Tumwater: 10,000; Olympia: 33,900   Elevation: 115 and 36 feet**

A year before the international boundary was set at the 49th parallel, optimistic Americans headed north into British territory and established the community of New Market. It later was changed to Tumwater, after a waterfall on the Deschutes River. That river provided power for a sawmill and other early industries. A few decades later, nearby artesian wells provided "tumwater" for one of the West's best-known breweries.

Olympia, on Budd Inlet at the head of Puget Sound navigation, was quick to follow Tumwater. In 1846, Americans Levi Smith and Edmund Sylvester platted Smithfield, later named Smithster. That sounded silly, so it became Olympia, after the mountains across the sound. The new shipping port grew quickly, and Governor Isaac Stevens picked it as the capital when Washington became a territory in 1853. Oddly, it didn't earn official status as the capital city until 1890, so it spent several decades fighting off theft attempts. It still is the capital, of course, and its 55-acre Capitol Campus is the focal point of this rather attractive city.

Although Washington is the West's second most populous state after California, Olympia is one of America's smaller capitals. It's a prim little package of well-tended homes tucked beneath mature trees, surrounding a rather old fashioned downtown area. The capitol building, sitting on a knoll, is something of a beacon for the area, particularly at night, when the Romanesque dome is lighted.

Tumwater and Olympia have blended together and generally are treated as one by visitors, although they're separate towns. Approaching from the south on I-5, one hits Tumwater first, guided by that familiar brewery sign that proclaims: "It's the water."

## Driving Tumwater/Olympia

☺ Freeway exit 103 takes you straight into the **Olympia Brewing Company,** which has been sitting on the banks of the Deschutes River since its founding in 1896. Tours are conducted daily; see "Attractions" below. Approaching the brewery, you'll pass the appealing little **Tumwater Falls Park,** with a playground and picnic areas. A few blocks beyond the beer company on Deschutes Way is **Tumwater Historical Park,** the original townsite. It has several yesterday buildings, including the **Henderson House Museum,** a Victorian with a witch's hat tower.

☺ From the historic area, curve left under the freeway, following Deschutes Parkway into Olympia and alongside the extensive greens and blues of **Capitol Lake Park.** This is a favorite haunt of Olympians. Among its appeals are a roadside jogging-biking trail, assorted other pathways, hidden picnic coves and the restful, duck-busy shores of ten-acre Capitol Lake.

*Visitors can find out what's cooking in giant copper and stainless steel kettles at Tumwater's Olympia Brewing Company.* — **Betty Woo Martin**

The state capitol building, perched upon a hillock across the lake, is a commanding presence.

At the north end of the park, turn right onto Fifth Avenue and corss between Capital Lake and Budd Inlet. After a few blocks, go right again onto Capitol Way and drive to the Capitol Campus. This is home to the nobly domed statehouse and most of Washington's other state buildings. Pass in front of the Capitol, turn right onto 14th Avenue and you're beside the **Capitol Visitor Center.** It's open weekdays 8 to 5 the year around, plus summer weekends from 10 to 4. In addition to providing material on the campus, it functions as a visitor center for the city, the region and the rest of the state.

You can park in a small visitor center lot, or any of several designated areas around the campus by getting a fifty-cent ticket from a vending machine. (Many parking spaces are reserved, so make sure the one you select is properly marked.)

*RV advisory:* If you're driving a long rig or pulling a trailer, you'll have trouble finding parking on the campus. It's plentiful along Deschutes Parkway in Capitol Lake Park, and you can catch a free shuttle to the campus and downtown area. Or, enjoy a walk through the park; it's less than a mile from there to the campus.

☺ The **Capitol Campus** is one of the most attractive legislative complexes in the country. Although the domed capitol—actually the Legislative Building—is hemmed in by a breastwork of other structures, the surrounding grounds are rather expansive. The area is immaculately landscaped, ablaze with rhododendrons, roses and other flowering flora. A replica of Denmark's Tivoli Fountain, a Winged Victory monument and a sunken garden add luster to this complex. (See "Attractions" below for details on individual buildings open to visitors.)

☺ The **Washington State Capital Museum** is off-campus, reached by continuing south on Capitol Way, and then turning right onto 21st Avenue. You'll first see the imposing **McCleary Mansion** at the corner of Capitol Way and 21st. This cut-stone turn-of-the-century edifice now houses office buildings. The State Capitol Museum is a block beyond, in a yellow brick California Spanish style structure.

Retrace your route on Capitol Way, drive several blocks past the campus, turn left onto Fourth Avenue and follow it down to Budd Inlet and **Percival Landing.** This is the town's original waterfront, now an aquatic park, offering a marina, a one-mile boardwalk and your first serious view of Puget Sound. The legendary **Olympia Oyster House** (listed below) is here, at Fourth and Sylvester.

Now, shift over to Fifth Avenue (since it's one-way the right way), take it downtown to Washington Street and turn right to attractive **Sylvester Park.** Opposite the park, at Washington and Legion, is the baronial, cut-stone **old capitol building.** It now houses the offices of the Superintendent of Public Instruction. Downtown Olympia, pleasantly old fashion with lots of brick and masonry, appears to be holding its own against urban business flight. Most of its low-rise store fronts are occupied. Overall, the area is a couple of cuts above scruffy.

Return to Fourth Avenue, follow it east about five blocks to Plum Street/East Bay Drive and turn left. East Bay Drive takes you past a yacht harbor and along the East Bay arm of Puget Sound. This landscaped boulevard is lined with elegant homes, most of which block your view of the bay. About a mile from downtown, turn right into **Priest Point Park,** a large, wooded area covering both sides of the boulevard.

If you'd like to admire a few more East Bay Boulevard homes, drive a few blocks beyond the park and eyeball assorted estates until the area becomes an ordinary neighborhood. Then return downtown; East Bay becomes Plum Street and signs will direct you to I-5.

## ATTRACTIONS
### In order of appearance

☺ *Olympia Brewing Company* ● *Deschutes Drive at Boston Street; (206) 754-5212. Tours daily 8 to 4:30; free.* ◻ Never mind your Colorado Kool-Aid. As soon as I attained the age of consent, my choice was "Oly." It has been the West's own beer since Leopold F. Schmidt founded the Olympia Brewing Company in 1896. Pabst bought it out in 1983, although the Olympia label survives. Tours take visitors past gleaming copper kettles that bubble and bubble (but no toil and trouble). You learn that it would take 340 years to empty one of the 1,000-gallon aging tanks, if you drank a quart a day. (By then of course, the beer would have gone flat.) The tour ends with samples of free suds for the grown-ups. A large gift shop is adjacent to the tasting room.

*Tumwater Historical Park* ● *Deschutes Way near Grant; (206) 753-8583. Henderson House open Thursday-Sunday noon to 4; Crosby House tours*

*Thursdays only 2 to 4, or by appointment. Donations appreciated.* ☐ The 1905 Henderson House, on Tumwater's original townsite, offers furnished rooms, pioneer displays and artifacts from the first post office. The Crosby House, furnished to its 1858 period, was built by Bing's grandfather, Captain Nathaniel Crosby III.

☺ **Capitol Campus** • *Legislative Building open daily 8 to 5, tours daily 10 to 3. Capitol Conservatory open weekdays 8 a.m. to 3:15 p.m. Temple of Justice open weekdays 8 to 5. Governor's Mansion tours Wednesdays only, by appointment. Call (206) 586-TOUR for tour information, 586-3460 for visitor services and 753-3269 for parking services.*

Most visitors to the Capitol Campus are drawn first to the sandstone **Legislative Building**, whose 287-foot cap is among the world's tallest masonry domed buildings. The interior is a striking study in glossy marble columns, stairways and sweeping balconies. Particularly impressive is the second-floor reception room with coffered barrel-arched ceilings, Tiffany chandeliers and 19th century furnishings. If you want to catch legislators in action, a 120-day session is held in odd years from January to April, and a 90-day session runs from January through March in even years.

The Grecian-style **Temple of Justice** also deserves a look, with lots of marble, coffered ceilings and polished woods. Visitors can enter the supreme court chambers, and even attend sessions. An interesting set of graphics on the second floor describes landmark rulings made by this court.

The opulent Capitol Campus gardens are nourished by the **Conservatory,** an elaborate greenhouse and potting shed. Plant lovers will love its warm, humid interior. The modern granite **State Library,** while not awesome, has a nice collection of murals and other artwork by state artists. It's open weekdays 8 to 5. The **Governor's Mansion,** is a red brick Colonial structure, a complete mismatch to the gray sandstone of the rest of the capital complex. The Wednesday-only tour (1 to 2:45 by reservation) takes visitors through several rooms with opulent early American furnishings.

☺ **Washington State Capital Museum** • *2111 W. 21st Ave.; (206) 753-2580. Tuesday-Friday 10 to 4, Saturday-Sunday noon to 4, closed Monday. Adults $2, kids and seniors $1, family groups $5.* ☐ Exhibits from Northwest Indian tribes are a strong focus in this fine museum, ranging from traditional weapons and basketry to modern Native American art. Other displays trace Olympia's early days; featured are a well-stocked apothecary shop and general store. The mansion was completed in early 1924 by Clarence J. Lord, a wealthy banker and Olympia mayor.

*Old state capitol* • *Legion Way and Washington streets; 753-6740. Weekdays 9 to 5.* ☐ This block-long Medieval style behemoth, with an octagonal tower, turrets, and gargoyles thrusting from its rough stone façade, was built in 1891. It served first as the Thurston County Courthouse, then as the capitol from 1903 until completion of the Legislative Building in 1928. Tours are available for groups only, although casual visitors can check out its surprisingly modern interior, done in light oak.

☺ **Priest Point Park** • *Off East Bay Drive.* ☐ This thickly wooded 250-acre park provides hiking trails, a playground and tucked-away picnic tables for those who want to be alone. Cross an overpass to the west side for nice views of Puget Sound. Among the hiking trails is a three-mile waterline path around the edge of Ellis Cove, with Puget Sound vistas from assorted angles.

## ACTIVITY

*Olympia Farmers Market* ● *401 N. Capitol Way at Percival Landing; (206) 352-9096. Open 10 to 3, weekends only in April, Thursday-Sunday May through September, Friday-Sunday in October and weekends only November to mid-December.* ⛶ The largest farmers market in the state, it features a variety of seasonal produce, baked goods, flowers, arts and handicrafts.

## ANNUAL EVENTS

For information on these activities, contact the Visitors Information Center at (206) 357-3370.

**Tumwater Bluegrass Festival,** third weekend in May at Tumwater High School; (206) 357-5153.

**Lakefair,** mid-July in Capitol Lake Park; entertainment, foods, crafts.

**Thurston County Fair**, early August at Thurston County Fairgrounds.

**Shakespeare Festival and Renaissance Faire,** last half of August in Sylvester Park.

**Fountain Festival,** late August; music in the Capitol Campus park.

**Olympia Harbor Days,** early September off Percival Landing; boat races, arts and crafts.

## WHERE TO DINE

If you haven't tried those famous Olympia oysters, you haven't dined properly in Olympia. These tiny succulent mollusks are found only in the mudflats in southern Puget Sound. Their numbers have been greatly depleted by pollution and the importation of Japanese oysters, although a few are still being harvested. Most local seafood houses have them on the menu; Olympia Oyster House is particularly noted for these delicacies.

*Budd Bay Café* ● ΔΔ $$$ Ø

⛶ *525 N. Columbia (at Percival Landing); (206) 357-6963. American, with seafood emphasis; full bar service. Monday-Saturday 11 to 10, Sunday 10 to 10. Major credit cards.* ⛶ Cleanly attractive restaurant with marina views and a varied menu ranging from local seafood to steaks, chicken and pasta. Try the shrimp madeira (sauteed shrimp with Dungeness crab and fruit in a papaya sauce) or broiled salmon filet in white wine with garlic and herbs. Good selection of international beers and Northwest wines. The place is something of a power lunch hangout. Tourists go to the Olympia Oyster House; locals come here. All non-smoking.

☺ *Carnegie's* ● Δ $ Ø

⛶ *Seventh and Franklin; (206) 357-5550. Light American fare; espresso bar. Monday-Tuesday 10 to 6, Wednesday-Friday 10 to 8, Saturday 10 to 6, Sunday noon to 5. MC/VISA.* ⛶ Appealing bookstore and café in a 1914 yellow brick Carnegie Library building. The menu mostly offers espressos and lattes, salads and interesting sandwiches such as Andy's Dandy (turkey, cream cheese and cucumbers) and the Timberjack (ham, pepperjack cheese, tomatoes and mustard).

*Columbia Street Public House* ● ΔΔ $

⛶ *200 W. Fourth Avenue (at Columbia); (206) 943-5575. American; wine and beer. Lunch and dinner daily until 10 p.m., breakfast from 9 on weekends. MC/VISA.* ⛶ Pleasantly funky back to the 60s place with doo-dads on its walls and high ceilings. Entrèes, all under $10, include daily vegetarian specials, chili, beef stew, salads, soups and sandwiches. Live Irish, jazz and bluegrass music several nights a week.

### ☺ Falls Terrace Restaurant ● ∆∆∆ $$

☐ 106 S. Deschutes Way (Tumwater Falls Park); (206) 943-7830. American; full bar service. Monday-Friday 11 to 9, Saturday 11:30 to 9, Sunday 11:30 to 8. Major credit cards. ☐ With picture windows overlooking the falls and Olympia Brewery, it's a special occasion place for locals and a required stop for tourists. Tables are at two levels, to maximize views for all. The menu, while not terribly creative, is versatile, jumping from lamb chops to steaks to seafood, including Olympia oysters and a rather good bouillabaisse. Reservations are essential.

### Genoas on the Bay ● ∆∆∆ $$$

☐ 1525 N. Washington Street (at the Port of Olympia); (206) 943-7770. American, mostly seafood; full bar service. Monday-Thursday 11 to 9, Friday 11 to 1, Saturday 4 to 10, Sunday 10 to 2:30 and 4:30 to 9. Major credit cards. ☐ One of Olympia's few water-view restaurants, featuring local fresh seafood, plus prime rib and a few chops and steaks. Try the oysters Rockefeller, blackened snapper with orange marmalade sauce, or baked scallops. The look is nautical modern, with light woods and drop lamps. Washington Street doesn't go through the port area, so you have to approach via the East Bay Marina, then go into the port and turn right.

### ☺ Olympia Oyster House ● ∆∆ $$

☐ 320 W. Fourth Ave. (at Sylvester); (206) 943-8020. American, mostly seafood; full bar service. Daily 11 a.m. to 11 p.m. Major credit cards. ☐ This is legendary home of the tiny Olympic oyster, available by the plateful for $22. Dating from 1925, it's Washington's oldest fish haus, offering a large seafood menu, excellent clam chowder and a few steaks and prime rib. Visitors can sit in comfortable paisley booths with a view across a parking lot to the sound; or dine outside when the weather cooperates.

### ☺ Spar Café and Bar ● ∆ $

☐ 114 E. Fourth Avenue (between Capitol Way and Washington); (206) 357-6444. American; full bar service. Monday-Saturday 6 a.m. to 9 p.m., Sunday 7 to 3. MC/VISA, AMEX. ☐ Great 1930s style café with an art moderne interior of slatted wooden walls, milk glass light fixtures and wooden counter chairs. Historic photos adorn the walls. The massive, rather inexpensive menu features everything from chicken, steaks, chops and seafood to hamburgers and bread pudding. A card room and pub are in back, reached via batwing doors.

## WHERE TO SLEEP

### Best Western Aladdin Motor Inn ● ⌂⌂⌂ $$ ∅

☐ 900 Capitol Way, Olympia, WA 98501; (800) 528-1234 or (206) 352-7200. Couples $57 to $68, singles $52 to $61. Major credit cards. ☐ A 100-unit motel with TV, rental VCRs, room phones; some refrigerators. Pool, coin laundry, **Dining room** serves 6:30 a.m. to 10 p.m.; dinners $9 to $20.

### Capital Inn Motel ● ⌂⌂ $$ ∅

☐ 120 College St. SE, Olympia, WA 98303; (206) 493-1991. Doubles and singles $47 to $62, kitchenettes $5 extra. Major credit cards. ☐ An 83-unit motel with TV movies, room phones; sauna, exercise room and coin laundry.

### Golden Gavel Motor Hotel • ⌂ $$ Ø

◻ *909 Capitol Way (Ninth), Olympia, WA 98501; (206) 352-8533. Couples $39 to $49, singles $37 to $42. Major credit cards.* ◻ Well-maintained 28-room motel with TV, room phones; some two-bedroom units.

### Harbinger Inn • ⌂ $$$

◻ *1136 E. Bay Dr., Olympia, WA 98506; (206) 754-0389. Couples $60 to $90, singles $55 to $85. Four rooms with private baths; full breakfast. MC/VISA, AMEX.* ◻ A restored 1910 mansion overlooking Olympia's capitol and the bay; with a mix of modern and traditional furnishings.

### Ramada Inn-Governor House • ⌂⌂ $$$ Ø

◻ *621 S. Capitol Way, Olympia, WA 98501; (800) 272-6232 or (206) 352-7700. Couples $68 to $98, singles $60 to $90. Major credit cards.* ◻ Attractive inn with 125 nicely-furnished rooms; TV movies, phones; some refrigerators; some efficiency units. Some units overlooking Capital Lake. Pool, sauna, exercise room, coin laundry. **Dining room** serves 6:30 a.m. to 10 p.m.; dinners $5 to $14; full bar service.

### Tyee Hotel • ⌂⌂ $$ Ø

◻ *500 Tyee Dr., Tumwater, WA 98502; (800) 648-6440 or (206) 352-0511. Couples $65 to $71, singles $62. Major credit cards.* ◻ Attractive hotel with landscaped grounds; 145 rooms with TV, phones; some refrigerators; some balconies and fireplaces. Pool, spas, tennis court. **Restaurant** serves 6:30 a.m. to 10 p.m.; dinners $6 to $16; full bar service.

## WHERE TO CAMP

**American Heritage Campground** • *9610 Kimmie St. SW, Olympia, WA 98512; (206) 943-8778. RV and tent sites; $16 to $18, sleeping cabin for $25. Reservations accepted; MC/VISA.* ◻ Wooded campground with showers, coin laundry, mini-mart, rec room with scheduled activities, pool, playground and rental bikes. To reach it, take I-5 exit 99, go east to 93rd and south to Kimmie.

**Olympia Campground** • *1441 83rd Ave. SW, Olympia, WA 98502; (206) 352-2551. RV and tent sites; $15 to $16, camping cabins $25. Reservations accepted; MC/VISA.* ◻ Nicely maintained campground with showers, mini-mart, pool, playground, and rec room. Take I-5 exit 99 east to 93rd, go a mile north on Kimmie Road, and a quarter mile east on 83rd.

# OLYMPIA TO TACOMA

As you head north from Olympia on I-5, you'll encounter considerable suburban sprawl, since you're on the outer rim of the greater Seattle metropolitan area. About the only open country left here has been captured in the massive Fort Lewis Army installation that's wedged between Olympia and Tacoma.

Much of southern Puget Sound's mudflats have been industrialized, although a significant slice is preserved in the **Nisqually National Wildlife Refuge.** To reach it, take either exit 111 or 114 from I-5 and drive west to the sound. You can follow a trail for five and a half miles through the wetlands and scope out more than 300 bird species. Blinds have been set up along the way for those with good binoculars, cameras and patience. The less focused can take shorter trails, including a half-mile interpretive loop. Best viewing is in the spring and fall when thousands of migratory

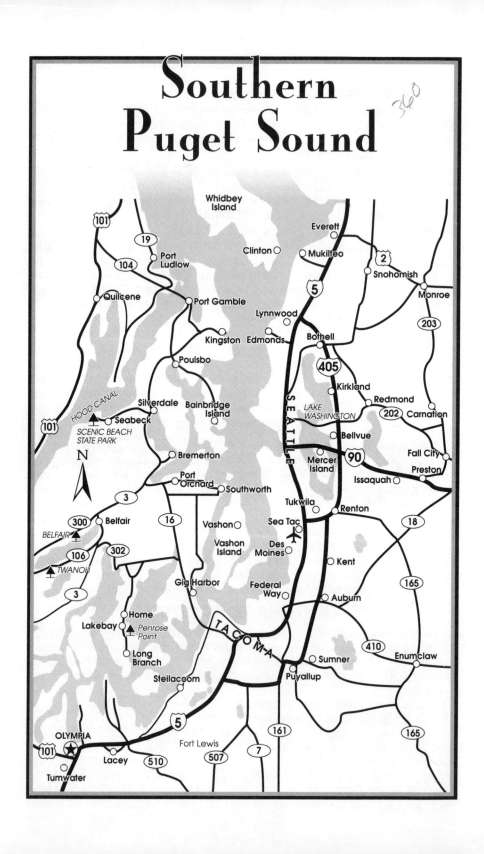

# Southern Puget Sound

water birds add to the local population. Refuge entry fee is $2 per carload.

Exit 111 also takes you five miles west to **Tolmie State Park** on Nisqually Reach, with swimming, fishing, an underwater park and several miles of hiking trails. There's picnicking but no camping. Nearby is the **Audubon Nature Center** on Luhr Beach at 4949 D'Milluhr Road NE; (206) 459-0387. The facility, open only weekends and Wednesday afternoons, offers a small natural history museum, picnic tables, a fishing area and boat launch. Call for details on guided tours, including raft trips out in Nisqually Reach.

Back on the freeway, you'll note a remarkably elaborate Swiss style structure off to your right. That's the **Fort Lewis Military Museum,** definitely worth a stop. To reach it, continue north for a couple of miles on the freeway and take exit 120. The stone main gate of the fort stands before you, but ignore that. Do a U-turn, cross back under the freeway to the North Fort Lewis Gate. Here, you'll be asked for your driver's license, vehicle registration and proof of insurance (but not your name, rank and serial number). The sentry will give you a map that will direct you back to the museum.

☺ **Fort Lewis Military Museum** ● *Fort Lewis; (206) 967-7206. Wednesday-Sunday noon to 4; free.* ❑ Old war dogs will love this place, with its indoor military exhibits and its yard full of olive drab tanks, howitzers, halftracks and an amphibian DUKW, a boat that looks like it can't float. The museum's focus is the American military presence in the Northwest, from Lewis and Clark to Stormin' Norman. General Norman Schwartzkopf was base commander and I Corps boss here in the 1980s, before going to the Pentagon and then to the sandy glory of the Gulf War. His jeep and several photos are on display. Our favorite museum exhibit is a full-scale tableau with a soldier using his cigar to light a punk, preparatory to firing his 1831 field gun. (The I Corps, should you wonder, is an elite military unit established during World War I and now based at Fort Lewis. A special exhibit traces its history.)

The large wooden museum building's Swiss look comes from its days as the Red Shield Inn, a Salvation Army-run lodge and social center during World War I. Camp Lewis was established in 1917. Tacoma citizens, eager for a military presence, passed a bond issue to purchase the land and donate it to the army. America's largest military facility during World War I, it was re-designated as Fort Lewis in 1927.

From the museum, return to the freeway, retreat a mile south to exit 119 and head northwest along the southern edge of the fort. For you vets who want to reminisce further, the highway passes acres and acres of mothballed military rigs. The road then enters a woodland and drops down to the Puget Sound bayfront and a real charmer of an old village.

# Steilacoom

**Population: 5,700**                      **Elevation: 50 feet**

☺ Established in 1854, Steilacoom was Washington's first incorporated community, and it looks its age. The small downtown area offers an enticing collection of false front and brick stores. With carefully-tended flower baskets hanging from vintage lamp posts, it's as prim as a pin. Not surprisingly, it has been declared a national historic district. Settlement in the area actually predates the town. Captain Lafayette Balch established Point Steilacoom just up the beach in 1851; later that year, John B. Chapman founded the rival community of Steilacoom City, on the town's current site.

The road to Steilacoom ends at a ferry dock, where infrequent service can get you to rural **Anderson** and **Ketron Islands**. There also are connections to **McNeil Island**, but you probably don't want to go there; it's a state prison.

To reach Steilacoom's tiny business district, swing to the right from the ferry dock around a small waterfront park, then go right again onto steeply uptilted Main Street to Lafayette Street. Steilacoom's appeals are within a short walk of one another, so park and start prowling. More than 30 of its homes and businesses are on the national historic register, and a walking map will direct you past them. Copies are available at your first stop:

☺ **Steilacoom Historical Society Museum** ● *112 Main Street (at Lafayette Street); (206) 584-4133. Tuesday-Sunday 1 to 4. Free; donations appreciated.* ❑ Located in the basement of the old clapboard town hall, the museum is a dedicated amateur effort and quite pleasingly done. Uncluttered, cohesive exhibits include a 19th century parlor, blacksmith shop and volumes from the original library. (As Washington territory's first incorporated town, Steilacoom boasted its first library, jail and courthouse.)

**Blair Historic Hardware and Drug** ● *Lafayette and Wilkes streets; (206) 588-9668. Weekdays 9 to 5 (Friday night dinner until 9), weekends 8 to 5. Free.* ❑ Built in 1895 as a combined hardware and drug store, it's now mostly a small café and ice cream parlor (see listing below). Many of the original hardware and drug items are on display, and the café's bakery lurks behind oldstyle post office boxes.

☺ **Steilacoom Tribal Cultural Center** ● *1515 Lafayette St.; (206) 584-6308. Tuesday-Sunday 10 to 4, closed Monday. Adults $2, seniors and kids $1.* ❑ This small museum has a dual appeal: It houses a nicely-arranged collection of Southern Puget Sound tribal arts, and it is housed in the 1903 Oberlin Congregational Church building. Native American displays are both historic and modern; it also has a small coffee shop.

Just north of downtown, a continuation of Lafayette Street takes you to **Sunnyside Beach,** with both sandy and grassy areas and a swimming bay.

## WHERE TO DINE

**Blair Historic Hardware and Drug** ● ΔΔ $

❑ *Lafayette and Wilkes streets; (206) 588-9668. Light American fare; wine and beer. Monday-Thursday 9 to 5, Friday 9 to 9, weekends 8 to 5. MC/VISA, AMEX.* ❑ The 1906 soda fountain in this ancient store serves fizzes, phosphates and sundaes, along with breakfasts and light lunches. Savory baked goods emerge from a back room. Dinner specials are available on Friday nights.

☺ **E.R. Rogers Restaurant** ● ΔΔΔ $$$ ∅

❑ *702 Commercial St. (at Wilkes); (206) 582-0280. Northwest cuisine; full bar service. Dinner nightly from 5:30 (from 5 on Sundays), plus Sunday brunch 10 to 2. MC/VISA.* ❑ Elegantly restored Queen Anne Victorian, gray with russet trim. The handsome interior features paisley table cloths, crystal chandeliers, cane-backed chairs and fine Puget Sound views. Some booths are in their own personal bay windows; great places for a cozy evening. The fare is innovative and tasty, including Drambuie chicken, Northwest salmon charbroil and prime rib specials. Our choice was halibut with vegetables, shrimp and Parmesan cheese, baked in a parchment packet.

From downtown Steilacoom, head uphill on Main Street to Rainier Street, go left for two blocks, then take a right and a left, which puts you onto Steilacoom Boulevard. It winds through a brief brace of woods, straightens out and takes you shortly to the site of **Fort Steilacoom.** It's now occupied by the extensive brick complex of **Western State Hospital,** established in 1954. One of Washington's first American facilities, the fort was built in 1849 to protect local settlers, and it remained active until 1868. A few wooden structures survive, rimming a grassy parade ground adjacent to the hospital complex. They house an interpretive center, sutler's store and small museum. Tours are given Saturdays in summer from 1 to 4; (206) 584-2368 or 582-5838.

Continue eastward on Steilacoom Boulevard for a few miles, passing through homes and businesses of Tacoma suburbia. Following signs to I-5 north, you'll T-bone into Custer Road and turn left; the route becomes 74th Street and takes you to the freeway. Climb aboard and head north to Washington's third largest city. (Tacoma is just a tad smaller than Spokane and may have become larger by the time you read this.)

# Tacoma

**Population: 176,700**                    **Elevation: 87 feet**

Like Oakland in San Francisco's shadow, Tacoma once suffered something of an ugly sister complex in the light of larger Seattle. These days, however, Tacoma isn't all that ugly. It has taken significant steps in recent years to spruce up its downtown and beautify its waterfront. Tacoma Dome, although lacking a major league tenant, rivals Seattle's Kingdome in architectural stature.

Tacoma has become a cultural center of some significance, booking important shows in that lofty dome and luring artists to subsidized quarters in old waterfront warehouses. Other cargo sheds are being restored for professional offices. Curiously, Tacoma—not Seattle or Olympia—is home to the fine Washington State Historical Museum. Revitalization is apparent it the new businesses and shops in the old downtown area, cantilevered above Puget Sound. New landscaping, parks and pedestrian overcrossings add to downtown's appeal. The vision is enhanced by the broad-shouldered mass of Mount Rainier, which can be as vivid as a painted backdrop on clear days.

The town has modernized and containerized its port in recent decades, stealing most of Olympia's shipping business and some of Seattle's. It also has diversified to avoid sister Seattle's roller coaster ride with the aircraft and electronics industries. Tacoma's rejuvenation is particularly impressive, considering the recession clouds that persist over Puget Sound.

This remarkable city has deep historic roots. Peter Puget navigated the present-day Tacoma Narrows in 1792 and made note of its strategic position. In 1833, members of the Hudson's Bay Company built Fort Nisqually at Point Defiance, the entrance to the Narrows. Eight years later, Captain Charles Wilkes began surveying the southern Puget Sound and called his starting point Commencement Bay, the name it still bears.

A few settlers came to the bay shore, although Tacoma didn't earn its present name until 1869. General Morton Matthew McCarver applied that moniker to a large tract of land he'd purchased for a townsite. If it sounds familiar, it's a derivation of *Tahoma* or "Mother of the Waters," the Native American name for Mount Rainier. The Northern Pacific Railroad reached

McCarver's Tacoma in 1873 and its future as a lumbering and shipping center was assured. In fact, it was the Puget Sound's leading city until the turn of the century, when the Yukon Gold Rush drew shipping and settlers north toward rival Seattle.

## Driving Tacoma

The city is a bit of a challenge to navigate. Its street patterns are dictated by the contours of Commencement Bay, Tacoma Narrows and the steep hills above them. We suggest that you first pilot yourself to the **Tacoma Visitor Information Center.** It occupies a small kiosk in a parking lot near a freeway overpass, at 130 Puyallup Avenue; open daily 9 to 5. To reach it, take the I-705 exit from I-5, then follow a visitor information sign to the left onto 26th Street, going past and turning away from the **Tacoma Dome.** Go right onto A Street for two blocks to 24th Street and turn right again. Twenty-fourth becomes Puyallup Avenue and you see the visitor center within a block, on your right. The nearby dome once offered tours, but they weren't available when we visited. Check with visitor center folk to determine if they've resumed.

One of the first things you may want to explore—not because it's awesome but because it's close—is a theme shopping complex called **Freighthouse Square Public Market.** It's a good example of the revitalization of Tacoma's older section near the waterfront. The Square is a collection of galleries, boutiques and cafès in a long freight shed, stretching for three blocks on 25th Street between D and F. To reach it, continue two blocks on 24th/Puyallup to D Street and turn right to 25th. From Freighthouse Square, follow 25th five blocks west and turn right onto Pacific Avenue, one of downtown Tacoma's main streets.

☺ You'll shortly see, on your right, the massive and architecturally curious beehive-domed **Tacoma Union Station** at Pacific and 19th. Just beyond, opposite a BP Station, take a half right onto Hood Street and follow it along the **Thea Foss Waterway.** Much of the city's port activity is focused along this narrow ship channel. Hood blends into A Street, then swings around to the right onto Ninth at **Fisherman's Park.** It's a pleasant patch of green offering picnic tables and port vistas. A bronze of a lumberman with his "misery whip" cross-cut saw and a 105-foot-high totem—one of the world's tallest—are the park's focal points. Nearby are exhibits and photos of the early-day waterfront. A **viewing tower** at the foot of Eleventh Street provides pleasing port vistas.

Ninth or Eleventh will return you to Pacific Avenue. To thoroughly explore downtown with its architectural mix of old and new, we're going to suggest backtracking on Pacific to 15th Street. Then, go a block uphill to Commerce Street and head downtown again. You might want to do it afoot; you'll be traveling ten to twelve blocks each direction. (A map available at the visitor center will help make sense of this.)

☺ During your downtown prowl, pause at the **Tacoma Art Museum** at Pacific and 12th Street, housed in the 1920 cut stone National Bank of Washington building. When you shift up to Commerce, you'll be in the heart of the revitalized downtown area. Sidewalks have been extended and landscaped and major stores have been linked by pedestrian crossings. From Commerce, take a left up Ninth Street for a peek at two impeccably restored early 20th century movie theaters—the **Pantages** at Broadway and the **Ri-**

alto near Market. Tacoma's **antique shop district** is just north of here, on Broadway. The **Children's Museum of Tacoma** is at 925 Court Street, a block south of Ninth. Also worthy of a peek is the old **Tacoma City Hall** with its clock tower and French Renaissance architecture, at Commerce and Seventh.

When you've finished with downtown, continue a few blocks up Ninth to Tacoma Avenue and turn right. After a dozen blocks, you'll enter the **Stadium District,** and old neighborhood undergoing gradual gentrification. Perched on a cliff overlooking Puget Sound, this was home to lumber and shipping barons a century ago. It now offers a few boutiques, cafès and galleries, tucked among old brick apartment houses. Take a right onto Third Street, which shortly curves into Stadium Way and presents you with two notable landmarks.

☺ The outstanding **Washington State Historical Society Museum** occupies a Greek-style structure overlooking the Sound. Opposite is the most imposing public school you'll ever see, the elaborate multi-spired French Renaissance **Stadium High.** It rises like a medieval castle above its own playing field, for which the neighborhood is named.

From the Stadium District, return to Pacific Avenue in the downtown area and head west. Pacific soon becomes Shuster Parkway, taking you to the newly landscaped **Commencement Bay shoreline.** Keep to the left on Shuster Parkway, avoiding a right-hand split onto an overpass that leads inland to 30th Street. Beyond the split, Shuster becomes Ruston Way.

You're now traveling along a pleasing park strip and jogging/biking trail that's interrupted occasionally by patches of green and restaurants on piers. This has become Tacoma's favorite haunt for dining out, working out and admiring vistas of Puget Sound and the ever-present (if often obscured) Mount Rainier. On a clear day, this is as nice as Tacoma ever looks: the waterfront in the foreground, downtown beyond and the mountain on the horizon.

You'll find parking, potties, a snack shop and public fishing pier at **Les Davis Park,** the largest swatch of green along here. It is, incidentally, a great place to watch the sunset. Beyond the park, the waterfront becomes briefly ugly and industrialized. Then you'll pass through a skinny tunnel and emerge in the tiny town of **Ruston.**

*RV advisory:* The tunnel is a tight squeeze for big rigs. Approach very slowly and sound your horn before entering.

☺ Hit a stop light at Pearl Street, turn right and you soon enter the crown jewel of Tacoma's many parklands, **Point Defiance Park.** Its 698 acres shelter a fine **zoo and aquarium,** restored **Fort Nisqually** and the **Camp 6 Logging Exhibit,** a kiddie attraction called **Never-Never Land,** a rose garden, marina and boathouse with boat rentals, grassy lawns, play areas, old growth forest and many miles of hiking and biking trails.

Roads through the park can be confusing and you may find yourself going in circles, although signs to assorted attractions are plentiful. If you stay close to the bayfront on **Five-Mile Drive,** you'll catch frequent vistas of Puget Sound. Signs and graphics at turnouts describe historical events such as the discovery of the Narrows (which borders on the park) and the establishment of Fort Nisqually.

Once you've found your way out of the park, pick up Pearl Street and head south through Ruston. It's a cute little old town with some false front stores housing cafès and antique shops. Follow Pearl about two miles south, then turn right onto Narrows Drive. It's lined with attractive homes perched above that slender waterway. Ahead, you'll see the **Tacoma Narrows Bridge,** a Golden Gate clone of a different color, stretched across the passage. With a central span of 2,800 feet, it's the world's fifth longest single-span suspension bridge. You've probably seen old newsreel footage of the original bridge. It earned the title of "Galloping Gertie" after it began swaying in a high wind and collapsed in 1940, just four years after it was completed.

You'll soon encounter Highway 16; the westbound lane will put you onto the bridge—which, fortunately, no longer gallops. A crossing of this 188-foot-high span delivers you to Gig Harbor on the **Kitsap Peninsula,** which we will visit shortly. This water-rimmed land mass stretches two-thirds of the way up Puget Sound. Avoid the bridge during rush hour, and particularly on a Friday evening.

## Attractions
### In order of appearance

**Freighthouse Square Public Market** ● *25th Street between D and F. Most shops open Monday-Saturday 10 to 7 and Sunday noon to 5; some restaurants open later.* ◻ A freight house, should you wonder, is different from a cargo shed in that it's long and skinny, permitting a train to pull up and unload several cars at once. Inside, the cargo is either stored or spirited away by waiting wagons. This freight house now houses shops, boutiques and several restaurants, mostly with international themes. Many of the cafès are open to the long central passageway, nice spots for people-watching.

☺ **Tacoma Union Station** ● *Pacific Avenue near 19th Street. Weekdays 8 to 5.* ◻ This huge 1911 beehive structure with red brick walls and arched windows was designed by the same architects who brought New York's Grand Central Station to life. Originally the terminus of the Great Northern Railway, it now houses the Federal Courthouse. Step inside the lofty waiting room to see what a multi-million dollar restoration can accomplish. The interior is surprisingly contemporary, with light woods and soft pastel colors.

**Tacoma Art Museum** ● *1123 Pacific Ave.; (206) 272-4258. Adults $3, teens and seniors $2, kids 6 to 12, $1. Tuesday-Saturday 10 to 5 (Thursday until 7), Sunday noon to 5, closed Monday.* ◻ Small and handsomely arrayed, the museum features American and European artists, with an accent on impressionism. It also has an impressive Asian collection, with Japanese woodblock prints and Chinese imperial robes. A rich variety of changing exhibits makes this nice little museum worthy of repeat visits.

**Children's Museum of Tacoma** ● *925 Court St. (between Ninth and Eleventh); (206) 627-2436. Tuesday-Saturday 10 to 5, Sunday noon to 4, closed Monday. Adults and kids $3, tots free.* ◻ Kids learn the basics of architecture with hands-on building blocks in this creative museum. Youngsters can climb through a tree house, explore an old English town and dabble with assorted arts and crafts.

☺ **Stadium High School and Bowl** ● *Stadium Way at Third Street.* ◻ The structure was intended to be a luxury hotel, a joint venture of the Northern Pacific Railroad and the Tacoma Land Company. However, both outfits went broke around the turn of the century, before it could be finished. The Tacoma School Board bought the building for a fraction of its worth, completed construction and opened it as a high school in 1906. It's still active, and the stadium is one of the oldest on the West Coast.

☺ **Washington State Historical Society Museum** • *315 N. Stadium Way; (206) 593-2830. Tuesday-Saturday 10 to 5, Sunday 1 to 5, closed Monday. Adults $2, seniors $1.50, kids $1, family groups $5.* ⌂ Easily one of Washington's finest museum, this archive combines leading edge mixed media with artfully placed artifacts to tell state's story. Begin with a computerized tableau that traces Washington's development, then stroll past a cubistic Plexiglas clutter of a time-line. The museum also has a gallery featuring works of state artists. All this will change in 1996, when the facility moves to new quarters beside Union Station.

## Point Defiance Park attractions

☺ **Point Defiance Zoo & Aquarium** • *Off Five-Mile Drive; (206) 591-5335. Daily in summer 10 to 7, the rest of the year 10 to 4. Adults $6.25, seniors and handicapped $5.75, kids $4.50, tots $2.25.* ⌂ Can you imagine eating 120 hamburgers a day? That's the equivalent of a sea otter's daily diet, since it consumes 25 percent of its weight. Clever graphics such as this, tied to creative exhibits, have taken Tacoma's zoo beyond the ordinary animal farm. Our favorite area focuses on critters next door—the wolves, puffins, walruses, dolphins, polar bears and others in the Northwest and Arctic tundra exhibits. Another fine display is the World of Adaptations, where one learns how animals conform to specific environments. The small aquarium offers the usual aquatic tanks, with a focus on sharks and their habitats.

**Fort Nisqually** • *5400 N. Pearl St.; (206) 591-5339. Daily 11 to 6, shorter hours in winter. Adults $1, kids 50 cents.* ⌂ This Hudson's Bay Company outpost, completed in 1833, originally stood near the Narrows. When fur trading declined a few years later, it was moved a mile inland, where its tenants could oversee agricultural activities. Today's version, reconstructed during the Depression by the Civilian Conservation Corps, is near the second site. The restored factor's house contains early-day furnishings, complete with Blue Willow china on a well-set table. A squared-log granary, shops, sleeping quarters and three-story bastion comprise the rest of the complex.

**Never-Never Land** • *Adjacent to Fort Nisqually; (206) 591-5845 or (206) 591-3690. Daily 11 to 7 in summer and 11 to 5 in April and May, weekends only 11 to 5 in March and September, closed the rest of the year. Adults $2, teens $1.50, kiddies $1.* ⌂ Say howdy to Humpty Dumpty and 41 other life sized storybook characters. They occupy 28 tableaux in this small kiddieland, where tree-shaded paths take visitors down assorted yellow brick roads.

☺ **Camp 6 Logging Exhibit** • *Off Five-Mile Drive; (206) 752-0047. Wednesday-Sunday in summer and major holidays, 10 to 6; shorter hours in the off-season. Train rides on weekends, noon to 6. Exhibits free; train rides $2 for adults and teens, $1 for seniors and kids.* ⌂ The great days of steam logging" are preserved in this rambling exhibit, with lots of lumber-hauling rolling stock and forest-focused memorabilia. Particularly interesting are mobile bunkhouses, mounted on skids so they could be dragged by horses or skidded aboard flatcars for movement from one forest camp to another. On weekends, steam or diesel logging locomotives offer brief rides through adjacent forests.

# ACTIVITIES

**Baseball** • Pacific Coast League Tacoma Tigers play at Cheney Stadium; (206) 752-7707.

**Boat and fishing tackle rentals** • Boathouse Marina at Point Defiance Park; (206) 591-5325.

**Bus tours** • Cascade Trailways Tours offers sightseeing trips from Tacoma to Mount St. Helens, Rainier and Kitsap Peninsula seaports, plus cruises to Victoria; (206) 383-5615.

**Farmers Market** • Held periodically in summer on Antique Row, Broadway between Seventh and Ninth streets; (206) 627-2836.

**Harbor cruises** • Tacoma Harbor Tours features dinner cruises and other Puget Sound tours aboard an old-fashioned passenger ferry. In summer, cruises are offered to the Tillicum Village salmon bake on Blake Island; (800) 974-8007 or (206) 572-1001.

**Hockey** • The Western Hockey League's Tacoma Rockets play at Tacoma Dome; (206) 627-3653.

**Live theater** • The restored Pantages Theater presents concerts, plays and such; (206) 591-5894. Tacoma Actors Guild presents a winter season of dramas and comedies; (206) 272-2145. Broadway Center for the Performing Arts has a varied season of theater, dance and concerts; (206) 591-5894. Dinner theater shows are presented at a restaurant called 565 Broadway; (206) 272-8118.

**Tacoma Dome events** • (206) 272-3663 for information and tickets.

## Transportation

**Airlines** • Sea-Tac International Airport, midway between Tacoma and Seattle, is served by most major U.S. carriers; call (800) 826-1147 for airlines and schedules.

**Amtrak** • The *Coast Starlight* offers daily service from Los Angeles, San Francisco and Portland, and the *Pioneer* cruises to Salt Lake City via Seattle. Tacoma's Amtrak station is at 1001 Puyallup Avenue; call (800) USA-RAIL.

**Bus service** • The Greyhound terminal is at 1319 Pacific Ave.; (206) 383-4621. Pierce Transit offers service between Tacoma, Puyallup, Gig Harbor, Steilacoom and other nearby communities; (800) 562-8109 or (206) 593-4500.

**Ferry service** • The Washington State ferry system ties Tacoma to Vashon Island and, from there, the rest of Puget Sound. The ferry terminal is at the north end of Pearl Street near Point Defiance Park. Call locally (206) 464-6400 (a Seattle number) or statewide (800) 84-FERRY for schedules and fares.

## ANNUAL EVENTS
### Tacoma and surrounds

**Tacoma Dome Boat Show** in early April; (206) 756-2121.

**Arts & Crafts Show** in mid-April at the Tacoma Mall; 475-4565.

**Living History Day** in mid-April at Fort Nisqually; (206) 591-5339.

**Gem Faire** in mid-May at the Tacoma Dome; (206) 272-6817.

**Tacoma Boat Show** in late May at the Tacoma Dome; 634-0911.

**Taste of Tacoma** food festival, early July in Point Defiance Park; (206) 232-2982.

**Gig Harbor Art Festival** in mid-July at Gig Harbor; (206) 851-6865.

Point Defiance Salmon Bake in late July and mid-August at Owen Beach; (206) 591-3690.

Fort Nisqually Brigade Encampment, early August; 591-5339.

Gig Harbor Jazz Festival in mid-August at Celebrations Meadow; (206) 627-1504.

Air Show in late August at McChord Air Force Base; (206) 984-5637.

Antique Show in early September at Tacoma Mall; (206) 627-7946.

Greater Northwest Antique Show and Sale in mid-September at Tacoma Dome; (206) 441-4290.

Port of Tacoma Free Boat Tours in late September at the waterfront; (206) 383-5841.

## WHERE TO DINE

### Boathouse Grill ● ΔΔ $ Ø

☐ Point Defiance Park, Ruston; (206) 756-7336. American; wine and beer. Sunday-Thursday 6:30 a.m. to 9 p.m., Friday-Saturday 6:30 to 9:30. MC/VISA. ☐ Recently remodeled restaurant (after a fire) offers picture-window panoramas of Puget Sound, Vashon Island and Gig Harbor. The interior is pleasingly simple with oilcloth tables and historic waterfront photos. While not gourmet, the fare is quite good and inexpensive, wandering from fresh seafood to Cajun chicken to liver and onions. All non-smoking.

### Fujiya ● ΔΔ $$

☐ 1125 Court (between Broadway and Market, downtown); (206) 627-5319. Japanese; wine and beer. Lunch weekdays from 11 a.m., dinner Monday-Saturday from 5:30. MC/VISA, AMEX. ☐ An open sushi bar is a focal point at this locally popular, chef-owned place. It's busy with business men at lunch, and it draws dinner crowds to its properly-done tempura, gyoza (pork-filled dumplings) and other Nippon fare.

### ☺ Guadalamama's Fajita Cantina ● ΔΔ $$ Ø

☐ 3327 Ruston Way; (206) 756-5611. Mexican-American; full bar service. Sunday-Thursday 11 to 11, Friday-Saturday 11 to midnight. Major credit cards. ☐ One of several new over-the-water restaurants along Ruston Way, this one's a formula Ameri-Mex place. Check out the bright yellow exterior and a lime green and yellow interior dressed in comic Mexican figures. A local critic accurately described it as a Mexican Toontown. The menu is predictable and generally good: Rockfish Vera Cruz, pork fajitas, charbroiled Pacific salmon, plus typical Mexican entrées. Indoor and outdoor dining.

### G.I. Shenanigans ● ΔΔ $$ Ø

☐ 3017 Ruston Way; (206) 752-8811. American, mostly seafood; full bar service. Sunday-Thursday 11 to 10, Friday-Saturday 11 to 11. Major credit cards. ☐ Despite the silly name, it's a remarkably handsome establishment dressed in river stone, polished woods, brass and frosted glass. Another of the Ruston Way group, it's very popular with locals; reservations are urged nights and particularly on weekends. An innovative menu ranges from citrus catfish and coconut strawberry prawns to more predictable steaks, chops and chickens. The nut and honey swordfish tastes better than it sounds. Indoor and outdoor dining.

### Harbor Lights ● ΔΔ $$ Ø

☐ 2761 Ruston Way; (206) 752-8600. American, mostly seafood; full bar service. Monday-Thursday 11 to 11:45, Friday-Saturday 11 to 12:45, Sunday

*11 to 9. Major credit cards.* ❏ The oldest of the Ruston Way cafès, it shares none of the gaudy or classy look of the others. It's dressed in ordinary nautical fishnet garb. However, it is on a culinary par with the rest, and it's and often packed. The menu is as unpretentious as the dècor—lots of fresh fish and shellfish, plus chickens and chops. This is your place if you don't care for strawberry sauce on your salmon.

### ☺ *Pacific Rim* • △△△△ *$$$* ∅

❏ *100 S. Ninth St. (at A, downtown); (206) 627-1009. Eclectic Asian; full bar service. Monday-Thursday 11 to 10, Friday-Saturday 10 to 11; reservations required. MC/VISA, AMEX.* ❏ Exceptional restaurant housed in old brick, with a lively open kitchen bistro downstairs and a more subdued polished mahogany dining room upstairs. The creative menu focuses on the countries of the Pacific Rim. However, entrèes are liberally laced with American *nouveau* touches, such as fish sausage appetizers, and grilled salmon in cucumber-*wasabe* sauce.

### *Ram American Grill* • △△ *$$* ∅

❏ *3001 Ruston Way; (206) 756-7886. American; full bar service. Breakfast Monday-Friday 6 to 11, Saturday 7 to 11 and Sunday 7 to 2; lunch and dinner Monday-Thursday 11 to 10, Friday-Saturday 11 to 11 and Sunday noon to 10. MC/VISA.* ❏ This is yet another Ruston Way pier place. The look is ivy league nautical with brass, polished woods and a rowing scull hanging from the open beam ceiling. The fare is American grill—turkey pot pie, roast turkey and fried seafood. Indoor and outdoor dining.

### *Ruston Inn* • △ *$$*

❏ *Pearl at 51st streets, Ruston; (206) 752-3288. American; full bar service. Daily 7 a.m. to 9 p.m. Major credit cards.* ❏ This is where you go for something more substantial than concession food at the zoo. Located a few blocks from Point Defiance Park, the simple family-style cafè serves essential American pork, chicken and beef, plus local oysters, prawns and seafood.

## WHERE TO SLEEP

### *Best Western Tacoma Inn* • ⌒⌒⌒ *$$$* ∅

❏ *8726 S. Hosmer, Tacoma, WA 98444; (800) 528-1234 or (206) 535-2880. Couples $64 to $74, singles $58 to $68, kitchenettes $69 to $79, suites $130 to $160. Major credit cards.* ❏ Nicely maintained 149-unit inn with TV movies, room phones, some refrigerators; pool, two spas, putting green, playground. **Copperfield's** serves American fare; dinners $10 to $16; full bar service; lounge adjacent with live entertainment.

### *Corporate Suites* • ⌒⌒⌒ *$$$*

❏ *219 E. Division Court (near B Street), Tacoma, WA 98404; (800) 255-6058 or (206) 473-4105. Couples and singles $45 to $79. Major credit cards.* ❏ Twenty-seven condo suites with complete kitchens, TV, room phones; pool. Some two-bedroom units.

### *Days Inn Tacoma Mall* • ⌒⌒ *$$$* ∅

❏ *6802 Tacoma Mall Blvd. (I-5 at 72nd Street), Tacoma, WA 98409; (800) 325-2525 or (206) 475-5900. Couples $55 to $85, singles $45 to $75, suites $75 to $120; rates include full breakfast. Major credit cards.* ❏ A 132-unit motel with TV movies, phones, free coffee and newspapers; passes to adjacent athletic club. **Calzone's Cafè** serves Italian fare; 7 a.m. to 10 p.m., dinners $5 to $13; full bar service.

**Executive Inn** • ⌂⌂⌂ $$$$ Ø

⌖ *5700 E. Pacific Hwy. (at 54th Avenue), Tacoma, WA 98424; (800) 938-8500 or (206) 922-0080. Couples $71 to $81, singles $66 to $78, suites $125 to $150. Major credit cards.* ⌖ Newly refurbished 140-room inn with TV movies, room phones; free airport shuttle; health club privileges. **Christie's Restaurant** serves daily 6 a.m. to 10 p.m.; American; dinners $9 to $17; full bar service. Also coffee shop and lounge with live entertainment.

**Friendship Inn** • ⌂⌂ $$ Ø

⌖ *9920 S. Tacoma Way (at 100th), Tacoma, WA 98499; (206) 588-5241. Couples and singles from $42, kitchenettes from $46. Major credit cards.* ⌖ A 103-room motel with TV, room phones and refrigerators. **Jim Moore's** restaurant offers an eclectic menu, open 24 hours; full bar service.

**Howard Johnson Lodge** • ⌂⌂ $$$

⌖ *8702 S. Hosmer, Tacoma, WA 98444; (800) 446-4656 or (206) 535-3100. Couples $64 to $69, singles $59; rates include continental breakfast. Major credit cards.* ⌖ A 143-unit inn with TV, room phones; pool.

**Royal Coachman Inn** • ⌂⌂⌂ $$$ Ø

⌖ *5805 E. Pacific Highway (I-5 exit 137), Tacoma, WA 98403; (800) 422-3051 or (206) 922-2500. Couples $58 to $68, singles $51 to $61, kitchenettes $75 to $85, suites $100 to $150. Major credit cards.* ⌖ Well-kept 94-unit inn with TV, room phones; some rooms with refrigerators; some with spa tubs; guest laundry, spa. **Castle Fife Restaurant** serves American fare 6:30 a.m. to 9 p.m.; dinners $5.50 to $14; full bar service.

**Sheraton-Tacoma** • ⌂⌂⌂ $$$$$ Ø

⌖ *1320 Broadway Place (at 13th Street), Tacoma, WA 98403; (800) 845-9466 or (206) 572-3200. Couples $102 to $125, singles $92 to $120, suites $140 to $400. Major credit cards.* ⌖ A 319-room hotel with TV movies, room phones; sauna and spa. **Wintergarden** and 26th-floor **Altezzo** restaurants serve American and continental fare; meal service 6 a.m. to 11 p.m.; dinners $8 to $20; full bar service.

**Sherwood Inn** • ⌂⌂ $$$ Ø

⌖ *8402 S. Hosmer (S. 84th), Tacoma, WA 98444; (800) 537-8483 or (206) 535-2800. Couples $49 to $54, singles $44 to $49, suites $54 to $64. Rates included full breakfast. Major credit cards.* ⌖ An 118-unit inn; large, comfortable rooms with TV, phones; pool. **Garden Café** serves American fare 6:30 a.m. to 9 p.m. (to 10 Friday-Saturday); dinners $6 to $14.

## Bed & breakfast inns

**Bay Vista Bed & breakfast** • ⌂⌂⌂ $$$

⌖ *4617 N. Darien Dr. (west of North Pearl), Tacoma, WA 98407; (206) 759-8084. Couples $55 to $75, singles $50 to $70. Two bedroom suite suitable for couples or families; private bath; continental breakfast. MC/VISA.* ⌖ Ranch style home with sweeping views of Puget Sound and the Cascades; fireplace; garden patio. In the north end near Point Defiance Park and the Ruston Way waterfront.

**Commencement Bay Bed & Breakfast** • ⌂⌂⌂ $$$$ Ø

⌖ *3312 N. Union Ave. (at N. 34th Avenue), Tacoma, WA 98407; (206) 752-8175. Couples and singles $70 to $105. Three rooms, one with private and two with share baths; continental or full breakfast. MC/VISA, AMEX.* ⌖

Colonial style home with "classically elegant furnishings"; each room individually decorated. Fireplace in reading room; game room; office for business travelers; spa in garden. Refrigerators and microwaves available.

## WHERE TO CAMP

We found no camping facilities within Tacoma; these are nearby:

**Dash Point State Park** • *5700 SW Dash Point Rd., Federal Way, WA 98002; (206) 593-2206. RV and tent sites, $10. No reservations or credit cards.* ☐ Flush and pit potties, picnic tables and barbecues, fishing, swimming and nature trails. To reach it, go five miles northeast of Tacoma on State Route 509 to the community of Federal Way.

**Gig Harbor Campground** • *9515 NW Burnham Dr., Gig Harbor, WA 98332; (206) 858-8138. RV and tent sites, $13.73 to $20.85, camping cabin $24. Reservations accepted.* ☐ Some pull-throughs, picnic tables; showers, coin laundry, mini-mart, volleyball, badminton and horseshoes. To reach it, cross the Tacoma Narrows Bridge, then take the North Rosedale Exit to Burnham Drive and follow signs.

**Majestic Manor RV Park** • *7022 River Rd., Puyallup, WA 98371; (800) 348-3144 or (206) 845-3144. RV sites, $14 to $18. Reservations accepted.* ☐ Several overnight sites within a mobile home park, near the Puyallup River. Showers, pool, rec hall, TV hookups, coin laundry, some grocery items; fishing nearby. To reach it, take exit 167 (River Road) from I-5 and follow it east along the Puyallup River; it's on the right, west of Puyallup.

## SIDE TRIP: THE KITSAP PENINSULA

Extending north from Tacoma, the Kitsap Peninsula is technically an appendage of the Olympic Peninsula, although it is demographically more related to Tacoma and Seattle. It's separated from the larger peninsula by the narrow inlet of Hood Canal, with a small connection northwest of Tacoma.

Reaching north past Seattle and Everett, the Kitsap is a low-lying land mass, rather thickly settled and offering little of visitor interest. Its commercial core is the blue collar community of Bremerton, home to a large naval facility. It does have some communities worth a peek, notably Gig Harbor just across from Tacoma, Port Orchard below Bremerton, and the old lumber town of Port Gamble, far to the north.

Our side-trip up the Kitsap begins by taking State Route 16 across that "green Golden Gate"—the Tacoma Narrows Bridge. The high span delivers nice views of this narrow waterway between the peninsula and mainland. (If you'd like to absorb the view slowly, you can take a pedestrian path across.) Highway 16 is a freeway here, whisking travelers northward through the center of the peninsula. However, we're going to direct you along water-side roads less traveled.

## Gig Harbor

**Population: 3,200**                    **Elevation: about 80 feet**

About four miles from the bridge, take the second Gig Harbor exit, following city center signs onto Pioneer Way. You'll drift downhill and hit Harborview Drive, the main commercial street. Gig Harbor presents a pretty picture, occupying a hillside above the wooded shoreline of Colvos Passage, which separates the Kitsap Peninsula from Vashon Island. Fishing boats and pleasure craft fill offshore marinas.

*A forest of masts decorates Gig Harbor, an attractive little community across the Narrows from Tacoma.* — **Betty Woo Martin**

For orientation, turn right from Pioneer Avenue onto Judson Street, a block before you reach Harborview, and drive a block to the Gig Harbor Peninsula Area **Chamber of Commerce** at 3125 Judson. It's open 9 to 5 weekdays. Then continue down to aptly-named Harborview Drive to explore the small business district, which stretches for three or four blocks along the waterfront. It's not a major tourist area, although it does offer a few boutiques, galleries and water-view cafès. A restaurant near Pioneer and Harborview is a handy lunch stop, and a small museum a few blocks north is worth a brief visit:

### Harbor Inn Restaurant ● △△ $$

□ *3111 Harborview Dr.; (206) 851-5454. American, mostly seafood; full bar service. Breakfast weekends from 8:30, lunch and dinner daily from 11. MC/VISA.* □ Harbor-view dining rooms upstairs and down, with nautical trim and comfortable upholstered captains chairs. Typical seafood menu ranges from red snapper and mixed grill to chioppino and calimari steaks, plus a couple of steak and chicken dishes.

### Puget Sound Mariners' Museum ● *3311 Harborview Drive; (206) 858-9395. Call for hours. Free; donations appreciated.* □ Housed in a clapboard cottage above the water, this cozy little museum exhibits things nautical, relating to the Puget Sound's seafaring history. Displays include old diving suits, seamen's uniforms, ships models and brassworks. By the museum's own admission, it displays "tons of paraphernalia relating to working, sailing and navigating ships."

From the museum, continue north on Harborview Drive and follow it around to the right after a mile, staying close to the water. Less than a mile later, it T-bones into Vernhardson Street; turn right and follow it past **Gig**

**Harbor Town Park,** along the banks of a small creek. At the next intersection, turn left onto Crescent Valley Road. This drive takes you quickly through the bucolic innards of the island.

After a few miles, as you enter Klikitat County, you'll return to waterside, along **Colvos Passage.** Cross a bridge over a narrow channel at the **Olalla boat ramp,** then turn right and uphill onto Banner Road. Follow its twisting course up a high bluff, with great views of Colvos Passage and **Vashon Island** across the way. The route soon swings away from the channel and takes you on a straight but roller coaster ride through the island's hilly midsection.

The highway T-bones into Sedgwick Road after about four miles. Turn right and drive into **Southworth** at the entrance to Colvos Passage. Here, ferries can take you either to Vashon Island or to Fauntleroy, on the mainland just below Seattle. You'll start getting impressive views of the distant Seattle skyline from here.

To continue up the Kitsap, take Cherry Street north from downtown Southworth; it's just above the ferry landing. After some twists and turns, it becomes Olympiad Drive, a narrow residential street offering *great* views of the Seattle skyline to the east and the Olympic Mountains to the west. The route shortly swings away from the beach. Take a sharp right to stay with Olympiad, then hit a stop sign after a few blocks and go right again to return to the beach, following signs toward Port Orchard.

The next town is **South Colby,** which is little more than a post office and a collection of shorefront homes. That green clump out in Puget Sound is **Blake Island,** a state park and the site of a popular Native American salmon bake. You'll learn all about that in the next chapter. The route, now called Colchester Drive, continues north to **Manchester,** a scruffily cute waterfront town. As you T-bone into its Main Street, turn uphill to Beach Drive East and follow signs to Manchester State Park. You'll travel along a lagoon, then into a wooded residential area. Go right onto Hilldale Road:

☺ *Manchester State Park* ● *P.O. Box 36, Manchester, WA 98353; (206) 871-4065. RV and tent sites, $10; hiker/biker sites $5; coin showers. No reservations or credit cards.* ⊓ This park encompasses a former coastal artillery defense post called Fortress Mitchell. Trails take you to some of the surviving batteries and to a large brick torpedo warehouse. The camping and picnicking area offers 3,400 feet of waterfront and a swimming beach. The park in closed in winter.

Turn right out of the park, and continue along this north-facing nub of the Kitsap on Beach Drive East. After several miles of mudflat beach—great for clamming—you'll encounter one of the Kitsap Peninsula's more appealing little towns.

☺ **Port Orchard** offers a good-sized collection of old fashioned storefronts, linked together by covered sidewalks. They give it a kind of nautical-Western look. Although this slightly scruffy town is cute enough to have tourist appeal, it offers little of visitor interest. Antiquers will want to pause at the large **antique mall** downtown at the corner of Rainier Street and Sydney Avenue. Sydney also takes you to the town's small **waterfront dock** with a few boats at bay and a shorefront walk.

Continue through Port Orchard and you'll finally rejoin State Highway 16, which takes you around **Sinclair Inlet** and merges with State Route 3. Just ahead is the largest town on the Kitsap Peninsula.

# Bremerton

**Population: 38,100**                              **Elevation: 10 feet**

The northern home of America's Pacific Fleet, Bremerton is the classic navy town, rimmed by gray-hulled ships and government housing projects. Spread over shoreline hills, it has occupied this key position on Sinclair Inlet since German immigrant William Bremer arrived in 1891. The brickfront downtown area has that weathered look of a tough old survivor.

To check out the town, take Highway 304, following "Bremerton Boardwalk and Naval Museum" signs. You'll shortly pass the **Puget Sound Naval Shipyard.** Stay with Highway 304 as it twist and turns through the town's residential district and—with any luck at all—you'll wind up on Burwell Street, and then you'll T-bone into Washington Avenue. Turn right and you'll encounter the two reasons for visiting Bremerton:

*Bremerton Naval Museum* • *130 Washington Ave. (near Second); (206) 479-7447. Tuesday-Saturday 10 to 4, Sunday 1 to 4, closed Monday. Free; donations appreciated.* ⧠ This old storefront is filled with nautical lore, relating to both military and civilian seamanship. Walk about its open spaces and peer at a cumbersome old diving suit, ship models, brassware and other artifacts in display cases, on the walls and hanging from the ceiling. This large museum is almost cluttered, yet close to being neatly arranged.

☺ *Bremerton Boardwalk* and the *Turner Joy* • *Boardwalk gift shop open daily 10 to 5;* Turner Joy *destroyer open for tours Monday-Thursday-Friday 11 to 4 and weekends 10 to 4. Adults $5, kids and seniors $4.* ⧠ Just below the museum, the Bremerton Boardwalk is quite concrete, providing access to the town's busy waterfront. Sitting at permanent anchor is the 1958 destroyer *Turner Joy*, which saw action off Vietnam and now sees thousands of annual visitors. If you're a reminiscing sailor or a landlubber who's never been to sea, you'll enjoy exploring its busy innards, walking narrow corridors and smelling a distinctive greasy metallic aroma that says "Navy ship."

Above the boardwalk is a handy place for a lunch break, with a nice harbor view, if you don't mind its rather smoky atmosphere:

*The Wheelhouse* • • △ $$

⧠ *116 First St.; (206) 377-0821. American, mostly seafood; full bar service. Daily from 11. MC/VISA, AMEX.* ⧠ It's a nautically simple place, appealing mostly for aquatic views from dining rooms upstairs and down. The menu is basic seafood—ling cod, halibut steak, scallops and such—plus a few steaks and chickens.

From downtown, go north on Washington Avenue, which curves to the left, away from the waterfront, and becomes Eleventh Street. After about six blocks, turn right at a stop onto Warren Avenue (north State Highway 303). You'll cross a bridge over **Dyes Inlet** and pass through the commercial suburban sprawl of Bremerton. You can go quickly north on Highway 303, or stay with the waterfront by following signs east on Sylvan Way (Route 306) to **Illahee State Park.** Sitting beside Port Orchard Channel, it offers standard campsites ($10), a swimming area, boat launch and fishing pier.

Follow Illahee Road north along the shorefront; it re-joins State Route 303 at the hamlet of **Brownsville.** Eight miles beyond is **Keyport.** It's home the **Naval Undersea Warfare Center** and a museum which sets out to prove, as they said in *The Little Mermaid*, life is better under the sea:

☺ **Naval Undersea Museum** • *610 Dowell St., Keyport (just outside the Undersea Warfare Center Gate); (206) 396-4148. Summer 10 to 4 Tuesday-Sunday, winter 10 to 4 Tuesday-Saturday. Free.* ⊓ Still being developed but with plenty to see now, this new museum focuses on the Navy's role beneath the sea, from the first Revolutionary War submarine called the "Turtle" to modern underwater research vehicles. Exhibits include modern and ancient diving gear, a rare Japanese World War II suicide torpedo, diving bells and mock-ups and models of submarines, subsea rescue vehicles and anti-sub aircraft. Self-guiding tours take visitors from displays on sea mythology and legends to the future of the undersea world. The first major phase was scheduled for opening in late 1994; a preview center focuses on exhibits yet to come.

From Keyport, head west on Highway 308, then drive eleven miles north on State Route 3 to the edge of **Hood Canal**. You'll shortly pass the entrance to the Hood Canal floating bridge, which links the Kitsap and Olympic peninsulas. Constructed of concrete floats with the roadbed on top, it's one of four in the world and the only one crossing saltwater. Two of the others span Seattle's Lake Washington. Just north of here, you'll encounter one of Washington's oldest communities.

# Port Gamble

☺ A deliberate New England transplant, Port Gamble offers a wonderful collection of old false front, early American and Victorian architecture. It was founded in 1853 as a sawmill town and lumber shipping port by Captain William Talbot, A.J. Pope and Cyrus Walker. They styled their settlement after their hometown of East Machias, Maine, even importing maples and other New England hardwoods. The Pope and Talbot lumber mill still turns out lumber; it's the oldest continuously operating sawmill in America.

Two museums occupy the Port Gamble Country Store building:

**Of Sea and Shore Museum** • *Port Gamble General Store; (206) 297-2426. Store open weekdays 8 to 5 and weekends 9 to 5; MC/VISA. Museum open daily 11 to 4 in summer, weekends only the rest of the year.* ⊓ The country store once served the needs of the lumbermen, and it still has the look of a general mercantile. However it caters more to tourists than workers today; which is to say it sells more souvenir T-shirts than lunch buckets. The museum consists of a large clutter of pioneer, lumbering and nautical regalia in a loft above the store.

**Port Gamble Historic Museum** • *Port Gamble General Store basement; (206) 297-3341. Daily 10 to 4 in summer, closed the rest of the year. Adults $1, seniors and kids, 50 cents.* ⊓ Walk down behind the general store and you'll encounter this museum, installed in former boarding rooms of mill workers. Exhibits, not professional but interesting, trace the town's lumbering and aquatic history. A Forest of the Future display focuses on reforestation.

The chuffing and whining **Pope and Talbot Lumber Mill** is a commanding presence, just downhill from the town. Across the street from the general store, note the unusual double false-front façade on a large yellow and white office building, now housing the town's post office. Walk to a waterfront bluff for a nice view of Hood Canal and adjacent Olympic Peninsula. A monument there discusses the town's history. From the downtown area, follow signs to the **Cyrus T. Walker Tree Nursery and Forest Research Center,** where you can visit millions of seedlings and watch a film on tree planting; (206) 297-3292.

From Port Gamble, head south and then east on Highway 104, about eight miles to **Kingston.** Here, Washington State ferries can take you to Edmonds, midway between Seattle and Everett. Kingston is kind of a cute little town, with a row of false front stores leading down to the ferry landing. They're handy for browsing while waiting for the next boat.

## SIDE TRIP: VASHON ISLAND

Despite its pivotal location in southern Puget Sound, Tacoma is served by only one ferry, which runs every few minutes to Vashon Island. There's no urgent reason for the casual tourist to visit Vashon, since it's more bucolic novelty than substance. It does offer a woodsy break from Tacoma's concrete and commerce, along with several bed and breakfast inns.

The island is pleasantly rural but not unpopulated. Homes line the wooded shorelines and few beaches are open to the public. The small towns of Burton, Vashon Center and Vashon offer folksy business districts. The island is popular with cyclists, since most of the roads are level after a steep pull from the Southend ferry terminal.

To reach Vashon from Tacoma, head for Point Defiance, turn north onto Pearl Street and drive a short distance to road's end at the ferry terminal. The 15-minute crossing offers pleasing views of the Tacoma waterfront and—on a clear day—an unobstructed gander at Mount Rainier. About a mile after you've left the ferry at Southend terminal, veer to the right onto Vashon Highway, which takes you shoreside along Quartermaster Harbor. Across the way are waterfront homes of adjoining **Maury Island** (actually a Vashon Island peninsula).

**Burton** has a pleasing Victorian look, with a few false front stores downtown. About a mile beyond, turn right onto Quartermaster Drive and take it to tiny **Portage,** then follow Point Robinson Road out to **Point Robinson Park** on Maury Island. One of the island's few public beaches, it offers picnic tables, beach walks and a glimpse at a Coast Guard lighthouse.

Retreat from Maury Island and resume your northward trek. In **Valley Center,** you might pause at the **Country Store and Farm,** a combination general store and produce mart. It specializes in natural foods, herbs, fruits and vegetables; open Monday-Saturday 9 to 6 and Sunday noon to 5; (206) 463-3655. Just beyond is the **Amondson Gallery,** featuring works of local artists. At the entrance, note the clever roadside sculpture of a family piled into a Model-T truck.

Farther along, you reach the towns of **Vashon Center** and then **Vashon.** It's the island's largest village with a fair-sized business district. A few miles north, Vashon Highway runs out of asphalt, ending at the **Northend Ferry Dock.** Ferries sail in three directions from this busy little terminal—east to the mainland in south Seattle, north to downtown Seattle (passengers only) and west to Southworth on the nearby Kitsap Peninsula.

## WHERE TO DINE

☺ *Sound Food Restaurant and Bakery* ● ▵▵ $ Ø

⧠ *20312 Vashon Highway, Valley Center; (206) 463-3565. Earthy American nouveau; wine and beer. Sunday-Thursday 7 a.m. to 10 p.m., Friday-Sat-*

urday 8 to 11. MC/VISA. ☐ Charming little rural American café with open beams, from which dangle wisteria and other greenery. Diners enjoy a garden view as they browse a menu featuring chicken dijon, fresh local seafood, vegetarian linguine and scallops poached in sherry. Weekend brunches are popular (and often mobbed), and the bakery issues exceptionally tasty breakfast rolls, breads, pies and cookies.

**Café Tosca ● ΔΔ $$**
☐ *9924 SW Bank Rd., Vashon Island; (206) 463-2125. Italian; wine and beer. Lunch and dinner Tuesday-Sunday from 11, closed Monday. MC/VISA.* ☐ This charming little bistro dishes up ample portions of fresh pasta, scampi, great minestrone and other Italian fare. The *capelli pomidoro*—angel hair pasta with tomatoes, garlic and basil in olive oil—is a specialty. For dessert, try the almond flour torts or homemade cheesecake.

## WHERE TO SLEEP

**Castle Hill Bed & Breakfast ● ⌂⌂ $$$ Ø**
☐ *26734 SW 94th Ave. (in the Dockton area), Vashon, WA 98070; (206) 463-5491. Couples and singles from $65. A private suite with TV, room phone and bath; full breakfast.* ☐ Victorian gingerbread cottage isolated from main house; kitchen with microwave. Newly built, with queen-sized sleigh bed and other Victorian style furnishings.

**Sweetbriar Bed & Breakfast ● ⌂⌂⌂ $$$$ Ø**
☐ *16815 SW 129th Lane, Vashon, WA 98070; (206) 463-9186. Couples $75 to $90, singles $65 to $90. Three units with room phones and private baths; full or continental breakfast.* ☐ Large Northwestern style cedar home perched atop a hill, offering views of the surrounding forest, Olympics and Puget Sound. Two suites and a cabin furnished with antiques and local art. Full kitchen in cabin; kitchenettes available for suites.

# SIDE TRIP: PUYALLUP-SUMNER-ENUMCLAW

Tacoma's agricultural neighbor, the Puyallup Valley is noted for its daffodils, rhubarb patches and berry farms. It's home to the Western Washington Fairgrounds, and it shelters some interesting 19th century style villages. To many residents, our side trip is a favorite approach to Mount Rainier National Park. It takes travelers through the valley, into the Cascade foothills, then south over Cayuse Pass into the park.

From downtown Tacoma, take Pacific Avenue (State Route 7) south about five miles to Freeway 12. (You can avoid the congestion of Highway 7 by taking I-5 to Route 12, although it's not as direct.) Once on Freeway 12, head east, following Puyallup-Mount Rainier signs.

## Puyallup

**Population: 23,900**                    **Elevation: 48 feet**

This town with the curious name (pu-YALL-up) was founded by one of the most colorful characters ever to hit the Oregon Trail. Ezra Meeker rode an ox cart west in 1852, then he settled in the Puyallup Valley ten years later and began raising hops. He platted a town and named it for a local Indian tribe. The word, like most tribal names, simply means "we, the people."

The hops and Meeker thrived and he soon became known as the world's hop king. But that was just the beginning. Before he passed from the scene in 1928 at the age of 98, he gained fame as an author, businessman, civic leader and philanthropist. He won and lost several fortunes and spent the last 20 years of his life traveling and marking the Oregon Trail. He crossed it five times—by oxen, automobile, train and airplane. His mansion, one of the most carefully preserved pioneer homes in the Northwest, offers a good reason to pause in Puyallup.

Keep to the freeway it swings northward and passes the large **Western Washington Fairgrounds** on the outer edge of Puyallup. Then take the Orting/Pioneer exit and go left under the freeway on Pioneer Way, following Meeker Mansion signs. The structure is within three blocks, off the street behind some ancient evergreens.

☺ *Meeker Mansion* • *321 Spring St. (just off Pioneer); (206) 848-1770. Open March through mid-December, Wednesday-Sunday 1 to 4. Adults $2, seniors and teens $1.50, kids $1.* ☐ This handsome 1890 Italianate mansion is resplendent with stained glass windows, ceiling murals, elaborate fireplaces and polished woods. The three-story edifice reflects the great wealth accumulated by its builder, who found time during his extensive travels to serve as Puyallup's first mayor.

If you'd like to explore more of the Puyallup Valley, pick up maps and brochures at the **Puyallup Chamber of Commerce.** To reach it, continue on Pioneer Avenue through the slightly tatty downtown area and turn left onto Second Street. It's in a white and green cottage on your right, at 322 Second; open weekdays 10 to 4. Opposite is **Pioneer Park,** a large swatch of green with picnic tables and a children's play area.

At the Chamber, you can get directions to **Western Frontier Museum,** which claims to display the world's largest collection of Western regalia, including lots of stuff on longhorns. It's at Trail's End Ranch, 2301 23d Avenue SE; (206) 832-6300. The museum is open Wednesday-Sunday 9 to 5; adults $3.50, seniors and kids $2.50.

After you've done Puyallup, retrace your route along Pioneer Way, then follow it two miles east until you hit the **Van Lierop Bulb Farm.** It's just off the road on the left, at 13407 80th Street E; (206) 848-7272, open daily 9 to 5. The public is welcome in its large daffodil, tulip, iris, crocus and hyacinth gardens; peak blooms are in March and April.

From the bulb farm, continue east about a mile to Highway 162, turn left and follow it a couple of miles north into **Sumner.** This small town offers an imposing collection of 19th century homes and a neat-and-prim brick business district. Historic murals decorate some of the buildings and flower baskets adorn oldstyle lamp posts. As you approach the village, turn left onto Main Street toward the historic district and watch on your left for an appealing little museum:

☺ *Ryan House* • *1228 Main St.; (206) 863-8936 or (206) 863-5567. Wednesday, Saturday and Sunday 1 to 4. Adults $1, seniors 50 cents, kids 25 cents.* ☐ The best way to enjoy this nicely-arranged little 1875 farmhouse museum is to take one of the docent's tours. You'll learn how to churn butter and run a hand-cranked washing machine. You'll also learn that the town was christened in 1878 when Massachusetts Senator Charles Sumner's name was drawn from a hat. Fleishmann's Yeast opened a plant here in 1914, and it's still a major employer. Exhibits from the old plant are featured in the museum.

Sumner's attractive downtown area is just beyond the museum. After admiring its murals and lamp post planters, reverse your route on Main Street.

Continue east through a couple of country turns and eventually you wind up on State Highway 410, headed toward Buckley. You'll soon begin climbing **Elhi Hill,** with views back to the farm patchwork of the Puyallup Valley.

☺ In mid-climb, you'll encounter **Manfred Vierthaler Winery and Restaurant.** This appealing Bavarian style complex offers wine tasting and that nice valley view from its picture-window dining room. The winery is open noon to 6, and restaurant hours are 11 to 10 (listed below). When the winery's closed, wine-tasting is sometimes conducted in the restaurant foyer.

The divided highway ends two miles east of Vierthaler as you complete your hill-climb. Just beyond, about to be swallowed up by swelling Puget Sound suburbs, is **Buckley.** It's another old charmer, with turn-of-the-century front porch homes and a brick and false front downtown. Turn right onto Main Street at the business district sign, then take a quick left onto River Avenue. Note the old **American Feed and Farm Supply** on your left. It's a classic rural American feed store, complete with an elevated loading dock. Just beyond is Buckley's archive:

☺ **Foothills Historical Museum** • *175 Cottage Street at River; (206) 829-1533. Sunday 1 to 4 and Thursday noon to 4. Donations appreciated.* ☐ It's a pity that this interesting complex doesn't offer longer hours. More than a museum, it's a collection of historic buildings brought to this spot, including a blacksmith shop, log cabin ranger station, lumber camp bunk house and saw shop on skids, and a logging display. The main wood-sided museum building has the usual pioneer displays and period furnished rooms.

The town's business district is just beyond the museum, back on Main Street. You'll find several antique shops, a gift shop or two and a couple of galleries. Note the brown and mustard cottage style **Buckley City Hall** at Main and A. Back on Highway 410, continuing east toward Mount Rainier, note the great old American graffiti **Wally's Drive-In** on your right. It has all the 1950s trappings except car hops on roller skates. You tuck the hood of your car under a sheltering shed and deliver your burger and soda order through a speaker-mike.

**Enumclaw,** four miles beyond Buckley, sits against wooded foothills, with Mount Rainier providing a dramatic backdrop. It occupies a transition zone between Puget Sound sprawl and the Cascades. The city center is appropriately old fashioned, although it lacks the charm of Sumner and Buckley. Downtown sits just off the highway; to drag main, take a half-left at the business district sign onto Cole Street. You'll shortly pass the **Enumclaw Chamber of Commerce** visitors information center, in a little cottage at Cole and Stevenson. It's open weekdays 9 to 5 and you can pick up a walking tour map of its old buildings—mostly turn of the century. Continue a few blocks, go right onto Griffin Avenue and you'll be back on the highway. Just beyond town is the **White River Ranger Station,** where you can load up on information for the coming Snoqualmie National Forest; it's open weekdays 8 to 4:30.

Since it occupies the fringe of the foothills, Enumclaw is a logical jumping-off place to explore the Cascades, and it's a gateway to Mount Rainier National Park. Among nearby attractions are:

**Mud Mountain Dam** • Seven miles east of town, south of State Highway 410, it's one of the country's highest earth and rock dams. The reservoir offers the usual boating and fishing.

**Federation Forest State Park** • It shelters more than 600 acres of virgin timber with displays, hiking trails, picnicking and fishing. The park is 18 miles east of Enumclaw on State Highway 410.

**Green River Gorge State Conservation Area** • This is a river preserve with hiking trails, caves and fossils, between Enumclaw and Black Diamond to the north, on State Highway 169. Also along this route are unusual methane-fed geysers at **Flaming Geyser State Park.** It offers hiking trails, picnicking and a boat dock.

## ANNUAL EVENTS IN THE PUYALLUP VALLEY

**Daffodil parade and Spring Fair,** mid-April in downtown Puyallup; (800) 634-2334 or (206) 845-6755.

**Ezra Meeker Days** civic celebration, late June to early July in Puyallup; (206) 845-6755.

**King County Fair** in late July, fairgrounds in Enumclaw; 825-7666.

**Western Washington Fair** in mid-September at Western Washington Fairgrounds, Puyallup; (206) 845-1771.

## WHERE TO DINE IN PUYALLUP VALLEY

**KC's Caboose** • ∆∆ $$ ∅
☐ *905 Main St., Sumner; (206) 863-8010. American; full bar service. Daily 6:30 a.m. to 11 p.m. MC/VISA.* ☐ Slightly scruffy but appealing family café. It has an old town façade with a model train on the roof, and a railroading theme inside, complete with a waitstaff in coveralls. Sit in highbacked wooden booths beneath simulated Tiffany lamps and order from a rather pedestrian menu of steaks, chicken and chops.

**Gast House Bakery** • ∆ $
☐ *1012 Main St., Sumner; (206) 863-4433. German-American bakery; no alcohol. Weekdays 8 to 6, Saturday 8 to 5:30, closed Sunday. No credit cards.* ☐ This is a handy breakfast or lunch stop for folks exploring historic downtown Sumner. Light entrées include goulash, knackwurst and bratwurst, plus American soups and sandwiches. From the bakery, try tasty strudels, Black Forest cake or the ultra-rich "beesting" pastry with a whipped cream and almond filling.

☺ **Manfred Vierthaler Restaurant** • ∆∆∆ $$
☐ *17136 Highway 410, between Sumner and Buckley; (206) 863-1633. German-Bavarian; wine and beer. Daily 11 to 10. Major credit cards.* ☐ Appealing Bavarian-style complex with a winery tasting room, dining room with impressive valley views and a roof garden. The dining room look is yesterday Bavarian: carved woods, maple chairs, red checkered tablecloths and a plate rail lined with wine bottles. The menu follows suit: *rindsrouladen* (beef rolled with ham, pickle and onion), chicken *cordon bleu* and *leberkäse* (veal loaf with fried egg). Several American dishes are on the menu as well.

# TRIP PLANNER

**WHEN TO GO** ● More than any other destination in Washington, Seattle is an all-year place. Although some attractions and activities reduce their hours in the off-season, virtually all are open. The performing art scene is as lively in winter as summer; perhaps livelier. Weather is never a problem since snow is rare and hard freezes are an occasional novelty. Do bring your bumbershoot and galoshes in winter, however.

**WHAT TO SEE** ● Chittenden Locks, Fishermen's Terminal, Klondike Gold Rush National Historical Park, Museum of Flight, Nordic Heritage Museum, Pacific Science Center, Pike Place Market, Seattle Art Museum, Seattle Museum of History and Industry, Seattle Aquarium and Woodland Park Zoo.

**WHAT TO DO** ● Ascend the Space Needle, of course, along with Smith Tower; take Bill Speidel's Underground Tour; cruise to Blake Island for the Tillicum Village salmon bake; explore the streets, boutiques and old brick of Pioneer Square; prowl the campus of the University of Washington; hike the length of Myrtle Edwards Park or the perimeter of Green Lake; ride the Monorail and Waterfront Streetcar; catch the *Spirit of Washington* dinner train; sail the *Victoria Clipper* to Victoria and have high tea at the Empress.

## Useful contacts

**Seattle-King County Convention & Visitors Bureau**, 520 Pike St., Suite 1300, Seattle, WA 98101; (206) 461-5800.

**Visitors Information Center** is in the Washington State Convention and Trade Center, Pike Street and Ninth Avenue; (206) 461-5840.

## Seattle radio stations

KBSG, 97.3-FM—oldies
KLTS, 95.7 FM—soft hits of 70s, 80s and 90s
KXRX, 96.5 FM—rock
KCLU, 90.3-FM, Tacoma-Seattle—National Public Radio.
KDSG, 94.3-FM—top 40
KOOL, 106-FM—vintage top 40 and rock
KYLM, 106.5-FM—soft rock and Christian
KMPS, 94.1-FM—country
KPBS, 88.5-FM, Tacoma-Seattle—National Public Radio
KBCS, 91.3-FM—jazz, blues and folk
KBSG, 1210-AM—oldies
KJRA, 950-AM—sports
KIRO, 710-AM—news, sports and talk (CBS)
KIXI, 880-AM—pops classic and swing
KVI, 570-AM—news and talk
KOOL, 770-AM—vintage top 40 and rock.

## Chapter four

# *SEATTLE*

## Cloudy city with a sunny disposition

---

**IF THERE'S SUCH A THING** as a totally civilized large city, it just might be Seattle.

Scientists and demographic experts have proven that the more tightly you pack white mice or people, the more surly and disagreeable they become. Yet, the half a million people snugly packed into the Northwest's largest city are remarkably polite and gracious. Seattle has won national awards as the most mannerly big city in America.

Sometimes, of course, Seattlites carry propriety *too* far. Residents wait patiently for the "walk" light to change, even though the street is empty. We've watched outsiders start across an intersection, then look curiously at these people and glance about nervously, looking for this unseen object that's kept the locals rooted to the sidewalk. (Of course, the fact that jaywalking laws are rigidly enforced may have something to do with this. The police are gentle, too, riding around on mountain bikes and politely issuing jaywalking citations.)

Seattle has, in recent years, been rated the most livable city in America (*Places Rated Almanac* and *USA Today*), the best American city for women (*Savvy* Magazine), the second best place to locate a business (Louis Harris survey) and number one as the "City of the Future" (*USA Today*).

Of course, the fact that people wait for traffic lights, smile and say "please" and "thank you" aren't compelling reasons for visiting a city. You want reasons? Seattle has a boatload of them.

It's one of the most beautifully situated cities in America, cradled between the Olympic and Cascade mountains, and resting beside the giant blue lagoon of the Puget Sound. It has excellent museums and galleries, fine shopping and the second best restaurant collection west of the Rockies, after San Francisco. Despite its drizzly reputation, it has a benign climate and the *Zagat Survey* says it has the best hotels in America. (Note that we've resisted any *Sleepless in Seattle* jokes.)

For fans of major league sports, it has America's most lovable football team (great helmet logos), the most pitied baseball team and one of the most aggressive basketball teams. For fans of the outdoors, it has a fine collection of parks and walking, hiking and biking trails. If you've brought anything that floats, it's a mecca for water sports. With Puget Sound, Lake Union, Lake Washington and assorted other waterways as playgrounds, Seattle has one of the highest per capita boat ownerships in the country.

It is thus not surprising that Seattle was once voted by *Rand McNally* as America's best vacation destination.

All of this and—refreshingly—not a single theme park.

## Here come the brides

The story of Seattle's founding sounds like a silly plot for a TV series and, for a mercifully brief period, it was one.

In 1851, the first settlers landed at Alki Point, a tip of land southwest of the present downtown area. This proved to be too windy, so they soon retreated to the sheltered shores of Elliott Bay. The settlement was named for local Indian Chief Sealth, who befriended the newcomers and helped them get established. Legend suggests that the settlers paid him $16,000 for the use of his name, although that's open to question. Native Americans of the period didn't have copyright laws and the settlers certainly could have used a derivative of the chief's name without his consent. It seems unlikely that struggling, hard-working pioneers would spend their money that freely.

Henry Yesler built a sawmill to harvest the thick forests surrounding the bay, and Seattle thrived. By 1856, the men felt the need for feminine companionship, so Asa Mercer went east and convinced eleven eligible women to brave the Western frontier. A second trip yielded 57 recruits, including Mercer's future wife. This brash experiment in population growth became the basis for the 1960s television series, *Here Come the Brides*.

Rimmed by timber, early Seattle was built almost entirely of wood. Then in 1889, a painter's glue pot boiled over on a hot stove and the city was burned back to the mud. As the town was rebuilt—this time of brick and masonry—mud and tides became its most serious problem. The bottomlands along Elliott Bay became bogs when it rained, and high tides caused the sewer system to go into reverse. (If you take the amusing Bill Speidel Underground Tour, you'll be regaled with stories of exploding Crappers.)

City fathers decided to elevate the streets in the lower section of town, and the sidewalks became trenches behind retaining walls. These later were bridged over, and then covered completely, creating a dark and musty basement city suited more to rats than people. After a plague outbreak in 1907, health officials condemned it. However, an underground of opium dens, brothels and moonshiners thrived there for several more years.

The arrival of the Northern Pacific Railroad in 1883 was a major boon to the new town. A second boost came with an event that occurred more than a thousand miles north. In 1896, three prospectors found rich placer deposits on creeks flowing into the Yukon River. As with the California gold rush, it took more than a year for word to get out. Then, thousands of '98ers flocked to the Northwest, seeking passage to the Klondike Gold Rush. Thanks to an ambitious chamber of commerce publicity committee, Seattle became the main outfitting center for Klondike-bound gold-seekers.

However, the trip north proved to be more of a trail of tears than a rush to riches. The only access to the Yukon River was up Alaska's Inside Passage to Skagway, then over one of two steep trails, the Chilkoot or White Pass. Canada's cautious Northwest Mounted Police required that each man entering Yukon Territory have a year's worth of supplies. That amounted to about a ton of gear. Prospectors had the choice of making dozens of hiking trips up the Chilkoot, or driving over-burdened horses over the treacherous White Pass. (So many pack animals perished on that route that it became known as Dead Horse Trail.) Finally, the adventurers had to build rafts or boats and face the icy rapids of the Yukon River to reach the gold fields.

By the time the '98ers got there, the good stakes had been claimed. Seattle outfitters made more money than most of the Klondikers. Many disappointed gold-seekers returned to become part of that growing city's future.

Historic footnote: Although many earlier prospectors did become rich, the Klondike was not large as gold rushes go. During California's bonanza, a single mine—the Empire in Grass Valley—yielded more gold than the entire Klondike rush. Bolstered by tales from the likes of Jack London and poet Robert Service, the Klondike generated more headlines than gold.

During the first half of this century, Seattle became a major aircraft manufacturing center, after William Boeing set up shop in a former boat-building shed in 1909. The area's waterways lured the U.S. Navy, and the city prospered during World War II and well beyond. Aircraft sales slumped sharply after the war, of course, then the Boeing company gambled on the development of America's first commercial passenger jet—and won. The Boeing 707 and later models put Seattle and its aviation industry back in the black. A world's fair—the only one ever to show a profit—was staged in 1962 to celebrate the city's good fortunes. The Space Needle and other Seattle Center fixtures are legacies of that Century 21 extravaganza.

Vulnerable as a two-industry town—aerospace and lumber—the area has suffered massive slumps in recent decades. Seattlites kept their sense of humor, however. Several years ago, someone erected this billboard south of town: "Will the last person to leave Seattle please turn out the lights?"

Seattle today is recovering from its most recent slump, and planners are pushing for more diversity. Tourism, convention business, electronics, computer firms such as the giant Microsoft and other industries are filling some of the potholes in its economic highway.

## Getting there

*By highway* • Interstate 5 is the main feeder into Seattle from the north and south. I-90 comes in from the east, crossing Lake Washington and merging with I-5 just south of the downtown area. For the uninitiated, Seattle's freeways are about as logical as spaghetti. If you don't remain alert, an off-ramp will blend you back onto the freeway, and away you go, bound for Canada. Also, rush-hour express lanes change direction from morning to night. If you merge onto one without intending to—an easy trick—you'll be expressed halfway to Everett or Tacoma before you can get off again.

All of this said, if you have a detailed map and approach the city during non-commute hours, you should be able to find your destination without winding up in Issaquah. The Madison Street exit will get you into the heart of downtown. Once there, you'll find a convenient grid of named streets (running southwest to northeast) and numbered avenues (northwest to southeast). These are one-way streets so again, you'll need a map. As you'll notice on that map, blocks of streets outside the downtown area are often skewed and truncated to accommodate the city's many lakes and waterways.

**RV advisory:** Big cities aren't RV country and Seattle is no exception. There are ample RV parks in the suburbs, however, and we've listed some of them below, under "Where to camp." If you have a tow-along or a fifth-wheel unit, unhitch and leave your mobile home immobilized at the RV park. There are several outdoor parking lots on the fringes of downtown, but few can accommodate large rigs. And you won't be a happy camper if you venture into the city center during the rush hour. Fortunately, the heart of Seattle is very compact and the downtown area is a free ride zone for municipal buses. So getting around is relatively easy.

**By air** ● Seattle-Tacoma International Airport—Sea-Tac—located midway between those cities, is served by most major airlines. Call (800) 544-1965 or (206) 431-4444 for information on parking, air and ground traffic, arrivals and departures. Of course, all the major rental car agencies are available. Passenger service downtown is provided by **Gray Line Airport Express,** serving nine hotels with half-hour departures, (206) 626-6088; **Shuttle Express,** a limo van service, (800) 942-0711 or (206) 622-1424; and by **Metro,** the city's public bus system; call (206) 553-3000 for route and schedule information. **Suburban Airporter** provides service to east side communities; (206) 455-5055. Shuttle Express also has service to Everett and Tacoma.

**By rail** ● The handsome old King Street Station near the Kingdome at Third Avenue and King Street is home to **Amtrak.** The *Coast Starlight* has daily service between Seattle and Los Angeles. The *Pioneer* links the city with the East, via Salt Lake and the *Empire Builder* takes the northern route through Montana to Chicago. Frequent service is provided between Seattle and Portland aboard the *Mount Rainier.* Call (206) USA-RAIL for information and reservations; the local number is (206) 464-1930.

**By bus** ● **Greyhound** operates from a terminal at Eighth Avenue and Stewart Street, serving most of the rest of the country via I-5 and I-90; (206) 624-3456. **Trailways,** at Sixth Avenue and Westlake, provides service to Everett, Whidbey Island and Vancouver, B.C.; (206) 728-5955.

**By ferry** ● Now, that's the *grand* way to come to Seattle! Washington State Ferries sail from Bremerton on the Kitsap Peninsula and from Bainbridge Island, arriving in the heart of town at Coleman Dock, Pier 52. Passenger-only ferries run between Bremerton and Seattle's Pier 50. Other nearby ferry routes are from Kingston on the Kitsap Peninsula to Edmonds, just north of Seattle; and from Southworth on the Kitsap and from Vashon Island, arriving at Fauntleroy, south of the city. Call locally (206) 464-6400 or statewide (800) 84-FERRY for schedules and information. The hearing-impaired number is (800) 833-6388.

Other cruise ships and boats take you all about Puget Sound and all the way to Victoria, B.C. We discuss them below, under "Tours and activities."

## Visitor services

The **Seattle-King County Convention and Visitors Bureau** operates a visitor information center on Level One of the new Washington State Convention and Trade Center, open weekdays 8 to 5; (206) 461-5840. The center is sandwiched against and under the freeway between Pike Street and Ninth Avenue. If you're coming into Seattle on I-5, take the Madison Street exit downtown, go northwest on Fourth or Sixth, turn right onto Pike and follow it back toward the freeway to the center's parking garage. If you're afoot, go up Pike Street, enter the Trade Center through its Galleria Shops (between Seventh and Eighth) and walk to the far corner of the ground floor.

The convention and visitors bureau's main office, which also offers visitor information, is at 520 Pike Street, Suite 1300, open weekdays 8:30 to 5; (206) 461-5800. You might want to request the free *Seattle/King County Visitors Guide* in advance by writing or calling the bureau. This thick and slick publication covers attractions, lodgings, restaurants, shopping, transportation and assorted other visitor services. It also contains some material on surrounding areas.

## Getting oriented

You'll need a good street map to find your way about. The *Seattle/King County Visitors Guide* contains downtown and area maps. Good, detailed street maps are produced by the American Automobile Association's **AAA Washington**, although you have to be a member to get one. There are two Seattle AAA offices—at 330 Sixth Ave., near Harrison Street just east of Seattle Center; open weekdays 8:30 to 6:30, (206) 448-5353; and in the Pacific First Centre lobby, downtown at 1420 Fifth Avenue near Pike, weekdays 8:30 to 5, (206) 623-6047. A retail version of that same map, produced by the H.M. Gousha Company, is available at book and travel stores and hotel newsstands and gift shops. A good source for maps, travel guides and other travel items is the **AAA Travel Store** at 330 Sixth Avenue N; it's open to the general public.

Free brightly colored *Seattle Tourmaps* and the *Guest Quick Guide* with locator maps are available at most hotel and motel desks. The *Tourmap* is cluttered with advertising logos, although it's useful for finding downtown points of interest.

## Getting around and getting parked

Seattle isn't *quite* as tight on parking as some cities, although available spots are scarce and you don't get much for a quarter on a meter. If you can find a meter, it'll be color coded according to its time limit: yellow for 15 minutes, green for 30 and silver for two to four hours.

Pay parking facilities are abundant and they generally don't fill up during business days. Diamond Parking operates several outdoor lots, and they have a free parking agreement with Budget Rent A Car customers. Most high-rise office buildings and hotels have subterranean parking, which is predictably expensive.

Knowledgeable Seattlites park cheaply or free on the periphery and catch a bus downtown, taking advantage of the free ride zone. You can find some longer time limit meters on the outer fringes of Pioneer Square and the International District, and on Alaskan Way along the waterfront.

## Public transit

Most of the downtown area is within Metro's free zone, which operates from 6 a.m. to 7 p.m. Simply hop on a bus, take it to your destination and hop off again, with a clear conscience. The fareless zone is bordered by Sixth Avenue, the freeway, Battery Street, the waterfront and Jackson Street. It includes the city's unusual underground bus tunnel, which runs from the International District to the convention center; 5 a.m. to 7 p.m. weekdays and 10 to 6 Saturday; no service Sunday. The tube was designed for eventual conversion to a light rail subway system.

Fares beyond downtown are $1.10 for the first zone and $1.60 for the second. Naturally, drivers don't make change, but the fare boxes do take dollar bills. Call (206) 553-3000 for route and fare information.

Two other forms of public transit are popular with visitors, and we've worked them into a downtown walking/transit tour, which we outline below. The **Monorail,** built for the Seattle world's fair, runs from Westlake Center shopping mall at Fifth Avenue and Pine Street to Seattle Center. It operates every 15 minutes, daily 9 to midnight in summer; the rest of the year, hours are Sunday-Thursday 9 to 9 and Friday-Saturday 9 to midnight. Fare is 75 cents; less for seniors, handicapped and kids.

**Waterfront Streetcars** are quaint 1927 trolleys imported from Australia. They run from Pier 70, along Elliott Bay and then inland to Pioneer Square at Fifth Avenue and Jackson Street. Departures are every half hour, weekdays from 7 a.m. to 6:15 p.m., and weekends and holidays from 10:30 to 5. Fare is a dollar, and you can get a transfer onto the Metro system, good for the next hour and a half.

Many downtown merchants offer "Easy Street" tokens, which are good for parking discounts and for free rides on Metro, the Monorail and Waterfront Streetcars.

Downtown Seattle is generally described as the area between Seattle Center (the World's Fair site), the Kingdome, the I-5 freeway complex and Elliott Bay. Within this area are several easily-defined sections. The **shopping, hotel and business district**, shaded by some of the tallest highrises west of Chicago, is concentrated between Eighth Avenue, Stewart Street, Third Avenue and Columbia Street. In fact, the 76-story Columbia SeaFirst Center at Fourth Avenue and Cherry Street *is* the tallest thing west of Chicago, topping out at 943 feet. When you look northwest from downtown toward the 605-foot Space Needle, that famous spire looks a bit squat.

Just south of downtown is the **Pioneer Square** area, site of Yesler's sawmill, the underground and other relics of Seattle's beginnings. Undergoing major rehabilitation, it is now home to shops, restaurants and galleries tucked into fine old brick buildings. Just above Pioneer Square is Chinatown, formally called the **International District** because of the influx of several other nationalities, primarily Asians. The Kingdome and historic King Street railroad station form its western border.

The **Waterfront,** just about everyone's favorite locale in Seattle, stretches for three miles along Elliott Bay, immediately below the downtown high-rises. Although Seattle is one of the West Coast's major shipping centers, most of the heavy cargo-handling activity has shifted south. The downtown waterfront offers a savory mix of restaurants, shops, parks, public piers and ferry terminals. Its centerpiece is lovable old Pike Place Market, at the

foot of Pike Street. North of the waterfront and inland is **Seattle Center.**
Here, leftover pieces of the world's fair are represented in the Space Needle,
Pacific Science Center, Seattle Opera House, Coliseum sports center and as-
sorted carnival rides and exhibit halls.

Downtown is built on a tilt, so a stroll will give you a good workout.
Most streets are one-way, so watch your intersection turns. Down at the waterfront, Alaskan Way will get you to its many attractions. To leave the area
quickly, get on the elevated Alaskan Way Viaduct.

## Shopping

The best shopping is centered in three areas of downtown Seattle—the
downtown core, the waterfront and Pioneer Square.

Most major department stores and specialty shops are concentrated
along Fifth and Sixth avenues in the heart of downtown. Four major shopping complexes are **City Centre** at Sixth and Union across from the Sheraton, **Rainier Square** at the base of several skyscrapers between Fourth
and Fifth avenues near Union Street, **Westlake Center** at Pine Street between Fourth and Fifth avenues, and **Century Square** at Fourth Avenue
and Pine Street. Downtown's two major department stores are **Nordstrom**
at 1501 Fifth Avenue between Pine and Pike and the **Bon Marche** at Third
Avenue and Pine.

If you must have a Seattle ashtray or made-in-Taiwan totem, head toward the waterfront, where most tourist-oriented shopping is based. The
main attraction, on a bluff above the waterfront, is **Pike Place Market.**
Hardly a tourist gimmick, it's a wonderful collection of produce stands, food
stalls, restaurants and eclectic shops. South of Pike, you'll find serious tourist shopping at **Bay Pavilion** on Pier 57, with more shops on piers 56 and
55, and the **Old Curiosity Shop** at Pier 54.

Pioneer Square offers the city's best selection of designer showrooms, antique stores, galleries and book stores, in addition to a good selection of restaurants. Elliott Bay Book Company at 101 S. Main near First, with
hundreds of thousands of books and a folksy café tucked between old brick
walls, is one of the great book stores of western America.

## Lodging

When visiting Seattle, we'd recommend staying were the action is—in
the downtown area—and commute to the peripheral activities. It's great to
be able to walk to Pike Place Market for breakfast and watch the city stretch
and yawn as it prepares for another day.

Three hotels that we used in researching this book all have their location
advantages, in addition to other assets. **Sheraton Seattle,** 1400 Sixth Avenue at Pike, is in the heart of the high-rise district and is in fact one of them.
The venerable **Alexis,** a boutique luxury hotel is at 1007 First Avenue near
Madison, the center of a convenient triangle between downtown, Pioneer
Square and the waterfront. The **Edgewater Inn** is just that, a low-rise hotel built onto Pier 69 at the waterfront, with views thereof; it's the city's only
waterside hotel. From here, a stroll or the waterfront street car can take you
along Elliott Bay. These three and many others are listed further on, under
"Where to sleep."

Many motels are grouped along Aurora Avenue in north Seattle, since
that's the original Highway 99, which served the city in pre-freeway days.
More lodgings are strung along Highway 99 to the south as it heads toward

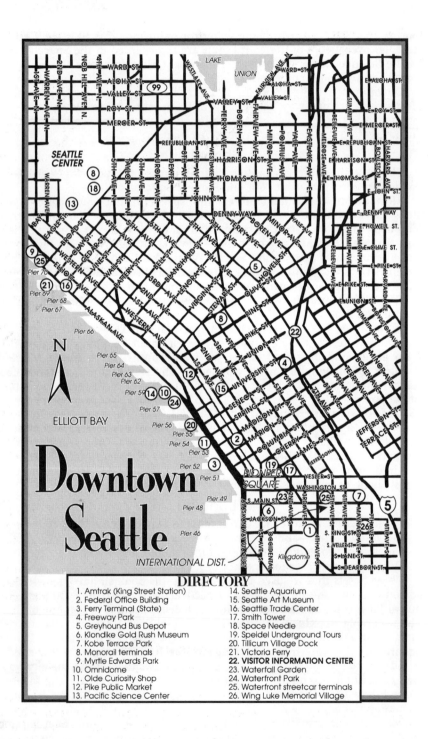

# Downtown Seattle

**ELLIOTT BAY**

**SEATTLE CENTER**

**INTERNATIONAL DIST.**

**DIRECTORY**

1. Amtrak (King Street Station)
2. Federal Office Building
3. Ferry Terminal (State)
4. Freeway Park
5. Greyhound Bus Depot
6. Klondike Gold Rush Museum
7. Kobe Terrace Park
8. Monorail terminals
9. Myrtle Edwards Park
10. Omnidome
11. Olde Curiosity Shop
12. Pike Public Market
13. Pacific Science Center
14. Seattle Aquarium
15. Seattle Art Museum
16. Seattle Trade Center
17. Smith Tower
18. Space Needle
19. Speidel Underground Tours
20. Tillicum Village Dock
21. Victoria Ferry
**22. VISITOR INFORMATION CENTER**
23. Waterfall Garden
24. Waterfront Park
25. Waterfront streetcar terminals
26. Wing Luke Memorial Village

Sea-Tac International Airport. And of course, Sea-Tac has the usual cluster of airport hotels and motels.

## The neighbors

Several interesting neighborhoods rim downtown Seattle. **Queen Anne Hill** is to the northeast, site of posh Victorian homes. The name, in fact, comes from its preponderance of Queen Anne style architecture. Farther north is **Ballard,** settled by Scandinavian fisherfolk and site of the **Chittenden Locks** that elevate boats from Puget Sound to the higher waters of Lake Union and Lake Washington. North of the locks is the fine Nordic Heritage Museum; to the northeast is Woodland Park Zoo, called the most humane in America because of its spacious animal compounds.

The **Eastlake** area encompasses Lake Union, rimmed by a commercial-residential district and tied to Puget Sound by a ship canal (along with Lake Washington). About two miles west, on that canal, is Fishermen's Terminal, home to the West Coast's largest commercial fishing fleet. Northeast of Lake Union is the **University District,** locally known simply as the "U District." Therein lies the large University of Washington campus, surrounded by venerable homes and student-focused shopping areas of coffee houses, book stores, earthy bakeries and small ethnic cafès. Also in this area is the Seattle Museum of History and Industry.

**Capitol Hill,** south of the U District, is a neighborhood of fine old homes—mostly restored—and stylish boutiques and cafès. It's also home to much of Seattle's gay and lesbian community. East of Capitol Hill is huge **Lake Washington,** surrounded by several water-oriented residential areas. The city of **Bellevue** occupies the far shore and **Renton** is at the bottom.

South of downtown—not a neighborhood but certainly a keystone to Seattle's development—is **Boeing Field,** where the Boeing Airplane Company is headquartered. The airstrip is used primarily for charter airlines and general aviation. The Museum of Flight there is one of the country's finest aviation archives.

Much of what Seattle has to offer visitors is focused in the downtown area and along the Elliott Bay waterfront. Other attractions are in something of a vague semi-circle around its outer edge. To help you find the best of the city, we've fashioned a downtown walking/transit tour, followed by a longer peripheral driving tour. The first covers about six miles. Don't panic; more than half of that is aboard public transit.

You *can* drive the downtown tour, although you won't see as much. Also, it's a bother to find parking places to check out attractions and shops along the way. Seattle has a wonderful collection of public art, and you'll miss most of it if you drive. Further, it's very difficult to make friends with a waterfront seagull from a moving vehicle.

## Walking/transit tour

Items marked with a ☺ are listed with more detail under "Attractions," below.

The tour begins with transit, at the **Monorail** terminal in Westlake Center at Fifth and Pine. Hop aboard and take it to **Seattle Center,** with its sundry attractions. This 74-acre complex looks like what it is—leftover pieces of a world's fair, with monumental Tinkertoy architecture, a permanent fun zone and large exhibit halls. The ● **Pacific Science Center** here is a good place to park the kids, and possibly yourselves. And *everyone* must ascend the ● **Space Needle.** The view from on high will help orient you to your upcoming exploration. A sophisticated locator system points out landmarks. (***Motoring note:*** If you drive this route, follow Sixth Avenue to Seattle Center, since Fifth is one way the wrong way.)

After you've finished with the center's attractions, exit through the Broad Street gate (southeast corner; walk between the Space Needle and Science Center), and make a right. Broad takes you down to the **waterfront.** It hits Alaskan Way just below the car barn and the first trolley stop of the **Waterfront Streetcars.** Before committing yourself to Alaskan Way, turn right and stroll to **Myrtle Edwards Park.** It extends a mile and a half north along the waterfront, offering great views, a walking/jogging/biking path and a public fishing pier. (Our tour route mileage doesn't include walking the length of the park.)

Opposite the streetcar barn, **Pier 70** houses shops and restaurants, and adjacent **Pier 69** is the launching pad for **Victoria Clipper** cruises. (See "Quick ship to Victoria" box on page 151.) Just beyond is the **Edgewater Inn** with the harbor-view Ernie's Restaurant, which you might consider as a lunch stop. From here, there's not much of interest for nearly a mile, which provides a perfectly good excuse to hop aboard a Waterfront Streetcar. The Vine Street station is near the Edgewater; you should get off at the Pike Street station.

● **Pike Place Market** is just above, reached by climbing 143 steps up the **Pike Hill Climb.** It's worth the exertion to visit this wonderfully weathered collection of produce stands, food stalls, shops and restaurants. Several shops are terraced into the hillside, offering opportunity to pause in mid-climb. (If the hill climb is too difficult, you can visit Pike Place from downtown Seattle simply by following Pike Street to the end.)

Return from Pike to the waterfront for visits to the excellent ● **Seattle Aquarium** and the ● **Omnidome** theater, which shows those wide-angle travel and adventure films. Both attractions are on Pier 59. **Waterfront Park** offers benches, picnic tables and public fishing at adjacent Pier 57. That pier also is home to the **Bay Pavilion,** with a collection of souvenir shops and seafood restaurants. **Gray Line** sightseeing boats depart from a dock between piers 57 and 56.

The bright yellow Pier 56 offers more shops and restaurants, plus the landing for boat cruises to the ● **Tillicum Village** Blake Island Indian salmon bake. Next door at Pier 54 is the **Old Curiosity Shop,** the waterfront's senior souvenir store, tracing its roots back to 1899. It's part curio shop and part museum, offering exhibits such as a pickled two-headed pig and the remains of Sylvester, a cowboy mummy found buried in the hot Arizona sand in 1895.

If all this works up an appetite, **Ivar's Acres of Clams** is next door. It's the first of a series of Seattle area seafood restaurants started back in 1938 by Ivar Haglund. A bronze of Ivar feeding the gulls stands near the entrance. (It's been said that one shouldn't trust the food at a restaurant that prints the history of its founder in the menu. We don't know if this applies to bronze statues.)

Waterfront fish and chips take-outs are Seattle's version of the San Francisco Fisherman's Wharf walk-away shrimp and crab cocktails. You'll find

*Most of the city's visitor attractions are focused around downtown and the Space Needle, which rises from the former world's fair site at Seattle Center.*
— **James Bell, Seattle-King County News Bureau**

several stalls between Seattle Aquarium and Ivar's. They're handy for quickie lunches, although they're mass-produced and—like those walk-away cocktails—are not memorable meals.

The waterfront becomes frankly industrial below here. Other than the **Washington State Ferry Terminal** at Pier 52, it offers little of interest. You can catch a Waterfront Streetcar across from the Old Curiosity Shop at Madison Street station and take it into **Pioneer Square.** Get off at the Main Street and Occidental stop. If you prefer to keep walking, stroll up Madison or Marion street to First Avenue and turn right. The ascent is considerably more gentle than the Pike Hill Climb since much of this area is landfill. Approaching the Pioneer Square district on First Avenue, you'll see the square itself at First and Yesler Way. Adjacent to this wedge of grass, concrete and benches is Bill Speidel's ◉ **Underground Tour** office, in Doc Maynard's Public House.

Yesler Way was the site of Henry Yesler's sawmill, and this street contributed a familiar phrase to the English lexicon. Logs were skidded downhill to the mill in a board trough called a skid road. When the city center shifted northward early in this century, this area became a slum, and "Skid Road" came to mean a hangout for down-and-outers. The term spread throughout the country, warped into "Skid Row."

Hardly a slum today, Pioneer Square is experiencing a metamorphosis as one of the city's better shopping and dining areas. Some weedy corners remain, and it's still the neighborhood of choice for Seattle's few derelicts and street people. However, more old buildings are being transformed into trendy mercantiles even as we write this. Gallery hoppers and antiquers will like this area, and the **Elliott Bay Book Company** at First and Main is a required stop for bookish browsers. Most of the area's shops are along First Avenue and Occidental, which has become a pedestrian mall.

We won't suggest specific routing through Pioneer Square; simply wander about at will. Among recommended stops is ☻ **Smith Tower** at Yesler Way and Second Avenue, Western America's first real skyscraper. A clanking, manually-operated elevator will take you 42 stories to the top for great views. Also, stroll through pretty little **Waterfall Park** at Main and Second Avenue. A fountain-fed stream cascades over boulders beside benches and tables in this appealing pocket park. Learn all about the Yukon Gold Rush at the storefront ☻ **Klondike Gold Rush National Historic Park** at Main and Occidental, opposite the Waterfront Streetcar stop. Pioneer Square was the main staging area for the rush to riches, and this small, well-done museum represents the Seattle element of the historic park, which also has units in Skagway, Alaska, and Dawson City in the Yukon Territory.

From Pioneer Square, follow Jackson Street past the ☻ **Kingdome** and brick clock-towered **King Street Station** to the **International District.** Although it lacks the colorful congestion of some other Chinatowns, it is busy with Asian restaurants and shops. Note the elaborate gate standing in the middle of **Wing Hay Park** at Jackson and Maynard Avenue. Pause at the ☻ **Wing Luke Asian Museum,** in a former garage at 417 Seventh Avenue, just south of Jackson.

A rather steep hike up Maynard Avenue or Seventh Avenue will take you to **Kobe Terrace Park** and the **Danny Woo Community Garden,** graded into a steep slope below the freeway. Neither is well-kept, although the concept of tiny family garden patches in a city is interesting.

From here, take the third element of Seattle's transit system to return to your starting point. The free **"tunnel bus"** disappears underground at Fifth Avenue and Jackson, with several station stops in the high-rise district. If you stay with it to the end, at Ninth Avenue between Olive Way and Pine Street, you can drop down to Eighth Avenue and then walk south about four blocks to **Freeway Park.** It's a series of terraces and landscaped patios built into the tanglework of the freeway system. While not particularly impressive as a park, it does offer an interesting study in land use.

## Driving tour

Items marked with a ☻ are listed with more detail under "Attractions," below.

This ambitious drive covers most of the appeals of the greater Seattle area. It stretches nearly 70 miles, so you may want to divide it into two days, particularly if you want to spend a reasonable amount of time at attractions en route. Try to avoid it during the rush hour. As you drive, you'll encounter occasional "Scenic Drive" signs with a trident. However, many have been taken down, so you'll get lost if you trust them to deliver you to the city's highlights.

Don't try this drive without a good, detailed map, since Seattle is a vast and complex city. To begin, head south along the waterfront on Alaskan Way—not the viaduct but the surface street.

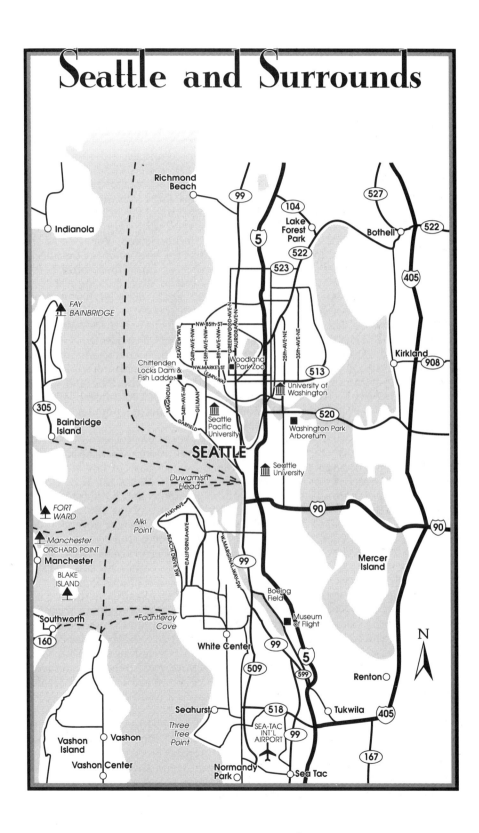

# Seattle and Surrounds

*Navigational note:* Most downtown streets stop short of the waterfront. If you're starting from downtown, go south to Madison, follow it down to Alaskan Way and turn left.

Heading south on Alaskan Way, you'll soon clear the "tourist section" of the waterfront and enter the working port district. To demonstrate their serious intent, pier designations are changed to terminals, although the sequential numbers continue. Near **Terminal 30,** a sign directs you to the right to **Jack Perry Memorial Viewpoint.** It's a postage-stamp park offering views of the **East Waterway** that brings ships into the cargo docks. Continuing south, your route south has changed its name to Marginal Way. Pass under a complex of freeway ramps and then turn right onto Spokane Street, following signs to West Seattle and Harbor Island. You'll cross the lower level of a viaduct over **Harbor Island** at the bottom of the port area.

Stay with Spokane Street through a couple of turns then, after a few blocks, fork to the right for Harbor Avenue/Avalon Way, ducking out from under the freeway. At a stoplight, turn right again onto Harbor Avenue. You'll pass through a scruffy woodsy area, with some nice views northeast to the city skyline. The route returns to the waterfront and travels alongside a series of parklands that mark the shoreline of **West Seattle.**

As your route bends around **Duwamish Head,** it changes its name to Alki Avenue SW. A walking/biking path extends for several miles along the shorefront, passing from **Don Armeni Park** through the long and skinny **Alki Beach Park** to **Alki Point,** where Seattle began. Alki Beach Park has one of the few sandy bathing beaches in the area and it's popular with the suntan crowd on rare warm summer days.

Stay alert and you'll see—on your right—a small obelisk at 63rd Avenue SW, marking the city's birthplace. A stone from Plymouth Rock, another significant American landing site, is embedded into its base. A few blocks beyond, Alki Avenue crosses the nub of Alki Point and passes the **U.S. Coast Guard Light Station.** It's open to visitors weekends and holidays noon to 4, with tours May through September by appointment; (206) 286-5423.

You're now on Beach Drive SW, which you'll follow for several miles through a mix of homes and shorefront parklands. Hit a stop sign and take a half left (to avoid a dead end), following Vashon Ferry/Scenic Drive signs. You'll shortly encounter another stop sign, opposite large **Lincoln Park,** a mix of woods and lawns covering the conical lump of Williams Point.

At this juncture, start heading back toward central Seattle by turning left and blending onto Fauntleroy Avenue SW. The main thoroughfare from the Fauntleroy ferry landing, it curves through a mix of homes and businesses and returns you to the upper level of that viaduct over Harbor Island. Now an expressway, it hurries you east to Interstate 5. Head south on I-5 for a mile to exit 162 and take the Corson Avenue/Michigan Street off ramp west across the top of **Boeing Field.** Continue straight ahead on Corson (avoiding a right-hand swerve onto Michigan) and you'll shortly T-bone into East Marginal Way.

Turn left and follow Marginal alongside Boeing Field a couple of miles to the excellent ☺ **Museum of Flight,** on your left. You'll first see the red and white "barn"—a reconstruction of the original Boeing plant. The modernistic greenhouse of the main museum is adjacent. Drive past it and turn left into the museum's parking area.

From the museum, continue south on Marginal for less than a mile, then turn left at a State Highway 900 sign. Cross over I-5 and get into the left lane for Martin Luther King Jr. Way (Highway 900). Drive north through a scruffy industrial area and, after less than a mile, hit a stop sign and turn right onto Henderson Street. This takes you to **Atlantic City Park** on the shore of **Lake Washington.** The park has picnic and swimming areas and a boat launch.

From here, Seward Park Avenue takes you north through an elegant old waterfront home district and eventually to large **Seward Park.** Occupying a lumpy, wooded peninsula on Lake Washington, it's one of the city's most versatile parks, with walking paths, kiddie play area, a Japanese Garden, picnic grounds, boat launch and swimming beach. As you leave the park, turn right onto Lake Washington Boulevard, which you'll take for several miles along the lakeshore. Like Alki Avenue, it follows a long park strip with a hiking/biking path. With boats at play on Lake Washington and Mercer Island across the way, it's one of the city's more attractive drives.

Two of the world's four floating bridges are along this route. Lake Washington Boulevard crosses under the west anchorage of **Lake Washington Floating Bridge,** which carries I-90 traffic to Mercer Island and beyond. Built on hollow concrete pontoons, the original was completed in 1939 as the first of its kind. It was replaced by two side-by-side bridges after it sank in a storm in 1991.

After passing under the bridge anchorage, your route brushes more lakeside parks and then swings inland to pass through long, skinny and large **Washington Park.** Stay with Lake Washington Boulevard, forking to the left to avoid eastbound State Route 520 freeway and **Evergreen Point Floating Bridge,** which spans upper Lake Washington. You'll shortly swing westward to parallel Freeway 520, then take a quick right across it, following signs to the ☻ **Seattle Museum of History and Industry.**

Return to Lake Washington Boulevard, go a block west and turn right onto Montlake Boulevard. You'll cross the freeway again and enter the extensive campus of the ☻ **University of Washington.** If you want to explore the grounds, pick up a map at the **Visitor Information Center** at 4014 University Way; (206) 543-2100. To reach it, fork to the left from Montlake onto NE Pacific Street, follow it to University Way and turn right. It's two blocks up, on your right at the corner of NE Campus Parkway.

The university's northern edge is bordered by NE 45th Street, which separates it from the old and mostly well-tended homes of the U District. Many are now fraternity and sorority houses. Reach 45th by turning left off Montlake or right off University Way, then turn north onto 17th Avenue NE. This handsome street with a park strip center divider passes several university frat houses, then hits NE Ravena, another landscaped boulevard. Turn left and follow it along the edge of **Ravena Park.** NE Ravena passes under I-5 and dovetails into Green Lake Drive, which takes you along the shoreline of the park-rimmed **Green Lake.**

You may be tempted to pause and play at this popular park which offers—among other things—a 2.8 mile walking/biking path around its shoreline. Or rent a canoe, kayak or rowboat at **Green Lake Boat Rentals** (527-0171) and go a-paddling. Unlike chilly Puget Sound, Green Lake's protected waters are warm enough for summer swimming.

From here, head for ☻ **Woodland Park Zoo,** which is fused into the southwestern edge of Green Lake Park, across Aurora Avenue expressway

(Highway 99). The easiest approach is to drop south from the park to North 50th Street, go west under the expressway and then north to the zoo.

Having talked with the animals, take 50th to Woodland Park's western edge, turn north onto Phinney Avenue, take it about half a mile to NW 65th Street, turn left and follow it west. You're now in the community of **Ballard,** settled by Scandinavians and boasting a fine ethnic archive. To reach the ❷ **Nordic Heritage Museum,** go north on 32nd Avenue NW to NW 68th Street and turn right.

Return to 32nd and continue north. At a stop sign at NW 85th Street, veer to the left toward **Shilshole Bay Marina** and **Golden Gardens Park.** The route takes you down through the park, in a looping spiral to the waterfront, while conveniently pointing you back toward downtown Seattle. More green than golden, the park is thickly wooded and laced with hiking trails. Its shoreline offers sandy beaches, boat ramps and great views of Puget Sound.

This puts you on the aptly-named Seaview Avenue NW; press southward through **Shilshole Bay Marina,** with its forests of masts and aquatic-view restaurants. You'll shortly curve around to the east onto NW 54th Street and arrive at ❸ **Hiram M. Chittenden Locks and English Gardens.** When you see the **Lockspot Café** ahead, turn right into a parking area alongside a railroad track and walk through the gardens to the locks.

Continue briefly east on 54th, which blends onto NW Market Street; follow it several blocks to 15th Avenue NW and turn right for the **Ballard Bridge.** This takes you across **Salmon Bay** and the **Lake Washington Ship Canal.** Down to your right, you'll see a great armada of commercial fishing boats, packed tightly against the piers of ❹ **Fishermen's Terminal.** To reach this interesting area, turn right onto West Emerson at the end of the bridge and follow signs.

As you leave the terminal, return to westbound Emerson, stay in the right hand lane and take a half right onto 22nd Avenue West. Turn left onto Commodore Way, passing through a waterfront industrial area. Hit 40th Avenue and go left into **Discovery Park.** Just beyond the park gate, turn right and downhill to a nice viewpoint and the modern pitched-roof **Daybreak Star Arts Center**; (206) 285-4425. Primarily a meeting hall and activity center for area Native Americans, it also displays contemporary Indian art. Discovery Park is a mix of woodlands, moors and sea cliffs, occupying the site of the former Fort Lawson army base. Facilities include kiddie play areas, self-guiding nature trails, a play field and tennis and basketball courts. Call (206) 386-4236 for information concerning conducted nature walks.

After exploring the park, drive along the its eastern and southern edges by following 36th Avenue south and then Emerson Street west. At the second stop sign on Emerson, turn left onto Magnolia Boulevard and follow it south through an attractive coastal residential area. The views are impressive from this landscaped boulevard—Puget Sound to your right and the city skyline ahead. Pretty little **Magnolia Park** along here has picnic shelters and more hillside views.

And just when you thought you'd never complete this loop, you drop down from these attractive heights into an industrial area. Cross a viaduct and turn right onto 15th Avenue. It becomes Elliott Avenue, taking you past **Myrtle Edwards Park** along Elliott Bay and toward the city center. To reach the waterfront, stay on Elliott to Broad Street, turn right and follow it down to Alaskan Way. If you're headed for the downtown area, veer to the left from Elliott onto Western Avenue.

# ATTRACTIONS
### In alphabetical order

☺ *Hiram Chittenden Locks and Carl S. English Jr. Botanical Gardens* • *3015 NW 54th St.; (206) 783-7059. Visitor area open 7 a.m. to 9 p.m. Guided tours daily at 1 and 3:30 in summer, weekends only at 2 the rest of the year.* ☐ We've always wondered why the Army Corps of Engineers didn't just pull the plug on the Lake Washington Ship Canal and let lakes Union and Washington drain down to sea level. Instead, the corps completed this system of locks in 1917. Among its distinctive features are a fish ladder and a special holding basin to prevent Puget Sound salt water from mixing with fresh water in the lakes. After watching the parade of pleasure boats and commercial craft rise and fall through the locks, visitors can adjourn to the adjacent garden, which was planted and nurtured by Corps of Engineer employee Carl English. He spent 43 years transforming once-barren ground into a botanical showplace, with 500 plant species from around the world.

☺ *Fishermen's Terminal* • *Salmon Bay Waterway, above Emerson Viaduct.* ☐ Washington fishing vessels harvest 2.3 billion pounds of seafood a year, more than half the total U.S. catch. A good many of them—more than 700—tie up here, at the West's largest commercial fishing dock. The terminal was established in 1913. Fishermen love the place because its fresh water cleans saltwater barnacles from the hulls of their boats. Step out onto the dock, where signs will help you identify the trollers, crab boats and huge factory ships that range the nearby seas. **Chinook's Restaurant** (listed below, under "Where to dine") offers views with its fish menu, and the small take-out has better fish and chips than those waterfront outfits. For take-home fresh fish, crabs and shellfish and a serious selection of white wine, step into **Wild Salmon Seafood Market,** open Monday-Saturday 10 to 6 and Sunday 11 to 6; it takes major credit cards.

☺ *The Kingdome* • Second Avenue South and South King Street; ticket office (206) 296-3111. Guided tours conducted from mid-April through mid-September, Monday-Saturday at 11, 1 and 3, except during daytime events. Adults and teens $3, seniors and kids $1.50; (206) 296-3128 or (206) 296-3100. ☐ While not the largest of America's domed stadiums, the Kingdome is hardly small, with a capacity of 80,000 for concerts and around 60,000 when the Seahawks and Mariners come to play. It's 250 feet high, 660 feet in diameter and covers more than nine acres. It's so big, the Space Needle will fit inside—if you tip it on its side. Tours take visitors out onto the playing field, into the locker rooms, through a sports museum, press section and VIP boxes.

☺ *Klondike Gold Rush National Historical Park* • *117 Main Street (near Occidental); (206) 553-7220. Daily 9 to 5; free. Guided tours of Pioneer Square offered in summer.* ☐ Small and handsomely arrayed, this storefront museum represents the Seattle end of an international historic park that includes elements in Skagway, Alaska, and Dawson City, Yukon. Several films recall the history of the rush to the Klondike. Particularly interesting is a film using colorized versions of old black and white photos. Exhibits include original and replica artifacts from the gold rush, and photo murals. Piled near the entrance is and an example of the ton of provisions that Mounties required for each man headed to the gold fields.

☺ **Museum of Flight** • *9404 E. Marginal Way (beside Boeing Field); (206) 764-5720. Daily 10 to 5 (Thursdays until 9). Adults $6, kids $3.* ❑ Simply put, this is Seattle's finest museum. If you're an aviation nut, it's the *Northwest's* finest museum. This imposing facility, housed in a modernistic six-story greenhouse, covers the full spectrum of flight, from earliest attempts at soaring through the jet age to the first moon landing. Full-sized aircraft, including an entire DC-3 "Gooney Bird," dangle from the rafters of the main building, like a close-formation squadron. Other aircraft—including a rare Boeing 1929 tri-motor, an F4U gull-wing Corsair and a wickedly sleek A-12 Blackbird—are parked below and outside. Movies trace the history of aviation, and videos in the large moon landing exhibit show those dramatic moments when man first set foot on the lunar surface. Visitors can crawl into the snug cockpit of an F-18, explore the innards of other aircraft and learn to make exceedingly airworthy paper planes. A large gift shop sells a startling variety of things avionic.

Adjacent to the main building is a replica of the "red barn," where William Boeing began building airplanes in 1909. It adds another dimension to this full-dimensional museum, focusing on the design and construction of early aircraft. In a full-scale mockup, mannequins stitch fabric over wooden wing frames.

☺ **Nordic Heritage Museum** • *3014 NW 67th St. (near 32nd Avenue NW); (206) 789-5707. Tuesday-Saturday 10 to 4, Sunday noon to 4, closed Monday. Adults $3, seniors and students, $2, kids $1.* ❑ Nearly three million Danes, Swedes, Finns, Norwegian and Icelanders came to America in the last half of the 19th century. This fine museum, housed in an old brick grade school, tells their story. Its particular focus is the Scandinavians who found their way to the Northwest. Professionally done exhibits follow the adventures and perils of immigrants from lurching ships to Ellis Island and across the country. Full-sized mockups depict an alien farm hand's hovel in a barn, an urban slum alley and—as the Vikings' lot improved—prim farms and a Scandinavian-American store. Looms, period costumes and modern and traditional Nordic art add more dimension to the museum.

**Omnidome** • *Pier 59; (206) 622-1868. Shows 10 to 6:45 Sunday-Thursday; until 9:30 Friday-Saturday. Single film $5.95, plus combination tickets for two shows and/or Seattle Aquarium admission. MC/VISA.* ❑ This is another of those super wide-angle movie theaters with tilt-back seats and surround sound. The Omnidome alternates the showing of two films. When we last checked, they were the Mount St. Helens eruption and a nicely-done environmental film called *Hidden Hawaii*, with the usual dramatic fiery lava footage.

☺ **Pacific Science Center** • *200 Second Avenue in Seattle Center; (206) 443-2001 or (206) 443-2880; IMAX theater (206) 443-IMAX; laser show schedule (206) 443-2850. Daily 10 to 6 in summer, weekdays 10 to 5 and weekends 10 to 6 the rest of the year. Adults $5.50, seniors and kids $4.50; separate fees for laser show and IMAX theater.* ❑ The science center is easy to find on the extensive Seattle Center grounds; just head for those five free-standing steel web arches. Directed mostly at kids but interesting for adults

*Full-sized aircraft, including an early DC-3, dangle from the greenhouse roof rafters of the outstanding Museum of Flight near Boeing Field.* — **Don W. Martin**

as well, it is many things under several roofs. The main center has 200 hands-on exhibits where folks can interact with science and technology. A planetarium does star shows, the IMAX theater has wide-screen films and the Boeing Spacearium features a "Laser Fantasy Light" show. If you have kids in tow and need to lose them for the afternoon, this is the place.

Other Seattle Center lures include the **Fun Forest** amusement park with thrill rides; **Children's Museum** with hands-on exhibits, bubble play area and art studio for toddlers; a **Food Court;** the **Seattle Opera House;** the **Coliseum,** home to the NBA's Seattle Supersonics; and of course, the **Space Needle** (listed below).

☺ *Pike Place Market* ● *At the foot of Pike Street, above the waterfront; (206) 682-7453. Most shops close in the evening, although restaurants remain open. Maps available at an information booth at First Avenue and Pike Place.* ☐ This wonderful conglomeration of fish and produce mongers, ethnic food stalls, cafés and curio shops is the heartbeat of Seattle. It rivals Seattle Center as the city's most popular attraction. Locals come as well as visitors—for fresh fish and produce, for morning coffee and conversation at Lowell's Café and for dinner at one of several harbor-view restaurants. The market started in 1907 to provide farmer-to-consumer groceries for Seattle housewives. It has survived to become the oldest farmers' market in America.

Mimes, street musicians and puppeteers compete with barking fish mongers for the attention of passersby. Despite this circus atmosphere, the market has resisted tacky carny attractions that have ruined other markets and waterfront tourist lures. (San Francisco's Fisherman's Wharf comes quickly to mind.) Franchise fast food parlors and national store chains cannot operate here. Instead, 90 farmers, fish and meat vendors and 200 artists and crafts people are licensed to sell their wares. More than 250 shops, stalls and cafès are crammed into this wonderfully cluttered space.

☺ **Seattle Aquarium** • *Pier 59; (206) 386-4300 or (206) 386-4320 for a 24-hour recorded message. Daily 10 to 7 in summer and 10 to 5 the rest of the year. Adults $6.75, seniors and disabled $5.25, students $4.25, kids $1.75; also combination tickets with the adjacent Omnidome.* ⊓ The aquarium's focus is the watery world of Puget Sound. It exhibits a goodly collection of finned, furred and feathered creatures who make the water or shoreline their home. Exhibits provide learning experiences for the curious. You not only see an electric eel; you hear its crackling voltage and learn how it uses this to stun is dinner entrèe. Two distinctive features here are a small salmon hatchery with a fish ladder (common elsewhere but unusual in aquariums) and the Fish Dome, where visitors are beneath the sea, looking up at the fish. It's like a glass bottom boat in reverse.

☺ **Seattle Art Museum** • *100 University Street (between First and Second avenues); (206) 625-8900 or (206) 654-3100. Tuesday-Sunday 10 to 5 (until 9 Thursday), closed Monday. Adults $6, seniors and students $4.* ⊓ Seattle's dramatic new masonry and glass museum building is terraced down the slope of University Street, with several galleries of permanent and changing exhibits and a fine little cafè. Out front is a monumental sculpture of a metal-working artist. Major exhibits feature artifacts from Northwest coastal Indians, African tribal art and an excellent collection of paintings, carvings, pottery and screens from several Asian countries. Providing international balance are small and select assemblies of European paintings, vases and glassware, and Egyptian tomb artifacts. Changing exhibits generally are more contemporary—often the blobs, scrawls and "formulations" of op art and pop art.

☺ **Seattle Museum of History and Industry** • *2700 24th Avenue East; (206) 324-1126. Daily 10 to 5. Adults $3, kids and seniors $1.50.* ⊓ The focal point of this older, nicely done museum is a Seattle boardwalk scene of the 1880s. It features a full-scale replica of Henry Yesler's Wharf, store façades and a batwing door saloon that doesn't bat. A nicely done video recalls that awful day in 1889 when the city burned, leaving the "hideous remains of the feast of fire." In a hands-on history room, visitors can operate model ship cranes and try on old fashioned hats. A "Seattle hits" display features items that originated here, from Almond Roca to Rainier beer to Boeing aircraft.

☺ **Smith Tower** • *Second Avenue at Yesler Way; (206) 622-4004. Elevator operates weekdays 9 to 11:30, 1:30 to 4:30 and 5:30 to 10; weekends 9 to 10. Adults $2, kids $1. Tickets at adjacent cigar store or from the elevator operator.* ⊓ L.C. Smith of typewriter and revolver (Smith and Wesson) fame wanted a monument to his success, so he financed this 500-foot tower, completed in 1914. It stood as the tallest building west of the Mississippi until 1959, and it was the most lofty structure in Seattle until the Space Needle topped it in 1962, at 605 feet. Step inside to admire its marble walls and wrought iron trim, then board one of America's few surviving manually operated elevators for a rattling ride to the top. Once there, you'll emerge into the Chinese Room, with some beautifully carved Chinese screens and furniture. Step onto the wrap-around observation deck to enjoy a predictable panorama of the city.

☺ **The Space Needle** • *In Seattle Center; (206) 443-2100. Observation deck hours: summer 8 to midnight; the rest of the year 9 to midnight. Adults $5.50, seniors $4.50, kids $3; free to restaurant patrons. For restaurant/cocktail lounge hours and details, see "Where to dine" below.* Four other Seattle structures now tower over the Space Needle, yet this skinny tripod remains the city's most popular high-rise landmark. Since its erection for the 1962 world's fair, it has become Seattle's logo, appearing on everything from souvenir ash trays to guidebook covers. (We purchased four Seattle guidebooks for reference; all displayed The Needle.) The slowly-revolving restaurant at the 500-foot level is a requisite stop for every Seattlite's visiting cousin, despite a lack of raves for culinary accomplishments. For considerably less than the price of a meal, you can ascend to the cocktail lounge or the observation deck for the same view. A sophisticated locator compass on the observation deck tells you what you're seeing.

☺ **Bill Speidel's Underground Tour** • *Meets at Doc Maynard's Public House, 610 First Ave.; (206) 682-1511 for information and (206) 682-4646 for reservations. Various tour hours; generally 11 to 6; call for reservations. Adults $5.50, seniors $4.50, students $4, kids $2.25. MC/VISA.* ☐ Some things are so corny they're appealing, and this is certainly the case with these underground tours, originated by the late Bill Speidel in 1964. Intrigued with the catacombs formed when the streets of Pioneer Square were elevated, he and teams of volunteers cleared away several tons of rubble and began conducting tours.

His light-hearted, irreverent style is maintained in today's outings. The guides' narratives are slightly bawdy, often politically incorrect and rich in history, anecdotes and harmless exaggerations. Visitors descend beneath the sidewalks in three different areas, exploring musty corridors, long-abandoned underground businesses and cobweb-draped corners that would make great sets for Alfred Hitchcock movies. The outing ends in a subterranean museum-gift shop.

☺ **Tillicum Village Salmon Bake** • *Departs from piers 55 and 56; (206) 443-1244. Lunch, mid-afternoon and dinner cruises; hours vary with the seasons; call for reservations. Adults $39.95, seniors $36.95, teens $25.95, kids 6 to 12, $15.95 and toddlers $7.95. Prices include cruise to Blake Island, salmon feed and show. MC/VISA.* ☐ Generations ago, settlers took Blake Island from Native Americans and eventually made it into a state park. Several decades ago, descendants of the original inhabitants were invited back to present Indian-style salmon bakes for tourists. The salmon feed has become the darling of the tour bus set and—like the Space Needle—a requisite outing for visiting relatives. (President Bill Clinton hosted Asian leaders at an economic summit with a salmon feed in late 1993.)

The boat cruises past Seattle's working waterfront and then across Elliott Bay to thickly wooded Blake Island. Views back at the skyline—day or night—are striking. On the island, visitors are ushered into a reconstructed longhouse for a meal featuring salmon baked over open fires. They then witness *Dance on the Wind,* an excessively slick and stagey portrayal of Indian dances and legends. (We preferred the simpler, earlier versions without the recorded thunder and strobe lightning.) After the show, there's time to stroll island paths or browse through a crafts display before catching the boat back to Seattle.

☺ **University of Washington campus** • *Visitor Information Center at 4014 University Way; (206) 543-2100. Visitor parking $3.* ☐ Occupying a peninsula shaped by Union Bay and Portage Bay, the wooded campus of Washington's senior university is one of the most attractive in the West. This was the site of the 1909 Alaskan-Yukon-Pacific Exposition and several structures were left for use by the school. Pick up a map at the information center at University Way and NE Campus Parkway and stroll this tree-shaded campus of brick and grass. Among its lures are the **Thomas Burke Memorial Washington State Museum** at 17th Avenue NE and NE 45th St., open daily, with Native American and natural history exhibits, 543-4490; and the **Henry Art Gallery,** 15th Avenue NE and NE 41st Street, daily except Monday, exhibiting 20th century American and European art, 543-2280. There's an neat little student coffee house in the basement of the Burke Museum called **The Boiserie**, 543-9854.

**Wing Luke Asian Memorial Museum** • *407 Seventh Ave. S (near Jackson); (206) 623-5124. Tuesday-Friday 11 to 4:30, Saturday-Sunday noon to 4, closed Monday. Adults $2.50, seniors and students $1.50, kids 75 cents.* ☐ This modest museum tells the story of Asian immigrants in America. Its most touching exhibit concerns the World War II relocation of loyal Japanese-American citizens to inland concentration camps. Other displays include examples of calligraphy, and arts and crafts of various Asian communities in the Northwest. The museum's name honors Seattle's first Chinese-American city councilman, who perished in a plane crash.

☺ **Woodland Park Zoo** • *Woodland Park, off Phinney Avenue between 50th and 59th streets; (206) 684-4800. Daily 9:30 to 6 (closes at 4 from mid-October to mid-March). Adults $5; seniors, handicapped and kids, $2.50.* ☐ One of the West Coast's best museums is getting better. Major improvements, which may be completed by the time you arrive, include an expanded Asian elephant exhibit, tropical rain forest and tropical Asia. This large, lushly landscaped complex shelters more than a thousand critters. Most are in open-air compounds, where they have room to roam. Among the zoo's better features are the African savanna and a nocturnal display, where time has been reversed so visitors can see night creatures on the prowl.

## TOURS AND ACTIVITIES

**Getting ticketed** • Pacific Northwest Ticket Service (232-0150) and TicketMaster Northwest (628-0888) are Seattle's major agencies for theater, concert and sports tickets. Both have credit card charge-by-phone service.

**Air tours** • Seaplane flights from Lake Union are offered by Kenmore Air, (800) or 543-9595 (206) 486-8400; and from Lake Washington by Sound Flight in Renton, (206) 255-6500.

**Airport tour** • Sea-Tac International Airport tours may be arranged by calling (206) 433-5386.

**Bike tours** • Guided bicycle trips around the Seattle area are conducted by Terrene Tours; (206) 369-4196.

**Brewery tours** • Rainier Brewing Company, 3100 Airport Way S., has free tours and tastings weekdays from 1 to 6; (206) 622-2600. Red Hook Ale Brewery, 3400 Phinney Ave. N., conducts free tours and tastings weekdays at 3 and weekends at 1:30, 2:30, 3:30 and 4:30; (206) 548-8000.

**Kingdome Tours** • Guided tours of Seattle's domed sports arena are conducted from mid-April through mid-September; see "Attractions" above.

# TEN THINGS YOU GOTTA DO IN SEATTLE

If your time is limited, try to accomplish these things to complete your Seattle experience. They're listed in our arbitrary order of personal importance. Feel fee to shuffle the sequence.

**1. Start your day at Pike Place Market** ● Watch one of America's few authentic public markets come alive as merchants array silvery fish on beds of shaved ice, and fashion turnips into geometric designs at the produce stands. Then fetch a donut from the bakery and share it with the gulls, or take breakfast on one of the floors of Lowell's cafeteria.

**2. Take Bill Speidel's Underground Tour** ● The late Bill Speidel had a barroom sense of humor and it survives in his new generation of tour guides. You'll learn more than you ever wanted to know about exploding Crappers as you tour the catacombs beneath Pioneer Square.

**3. Have a caffè latte at Elliott Bay Book Company** ● Located in Pioneer Square, it's Seattle's penultimate book store. Select from thousands of titles and adjourn to the sanctity of the brick-walled cellar cafe. Don't forget to buy the book on your way out.

**4. Do the Tillicum Village Indian salmon bake thing** ● The salmon is overdone and the accompanying ritual dances are a bit too theatrical, but this is still a fine outing. Tour boats first skim Seattle's working waterfront, then cruise across Puget Sound to wooded Blake Island, a state park within sight of the distant city skyscrapers. After the salmon feed and show, there's time to walk wooded hiking trails and quiet shores.

**5. Earn your historic wings at the Museum of Flight** ● The only way to find a more comprehensive aviation archive is to fly to Washington and visit the Smithsonian's Air and Space Museum.

**6. Take the elevator to the top of Smith Tower** ● There certainly are taller structures in the city with panoramic views. The Space Needle, for instance. However, the marble and brass interior of Seattle's first skyscraper and the ride up the manually operated elevator make this a special experience.

**7. Ascend the Space Needle** ● For a hefty tab, you can dine at one of two Space Needle restaurants and watch the city and countryside revolve in slow motion. For considerably less, you can take the elevator to the observation deck and enjoy the same views. If you like the idea of rotating, walk in a slow circle.

**8. Visit the Nordic Heritage Center** ● Since you're nearly all immigrants, if you go back enough generations, you'll enjoy the displays at this splendid museum. Exhibits trace immigration of the Nordic peoples from their homelands through the uncertainty of Ellis Island to the farms, timberlands and fisheries of the West.

**9. Watch boats and fish rise and fall at Chittenden Locks** ● We don't know why it's fascinating to stand alongside the locks, watching boats pass in and out of the ship channel to lakes Union and Washington. But we *were* fascinated. You also can watch salmon make the same passage through fish ladder viewing windows.

**10. Generate your own personal lightning bolt at Pacific Science Center** ● This large facility at Seattle Center is mostly for kids, so become one and play with the more than 200 hands-on exhibits.

**Major league sports** ● The Seattle Mariners play baseball in the King-dome to small but enthusiastic crowds; for tickets, call 628-3555. The National Football League's Seattle Seahawks are a much tougher ticket; most of their games at the Kingdome are sold out, but try anyway: 827-9766. Also popular are the Supersonics, although seats for their games at the Coliseum generally are available a few days before game time; 281-5850.

**Minor league, college and other sports** ● The Western Hockey League's Thunderbirds play at the Seattle Center Arena; (206) 728-9124. The football Huskies of the University of Washington, perhaps even more adored than the Seahawks, also are a difficult ticket buy; it's easier to get UW basketball tickets; (206) 543-2200 is the phone number for both. Auto and motorcycle racing are held at the Seattle International Raceway at 31001 144th in nearby Kent; (206) 631-1550.

**Newspaper tour** ● The **Seattle Times** at Fairview Avenue and John Street has free tours of its editorial offices, pressroom and composing room Tuesday-Friday 9:30 to noon, by reservation only, from September through June; (206) 464-3237.

**Performing arts** ● The prestigious Seattle Opera sings at the Seattle Center Opera House from September to May; (206) 443-4711. Sharing that hall is the Seattle Symphony, with concerts October through April; (206) 362-2300. Pacific Northwest Ballet features the *Nutcracker* during the holidays as part of its October to May season; (206) 628-0888. Seattle Repertory Theater hits the boards at the Bagley-Wright Theater in Seattle Center, with an October-May season; (206) 443-2222. Pioneer Square Theater preforms at the Mainstage, a former strip parlor at 512 Second Ave.; (206) 622-2016. A Contemporary Theatre (ACT) performs at 100 W. Roy Street from May through September; (206) 285-5110. Seattle Center's Intiman Playhouse hosts classic drama from June through November; (206) 626-0782.

**Sea kayak rentals and tours** ● NW Outdoor Center has sea kayak rentals, classes and guided tours on Elliott Bay, Lake Union and the San Juan Islands; (206) 281-9694.

**Seattle City Light Skagit tours** ● The Seattle utility company offers tours to its hydroelectric dam in the North Cascades (see Chapter 7). Although tours originate at the dam, they can be booked at Seattle City Light, 1015 Third Avenue downtown; (206) 684-3030. Outings range from four-hour meal tours for $25 to dam and power plant tours for $5. Meal tour reservations are required at least two months in advance.

**Sightseeing tours** ● Bus tours of the town and surrounds are offered by several firms. Gray Line of Seattle books a variety of tours in the city, on Elliott Bay and Puget Sound, plus excursions to the Boeing plant in Everett, Mount Rainier National Park and Victoria, B.C.; (800) 426-7532 or (206) 626-5208. Seattle Tours has trips around town and to Hurricane Ridge in Olympic National Park, Bainbridge Island, Mount Rainier and Snoqualmie Falls; (206) 660-TOUR. Seattle Name-Dropper Tours take visitors to "personality spots" where famous people lived, performed or visited in Seattle; (206) 625-1317. Chinatown Discovery Tours guides folks through the streets of the International District; (206) 236-0657. Seattle's Best Walking Tours conducts behind-the-scenes strolls of the city's major and offbeat attractions; (206) 236-2060.

**Sport fishing/whale watching** ● Among outfits that offer fishing and/or whale watching trips in Puget Sound are Sport Fishing of Seattle, (206)

# QUICK SHIP TO VICTORIA

I say! While you're visiting Seattle, why not pop over to Victoria for a spot of tea at the Empress? That wonderfully British city on Canada's Vancouver Island is within easy reach—right across Puget Sound.

The high speed catamaran *Victoria Clipper* makes the 75-mile trip in two and a half hours, with plenty of Puget Sound scenery en route. Food and beverage service and duty-free shopping are available in the airline-style cabin. Unlike the ferry boats that put ashore up-island, the *Clipper* delivers travelers right to the Inner Harbour, within walking distance of the legendary Empress Hotel and downtown Victoria.

Cruises depart Pier 69 on the Seattle Waterfront, an easy cab ride or brisk walk from downtown. You can make the round trip in one day, with several hours to explore Victoria, or book one of several overnight packages. There are several departures daily in summer, and at least one daily round trip the rest of the year that allows several hours ashore. Round trip fares are $85 for adults, $75 for seniors and $42.50 for kids, with discounts for advance purchases. Fares are less in the off-season.

Clearing Canadian customs is simple. American citizens need only two forms of identification, such as a driver's license and credit cards. Citizens of other countries visiting America should carry their passports.

Visitors can pack a lot of sightseeing into a few hours ashore. The venerable Empress Hotel is just a few hundred yards from the ferry dock, and $17 will get you the famous mid-afternoon high tea ceremony. **Miniature World,** with tiny working replicas of sawmills, railroads and other constructions, is in the Empress north wing, and the **Crystal Garden** tropical atrium is just behind. A block south of the hotel is the superb **Royal British Columbia Museum,** with full-scale mock-ups tracing the history of Canada and B.C. The **Maritime Museum of British Columbia** is just north of the Empress, in Bastion Square. **Undersea Gardens** and the **Royal London Wax Museum** occupy the Inner Harbour's southern arm.

A short walk delivers visitors to the heart of old Victoria, a virtual outdoor museum of English architecture. Within a few blocks are a compact **Chinatown**, an array of antique shops, boutiques, restaurants and tearooms. Inexpensive tours will take you to the Shakespearean-era **Ann Hathaway's Cottage** and the legendary **Butchart Gardens.**

Try the harbor-view **Spinnakers Brew Pub** for lunch and a hand-crafted beer. It's a brief stroll or quick cab ride from the Empress, at 308 Catherine Street. And then it's back on the ship and back to Seattle—even before you've had time to cultivate a proper British accent.

For information, contact Clipper Navigation, Inc., 2701 Alaskan Way, Pier 69, Seattle, WA 98121; (800) 888-2535 or (206) 488-5000. To learn about your destination, contact Tourism Victoria, 710-1175 Douglas St., Victoria, B.C. V8W 2EI; (604) 382-2127. Once in Victoria, stop by the Info Center at 812 Wharf Street.

623-6364; Orca Adventures in Edmonds, (206) 774-4374; and Sea Charters in Edmonds, (206) 776-5611 or (206) 771-2172.

☺ *Spirit of Washington Dinner Train* • *P.O. Box 835, Renton, WA 98057; (800) 876-RAIL or (206) 277-RAIL. Lunch and dinner excursions throughout the year; call for schedules and reservations. Regular seating $57 for dinner and $47 for lunch or brunch; dome car seating $69 for dinner and $59 for brunch.* ◻ Unlike some dinner trains that employ tired old rolling stock, this operation in the nearby city of Renton uses sleek aluminum cars pulled by a diesel electric locomotive. Dome dining cars provide the best seating, offering wide-angle views as the train cruises along the shores of Lake Washington and then across a long wooden trestle and into the hills to Columbia Winery. Here, passengers have time to tour and sip before returning to the train. Dessert and after-dinner drinks are served on the way back.

**Steamship Virginia V** ● *901 Fairview Ave. N., berth A-100, Chandlers Cove (south end of Lake Union); (206) 624-9119.* ⊓ Built in 1922, this wooden-hulled vessel is the last of Puget Sound's "Mosquito Fleet" and the only operating reciprocating steam engine vessel on the Pacific Coast. Although it doesn't yet offer regular excursions, it can be seen at berth in Chandler's Cove. Also, visitors can book cruises during special Christmas-New Years holiday outings, and it's available for charter.

**Water tours** ● Several firms offer cruises in Elliott Bay and Puget Sound. The sleek *Spirit of Puget Sound* has lunch, dinner, dancing and excursion cruises, leaving from Pier 70; (206) 443-1442. Seattle Harbor Tours makes daily one-hour harbor cruises, plus longer trips through the Chittenden Locks and up the Lake Washington Ship Canal and cruises around Lake Washington; (206) 623-4252. Among Gray Line's many outings is a loop tour that begins with a cruise from Pier 57 through the locks to Chandler's Cove on Lake Union, then a bus tour across town; (206) 623-4252.

## ANNUAL EVENTS

The big event in Seattle is **Seafair,** spread over three weeks from mid-July into early August. It's a busy dazzle of parades, craft shows, sports events, food fairs and ethnic festivals, climaxed by unlimited hydroplane races across Lake Washington. Book your lodgings early if you plan to be in town during this lively time. For event information, call (206) 728-0123.

To learn more about events listed below—and others—call the Seattle-King County Convention and Visitors Bureau at (206) 461-5800.

**Chinese New Year,** sometime in January or February (based on the Chinese lunar calendar), in the International District; (206) 623-8171.

**Fat Tuesday,** a week-long mardi gras style celebration in Pioneer Square, late winter to early spring; (206) 461-5800.

**Cherry Blossom Festival,** Japanese-American celebration in Seattle Center, early April.

**Opening Day of Yachting Season,** first weekend of May on the waters around Seattle.

**University Street Fair,** third week of May in the U District.

**Northwest Folklife Festival,** featuring dances, crafts and ethnic foods, Memorial Day Weekend in Seattle Center; 684-7300.

**Pike Place Market Festival,** in May at the market.

**Summer Arts Magic Fair**, June at the Seattle Art Museum; (206) 625-8900.

**Emerald City Marathon,** July, through city streets; (206) 285-4847.

**Lake Union Wooden Boat Festival** in July.

**Bumbershoot Festival,** perhaps anticipating the coming of the rainy season, Labor Day weekend in Seattle Center with performing arts, crafts and foods; (206) 684-7200.

**Seafoodfest,** September, Bergen Place Park, Ballard; (206) 784-9705.

**Christmas Ships Parade,** mid-December, with lighted boats cruising Lake Washington.

# WHERE TO DINE

In the entire West, Seattle ranks close behind San Francisco for its number and variety of restaurants. Dining is a delight for visitors, who can pay high prices for high views atop the Space Needle, enjoy waterfront vistas and fish along Elliott Bay, get good fish and chips at Fishermen's Terminal, dine with class and high-rise views in downtown hotel restaurants, or go for ethnic variety in the International District. Many places feature "Northwest cuisine," which essentially is California *nouveau* with salmon. Like other regional American cuisines, Northwest fare is influenced by fresh local ingredients and ethnic accents. Much of this, of course, is centered on seafood.

The city also is famous for its coffees, with an abundance of espresso machines, coffee carts and long lists of specialty coffees on most good menus. Seattle has ten commercial roasting companies and "few restaurants dare serve a national brand coffee," wrote one visiting writer.

We can do little more than scratch the city's culinary surface in our limited space. So, we'll focus on interesting restaurants in areas frequented by visitors. For a much more comprehensive list, pick up a copy of the thick *Seattle Best Places* at any bookstore. Its reviews are unbiased and we admit to frequently peeking into its pages for guidance.

Virtually all establishments have non-smoking areas, so we use our Ø symbol only to indicate that places have separate smoke-free dining rooms.

## Downtown

### ☺ *The Brooklyn* ● ∆∆∆ $$$

◻ *1212 Second Ave. (at University); (206) 224-7000. American; full bar service. Weekdays 11 to 3 and 5 to 10, Saturday 5 to 11, closed Sunday. MC/VISA, AMEX.* ◻ This 1890s style restaurant installed behind old brick is the city's power lunch venue, with lots of brass, beveled glass and high-backed booths. From the steak-and-seafood-focused menu emerges the Carpetbagger (filet mignon stuffed with fresh oysters and wrapped with bacon), Northwest prawn sautè and Louisiana pan-fried oysters.

### *Campagne* ● ∆∆∆ $$$$ Ø

◻ *86 Pine Street near First (the Inn at the Market); (206) 728-2800. French; full bar service. Dinner nightly 5:30 to 10; lighter cafè fare until midnight. Major credit cards.* ◻ Crisp white linens and tiny flower vases accent the clean, simple lines of this elegant little cafè. Menu offerings include the classic southwestern French cassoulet with pork, duck confit, sausages and white beans in a savory sauce; pan-roasted scallops with potato purèe and green peppercorn, tarragon and lemon; and rabbit marinated in mustard.

### *Cascade Gardens* ● ∆∆ $$

◻ *96 Union (at First); (206) 292-8889. Chinese, mostly Mandarin. Monday-Thursday 11:30 to 2:30 and 5 to 9:45, Friday 11:30 to 2:30 and 5 to 10:45, Saturday noon to 10:45, Sunday noon to 8:45. Wine and beer. MC/VISA, AMEX.* ◻ Start with potstickers and then move on to an assortment of spicy Szechuan, Mandarin and Hunan dishes in this cellar restaurant. You'll find a few calmer Cantonese entrèes as well. The look is sort of Chinese art deco, with fluted chandeliers and Oriental accents.

### ☺ *Fullers* ● ∆∆∆∆ $$$$ Ø

◻ *Seattle Sheraton, 1400 Sixth Ave. (at Pike); (206) 447-5544. Northwest cuisine; full bar service. Lunch weekdays 11:30 to 2, dinner Monday-Saturday*

*5:30 to 10. Major credit cards.* ◻ Fullers may be the ultimate Northwest dining venue, both in art and cuisine. Works of Northwest artists grace the walls of this softly elegant restaurant. Skillfully prepared and artfully presented dishes emerge from the kitchen. The accent is continental-Asian, with creations such as oysters in ginger *mignonette*, grilled sea scallops in puréed sorrel with lemon fettuccine, or pork loin in an apple brandy-blue cheese sauce.

### ☺ *Mangeamo* • ΔΔΔ $$

◻ *1501 Fourth Ave. (third floor of Century Square); (206) 622-8955. Southern Italian; full bar service. Monday-Thursday 11:30 to 9. Friday 11:30 to 10, Saturday 5 to 10, closed Sunday. Major credit cards.* ◻ The look of this stylish place is pleasantly difficult to describe: a kind of art deco *nouveau* with globe chandeliers, high back booths, natural woods and modern art on the walls. From the open kitchen emerges innovative Italian fare with American *nouveau* touches. Try the linguine Marco Polo in light curried cumin stock, shallots and grilled vegetables; sausage ragout with provolone and mozzarella cheese wrapped in eggplant; or one of several interestingly spiced seafood dishes. The seafood salad with prawns and lox is excellent.

### ☺ *McCormick & Schmick's* • ΔΔΔ $$$ Ø

◻ *1103 First Ave. (Spring Street); 623-5500. American, mostly seafood; full bar service. Weekdays 11 to 11, weekends 5 to 11. Major credit cards.* ◻ This handsome establishment may be downtown Seattle's most serious seafood restaurant, with more than two dozen finned entrées. Emerging from the busy menu are Dungeness crab cakes, Hawaiian mahi mahi, clams linguine, Florida rock shrimp popcorn and so on. It's a popular business lunch establishment with a pleasant oldstyle look: brass and beveled glass, an island bar and an open kitchen.

### ☺ *The Painted Table* • ΔΔΔΔ $$$ Ø

◻ *In the Alexis Hotel, 92 Madison near First Avenue; (206) 624-3646. Northwest cuisine; full bar service. Daily 6:30 a.m. to 10 p.m. Major credit cards.* ◻ Opened in 1992 to replace the Alexis Restaurant, the Painted Table is finding quick success among foodies. The fare focuses on fresh fish, meats and vegetables of the *nouveau* movement, yet with classic touches. The changing menu may feature venison *osso bucco*, grilled smoked duck with *soba* noodles, a classic roasted prim rib, or black pepper roasted loin of pork with rosemary bread pudding. The look is elegantly simple, with art deco light fixtures and paneled walls adorned with modern art.

### *Palomino Café* • ΔΔΔ $$$

◻ *1420 Fifth Ave. (in City Centre); (206) 623-1300. Italian-Mediterranean; full bar service. Lunch Monday-Saturday 11:15 to 2:30, lighter café lunch Monday-Friday 11:15 to 3, dinner Sunday-Monday 5 to 9:30, Tuesday-Thursday 5 to 10, Friday-Saturday 5 to 10:30. Major credit cards.* ◻ Open to the City Centre shopping complex, this stylish Milanese café is a designer's vision of rose marble, hanging garlic garlands, glass sconces and potted palms. Two open kitchens keep diners busy with Mediterranean spiced seafoods, roasts and chickens. The wood-fired pizza is excellent.

### *Space Needle* • ΔΔ $$$$ Ø

◻ *Seattle Center; Emerald Suite reservations (206) 443-2150; Space Needle Restaurant reservations (206) 443-2100. American-continental; full bar* service. *Lunch 11 to 3, dinner 5 to 11, Sunday brunch 8 to 3. Major credit cards.* ☐ C'mon guys, stop making fun of the poor Space Needle! The food isn't *that* bad (although it's quite pricey), and the views are great. The outer rim of tables revolves slowly, giving diners the full sweep of city and Puget Sound every hour. The Needle has dressed up its image by dividing into two restaurants. The Emerald Suite is a bit more stylish, with a focus on continental fare, while the Space Needle Restaurant is more of a family venue with Northwest cuisine. Prices, which range into the high $30s, include the vertical passage.

### Waterfront/Pike Place Market

Few restaurants along the waterfront have earned culinary raves, although the dining room views are great. You can generally get decent seafood by asking what's fresh, and then insisting that it not be overcooked.

#### ☺ *Elliott's Restaurant* ● ∆∆∆ $$

☐ *Pier 56 (near Seneca); (206) 623-4340. American, mostly seafood; full bar service. Sunday-Thursday 11 to 10, Friday-Saturday 11 to 11. Major credit cards.* ☐ Perhaps the best waterfront *fishhaus*, Elliott's has the most extensive oyster bar in the city, and *nouveau* touches are found in its seafood entrées. F'rinstance: prawn linguine with sun-dried tomatoes and olive oil, salmon with raspberry soy glaze, and smoked salmon fettuccine. The look is bright, light and cheerful, with natural woods, greenhouse roof dining area and an open kitchen.

#### *Fisherman's Restaurant* ● ∆∆ $$$

☐ *Pier 57 in Bay Pavilion; (206) 623-3500. American, mostly seafood; full bar service. Daily 10 to 10. Major credit cards.* ☐ The inside look is predictably nautical, with the usual brass and polished wood; the outside view is excellent, since part of the dining area occupies a loft. The menu features mesquite grilled salmon, halibut, swordfish, prawns and such. If you've brought a big appetite, try the "Fisherman's Feast" for two or more, with chowder, salad, sourdough bread and an entrée.

#### *Ivar's Acres of Clams* ● ∆∆ $$

☐ *Pier 54 (at the foot of Madison); (206) 624-6852. American, mostly seafood; full bar service. Daily 11 to 10. MC/VISA, AMEX.* ☐ The late Ivar Haglund started frying fish here in 1938, and his restaurants have since spread throughout the area. The company has made this place something of a museum, with historic photos on the walls and a bronze of Ivar out front, feeding the seagulls. The mostly seafood menu isn't particularly innovative but you can get good fish by being selective. And the polished wood and brass and great views provide a nice setting.

#### ☺ *Lowell's* ● ∆ $

☐ *In Pike Place Market; (206) 622-2036. Monday-Friday 7 to 5, Saturday 7 to 5:30, Sunday 8 to 3. Major credit cards.* ☐ A single ∆ with a ☺ tells you that this slightly scruffy food parlor must have character. We like to start a Seattle day here, eating a high-cholesterol breakfast and watching the market awaken. It's also a handy and inexpensive lunch stop. Place your order at the busy counter and adjourn to one of three bare-bones dining rooms with views of Elliott Bay. A few Pike Place Market scenes adorn dining room walls and not much else. But the prices (grilled silver salmon in dill butter for under $8) are hard to beat.

### Maximilien-in-the-Market • ΔΔ $$$

☐ *Pike's Place Market; (206) 682-7270. French-continental; full bar service. Breakfast 7:30 to 11, lunch 11:30 to 4, dinner from 5. Major credit cards.* ☐ Dark woods, beamed ceilings and artwork create a pleasant French bistro setting; only the view of Elliott Bay says it's tucked into a corridor of Pike's Place. Fish stew is a specialty; other offerings from its changing menu may include beef tenderloin with bearnaise sauce, grilled sweetbreads and salmon fillet stuffed with shrimp and sole. Family-style *prix fixe* dinners are served week nights for under $15.

### Old Spaghetti Factory • ΔΔ $$

☐ *Elliott and Broad; (206) 623-3520. Italian; full bar service. Lunch weekdays 11:30 to 2, dinner Monday-Thursday 5 to 10 and Friday 5 to 11, Sunday hours noon to 10. MC/VISA, DISC.* ☐ This formula spaghetti house, in an old warehouse just in from the waterfront, looks more Gay Nineties than Italian. Assorted pastas, pizzas and an occasional cacciatore reveal the menu's roots.

### Panos Greek Cuisine • ΔΔ $$

☐ *Pier 70; (206) 441-5073. Greek; wine and beer. Lunch Monday-Friday 11:30 to 2:30, dinner Monday-Saturday 5:30 to 9:30, closed Sunday. Major credit cards.* ☐ Appropriate to its waterfront setting, this small Greek cafè features several seafood dishes, plus the usual *moussaka, dolmades* and *gyros.* If you like lamb, try the boneless leg with garlic and thyme. It's a cheerful white and blue space with floral border paintings on the walls and white bentwood chairs. There are bay views, of course.

### ☺ Place Pigalle • ΔΔΔ $$

☐ *Pike Place Market; (206) 624-1765. French-continental-Northwest; full bar service. Lunch Monday-Friday 11:30 to 3, Saturday to 3:30; dinner Monday-Thursday 5:30 to 10, Friday 6 to 11 and Saturday 6 to 10:30. Major credit cards.* ☐ Like Gaelic bookends, Maximilien's and Place Pigalle flank the marketplace. Pigalle offers similar warm woods, artwork and Elliott Bay views. The menu is considerably more versatile, however, touching on a variety of cuisines. Examples are pan-roasted rabbit with kale, red bell pepper, orange zest and pecans; sturgeon with prawn tomato cream sauce, jicima and pink grapefruit salad; and roasted duck served with roasted fennel, garlic purèe, prosciutto and Cabernet sauce.

### Red Robin • Δ $

☐ *Pier 55; (206) 624-3969. American; full bar service. Sunday-Thursday 11 to 10, Friday-Saturday 11 to 1 a.m. MC/VISA.* ☐ This where you take the kids for a quick lunch or light supper, with an Elliott Bay View. The look glitzy back-to-the-fifties nautical pizza parlor, although hamburgers are the main menu boast. It claims to serve gourmet 'burgers, but that, of course, is a self-canceling phrase. There are several other Robins Red in town.

## Pioneer Square

### Guido's Bakery • Δ $

☐ *807 First (near Columbia); (206) 340-5966. American-Italian; no alcohol. Weekdays 6:20 to 5:30. No credit cards.* ☐ This bakery, with an unusual interior Spanish tile roof, is a handy quickie breakfast or lunch stop during an exploration of Pioneer Square or the International District. It serves up bakery goods, calzones, lasagna, sandwiches, soups and salads.

### ☺ *G.V. Underground* • ΔΔ *$$*

⛶ *88 Yesler Way; (206) 343-9988. Chinese; wine and beer. Monday-Thursday 11 to 9, Friday 11 to 10, Saturday 4 to 10, closed Sunday. MC/VISA.* ⛶ Despite the sinister sounding name, this is a locally popular Chinese restaurant, tilted toward Mandarin and Szechuan cuisine. It *is* underground, appropriate to its Pioneer Square location, with simple furnishings, floral tablecloths and earthy cut-stone walls. Enliven your palate with hot pepper prawns, pepper spiced chicken or—for you vegetarians—hot broccoli with garlic sauce. The extensive menu also offers are milder dishes.

### *J&M Café* • Δ *$*

⛶ *201 First Ave. (Washington); (206) 624-1670. American; wine and beer. Lunch and dinner daily. AMEX.* ⛶ This cavernous, smoky cafè with pressed tin ceilings is one of two claiming to be Seattle's oldest restaurant, dating from 1890. It has occupied its current spot since 1902. Walls are decorated with hundreds of Hollywood publicity stills and photos of long-time patrons. The fare is simple and ordinary—salads, hamburgers and other sandwiches.

### ☺ *Merchant's Café* • ΔΔ *$$*

⛶ *109 Yesler Way (First Avenue); (206) 624-1515. American; full bar service. Sunday-Thursday 11 to 8, Friday-Saturday 11 to 11. Major credit cards.* ⛶ The second claimant to the oldest restaurant title, the 1890 Merchants goes a step further, insisting it's the oldest restaurant on the West Coast occupying its original spot. Whether or not, it's an appealing old fashioned diner with a long weathered bar, bentwood chairs and marble-topped tables. The menu is small and simple: fettuccine Alfredo, Chicken dijon, pepper steak and broiled salmon, plus sandwiches and salads. A basement pub is one of the few businesses still alive in the underground.

### *New Orleans* • ΔΔ *$$*

⛶ *114 First Ave.; (206) 622-2563. Creole-Cajun; full bar service. Lunch and dinner daily. MC/VISA.* ⛶ More of a jazz club than a restaurant, New Orleans nevertheless fills a niche as Pioneer Square's Southern-style cafè. Red beans and rice, seafood *etouffe* and jambalaya are on the menu to prove it. The look is yesterday Seattle or maybe Bourbon Street—raw brick walls, high ceilings and bentwood chairs.

### ☺ *Pacific Northwest Brewing Company* • ΔΔ *$$*

⛶ *322 Occidental (Jackson); (206) 621-7002. Brewpub; full bar service. Monday 4 to 10, Tuesday-Thursday 4 to midnight, Friday 4 to 2 a.m., Saturday 11:30 to 2, Sunday 12:30 to 9. Major credit cards.* ⛶ A huge copper brewing kettle forms a striking backdrop for the circular bar in this stylish brewpub. Black lacquer furniture and replica brew barrels along the seating area add visual impact. Brews range from bitter English styles to milder but full-flavored Northwest beers. The food is geared to the suds: pork chops over Mexican black beans, bratwurst steamed in ale and a hot sausage and shellfish gumbo.

## International District

### *Bangkok House* • ΔΔ *$$*

⛶ *606 Weller; (206) 382-9888. Thai; wine and beer. Sunday-Thursday 11 to 10, Friday-Saturday 11 to 11. MC/VISA, AMEX.* ⛶ It's a cozy little cafè, simply decorated with a few Thailand ornaments and pictures. The menu is typically Thai-spicy—curried crab, garlic calamari and sweet and sour chicken. Curiously tasty is the sautèed Southern Comfort chicken, stir-fried with bamboo shoots, peanuts, mushrooms and wine.

### ☺ Bush Garden • ΔΔΔ $$

□ 614 Maynard; (206) 682-6830. Japanese; full bar service. Lunch weekdays 11:30 to 2, dinner Monday-Sunday 5 to 10. Major credit cards. □ Step off the busy street into a quiet refuge of bamboo, painted screens, tatami mats, low tables and even a babbling brook. Sukiyaki is a feature, although there are more interesting things on the menu. Try the tableside-cooked teppenyaki dinner or fresh and tasty sushi.

### ☺ China Gate • ΔΔΔ $$ Ø

□ 516 Seventh Ave. (Weller); (206) 624-1730. Chinese; full bar service. Weekdays 11 a.m. to 2 a.m., weekends 10 to 2. Major credit cards. □ This wonderfully overdone place is a visual feast, with its red and green tile roof, dragon-entwined columns and temple-like interior. The menu leans toward spicy Mandarin, featuring duck hot pot, fried chicken with curry sauce and champagne pork chops or prawns. Local critics rave about the dim sum.

### House of Hong • ΔΔ $$

□ 409 Eighth Ave. (Jackson); (206) 622-7997. Chinese; full bar service. Monday-Thursday 11 to 10, Friday 11 to midnight, Saturday 10:30 to midnight. Major credit cards. □ More subdued than China Gate in both dècor and menu, this quietly attractive restaurant specializes in milder Cantonese dishes. Its daily dim sum lunch is popular with locals, with more than three-score items available. For dinner, steamed fish dishes are excellent, as are prawns in lobster sauce.

### Ichiban • Δ $$

□ 601 Main Street (Sixth); (206) 623-8868. Japanese; wine and beer. Lunch Monday-Friday 11:30 to 2 and Saturday noon to 2, dinner Monday-Saturday 5 to 8:15, closed Sunday and Wednesday. MC/VISA. □ Not fancy but inexpensive and generally tasty, this is a simple Naugahyde booth cafè. It's handy for a noodle soup lunch break during an International District exploration.

### ☺ Koto Sushi Bar and Dining Room • ΔΔΔ $$

□ 520 Main (in the Imperial House, near Sixth); (206) 622-1217. Japanese; wine and beer. Lunch and dinner daily. MC/VISA, AMEX. □ This exceptionally attractive place is dressed in Japanese screens and light woods, with black lacquer and gold accents. The sushi bar offers an imposing variety of fresh, carefully crafted morsels. The dinner menu is extensive, covering the usual range of teriyakis, domburis, teppenyakis and tempuras.

### Pho Hoa • Δ $

□ 618 Weller; (206) 624-7189. Vietnamese; wine and beer. Daily 9 to 9. No credit cards. □ This Formica cafè is tiny but neat and it serves tasty food at remarkable prices. Try the grilled chicken and spring rolls; grilled roast pork chop and shredded roast pork rice; or vermicelli with marinated prawns and grilled pork slices—each for under $5.

### ☺ Sea Garden Restaurant • ΔΔΔ $$

□ 509 Seventh Avenue (King); (206) 623-2100. Chinese; full bar service. Monday-Thursday 11 to 2 a.m., Friday-Saturday 11 to 3 a.m., Sunday 11 to 1 *a.m. MC/VISA.* ☐ Local critics call this one of Seattle's best Chinese restaurants; a meal there put us in contented agreement. You're greeted on entry by a tank stuffed with squirming crabs who are obviously less excited about dinner than you. The dècor is neat and prim, almost utilitarian, done in a soft mauve. The focus is on seafood and vegetables, Cantonese style—which means perfectly fresh and lightly cooked.

## Lake Union and Beyond

### ☺ *Chandler's Crabhouse* ● ∆∆∆ $$ Ø

☐ *901 Fairview Ave. (in Chandler's Cove on Lake Union) (206) 223-2722. American, mostly seafood; full bar service. Lunch weekdays 11:30 to 2, Saturday 11:30 to 3 and Sunday 10:30 to 3; dinner Sunday-Thursday 5 to 10, Friday-Saturday 5 to 11. Major credit cards.* ☐ The look is East Coast fishhaus, with a high domed ceiling and aquatic mural, although there's a Northwestern slant to the menu. Picture windows provide fine views of Lake Union. If the huge menu leaves you hungry with indecision, here are some suggestions: smoked seafood sampler, prosciutto-wrapped scallops in a Szechuan sauce, sautèed crab legs with garlic and lemon; or a salmon mixed grill with the fish prepared in a variety of ways. Start with an excellent hot Dungeness crab dip with corn tortillas.

### *Chinook's* ● ∆∆∆ $$

☐ *At Fishermen's Terminal (900 W. Nickerson St.); (206) 283-4665. Lunch and dinner weekdays from 11 a.m.; breakfast, lunch and dinner weekends from 7:30 a.m. Major credit cards.* ☐ This cavernous cafè, looking more like a cargo shed than a restaurant, offers great views of Fishermen's Terminal, plus an extensive selection of seafood at modest prices. There are *nouveau* touches to some of the dishes, although the simply cooked just-off-the-boat fish are best. For the kids, convince them that Chinook's salmon burgers are more interesting and healthier than a Big Mac and fries. Speaking of fries, nearby ☺ **Little Chinook** serves the best fish and chips in town; order the halibut version. It's open weekdays from 8 and weekends from 11; with inside and outside tables.

### ☺ *Cucina! Cucina!* ● ∆∆ $$ Ø

☐ *901 Fairview Ave. (near Chander's Crabhouse); (206) 447-2782. Italian; full bar service. Lunch weekdays 11 to 4; dinner Monday-Thursday 4 to 11, Friday-Saturday 4 to midnight and Sunday 4 to 10. Major credit cards.* ☐ One of several exclamatory Cucinas in the area, this is a busy, affably noisy place dishing up good-sized portions of things Italian. High ceilings help absorb the clamor and picture windows offer views of Lake Union and Chandler's Cove marina. Among its more interesting offerings are prawns sautèed with garlic, lemon, white wine and butter; and chicken breast done with prosciutto, cheese and dijon mustard. There are crayons each table for testing your artistic skills on the white paper table covers. Diners can adjourn outside in warm weather.

### *Hiram's at the Locks* ● ∆∆ $$$

☐ *5300 34th Ave. NW (near Hiram Chittenden Locks); (206) 784-1733. American; full bar service. Lunch Monday-Saturday 11 to 3, Sunday brunch 9 to 2:30, dinner Monday-Saturday 4 to 11 and Sunday 4:30 to 9:30. MC/VISA.* ☐ Instead of joining the plebeians watching the passage of boats down on the locks, you can get a window seat in the Hiram's and watch in comfort.

Be not misled by the corrugated exterior; the dining room is rather stylish—with prices to match. Views of the locks are impressive at night when they're floodlighted, The mostly steak and seafood menu has a Northwest accent.

☺ **Ray's Boathouse** ● ∆∆∆ $$$ Ø

⌂ *6049 Seaview Ave. NW (north of downtown, on Shilshole Bay); (206) 789-3770. American, mostly seafood; full bar service. Lunch weekdays 11:30 to 2, dinner Monday-Thursday 5:30 to 9 and Friday Saturday 5 to 10. Major credit cards.* ⌂ Visitors who take the trouble to drive north to Shilshole Bay will find sterling views, faultlessly fresh seafood and lots of locals in this attractive restaurant. The vista is exemplary, across Puget Sound to the Olympics—a great locale for sunsetting. When you've finished with the view, scan the menu for smoked black cod, rockfish in white wine, perfectly cooked scallops or salmon prepared in a variety of ways.

☺ **Salty's on Alki Point** ● ∆∆ $$$

⌂ *1936 Harbor Ave, SW; (206) 937-1600. American, mostly seafood; full bar service. Lunch weekdays from 11:30, dinner nightly. Major credit cards.* ⌂ Our little ☺ is for the view, not the food. The seafood-focused fare is okay but not exceptional. The view, however, is splendid: a great panorama of the Seattle skyline, Elliott Bay and Puget Sound. It's a popular restaurant, so make reservations.

## WHERE TO SLEEP
### Downtown and the waterfront

☺ **Alexis Hotel** ● ⌒⌒⌒ $$$$$ Ø

⌂ *1007 First Ave. (Madison), Seattle, WA 98104; (800) 426-7033 or (206) 624-4844. Couples $185 to $340, singles $170 to $325, kitchen units $165 to $235, suites $235 to $340. Rates include continental breakfast. Major credit cards.* ⌂ Opulent boutique hotel fashioned from a turn-of-the-century brick commercial building. The 54 elegantly furnished rooms have TV movies, phones, mini-bars, some refrigerators. Tennis court and health club privileges. Attractive **Bookstore** pub and **Volcano Cafè** have food service from 6:30 a.m. to 10:30 p.m. **Painted Table** restaurant listed above. Hotel has a no-tipping policy.

**Days Inn Town Center** ● ⌒⌒ $$$$ Ø

⌂ *2205 Seventh Ave. (Blanchard), Seattle, WA 98121; (800) 225-7169 or (206) 448-3434. Couples $79 to $85, singles $76 to $80. Major credit cards.* ⌂ A 90-unit inn; attractively furnished rooms with TV and phones. **Green House Cafè & Bar** serves American fare; 6:30 a.m. to 10 p.m.; dinners $8 to $13; full bar service.

☺ **The Edgewater** ● ⌒⌒⌒ $$$$$ Ø

⌂ *2411 Alaskan Way (Pier 67), Seattle, WA 98121; (800) 624-0670 or (206) 728-7000. Couples and singles $109 to $200, suites $200 to $300. Rates include continental breakfast. Major credit cards.* ⌂ Seattle's only waterfront hotel, built on a pier overlooking Elliott Bay. The recently remodeled inn has an appealing Western-nautical look; 237 units with TV movies and room phones; most with mini-bars and/or room refrigerators, microwaves. Pool, spa, sauna, heath club available; shuttle service to downtown Seattle. Bayview **Ernie's Grill** serves American fare, mostly seafood; dinners $12 to $25; 6:30 a.m. to 10 p.m. full bar service.

### Four Seasons Olympic Hotel ● ⌂⌂⌂ $$$$$ ∅

⌂ *411 University St., Seattle, WA 98101; (800) 821-8106 or (206) 621-1700. Couples $130 to $290, singles $130 to $260. Major credit cards.* ⌂ Beautifully restored Italian Renaissance hotel with opulent décor and full resort facilities; 450 rooms with TV movies, mini-bars and other amenities; some refrigerators. Indoor pool, saunas, spas, exercise room, massages. **Georgian Room** is one of the city's most accomplished restaurants, serving Northwest cuisine; other restaurants and cafeteria serve from 6 a.m. to 10 p.m.; full bar service.

### Holiday Inn Crowne Plaza ● ⌂⌂ $$$$$ ● ∅

⌂ *1113 Sixth Ave. (Seneca), Seattle, WA 98101-3058; (800) 858-0511 within Washington and (800) 521-2762 elsewhere; (206) 464-1980. Couples $160 to $180, singles $140 to $160, suites $250 to $500. Major credit cards.* ⌂ Stylish 415-room high-rise hotel with TV movies, phones; spa, sauna, exercise room and gift shop. **Seneca Square Cafe** serves 6:30 a.m. to 11 p.m.; dinners $15 to $20; full bar service.

### Hotel Seattle ● ⌂⌂ $$$$ ∅

⌂ *315 Seneca St. (between Third and Fourth), Seattle, WA 98101; (800) 426-2439 or (206) 623-5110. Couples $72 to $76, singles $66 to $70, suites $80 to $98. Major credit cards.* ⌂ An 81-room hotel with TV, room phones and some refrigerators. **Bernard's on Seneca** serves American-German fare; weekdays 6 a.m. to 8 p.m., Saturday 7 to noon; dinners about $20; full bar service.

### Inn at the Market ● ⌂⌂⌂ $$$$$ ∅

⌂ *86 Pine St., Seattle, WA 98101; (800) 446-4484 or (206) 443-3600. Couples $105 to $165, singles from $95, suites from $155. Major credit cards.* ⌂ Splendid small French country hotel with an inner courtyard, near Pike Place Market; 79 units with TV movies, phones, other amenities; many view rooms. Laundry, rooftop deck. **Campagne** restaurant listed above.

### Mayflower Park Hotel ● ⌂⌂⌂ $$$$$ ∅

⌂ *405 Olive Way (Fourth Avenue), Seattle, WA 98101; (800) 426-5100 or (206) 623-8700. Couples $120 to $150, singles $110 to $140. Suites $160 to $140. Major credit cards.* ⌂ Elegant 173-room hotel with attractive European décor; TV movies, room phones, some refrigerators. Lobby access to Westlake Center shops. **Clippers** restaurant serves Northwest cuisine; 6:30 a.m. to 10:30 p.m.; dinners $13 to $20; full bar service. Less formal **Olivers Lounge** has lunch and cocktails, open 11:30 a.m. to 1:30 a.m.

### Pacific Plaza Hotel ● ⌂⌂ $$$$ ∅

⌂ *400 Spring St. (Fourth), Seattle, WA 98104; (800) 426-1165 or (206) 623-2059. Couples and singles $74 to $94. Rates include continental breakfast. Major credit cards.* ⌂ Well-kept older hotel; 160 rooms with TV movies and phones. **Red Robin** and **Pizza Brava** serve 10:30 a.m. to 10 p.m.; meals $4 to $15; full bar service in Red Robin.

### Seattle Hilton ● ⌂⌂⌂ $$$$$ ⌂ ∅

⌂ *P.O. Box 1927 (Sixth at University), Seattle, WA 98101; (800) 542-7700 or (206) 624-0500. Couples $144 to $194, singles $129 to $179, suites $295 to $395. Major credit cards.* ⌂ Nicely appointed 237-room hotel with TV movies and room phones; tennis courts. **McCaulay's** serves American fare, 6 a.m. to 10 p.m.; American fare; dinners $10 to $20; full bar service.

### ☺ *Sheraton Seattle* • ⌂⌂⌂ $$$$$ ∅

⎚ *Sixth Avenue at Pike Street, Seattle, WA 98101; (800) 325-3535. Couples and singles $114 to $185, suites $250 to $575. Major credit cards.* ⎚ Full service high-rise hotel attired with an impressive collection of contemporary Northwest art; 880 rooms with TV movies, phones, mini-bars or refrigerators and other amenities; most with imposing views. Tower Rooms include continental breakfast, afternoon tea and snacks and soft drinks. Indoor pool, sauna, spa, health club. Three **restaurants** and two lounges; food service from 6 a.m. to midnight. **Fullers Restaurant** listed above.

### *Sixth Avenue Inn* • ⌂⌂ $$$ ∅

⎚ *2000 Sixth Ave. (Virginia Street), Seattle, WA 98121; (800) 648-6440 or (206) 441-8300. Couples $62 to $98, singles $59 to $88, suites $95 to $130. Major credit cards.* ⎚ A 166-unit hotel across from the Westin; TV movies and room phones. **Sixth Avenue Bar & Grill** serves American fare; 7 a.m. to 10 p.m.; dinners $7.50 to $15; full bar service; sports lounge.

### *Stouffer Madison Hotel* • ⌂⌂⌂ $$$$$ ∅

⎚ *515 Madison St., Seattle, WA 98101; (800) 468-3571 or (206) 583-0300. Couples $174 to $134, singles $154 to $214. Major credit cards.* ⎚ Stylish high-rise hotel with 554 units; TV movies, phones, mini-bars and other amenities; many two-room units; most rooms with imposing views. Rooftop fitness center, indoor pool. **Dining room** and coffee shop serve from 6 a.m. to 11 p.m.; American-continental; dinners $10 to $16; full bar service.

### *WestCoast Camlin Hotel* • ⌂⌂ $$$$ ∅

⎚ *1619 Ninth Ave. (Pine), Seattle, WA 98101; (800) 426-0670 or (206) 682-0100. Couples $90 to $101, singles $80 to $91, suites $175. Major credit cards.* ⎚ Nicely appointed older 140-room hotel with TV movies, room phones; pool. The rooftop **Cloud Room** serves Northwest and continental fare; 7 a.m. to 10:30; smoke-free dining room; full bar service; city views.

### *WestCoast Roosevelt Hotel* • ⌂⌂ $$$$$ ∅

⎚ *1531 Seventh Ave. (Pine), Seattle, WA 98101; (800) 426-0670 or (206) 621-1200. Couples $150 to $170, singles $125 to $150, suites $160 to $170. Rates include continental breakfast. Major credit cards.* ⎚ Handsome older hotel completely renovated in 1993; TV movies, room phones, refrigerators available. Attractive lobby with piano entertainment, workout room. **Von's Grand City Café** serves Northwest cuisine; 6:30 a.m. to 10 p.m.; dinners$14 to $22; full bar service.

### *Westin Hotel, Seattle* • ⌂⌂⌂ $$$$$ ∅

⎚ *1900 Fifth Ave., Seattle, WA 98101; (800) 228-3000 or (206) 728-1000. Couples $180 to $220, singles $155 to $195. Major credit cards.* ⎚ Dramatic landmark hotel with twin silo towers; 865 units with TV movies, phones, mini-bars and other room amenities. Indoor pool, saunas, spa, fitness center. **Palm Court** is a glass pavilion dining room serving Northwest cuisine; other restaurants and coffee shop serve from 6:30 a.m. to 11 p.m.; dinners $8 to $20; full bar service.

## Seattle north

### *Aurora Seafair Inn* • ⌂⌂ $$ ∅

⎚ *9100 Aurora Ave. N., Seattle, WA 98103; (206) 522-3754. Couples and kitchenette units $52 to $56, singles $48 to $52. Major credit cards.* ⎚ A 42-unit motel with TV movies, phones, refrigerators, microwaves; coin laundry.

### Best Western Evergreen Motor Inn • △△△ $$$ ∅
◻ 13700 Aurora Ave. N., Seattle, WA 98133; (800) 528-1234 or (206) 361-3700. Couples $72, singles $64. Major credit cards. ◻ Very attractive 72-unit inn with TV movies, phones, rental VCRs; some efficiency units. Sauna, spa, coin laundry. **Restaurant** opposite.

### Rodeside Lodge • △△ $$ ∅
◻ 12501 Aurora Ave. N. (at 125th), Seattle, WA 98133; (800) 227-7771 or (206) 364-7771. Couples $45 to $65, singles $39 to $60, suites $55 to $75. Major credit cards. ◻ An 87-unit motel with TV movies, room phones; room refrigerators available, pool, spa and sauna. **Rodeside Broiler** serves American-Northwest fare; Monday-Saturday 7 to 10 and Sunday 7 to 2; dinners $6 to $12; full bar service.

### University Motel • △△
◻ 4731 12th Ave. NE (near NE 47th), Seattle, WA 98105. Kitchenettes $55 to $58, singles $49. Major credit cards. ◻ A 21-unit apartment hotel; all have full kitchens, TV and room phones; coin laundry.

## Seattle south (including Sea-Tac)

### Comfort Inn at Sea-Tac • △△△ $$$ ∅
◻ 19333 Pacific Hwy. S., Seattle, WA 98188; (800) 826-7875 or (206) 878-1100. Couples $65 to $80, singles $65 to $75, suites $135 to $150. Rates include continental breakfast. Major credit cards. ◻ A 119-unit inn with TV movies, room phones; spa; 24-hour airport transportation.

### Econo Lodge Seattle Airport • △△ $$$ ∅
◻ 13910 Pacific Hwy. S. (S. 139th), Seattle, WA 98168; (800) 444-6661 or (206) 244-0810. Couples $55 to $65, singles $50 to $60, suites $80. Rates include continental breakfast. Major credit cards. ◻ A 65-unit motel with TV movies, room phones, refrigerators; weight room. **Country Vittles** restaurant adjacent; 7 a.m. to 9 p.m.; dinners $6 to $10; no alcohol.

### Hampton Inn Seattle Airport • △△△ $$$$ ∅
◻ 19445 International Blvd., Seattle, WA 98188; (800) 426-7866. Couples $75 to $77, singles $65 to $67. Major credit cards. ◻ A 130-unit inn with TV movies and room phones; free airport transportation.

### Holiday Inn Sea-Tac • △△△ $$$$$ ∅
◻ 17338 Pacific Hwy. S. (near 170th), Seattle, WA 98188; (800) HOLIDAY or (206) 248-1000. Couples $106 to $126, singles $96 to $116. Continental breakfast in business class level. Major credit cards. ◻ A 260-unit hotel with TV movies, phones; Pool, spa, gift shop, airport transportation. **Top of the Inn** revolving rooftop restaurant serves 7 a.m. to 2 and 5:30 to 10; dinners $16 to $30; full bar service.

### Jet Motel Park 'N Fly • △ $$ ∅
◻ 17300 Pacific Hwy. S. (between 170th and 176th), Seattle, WA 98188; (800) 233-1501 or (206) 244-6255. Couples $43 to $47, singles $40 to $43. Major credit cards. ◻ A 51-unit motel with TV, room phones and a pool. **Denny's Restaurant** nearby.

### Red Lion Hotel Seattle Airport • △△△ $$$$$ ∅
◻ 18740 Pacific Hwy. S. (188th), Seattle, WA 98188; (800) 547-8010 or (206) 246-8600. Couples and singles $125 to $155, suites $295 to $495. Major credit cards. ◻ Attractively appointed hotel within view of the airport;

850 rooms with TV movies, phones; gift shop and spa. Three **restaurants** serve from 6 a.m. to 11 p.m.; dinners $5 to $20; full bar service.

**Seattle Airport Hilton** ● ⌂⌂ $$$$$ Ø

☐ *17620 Pacific Hwy S. (176th), Seattle, WA 98188; (800) HILTONS or (206) 244-4800. Couples and singles $109 to $129, suites $250 to $350. Major credit cards.* ☐ Very attractive courtyard style hotel; 173 units with TV movies, phones. Courtyard pool, spa, sauna and exercise room; gift shop and coin laundry. **Great American Grill** serves 6 a.m. to 11 p.m.; dinners $9 to $20; full bar service.

**Travelodge Seattle Airport** ● ⌂⌂ $$$ Ø

☐ *2900 S. 192nd St. (International Boulevard), Seattle, WA 98188; (800) 578-7878 or (206) 241-9292. Couples $50 to $80, singles $40 to $50. Major credit cards.* ☐ A 104-unit motel with TV movies, room phones, refrigerators and in-room coffee; sauna and coin laundry.

**Wyndham Garden Hotel** ● ⌂⌂ $$$$ Ø

☐ *18118 Pacific Hwy. S., Seattle, WA 98188; (800) WYNDHAM or (206) 244-6666. Couples $99 to $119, singles $89 to $109, suites $129. Major credit cards.* ☐ Well-kept hotel at airport entrance; 204 rooms with TV movies, phones, work areas; pool, sauna, spa and coin laundry. **Garden Cafe** serves 6:30 a.m. to 2 p.m. and 5 to 10; dinners $7 to $19; full bar service.

## Bed & breakfast inns

☺ **Chelsea Station Bed & Breakfast Inn** ● ⌂⌂ $$$$ Ø

☐ *4915 Linden Ave. N. (N. 150th), Seattle, WA 98103; (206) 547-6077. Couples $69 to $104, singles $64 to $99. Six units with private baths; full breakfast. Major credit cards.* ☐ Restored 1920 brick colonial style home across from Woodland Park and Zoo; short walk to Green Lake Park. Rooms furnished with American antiques. Guest kitchen and guest telephones are available.

**Gaslight Inn** ● ⌂⌂ $$$ Ø

☐ *1727 15th Ave. (Capitol Hill area), Seattle, WA 98122; (206) 325-3654. Couples and singles $62 to $98. Nine rooms; some private and some share baths; continental breakfast. MC/VISA, AMEX.* ☐ Restored turn-of-the-century home; attractive, comfortable rooms furnished with American antiques and Northwest Indian art; some with fireplaces, decks and/or views. Heated seasonal pool.

**Queen Anne Hill Bed & Breakfast** ● ⌂⌂ $$$ Ø

☐ *1835 Seventh Ave. W. (Howe Street), Seattle, WA 98119; (206) 284-9779. Couples and singles $55 to $75. Five units; two with private baths; continental breakfast. MC/VISA.* ☐ Turn-of-the-century shingle-sided home on Queen Anne Hill with views of Elliott Bay and the Olympics. Rooms furnished with American antiques; decorated with art and collectibles.

**Salisbury House** ● ⌂⌂ $$$$ Ø

☐ *750 Sixteenth Ave. E. (Aloha Street), Seattle, WA 98112; (206) 328-8682. Couples $70 to $95, singles $60 to $85. Four units with private baths; full breakfast. Major credit cards.* ☐ Early 20th century Victorian on landscaped grounds, near the University of Washington. Rooms furnished with American and English country antiques and reproductions. Sun porch, library, self-service refrigerator.

☺ **The Shafer-Baillie Mansion** ● △△△ **$$$** Ø

☐ 907 14th Ave. E. (at Aloha), Seattle, WA 98112; (206) 329-4654. Couples and singles $65 to $125. Thirteen units; eleven with private baths; continental breakfast. MC/VISA, AMEX. ☐ Large English manor mansion on Seattle's "Millionaires' Row" in the Capital Hill area. Elegant 15,000-square foot home furnished with antiques, linen padded walls, chandeliers and sconces; all rooms have TVs and refrigerators

☺ *Tugboat Challenger* ● △△ **$$$$** Ø

☐ *809 Fairview Place N., Seattle, WA 98109; (206) 340-1201. Couples $75 to $135, singles $55 to $135. Eleven units; shared and private baths; some room TVs and phones; full breakfast. Major credit cards.* ☐ *Nautically styled units built into a trawler, yacht and vintage tugboat on Lake Union.*

**Villa Heidelberg** ● △△ **$$$** Ø

☐ *4845 45th Ave. W. (Erskine Way), Seattle, WA 98116; (206) 938-3658. Couples $55 to $85, singles $45 to $75. Four rooms with shared baths; full breakfast. MC/VISA, AMEX.* ☐ A 1909 Craftsman clinkerbrick home with a covered wrap-around porch, gardens, fish pond and decks. Rooms furnished with a mix of antique and modern.

**Williams House Bed & Breakfast** ● △△△ **$$$$** Ø

☐ *1505 Fourth Ave. N (near Galer), Seattle, WA 98109; (800) 880-0810 or (206) 285-0810. Couples $85 to $105, singles $70 to $90. Five units; room phones available; private or semi-private baths; full breakfast. Major credit cards.* ☐ Turn-of-the-century Craftsman home atop Queen Ann Hill, with original gas light fixtures converted to electricity, ornate wood paneling; furnished with American antiques. In a quiet neighborhood near downtown.

## Where to camp

We found no RV parks within Seattle; these are in nearby communities.

**Aqua Barn RV Park** ● *15227 SE Renton Maple Valley Rd., Renton, WA 98058; (206) 255-4618. RV and tent sites; $12.50 to $21.50. Reservations accepted; MC/VISA.* ☐ Showers, coin laundry, mini-mart; small indoor pool, sauna, spa, fishing. From I-405, take northbound exit 4A or southbound 4E and go east 3.5 miles on State Route 169.

**Saltwater State Park** ● *Two miles south of Des Moines on Puget Sound; (206) 764-4128. RV and tent sites; $10. No reservations or credit cards.* ☐ Sites near the water with flush and pit potties and showers; no hookups. Boat dock, scuba diving, nature trails, mini-mart.

**Seattle South KOA** ● *5801 S. 212th, Kent, WA 98032; (206) 872-8652. RV and tent sites; $19 to $23.50. Reservations accepted; MC/VISA.* ☐ Some pull-throughs; showers, coin laundry, mini-mart, car rentals. Clubhouse, pool, playground, game room. Take I-5 exit 152 or Highway 167 exit to 212th Street, 1.25 miles west.

**Trailer Inns, Inc.** ● *15531 SE 37th, Bellevue, WA 98006; (206) 747-9181. RV sites; $19.50 to $23.50. Reservations accepted; MC/VISA.* ☐ Showers, coin laundry, indoor pool, sauna, spa, rec room and playground. Take I-90 exit just under a mile on a service road.

**Vasa Park** ● *3650 W. Lake Sammamish Rd. SE, Bellevue, WA 98008; (206) 746-3260. RV and tent sites; $12. Reservations accepted.* ☐ On Lake Sammamish with showers, swimming, fishing, boat ramp and kids' playground. One mile north of I-90 from exit 13.

# TRIP PLANNER

**WHEN TO GO** ● Best of all, you'll love the fall in northern Puget Sound. Summer is fine, although tourists love Whidbey and the San Juan Islands to death; ferries, lodgings and restaurants are crowded. If you do plan a summer visit, make lodging or camping reservations as far in advance as possible, particularly for the San Juan Islands.

**WHAT TO SEE** ● Historic Langley and Coupeville and Ebey Island National Historic Preserve on Whidbey Island; downtown Anacortes' "people murals," the Whale Museum in Friday Harbor; San Juan Island National Historic Park; International Peace Arch at Blaine; Whatcom County Historical Museum and Fairhaven historical district in Bellingham; old La Conner and its Skagit County Historical Museum; Everett Museum and "millionaires' row" in Everett.

**WHAT TO DO** ● Take a sea kayak tour in the San Juan Islands; hike the trails to enjoy the vistas at Deception Pass State Park; drive or hike to the top of Mount Constitution at Moran State Park on Orcas Island; have lunch with a view at Rosario Resort on Orcas Island; drive scenic routes in Anacortes' Washington Park and Chuckanut Drive below Bellingham; take a cruise on Everett's *River Queen;* tour the huge Boeing assembly plant.

## Useful contacts

**Anacortes Chamber of Commerce,** 819 Commercial Ave., Anacortes, WA 98221; (206) 293-3832.

**Bellingham/Whatcom County Visitor's and Convention Bureau,** 904 Potter St., Bellingham, WA 98226; (800) 487-2032 or (206) 671-3990.

**Central Whidbey Chamber of Commerce,** P.O. Box 152, Coupeville, WA 98239; (206) 678-5434.

**Everett/Snohomish County Convention & Visitor Bureau,** P.O. Box 1086 (1710 Marine View Dr.), Everett, WA 98206; (206) 252-5181.

**Greater Oak Harbor Chamber of Commerce,** P.O. Box 883, Oak Harbor, WA 98227; (206) 875-3535.

**La Conner Chamber of Commerce,** P.O. Box 1610, La Conner, WA 98257; (206) 466-4778.

**Langley Chamber of Commerce,** P.O. Box 403, Langley, WA 98260; (206) 221-6765.

**Orcas Island Chamber of Commerce,** P.O. Box 252, Eastsound, WA 98245; (206) 376-2273.

**San Juan Island National Historic Park,** P.O. Box 429, Friday Harbor, WA 98250; (206) 378-2240.

**San Juan Island Chamber of Commerce,** P.O. Box 98, Friday Harbor, WA 98250; (206) 378-5240.

## Northern Puget Sound radio stations

KRWM, 106.9-FM, Seattle—soft hits, easy listening
KPLU, 88.5-FM, Seattle-Tacoma—PBS
CBC, 92.3-FM, Vancouver B.C.—music, news and talk
KISM, 92.9-FM, Bellingham—rock
KMPS, 94.1-FM, Seattle—country
K-LITE, 95.7-FM, Seattle—soft hits (70s, 80s, 90s)
KAFE, 104.3-FM, Bellingham—light rock, top 40
CJJR, 93.7-FM, Vancouver—country.
KPLU, 88.5 and 91.3-FM, Tacoma-Seattle—NPR with jazz, news and talk
CKLG, 730-AM, Vancouver—mostly news and talk
KIXI, 880-AM, Seattle—swing era and other pops oldies
CKVI, 900-AM, Victoria—pops and rock oldies
KLKI, 340-AM, Anacortes—top 40, news and sports

## Chapter five

# *PUGET SOUND NORTH*
### Whidbey and the San Juans: islands in the sun

---

*UNIQUE IS A WORD* that good writers rarely use, for it means the only one of its kind. (Those who write ad copy and chamber of commerce brochures apparently have never looked it up in a dictionary.) For travelers seeking discoveries, the northern Puget Sound area is unique. Nowhere else in the world is there a more fascinating meeting of land and sea.

Here, clumps of velvety green have drifted from the shore and scattered over water, forming emeralds on a base of sapphire blue. Other states and nations have inland waterways, wooded shorelines and offshore islands. None have anything to compare with the hundreds of isles sheltered by the Olympic Peninsula. Thus protected, Whidbey Island and the San Juans reside in a rather calm sea. Surrounded by water yet linked by ferries or bridges, the larger islands are thinly populated but easy to reach. They bask in a mini-rainshadow of the Olympic Mountains and Vancouver Island, receiving only half the rainfall of neighboring Seattle.

Those seeking absolute escape can find it here, providing they have a boat. There are 428 to 743 islands in the San Juan archipelago, depending on the tides. Only 172 have names and only four of these are served by ferries. Where else in the world can one put ashore on an unnamed, uninhabited island and still see the lights of civilization?

The northern Puget Sound is one of the best reasons for travelers to come to the Northwest, for it does make Washington unique. Captain George Vancouver, one of the first to thoroughly explore the area, agreed with us, commenting in his ship's log: "There is no country in the World that possesses waters equal to these."

Glaciers buried Washington 15 million years ago and shaped the future islands by carving valleys and scouring off mountain tops. Then they raised the level of the ocean as they melted, leaving hundreds of hillocks and high plateaus exposed. Thus, the terrain of most of these islands is lumpy, but with few high promontories.

In a sense, the state's history began in the San Juans. Earliest navigators along the Pacific Coast were intrigued by this great inland sea, thought to be the fabled Inside Passage. They probed its coastal inlets, noted its abundant natural wealth and thus spurred the interest of the outside world. Greek navigator Juan de Fuca, sailing under a Spanish flag, may have sighted this passageway as early as 1592. There is no evidence that he entered it. Others came and saw, but did not conquer the inland waters: Juan Pèrez and Bruno Heceta in 1774 and peripatetic James Cook in 1778.

Finally, in 1788, Captain James Meares found the major passageway between Vancouver Island and the mainland, and named it in honor of de Fuca. Spain's Francisco Eliza followed Meares in 1791, charted the San Juan Islands and gave them their Spanish names. The next year, Captain Vancouver began a detailed exploration of northern Puget Sound. He named practically everything in sight for his peers: the sound for Peter Puget, mountains for George Baker and Peter Regnier (Rainier), and a big island for Joseph Whidbey. The largest island, Vancouver, he saved for himself.

### A mystery from history

There is an historic mystery here. Although Whidbey, the skipper of Vancouver's flagship *HMS Discovery,* was apparently the first outsider to explore that island, he found rotting fragments of another ship. Oxen, definitely not indigenous, were roaming wild here. Indians he encountered could offer no explanation.

Fur traders hurried to this rich inland sea and employed the natives to trap its wildlife. When the fur was gone, settlers and lumbermen came to push these original residents off their land. Although the first pioneers came by land, it was stories of the navigators that drew them toward the Puget Sound. The area figured prominently in the lengthy boundary dispute between Great Britain and the United States. Although they finally agreed on the 49th parallel, with Great Britain keeping Vancouver Island, boundaries were vague through the northern Puget Sound. A war nearly erupted over possession of the San Juan Islands, stemming from a jurisdictional dispute over the shooting of a potato-loving pig. (See box on page 196.)

In another boundary fluke, the tiny nub of Point Roberts below Vancouver, which extends south of the 49th parallel, became part of the United States. It remains an American enclave—an isolated scrap of Washington's Whatcom County.

We will begin our exploration of Puget north with a short ferry ride to from Mukilteo to Whidbey Island. After prowling its protracted countryside (it's the longest island in America), we'll cross the bridge at Deception Pass State Park to small Fidalgo Island and Anacortes, and then go island-hopping in the San Juans. To complete our loop, we'll catch a ferry to Canada, visit the American nub of Point Roberts, and then travel the dry land side of the sound, back to Everett and Mukilteo.

Whidbey, adjacent Camano and six smaller islands, make up Island

County. It shares geographic distinctions with neighboring San Juan. They are the state's only counties comprised entirely of islands, and they're its two smallest. Island County is less than 250 square miles; the collective San Juans a mere 57. Despite its bridge link to Whidbey, Fidalgo Island is part of large Skagit (*SKA-jit*) County, which stretches eastward into the Cascades.

After droning northward from Seattle on I-5, take exit 182 onto State Highway 525 and head northwest. You'll swerve briefly north on old Highway 99, then shift to the left to stay with Route 525, following signs to **Mukilteo**. This old waterfront town, gathered around the ferry terminal, offers a few shops and boutiques, so you might want to arrive an hour or so before you catch the ferry. **Mukilteo State Park,** next to the Whidbey Island ferry terminal, offers picnicking, a beach and boat launch. **Mukilteo Lighthouse,** built in 1905 and still operating, is open to visitors Saturday and Sunday afternoons; (206) 355-2611. Coming in the future—perhaps by the time you arrive—is a **Mukilteo Maritime Museum** with ship models, photos and other exhibits on the ferries and the maritime history of Puget Sound; call (206) 353-4151.

Of the handful of restaurants in Mukilteo, one provides a fine view of Puget Sound:

### *Ivar's Mukilteo Landing* • ∆∆ **$$**

☐ *710 Front Street (next to the ferry dock), Mukilteo; (206) 742-6180. American; full bar service. Daily 7 a.m. to 11 p.m. MC/VISA, AMEX.* ☐ Watch the ferries come and go—and perhaps kill time while waiting to catch one—at this nautically decorated place next to water's edge. In summer, dine outside at the fishbar. The menu focuses on Northwest seafood, featuring fresh and smoked fish and shellfish, plus the usual array of fresh fish, chicken, steaks and chops. Among its specialties are halibut au gratin and several alder-barbecued selections, including seafood brochettes, salmon, chicken, prawns and prime rib.

# WHIDBEY ISLAND

Whidbey-Fidalgo are linked to the mainland at Anacortes. However the southern end, vulnerable to the spreading population mass of Seattle-Everett, is served only by ferryboat. Thus it remains for the most part a rather bucolic enclave on the edge of suburbia, with more woodlands and pasturelands than subdivisions. It is, among other things, a serious Loganberry producing area. Other than Anacortes, the towns are small; some would call them quaint. Visions of coastal New England villages may come to mind as you explore old Langley, Coupeville and Oak Harbor. This rustic look is changing, however. In the last decade, Island County was the second fastest-growing area in the state.

Rainfall is only 17 inches a year here. Summer and fall days are generally sunny, so the islands are immensely popular with folks seeking sanctuary from the crowded—and wetter—mainland. Thus you will note, if you visit on a summer weekend, that they do a good job of bringing their crowds with them. Deception Pass is the most-visited state park in Washington, attracting as many as five million people a year. That rivals the crowds at Mount Rainier and Mount St. Helens.

From the Mukilteo ferry dock, a 20-minute crossing deposits you at Whidbey Island's **Clinton,** which is a ferry terminal but not really a town. You're still on Highway 525, which travels the island's middle, merging into

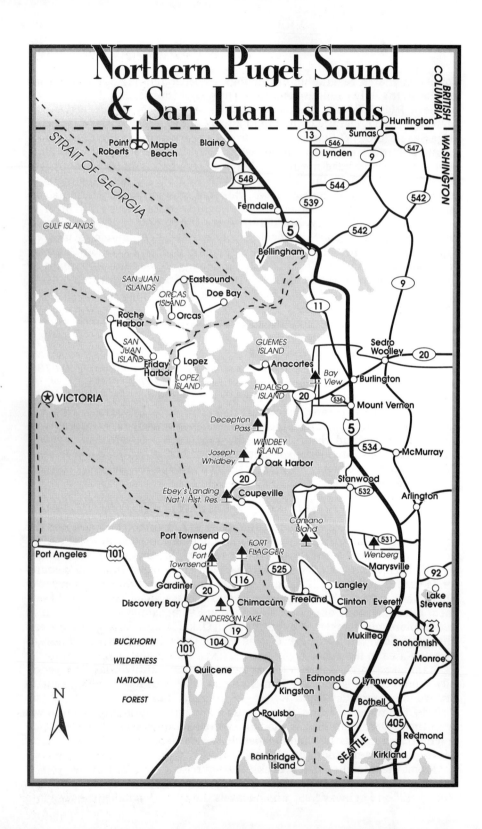

State Highway 20 below Coupeville. If you were to stay with Route 20, it would take you clear across the state, into Idaho.

Although this rather low-lying island is certainly green and pleasant, you'll be disappointed if you expect a lot of awesome seascapes as you drive. For the most part, the highway remains inland and much of the shoreline is privately owned. However, you can capture imposing visual moments at some of the island's many state parks; there are seven of them! South Whidbey, Fort Casey, Fort Ebey, Joseph Whidbey and Deception Pass offer the best aquatic views. Incidentally, the island's gentle contours are great for bike riding.

To catch a Whidbey water vista, turn left a few miles north of Clinton, opposite the road to Langley. Follow signs six miles to **Possession Beach Waterfront Park** at Possession Point. The park isn't that impressive; just a few picnic tables set in mowed weeds, and a boat launch. However, the view across the sound to Port Townsend and the Olympics is impressive.

Return to the highway and cross it, taking Langley Road to the most appealing little town on the island. En route, you'll encounter **Whidbey Island Vineyards,** with a tasting room open Friday 2 to 6 and weekends noon to 5; (206) 221-2040. Although most of its grapes come from eastern Washington, this small winery manages to grow a few cool-weather tolerant varieties, such as Madeleine Angevine and Madeleine Sylvaner.

# Langley

**Population: 300**                                          **Elevation: 50 feet**

☺ This tiny town is a perfect vision of a New England coastal community, with its wood-frame buildings perched above a small harbor. Boutiques, galleries and cafés are tucked behind lace-curtain windows. Not surprisingly, it's a lively little art colony, and works of local artists can be found in the shops.

Langley was established in 1890 by an enterprising teenager, German immigrant Jacob Anthes. He was too young to file a homestead claim, so he scraped up $100, bought 120 acres of land and started selling cordwood to passing steamers. When he hit 21, he did file a homestead, then formed a corporation and laid out the town. It was named for one of his partners, Seattle judge J.W. Langley. The town thrived until the extension of the Northern Pacific Railroad to Bellingham undercut Puget Sound shipping business. Langley was lulled to sleep and thus many of its old buildings were preserved for lack of progress.

The business district is tucked against the shore, overlooking Roosevelt Passage opposite Camano Island. Follow signs from the main highway, which will take you to the right onto Cascade Avenue (at a stop sign) and along the waterfront to First Street in the cozy downtown area. Weekend visitors crowd the shops along First Street and the courtyard shopping complex called **Langley Village.**

The **Chamber of Commerce**, open weekdays 9 to 4, is easier to find on foot than by car. It's on Second Street, a small alley parallel to First, behind **Café Langley** and the **Garden Path Inn.** Follow a brick path past the inn and you'll walk right into it. **Seawall Park** is a stretch of rocky beach below a boardwalk, a pleasing place for strolling and seaweed-scuffing. The small **South Whidbey Historical Museum** at 312 Second Street is housed in a restored bunkhouse built by Anthes for his wood-cutting crew. It displays an early-day kitchen, Native American objects, old time photos and the usual pioneer artifacts; open weekends only, 1 to 4 or by appointment; (206) 321-4696 or (206) 221-3519.

After you've finished browsing Langley, continue along the waterfront, hit a stop sign and turn inland to get back to the highway. **Freeland** is mostly a residential area with a small waterfront park, picnic area and boat launch. Just beyond, take Bush Point Cove Road west.

☺ It blends onto Smugglers Cove Road, which takes you to **South Whidbey State Park,** with a rugged shoreline, picnic area, nature trails and camping (listed below). Take time to stroll a 1.5 mile trail through a hushed old growth forest. From the park, stay on Smugglers Cove Road, enjoying some nice water views, and you'll wind up in **Greenbank** back on Highway 525. It's another residential community perched near the water.

Continue north on the highway and you'll shortly encounter **Whidbeys Greenbank Berry Farm and Winery,** open daily 10 to 5; (206) 678-7700. Only Loganberry wine is produced at this attractive red and white complex. However, it's owned by the parent company of Chateau Ste. Michelle, Washington's largest winemaker, so sips of both Loganberry and table wines are available in the tasting room. A self-guiding tour will take you past aging and storage tanks and the Loganberry wine bottling line.

# Coupeville

**Population: 1,400**                                    **Elevation: sea level**

☺ The next town in line, the oldest on the island, dates from 1853. It was founded by Captain Thomas Coupe, one of the first sailors to navigate Deception Pass. Coupeville was home to sea captains and farmers, who built blockhouses as protection from the Skagit Indians who resented their intrusion. Two of them still stand. Before entering the town proper, turn left to follow signs toward the **Keystone ferry terminal,** which offers service to Port Townsend. Continue past it to:

☺ *Ebey's Landing National Historic Reserve* and *Fort Casey State Park* • *P.O. Box 774, Coupeville, WA 98239; (206) 678-6084.* ☐ America's first and one of its largest national historic parks, Ebey's Landing is spread over 17,000 acres. It encompasses Fort Casey and Fort Ebey state parks and historic sections of Coupeville. Fort Casey was established in 1900, one of several coastal artillery bases designed to defend Puget Sound. Several of its wooden buildings have been restored; some are occupied by a bed and breakfast inn and by Seattle Pacific University.

**Fort Casey State Park** is at the southern part of the complex, with a campground (listed below), an interpretive center in Admiralty Head Lighthouse, and an extensive set of coastal artillery bunkers. Some have five-inch disappearing carriage guns still in place. The guys manning those weapons had a spectacular view—across Puget Sound to the Olympics and the Strait of Juan de Fuca. Other lures include nature trails, picnic areas and an underwater park.

Driving north from Fort Casey, you'll see more striking coastal views along Ebey's Landing. Follow Fort Ebey Road through farmlands to a small parking area, then take a one-mile trail to **Parego's Lake.** If you don't mind getting your tootsies wet, shed your shoes and cross the shallow lagoon to **Parego's Bluff** for more imposing vistas.

From Ebey's Landing, follow Engle Road north across the island; it enters Coupeville's side door and becomes Main Street. Start your exploration with a stop at the **Chamber of Commerce** at Five South Main; open weekdays 9 to 5. Pick up a walking map that directs you past 30 historic buildings, including those surviving blockhouses. Like Langley, Coupeville has several boutiques and galleries tucked into its ancient wood frame buildings.

Continue down Main to Front Street, turn left and follow it to the **Island County Historical Museum** at Alexander and Front, just past the wharf. This relatively new archive traces the shipping and agricultural history of the area, with the usual Native American and pioneer artifacts. It's open 11 to 5, April through October and noon to 5 the rest of the year.

A mile east of Coupeville, **Rhododendron State Park** offers an impressive bloom display in late spring to early summer. Just beyond, a sign will point you to the left to yet another state park:

☺ *Fort Ebey State Park* ● *Highway 20, Coupeville; (206) 678-4636.* ⊓ The park occupies a pretty wooded enclave just off the beach at Partridge Point. In these chilly coastal climes, it offers one of the few places with a good swimming hole. Lake Pondilla gets warm enough for dipping in summer and it's a popular bass fishing spot. During low tide, you can walk the beach five miles south to Ebey's landing and Fort Casey State Park. The gravelly shore often yields jade, quartz, agate and petrified wood. Like Fort Casey, the park has several bunkers with Puget Sound vistas, and a campground (listed below).

Yet another state park, **Joseph Whidbey,** can be reached by following West Beach Road north from Fort Ebey State Park. You'll be rewarded with nice aquatic views along the way. Whidbey is a day use facility, with picnic areas and a mile-long stretch of sandy beach. From here, follow Swantown Road south and then east to the island's largest town.

## Oak Harbor

**Population: 17,500**                                    **Elevation: 84 feet**

The only metropolitan area on the island, Oak Harbor is a bustling community supported primarily by the adjacent Whidbey Island Naval Air Station, and by the flow of tourists toward nearby Deception Pass State Park. First settlers came here in the 1850s, then a colony from Holland migrated from the Midwest to establish farms and tulip gardens.

Most of Oak Harbor's growth came after 1935, when completion of the Deception Pass Bridge linked it to Fidalgo Island and therefore to the mainland. The air station followed in 1941. Today, it's home to the Navy's tactical electronic warfare squadrons. The town's name, incidentally, comes from the Garry oaks, which are native to the Northwest and once grew in profusion here. Most have been cut down, and the city is protecting the few survivors. You'll find a some centuries-old examples around town. **Smith Park** on Midway Boulevard near Oldtown is canopied with them.

Tulips are still grown in the countryside and Oak Harbor celebrates its Dutch heritage in April. Catch the spring blooms at **Holland Gardens,** landscaped around a traditional Dutch windmill, at 500th Avenue West and 80th Northwest. You'll find another windmill at City Beach Park; go right off Highway 20 (Pioneer Way) onto 80th Southwest. The **visitor information center** of the Greater Oak Harbor Chamber of Commerce at 6506 Highway 20, about a mile from the heart of town, toward Deception Pass.

Despite its growth—including a recent spate of new condos—Oak Harbor still has a somewhat appealing downtown area. It lacks the 19th century charm of Langley and Coupeville however; the look is more 1930s and 1940s. Its most attractive area is **Oldtown,** down at the waterfront, where galleries and boutiques are tucked behind false fronts. You can admire the boats at the busy harbor and take a stroll along the adjacent beach. **Old Town Mall,** on the main highway through town, has a few shops and cafès fashioned around an atrium. The suburbs are aswarm with the service stations, Safeways and fast food take-outs of any ordinary community.

As you approach the north end of the island, thick subdivisions yield to thick forests. Just beyond is Whidbey-Fidalgo's most striking physical feature and Washington's most-visited state park.

☺ **Deception Pass State Park** ● *5175 N. State Highway 20, Oak Harbor, WA 98277; (206) 657-2417. Park hours (other than the campground) are 6:30 to dusk from April to mid-October and then 8 until dusk.* ☐ Although most of Whidbey Island flows gently to the water, craggy sea cliffs separate it from Fidalgo Island at Deception Pass. More than 3,000 acres of wilderness coast and thick forest are within this state park, on both sides of the pass. Hiking, fishing, clamming and camping (see below) draw visitors by the droves. Deception Pass Bridge—actually twin bridges that leapfrog from Whidbey to craggy little Pass Island and then to Fidalgo—provides one of the state's most photographed settings.

More than eighteen miles of hiking trails wind through forest thickets and crawl along dramatic sea cliffs. The park offers the best hiking in the northern Puget Sound area. For a nice short walk, drive across the bridge, go left down to **Bowman Bay** and pick up the **Lighthouse Point Trail.** It winds back toward the bridge for great views of the narrow, island-dotted passage, above a lighthouse. The approach to the light is closed to the public. Another popular walk is the shoreside trail between Bowman Bay and Rosario Beach. Once at Rosario, hike out to **Rosario Head** for an awesome view of the San Juan Islands, Rosario Strait and the Strait of Juan de Fuca.

Deception Pass was one of the many American parks improved by the willing hands of Civilian Conservation Corps workers during the Great Depression. They built picnic shelters, potties, hiking trails, park residences and the Deception Pass bridge. A **CCC Interpretive Center** at Bowman Bay tells the CCC story; it's open only in summer. Local residents who once worked with the "Three-Cs" did much of the work on the center, and they often staff it as volunteers. "We got $30 a week, and $25 of that was sent home," one of them recalled.

Captain Vancouver named the narrow passage here in 1792. Thinking it was an inlet, he first called it Port Gardner. He renamed it Deception Pass after realizing it was a strait between two islands.

## WHIDBEY ISLAND ACTIVITIES

*Bicycle rentals* ● The Pedaler, 5603 1/2 S. Bayview Rd., Langley, WA 98260; (206) 321-5040. All Island Bicycles, 302 N. Main St., Coupeville, WA 98239; (206) 678-3351.

*Bus touring* ● Whidbey Island Transit offers fare-free public bus service around the island; call (206) 678-7771 or (206) 321-6688 for schedules.

*Clamming* ● Some beaches on Whidbey Island are popular for clamming. Contact the Washington Department of Wildlife at (206) 775-1311 or

(206) 753-5700 for a booklet with information on catch limits and seasons.

**Sailboat rides and charters** • North Isle Sailing; (206) 675-8360. Beachcomber Charters, 221 Cornet Bay Rd., Deception Pass, WA 98277; (206) 675-7900.

**Sightseeing flights** • Island Air, Langley Airport; (206) 341-1505.

**Theater** • Whidbey Playhouse has a September-April season of dramas, musicals and comedies in the old First Reformed Church building at 1094 Midway Blvd., Oak Harbor; (206) 679-2237.

## ANNUAL EVENTS

**Holland Happening** tulip festival, April in Oak Harbor; (206) 675-3535.

**Loganberry Festival,** mid-July at Whidbeys Greenbank Berry Farm near Greenbank; (206) 678-7700.

**Choochokam** July art festival in Langley; (206) 321-6765 or 221-7494.

**Old Town Waterfront Street Fair,** mid-July in Oak Harbor; (206) 675-3535.

**Whidbey Island Race Week** in July, boat races off Oak Harbor; (206) 675-1314.

**Island County Fair,** August in Langley; (206) 321-4677.

**Arts and Crafts Festival,** mid to late August in Coupeville; (206) 678-5434 or 678-6116.

**Squash Festival,** October in Coupeville; (206) 678-5434.

## WHERE TO DINE ON WHIDBEY ISLAND
### (In order of appearance)

☺ *Café Langley* • ∆∆∆ $$$ Ø

☐ *113 First St., Langley; (206) 221-3090. Greek-continental; wine and beer. Sunday-Monday and Thursday 11:30 to 2:30 and 5 to 8, Friday-Saturday 11:30 to 2:30 and 5 to 8:30, closed Tuesday-Wednesday. MC/VISA.* ☐ Regarded by many as the island's best cafè, this cozy little place features fine fare from the Mideast, such as *spanakopita (spinach and cheese pie in phyllo), moussaka* and lamb kebob, plus nicely seasoned chops and chickens. Try the Mediterranean seafood stew with tomato sauce, herbs, spices and olive oil. The dècor is pleasingly simple: bleached ceiling beams, Mediterranean floor tiles and stucco walls adorned with fish prints. It's all smoke-free.

☺ *Star Bistro Café* • ∆∆ $$

☐ *201 1/2 First St. (above Star Market), Langley; (206) 221-2627. American nouveau; full bar service. Sunday 11 to 8, Monday 11:30 to 3, Tuesday-Thursday 11:30 to 8:30, Friday-Saturday 11:30 to 10. MC/VISA, AMEX.* ☐ This trendy place has an upbeat art deco look of black and white floor tiles, with walls accented by artworks and swatches of color. An outdoor deck with a view of the water is a great place for a sunny summer lunch. The menu is trendy, too, featuring salmon Florentine with whole wheat linguine, and baby back ribs or king salmon done with whiskey barbecue sauce. San Francisco style *gateau* is a dessert specialty.

*Mike's Place* • ∆∆ $$

☐ *First and Anthes, Langley; (206) 221-6575. American; wine and beer. Monday-Thursday 10 to 2, Friday 7 a.m. to 8 p.m., Saturday 8 to 8 and Sun-*

day 9 to 2, closed Tuesday-Wednesday; longer hours in summer. MC/VISA. ☐
This light and bright corner cafè has light-wood wainscotting and framed
prints on its walls. The menu is essential American, with simple entrèes
such as chicken fried steak, shrimp and chips and captain's seafood plate.

### ☺ Whidbey Fish Market & Café • ΔΔ $$

☐ *Highway 525 (just south of Whidbeys Greenbank Farm), Greenbank;
(206) 678-3474. American, mostly seafood; wine and beer. Lunch and dinner
Friday-Sunday, "fish feed" Monday night. MC/VISA.* ☐ Large outdoor aquatic
murals draw people to this funky little seafood market turned cafè, and a
busy, inexpensive seafood menu keeps them there. Pull up chairs at a family-style table and order the freshest seafood on the islands. Locals like to
bring their appetites for the all-you-can-eat fish feed on Monday night.

### Tyee Hotel • ΔΔ $$

☐ *405 S. Main St., Coupeville; (206) 678-6616. American; full bar service.
Daily 6:30 a.m. to 8 p.m. MC/VISA.* ☐ This American style cafè dwells in an
old false-front inn, with knotty pine walls and maple furniture. The menu is
early Gringo as well: chicken fried steak, breaded veal cutlets and several
seafood dishes. Hotel and motel rooms available.

### China Harbor • ΔΔ $$

☐ *1092 W. Pioneer Way (in Old Town Mall), Oak Harbor; (206) 679-
1557. Sunday-Thursday 11 to 10, Friday-Saturday 11 to 11. Chinese; full bar
service. MC/VISA.* ☐ This airy cafè is open to the mall atrium. The menu
runs the Asian gamut from mildly spiced Cantonese to peppier Szechuan,
plus some American entrèes. Try the orange beef, crab and garlic in black
bean sauce. The restaurants cocktail lounge is upstairs, with views down
into the atrium.

### Dave's Bakery • Δ $

☐ *116 W. Pioneer Way, Oak Harbor; (206) 679-4860. American, no alcohol. Breakfast and lunch daily from 7 a.m. No credit cards.* ☐ This handy
lunch stop in downtown Oak Harbor serves good French dip sandwiches,
hamburgers and assorted salads, plus breakfast fare and baked goodies.

### Lucy's Mi Casita • ΔΔ $

☐ *1380 Pioneer Way, Oak Harbor; (206) 675-4800. Mexican; full bar
service. Daily 11 to 11. MC/VISA, AMEX.* ☐ Are you ready for a Turbo Godz-
illa margarita? You'll need plenty of smashed beans and rice to absorb the
impact of the huge margaritas at "My Little House." All the food and most of
the wonderfully tacky Latino decorations are homemade in this lively little
cantina. The menu offers the usual range of taco-wrapped things.

## WHERE TO SLEEP
### In order of appearance

### ☺ The Inn at Langley • ⌂⌂⌂⌂ $$$$$ Ø

☐ *P.O. Box 835 (400 First St.), Langley, WA 98260; (206) 221-3033.
Couples and singles $165 to $185, suites $245. Rates include continental
breakfast. MC/VISA, AMEX.* ☐ Elegant Northwest style inn on a bluff overlooking Saratoga Passage. Twenty-four rooms, all facing the passage, with
balconies, TV, fireplaces, spa tubs, refrigerators and coffee makers. **Country
Kitchen** serves a *prix fixe* "Northwest island supper" Friday and Saturday
for about $40 per person. Beach and Langley village shops within walking
distance.

### Harbour Inn Motel ● ⌂ $$$ Ø

⧠ *1606 Main St., Freeland, WA 98249; (206) 331-6900. Couples $50 to $66, singles $45 to $61. Rates include continental breakfast. MC/VISA, AMEX.* ⧠ A 20-unit motel with TV, room phones; some refrigerators and microwaves.

### ☺ Captain Whidbey Inn ● ⌂⌂ $$$$ to $$$$$ Ø

⧠ *2072 Captain Whidbey Inn Rd. (Madrona Lane), Coupeville, WA 98329; (800) 366-4097 or (206) 678-4097. Couples $85 to 195, singles $75 to $185, kitchenettes $155 to $195, suites from $145. Rates include full breakfast. Major credit cards.* ⧠ Restored madrona log inn on Penn Cove; 32 rooms and cottages with antique furnishings and share baths, most with phones and in-room coffee; two TVs in public areas. Comfortable sitting room with a stone fireplace, **Dining room** for guests serves dinner 6 to 9:30, plus lunch during peak season; Northwest cuisine, dinners $20 to $30. Dining room and lounge overlook Puget Sound.

### Colonel Crockett Farm ● ⌂⌂ $$$ Ø

⧠ *1012 S. Fort Casey Rd., Coupeville, WA 98239; (206) 678-3711. Couples and singles $65 to $95. Five units with private baths; full breakfast. MC/VISA.* ⧠ Refurbished 1855 Victorian farmhouse amidst lawns and flowers on two acres. Rooms are furnished with a mix of American, Victorian and Edwardian antiques. Guest can gather in an oak-paneled library with a slate fireplace and solarium furnished with Victorian wicker.

### Coupeville Inn ● ⌂⌂ $$$ Ø

⧠ *P.O. Box 370 (200 Coveland St.), Coupeville, WA 98329; (800) 247-6162 or (206) 678-6668. Couples $54 to $95, singles $50 to $85. Rates include continental breakfasts. Major credit cards.* ⧠ Modern 24-unit inn overlooking the Coupeville historic district. TV, room phones. Near beach and restaurants.

### Acorn Motor Inn ● ⌂⌂ $$$ Ø

⧠ *8066 Highway 20 (at Third Avenue), Oak Harbor, WA 98277; (206) 675-6646. Couples $48 to $56, singles $41 to $46, kitchenettes $48 to $85, suites $65 to $95. Rates include continental breakfast. Major credit cards.* ⧠ A 30-unit motel with TV, room phones and refrigerators; microwave in lobby.

### Auld Holland Inn ● ⌂⌂ $$$ Ø

⧠ *5861 N. Highway 20, Oak Harbor, WA 98277; (800) 228-0148 or (206) 675-2288. Couples and singles from $55, kitchenettes $44, suites $135. Major credit cards.* ⧠ Attractive European-style inn with antique furnishings; TV movies, room phones, refrigerators and microwaves. Pool, spa, sauna, tennis courts, gift shop and coin laundry. **Kasteel Franssen** restaurant serves French and Northwest cuisine Monday-Saturday 5:30 to 9:30; dinners $12 to $19; country Dutch décor; full bar service.

### ☺ Best Western Harbor Plaza ● ⌂⌂⌂ $$$$ Ø

⧠ *5691 State Route 20 (Midway Boulevard at Goldie Road), Oak Harbor, WA 98277; (800) 527-9478 or (206) 679-4567. Couples $80 to $120, singles $70 to $95. Rates include continental breakfast. Major credit cards.* ⧠ A luxury 80-unit inn with TV movies, phones, refrigerators and microwaves. Amenities include pool, spa, tanning and fitness center and game room. **Mitzel's American Kitchen** serves Sunday-Thursday 6 a.m. to 11 p.m., Friday-Saturday 6 to midnight. American; full bar; dinners $7 to $15.

**Queen Ann Motel** • ◠◠ **$$** Ø
◻ *1204 W. Pioneer Way (70th NW), Oak Harbor, WA 98277; (206) 679-2720. Couples $45 to $51, singles $42 to $47, kitchenettes $58 to $60, suites $51 to $56. Major credit cards.* ◻ A 21-unit motel with TV, room phones; some with refrigerators. **Henderson's** serves American fare 7 to 9 weekdays and 8 to 10 weekends; dinners $8 to $16; full bar service.

## Bed & breakfast inns

**Kittleson Cove Cottage** • ◠◠◠ **$$$$$** Ø
◻ *P.O. Box 396 (4891 E. Bay Ridge Drive), Clinton, WA 98236; (206) 341-2734. Couples $125 to $175, singles $100 to $130. Two units with private baths; continental breakfast.* ◻ Contemporary home with a cottage and suite, located on the beach. Both units have full kitchens, TV and room phones. Fireplace and spa tub in the suite.

☺ **Eagles Nest Inn** • ◠◠◠ **$$$$** Ø
◻ *3236 E. Saratoga Rd., Langley, WA 98260; (206) 221-5331. Couples $95 to $115, singles $75 to $95. Four units with private baths; full breakfast. MC/VISA, DISC.* ◻ Distinctive multi-level octagonal home on a hilltop perch with views of Saratoga Passage and Camano Island. "Casually elegant" furnishings; decks, spa; on two and a half acres.

**Lone Lake Cottage & Breakfast** • ◠◠◠ **$$$$$** Ø
◻ *5206 S. Bayview Rd., Langley, WA 98260; (206) 321-5325. Couples and singles $110. Four units with private baths; expanded continental breakfast. No credit cards.* ◻ Four separate cottages on Lone Lake with kitchens, fireplaces, spa tubs, TVs and VCRs. Oriental décor with modern amenities; boats and canoes available. Smoking on outside decks only.

☺ **The Inn at Penn Cove** • ◠◠◠ **$$$ to $$$$** Ø
◻ *P.O. Box 85 (702 N. Main St.), Coupeville, WA 98239; (800) 688-COVE or (206) 678-8000. Couples and singles $60 to $125, singles $55 to $120. Six units; four private and two share baths; full breakfast. Major credit cards.* ◻ Two elegant 19th century homes—one Victorian and one Italianate—furnished with American European antiques, with touches of modern and Oriental. Three rooms have fireplaces; one has a spa tub.

**The Victorian** • ◠◠◠ **$$$ to $$$$** Ø
◻ *P.O. Box 761 (Main and Sixth), Coupeville, WA 98239; (206) 678-5305. Couples $65 to $95, singles $60 to $90. Three units with private baths; full breakfast. MC/VISA.* ◻ Imposing Italianate Victorian built in 1889 and listed on the National Register of Historic Places. Two rooms and a guest cottage, furnished with Victorian antiques. Near Coupeville historic district.

## WHERE TO CAMP

Four state parks on Whidbey Island offer camping. They are, in order of encounter:

**South Whidbey State Park** • *Smuggler's Cove Road; (206) 321-4559. RV and tent sites, no hookups; $10. No reservations or credit cards.* ◻ Well-spaced sites with barbecues and picnic tables; near the beach. Flush potties, showers, sheltered picnic area; hiking trails. Closed in winter.

**Fort Casey State Park** • *Above Camp Casey, near Coupeville; (206) 678-4519. RV and tent sites, no hookups; $10. No reservations or credit cards.* ◻ Sites are mostly unshaded but nicely situated, near the water's edge adjacent to the Keystone ferry terminal. Flush potties, showers, barbecues and picnic tables. Other park facilities listed above.

**Fort Ebey State Park** • *Off Libbey Road north of Coupeville; (206) 668-4636. RV and tent sites, no hookups; $10. No reservations or credit cards.* ☐ Shaded sites on Partridge Point above the beach; barbecues and picnic tables; flush potties and showers. Closed in winter.

**Deception Pass State Park** • *5175 N. State Highway 20, Oak Harbor, WA 98277; (206) 657-2417. RV and tent sites, no hookups; $10. No reservations or credit cards.* ☐ Shaded and open sites on the Whidbey Island side of the park, near Deception Pass. Picnic tables, barbecues, flush potties and showers; seasonal concession stand and amphitheater.

### Other RV parks

**Mutiny Bay Resort** • *5856 S. Mutiny Bay Rd. (P.O. Box 249), Freeland, WA 98249; (206) 321-4500. RV sites only; $10 to $18.50. Reservations accepted; MC/VISA.* ☐ On Puget Sound, with showers and full hookups. Boat dock and launch, fishing, tackle rentals, swimming, rec field, shuffleboard. Also rental cabins.

**North Whidbey RV Park** • *565 W. Cornet Bay Rd. (at Highway 20), Oak Harbor, WA 98277; (206) 675-9597. RV and tent sites; $16. Reservations accepted; MC/VISA.* ☐ Some pull-throughs; showers, full hookups, picnic tables and fire pits; playground, volleyball, horseshoes, rec field. Near Deception Pass State Park.

**Oak Harbor City Beach** • *80th SW, off Pioneer Way; (206) 679-5551. RV and tent sites; $10. No reservations or credit cards.* ☐ Water and electric; showers. Playground, boat ramp, swimming and fishing.

# Anacortes

**Population: 12,100**                                                    **Elevation: 75 feet**

Although not a major tourist center, Anacortes is one of our favorite little Washington towns. The thousands of travelers who pass through here en route to the San Juan Islands or Deception Pass would do well to take pause and look about.

Laid out in a logical, low-lying grid, the town occupies the northern tip of Fidalgo Island, surrounded by the beauty of northwest Washington. The San Juans lie just to the west, the Olympics to the southwest and the Cascades to the east. On a good day, from the crest of Mount Erie above the city, all of these can be seen. Murals, including smaller paintings of local characters past and present, grace business buildings in the tidy, clean-swept downtown area.

Anacortes was established in 1879, when one Amos Bowman built a wharf and store and named the settlement for his wife Anna Curtis. The name later was given a Latin lilt to harmonize with the Spanish names of the San Juans. (A self-proclaimed "King of Fidalgo Island," William Munks, may have been the area's earliest resident; records trace him back to the 1850s.) Bowman and others tried mightily to interest a railroad into crossing the narrow channel from the mainland. Several potential depots were built before Burlington Northern finally arrived at the turn of the century. It pulled out after a few years, but lumber mills and fish canneries kept the village going. Today, the presence of two large oil refineries, which process Alaska crude, ensure the town's future.

## Driving Anacortes

Oil refineries are hardly tourist attractions, although the mudflat peninsula that they occupy provides views of Puget Sound and offshore islands, plus free overnight RV parking. We suggest beginning your driving tour with a skim around its perimeter.

Crossing Fidalgo Island from Deception Pass, you'll hit a stoplight at a T-intersection. Instead of going left into town, take a right toward Mount Vernon. Then take the next left at a signal, onto March's Point Road, for a shoreline spin around the edge of the Shell and Texaco refineries. The free RV parking is on the outer rim, opposite Shell (see below).

After completing your loop, you may want to go briefly east to the **Swinomish Smoke Shop** on the adjacent reservation. It offers a good selection if Native American art and artifacts, open Monday-Saturday 9 to 7 and Sunday 10 to 6. Otherwise, pick up Highway 20 and head west toward Anacortes. Just beyond the T-intersection where you made your initial turn, drop down to Fidalgo Bay Road. It parallels the main highway into town, hugging the shoreline to provide more interesting views.

At the edge of town, you'll swing away from the shore briefly and hit a stop sign at R Avenue. Turn right and you're on the Fidalgo Island Scenic Drive, marked by signs. It takes you along the working waterfront and yacht harbor, past the **W.T. Preston** paddlewheeler, now an aquatic museum, and the old **Burlington Northern Depot,** the town's art center. A **Saturday Market** is held here each week May through October, featuring produce and local crafts. Also in this area is the **Anacortes Railway,** where a scale model steam engine offers rides on summer weekends.

Continue along R to a stop sign at Fourth Street and turn right. Go uphill briefly and turn right again, following signs through an attractive hillside residential area to **Cap Sante Viewpoint.** The first of two sterling vista points on the island, it offers a low-level panorama of the town and surrounding Puget Sound. Retrace your route back to Fourth Street and follow it to Commercial Avenue, beside the elegant four-story clapboard **Majestic Hotel.** Turn left up Commercial, into the town's main business center. To stock up on local tourist information, visit the **Anacortes Chamber of Commerce,** in a small nautical-style complex on your left at Ninth and Commercial. It's open weekdays 9 to 4.

While on the main drag, you may want to browse a few boutiques, antique shops and galleries in turn-of-the-century storefronts. On various buildings, note the small "volksmurals", which are distinctive to Anacortes. Then turn west onto Eighth Street and you'll enter a neighborhood of modest-to-elaborate turn-of-the-century homes.

☺ Pause for a stroll around **Causland Memorial Park,** on N Avenue between Seventh and Eighth. Curiously ornate river stone walls gird this park, which is a memorial to veterans of past wars. The main structure looks like a pebbly version of Darth Vader's helmet. A block beyond, at Eighth and M Avenue, is the **Anacortes Museum,** housed in the 1909 Federalist style former Carnegie library. Some of the town's more elaborate homes are along Seventh and Eighth, on a gentle slope above the water.

If you'd like to visit small **Guemes Island** just offshore, drive down to the base of I Avenue and catch a small ferry. The round-trip crossing is $5.25 and it departs about every hour; more frequently during morning and afternoon commute times. This is hardly an awesome trip, since the island is primarily a residential area, although some of the offshore views are pleasant. Its relatively level roads are good for bike touring.

Back in Anacortes, drive up Commercial Avenue to 32nd Street, turn right, follow it to H Avenue and turn left. This takes you onto Heart Lake Road, carrying you into a pleasant swatch of lake-dotted forest. Just past Heart Lake, fork to the left, following signs to **Mount Erie Park.** This, the highest promontory on Whidbey-Fidalgo, offers a sweeping panorama of the aquatic countryside. On a clear day, you can see the Olympics, the Cascades peaks and even faraway Oregon's Mount Hood. There's also a hiking trail to these heights.

Drop down from your perch, continue south on Heart Lake Road for about a mile, then turn right (west) onto Rosario Road. After you pass **Lake Erie,** go to the right onto Marine Drive. This route takes you along the island's shoreline, and then inland (it becomes Anaco Beach Road) to Sunset Avenue. Turn to the left into island's most beautiful spot.

☺ Handsome 200-acre **Washington Park** occupies the wooded nub of **Fidalgo Head.** A 2.3-mile scenic loop takes you around this thickly wooded promontory, offering great views of the sound, Rosario Strait, the San Juans and Olympics. Many folks park and walk or bike this scenic route. The park also offers other hiking trails, picnic areas and camping (listed below). From here, a short drive east on Sunset Avenue and then north (left) on Ferry Terminal Road will take you to Ship Harbor and the San Juan ferry dock.

*RV advisory:* The scenic loop in Washington Park is narrow in spots with some sharp turns, although larger rigs and trailers can make it. The road up to Mount Erie is even more steep and winding. It's a tough climb for a big rig, although there is an ample turn-around at the top. (If you have a trailer rig or tow-along, you might prefer to unhitch at the bottom.)

## ATTRACTIONS

☺ *W.T. Preston paddlewheeler* ● *R Avenue at Eighth Street; (206) 293-1916. Memorial Day through Labor Day, Friday-Monday noon to 5. Free; donations appreciated.* ◻ Despite its stately look, the *Preston* was not a passenger boat but a snag boat that cleared flotsam from Puget Sound. It was retired in 1981 and is now a maritime museum, with most of its engines and original hardware intact.

*Burlington Railway Depot* ● *R Avenue at Seventh Street; (206) 293-2670. Gallery hours Sunday and Tuesday-Friday 1 to 4, Saturday 10 to 4; closed Monday.* ◻ Works of local artists and traveling exhibits are displayed in galleries built into the turn-of-the-century railway passenger station. When not looking at art, you can admire the original furniture and other fixtures in the restored depot.

☺ *Anacortes Museum* ● *1305 Eighth St. (at M Avenue); (206) 293-5198. Thursday-Monday 1 to 5 from April through September; Friday-Sunday 1 to 5 the rest of the year. Free; donations appreciated.* ◻ Artifacts, photos and furniture in three galleries of this well-kept museum recall Fidalgo Island's earlier days. Among its displays are a Victorian living room, doctor's and dentist's offices and replica of an old cannery office. It also contains an extensive archive of photos and records. Note the multi-level drinking fountain out front, with basins at proper heights for people and animals.

## ACTIVITIES

**Bicycle rentals** • Ship Harbor Inn Bicycle Rental, 5316 Ferry Terminal Rd., Anacortes, WA 98221; (206) 293-5177.

**Boat charters** • Several firms offer crewed boats and/or rental boats for fishing, whale watching and sightseeing in the San Juans. Among them: ABC Yacht Charters, 1905 Skyline Way, Anacortes, WA 98221, (800) 293-9533 or (206) 426-2313; Anacortes Yacht Charters, 2413 T Avenue, Anacortes, WA 98221, (800) 233-3004 or (206) 293-4555; Charisma Charters, 5708 Kingsway West, Anacortes, WA 98221, (206) 293-0677; Highliner Charters, 245 Sharpe Rd., Anacortes, WA 98221, (206) 293-3072; and Penmar Marine Charters, 2011 Skyline Way, Anacortes, WA 98221; (800) 828-7337 or (206) 293-4839.

**Cruises** • The sailing schooner *Sophia Christina* offers daily and longer sightseeing cruises out of Anacortes; (800) 882-4761.

**Theater** • Anacortes Community Theater presents dramas, comedies and musicals; (206) 293-6829.

## ANNUAL EVENTS

**Anacortes Waterfront Festival** and boat show in late May; (206) 293-3832.

**Shipwreck Days,** mid-July merchants' festival; (206) 293-3832.

**Anacortes Arts and Crafts Festival** in early August; (206) 293-6211.

**King Salmon barbecue** in late August; (206) 293-3832.

## WHERE TO DINE

### ☺ *La Petite Café* • ∆∆∆ $$$ ∅

❑ *3401 Commercial Ave. (at 34th, in Islands Inn); 293-4644. French-Dutch; full bar service. Breakfast daily, plus dinner Tuesday-Sunday 5 to 10. Major credit cards.* ❑ Although it occupies a corner of the Islands Inn, this is hardly a motel coffee shop. It's a fetching little French-style café with crisp white nappery, potted plants, wall prints and properly subdued lighting. The menu includes local fresh fish such as salmon in balsamic sauce, plus sweetbreads, chicken breast in garlic sauce over Parmesan pasta and the very Dutch *varkens haas* (pork tenderloins in a mustard sauce.) The dining room is smoke-free.

### *Boomer's Landing* • ∆∆ $$

❑ *209 T Ave. (near Wyman's Marina); (206) 293-5108. American; full bar service. Lunch and dinner daily, Sunday brunch 10 to 2. MC/VISA.* ❑ Cantilevered over Guemes Channel, this nautical dining room offer a typical American menu of steak, chicken, chops and locally fresh seafood. The best thing here is the view of the San Juans. This is a great place to watch the sunset.

### *El Jinéte* • ∆∆ $ ∅

❑ *509 Commercial Ave.; (206) 293-2631. Mexican; wine, beer and margaritas. Sunday-Thursday 11 to 9, Friday-Saturday 11 to 10. MC/VISA.* ❑ Bright, flare-skirted Mexican dresses tacked to the walls add cheerful accents to this attractive Mexican cantina. It serves a wide range of Latino dishes at modest prices, from chicken molè to a very good chilè Colorado. One dining room is smoke-free.

☺ *Janot's Bistro* • ∆∆∆ *$$$* Ø

⎕ *In the Majestic Hotel, 419 Commercial Ave.; (206) 293-3355 or (206) 299-9163. Northwest regional; full bar service. Sunday brunch 9 to 3; lunch daily 11:30 to 2:30, dinner 5:30 to 9:30. Major credit cards.* ⎕ The ornate, square-shouldered 1889 Majestic Hotel has been restored to Victorian splendor, with lots of brass, painted glass and marble. The restaurant, much more glamorous than its bistro name, offers interesting *nouveau* creations, such as grilled salmon with Chinese pesto and mango salsa; peppercorn beef; prosciutto-wrapped prawns; and a vegetarian dish of curry, potatoes, eggplant, squash, tomatoes and peppers with rice and pita.

## WHERE TO SLEEP

**Anacortes Inn** • ⌂⌂ *$$$* Ø

⎕ *3006 Commercial Ave. (30th), Anacortes, WA 98221; (800) 327-7976 or (206) 293-3153. Couples $48 to $88, singles $48 to $75, kitchenettes $55 to $95, suites $125 to $135. Major credit cards.* ⎕ A 44-unit motel with TV movies, room phones, refrigerators and microwaves; pool and barbecues.

**Channel House** • ⌂⌂⌂ *$$$$* Ø

⎕ *2902 Oakes Ave., Anacortes, WA 98221; (206) 293-9382. Couples $69 to $95, singles $59 to $95. Six units with private baths; full breakfast. MC/VISA, DISC.* ⎕ Early-American Craftsman style 1902 home, with a mix of antique and contemporary furnishings. Two units have fireplaces. Hot tub, comfortable sitting rooms; on Guemes Channel with Puget Sound views.

**Guemes Island Resort** • ⌂⌂ *$$$$*

⎕ *326 Guemes Island Rd., Anacortes, WA 98221; (206) 293-6643. Kitchenette units $75 to $175. MC/VISA.* ⎕ Seven fully furnished housekeeping units on Guemes Island's north shore. Country store, boat rentals, fuel, pool, gift shop, coin laundry and barbecue area. Also campsites with showers.

**Island Inn** • ⌂⌂ *$$$* Ø

⎕ *3401 Commercial Ave. (at 34th), Anacortes, WA 98221; (206) 293-4644. Couples and singles $48 to $80, suites $85 to $110. Rates include a Dutch breakfast. Major credit cards.* ⎕ Attractive, well-kept inn with TV, room phones and some room refrigerators and coffee makers; many rooms with views of Fidalgo Bay. Pool and spa. **La Petite Cafè** listed above.

☺ **Majestic Hotel** • ⌂⌂⌂ *$$$$* Ø

⎕ *419 Commercial Ave., Anacortes, WA 98221; (206) 293-3355. Couples and singles $89 to $138, suites $177. Rates include club breakfast. Major credit cards.* ⎕ Beautifully restored four-story hotel in downtown Anacortes. Rooms furnished with antiques; TV movies and phones; some with refrigerators and wet bars; some with Puget Sound views. **Restaurant** listed above.

**Marina Inn** • ⌂⌂ *$$$$* Ø

⎕ *3300 Commercial Ave. (23rd Street), Anacortes, WA 98221; (206) 293-1100. Couples $71 to $89, singles $65 to $89, kitchenettes $70. Major credit cards.* ⎕ A 32-unit motel with TV and room phones; some refrigerators and microwaves. Large attractively furnished lobby and game area; spa.

**San Juan Motel** • ⌂⌂ *$$* Ø

⎕ *1103 Sixth St. (O Street), Anacortes, WA 98221; (800) 533-8009 or (206) 293-5105. Couples and kitchenette unites $43 to $65, singles $40 to*

*$38. Major credit cards.* ◻ A 29-unit motel with TV, room phones, most with refrigerators; coin laundry.

### Ship Harbor Inn ● ⌂⌂ $$$ Ø

◻ *5216 Ferry Terminal Rd. (Sunset), Anacortes, WA 98221; (800) 852-8568 or (206) 293-5177. Couples $58 to $75, singles $52 to $62, kitchenettes $72 to $82, suites $65 to $75. Major credit cards.* ◻ A 26-unit motel with TV, room phones; some refrigerators and microwaves; coin laundry. All rooms have water views.

## Bed & breakfast inns

### ☺ Albatross Bed & Breakfast ● ⌂⌂⌂ $$$$ Ø

◻ *5708 W. Kingsway (Skyline Marina), Anacortes, WA 98221; (206) 293-0677. Couples $85, singles $80. Four units with private baths; full breakfast. MC/VISA.* ◻ Cape Cod style Craftsman home near the ferry terminal; with ornate wood moldings, crystal chandeliers and wall sconces. Rooms furnished with "Southern mansion" and Victorian antiques. Living room with fireplace, TV and stereo; large yard with barbecue; sailboat available.

### Hasty Pudding House ● ⌂⌂⌂ $$$ Ø

◻ *1312 Eighth St. (M Street), Anacortes, WA 98221; (206) 293-5773. Couples and singles $60 to $85. Four units with private baths; full breakfast. Major credit cards.* ◻ Handsomely decorated 1913 Craftsman style home built by a former Anacortes mayor. Rooms furnished with Victorian and American country antiques; fireplace in the common room. In one of the town's historic neighborhoods, near downtown.

## WHERE TO CAMP

**Deception Pass State Park** camping facilities are listed above.

**March Point** ● *West of Anacortes, off March Point Road. Free; no facilities or hookups.* ◻ Roadside parking for self-contained RVs only, opposite the Shell Oil Refinery; nice views of the Puget Sound; boat launch nearby.

**Washington Park** ● *End of Sunset Avenue; (206) 293-1918. RV and tent sites, $12 with water and electric, $8 with none. No reservations or credit cards.* ◻ Nice campsites between evergreens, near the water. Showers, barbecue pits and picnic tables; coin laundry. Hiking trails, picnic areas, boat launch and playground.

# THE SAN JUAN ISLANDS

You will be delighted or disappointed by the San Juans, depending on whether you seek quietude or tourist gimmicks. The islands' charm lies in their isolation, their farmlands and forests and quaint villages. There are plenty of things to do, although they are quiet sorts of things. Folks come here to drive or pedal country lanes, prowl pebbly beaches and rocky inlets, and watch for whales, orcas and offshore bird life.

The islands are a boaters' paradise, for one can cruise to perfectly private little places for a picnic, or from one waterfront village to another. Several uninhabited islands are state parks, with primitive campgrounds and hiking trails. Sea kayaking is popular in these sheltered, relatively calm waters, and several outfits offer trips and rentals (see "Activities" below).

Diving is another prevalent pastime, and the San Juans are a favorite hangout of Jacques Cousteau. The walls of these submerged mountains shelter large colonies of sea anemone, and giant kelp forest rise from the ocean

# HAVE A FERRY NICE DAY

During the formative years of the American West, water provided the cheapest, most reliable means of transportation. In Washington's Puget Sound, it still does. Driving or hopping aboard a ferryboat is a way of life for area residents, and an appealing novelty for visitors.

In fact, Washington State Ferry System officials say that ferries are the state's biggest tourist attraction. Many of the nearly 25 million passengers carried each year are visitors. Daily ridership jumps from an average of 57,000 in winter to 86,000 in summer. The route through the San Juan Islands is particularly popular with visitors. Travelers can call (206) 464-6400 or toll-free (800) 84-FERRY (within Washington only) for schedule information; the hearing-impaired number is (800) 833-6388. Ferry schedules are available at all terminals and at many visitor centers.

The state's public ferry service began in 1889 when the city of Seattle provided service to west Seattle for a nickel a ride. Several private ferryboats soon emerged. From the turn of the century and beyond, a squadron of mail, freight and passenger ferries called the Mosquito Fleet swarmed over Puget Sound.

The state entered the ferry business in 1951 when it purchased the Puget Sound Navigation Company. It expanded rapidly, using some of the old ferryboats from the San Francisco Bay, which had been put out of business by the Golden Gate and Oakland Bay bridges. Today, those green and white Washington State ferries are as familiar as seagulls as they criss-cross Puget Sound. The system has nine routes serving 20 terminals, including an international run through the San Juans to Sidney on Vancouver Island.

Vehicle reservations are required on the routes between Orcas Island or Friday Harbor (on San Juan Island) and Sydney, B.C. They must be made at least 24 hours ahead; call Orcas at (206) 376-2134 or Friday Harbor at (206) 378-4777. During the summer, ferries will accept reservations between Anacortes and Sidney. They aren't required, although a reservation will guarantee space for your vehicle. Foot and bicycle passengers never need reservations.

For all other routes, it's first come, first served. One simply gets in line and drives or walks on board. However, it's always a good idea to arrive well before departure time—an hour or more during busy summer periods. The ferries can accommodate everything from 18-wheel cargo trucks to kayaks.

The state's 25 boats comprise the largest ferry fleet in the United States and one of the largest in the world. Ferries range in size from the *Walla Walla* and *Spokane*, capable of carrying 2,000 passengers and 206 vehicles, to the little *Hiyu*, with a capacity for 40 cars and 200 people. Larger ones have cafeterias and elevators; all have comfortable indoor lounges, outdoor deck space, restrooms and food vending machines. All interior spaces are smoke-free. The ferries are well-maintained, spotlessly clean and remarkably prompt, considering the uncertainties of fog and open water.

Ferry users need only remember a few simple rules and suggestions:

• Vehicle Propane tanks must be sealed while on board; use of Propane in RVs while en route is strictly prohibited.

• Drivers should stay with their vehicles while waiting to board. There's a $100 fine for leaving an abandoned vehicle in line when boarding starts.

• If possible, travelers should avoid using the ferries during commute hours (westbound in the morning and eastbound in the evening).

By necessity of design, the double-ended ferries are hardly sleek. However, as they cruise through the water—usually with an impressive Puget Sound backdrop—they exhibit a kind of dumpy grace. They're particularly appealing at night, all lit up and gliding silently along on their own reflections.

floor. Divers may find themselves playing tag with playful dolphins.

Cyclists like to take to the country lanes, perhaps with a picnic hamper strapped behind. A word of caution, however: the roads are very narrow, usually with no shoulders. Both bike and car traffic can become quite thick in summer.

In touring the San Juans, you will find no craggy promontories, awesome ravines or rugged cliffs. The green countryside looks pretty much the same—island to island and country lane to country lane. You will find some hideaway resorts, a few good restaurants, lots of pretty coastal vistas and one grand panorama—from Mount Constitution on Orcas Island.

Only four of the many islands are served by ferry and only two of these, Orcas and San Juan, have any towns to speak of. Friday Harbor on San Juan is the largest with about 3,000 people; it's the county seat and the only incorporated community.

***Ferry facts:*** Life moves at a slow pace on these islands, perhaps because it is set by the ferries, which move slowly and resolutely from one to another. As a visitor you, too, must attune your schedule to these lumbering green and white boats. (See box on page 185.)

Ferries depart every hour or so from Anacortes, docking at Lopez, Shaw, Orcas and San Juan islands, with international runs on to Vancouver Island. Not all trips hit all islands, so keep a schedule handy. Fares are collected westbound only. You can get a free transfer, good for 24 hours, that allows you to get off at one island and catch a later boat to the next.

Get to the terminals *early,* particularly in summer. Walk-ons can always hop aboard, but vehicles must wait in lines and they can become ridiculously long on weekends. Ferries can accommodate bicycles and kayaks. Some of the smaller terminals, such as Lopez and Shaw, are manned only by one person, so get there in plenty of time to purchase your ticket, even during the slow season. Buy it at the ticket office and return to your vehicle, since the attendant will be too busy to sell you one as you drive aboard.

***RV and general vehicle advisory:*** Fuel is much higher on the islands, as much as 40 cents more a gallon, so tank up in Anacortes. RV parks are scarce on the islands and state and county park sites fill up quickly in summer. Where reservations are accepted, make them as early as possible.

Incidentally, you can fly to the islands. West Isle Air serves Friday Harbor from Anacortes, with connections to Sea-Tac; (800) 874-4434. San Juan Airlines flies from Seattle, Bellingham and Vancouver, B.C., to Friday Harbor; call (800) 438-3880 in Washington only, or (206) 452-1323.

## Lopez Island

This may be the only place in the world (we can use that word "unique" again) where strangers routinely wave at one another from passing vehicles. Lopez Island is *that* friendly. Some motorists look hurt when you fail to return their greeting.

After you've gotten used to this sensitivity training, you can adjourn to **Lopez Village** to poke around its few shops, and then just wander the island's roads at will. Lopez is laced with them, so expect to get lost. You won't stay astray for long, however. Your route will either dead-end at a beach, or loop you back to where you started. With few steep grades, Lopez is one of the more popular islands for cyclists.

Lopez Village is about five miles in from the ferry terminal. Just follow

Ferry Road south; it becomes Fishermans Bay Road. En route, you'll see signs to **Odin County Park** to your right and **Spencer Spit State Park** to your left. Both offer hiking trails, picnic areas and shoreline camping (listed below). Spencer Spit's mile-long beach is popular for clamming.

You'll also encounter **Lopez Island Vineyards,** with a tasting room open noon to 5, Wednesday-Sunday in summer and Friday-Saturday only the rest of the year; (206) 468-3644. Like other Puget Sound wineries, it makes whites from the little-known Madeleine varieties, and it imports other grapes from eastern Washington.

Lopez is a village in every stretch of the word: no sidewalks, stoplights or streetlights. It offers a couple of good restaurants (listed below), a few shops and the small **Lopez Historical Museum** at Weeks Road and Washburn Place. You'll find a couple of farm implements parked outside and glimpses of the island's past inside. Among its casually arrayed exhibits are pioneer relics, a fish trap and models of steamboats that once chugged among the islands. Hours are noon to 4, Wednesday-Sunday in July and August, and Friday-Sunday in May, June and September; (206) 468-3447.

From Lopez Village, you can continue north on Fisherman's Bay Road, skimming past the bay. You'll pass through rolling pasturelands and an occasional forest. There's nothing imposing out there, although it's a pleasant drive that—when you get lost—tends to circle back on itself.

Don't forget to wave.

## WHERE TO DINE

### ☺ *Bay Café* ● △△△ *$$* Ø

☐ *Lopez Village; (206) 468-3700. Eclectic; wine and beer. Dinner nightly except Monday from 5:30. MC/VISA, DISC.* ☐ Housed in an old false front store, this cheery little café is decked out in floral table cloths, drop lamps and watercolor paintings. The menu changes frequently, reflecting chef-owner Bob Wood's ingenuity and curiosity about ethnic dishes. Local crab and seafood is featured, often enlivened with Mediterranean or Southeast Asian spices. He generally has one vegetarian dish.

### *Bucky's Lopez Island Grill* ● △△ Ø

☐ *Lopez Village; (206) 468-2595. American; wine and beer. Sunday-Thursday 8 to 8, Friday-Saturday 8 to 9. MC/VISA.* ☐ Cozy little place with a 1930s look: chromed rimmed bar stools at a counter, and historic prints on the walls. The menu lists fish and chips, fish fettuccine and baby back ribs.

## WHERE TO SLEEP

### ☺ *Inn at Swift's Bay* ● ⌒⌒⌒ *$$$$ to $$$$$* Ø

☐ *Route 2, Box 3402 (Port Stanley Road), Lopez Island, WA 98261; (206) 468-3636. Couples and singles $75 to $140, suites $110 to $140. Five rooms; three private and two share baths; full breakfast. Major credit cards.* ☐ Casually elegant Tudor style retreat on a private beach, with comfortable rooms and suites; one is an attic hideaway with skylights. Secluded hot tub; comfortable sitting room with large film and music library. The inn is noted for its breakfasts.

### *Marean's Blue Fjord Cabins* ● ⌒⌒⌒ *$$$$*

☐ *Route 1, Box 1450 (Elliott Road), Lopez Island, WA 98261; (206) 468-2749. Two individual cabins, $78; with private baths. No credit cards.* ☐ Nordic style log chalets tucked amidst the trees on a small bay; each is isolated

188 — CHAPTER FIVE

from the other, with patio decks and full kitchens with appliances and utensils, plus TVs and radios. Trails lead into the surrounding forest and to a nearby beach with a picnic gazebo

## WHERE TO CAMP

*Hummel Haven Bicycle Camp* • *Center Road at Hummel Lake; (206) 468-2217. Sites $2.50. No credit cards.* ☐ Campground for cyclists only; cars may park on the perimeter. Picnic tables and fire pits; fee trout fishing. Bike rentals, $10 a day.

*Odin County Park* • *Ferry Road (north end). RV and tent sites, no hookups; $10 ($5 November through February). No reservations or credit cards.* ☐ Small park with shaded sites, some with water views; barbecues and picnic areas, playground, boat launch.

*Spencer Spit State Park* • *East side, Lopez Island; (206) 468-2251. RV and tent sites, no hookups, $10. Closed in winter. No reservations or credit cards.* ☐ Shaded, well-spaced sites near the water; barbecues, picnic tables; nature trails.

# SHAW ISLAND

A few Franciscan Nuns runs things on tiny Shaw Island, including the ferry dock and a general store and curio shop called Little Portions. (This supposedly is the only nun-run ferry terminal in the world.)

Although hills are a bit hillier, you might prefer Shaw for biking because of the lack of traffic. As you pedal or drive about, follow Shaw Island Road two miles south from the ferry dock to **South Beach County Park,** offering picnicking and camping. From here, take Squaw Bay Road east and then turn north on Hoffman Cove Road to a fetching **little red schoolhouse.** Close by is the **Shaw Island Historical Museum,** with an undisciplined clutter of pioneer relics in a small log cabin. Hours are irregular; try your luck on a summer weekend or call (206) 468-3351.

# ORCAS ISLAND

Shaped like a clutching, stubby-fingered hand, Orcas is our favorite of the San Juan group. It's not quite as crowded as San Juan Island in summer, although it has more resorts than the more populated San Juan. It offers some pleasing scenic drives and the best vista point in the archipelago. Rocky and wooded shorelines of the narrow fjords between its chubby fingers provide imposing waterscapes. This island is so hilly that you may think you're in the Cascades instead of Puget Sound.

The only town of note, Eastsound, is a pleasing compromise between too-tiny Lopez Village and sometimes too busy Friday Harbor. This island community also is something of an art colony.

When you put ashore at the ferry dock at **Orcas,** steer to your left and you'll see a mural map that will help orient you to the island. Also here are the attractive Victorian **Orcas Hotel** (listed below) and the **Orcas Wine Company** tasting room, where you can sip some imported eastern Washington wine.

You'll find another orientation sign about four miles inland. Take a right at a fork in the highway, following signs toward Eastsound. As you approach, watch on your left for the **Crow Valley School Museum,** an early one-room school house that's been restored and furnished. It's open

*Charming little Eastsound on Orcas Island peeks through the trees from its perch at the head of a deep, fjord-like inlet.* — **Betty Woo Martin**

from Memorial Day through mid-September, Tuesday 2 to 4, Thursday 10 to noon and Saturday 2 to 4; (206) 376-4260.

☺ **Eastsound** is a fetching little hamlet wrapped around the base of the deep Eastsound inlet. The town is comprised mostly of a few gift shops, galleries and cafès, housed in tidy wood frame buildings. Like the other islands, Orcas has its requisite historical archive; this one is reach by turning north off the highway:

☺ *Orcas Island Historical Museum* ● *North Beach Road, Eastsound; (206) 376-4840. Open May 1 through Labor Day, Tuesday-Friday 1 to 4 and Saturday 10 to 4. Donations appreciated.* ⊓ This is a museum *complex,* with six homestead cabins, linked and clustered around an old water tower. One has typical pioneer furnishings; others display extensive collections of Native American lore, historic photos, early day artifacts and exhibits concerning philanthropist Robert Moran, the island's most prominent citizen, who you will shortly meet.

After exploring Eastsound, head southeast on Horseshoe Highway, following signs to Moran State Park and Rosario.

☺ **Rosario Resort,** a handsome and historic retreat on its own sheltered bay, comes up shortly. Even if you aren't staying, drive the winding road down to this copper-roofed classic, set amidst lushly landscaped grounds. Former Seattle mayor and shipbuilder Robert Moran built the main structure as his mansion early in this century. Told by Seattle doctors that he had only six months to live, he came here in 1905, bought this land and thousands more acres. He gave most of his holdings to Moran State Park. He didn't accomplish all this in six months; Moran lived another 38 years.

You may want to schedule lunch or dinner in the Rosario Resort dining room (see below), where tables are terraced to give everyone a view of the bay. A marina is adjacent, and its small Cascade Bay Cafè is more casual than the dining room. From Rosario, a short drive delivers you to the park named for its founder:

☺ **Moran State Park** ● *Star Route, Box 22, Eastsound, WA 98245-9603; (206) 376-2326. Grounds open in summer 6:30 to dusk, the rest of the year from 8 to dusk. Camping listed below.* ☐ This 4,934-acre park rivals Deception Pass for its scenery and versatility. A freshwater lake invites fishing, swimming, boating and picnicking. Several miles of hiking trails wind past waterfalls and into thick forests. A steep four-mile trail leads to park's crowning glory, figuratively and geographically. At 2,409 feet, **Mount Constitution** is the highest promontory on any of the Puget Sound islands. You don't have to hike it, however. A winding road leads to the top. From there, you can climb another 50 feet up a stone lookout tower, for one of the most imposing views in the Northwest. The San Juans spread far below, as detailed on a clear day as a *landsat* photo. You can see much of northwestern Washington and Vancouver Island from here—from the Strait of Georgia to the Cascades to the Olympics. One of several park buildings constructed by the Depression-era Civilian Conservation Corps, the tower was styled after lookout towers of southeastern Europe's Caucasus Mountains.

*RV advisory:* The steep, winding road to Mount Constitution is not recommended for large motorhomes and trailers. You can drive part way to a turnout, where another road branches to the right, and then pick up a the hiking trail or walk the winding road to the top.

☺ Continue through the park on Horseshoe Highway, and fork right after two miles to **Olga,** a tiny waterfront community. Before you run out of road, stop at **Cafè Olga** on your left. It has an American folkcraft shop downstairs, and a new age book and music store in a loft above the restaurant. The road ends about two blocks beyond the cafè. You can park and explore a sheltered beach or stroll onto a skinny fishing pier.

From the Olga turnoff, Point Lawrence Road goes about eight miles northeast to **Doe Bay.** Other than a couple of resorts, this route doesn't offer much more than thick forest. It stays mostly inland, so you'll catch few aquatic views. For some exceptionally fine marine scapes, retrace your route to Eastsound, head back toward the ferry terminal, then hang a right at the Westsound/Deer Harbor Road sign. You shortly enter **Westsound,** which has a small marina and not much else. However, the views of rocky shoreline, inlets and tiny offshore islands are splendid.

☺ After winding around the Westsound inlet, the road takes you to **Deer Harbor.** Tucked snugly against its own rocky, island-dotted cove, it presents perhaps the prettiest picture in all of the San Juans. The road swings inland from here, through thick forests. You may be tempted to follow this attractive route, but there is no outlet.

## WHERE TO DINE

☺ *Bilbo's Festivo* ● ∆∆∆ *$$*

☐ *North Beach and A, Eastsound; (206) 376-4728. Mexican-Southwestern; full bar service. Dinner nightly in summer, Tuesday-Sunday in the off-sea-*

son. *MC/VISA.* ⊓ Taos comes to the islands in this charming little cafè, with adobe textured walls hung with Navajo and Chimayo weavings. A fireplace and handmade furniture add a proper level of cozy charm. From the kitchen emerges creative cuisine from both sides of the border—fresh seafood, mesquite-grilled carne asada, chicken in orange sauce, and the full range of things wrapped in tortillas.

### Bungalow Restaurant ● ∆∆ $$

⊓ *Eastsound; (206) 376-4338. Chinese-American-Italian; wine and beer. Lunch and dinner daily. MC/VISA.* ⊓ What you want is what you get at this versatile restaurant. The menu prances from fresh fish to chicken piccata to the "Triple Dragon Delight" of shrimp, chicken and beef in a spicy sauce. A Chinese buffet goes for $9.95. It's a cozy cafè with a fireplace and views of the sound.

### ☺ Café Olga ● ∆∆ $ ∅

⊓ *Point Lawrence Road, Olga; (206) 376-5098. Whole earth; wine and beer. Daily 10 to 6 (10 to 5 in November and December). MC/VISA.* ⊓ This charming spot is a cafè, art co-operative, cultural center and gift shop, tucked under one rustic roof—which used to house a strawberry packing shed. The health-conscious menu has international touches in entrèes such as Chilean artichoke pie, cashew chicken salad and mushroom-leek tart. The homemade cinnamon rolls and sour cream coffee cakes are excellent; grab a couple to go if you don't have time for breakfast for lunch. Olga's is smoke-free.

### Christina's ● ∆∆∆ $$$ ∅

⊓ *One Main Street (at North Beach Road), Eastsound; (206) 376-4904. American regional; full bar service. Dinner nightly from 5:30 in summer, Thursday through Monday in the off-season, closed January to mid-February. MC/VISA, DISC.* ⊓ This award-winning waterfront restaurant is perhaps the best all-around cafè in the islands, serving creative Northwest regional fare. Fresh seafood is a specialty, and the artfully seasoned lamb and beef dishes are tasty. Save space for ice cream puffs, assorted cheesecakes and other in-house desserts. This fine fare is served in an elegantly simple dining room, on an enclosed porch or—weather willing—on a rooftop terrace. All offer water views.

### ☺ Deer Harbor Inn ● ∆∆∆ $$

⊓ *Deer Harbor; (206) 376-4110. American; wine and beer. Dinner nightly; weekends only in the off-season. MC/VISA, AMEX.* ⊓ Come on a sunny day and relax on the outside deck of this charming old inn to enjoy splendid views of Deer Harbor. The dining room, properly wood and rustic, is a pleasant retreat as well. The inn serves excellent seafood, focusing on what's just been caught and surrounding it with locally fresh ingredients. The frequently changing menu also features chicken, chops and steak entrèes and at least one vegetarian dish.

### Orcas Fish Company ● ∆ $

⊓ *At the ferry landing; (206) 376-5755. American, mostly seafood; espresso, no alcohol. Breakfast and lunch daily. MC/VISA.* ⊓ It's a nice little spot for breakfast or lunch, perched right over the water, with view tables indoors and out. Stoke up on fish, scallops, oysters or calamari and chips (or a combination thereof), with coleslaw for about $7.

# WHERE TO SLEEP

### Beach Haven Resort ● ⌂⌂ $$$$
⌑ *Route 1, Box 12 (Beach Haven Road), Eastsound, WA 98245; (206) 376-2288. Cabins $85; MC/VISA.* ⌑ Thirteen rustic cabins and four modern apartments, on the beach, fully furnished with wood stoves and electric kitchens. Quiet area, surrounded by virgin forest.

### Kangaroo House ● ⌂⌂⌂ $$$$ Ø
⌑ *P.O. Box 334 (North Beach Road), Eastsound, WA 98245; (206) 376-2175. Couples $70 to $110, singles $60 to $100. Five units; two with private and three with share baths; full breakfast. MC/VISA.* ⌑ Turn-of-the-century Craftsman house, restored and furnished with American and Victorian antiques. Sitting room with a large stone fireplace; game room. Outside decks lead to extensive yard and gardens. Within walking distance of Eastsound shops and restaurants.

### ☺ Orcas Hotel ● ⌂⌂⌂ $$$$ to $$$$$ Ø
⌑ *P.O. Box 155 (at the ferry landing), Orcas, WA 98280; (206) 376-4300. Couples and singles $69 to $170. Shared baths; full breakfast. Major credit cards.* ⌑ Nicely restored 12-room 1904 hotel, with print wallpaper, antique wardrobes and other period furnishings. Comfortable parlor with fireplace. Attractive Victorian-style **Fireside Lounge** and bakery café have views of the sound and ferry terminal; they serve American fare 6:30 a.m. to 10 p.m.; full bar service. Restaurant closes in winter; hotel remains open.

### ☺ Outlook Inn ● ⌂⌂⌂ $$$$ Ø
⌑ *P.O. Box 210 (Main Street), Eastsound, WA 98245; (800) 767-9506 or (206) 376-2200. Couples $99 with private bath and $69 for shared baths, singles $94 and $64; half-off in winter. Major credit cards.* ⌑ Renovated 1888 inn with rooms furnished with American antiques, plus adjoining motel-style units. Inn rooms have shared baths and phones; motel units have private baths, phones and TV. Handsome Victorian-style **dining room** serves breakfast, lunch and dinner daily in summer; weekends only in the off-season; dinners $10 to $15; full bar service.

### ☺ Rosario Resort and Spa ● ⌂⌂⌂ $$$$$ Ø
⌑ *One Rosario Way, Eastsound, WA 98245; (800) 562-8820 or (206) 376-2222. Couples and singles $95 to $210 on weekends, $63 to $160 weekdays. Major credit cards.* ⌑ Handsomely-maintained historic resort on Cascade Bay. Waterfront and hillside units have TV movies and phones; some have fireplaces and balconies. Complete resort facilities include a health club, tennis courts, three swimming pools, sauna and spas. Marina adjacent with boat launch, rental boats and fishing. **Dining room** and coffee shop; serving breakfast, lunch and dinner daily 7:30 to 2 and 6 to 9 (until 10 Friday-Saturday); shorter off-season hours; American-continental; dinners $14 to $30; full bar service; views of Puget Sound.

### ☺ Turtleback Farm Inn ● ⌂⌂⌂⌂ $$$$ Ø
⌑ *Route 1, Box 650 (Crow Valley Road), Eastsound, WA 98245; (206) 376-4914. Couples $70 to $150, singles $60 to $140. Seven units with private baths; full breakfast. MC/VISA.* ⌑ Comfortable and elegantly cozy country inn on eighty acres of forest and farmland; with a mix of antiques and modern furnishings. Housed in a restored 19th century farmhouse, the inn was

voted one of the 12 most romantic spots in the country by a Los Angeles *Times* travel writer.

### West Beach Resort ● ⌂⌂ $$$$$

◻ *Route 1, Box 510 (Enchanted Forest Road), Eastsound, WA 98245; (206) 376-2240. Beachfront cabins $90 per night from mid-June through September, reduced rates the rest of the year. MC/VISA.* ◻ Rustic resort on a sandy beach with a marina, boat launch and rentals. Cabins have full kitchens, with wood stoves, electric heat and view decks. RV sites; see below.

## WHERE TO CAMP

### Moran State Park ● *Star Route, Box 22, Eastsound, WA 98245-9603; (206) 376-2330 or (206) 376-2326. RV and tent sites, $10. Hiker-biker sites $5. Reservations available in summer by requesting a form from the park; no credit cards.* ◻ Well-spaced, mostly shaded sites, some near a freshwater lake. Flush potties and showers, barbecues and picnic tables; no hookups. Swimming, boating, fishing and hiking trails (see above).

### West Beach Resort ● *Route 1, Box 510 (Enchanted Forest Road), Eastsound, WA 98245; (206) 376-2240. RV sites $20, tent sites $14. Reservations accepted; MC/VISA.* ◻ Grassy sites near the water; showers, coin laundry, mini-mart, playground. Marina with fishing tackle, boat launch and rentals. Also beachfront cabins (listed above).

## SAN JUAN ISLAND

Friday Harbor spills down from wooded hills and gathers around a narrow bay on San Juan Island. Sailboats in a marina add splashes of color and expensive homes peak from tree-shrouded cliffside perches. All this presents an appealing vision as your ferryboat moves purposefully toward the terminal.

San Juan is the second largest of the islands, slightly smaller than Orcas, yet its 6,000 people comprise more than half the archipelago's total population. And nearly half of these live in Friday Harbor. San Juan also is the only island on which the main town is at the ferry terminal. That's a handy condition if you're afoot or if you're biking it and want to park your gear in a motel before setting forth.

Although large on a San Juan Islands' scale, Friday Harbor is an appealing little town busy with galleries, boutiques and restaurants. You can begin your browsing at **Cannery Landing,** a gathering of shops beside the ferry slip. **Island Wine Company,** at Two Cannery Landing, offers gratis sips of its products, which are made in eastern Washington and therefore quite palatable; (206) 378-3229. For orientation, the **San Juan Island Chamber of Commerce** has a brochure rack in the Arcade Shops on lower Spring Street, just up from the harbor (beside the China Pearl restaurant).

Most of Friday Harbor's old, well-kept storefronts are along Spring Street, tilting upward from the ferry dock. Before tilting too far, take a right onto First Street for a visit to an excellent museum who's primary focus is marine mammals:

### ☺ The Whale Museum ● *62 N. First St.; (206) 378-4710. Daily 11 a.m. to 4 p.m. Adults $3, seniors and students $2.50, kids under 12, $1.* ◻ This is a museum with a mission, dedicated to nurturing compassion and understanding for the marine mammals that roam the Puget Sound and the rest of the globe. You enter the museum to the sound of orcas at play, and then you

*Washington State ferries carve liquid highways through the San Juan Islands. This one is gliding through Wasp Passage.*                    © — **Bob & Ira Spring**

can learn everything you ever wanted to know about whales, orcas and dolphins—and then some. Exhibits include shags of baleen, skeletons and models of whales and graphics about their habits and wiles. You learn that *spermaceti*, found in the foreheads of sperm whales, lit much of the world before the development of electricity, and nearly led to their extinction. And you probably wanted to know that marine mammals are descended from a a dog-like carnivore called *creodonta*, which apparently took a swim about 45 million years ago and never came back.

**San Juan Historical Museum** ● *405 Price Street (off upper Spring Street); (206) 378-3949. Wednesday-Saturday 1 to 4:30 Memorial Day through Labor Day; shorter hours or by appointment the rest of the year. Donations appreciated.* ⊐ A white clapboard 19th century farmhouse preserves past relics of the San Juans in a series of period furnished rooms. Objects of interest include a stereoptican, wind-up phonograph, kitchen utensils, butter churns and an unusual "spool bed" with an antique quilt.

San Juan Island, of course, is famous for the "Pig War" (see box on page 196), a boundary dispute between America and Great Britain. The two elements of San Juan Island National Historic Park are on opposite sides of the island, marking sites of the British and American camps. Before heading out, you can pick up information at a national park office on Spring and near First Street, open Monday-Friday 8 to 4; (206) 378-2240.

Armed with historical park information, head northeast on Second Street. It becomes Roche Harbor Road and takes you ten miles, mostly offshore through woods and pasturelands, to **Roche Harbor,** once a shipping port for the island's lime industry. Like Orca's Rosario, Roche Harbor shelters an old resort—perhaps less elegant but equally historic. Its focal point is the Victorian style **Hotel de Haro** (listed below). It's closed during winter. However, off-season visitors can wander the landscaped grounds, poke about a marina and peek into the 1886 company store of the Roche Harbor Lime and Cement Company. The store still functions as sort of an oversized mini-mart. The hotel was built in 1886 by company founder John S. McMillin, to house and entertain clients.

☺ Backtrack briefly from Roche Harbor to West Valley Road, turn right and drive just over a mile to **British Camp** of San Juan Island National Historic Park. When the American and British governments decided to send troops and begin the Pig War standoff, the Britts chose an attractive, sheltered spot above Garrison Bay. All that remains of the camp are a four restored buildings and a properly formal British garden, planted and tended by officers' wives to remind them of faraway home. Among the structure are a blockhouse, barracks with an interpretive center, commissary and hospital. They're open in summer from 8 to 6, closed the rest of the year. A short trail leads from the garrison out to Bell Point for views of the sound. Another leads up to Mount Young, offering a panorama of the San Juans.

From British Camp, continue along West Valley Road for just under three miles and turn right onto Mitchell Bay road. **San Juan County Park** appears on your right after three more miles. It has a beach, playground, picnic area and camping (listed below). The glimmer you see across the Haro Strait is the town of Saanichton on Vancouver Island.

Continue through thickening woods for another 2.5 miles and you reach the shoreline again at **Limekiln Point State Park.** This small day-use facility has picnic areas and an attractively rocky shoreline. A short hiking trail leads to a lighthouse that guides ships through Haro Strait; it's closed to the public. The point is a good place to spot offshore orcas and other sea mammals.

Continue around the island on scenic, cliff-hugging West Side Road, which offers fine views of the strait. It eventually swings inland, becomes Bailer Hill Road and cuts straight across the island. Shortly after it makes a 90-degree left turn onto Douglas Road, turn right onto Little Road and right again onto Cattle Point Road. This will take you to the American side of the historic park. (It isn't signed, so you may miss it. If so, continue back toward Friday Harbor and take a right onto Mullins Road toward the airport, just short of town.)

☺ Occupants of **American Camp** had a better view than the British, although their camp was rather stark. It occupied a grassy knoll overlooking the Strait of Juan de Fuca, on the island's skinny southeastern rim. The interpretive center has a fine graphics display of events leading to American independence and the subsequent dispute over the boundary with Canada. It's open Thursday-Sunday 8:30 to 4:30; hours may be longer in summer. From the visitor center, a trail leads across the moors to the few surviving buildings of American Camp. A spur trail heads for a coastal overlook, and you can scramble down to explore the rocky shoreline or loop back to the visitor center.

From the camp, drive about four miles to the island's southeastern tip at **Cattle Point Interpretive Area,** another good vista point. That's Lopez Island just across a narrow channel. This was an important fishing grounds

# THE OINK HEARD AROUND THE WORLD

"Upon the impulse of the moment, I seazed my rifle and shot the hog."

That impulse, by San Juan Island settler Lyman Cutlar, nearly led to war between the United States and Great Britain. Actually, the British considered Lyman to be a squatter and therein lay the problem.

When the border between the United States and Canada was established at the 49th Parallel in 1846, the boundary line through Puget Sound was vaguely worded. It was to be "in the middle of the channel which separates the continent from Vancouver's Island; and thence southerly through the middle of the said channel, and Fuca's straits to the Pacific Ocean."

However, there were two main channels: Haro Strait between the San Juan Islands and Vancouver, and Rosario Strait between the San Juans and the mainland. Both sides claimed the islands. The British established a salmon curing station and sheep ranch called Bellevue Farm on San Juan. Oregon's territorial legislature encouraged American settlement and tried to tax British property.

For the most part, American British settlers go along. However, a hog from Bellevue farm kept rooting in Lyman Cutlar's potato patch. When he complained, farm superintendent Charles Griffin snorted that it was up to Cutlar to "keep his potatoes out of the pig." Besides, he huffed, Cutlar had squatted on some of his best land.

## San Juan's Bay of Pigs

A crisis erupted on June 15, 1859, when Lyman got mad, grabbed his rifle and shot the hog. Then, regretting his temper tantrum, he went to Griffin and offered to pay restitution. But the British superintendent set too high a price. Cutlar refused to pay and Griffin threatened to have him hauled before a magistrate in Victoria. Alarmed American settlers petitioned General William S. Harney of the Department of Oregon, who sent an infantry detachment under command of George E. Pickett. (He later led the famous Civil War charge.) The British responded by sailing several warships into San Juan Harbor, and the stalemate began.

Fortunately, leaders of both sides called for cool heads in the crisis. British naval commander Rear Admiral Robert L. Baynes said he would not "involve two great nations in a war over a squabble about a pig." When word of Harney's occupation reached President James Buchanan, he was stunned. He ordered the hot-headed Harney relieved and sent his general of the armies, Winfield Scott, to seek a solution. Both sides agreed to send small military detachments, occupying opposite ends of the island until the issue could be resolved. It wasn't settled until 1872 when Germany's Kaiser Wilhelm I was asked to arbitrate. He ruled in favor of the Americans and the boundary was set between San Juan and Vancouver islands.

The opposing forces got along rather well during the 12-year occupation. Records show that the British were hosted to a "splendid affair" during an American Independence Day celebration. The British repaid the compliment by inviting them to a party in honor of Queen Victoria's birthday.

for Indians and later American settlers, since currents drove migrating salmon close to the shoreline. This is still a popular fishing ground for seekers of salmon. You'll see a lighthouse out on the point, although there is no public access. The road ends just beyond the interpretive area.

# WHERE TO DINE

### China Pearl Restaurant • ∆∆ $$

◻ *51 Spring St., Friday Harbor; (206) 378-5254 or (206) 378-5269. Chinese; full bar service. Monday-Thursday 11:30 to 10, Friday 11:30 to 10:30, Saturday noon to 10:30, Sunday noon to 10. MC/VISA.* ◻ The versatile menu covers all Chinese venues: Mandarin, Cantonese and Szechuan, with a special emphasis on seafood, including fresh-caught steamed fish. Shrimp comes in several versions: spicy Szechuan, *kung pao, moo shu*, sizzling rice, or sweet and sour. The look is essential Chinese, with comfortable high-backed booths and tables.

### Downrigger • ∆∆ $$

◻ *Front and Spring streets, Friday Harbor; (206) 278-2700. American, mostly seafood; full bar service. Lunch from 11 and dinner from 5 daily, breakfast from 8 a.m. on weekends. MC/VISA.* ◻ The dècor is nautically simple, but most diners prefer to look out the window, since this restaurant is perched over the harbor. Farm-raised baby coho salmon is a specialty, along with halibut and chips served with thick skins-on fries. Other offerings include shrimp and scallop fettuccine and assorted fresh fish. The clam chowder is excellent, with a nice herbal flavor.

### ☺ Duck Soup Inn • ∆∆ $$$

◻ *3080 Roche Harbor Rd. (between Friday Harbor and Roche Harbor); (206) 378-4878. American; wine and beer. Dinner Wednesday-Sunday; closed in winter. No credit cards.* ◻ It's an appealing little country place—both in dècor and location—with a continental tilt to its menu. In addition to properly cooked fresh fish or shrimp, the small menu features grilled pork tenderloin with port and apricots, Baja seafood stew with cheese and *crème fraise*, and steak Diane.

### Electric Company Restaurant and Pub • ∆∆ $$

◻ *175 First St. Friday Harbor; (206) 378-4118. American; full bar service. Lunch and dinner daily. MC/VISA.* ◻ The look is pleasant rural funk, with barnboard walls, wooden ceilings and maple chairs. An island bar between the dining areas adds a nice accent. The menu is reliable if not imaginative: chicken Parmesan, poached salmon, crab cakes and fresh seafood. The hot seafood salad is rather good.

### ☺ Springtree • ∆∆∆ $$$

◻ *310 Spring Street, Friday Harbor; (206) 378-4848. American-continental; wine and beer. Lunch Tuesday-Saturday 11:30 to 2:30, dinner Tuesday-Sunday from 5:30, Sunday brunch 9 to 2, closed Monday. MC/VISA.* ◻ Look for the elm out front, then step through the patio into this homey little cafè with a light Victorian look. The fare is generally excellent, ranging from linguine with grilled eggplant and artichoke to a seafood medley of shrimp and smoked mussels with basil. Our favorite was the sautèed chicken breast with mushrooms and brandy. It's all smoke-free. Diners can adjourn to that out-front patio during warm weather.

## WHERE TO SLEEP

### Duffy House • ⌂⌂⌂ $$$$ Ø

◻ *760 Pear Point Rd., Friday Harbor, WA 98250; (206) 378-5604. Couples $75 to $85, singles $70 to $80. Five units with share baths; full breakfast. MC/VISA.* ◻ Stylishly restored 1920s Tudor style home with leaded glass windows, coved ceilings and mahogany woodwork. Rooms furnished with antiques, accented by Navajo rugs and quilted wall hangings. Guest refrigerators, private beach, English garden and orchards.

### Friday's Historical Inn • ⌂⌂⌂ $$$$ to $$$$$ Ø

◻ *35 First St. (West Street), Friday Harbor, WA 98250; (206) 378-5848. Couples and singles $70 to $155. Ten units; three private and seven share baths; expanded continental breakfast. MC/VISA, AMEX.* ◻ Comely 1891 false-front hotel, carefully restored and finished with "casual Victorian" dècor. It offers a mix of traditional furnishings and modern conveniences, with leaded glass accents, oak antiques, spa tubs and radiant heating. Limited edition wildlife prints accent the walls.

### ☺ Hillside House Bed & Breakfast • ⌂⌂⌂ $$$ to $$$$$ Ø

◻ *365 Carter Ave., Friday Harbor, WA 98520; (800) 232-4730 or (206) 378-4730. Couples $65 to $145, singles $55 to $135. Seven units; some private and some share baths; full breakfast. MC/VISA, AMEX.* ◻ Modern multi-level home cresting a hill with a view of the port of Friday Harbor and Puget Sound. Furnishings are "contemporary casual"; one unit in the "Eagles Rest" penthouse features a spa tub. Wooded grounds and gardens with a two-story aviary stocked with exotic birds.

### ☺ Lonesome Cove Resort • ⌂⌂ $$$$ Ø

◻ *5810 Lonesome Cove Rd., Friday Harbor, WA 98520; 378-4477. Six individual cabins from $85 to $140. MC/VISA.* ◻ Rustic housekeeping cabins with stone fireplaces, fully equipped kitchens and open decks. Located on six acres of forest with 1,500 feet of beach on Puget Sound; barbecue area.

### Mariella Inns & Cottages • ⌂⌂⌂ $$$$ to $$$$$ Ø

◻ *630 Turn Point Rd., Friday Harbor, WA 98520; (206) 378-3622. Couples $85 to $160; Some private, some share baths; full breakfast in season, continental off-season. MC/VISA.* ◻ Victorian inn with eleven units; antique furnishings and two parlors with fireplaces. Also seven cottages with private decks over the water. Extensive gardens and beachfront on nine acres; volleyball; kayaks and bikes for rent.

### Moon & Sixpence • ⌂⌂⌂ $$$$ Ø

◻ *3021 Beaverton Valley Rd., Friday Harbor, WA 98520; (206) 378-4138. Couples $85 to $105, singles $80 to $100. Three units with private baths; full breakfast. No credit cards.* ◻ Nicely remodeled turn-of-the-century Victorian style farmhouse on an old dairy. Eclectic furnishings with antiques, artwork and collectibles. The complex includes a weaving studio, flower and dyestuff garden, picnic tables and private decks.

### Olympic Lights • ⌂⌂⌂ $$$$ Ø

◻ *4531-A Cattle Point Rd., Friday Harbor, WA 98520; (206) 378-3186. Couples $70 to $105, singles $65 to $100. Five units; one private and four share baths; full breakfast. No credit cards.* ◻ Restored 1895 American farmhouse with views of Puget Sound and the Olympic mountains. Rooms are furnished with antiques and contemporary wicker furniture, set off by soft colors. Outdoor amenities include a wildflower garden, croquet and horseshoes.

### San Juan Inn Bed & Breakfast ● ⌂⌂⌂ $$$ Ø

⌂ *P.O. Box 776 (50 Spring St.), Friday Harbor, WA 98250; (800) 742-8210 or (206) 378-2070. Couples $75 to $92, singles $65 to $92. Ten units with private baths; expanded continental breakfast. Major credit cards.* ⌂ Restored 1873 Victorian-style inn furnished with brass, wicker and other antiques. Comfortable parlor with over-stuffed furniture; secluded garden area. In downtown Friday Harbor, half a block from the ferry landing.

### Tucker House B&B and cottages ● ⌂⌂⌂ $$$$ Ø

⌂ *260 B St. (Nichols Street), Friday Harbor, WA 98250; (800) 742-8210 or (206) 378-2783. Couples $75 to $115, singles $65 to $85. Two inn rooms and three cottages; three private and two share baths; full breakfast. Major credit cards.* ⌂ An 1898 Victorian near downtown shops and restaurants. Main house furnished with antiques; contemporary dècor in cottages, with TV. Solarium, hot tub, decks and picket-fence yard with garden.

## WHERE TO CAMP

**Lakedale Campground** ● *2627 Roche Harbor Rd., Roche Harbor, WA 98250; (206) 378-2350. RV and tent sites; $15 to $18. Reservations accepted; MC/VISA.* ⌂ Some shaded and some open sites near small lakes; water and electric, flush potties and showers, mini-mart. Beach with swimming and boat dock; fee fishing; rental boats, canoes, paddleboats and bicycles.

**San Juan County Park** ● *Westside Road; (206) 378-2992. RV and tent sites, $13 ($6.50 in winter), hiker-biker $4.50, day use $4. No reservations or credit cards.* ⌂ Grassy sites near the water with picnic tables and barbecue pits; flush potties and showers. Beach with swimming bay, fishing.

## ACTIVITIES

### Including all the islands

**Bicycle rentals, sales or repair** ● Island Bicycles, 380 Argyle Ave. (P.O. Box 1609), Friday Harbor (San Juan Island), WA 98250; (206) 378-4941. Lopez Island Bike Shop, Fishermans Bay Road near Lopez Village; (206) 468-3497. Orcas Bicycle Company, Orcas Island; (206) 376-4517. Wildlife Cycles, Eastsound, Orcas Island; (206) 376-4708.

**Day cruises and boat tours** ● Western Prince Cruises (specializing in whale-watching and wildlife sighting), Friday Harbor; (206) 378-5315. San Juan Boat Tours, Port of Friday Harbor; (800) 232-ORCA or (206) 378-3499. Wildlife Whale Watch Tours, at the Main Dock, Friday Harbor; (206) 378-5315.

**Longer cruises** ● Catalyst Cruises, 515 S. 143rd St., Tacoma, WA 98444, (206) 537-7678; five-day to two-week motor cruises, sailing out of Seattle. Gallant Lady Cruises, P.O. Box 1250, Vashon Island, WA 98070, (206) 463-2073; six-day cruises aboard a yacht, departing Vashon Island. *J. Marie* Sailing Cruises, P.O. Box 722, La Conner, WA 98257, (206) 466-4292; six-day sailboat cruise departing La Conner, southeast of Anacortes. Norden Cruise, P.O. Box 10642, Bainbridge Island, WA 98110, (206) 842-2803; week long sailboat cruises, departing Friday Harbor. Sailing schooner *Sophia Christina*, Anacortes, (800) 882-4761; daily and longer sightseeing cruises out of Anacortes.

**Fishing charters** ● Buffalo Works Fishing Charters, (206) 378-4612. Moby Max Charters (salmon fishing), Route 1, Box 1065, Eastsound, WA 98245; (206) 376-2970. Captain Clyde's Charters, P.O. Box 1212, Friday Harbor, WA 98250; (206) 378-5661. Trophy Charters, P.O. Box 2444, Friday Harbor, WA 98250; (206) 378-2110.

**Kayak tours and rentals** ● Island Kayak Guides, Doe Bay Village Resort, Star Route 86, Olga, WA 98279; (206) 376-4755. Osprey Tours, Orcas Island; (206) 376-3677. Shearwater Adventures, P.O. Box 787, Eastsound, WA 98245; (206) 276-4699.

**Sailing charters and boat rentals** ● Cap'n Howard's Sailing Charters, P.O. Box 2993, Friday Harbor, WA 98520; (206) 378-3958. Deer Harbor Charters, P.O. Box 303, Deer Harbor, WA 98243; (800) 544-5758 or (206) 376-5989. Wind 'n Sails, P.O. Box 337, Friday Harbor, WA 98250; (800) 752-4121 or (206) 378-5343. Charter Northwest, P.O. Box 915, Friday Harbor, WA 98250; (206) 378-7196. Bon Accord Charters, Main Dock (P.O. Box 472), Friday Harbor, WA 98250; (206) 378-5921. Orcas Island Eclipse Charters, P.O. Box 290, Orcas, WA 98280; (206) 376-4663. Captain Clyde's Charters, P.O. Box 1212, Friday Harbor, WA 98250; (206) 378-5661. Trophy Charters, P.O. Box 2444, Friday Harbor, WA 98250; (206) 378-2110. San Juan Boat Rentals and Tours, P.O. Box 2281, Friday Harbor, WA 98250; 378-3499.

**Scenic and charter flights** ● West Isle Air, Friday Harbor; (206) 378-2440. Magic Air Tours, Eastsound Airport on Orcas Island (biplane flights); (206) 376-2733.

**Scuba diving** ● These outfits offer rental diving gear and/or conduct charter dives: Emerald Seas Diving Center, 180 First St. (P.O. Box 476) Friday Harbor, WA 98250; (206) 378-2772. Snug Harbor Resort on San Juan Island; (206) 378-4762. West Beach Resort on Orcas Island; (206) 376-2240. Bon Accord Charters, Main Dock (P.O. Box 472), Friday Harbor, WA 98250; (206) 378-5921.

**Theater** ● Life plays and concerts presented at Orcas Theatre and Community Center in Eastsound; (206) 376-4873. San Juan Community Theater presents dramas, comedies and musicals in Friday Harbor; (206) 378-3210.

## ANNUAL EVENTS

**Chamber Music San Juans,** mid-July at the San Juan Community Theatre in Friday Harbor; (206) 378-3210.

**San Juan Island Good Time Jazz Festival,** late July at the San Juan Island Fairgrounds; (206) 378-5509.

**San Juan County Fair,** mid-August at the San Juan Island Fairgrounds; (206) 378-5240.

**International Music Festival,** late August at Orcas Center, Eastsound; (206) 376-2787.

## CANADA SOUTH TO EVERETT

The mainland shore of northern Puget Sound is not a tourist area. However, its major cities of Bellingham and Everett offer lures that are worth a diversion from Interstate 5. For the most part, in fact, we'll avoid I-5, preferring the shoreline drive, which passes through a rather fertile farm belt. To add further novelty, we'll suggest looping through Canada instead of taking the eastbound ferry back to Anacortes.

As mentioned earlier, a 24-hour notice is required to catch the ferry from Friday Harbor to Vancouver Island; call (206) 378-4777. The crossing from Friday Harbor to **Sidney** on the Canadian side takes about an hour and a half. From Sidney, drive briefly north through Vancouver Island's lush green countryside to **Swartz Bay** to catch a B.C. Ferry to Tsawwassen on the British Columbia mainland. (And no, we don't know why the ferry terminals aren't in the same place.)

Vehicle reservations aren't required for this run, although you should get to the terminal early during the summer. Simply get into your assigned line and buy the ticket at a kiosk as you board. American and Canadian currency are accepted. During peak periods, ferries run hourly from 7 a.m. to 10 p.m. Call (604) 656-0757 for recorded schedule information or (604) 386-3431 to speak to a real person.

This hour-and-a-half passage takes you through the **Gulf Islands,** Canadian cousins to the San Juans and in reality, part of the same archipelago. B.C. Ferries call on these islands, which are less settled and equally as fascinating as the San Juans. That, of course, is another chapter in someone else's book.

# Point Roberts

**Population: 450**                    **Elevation: sea level**

When you touch mainland Canada soil, drive the long sandspit from the ferry terminal to the town of **Tsawwassen**, and then turn right onto 56th street at the sign for Point Roberts. This is the five-square-mile American enclave on the B.C. mainland, and you do, indeed, pass through a customs gate. Point Roberts is totally American, from its currency to its liquor laws (more lenient than Canada's, which results in a brisk trade) to the American brands in the town's one supermarket (no bilingual French-Canadian labels).

Although it offers nothing of real visitor interest, other than a nice vista of the Strait of Georgia, Point Roberts does a brisk "curiosity tourist" business with next-door Canadians. We suspect a that a lot of American wine from the surprisingly large liquor section in the Point Roberts market departs in the trunks of Canadian cars.

To tour Point Roberts, pass through the customs gate and continue straight ahead through the small business district. You'll soon hit the beach at **Lighthouse Park,** with great views of the sound, picnic tables, a beach and a campground. Campsites are $7 for Washington's Whatcom County residents, and $12 for the rest of us. Continue along the beach and you'll loop back to the international boundary on a road that parallels the custom stations. Return to Tsawwassen, pick up the main highway and follow it west through this flat delta land, staying with I-5 signs. You'll blend onto the interstate and shortly return to American soil through the international border crossing at **Blaine.**

*General driving advisory:* Border delays can be horrendous on Friday and Sunday nights as Canadians and Americans switch nations for weekend trips. Incidentally, once you've crossed into Washington, Blaine offers some of the cheapest fuel we've found in the Northwest.

☺ The **International Peace Arch** that straddles the border is certainly worth a close-up look. You can stand in its shadow and read its inscriptions by crossing through American customs, and then taking the

Blaine exit and branching to your left, following signs into **Peace Arch State Park**. (It's the third left; bypass the turn-in to U.S. Customs parking and the on-ramp to northbound I-5.) The arch, standing in a nicely landscaped park, was erected in 1921. It salutes the spirit of friendship between the U.S. and Canada, symbolized by their thousands of miles of open border. "Brethren dwelling together in unity," it reads on the Canadian side, and "Children of a Common Mother" on the American side. Washington and British Columbia school children pooled their pennies and nickels to buy land for the arch. The monument was proposed by good old Samuel Hill of Seattle, creator of the Columbia River Gorge Highway.

From Blaine, you can head south briskly on I-5, or detour west to Birch Point for more Strait of Georgia Views. **Semiahmoo County Park,** on a narrow sandspit aimed toward Canada, has a restored salmon cannery and small interpretive center, open noon to 5, Wednesday-Sunday in summer and weekends only the rest of the year. Just below is the planned resort community of **Birch Bay** with a fancy resort hotel, **The Inn at Semiahmoo**; (800) 854-2608 or (206) 371-2000). Nearby is the **Wild 'n' Wet** water park, open daily in summer 10:30 to 7:30; (206) 371-7911.

Continuing on around the point, you encounter **Birch Bay State Park,** offering camping for $14 (water and electric) and $10 (no hookups), plus a mile-long waterfront, underwater park, picnic area, playground and some short nature trails. Reservations may be made during summer by requesting an application form from: Birch Bay State Park, 5105 Helwig Rd., Blaine, WA 98230-9625; (206) 371-2800.

As you continue around the point, the highway swings you back to I-5. To avoid the freeway, you can follow signs to **Ferndale,** although this tidy town offers little of visitor interest. Incidentally, that imposing white mass on the eastern horizon is **Mount Baker.** Offering a bit more for visitors is the largest town in these parts:

# Bellingham

**Population: 52,200**                               **Elevation: 60 feet**

This old, rather prosperous and nicely-kept city is actually a blend of four earlier towns, dating back to the 1850s. It's a repository of early-day architecture, and some of the best examples are in its suburb of **Fairhaven,** an historic district busy with boutiques, antiques and cafès.

To see Bellingham/Fairhaven highlights, take I-5 exit 258, turn right at a stop sign, pass through another stop sign and drive a mile or so past the Bellingham Airport. At a T-intersection, turn left onto Marine Drive. It takes you along the Puget Sound waterfront, lined with nice homes that have a better view of the water than you do. The street then passes through the busy port section, through a neighborhood of nicely-kept older homes and into the downtown area. (The route becomes Eldridge Avenue and then Holly Street.) Looking to your left, you can't help noticing a four-story red brick building with a clock tower atop. To reach this fascinating structure, once the Bellingham city hall and now a museum, tale a half left onto West Champion Street and go left again onto Prospect and park.

☺ *Whatcom County Historical Museum* ● *121 Prospect St.; (206) 676-6981. Tuesday-Sunday noon to 5. Adults $2, seniors and kids $1.* ☐ This facility is outstanding on two fronts. The ornate brick 1892 former city hall is one of Washington's most visually appealing buildings, and the museum inside is one of the best in the state. Its grand centerpiece is a full-scale 1910 Bellingham street scene, with a boardwalk and windows dressed merchandise of the day. Recorded voices from the past discuss future prospects of this up-and-coming young city. Other rooms have smaller exhibits, focusing on Native American lore, women's costumes of the turn-of-the-century, and an extensive exhibit of children's toys.

**Children's Museum of the Northwest** ● *227 Prospect; (206) 733-8769. Thursday-Saturday 10 to 5, Wednesday and Sunday noon to 5; $2.* ⌑ Next door to the historical museum, this small facility has hands-on interactive stuff for kids, plus a puppet theater and walk-through train.

Bellingham has some very attractive public parks and historic districts and a well-maintained downtown shopping area. To see more of this handsome old city, stop by the Bellingham/Whatcom County **Convention and Visitors Bureau** at 904 Potter St., up near freeway exit 253.

From the museum, head south on Prospect, which angles into Bay Street and then swings left onto Chestnut. Go three blocks to North State Street, turn right and follow it along the waterfront. (Harbor Loop Route signs will help direct you.) You'll clear the waterfront after a few blocks and then travel alongside **Boulevard Park** for about a mile. Turnouts may tempt you to pause and enjoy views of Puget Sound. As you approach Fairhaven, just beyond Boulevard Park, take a half left onto 11th street.

## Fairhaven Historic district

☺ This fine collection of old brick and masonry dates back to the turn of the century. This once was a bawdy district, where railroad crews worked on the grade into Bellingham from the Skagit Valley. It's considerably more respectable now. Shops, boutiques, galleries and cafès have replaced bordellos and Shanghai saloons. Park and start exploring its more than 50 stores. Most are along 11th and Harris Avenue, with a few more on the fringes of this six-block area. Several interesting cafès here may tempt you to take a lunch or dinner break:

☺ *Colophon Café and Deli* ● △△ $ ∅

⌑ *1208 Eleventh St. (at Harris); (206) 647-0092. American; no alcohol. Monday-Saturday 10 to 10, Sunday 10 to 6. MC/VISA.* ⌑ Clothed in old brick, this North Beach-style cafè is part of an extensive bookstore that rambles over a couple of floors. The menu is appropriate for light reading—bagel melts, whole earth salads, a hummus platter, quiche and such.

☺ *Dirty Dan Harris's* ● △△△ $$

⌑ *1211 Eleventh St. (at Harris); (206) 676-1011. American; full bar service. Monday-Thursday 5 to 9, Friday-Saturday 5 to 10, Sunday 4 to 9. Major credit cards.* ⌑ Dan Harris, described by associates as being "as unreasonable as a pig," built a cabin here, then platted the town, opened a waterfront dive and made a fortune. This namesake place is considerably cleaner, a typical treatment of turn-of-the-century brass and brick with a typical menu. Offerings include ribs, teriyaki sirloin and chicken, scallops sautè and Alaskan king crab legs.

*Dos Padres* ● △△ $

⌑ *1111 Harris St.; (206) 733-9900. Mexican; full bar service. Monday-Thursday 11 to 10; Friday-Saturday 11:30 to 11, Sunday 11:30 to 10.* ⌑ This popular family-owned place concentrates more on the food than the dècor.

A few doo-dads on the wall say it's Mexican, and the menu underlines it, with the full range of fajitas, burritos and such, plus southern style barbecued chicken.

### Tony's ● ΔΔ $

☐ *1101 Harris at Eleventh; (206) 733-6319. Wine and beer. Daily 7 a.m. to 10:30 p.m. MC/VISA.* ☐ This funky Bohemian style coffee shop serves plowman's lunch, soups, salads and sandwiches. You can dine inside or on a sidewalk patio. An attractive tea, coffee and spice shop is next door.

The **Alaska Ferry Terminal** is at the foot of Harris Avenue, offering vehicle and passenger service through the state's scenically spectacular Inside Passage; (800) 642-0066. After you've finished exploring Fairhaven, head south on 12th Street—ignoring Harbor Loop and I-5 signs—and continue straight ahead for a short distance.

☺ Take a half left onto **Chuckanut Drive.** This is one of the most popular scenic drives in the state, winding at cliffside along Puget Sound. As you enter Chuckanut, note the lushly landscaped **Fairhaven Park** and extensive **rose gardens** on your left. Beyond here, the drive takes you through an upscale neighborhood and then along the tilted shoreline of a thickly wooded inlet.

*RV advisory:* Trailers aren't permitted on this narrow, winding drive, and operators of large motorhomes might hesitate as well. However, large rigs *can* make it part way through, to **Larrabee State Park**, and catch at least some of the scenery.

The route passes through a residential area terraced above the sound, and then enters thick woodlands at the state park. Larrabee offers a boat launch in a pretty little cove and—a bit farther along—a campground, picnic area, beach access and hiking trail. The campground has hookups for $14 and dry camping for $10, with showers, picnic tables and barbecues; (206) 676-2093.

Beyond the park, the forest thickens and the road becomes a real cliffhanger. You soon encounter a cute little café teetered on a ledge above a wooded creek ravine.

### ☺ Oyster Creek Inn ● ΔΔΔ $$

☐ *240 Chuckanut Dr.; (206) 766-6179. Northwest cuisine; wine and beer. Lunch and dinner daily. MC/VISA.* ☐ Drop lamps, warm woods and white napery accent this cozy dining room and the view down to the creek is pleasant. The menu is quite creative, offering charbroiled lamb, seafood stew with king crabs and prawns in ginger garlic sauce, pepper-crusted lamb loin, and Samish Bay oysters fetched up fresh from a nearby oyster farm.

To reach the **Samish Bay Shellfish Farm,** take a narrow, winding road down to the bay from the restaurant. You can watch folks shuck and prepare oysters, and then buy some smoked or fresh ones. The sales room is open Monday-Friday 8 to 5, Saturday 10 to 5 and Sunday 1 to 5; MC/VISA; (206) 766-6002.

A short distance south of the oyster inn farm, you shuck the thick woods and enter a delta flat, rich with row crops and commercial flower farms. It's a great drive in spring when the blossoms are a-bloom. Mount Baker and others of the Cascade Range add a dramatic backdrop to this bucolic scene. Take a right at a sign indicating Bayview State Park. You'll pass through the

1869 farm community of **Edison,** which looks its age in a prim sort of way.

Less than a mile out of town, just beyond the cottage style Edison Liquor Store, turn right at the Samish Island sign onto Bayview-Edison Road. Go about a mile and a half and turn left, staying with Bayview-Edison. If you continue straight ahead, you'll wind up on **Samish Island**, a low-lying agricultural patch that offers little of visual interest. Follow Bayview-Edison through this lush farmland and you'll eventually return to shoreside. **Bayview State Park** is basically a picnic area and campground and—of course—a view of the bay; $14 with hooklups, $10 without; (206) 757-0227. The community of **Bayview** just beyond is a gathering of shoreside homes. That familiar looking town you see across the water is Anacortes.

If you'd like to stretch your legs or unleash your bike, stop at a parking area on your left for **Padilla Bay Shore Trail.** The trail itself is just ahead on the right. After four miles beyond, the highway crosses State Route 20; just beyond, follow signs into a particularly fetching little town.

# La Conner

**Population: 700**                                    **Elevation: 75 feet**

☺ La Conner is a wonderfully preserved example of a rural turn-of-the-century village—not Victorian but no-nonsense wood-frame American. It sits prettily along the narrow Swinomish Channel between the mainland and Skagit Island. The downtown area offers an impressive assortment of shops, boutiques, galleries and trendy cafès. To get there, follow the highway into town until it bumps into First Street, then find a place to park.

Shops scamper off in both directions, offering a good mix of artwork, antiques and American folk crafts. Pause to nibble samples at the **Swinomish Smoked Salmon** stall; it's excellent and the prices are fair. The stuff is prepared at the **Swinomish Indian Reservation** on adjacent Skagit Island. From First Street, a set of stairs will lead you to a tilted neighborhood of fine old homes and to an historic museum. It's not in one of those handsome houses, but in a cinderblock building.

☺ *Skagit County Historical Museum* ● *501 Fourth St.; (206) 466-3365. Wednesday-Sunday 1 to 5. Adults $1, kids 50 cents.* ⊡ This is a nicely assembled museum, with artifacts in uncluttered display cases. Exhibits include a farmhouse kitchen scene with a plate of gingerbread cookies and canning jars, a 1912 Easy automatic washer, lots of women's costumes, a detailed general store, blacksmith shop and tack room, and—something we've not seen before in a museum—a moonshiner's still.

## WHERE TO DINE

☺ *Calico Cupboard Café* ● ∆∆ $ ∅

⊡ *720 S. First St.; (206) 466-4451. American; no alcohol. Weekdays 8 to 4, weekends 8 to 5. No credit cards.* ⊡ This exceedingly adorable place looks like a movie set for grandmaw's kitchen, with lace curtains and maple furniture. The bakery is excellent, and the place serves tasty lunches, such as chicken pot pie, Oriental chicken salad and smoked salmon scramble.

*China Pearl* ● ∆∆ $$

⊡ *505 First St.; (206) 466-1000. Chinese; wine and beer. Tuesday-Sunday 11:30 to 9:30. MC/VISA.* ⊡ Appropriate to its La Conner locale, China Pearl is a blend of Asian and rural American; would you believe wainscotting and red tasseled lanterns? The menu does the Mandarin-Szechuan-Cantonese thing, with a couple of specials, such as sizzling beef with scallops and a stir fry of shrimp, chicken bits, snow peas, baby corn and bamboo shoots.

**Lighthouse Inn** ● △△ $$ ∅

◻ *First Street at Morris; (206) 466-3147. American, mostly seafood; full bar service. Lunch and dinner Sunday-Friday, dinner only Saturday. MC/VISA, DISC.* ◻ The Lighthouse menu is an interesting mix: fresh seafood, curried Thai chicken, steak teriyaki, sweet and sour prawns and veal Oscar. The nautical wood-paneled dining has picture windows over the channel.

From La Conner, retrace your route out of town and fork to the right, following Conway signs. You'll pass through more farm country and cross the Skagit River. You reach the edge of small **Conway** at Interstate 5, where you can hop aboard and head briskly south to Everett. If you want to explore **Camano Island,** shun the freeway and go south to **Stanwood** and follow State Route 532 onto the island. This is a pleasant but not arousing route, through a mix of woods and rural homes. **Camano Island State Park** occupies a wooded shoreline, with hiking, picnicking and camping; flush potties and showers, no hookups, for $10.

Coming off the island, you can take a right turn and hug the shoreline, passing through the **Tulalip Indian Reservation,** a mix of farms and woods. If you miss the turn (it isn't marked), you'll wind up back at the freeway. The Tulalip route also returns you to I-5, at **Marysville.** It's an attractive community that's being absorbed into the growing Everett-Seattle megalopolis. Just below is the leading edge of that megalopolis.

# Everett

**Population: 70,000**                    **Elevation: 21 feet**

This sturdy working community offers several items of visitor interest, including some fine examples of turn-of-the-century mansions and an attractive marina. Particularly popular with visitors is the giant Boeing assembly plant, where the world's largest airplanes are pieced together.

Everett began as an elaborate planned community in 1891, funded by John D. Rockefeller. He and his New York cohorts wanted to build a grand city at the end of the Great Northern Railroad. Most of the rail traffic went south to Seattle, which came alive as the gateway to the 1900 Yukon Gold Rush. However, Everett thrived as a lumber center, primarily through the efforts of Frederick Weyerhauser. This German-born immigrant started with pennies and hard work and, in 1903, built the world's largest lumber mill in Everett. Although later mills eclipsed it, Weyerhauser is still one of the world's biggest lumber companies.

Everett is the largest city between Seattle and the Canadian border. Once a rather tatty town, it has started dressing up its old business district, including work on Colby Square, a theme shopping complex. The town's future growth is definitely assured. The adjoining U.S. Naval Station Puget Sound is getting most of the ships and shore operations from naval bases being closed in California during this decade. Also, orders are coming in for Boeing's new 777 airliner.

To catch the city's highlights, take exit 198 just below Marysville, and follow Marine View Drive (State Highway 529 south) toward the Port of Everett. Follow it across the Snohomish River and assorted other waterways to the waterfront. When you see signs indicating the Port of Everett North

Marina and Hat Island Ferry, turn right into the waterfront (13th Street) for a peek at the **Firefighters Museum.** It's more of an exhibit hall that a museum; doors are locked, although you can look through large windows at some vintage fire engines.

Five blocks farther along, at 18th and Marine View Drive, you'll see an imposing oversized Swiss chalet on your right. Once the elaborate business office for the Weyerhauser lumber operation, it now houses the **visitor center** of the Everett/Snohomish County Convention and Visitor Bureau; open weekdays 9 to 5. Even if you don't need Everett information, this grand edifice is worth a peek.

☺ The attractive new **Everett Marina** is just west of the visitor center, with a few shops and harbor-view restaurants in its **Marina Village.** From here, you can catch shuttle boats to **Jetty Island.** Although it's manmade, the island has become a popular bird refuge. If you'd like go cruising, the sidewheeler **River Queen,** berthed nearby, offers voyages up the Snohomish River (listed below). Its ticket office, behind the convention and visitor bureau, functions as a visitor center when the bureau is closed.

Continue along the waterfront, past the entrance to **Naval Station Everett,** over a viaduct and past the large steam-chuffing **Scott Paper Company** plant. Then go left one block up Everett Avenue (at the I-5 sign) and left again onto Grand Avenue. Grand and Rucker—a block above and parallel—are lined with stately turn-of-the-century homes, built by lumber barons and merchants. Follow Grand several blocks until it curves to the right up Alverson, then double back onto Rucker for more fancy homes.

As you near the business district, turn left up California Street and follow it five blocks to Rockefeller. Then go right to the **Snohomish County Museum,** on the left at 2817 Rockefeller. Just beyond, turn left onto Hewitt Avenue and follow it half a mile, over a viaduct, to the **Everett Museum.** It's in a handsome old brick and stone building, 2915 Hewitt at Maple Street. Head back downtown and explore the old but well-maintained business district. A required stop for shoppers and browsers is the Everett Publick Market, 284 Grand. This homely old masonry structure contains more than a dozen shops, galleries and cafés. The upper level features a 36-dealer antique mall.

To see the world's largest assembly plant, head south on Rucker through a couple of miles of Everett business and residential areas. It becomes Evergreen Way and hits State Route 526 freeway above Mukilteo. Turn right and drive about a mile west to the **Boeing Airplane Company's** massive complex at Paine Field. Note the rows of freshly painted 747s, 757s and perhaps even a new 777 parked on the tarmac. Take the third Boeing plant exit, following signs to the tour center.

**Suggested shortcut**: If you want to bypass downtown, take Maple Street south from the Everett Museum; it crosses Pacific Avenue and blends onto I-5. A few miles below, at exit 189, turn west onto State Route 526 and follow it to Paine Field.

## ACTIVITIES, TOURS AND ATTRACTIONS
### In order of appearance

☺ *The River Queen* • *1712 W. Marine Dr.; (206) 259-2743.* ⬜ This authentic replica of a 19th century sidewheeler offers historic and nature cruises and lunch and dinner voyages along the Everett waterfront and up the Snohomish River. The nature cruise passes through one of the state's largest wetland preserves. On-board features include a bar and Dixieland jazz band.

**Jetty Island tours** ● *Adjacent to Everett Marina; (206) 259-0300.* ☐ During summer, a free ferry takes visitors to man-made Jetty Island, where the Everett Parks and Recreation Department sponsors nature walks, campfire programs and concerts. It's a nice place for picnicking, birdwatching and viewing offshore boat races.

**Snohomish County Museum** ● *2817 Rockefeller; (206) 259-2022. Thursday-Saturday 1 to 4. Donations appreciated.* ☐ This storefront museum exhibits pioneer artifacts and photos recalling the county's early developments in lumber, railroading and shipping.

☺ **Everett Museum** ● *2915 Hewitt Ave.; (206) 259-8849 or (206) 259-8873. Wednesday-Sunday 1 to 4. Donations appreciated.* ☐ This well-organized museum is interesting inside and out. It's housed in 1906 brick, one of Everett's oldest commercial buildings. Within are turn-of-the-century room groupings, Native American artifacts and historic photos of Everett's developing years, including early pix of Weyerhauser's lumber mill.

☺ **Boeing assembly plant tour** ● *Paine Field, State Highway 526; (206) 342-4801. Tours weekdays 8:30 to 4; free. Reservations aren't required but tours fill up quickly in summer, so arrive early to get a ticket for the next departure. Children under 10 not permitted. Gift shop with Boeing logo items; it accepts MC/VISA.* ☐ Even those who hate to fly will be fascinated by this 90-minute tour of Boeing's 747, 757 and 777 assembly plant. Here, the superlatives flow as freely as a jetfoil. It's the world's largest assembly plant, where the world's largest commercial airplanes are assembled. The huge new Boeing 777 facility was recently added to the tour. This versatile medium-sized jetliner goes into service in mid-decade. After a video on Boeing's history, visitors are taken through an underground utility tunnel and then by elevator to a catwalk in the mile-long building. Here, they look down upon wings and fuselages being stitched together by giant cranes and an ant-swarm of workers. Later, the tour bus buzzes the flight line, where an international lineup of aircraft await delivery.

## Other tours

**Millstone Coffee Plant tour** ● *729 SE 100th St.; (206) 347-3848. Thirty-minute tours; call for hours.* ☐ You'll learn how fancy coffees are roasted, blended and packaged in this aromatic tour.

**Heritage Flour Mills tour** ● *2925 Chestnut St.; (206) 258-1582. Tours Tuesday-Friday; call for schedule.* ☐ Have a look at the state's largest stone flour grinding wheel, and then browse through the adjacent country store.

## WHERE TO DINE

**Anthony's Home Port** ● ∆∆ $$$ ∅

☐ *1726 W. Marine Drive at Marina Village; (206) 252-3333. American, mostly seafood; full bar service. Lunch Monday-Saturday 11 to 3, dinner nightly from 5, Sunday brunch 9:30 to 2:30. MC/VISA, AMEX.* ☐ This attractive place offers ample harbor views, either from the open-beam ceiling dining room or from an outside deck. Fresh sautéed fish is a feature, along with a good shellfish selection, plus medallions of beef and a couple of chickens and chops.

### ☺ *Buck's American Café* • ΔΔ $$

⊓ *2901 Hewitt Ave, (at Pine, near Everett Museum); (206) 258-1351. American; wine and beer. Lunch weekdays from 11, dinner Monday-Saturday from 5; closed Sunday. MC/VISA, DISC.* ⊓ Housed in handsome brick, Buck's has a pleasing yesterday look with tile floors, milk glass lighting, a long marble bar and a couple of moose heads staring morosely from the walls. The small, busy menu ranges from peppercorn steak to seafood sauté to assorted pastas. There's also an extensive raw bar for lovers of the slippery.

### *Portobello* • ΔΔ $$$

⊓ *1128 Marine View Drive at Marina Village; (206) 258-6254. American-continental, mostly seafood; full bar service. Dinner nightly from 5, lunch weekdays 11 to 4, weekend brunch 9 to 2. MC/VISA.* ⊓ The nautically simple dining room focuses mostly on the waterfront, offering views of Puget Sound and the far-away Olympics. The menu has a dual focus: seafood and European specialties. Try the tiger prawns sautéed with tomatoes, garlic and basil with fettuccine; the chicken Portobello with mushrooms, tarragon, brandy, wine and cheese sauce; veal Marsala; or an assortment of pastas.

### ☺ *The Sisters* • ΔΔ $ ∅

⊓ *2804 Grand Ave. (in Everett Public Market); (206) 252-0480. American; no alcohol. Breakfast and lunch daily 7 to 4.* ⊓ Funkily appealing family café in the town marketplace, featuring an interesting assortment of home-made soups and quiche. Vegans will like the bountiful salads and vegetarian burger with a cashew finish. Pancakes smothered in blueberry sauce are a morning specialty. Also, one could be tempted to start the day decadently with the excellent blackberry pie.

## ANNUAL EVENTS

### Bellingham to Everett

**Tulip Festival,** first two weeks of April in La Conner; (206) 466-4778.

**Salty Sea Days** boat festival at the Everett Marina in early June; (206) 252-5181.

**Ski to Sea Festival,** Memorial Day Weekend with street fairs, carnival and parades in Bellingham and Fairhaven, plus an 85-mile endurance run from the Cascades to Fairhaven; (206) 734-8180.

**Lummi Stommish Water Festival,** mid-June, with Native American canoe races and such, at the Lummi Indian Reservation near Bellingham; (206) 734-8180.

**Strawberry Festival,** early June in Marysville; (206) 659-7700.

**Jetty Island Days** July to September, with free ferry rides, regattas and guides nature walks on Everett's offshore island; (206) 259-0300.

**Northwest Washington Fair,** mid-August at Whatcom County Fairgrounds in Lyndon, northeast of Bellingham; (206) 354-4111.

**Washington State International Air Fair,** late August at Everett's Paine Field; (206) 355-2266.

**Harvest Fest,** October in Marysville; (206) 659-7700.

**Arts Alive** art festival, early November in La Conner; (206) 466-4778.

# TRIP PLANNER

**WHEN TO GO** ● The Olympic Peninsula is a spring-summer-fall place. Many national and state park facilities and museums are closed in winter, or they operate on reduced hours. Exposed to the open sea, the western face of the peninsula catches the brunt of winter storms. They're beautiful to watch from coastal vantage points, but not much fun to navigate.

**WHAT TO SEE** ● Fort Flagler and Fort Worden state parks, Jefferson County Museum in Port Townsend, Sequim Dungeness Museum in Sequim, Port Angeles waterfront and Clallam County Museum, drive-through bunkers at Salt Creek Recreation Area west of Port Angeles, Makah Cultural and Research Center museum at Neah Bay, Grays Harbor Historical Seaport in Aberdeen, the cute old waterfront town of Westport.

**WHAT TO DO** ● Explore Olympic National Park afoot at the Staircase Rapids Trail and Hoh Rain Forest trails; drive to the Olympic heights of Hurricane Ridge above Port Angeles; catch a cruise to Victoria from Port Townsend or Port Angeles; walk the wonderful old streets of Port Townsend; stroll the Waterfront Trail at Port Angeles; take a wilderness beach hike from Lake Ozette or La Push; catch a whale with your camera off the coast of Westport.

## Useful contacts

**Forks Chamber of Commerce,** P.O. Box 1249, Forks, WA 98331; (800) 44-FORKS or (206) 374-2531.

**Grays Harbor Chamber of Commerce,** 506 Duffy St., Aberdeen, WA 98520; (800) 321-1924 or (206) 532-1924.

**Grays Harbor Tourism Council,** 2109 Sumner Ave., Suite 202, Aberdeen, WA 98520; (206) 532-8857.

**Olympic National Park,** 600 E. Park Ave., Port Angeles, WA 98362; (206) 452-0330.

**Port Angeles Chamber of Commerce,** 121 E. Railroad Ave., Port Angeles, WA 98362; (206) 452-2363.

**Port Townsend Chamber of Commerce,** 2437 E. Sims Way, Port Townsend, WA 98368; (206) 385-2722.

**Olympic Peninsula Travel Association,** P.O. Box 625, Port Angeles, WA 98362-0112.

**Sequim/Dungeness Valley Chamber of Commerce,** P.O. Box 907 (1192 E. Washington St.), Sequim, WA 98382; (206) 683-6197.

**Westport-Grayland Chamber of Commerce,** P.O. Box 306, Westport, WA 98595; (800) 345-6223 or (206) 268-0991.

## Olympic Peninsula radio stations

You'll get lots of Canadian stations here, particularly in the northern part, since Victoria sits across the strait. Seattle stations (see Chapter four) carry over here as well.

QMFM, 103.5-FM, Victoria—soft hits
KBAC, 104-FM, Forks—country and popular
KAYO, 99.3-FM, Aberdeen—country
KGSO, 95.3-FM, Hoquiam—popular and news
KJTT, 110-AM, Oak Harbor—popular oldies
CKWX, 1130-AM, Victoria—country
KAPY, 1290-AM Port Angeles—70s, 80s and 90s pop
CKBA, 1200-AM, Victoria—oldies, mostly rock
KBAC, 1490-AM, Forks—country and popular
KAYO, 1450-AM, Aberdeen—country
KSGO, 1490-AM, Hoquiam—popular and news
KDUX, 1300-AM, Aberdeen—hard rock

### Chapter six
# *OLYMPIC PENINSULA*
**Snowy summits, rocky beaches, soggy forests**

---

***WASHINGTON IS A STATE OF EXTREMES,*** and nowhere are they expressed more dramatically than on the Olympic Peninsula. It's one of the few places on earth where two hours' travel can take you from a rock-bound seacoast through a moss-draped rain forest into granite peaks graced with glaciers. It's the equivalent of driving 1,500 miles from the Washington coast toward the North Pole.

The Olympic Mountains dominate the peninsula, running northwest to southeast, forming a striking snow-streaked ridge line. At their base, alluvial skirts of forests tilt gently toward the water. The combination of a temperate lowland next to the ocean and the cool mountain mass create ideal conditions for rainfall. Washington's west coast is the wettest area in America—with the exception of a few isolated regions of Hawaii. The mountains are both a blotter and a barrier, soaking up most of the moisture and creating a rainshadow for the northern Olympic Peninsula and Puget Sound. The area around Sequim (*squim*) receives only about 17 inches of rain a year, compared with more than 140 on the west coast. Contrary to what some other guidebooks suggest, however, Sequim is hardly a desert. The area is a mix of forests and meadowlands.

The peninsula's watery borders are the Pacific Ocean, the Strait of Juan de Fuca and Puget Sound's Hood Canal. Despite its name, the "canal" is a natural waterway that separates the Olympic and Kitsap peninsulas. Crossed by a single bridge, Hood Canal effectively isolates the Olympic Peninsula from the rest of Washington. It is thus relatively unsettled, even though the area to the east is the state's most densely populated region. Port Angeles, the peninsula's largest city, has fewer than 18,000 residents.

Most of the peninsula's mountainous heart and its Pacific coast wilderness are enclosed in Olympic National Park, ensuring continued protection from development. That doesn't mean it's ignored by the world outside. Hundreds of thousands of visitors explore its beaches and rain forests, nibble at the edges of its mountains and follow hiking trails to their heights. Olympic National Park is the tenth most popular unit of the federal parks system, receiving about three million visitors a year.

Our driving tour skirts the edges of the mountainous peninsula, with forays inland where roads permit. Further exploration requires hiking, which we certainly recommend at several Olympic National Park trailheads. Since it dominates the peninsula's landscape and provides much of its recreation, the park is the first thing to consider in planning a visit to the area.

## OLYMPIC NATIONAL PARK

Man has lived on the peninsula's perimeter for centuries. Thriving on a plenitude of berries, roots and fish, and building elaborate wood plank houses, the coastal Indians were among the most sophisticated tribes in the West. Their descendants still occupy several reservations here.

The Washington coast's earliest visitors—Juan de Fuca, Juan Perez, Robert Gray and George Vancouver—made note of this wild peninsula and its imposing mountain spine. However, it wasn't explored by land until 1885, when Lieutenant Joseph P. O'Neil led the first trek into its interior. James Christie accomplished a north to south crossing in 1889-90, then O'Neil returned in 1890 and crossed east to west.

Their reports of this stunning wilderness moved President Grover Cleveland to create the Olympic Forest Reserve in 1897. Part of it was upgraded to national monument status in 1909 by Teddy Roosevelt, and then Franklin D. Roosevelt elevated it to national park status in 1938. An important motivation for the area's preservation was to protect its great herds of native elk. The Roosevelt elk, which was named for Teddy, still thrives, with a population of about 5,000, mostly on the western slope.

Today, four-fifths of the Olympic Peninsula is either national park or national forest land. The park encompasses 923,000 acres, including skinny coastal stretches that protect 57 miles of wilderness beach. Despite their craggy, glaciated ramparts, the Olympic Mountains aren't particularly high. Mount Olympus is a mere 7,965 feet, lower than many peaks in the Cascades. However, incessant precipitation keeps its glaciers fed and watered; the heights are never free of snow.

### The essentials

A $5 per car entrance fee is collected in summer at **Elwha, Heart o' the Hills** (entrance to Hurricane Ridge), **Hoh Rain Forest, Staircase** and **Sol Duc.** Other entrances are free in summer, and all are free from mid-September to mid-May.

**Visitor facilities:** Services are scattered in an arc about the park's wide perimeter. Roads crawl into its flanks in several areas, often ending at trailheads for access to more than 600 miles of backcountry hiking.

The main visitor center is just above **Port Angeles** at 3002 Mount An-

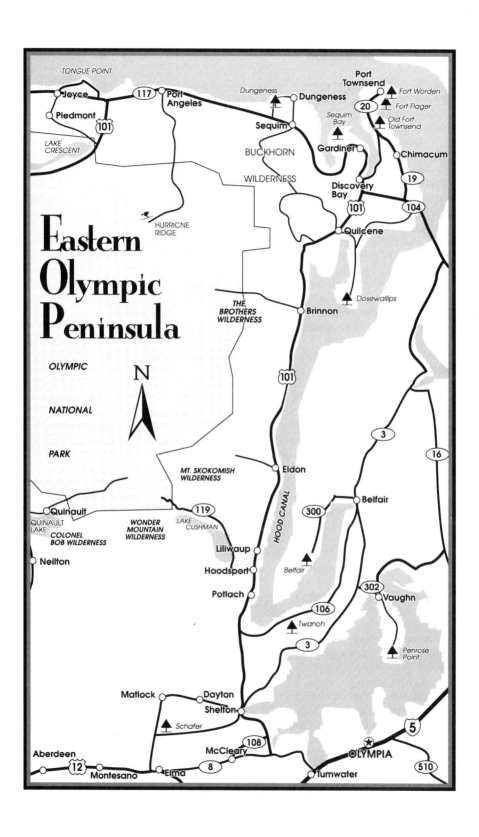

# Eastern Olympic Peninsula

N

OLYMPIC NATIONAL PARK

TONGUE POINT

Joyce
Piedmont
LAKE CRESCENT
117
Port Angeles
101

Dungeness
Dungeness
Sequim
Sequim Bay
Gardiner
BUCKHORN
WILDERNESS

Port Townsend
Fort Worden
20
Fort Flager
Old Fort Townsend
Chimacum
19

HURRICNE RIDGE

Discovery Bay
101
Quilcene
104

THE BROTHERS WILDERNESS
Dosewallips
Brinnon

101

3
16

MT. SKOKOMISH WILDERNESS
Eldon

Quinault
QUINAULT LAKE
COLONEL BOB WILDERNESS
Neilton
WONDER MOUNTAIN WILDERNESS
LAKE CUSHMAN
119
Liliwaup
Hoodsport
Potlach
HOOD CANAL

Belfair
300
Belfair
302
Vaughn
106
Twanoh
3
Penrose Point

Matlock
Dayton
Shelton
Schafer
108
McCleary
8
Elma
Aberdeen
12
Montesano
Tumwater
OLYMPIA
5
510

geles Road. Its museum and interpretive center is open daily 8:30 to 5:30 in summer and 9 to 4 the rest of the year. Park headquarters and the park's mailing address is: 600 E. Park Ave., Port Angeles, WA 98362; (206) 452-4501 or (206) 452-0330.

The park's deepest highway penetration is 17 miles, from the interpretive center to **Hurricane Ridge,** high on the mountain's flanks at 5,200 feet. It's open daily in summer, and Friday through Monday the rest of the year. The road may be closed temporarily by winter snow. Facilities include a ranger station, exhibit center and cafè. The gate is at **Heart o' the Hills** entrance station, five miles above the interpretive center. A campground at Heart O' the Hills is kept open the year around.

**Hoh Rain Forest** visitor center on the park's western edge is open daily 9 to 6:30 in summer and 9 to 4 the rest of the year. (It may not always be staffed in winter.) Other facilities, with summer ranger stations, are at **Staircase** in the southeastern corner, **Dosewallips** on the eastern edge, **Deer Park** on the northeastern edge, and **Elwha, Storm King,** and **Sol Duc** to the northwest. In the west, there are ranger stations at **Ozette, Mora** (near La Push)**, Kalaloch, Queets** and **Quinault.**

**Activities:** Hiking, backpacking, beachwalking, rain forest strolls and fishing draw three million visitors each year. Boat ramps are available at **Lake Crescent** to the north, **Ozette** to the northwest and **Willaby** (on Quinault Lake) to the southwest. For a list of naturalist activities and other park essentials, pick up a free copy of the *Olympic National Park* newspaper, available throughout the park during the summer.

**Food and lodging:** Several concessionaires operate lodges and motels within the park and there's a snack bar at **Hurricane Ridge.** Park concessionaires are **Kalaloch Lodge,** HC 80, Box 1100, Forks, WA 98331, (206) 962-2271; **Lake Crescent Lodge,** HC 62, Box 11, Port Angeles, WA 98362, (206) 928-3211; **Log Cabin Resort,** 6540 E. Beach Rd., Port Angeles, WA 98362, (206) 928-3245; and **Sol Doc Hot Springs Resort,** P.O. Box 2169, Port Angeles, WA 98362, (206) 327-3583. (Some are listed with more detail under their nearest towns, below.)

**Camping:** Seventeen campgrounds are within the park, most with flush potties, barbecue pits and picnic tables; no hookups or showers. Most are $8 a night, and accommodate both RVs and tents. Some are closed in the winter while others remain open, with no fees if cold weather requires that water be shut off. Several Olympic National Forest campsites are just off the fringes of the national park, offering the usual thickly wooded, no-hookup campsites.

**When to go:** The park is best visited from spring through fall. The lower elevation climate is mild enough for winter visits, although several facilities are closed or operate on reduced hours. And you should expect to get wet on the western slope. Hikers headed for the high country should wait for trails to clear of snow, generally mid-June to early July; they can be closed again as early as November.

**Winter activities:** Hurricane Ridge has a poma, rope tows and cross country ski trails, open weekends and holidays from December through March, weather permitting. For snow conditions, call (206) 452-0329.

*RV advisory:* Roads around the park's periphery are gently inclined with easy curves, posing no problem for large rigs or trailers. The route to **Hurricane Ridge** is a seven-percent climb with some switchbacks, but it can be negotiated by a carefully-driven rig, and there's ample turn-around and parking at the top. Long, winding roads from Highway 112 in the northwest to **Ozette** and from Highway 101 in the southwest to **Queets** can be handled by RVs, although trailers and big rigs will find them to be a chore, and they should be avoided in foul weather.

## OLYMPIA TO PORT TOWNSEND

If you're approaching the Olympic Peninsula from Interstate 5, take exit 104 just south of Olympia and head west on a freeway, following U.S. 101 North signs. The highway rims the entire peninsula before fleeing south to Aberdeen and on to Oregon. Heading west, you'll shortly shed Olympia's suburbia and enter a woodland, skimming the mudflats of Puget Sound's southern reaches.

At a junction with State Highway 8, stay on 101 north toward Shelton. The freeway ends just beyond and you'll soon see the **Olympic Peninsula Visitors Information Center** on your right (near a Texaco station). **Shelton** is an industrialized scatter of a working person's town; population 7,620. To pass through its ordinary low-rise downtown area, take Highway 3 and follow city center signs. At mid-town, turn left onto Railroad Avenue and take it past a small park with an old steam logging train on display. Another **visitor information center** occupies a caboose, open Monday-Friday 9 to 4. Follow Railroad Avenue for about a mile and you'll rejoin Highway 101.

This initial stretch of highway through second growth forest and scattered homes offers little of interest. About eighteen miles will deliver you to the hamlet of **Potlatch,** where you begin a long roadside relationship with **Hood Canal**. Nearby **Potlatch State Park** has RV and tent camping ($14 with hookups, $10 without), an underwater park and a nice picnic area on a sandspit reaching into Hood Canal; (206) 877-5361. It's closed in winter.

**Hoodsport** isn't a brand of athletic shoe for kids in south central Los Angeles; it's another small town with a café or two and a motel or two. At the far end of town, you can gather material on Olympic National park and forest at the **Hood Canal Ranger Station.** It's open daily in summer 8 to 4:30 and weekdays the rest of the year 7 to 4:30.

Head inland past the ranger station for your first encounter with Olympic National Park, at Staircase. The route takes you past **Lake Cushman,** a reservoir and recreation area busy with summer cabins. **Lake Cushman State Park** offers campsites with or without hookups ($14 or $10), showers, nature trails, a boat launch and swimming areas; (206) 877-5491. It's closed in winter.

Continuing beyond the lake, you'll catch occasional views of the craggy Olympics ahead and the long and slender blue finger of Hood Canal behind. Four miles of level and only slightly potholed gravel road takes you to **Staircase,** with a national park campground and picnic area. From here, trails follow the north fork of the Skokomish River deep into Olympic wilds.

☺ Take a 1.9-mile trail through thick, moss-draped forest to **Staircase Rapids,** for a scenic and relatively easy hike. It follows a busy stream to a wild brace of rapids, crosses and arched bridge and then returns through a quiet forest glen. The odd name, incidentally, comes from stair-step trails carved up these steep slopes for pack mules during explorations in the 1890s.

Back on Highway 101, you'll pass through several miles of pleasantly monotonous scenery along Hood Canal. No wilderness here; the route is busy with homes, RV parks and small motels. **Lilliwaup** consists of a motel and grocery store occupying a pretty inlet at the base of steep, wooded slopes. **Hamma Hamma Recreation Area** is just beyond, an Olympic National Forest facility with picnic tables and hiking trails. About 20 miles north of Lilliwaup, **Dosewallips State Park** has camping inland, on the banks of the Dosewallips River ($14 and $10), and a nice picnic area and beach access on the canal side; (206) 796-4414; closed in winter. Nearby, another road penetrates Olympic National Park, to a Dosewallips campground, seasonal ranger station and trailheads. It, too, is closed in winter.

A few miles beyond on Highway 101, watch on your right for the **Mount Walker Viewpoint**, offering nice images of Hood Canal and the Olympics. It's four miles off the highway, opposite the entrance to Rainbow Campground. Continuing on, **Quilcene**, population 100, has a ranger station and a few shabby businesses.

Fork to the right here, forsaking Highway 101 and head for **Chimacum**. You'll enter a mix of second growth forest and farmlands. When you reach Chimacum, start following signs toward Fort Flagler State Park. At **Port Haddock,** turn right at a stop sign onto State Highway 116 to stay on course for the park. The route takes you the length of a slender, exceptionally pretty peninsula of farm and forest, with water views on both sides. Wooded islands stand just offshore. Along the way, you'll pass an appealing resort, marina and restaurant:

☺ **The Old Alcohol Plant** ● ⌂⌂⌂ **$$$** ∅

☐ *310 Alcohol Loop Rd. (P.O. Box 1369), Port Hadlock, WA 98339; (206) 385-7030. Hotel rooms $49 to $85, townhouses $100 to $130, penthouse $250. MC/VISA.* ☐ Sitting at the head of Port Townsend Bay, this concrete and brick structure was built in 1911 to process alcohol from sawdust. The firm went broke after two years and the large, square-shouldered structure stood vacant for decades. It's now a distinctive resort with a locally-popular restaurant. Fabric wall hangings and art dress up the lofty interior spaces. The restaurant, an elevated bar and outdoor deck offer impressive views of the bay. It's open daily from 6:30 a.m., serving American-continental fare.

Just beyond the Alcohol Plant, follow Highway 116 across a bridge onto Marrowstone Island. This puts you on Fort Flagler Road, passing through a pleasing landscape of thin forests, pasturelands, moors and rural homes. Tiny **Nordland** presents a scruffily pleasant New England seacoast scene, with a weathered country store and sailboats at anchor. Just beyond, the highway passes postage stamp-sized **Mystery Bay State Park** with picnic tables and a boat launch. It then ends at a much larger park:

☺ **Fort Flagler State Park** ● *Nordland, WA 98358-9699; (206) 385-1259. RV and tent sites; $15 with hookups, $11 without. Reservations accepted in summer; write to the park for a form. No credit cards. Also a youth hostel; write for information.* ☐ Flagler was part of the "Iron Triangle," one of three forts constructed in the late 19th century to defend the Admiralty Inlet entrance to Puget Sound. The others were Fort Worden at Port Angeles and Fort Casey on Whidbey Island. Between the three, they could have directed a wicked field of cross-fire into an enemy fleet. There's much to see here today. Two three-inch guns are still in place and several original fort buildings survive. One contains an interpretive center focusing on the history of the fort and the region. Others house park employee residences, the park office and a youth hostel. A National Fisheries Research Center sits down at the waterfront. Views from this tip of Marrowstone Island are splendid—across the Strait of Juan de Fuca to Whidbey Island and the San Juans.

Retrace your route from Marrowstone Island, pass the Alcohol Plant again and continue straight ahead, following signs to Port Townsend on Highway 116. When you hit a T-intersection, turn right and then veer to the left onto State Highway 19, which shortly blends into route 20. It's less confusing than it sounds.

# Port Townsend

**Population: 7,500**                    **Elevation: sea level**

☺ Gracefully aging Port Townsend is one of the most appealing towns in Washington and certainly the most intriguing on the Olympic Peninsula. Its main street, on a low coastal shelf, is an outdoor architectural museum, with one of the West's largest collections of 19th century brick, cut stone and false front buildings. They house boutiques, galleries and several restaurants. Cluster globe street lamps add a final touch to this Gay Nineties scene. Elegant Victorian homes stand in neighborhoods on the bluff above.

Preening contentedly with its yesterday look, this small town has more than 70 preserved buildings. This structural treasure trove came from a brief and prosperous career as a key shipping point in the Strait of Juan de Fuca.

Port Townsend was established in 1851 as a lumber shipping center. Within three decades, it had become the chief port of entry for Puget Sound, hosting consulates from several nations. Toward the end of the century, cargo ships began bypassing the town, steaming straight to new transcontinental railheads in Tacoma and Seattle. Port Townsend soon went to sleep. As Rip Van Winkle discovered, in hibernation there is preservation.

Approaching Port Townsend on Highway 20, you'll see the Chamber of Commerce **Visitor Information Center** in a salmon and blue cottage on your right, in front of Harborside Inn. It's open weekdays 9 to 5, Saturday 10 to 4 and Sunday 11 to 4. Pick up a walking tour map that lists 72 old homes, businesses and other points of interest.

Just beyond the visitor center, the highway swings onto Water Street and passes the ferry landing. Two ferries sail from Port Townsend. The Washington State Ferries link the community to Keystone on Whidbey Island. Swift catamarans of Seattle's Clipper Navigation provide passenger service to Seattle and the San Juan Islands from late spring through fall. (See details below, under "Activities.")

As you drive along the waterfront, you'll see an unfortunate mistake by town planners—an incongruously modern Bay Variety shopping center. Just beyond are five fine blocks of the 19th century business district. Park and start walking, since the compact historic area is best seen afoot. The town's archives are stuffed into the three-story 1891 city hall toward the west end:

☺ *Jefferson County Historical Museum* ● *Water and Madison; (206) 385-1003. Monday-Saturday 11 to 4 and Sunday 1 to 4 in summer; weekends only in the off-season. Adults $2, families $5.* ☐ The old city hall's floors brim and possibly sag with a large, pleasantly cluttered collection of pioneer relics, Indian artifacts, nautical and military memorabilia and thousands of old photos.

As you prowl downtown, don't overlook Washington Street, paralleling Water Street and tucked against the base of the coastal shelf. It also has several interesting old buildings. If you're a car buff, check out the **Bergstrom Antique and Classic Automobiles** showroom on Washington near Adams. It's not a museum, but a sales and restoration shop displaying such mechanical nifties as a bullet-nose Studebaker, Depression-era Plymouth and a vintage racing Alfa Romeo. Across Washington Street is the large **Port Townsend Antique Mall.**

## Driving Port Townsend

After doing downtown, a quickie drive will take you past other points of interest, and to Fort Worden State Park. Begin by taking Washington Street east and uphill to the ornate cut-stone **post office** at 1322 Washington near Van Buren. It originally contained the port's customs house. A few historical exhibits are in the lobby.

☺ Go up Van Buren to Jefferson and follow it west about five blocks along the bluff to the **Rothschild House** at Jefferson and Taylor. It's a beautifully restored 1868 Victorian, complete with original furnishings. Now a state park property, the mansion is open for tours in spring and summer, daily 10 to 5 by reservation the rest of the year; (206) 385-2722. If it's closed, you can still admire the elaborate flower and herbal gardens.

☺ Retrace your route on Jefferson, going about nine blocks east to the resplendent **Jefferson County Courthouse** at Walker. Built in 1892 and still in use, this Romanesque-Gothic cut stone creation looks more like a medieval castle than a county office building. During business hours, you can pass beneath its cut stone archway, step inside and admire the dark wood wainscotting and inlaid tile floors. There's a visitor information desk in the hallway; inquire about a tour to the clock tower.

Head inland on Walker, which becomes Cherry Street and takes you about a mile and a half to Fort Worden. (After about a mile, take a slight jog to the right to stay on Cherry.)

☺ *Fort Worden State Park and Conference Center* ● *200 Battery Way, Port Townsend, WA 98368; (206) 385-4730. Puget Sound Coast Artillery Museum open daily 11 to 5 in summer, weekends and holidays noon to 4 the rest of the year; free. Port Townsend Marine Science Center open Tuesday-Sunday noon to 6 in summer, weekends noon to 4 the rest of the year; suggested donation $1. Vacation Housing information is listed below under "Where to sleep."*

Fort Worden is a busy historical package. Established as part of the Iron Triangle coastal defense system, it's one of the most intact late 19th century military installations in the Northwest. The parade ground is lined with restored plantation-style buildings, housing a conference center, vacation housing units and other facilities. The Coast Artillery Museum recalls that era from the late 19th century through World War II when big guns were trained on Admiralty Inlet to forestall enemy invasions that never came. Exhibits include 16-inch shells that are heavier than a small car, a scale model of a coastal battery, military weapons, uniforms and regalia. Several coastal batteries are scattered about the fort. The small Marine Science Center, perched on Fort Worden's dock, exhibits aquariums with critters from surrounding waters, and a touchy-feely tank. Programs include beach walks, sand sculpturing and workshops.

From Fort Worden, retrace your route on Cherry/Walker until you hit Washington Street. Turn right and you'll blend onto Highway 20, pointed out of town. Stay to the right to avoid the fork back onto Highway 19, and Route 20 shortly will take you to U.S. 101. Turn right to head for Sequim and Port Angeles.

## Activities

**Ferry service** • Washington State Ferries depart several times daily from Port Townsend to Keystone on Whidbey Island. Clipper Navigation, based in Seattle, offers quick catamaran service from Port Townsend to Victoria and to Seattle, with at least one departure daily from late April to mid-October. For schedules and fares, call (800) 888-2535 or (206) 448-5000 in Seattle.

**Historical tours** • Sidewalk, waterfront and historic homes tours are conducted in summers by Guided Historical Tours, 820 Tyler St., Port Townsend, WA 98368; (206) 385-1967.

**Fishing trips and marine wildlife tours** • Sea Sport Charters, P.O. Box 805, Port Townsend, WA 98368; (206) 385-3575.

**Scenic flights and charters** • Ludlow Aviation at Jefferson County International Airport, P.O. Box 719, Port Hadlock, WA 98339; 385-6554.

**Sea kayaking** • Tours are conducted by Kayak Port Townsend, P.O. Box 1387, Port Townsend, WA 98368; (206) 385-6240.

**Theater** • Drama with an entrèe is presented by Water Street Dinner Theatre, 926 Water Street; (206) 385-2422. The Centrum Foundation presents dramas and other creative arts in the summer at Fort Worden State Park; (800) 733-3608 or (206) 385-3102. Other local drama groups are Port Townsend Community Playhouse and the Key City Players.

**Van tours** • Peninsula Tours offers van trips in Port Townsend and surrounding areas; P.O. Box 1923, Port Townsend, WA 98369; (206) 385-6346.

## Annual events

For details on these and other functions, contact the chamber of commerce at (206) 385-2722.

**Hot Jazz Port Townsend,** jazz festival in late February.

**Rhododendron Festival,** third weekend in May.

**Wooden Boat Festival,** weekend after Labor Day; the largest celebration in the country featuring wooden boats.

**Victorian Homes Tour,** self-guiding tours of 10 historic sites, third weekend in September.

**Kinetic Sculpture Race,** early October, with people-powered vehicles running a land, water and bog obstacle course.

## WHERE TO DINE

☺ **Belmont Restaurant and Saloon** • △△△ $$

☐ *925 Water St. (between Taylor and Tyler); (206) 385-3007. American; full bar service. Lunch daily from 11, dinner Sunday-Thursday 5 to 9 and Friday-Saturday 5 to 10. Major credit cards.* ☐ Dating back to 1889 and looking the part, this stylish establishment is done up in globe chandeliers, high backed booths and other period furnishings. There's a deck over the waterfront for warm-weather dining. The menu, mostly seafood, features broiled salmon, pepper prawns served with jalapeno jelly, steamed clams and mussels, plus chickens, steaks and chops. For light fare, pause at the handsome marble-topped soda fountain.

### ☺ *Blackberries* ● ∆∆ $$ Ø

◻ *Building 210, Fort Worden State Park; (206) 385-9950. Northwest regional. Dinner nightly 5 to 10, Sunday brunch 10 to 2, shorter hours in the off-season. MC/VISA.* ◻ This Northwest style restaurant recently was installed in one of Fort Worden's historic buildings. The fare draws from fresh regional seafood, meats and veggies, prepared with innovating spicing.

### ☺ *El Sarape* ● ∆∆ $$

◻ *628 Water St. (Madison); (206) 379-9343. Mexican; full bar service. Monday-Thursday 11:30 to 9, Friday-Saturday 11:30 to 10, Sunday noon to 8. MC/VISA, DISC.* ◻ Bright serapes and Mexican murals decorate raw brick walls in this cozy place. The Latino menu focuses on seafood, with specialties such as *picato del dia* (catch of the day served in a tomato, green onion and mushroom sauce), plus the usual burritos, tacos and fajitas.

### *Public House Grill* ● ∆∆ $$

◻ *1038 Water St. (Polk); (206) 385-9708. American; full bar service. Daily from 11; full menu until 9 p.m., light fare until closing. MC/VISA.* ◻ This lofty space, once an automobile showroom, has the look and energy of a collegiate Bohemian ale house, with several micro-brews on tap to prove it. The pressed tin ceiling is decorated with banners and hung with fans. The menu is busy with grilled baby back ribs, lamb chops, chioppino, serious hamburgers, Caribbean chicken sausage and such.

### *Khu Larb Thai* ● ∆∆ $

◻ *225 Adams Street (between Water and Washington); (206) 385-5023. Thai; wine and beer. Daily 11 to 10. MC/VISA.* ◻ Thai cuisine in a 19th century town? Why not? Locals love this place and visitors will find the spicy fare tasty and inexpensive. Try the red snapper with coconut milk sauce, bell peppers and lime leaves; or prawn curry with bamboo shoots, fresh basil and pineapple in coconut milk. The large, open dining room is brightened with green nappery, hanging plants and globe chandeliers.

### *Salal Café* ● ∆∆ $

◻ *Water at Quincy; 385-6532. American; wine and beer. Breakfast and lunch Wednesday-Sunday 11 to 2, dinner Wednesday-Saturday. No credit cards.* ◻ It's a fetching little café with blonde bentwood chairs, brick and stone walls and a solarium ceiling. The eclectic menu skips spicily from quesadillas and burritos to oysters sautéed in garlic butter; there's a tofu-vegetable entrée sautéed in garlic butter for vegans.

## WHERE TO SLEEP

### *Fort Worden Vacation Rentals* ● ⌒⌒ $$ to $$$$ Ø

◻ *Fort Worden State Park, 200 Battery Way, Port Townsend, WA 98368; (206) 385-4730. Refurbished former military apartments and houses $72 to $193, unrefurbished units $59.45 to $89.45. Reservations accepted; no credit cards.* ◻ Lodgings are former officers and non-commissioned officers quarters, many with kitchens and fireplaces; some refurbished and furnished with Victorian reproductions. Unit are available with one to six bedrooms. Reservations should be made very early.

### *Harborside Inn* ● ⌒⌒⌒ $$$ Ø

◻ *330 Benedict St. (Washington), Port Townsend, WA 98368; (800) 942-5960 or (206) 385-7909. Couples and singles from $64, kitchenettes $104,* *suites $130. Rates include continental breakfast. Major credit cards.* ☐ Attractive waterfront inn with TV, rental movies, phones; some microwaves; coin laundry; pool and spa. All rooms have private patios or balconies.

### James G. Swan Hotel ● ⌂⌂ $$$ ∅

☐ *Water at Monroe, Port Townsend, WA 98368; (800) 776-1718 or (206) 385-1718. Couples, singles and suites $65 to $250.* ☐ Attractive nine-unit resort hotel with TV and room refrigerators; some room phones. Spa, coin laundry. Beach, park, marina and shopping within a block.

### ☺ Palace Hotel ● ⌂⌂ $$ to $$$$ ∅

☐ *1004 Water St., Port Townsend, WA 98368; (800) 962-0741 or (206) 385-0773. Couples $63 to $95 with private baths, $54 without; singles $58 to $90 with baths and $49 without. Major credit cards.* ☐ Restored century-old hotel with attractive Victorian décor. Fifteen rooms with TV; some refrigerators; many have views of the waterfront. **Casablanca Restaurant** serves American-Mediterranean fare 8 to 8; dinners $10 to $11; wine and beer.

### ☺ Point Hudson Resort ● ⌂⌂ $$ ∅

☐ *Point Hudson Harbor, Port Townsend, WA 98368; (800) 826-3854 or (206) 385-2828. Couples and singles $59 to $70 with full bath, $50 with half bath and $46 with shared bath. MC/VISA.* ☐ "Resort" is an overstatement, although it's an intriguing place to sleep—a restored 1934 Coast Guard station. Rooms are prim, clean and comfortable. The facility also has a marina with boat moorage available and 2,000 feet of beach frontage.

### Port Townsend Motel ● ⌂⌂ ∅

☐ *2020 Washington St. (Highway 20), Port Townsend, WA 98368; (800) 822-8696 or (206) 385-2211. Couples and singles $68 to $98, kitchenettes and suites $88 to $98. Rates include continental breakfast. Major credit cards.* ☐ Attractive 25-room motel with TV, phones; some refrigerators and microwaves. Spa and barbecue area.

### Waterstreet Hotel ● ⌂ $$$ ∅

☐ *635 Water St., Port Townsend, WA 98368; (800) 735-9810 or (206) 385-5467. Couples $50 to $75, singles $50 to $65, kitchenettes $75 to $125, suites $100 to $125. Some private and some shared baths; rates include continental breakfast. MC/VISA, AMEX.* ☐ Restored 1889 hotel near the Quincy Street Dock. Thirteen units with TV, refrigerators; some water-view rooms. Gift shop and coin laundry. **Silverwater Café** in the same building; lunch and dinner daily, Sunday brunch; health-conscious menu; wine and beer.

## Bed & breakfast inns

### ☺ Ann Starrett Mansion Victorian Inn ● ⌂⌂⌂ $$$$ ∅

☐ *744 Clay St. (Adams), Port Townsend, WA 98368; (206) 385-3205. Couples and singles $70 to $185. Major credit cards.* ☐ Elegantly restored 1889 towered mansion on a bluff overlooking Puget Sound. Beautifully furnished with museum quality American and European antiques. Frescoed ceilings, elaborate moldings and print wallpaper; dramatic spiral staircase in the octagonal tower.

### Bishop Victorian Guest Suites ● ⌂⌂⌂ $$$$ ∅

☐ *714 Washington St. (Quincy), Port Townsend, WA 98368. Couples $68 to $89, singles $54 to $89. Thirteen rooms with TV, room phones and private baths; continental breakfast. MC/VISA, AMEX.* ☐ Former 1890 tobacco warehouse converted into an office building with a Victorian inn upstairs. Rooms furnished with antiques and period reproductions. In downtown historic district, near shops, restaurants and waterfront.

**Heritage House** ● ⌂⌂⌂ *$$$ to $$$$$* Ø

☐ *305 Pierce St. (Washington), Port Townsend, WA 98368; (206) 385-6800. Couples and singles $55 to $115. Six units; four shared and two private baths; full breakfast. Major credit cards.* ☐ Italianate Victorian on the bluff above town with views of the strait and Olympics. Furnished with Victorian antiques, clawfoot tubs, period wallpaper; some original furnishings.

☺ **The James House** ● ⌂⌂⌂⌂ *$$$$* Ø

☐ *1238 Washington St., Port Townsend, WA 98368; (206) 385-1238. Twelve units, some private and some full baths; full breakfast. MC/VISA.* ☐ Grand Victorian mansion on the Port Townsend bluff, with sweeping views of the water and mountains. Furnished with period antiques and armoires; some rooms with fireplaces. Original parquet floors, ornately carved woodwork, carved mantles. Sitting amidst attractively landscaped gardens.

**Quimper Inn** ● ⌂⌂⌂ *$$$$* Ø

☐ *1306 Franklin St. (Harrison), Port Townsend, WA 98368; (206) 385-1060. Couples $70 to $130, singles $65 to $125. Five units, three with private baths; full breakfast. MC/VISA.* ☐ Victorian-era Georgian style home on the Uptown District bluff with views of water and mountains. Rooms furnished with turn of the century antiques. Large fireplace and library; mountain bikes and athletic club privileges.

## WHERE TO CAMP

**Fort Worden State Park** ● *200 Battery Way, Port Townsend, WA 98368; (206) 385-4730. RV and tent sites, $10 to $14. No reservations or credit cards.* ☐ Shaded sites at historic coastal battery; flush and pit potties, showers, picnic tables and barbecues; swimming, fishing, scuba diving, boat ramp, nature trails.

**Old Fort Townsend State Park** ● *Three miles south, off State Route 20; (206) 385-3595. RV and tent sites, $10. No reservations or credit cards.* ☐ On the site of a former fort; shaded spaces with picnic tables and barbecues, no hookups. Flush potties, showers, swimming, boat dock, fishing, trails.

**Point Hudson Resort** ● *Point Hudson Harbor, Port Townsend, WA 98368; (800) 826-3854 or (206) 385-2828. Full hookups $16, dry camping $13. Reservations accepted; MC/VISA.* ☐ Beachside sites at former Coast Guard station (listed above); flush potties, showers at the adjacent motel.

# PORT TOWNSEND TO PORT ANGELES

As you follow Highway 101 west toward Sequim, you'll catch some nice views of Discovery Bay and, once you've cleared the bay, the distant San Juan Islands.

For a peek at an overlooked bayside community and a striking collection of outdoor wooden sculptures, fork to the right onto Gardener Road, about half a mile past mileage marker 279. After a couple of miles, note the Victorian style red and white **Discovery Bay Volunteer Fire Department** structure on your left. Just beyond, turn right onto Gardener Beach Road and follow it about half a mile to the remote, upscale beachside residential community of **Gardener Bay.**

☺ The road skims the beach, then swings inland at a "local traffic only" sign and takes you past **Randy's Troll Haven.** It's an elaborate ranch complex trimmed with tiki fence posts, whimsical carvings of trolls and other curious critters. Note the castle-like mauve and gray ranch house. This area is *not* open to the public, so please drive on by. Turn left at the ranch house onto a country lane lined with more carvings. You'll shortly return to Gardiner Beach Road, which takes you back to Highway 101.

The highway heads west through a mix of pasturelands and frequently-cut forest and into the small **S'Klallam Indian Reservation** at **Blyn.** For some outstanding examples of modern Native American art, stop at the **Northwest Native Art Gallery** beside the S'Klallam Tribal Center; it's on a frontage road to your right. The gallery displays and sells intricately carved tribal masks and striking serigraphs and watercolors. It's open daily 10 to 6; (206) 681-4640; MC/VISA.

The landscape becomes increasingly attractive as you press westward, with deep inlets, thick stands of trees and emerald pasturelands. If you're here in summer, you may see some touches of brown, since you're beneath the unusual "blue sky hole" of the Sequim Peninsula, the driest area in western Washington. Just outside the town of Sequim, you'll encounter **Sequim Bay State Park,** with a wooded campground. It's a beautiful spot, with a picnic area and some campsites suspended over the water (listed below).

# Sequim

**Population: 4,019**                                    **Elevation: sea level**

That "blue hole" has made Sequim a popular retirement community, although the town itself is rather ordinary looking. It sits inland, failing to take advantage of the peninsula's fine views of the Strait of Juan de Fuca and Vancouver Island across the way.

Before reaching the downtown area, leave Highway 101 and follow White Feather Way to **John Wayne Marina,** which of course *is* at water's edge. It's a beautiful spot, occupying a crescent bay, with a small cafè, pleasure boats at anchor, green lawns and a few picnic tables. Why John Wayne? The Duke often visited this area in his converted Navy minesweeper yacht *Wild Goose.* Hearing that Clallam County needed a small craft harbor, he generously bought and donated this land in 1975. A small bronze and some Wayne memorabilia are displayed in a case in the main marina building. The small downstairs cafè is, of course, called **True Grits** (listed below).

Continuing west past the marina, you'll soon return to Highway 101. If you want to stop at the Sequim/Dungeness Valley Chamber of Commerce **visitor center,** backtrack briefly on the highway; it's on the north side, at 1192 E. Washington Street. To sample some local wine, follow signs south from Highway 101 to **Neuharth Winery,** housed in a weathered old former dairy barn; open Wednesday-Sunday 9:30 to 5:30; (206) 683-9652.

Downtown Sequim, just down the road, has a kind of ordinary 1950s look. It does offer a couple of attractions, and there's more to see if you head north out the Sequim Peninsula toward the shorefront.

When you hit a stoplight at Sequim Avenue, turn left and drive a short distance past the **Old Sequim Depot** to **Cedarbrook Herb Farm.** It's open daily, March to Christmas, 9 to 5; (206) 683-7733. Browse through an aromatic garden of herbs and sweet-smelling flowers. The farm's sales room has an extensive variety of plants and decorative plant items.

Reverse directions on Sequim Avenue, cross the highway, go one block to Cedar Street and turn left for the town museum:

☺ **Sequim Dungeness Museum** • 175 W. Cedar; (206) 683-8110. Daily 9 to 4; donations appreciated. ❑ This tidy little museum's most interesting display concerns the Manis mastodon. Its bones were unearthed nearby in 1978, as a local couple dug a hole for a pond in their yard. The dig drew national attention for the next several years, and many of the relics are on display at the museum. Other exhibits include the usual Native American relics, pioneer artifacts and period costumes.

## Driving the Sequim Peninsula

A marked 12-mile Dungeness Loop will take you around the grassy, low-lying Sequim Peninsula. The scenery isn't awesome, although you can visit a private game farm and a national wildlife refuge. Maps published by Home Realty, 618 E. Washington Avenue (Highway 101 downtown), will help you find your way; they're also available at the chamber.

Head north out Sequim Avenue (which becomes Sequim-Dungeness Way), following it past modest rural homes, moors and pasturelands. After a bit more than three miles, turn right at the "Three Crabs Restaurant" sign and drive to a small marina and the site of the old town of **Dungeness.** Back on the main road—now called Marine Drive—note the 1892 **Dungeness School** on your left, with an interesting domed bell tower. Just beyond, turn left onto Lotzgesell Road and follow signs to an outdoor zoo:

☺ **Olympic Game Farm** • Ward Road; (206) 683-4295. Open daily, 9 to 7 in summer and 10 to 4 the rest of the year. Adults $5, seniors and kids $4; combined walking-driving tour $7. ❑ This 90-acre game farm has a dual purpose—to train animals for Hollywood roles and to breed endangered species. Visitors can drive through enclosures where various critters roam, then walk the central compound, with a few animal pens, Hollywood sets and an aquarium. You might see some creatures being filmed for upcoming roles.

Return to Marine Drive, which takes you along the shoreline, past some attractive waterfront homes and a couple of small motels (see below). The route swings to the left onto Cays Road, which hits the other end of Lotzgesell Road. Turn right and follow signs toward Dungeness Spit and Recreation Area. Pass a gravel pit, then within a mile, watch for the gray and white sign on your right, pointing you north onto Voice of America Road.

**Dungeness Recreation Area** and **Dungeness National Wildlife Refuge** • Voice of America Road; (206) 683-5847 for the park and (206) 457-8451 for the wildlife area. Recreation area camping $8; wildlife refuge access $2 per family. ❑ Dungeness Spit is a skinny, 5.5-mile long finger of land extending into the Strait of Juan de Fuca. It forms Dungeness Bay, an ideal sanctuary for shorebirds, shellfish and breeding salmon. Its base is occupied by Clallam County Parks' Dungeness Recreation Area, while the seaward digit is part of Dungeness National Wildlife Refuge. You pass through the first to get to the second. The county park has picnic areas, campsites (see below), hiking trails and beach access. At the refuge, you can stroll half a mile through a forest for an overlook of the low-lying spit. The really ambitious can walk the spit's beach for an eleven-mile round trip. Views across the strait to Vancouver Island and the San Juans are fine. This is prime bird-watching area, since 30,000 waterfowl pause here in autumn and spring during their migration. Another 15,000 hang out for the entire year.

Beyond the recreation area/refuge, Lotzgesell Road makes a 90-degree turn to become Kitchen-Dock Road. After a mile or so, you'll hit a stop sign at Old Olympic Highway. Turn right and head west; it soon blends back into Highway 101, just short of Port Angeles.

## WHERE TO DINE

### ☺ Casoni's ● ΔΔ $$

□ *104 Hooker Road (1.5 miles west, Highway 101 at Carlsborg Junction); (206) 683-2415. Italian-Mediterranean; full bar service. Dinner nightly 4 to 9 in summer, Wednesday-Sunday the rest of the year. MC/VISA, DISC.* □ This cozy and tidy little Italian café is the domain of local culinary legend Mamma Casoni. It features fresh pasta with savory sauces, often innovatively spiced. Italian accented seafood, chicken and veal dishes round out the menu; the homemade cheesecake is excellent.

### The Three Crabs ● ΔΔ $$ ∅

□ *101 Three Crabs Rd.; (206) 683-4264. American, mostly seafood; full bar service. Daily from 11:30. MC/VISA.* □ In business for 35 years, this café with a nautical knotty pine interior specializes in local Dungeness crab. Assorted other seafoods—generally fried—and a few steaks round out the menu. If you like fish lightly cooked, tell the kitchen to go easy. The restaurant is on the waterfront at old Dungeness; unfortunately, planners put a parking lot between the café and the waterfront.

### True Grits Café ● ΔΔ $$

□ *John Wayne Marina; (206) 681-0577. American, mostly seafood; wine and beer. Lunch and dinner daily in summer from 11; open fewer days the rest of the year. MC/VISA.* □ This prim café overlooks the boat slips at the marina east of town. The small menu features a catch of the day, a few other fresh flippers, plus a couple of chickens and chops. On warm days, diners can adjourn to an outdoor patio.

## WHERE TO SLEEP

### Best Western Sequim Bay Lodge ● ⌂⌂⌂ $$$$ ∅

□ *268-522 Highway 101, Sequim, WA 98382; (800) 622-0691 or (206) 683-0691. Couples from $69, singles from $49, kitchenettes $89 to $139, suites $79 to $139.* □ Attractive 54-unit resort on 17 forested acres, three miles east of Sequim. Rooms with TV movies, phones; some refrigerators and microwaves. Nine-hole putting course, pool, barbecue area. Continental breakfast from October through March. **Buckhorn Grill** serves American fare; 7 a.m. to 9 p.m.; dinners $12 to $18; full bar service.

### Dungeness Bay Motel ● ⌂⌂ $$$$ ∅

□ *140 Marine Dr., Sequim, WA 98382; (206) 683-3013. Couples and singles $70 to $85. MC/VISA.* □ Five simple, well-kept housekeeping units with full kitchens; on Dungeness Bay across the road from the beach. Picture window views of Dungeness Spit and the Strait of Juan de Fuca. All non-smoking.

### Greywolf Inn Bed & Breakfast ● ⌂⌂⌂⌂ $$$ ∅

□ *395 Keeler Rd., Sequim, WA 98382; (800) 500-5889 or (206) 683-5889. Couples $62 to $98, singles $52 to $88. Six units with private baths; full breakfast. MC/VISA, AMEX.* □ Modern country home on five acres overlooking Sequim; courtyard with umbrella tables, sun decks, gazebo and Japanese-style spa. A mix of modern and antique furnishings; some canopy and four-poster beds.

☺ *Juan de Fuca Cottages* ● ⌂ *$$$$*

⌂ *182 Marine Dr., Sequim, WA 98382; (206) 683-4433. Cottages $90 to $150. MC/VISA.* ⌂ Six attractive and cozy, completely equipped family cottages, all with views of Dungeness Spit and the strait. Full kitchens, TV, spa tubs, fireplaces; landscaped grounds; beach and boat ramp across the road.

*Red Ranch Inn* ● ⌂ *$$$* ∅

⌂ *830 W. Washington, Sequim, WA 98382; (800) 777-4195 or (206)683-4195. Couples and singles from $60, kitchenettes $76, suites $80 to $90. Major credit cards.* ⌂ A 55-unit inn with TV, room phones; some with microwaves and refrigerators. **Red Ranch Restaurant** serves American fare from 3 p.m.; dinners $6 to $16; full bar service.

## WHERE TO CAMP

**Dungeness Recreation Area** ● *232 Voice of America Rd., Sequim, WA 98382; (206) 683-5847. RV and tent sites $8. No reservations or credit cards.* ⌂ Attractive sites near the beach; some shaded; barbecues and picnic tables; no hookups. Park facilities include hiking trails, picnic shelter and beach access.

**Rainbow's End RV Park** ● *261831 Highway 101, Sequim, WA 98382; (206) 683-3863. RV and tent sites, $17.50. Reservations accepted; no credit cards.* ⌂ Nicely landscaped park with creek and pond; showers, picnic tables and barbecues, coin laundry, cable TV. A mile and a half west.

**Sequim Bay State Park** ● *Four miles southeast on Highway 101; (206) 683-4235. RV and tent sites; water and electric $14; no hookups $10. No reservations or credit cards.* ⌂ Beautifully situated on Sequim Bay, some sites near the water; picnic tables and barbecues, flush and pit potties, showers. Boating, boat dock, swimming, fishing and scuba diving; nature trails. Minimart nearby.

**South Sequim RV Park** ● *282 Old Olympic Highway, Sequim, WA 98382; (206) 683-8048. RV and tent sites; full hookups $13.50, no hookups $6, tent sites $8. Reservations accepted; no credit cards.* ⌂ Some pull-throughs; showers, picnic tables and fire pits; bocci ball and horse shoes.

# Port Angeles

**Population: 17,710**                    **Elevation: sea level**

As you approach the peninsula's largest town, you pass through a typical string of suburban commercialism, then a sign proclaims: Where the Olympics greet the sea.

And indeed they do. Port Angeles occupies an imposing setting, sandwiched between the snow-dusted Olympics and the Strait of San Juan de Fuca. Ediz Hook forms a natural harbor, so it's natural that Port Angeles started as a shipping center. Out on that hook, the views back to the city and up to Hurricane Ridge in the Olympics are quite grand. Since Hurricane Ridge is one of Olympic National Park's most popular areas, Port Angeles is a series gateway, with strings of motels on its outskirts.

The view across the strait to Victoria and Vancouver Island is impressive as well. It's also an easy reach, aboard auto ferries of Black Ball Transport's *MV Coho*, and Victoria Rapid Transit passenger ferries (see below, under

"Activities"). Eighteen miles away, Victoria is vaguely visible in daytime, although it issues an inviting glow on the horizon at night.

Port Angeles lacks Port Townsend's Victorian charm; however, the 1950s style downtown seems reasonably prosperous. Think of it as a sturdy blue collar town between scenic bookends. Like Port Townsend, Port Angeles' business district sits on a low coastal shelf and most of its homes are on a sea cliff above. Its name dates back to 1791 when Mexican navigator Francisco Eliza called the natural harbor *Port of Our Lady of the Angels*. The town itself wasn't founded until 1890. Earlier, in 1862, it was picked as a U.S. naval base because of its natural deep harbor and pivotal site on the Strait of Juan de Fuca. Elements of America's fleet where anchored there periodically through the 1930s.

## Walking and driving Port Angeles

A tour of Port Angeles is short and relatively simple. After you've entered the one-way grid on Front Street, drive into the heart of town, turn right at Lincoln Street and drop down a couple of blocks to the waterfront. Park and start exploring on foot. The **Port Angeles Chamber of Commerce** is just to the left, in a Spanish tile-roofed building at 121 East Railroad. It's open weekdays 10 to 4 and weekends noon to 4. Most of the towns attractions are in this area as well.

**Arthur D. Feiro Marine Laboratory** ● *Port Angeles City Pier; (206) 452-9277, extension 264. Summer 10 to 5 daily, the rest of the year noon to 4 weekends. Adults $1, kids 50 cents.* ☐ This small facility is primarily a hands-on aquatic study lab, where instructors and student volunteers teach visitors about offshore marine life. A mural on the wall outside looks suspiciously like a casting call for *The Little Mermaid.*

**Waterfront observation tower** ● Perched on the end of a small pier, the four-story tower improves the already impressive views across the strait and over the city to the Olympics.

☺ **Waterfront trail** ● This hiking/biking trail extends for six miles along the Port Angeles shorefront, past the port district and out onto Ediz Hook. From the marina, you can take the trail west and north onto the mile-long hook, or east along the waterfront, following a former railroad bed. Parklands, picnic sites and a kiddies play area mark its path.

**The Landing** ● Several shops and restaurants occupy this old cargo shed, just west of the city pier. It's still being developed and many of the spaces are empty. The Victoria ferry puts into port just outside.

A 1.75-mile walking tour map available from the chamber will guide you past the city's older buildings. During your strolls, go up Lincoln to Fourth Street for a visit to the brick and bold 1914 **Clallam County Courthouse,** which shares is rooms with a museum:

☺ **Clallam County Historical Museum** ● *319 Lincoln (at Fourth); (206) 452-7831, extension 364. Open 10 to 4, Monday-Saturday in summer and Monday-Friday the rest of the year. Donations appreciated.* ☐ The best museum piece is the building, a baronial Georgian Revival structure with a vaguely Byzantine clock tower. A marble staircase leads to several rooms where interesting and only slightly cluttered displays tell of the area's past. Among exhibits are a diorama extolling the virtues of logging, and country store and post office façades.

After you've finished walking downtown, drive west on Front Street. It becomes Marine Drive as you approach the working waterfront, with a large commercial fishing fleet and a larger pile of wood chips. The road ends at the Daishowa-America paper mill.

To avoid the Daishowa dead end and to see some fine old Victorians mixed with a lot of ordinary homes, fork to the left from Marine Drive onto Hill Street. Follow it up to the residential bluff above town and slant to the right onto Fourth Street. You'll shortly reach **Crown Park,** a small patch of green with a waterfront view—mostly of that paper mill. Reverse your route on Fourth and—as you explore the neighborhood—work your way to Eighth Street and head east to Race Street. Eighth is the only street that goes all the way through to Race; the others are cut off by a shallow ravine.

Turn right on Race Street, follow it uphill to a stop light at Lauridsen Boulevard and turn left. You'll shortly see a turn off to the parking lot for **Port Angeles Fine Art Center,** open Thursday-Sunday 11 to 5; (206) 457-3532. The center, offering one of the city's best views, occupies a knoll just beyond a water tower. This small, attractive gallery usually exhibits the works of regional artists. If you don't care for what's currently stuck on the walls, you can enjoy the harbor view through large picture windows.

Return to Race and continue uphill for an encounter with Hurricane Ridge, one of Olympic National Park's most popular areas.

## ACTIVITIES
### Sequim and Port Angeles

*Air Service* ● Horizon Air has daily flights to Seattle, Victoria and Portland from Fairchild International Airport, west of the city; (800) 547-9308.

*Amusement Park* ● Family Entertainment Park, five miles east on U.S. 101, has mini-golf, go-cart rentals and other activities; (206) 452-4666.

*Auto Racing* ● Summer Saturdays at Port Angeles Speedway; 452-4666.

*Ferry service* ● Black Ball Transport's *MV Coho* auto ferry makes several daily trips to Victoria; (206) 457-4491. Passenger service is offered from spring through fall by Victoria Rapid Transit; (800) 633-1589 (in Washington only) or (206) 452-8088.

*Fishing charters* ● Admiralty Charters, John Wayne Marina, Sequim; (206) 683-1097. Doug's Charters, Port Angeles, (206) 457-1663; Port Angeles Charters, (206) 457-7629.

*River float trips* ● Olympic Raft and Guide Service at Elwha Resort, eight miles west of Port Angeles, has two-hour trips down the Elwha River in summer; (206) 457-7011.

*Scenic flights and charters* ● Rite Brothers Aviation, Fairchild International Airport; (206) 452-7227.

## WHERE TO DINE

### China First ● ΔΔ $

❑ *214 Lincoln (near the harbor) (206) 457-1647. Chinese, full bar service. Monday-Saturday 11 to 10, closed Sunday. MC/VISA.* ❑ This small café offers a variety of spicy Mandarin and milder Cantonese dishes. For a departure from typical Chinese fare, try the Mongolian barbecue, in which you pick the ingredients, to be cooked in an open kitchen and served.

### ☺ Coffeehouse Restaurant and Gallery ● ΔΔ $$

❑ *118 E. First St.; (206) 452-1459. American whole earth; no alcohol. Breakfast, lunch and dinner daily. No credit cards.* ❑ This is where Port Angeles' young and restless hang out—a Berkeley style coffeehouse with local artwork and potted plants. Some of the meals are fairly substantial—New York strip steak, fish of the day with *basmati* rice, or shellfish in butter and flamed with brandy and served over angel hair pasta. Vegans can order a little tofu or eggplant Parmesan.

### The Downrigger ● ΔΔ $$$

⊓ *In the Landing shopping center at 115 E. Railroad Ave.; (206) 452-2700. American, mostly seafood; full bar service. Lunch from 11:30, dinner from 5, Sunday brunch 10 to 2. Major credit cards.* ⊓ Located on the second floor of the Landing with nice views of the waterfront, it's a formula nautical-modern place with exposed beams and track lighting. Among its specials are salmon Wellington in puff pastry, tiger prawns sautèed with garlic cream, and halibut deep fried in Red Hook Ale batter.

### ☺ The Greenery ● ΔΔΔ $$$ Ø

⊓ *117-B E. First St.; (206) 457-4112. American-continental; full bar service. Lunch Monday-Saturday 11 to 3, dinner Monday-Thursday 5 to 8 and Friday-Saturday 5 to 9, closed Sunday. Major credit cards.* ⊓ This attractive turn-of-the-century style restaurant is dressed nicely in polished hardwoods, tasseled lamps and high-backed booths; a barnboard exterior creates an interestingly rustic accent. The fare is American, drifting toward continental, with a selection of locally fresh seafood, pastas, prime rib and poultry. The **Country-Aire** just above is an appealing health food and specialty foods place, with a similar old-time dècor. It's open Monday-Friday 9:30 to 5:30, Saturday 10 to 5:30, closed Sunday; (206) 452-7175.

### Harbor Deli ● Δ $

⊓ *102 W. Front (at Laurel); (206) 452-8683. American; wine and beer. Daily 7:30 a.m. to 9:30 p.m. MC/VISA.* ⊓ This neat, airy and inexpensive place is a deli and then some. It issues the usual sandwiches and salads, plus dinner entrèes such as chicken Riesling, chicken *cordon bleu* and sirloin scaloppine; they're all under $10. The dècor is simple: blue checkered oilcloth on the tables and a few hanging plants.

### La Casita Restaurant ● ΔΔ $$

⊓ *203 E. Front St.; (206) 452-2289. Mexican-American, full bar service. Sunday noon to 10, Monday-Thursday 11 to 10, Friday-Saturday 11 to 11. MC/VISA, AMEX.* ⊓ Tacos with a view? This attractive Mexican restaurant draped with bright Latin trappings is perched over the waterfront. In addition to smashed beans and rice, it offers steaks, chicken and prawn fajitas, and seafood entrèes such as Icelandic cod stuffed with Dungeness crab and prawn and scallop sautè.

## WHERE TO SLEEP

### All View Motel ● ⌂⌂ $$ Ø

⊓ *214 E. Lauridsen Blvd. (Lincoln), Port Angeles, WA 98362; (206) 457-7779. Couples $37 to $42, singles $35 to $40, kitchenettes $50 to $60, suites $60 to $65. MC/VISA, AMEX.* ⊓ A 19-unit motel with TV movies, phones; some refrigerators; coin laundry.

### Flagstone Motel ● ⌂⌂ $$ Ø

⊓ *415 E. First St. (Peabody), Port Angeles, WA 98362; (206)457-9494. Couples $49 to $52, singles $42 to $46. Rates include continental breakfast. Major credit cards.* ⊓ A 45-unit motel with TV and phones; pool and sauna.

### The Pond Motel ● △ $$ Ø

☐ *196 Highway 101 W. (near Bean Road), Port Angeles, WA 98362; (206) 452-8422. Couples $42 to $57, singles $39 to $51, kitchenettes $6 to $8 extra. MC/VISA.* ☐ A 10-unit motel on the town's outskirts with TV, room refrigerators; barbecue area.

### Portside Inn ● △△ $$$ Ø

☐ *1510 E. Front St., Port Angeles, WA 98362; (206) 452-4015. Couples from $60, singles from $53, suites from $74. Major credit cards.* ☐ A 109-unit motel with TV and room phones; some microwaves. Pool, spa, coin laundry.

### ☺ Red Lion Bayshore Inn ● △△△ $$$$ Ø

☐ *221 N. Lincoln (Front), Port Angeles, WA 98362; (800) 547-8010 or (206) 452-9215. Couples $95 to $125, singles $80 to $110, sites from $145. Major credit cards.* ☐ Attractive waterfront inn near downtown and Victoria ferry; 187 rooms with TV and phones, some in-room movies. Pool and spa. **Dining room** and coffee shop serve American fare; 5:30 a.m. to midnight; dinners $5 to $20; full bar service.

## Bed & breakfast inns

### Anniken's Bed & Breakfast ● △△ $$$ Ø

☐ *214 E. Whidby (between Chase and Lincoln), Port Angeles, WA 98362; (206) 457-6177. Couples $55 to $60, singles $50 to $55. Two units with shared baths; full breakfast. MC/VISA.* ☐ Comfortable 1930s Scandinavian style home. Two rooms share a bath and sitting room. Views of the Olympics and Strait of Juan de Fuca.

### Bavarian Inn Bed & Breakfast ● △△△ $$$$ Ø

☐ *1126 E. Seventh St., Port Angeles, WA 98362; (206) 457-4098. Couples $75 to $95, singles $70 to $90. Three units with private baths; full breakfast.* ☐ Modern Bavarian chalet style home with a mix of European antiques and modern furnishings; Bavarian dècor in the guest rooms. Just off Race Street on the road to Hurricane Ridge, with views of the city and strait.

### Tudor Inn ● △△△ $$$ Ø

☐ *1108 S. Oak St. (Eleventh), Port Angeles, WA 98362; (206) 452-3138. Couples $55 to $90, singles $50 to $85. Five units; two private and three shared baths; full breakfast. MC/VISA.* ☐ Turn-of-the-century Tudor style home furnished with European antiques. Rooms have views of the Olympics or strait; comfortable lounge and library, each with fireplaces.

## Olympic park lodging & camping near Port Angeles

### Log Cabin Resort ● △ $$ to $$$$

☐ *Mailing address: 6540 E. Beach Rd., Port Angeles, WA 98362; (206) 928-3211. Couples and singles $38.40 to $93.25, kitchenettes $73.50. MC/VISA. RV sites; full hookups $22.40.* ☐ Rustic resort on Lake Crescent west of Port Angeles, with cabins and lodge rooms. Gift shop, coin laundry, barbecue area, room refrigerators. Hiking trails; lake for swimming and boating. **Restaurant** serves breakfast 8 to 11 and dinner 6 to 8:30; dinners $8 to $17; wine and beer.

### ☺ Sol Doc Hot Springs Resort ● △△ $$$$ Ø

☐ *Mailing address: P.O. Box 2169, Port Angeles, WA 98362; (206) 327-3583. Cabins $75 per couple, cabins with kitchens $85; additional people $10 each. Major credit cards. RV sites $15. Adjacent national park tent and RV* *sites with no hookups $8.* ☐ Woodsy, Western-style hot springs resort with 32 single or duplex cabins. Designated smoking areas on decks. Swimming and hot springs mineral pools; message therapy; gift shop and grocery store. RV sites (listed below). **Restaurant** serves 8 to 11 and 5 to 9; dinners $10 to $20; wine and beer. Poolside deli open 11 to 4.

## WHERE TO CAMP

In addition to facilities listed below, **Log Cabin Resort** and **Sol Doc Resort** in **Olympic National Park** have RV hookups; see listings above.

**Al's RV Park** • *522 N. Lee's Creek Rd., Port Angeles, WA 98362; (206) 457-9844. RV sites $17. Reservations accepted; no credit cards.* ☐ Off-highway park with mountain and water views; showers, picnic tables, coin laundry, TV and phone hookups. Three miles east of Port Angeles, one-fourth mile off U.S. 101.

**Conestoga Quarters RV Park** • *40 Siebert's Creek Rd. (Highway 101), Port Angeles, WA 98362; (206) 452-4637. Full hookups $18.30, tent sites $13.50. MC/VISA.* ☐ Showers, picnic tables and fire rings; rec hall, volleyball, horseshoes and nature trails. Tours to nearby attractions arranged. Park is six miles east of Port Angeles.

**Port Angeles/Sequim KOA** • *80 O'Brien Rd., at Highway 101 East, Port Angeles, WA 98362; (206) 457-5916. RV and tent sites; $16 to $17; "Kamping Kabins" $30. Reservations accepted; MC/VISA.* ☐ Showers, swimming pool and hot tub, game room, playground, volleyball and horseshoes; mini-mart, coin laundry. Seven miles east of town.

**Shady Tree RV Park** • *47 Lower Dam Rd., Port Angeles, WA 98362; (206) 452-7054. RV sites $15, tents $10. Reservations accepted; MC/VISA.* ☐ Shady sites with picnic tables, showers, mini-mart, children's playground. Grassy, shaded open field for tenters. Park is half mile west of U.S. 101 at the Highway 112 junction.

**Welcome Inn Trailer Park** • *Highway 101 W., Port Angeles, WA 98362; (206) 457-1553. RV sites only; $10 to $15. Reservations accepted; no credit cards.* ☐ Showers and coin laundry. Two miles west.

# Hurricane Ridge

Each year, hundreds of thousands of fans of scenery, wildlife and craggy peaks beat a busy path up to Hurricane Ridge. It's the most-visited element of Olympic National Park.

From downtown Port Angeles, Race Street leads to a logical first stop, the **park visitor center** open 8:30 to 5:30 (shorter off-season hours). It contains fine interpretive exhibits, focusing on the Olympics and the wildlife therein. An imposingly large stuffed Roosevelt elk is a focal point. A 20-foot-long Native American canoe is nearby, typical of the frail craft these hardy folk once used to hunt whales. Their weapons were wooden harpoons.

Park headquarters is just below here and to the west, at 600 E. Park Avenue. However, the visitor center should be able to provide you with all the information you need. Above the visitor center, Race Street becomes Heart O' the Hills Parkway and begins a steep climb into the heart of the park. There's a shady campground at **Heart O' the Hills,** the entrance station a few miles above the visitor center. Campfire programs and naturalist walks are conducted here in summer. It's another 12 miles to Hurricane Ridge. The upper facilities are on limited hours in winter, generally Friday through

Monday, and the road is sometimes closed by snow, although the lower campground is kept open.

*RV Advisory:* The route to Hurricane Ridge is a steep, tough climb with switchbacks and a noticeable lack of guard rails. Larger rigs should be able to make it without too much driver anxiety.

Once you've achieved the top, the view is spectacular—a magnificent sweep of rocky, snow-streaked crests above and the Olympic Peninsula coast, Strait of Juan de Fuca and Vancouver Island below. Hiking trails reach even deeper toward the granite heights and shorter nature trails probe nearby forest and meadow. Some of these trails become cross-country ski routes in winter, and rope tows pull downhillers up to a few modest slopes. Facilities here are focused at the Hurricane Ridge visitor center, with naturalist programs, interpretive exhibits and food service.

From here, a narrow gravel road twists along the ridge for eight miles for even more impressive views. This route is not recommended for RVs and trailers; turnaround space at the end is limited.

## PORT ANGELES TO LA PUSH

As you push westward from Port Angeles and then southward toward La Push and Forks, you'll enter one of the least populated areas of the peninsula—in fact, of the entire state. This doesn't mean that it's a wilderness. Forests outside Olympic National Park have been visited frequently by logging crews, and they will be visited again. Much of this lowland woodland is owned by timber companies. Signs posted on various patches announce when they were last—to use that wonderful logging euphemism—harvested.

*General driving advisory:* There are no vehicle services or fuel west of Port Angeles for about 55 miles, until you reach Clallam Bay.

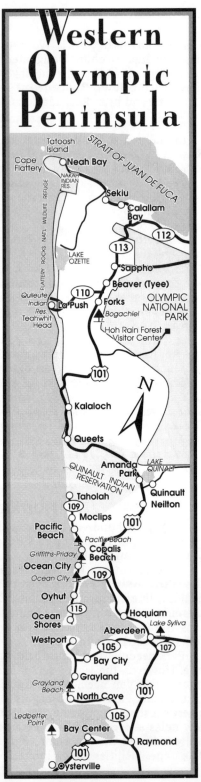

Westbound Highway 101 passes Lake Crescent on the northern edge of the national park. Summer homes are scattered along its shoreline, along with a couple of park ranger stations—Storm King to the east and Fairholm with a campground and boat launch to the west.

However, we're going to suggest bypassing all this and heading for the state's northwest tip, along the Strait of Juan de Fuca. A few miles after you leave Port Angeles, turn right from U.S. 101 onto Highway 112, following Sekiu/Neah Bay signs. After about eight miles, go right at the Salt Creek/Tongue Point/Crescent Beach recreation area sign. The road will take you four miles north to the shoreline, for a rather dramatic vista point.

☺ **Salt Creek Recreation Area** is a Clallam County Park near Tongue Point, offering a fine view over the strait to the mountains of Vancouver Island. It once was a coastal artillery battery and you can drive through the concrete arch of a World War II bunker on the park's west side. The beach is sandy, drift-wood littered and inviting. Park facilities include campsites with no hookups ($8 for visitors, $6 for Clallam County residents), a fine picnic area on a grassy terrace overlooking the strait and a kids playground.

From here, the side road loops back to State Highway 112 at **Joyce.** You may, if you choose, cross the highway and visit **Lake Crescent.** Continuing west on 112, you'll reach the **Lyre River,** where short roads lead to a pair of campgrounds near its mouth. **Lyre River Campground** on the east side is one of several in the north and west peninsula run by the Washington State Department of Resources. They have no hookups and only pit potties but the price is right—free. This one is in a nice wooded area just off the strait, with a trail leading to the beach. **Lyre River RV Park,** a commercial campground, is on the west side, with RV and tent sites for $13 to $20. It has full hookups, with some sites overlooking the strait; 928-3436.

About six miles beyond Lyre River, the highway emerges from logged-over forest to travel dramatically along the edge of the strait. **Pillar Point County Park** has camping with no hookups for $8 (outsiders) and $6 (insiders), with a picnic area and mudflat beach. Just beyond is **Pysht.** (Excuse me?) It's a company complex for the Merrill and Ring tree farm, with no services. The firm owns much of this frequently-harvested forest. From Pysht, the highway swings inland to a junctioin with Route 113 and then returns to the strait, at Clallam Bay and Sekiu. **Clallam Bay** is little more than a break in the road, with a couple of motels and cafès. **Sekiu** is slightly larger and kind of cute, tucked into the arm of the bay.

Beyond Sekiu, the long and winding Lake Ozette Road branches to the left, leading southwest to a coastal section of Olympic National Park. The road ends three miles short of the beach at **Lake Ozette**, a large lagoon; reaching the beach requires a three-mile hike. From here, serious backpackers like to do a multi-day stroll down the wilderness beach to Mora and La Push, 25 miles south. It's an impressive trip, past steep headlands, sea stacks and cozy coves, along a lonely coast littered with driftwood and other things cast up from the sea. Some lucky hikers find glass Japanese fish net floats.

Continuing northwest on Highway 112, you'll reach Washington's northwestern tip, Cape Flattery on the **Makah Indian Reservation.** It's a dramatic drive, since the road hugs the Juan de Fuca shoreline most of the way.

*RV advisory:* The road is narrow and winding, but negotiable by large rigs and trailers. The side-road to Lake Ozette is even more demanding and quite narrow, although it's paved.

*The lonely lighthouse keeper would feel right at home on remote Tatoosh Island, off Washington's northwestern most tip.* **— Betty Woo Martin**

The village of **Neah Bay** occupies a natural harbor just inside the entrance to the strait. Although the town is rather shabby, the setting at the base of a wooded headland is imposing. And it offers several reasons for a visit, including an excellent museum and some inexpensive lodging:

☺ *Makah Cultural and Research Center* ● *(206) 645-2711. Daily 10 to 5 (Wednesday-Sunday in the off-season). Adults $4, seniors and students $3.* ⧠ This $2 million facility paints imposing portraits of the Makah tribe's past and present. Exhibits include a 40-foot canoe used for whaling, a complete longhouse and a life-like sea lion diorama. Among its relics are wooden tools, carved cedar boxes and baskets unearthed from a village buried 300 years earlier by a mud slide.

*Cape Flattery Center* ● △ *$ to $$*

⧠ *P.O. Box 117, Neah Bay, WA 98357; (206) 645-2251. Rooms with shared bath $35; dormitory bunks $12.50.* ⧠ The Makah Nation has converted a former air force facility into a resort and conference center, available for groups and individual families. Among its recreational facilities are a gym, racquetball court, tennis court and bowling alley.

Since the village occupies an inshore niche, you'll need to drive another eight miles to get to the western edge of the continent. Once out there, you can see offshore **Tatoosh Island,** a windswept bit of rock occupied by a lonely lighthouse. To get there, pass through the village and turn left at a sign indicating the Cove Trails and Makah National Fish Hatchery. The route starts out being paved and bumpy, then becomes dirt and bumpy. Ignore the turnoff to the fish hatchery (five miles away and not that interesting) and continue five miles to the Cove trailhead. (Paths lead from here through thick woods down to the beach.)

From the trailhead sign, fork to the right, drive uphill briefly and then take the next right (unmarked). Climb steeply upward for half a mile and turn right again, into a parking area. Below you stands lonely little Tatoosh Island and the entire Pacific Ocean.

*RV advisory:* This is a steep climb with limited turn-around at the top. It's best to park at Cove trailhead and hike to the lookout.

From Neah Bay, backtrack to the junction of highways 112 and 113 southeast of Clallam Bay. Take 113 south through heavily logged slopes for a reunion with U.S. 101 at **Sappho,** and head west.

Just beyond tiny **Tyee,** you'll encounter a national park/national forest information station, and just below that, a turnoff to La Push and Mora, on the coastal segment of Olympic National Park. As you head westward, look in your rear view mirror for nice glimpses of Mount Olympus and Mount Toms. At **Mora Junction** (with a store, small resort and cafè, listed below), you can continue on the main road to La Push, or branch to the right for Mora, which isn't a town, but a national park campground and beach.

**La Push** is a small Quileute village occupying a nice setting at the mouth of the Soleduck River, beside several tree-thatched sea stacks. The largest, **James Island,** was used centuries ago by locals to escape slave-grabbing enemies. Modern La Push, while not a model of urban renewal, is considerably less scruffy than Neah Bay. Visitors can stay at the attractive Quileute-run Ocean Park Resort or adjacent campground (listed below).

Three national park beaches are near here, simply called **First, Second** and **Third**. First Beach is near the village, while the more remote Second and Third are reached by hiking trails: half a mile to Second Beach, 1.3 miles to Third in a beautiful sheltered cove. **Mora,** on the northern side of the Soleduck River's mouth, has a ranger station, campground (listed below) and picnic area. You can hike over great piles of driftwood to **Rialto Beach,** covered with a lifetime supply of perfectly flat skipping rocks. The views across the river's mouth to James Island and La Push are among the best along the Washington coast.

Return to Highway 101 and drop south a short distance to a town named for the merger of the Soleduck, Bogachiel and Calawah rivers:

# Forks

**Population: 3,310**                    **Elevation: 375 feet**

The only settlement of any size on the peninsula's western slope, Forks is fed by a busy lumber industry and by visitors to the national park. For you trivia lovers, it was founded in 1870 and its the western-most incorporated city on the American mainland. Mostly, it's a one-street hamlet strung with a few stores, cafès, motels and a museum.

*Forks Timber Museum* • *U.S. 101, just south of town; (206) 374-9663. Tuesday-Saturday 10 to 6 and Sunday 1 to 5, closed January to late April.* ☐ Built by the Forks High School carpentry class (no snide remarks, please), the wood frame museum exhibits a pioneer kitchen, lumbering displays, farm equipment and Native American artifacts. A nature and fitness trail leads into the trees behind.

## WHERE TO DINE

*Shop-Rite Coffee Shop* • ∆ **$**

☐ *Forks Avenue (Highway 101), Forks (in Pay 'n' Save Shop-Rite Supermarket); (206) 374-6321. American; no alcohol. Daily 5 a.m. to 9 p.m. MC/VISA.* ☐ Ya say ya wanna eat cheap and substantial? Follow the locals into this narrow slot of a cafè and load up on chicken fried steak, breaded veal cutlets or country sausages. Everything except steaks is under $10.

### South North Garden ● ∆∆ $$

◻ *210 Sol Duk Way, Forks (behind the Chevron station, just off the high-way); (206) 374-9779. Chinese; wine and beer. Tuesday-Thursday 11 to 9, Friday 11 to 10, Saturday noon to 10, Sunday noon to 9, closed Monday. MC/VISA.* ◻ It's a long way from anybody's Chinatown, although this place services fine Asian food. The menu focus is Mandarin/Szechuan; try the Szechuan dinner for a good sampler. About $10 gets you hot and sour soup, egg roll, barbecued pork, Hunan chicken, twice cooked pork, Mongolian beef and fried rice. Milder Cantonese-style dishes are available as well.

### Three Rivers Resort Café ● ∆∆ $

◻ *At Mora Junction; (206) 374-5300. American-Mexican; wine and beer. Daily 9 to 7. Major credit cards.* ◻ It's a cutely rustic café with barnboard walls from which hang a couple of game trophies. The menu displays a few Mexican dishes, steaks, "River Burgers" and other sandwiches.

### Vagabond Restaurant ● ∆∆ $$

◻ *142 Forks Avenue N, Forks; (206) 374-6904. American; full bar service. Monday-Thursday 11 to 9, Friday-Saturday 6 to 2 a.m., Sunday 6 to 9. MC/VISA.* ◻ This is a light and airy place with a greenhouse-style dining room, bamboo chairs and wood paneling. Menu offerings include a loggers' rib steak, chicken teriyaki, fried prawns and such.

## WHERE TO SLEEP

### Miller Creek Inn Bed & Breakfast ◠◠ $$$ ∅

◻ *P.O. Box 593 (654 E. Division St.), Forks, WA 98331; (206) 374-6806, Couples $50 to $55, singles $35 to $40. Six rooms; some half-baths; some shared; full breakfast. MC/VISA.* ◻ Restored homestead farmhouse with wrap-around porch; on three acres, eleven miles from the ocean. Rooms furnished with an antique-modern mix; "comfortable and unpretentious." Fireplace in living room; hot tub on back deck.

### Ocean Park Resort ● ∆∆ $$ to $$$$

◻ *P.O. Box 67, La Push, WA 98350; (800) 487-1267 or (206) 374-5267. Motel units $50 to $57, cabins $65, campers' cabins (beds but no bedding) $36, fireplace cabins $59 to $125. Camping listed below. MC/VISA, DISC.* ◻ Attractively rustic oceanside resort with cabins and motel units among the trees; all equipped for light housekeeping; some with sea views. Mini-mart and beach frontage. Reservations should be made early for summer visits.

### Olympic Suites ● ◠ $$$

◻ *Route 1, Box 1500, Forks, WA 98331; (800) 262-3433 or (206) 374-5400. Couples and singles $70 to $85, singles $50 to $55. Major credit cards.* ◻ Thirty suites with kitchenettes; TV, refrigerators and microwaves; private balconies or patios. Just north of Forks, two blocks off the highway.

### Pacific Inn Motel ● ◠◠ $$$ ∅

◻ *P.O. Box 1997 (352 Forks Ave. S.), Forks, WA 98331; (800) 235-7344 or (206) 374-9400. Couples $48 to $52, singles $43. Major credit cards.* ◻ Nicely-kept 34-unit motel with TV, phones; coin laundry. **Pacific Pizza** serves 11 a.m. to 10 p.m.; salad bar; wine and beer.

### River Inn ● ◠◠ $$$ ∅

◻ *2596 Bogachiel Way, Forks, WA 98331; (206) 374-6526. Couples $60, singles $50. Two rooms with TV and private baths; full breakfast. No credit* *cards.* ☐ Modern A-frame riverside home with two guest rooms, living room with fireplace and spa next to the river.

### Three Rivers Resort ● △ $$

☐ *7764 La Push Rd. (Mora Junction), Forks, WA 98331; (206) 374-5300. Doubles and singles $30 to $40. Major credit cards.* ☐ Small, rustic resort with cabins, café (listed above), mini-mart and coin laundry. Five simply furnished units with TV movies; kitchenettes. Fishing tackle and guide service available. Three Rivers Café listed above.

### Town Motel ● ◠◠ $$ Ø

☐ *HC 80, Box 350, Forks, WA 98331; (206) 374-6231. Couples $37, singles $27, kitchenettes $30 to $38. Major credit cards.* ☐ Cutely furnished rooms with TV; some kitchen units. Gift shop, barbecue and picnic tables in an attractive garden.

## WHERE TO CAMP

**Forks 101 RV Park** ● *P.O. Box 1041 (on the highway), Forks, WA 98331; (800) 962-9964 or (206) 374-5073. RV and tent sites, $14. Reservations accepted; no credit cards.* ☐ Some pull-throughs; showers, picnic tables, TV hookups, coin laundry and mini-mart; fishing nearby.

**Ocean Park Resort** ● *P.O. Box 67, La Push, WA 98350; (800) 487-1267 or (206) 374-5267. RV and tent sites, $13 with hookups, $11 without. No reservations.* ☐ Shaded sites just off the beach, with showers; mini-mart.

**Rialto Beach, Mora** ● *Olympic National Park campground, $8 in summer, free in winter. No reservations or credit cards.* ☐ Attractive shaded sites near the beach with barbecues, picnic tables and flush potties.

**Three Rivers Resort** ● 7764 La Push Rd. (Mora Junction), Forks, WA 98331; (206) 374-5300. RV sites $12 with full hookups, $10 with water and electric and $8 with no hookups. Major credit cards. ☐ Several RV hookups at a small resort (listed above), with showers, coin laundry and mini-mart.

## HOH RAIN FOREST

The road to America's largest and most beautiful temperate-zone rain forest branches inland from Highway 101, about 20 miles below Forks. The drive is a pleasant twelve and a half miles up the Hoh River Valley, under a canopy of ever-thickening, moss-draped woods. En route, you'll pass a couple of free State Department of Resources campgrounds, **Willoughby Creek** and **Minnie Peterson.** Just beyond Minnie, you'll re-enter the national park and shortly reach a campground and the Hoh Rain Forest visitor center. The campground ($8 a night in summer, free the rest of the year) isn't in a rain forest, but a hardwood grove.

Step from your vehicle, walk into the forest, look upward at a hundred shades of green and start conjuring comparative adjectives. It's the Amazon without alligators and macaws; grotesque forms from the forest flight in *Snow White;* green and furry icicles; woolly green mammoths; shag rugs draped over limbs; moldy lace.

The Hoh is soaked with more than 140 inches of rainfall a year and—as in the Amazon—much of it never reaches the ground. It's captured in the high canopy to nurture air plants (*epithytes*) and assorted mosses. The rain forest trees of choice are Sitka spruce, western hemlock, Douglas fir, western redcedar and red alder. All grow to record sizes under these soggy conditions. The Sitka, Alaska's primary tree, is nearly twice its normal size

*This is what happens if you park your truck too long in the same place along the rainy, lush western slope of the Olympic Peninsula.* — **Betty Woo Martin**

down here. You'll learn all of this at the visitor center, then you can hike one of three short trails into this chartreuse wonderland.

☺ The **Mini-Trail** is a quarter-mile loop that's handicapped accessible. From this branches the 1.25-mile **Spruce Trail** and the three-quarter-mile **Hall of Moss.** The Spruce Trail provides the best sampling of a rain forest at work. Serious hikers can continue into the upper wilds. Most assaults on Mount Olympus—which require a permit and should be tried only by skilled, well-equipped climbers—begin here.

## KALALOCH TO GRAYS HARBOR

Just beyond the Hoh Rain Forest turnoff, a narrow road follows the Hoh River to the coast at the **Hoh Indian Reservation.** Backpackers often use this as a starting point for a coastal hike north to La Push. Some say this shoreline is even more impressive than the stretch from Mora to Ozette.

Highway 101 also returns to the coast here, traveling on the opposite bank of the Hoh. The stretch from Ruby Beach to Kalaloch is busy with sea stacks, sheltered coves and wild surf. It's one of the prettiest drives on the peninsula, with frequent beach access and turnouts.

**Kalaloch** is a small, attractive settlement with a park ranger station, campground and a rather striking coastal resort:

☺ *Kalaloch Lodge* ● ⌂⌂⌂ *$$ to $$$$* ∅
  ☐ *HC 80, Box 1100, Forks, WA 98331; 962-2271. Couples and singles $48 to $120. Major credit cards.* ☐ Perched above a cozy little inlet, Kalaloch has several lodge rooms, cabins perched on the bluff, and a bay window dining room. A path leads down to the beach. The wood paneled **dining room** serves American fare from 7 a.m. to 9 p.m.; dinners $9 to $20; full bar service and great views. Other facilities include a gift shop, general store and service station.

The **national park campground** nearby also is beautifully situated, with some spaces right over the ocean; RV and tent sites are $8.

Below Kalaloch, the highway swings inland, shortly passing a turnoff into the **Queets Valley,** decorated with another rain forest. At the end is the park's largest Douglas fir, rivaling California's redwoods. The forest is similar to the Hoh, so this drive may be worth the effort only if you like large Douglas firs. It *is* nice and quiet back in there, compared with the summer hubbub at the Hoh.

Highway 101 skims past one final piece of the national park, at **Quinault Lake,** before dropping south to Aberdeen. This attractive pond is rimmed with evergreens, vacation homes and a scenic drive. At shoreside is a particularly appealing old fashioned resort:

☺ *Lake Quinault Lodge* ● △△△△ *$$$$ Ø*

⬜ *P.O. Box 7, Quinault, WA 98575; (800) 562-6672 or (206) 288-2571. Couples and singles $80 to $110, suites $210. Major credit cards.* ⬜ This handsomely restored lodge, built in 1926, is a grand retreat, with lofty ceilings, French windows on the lake and a crackling fireplace in the spacious lobby. Paths lead through landscaped grounds to a gazebo at lakeside, where visitors can have a picnic or launch a canoe. Many rooms have lake views; some have fireplaces and balconies. Facilities include an indoor pool, spa, saunc and gift shop. The **dining room** serves Monday-Saturday 7 to 3 and 5 to 9 and Sunday 7 to 9; dinners $10 to $20; full bar service.

Below Quinault, the townlet of **Neilton** passes in a flash. Just beyond, you have the option of visiting a little-visited (but not unpopulated) stretch of coast, or staying with Highway 101 for a quicker drive to Aberdeen. To visit the coast, head southwest on the Moclips-Olympic Highway. The first and last five miles of this 20-mile stretch are paved, with ten miles of well-graded gravel in the middle. Once you hit the coast at State Highway 109, you can drive eleven miles north to the village of **Taholah** on the Quinault Indian Reservation, although it offers little of interest. Heading south on 109, you'll pass several pleasantly ordinary coastal hamlets of **Moclips, Pacific Beach, Copalis Beach** and **Ocean City.** Views of sloping headlands and rocky beaches may make this detour worthwhile. There are shoreside state park campgrounds near Pacific Beach and Ocean City. What probably isn't worthwhile is continuing on to **Ocean Shores** at the end of the highway. It's a scattered residential and retirement community along a narrow sandspit, which forms the upper arm of **Grays Harbor.**

Rejoin Highway 101 by heading east on State Route 109 from Ocean City. You'll soon encounter the twin cities of Hoquiam and Aberdeen, strung along the north shore of Grays Harbor. (They're too far south to be Olympic Peninsula cities, although this is a logical completion of an Olympic driving loop.) En route, birders can get off at **Grays Harbor National Wildlife Refuge,** just south of the highway. Good-sized herds of shorebirds congregate here and the best viewing is April and May; (206) 532-6237.

# Aberdeen-Hoquiam

**Aberdeen: 19,000; Hoquiam 9,000**　　　　　　**Elevation: 10 feet**

Built on the mudflats of Grays Harbor, Aberdeen and Hoquiam aren't tourist boroughs, although they do offer some items of interest. They're primarily lumbering towns—witness all that harvested forest you drove through—and shipping ports.

You first encounter Hoquiam, popular with some visitors for its ornate **Hoquiam's Castle** at 515 Chenault Avenue. Built in 1897 by a lumber baron, this 20-room mansion has been restored and is open for tours daily in summer, and weekends the rest of the year, 11 to 5; adults $4, kids $1; (206) 533-2005. If you're approaching from the coast on Route 109, follow a castle sign to the right up Garfield; if you've come down Highway 101, you'll have to backtrack several blocks on 109.

Heading west through Hoquiam, Highway 101 becomes one-way Simpson Avenue. After crossing the Hoquiam River, you can follow signs to the **Polson Park and Museum,** which requires a double-back on one-way Sumner Avenue to 1611 Riverside Avenue. Another former lumber baron's mansion, the Polson house exhibits artifacts and photos of the area's past; a rose garden and steam train decorate the park. The house is open Wednesday-Sunday 1 to 4 in summer and weekends noon to 4 the rest of the year; (206) 533-5862.

Back on westbound Simpson, you'll enter Aberdeen's city limits. To gather some material on the area, turn left onto Duffey Street and take an immediate right into a parking lot for the **Aberdeen Visitors Information Center,** open weekdays 9 to 5. Just beyond, a left turn onto Third Street will take you several blocks to the **Aberdeen Museum of History** at 111 E. Third. It has the same hours as the Polson Museum; (206) 533-1976. A nice display of fire fighting equipment and early 20th century room groupings are the museum's best features.

From here, head south for several blocks into the heart of downtown, where you'll find a good collection of old brick along the waterfront. You'll cross one-way westbound Wishkah, hit one-way eastbound Herron and turn left. Once you hit Herron, get into the middle lane and go straight ahead onto Highway 12 east, staying with Herron and following "Tall ship" signs. Cross the Wishkah River, turn right at a Texaco station and drive into a port industrial area. Your destination, difficult to see from the street, is Aberdeen's ambitious waterfront history project.

☺ *Grays Harbor Historical Seaport* ● *P.O. Box 2019 (813 E. Herron St.), Aberdeen, WA 98520; (206) 532-8611. Daily 10 to 5; shorter hours in the off-season. Adults $3, seniors and students $2, kids $1* A former shipyard and lumber mill at the confluence of the Wishkah and Chehalis rivers is being fashioned into a 19th century seaport. When we last checked, the star attraction was the brig *Lady Washington,* a full-scale replica of one of Captain Robert Gray's ships. Recently added to the maritime collection were two longboats. A reproduction of Gray's famous *Columbia Rediviva* is hoped for the future. Other plans include period seaport buildings and a river walk.

Wanna-be sailors can sign up for Grays Harbor cruises in the *Lady Washington* or the longboats. The *Lady* takes more ambitious trips up the Olympic Peninsula and into Puget Sound, retracing the journey of early voyagers. The grand little ship even schedules trips to Hawaii. To receive schedules of her sailings, write to the seaport and inquire about membership.

From the historic seaport, cross back over the river on westbound Wishkah Street and then follow Highway 101 signs south across the wide Chehalis River. Get into the right lane and take State Highway 105 south and east toward Westport and Raymond. The highway skims the edge of Grays Harbor between delta pasturelands and mudflats. Fork to the right for your final port of call in this area.

# Westport

**Population: 1,900**                          **Elevation: sea level**

Tiny, scruffy and completely charming, Westport clings to the absolute tip of Grays Harbor's southern appendage. Despite its appealing peninsular location and weathered seaport atmosphere, it has been bypassed by the tourist mainstream—or at least by fancy resorts. Mom and pop motels are abundant; major hotels are missing. This may be an undisguised blessing. It has been spared the commotion and tackiness of more popular coastal retreats. Westport is primarily a fishing port, both commercial and pleasure, and the town justifiably calls itself the Salmon Capital of the World. It's also popular for whale watching when the great beasts pass just offshore, southbound from November through February, and north in March and April.

As you cruise along the bottom of Grays Harbor, a sign will direct you to the right toward Westport. Right in the notch of the Y-intersection and somewhat difficult to reach from this direction is the Westport-Grayland Chamber of Commerce **visitor center**, open weekdays 9 to 5. As you drive into town, don't be put off by the drab looking scatter of small homes, businesses and motels along the main road. The appealing part comes at the very end.

Before you get there, follow a sign to the left to **Westport Light State Park**. The slender candlestick of a lighthouse still operates, although it's closed to the public. The closest you can get is a roadside viewing platform. Beyond the light, the street blends into a drive-upon beach. Use caution and avoid soft spots if you venture out. If your vehicle has skinny tires, you might want to plan on getting stuck.

The real Westport, along Westhaven Drive, is a small business district that looks out over a small marina to Grays Harbor. A good sized squadron of pleasure and commercial boats doze in their slips. Small wood frame storefronts house the usual shops, boutiques, cafès and requisite frozen yogurt outlets. One gift shop, at Harbor near Westhaven, has installed a big fish tank and expanded itself into the **Westport Aquarium.** It's open daily from April through December; (206) 268-0471.

Westport's look, except for the frigid yogurt, is 1950s seaside. At the northwestern end of Westhaven, you can climb a viewing tower, where a bolted-down set of binoculars will help you scan the harbor and open sea. At the opposite end of the street is a fine museum:

☺ *Westport Historical Maritime Museum* ● *2201 Westhaven Dr.; (206) 268-0078. Wednesday-Sunday noon to 4 in summer, weekends noon to 4 in spring, by appointment only the rest of the year. Donations appreciated.* ☐ Housed in a Nantucket-style 1939 Coast Guard station, the museum displays historic seafaring regalia, pioneer artifacts and old photos. The complete skeleton of a gray whale and several other aquatic bones are strung along an outside corridor. They're visible when the museum is closed.

For a brief cruise on Grays Harbor, catch the **Westport-Hoquiam Ferry** which provides passenger service from the waterfront to Hoquiam and Ocean Shores; (206) 268-0047.

As a final optional leg in your Olympic Peninsula loop, you can press south on Highway 105 from Westport to and through **Grayland**. It's a well-kept beach community that's strung out for several miles. Between homes are the bogs of Washington's cranberry industry, plus a few beach accesses and picnic areas. Beyond tiny **North Cove,** you can take a half right into **Tokeland** and follow the road a few miles through beachside homes to the weathered old **Tokeland Pier** at the end of a sandspit. There isn't much here, but the view across **Willapa Bay** to some mid-bay islands and **Leadbetter Point** is nice. Continuing south, Highway 105 curves around the upper shoreline of Willapa Bay. It offers more pleasant views aquatic, before terminating in **Raymond,** which we visited back in Chapter two.

## ACTIVITIES

*Beach rides* ● Tranquility Farms Rentals, Grayland Beach, 267-1037.

*Fishing charters* and *whale-watching* ● Most of these outfits offer both: Westport Charters, P.O. Box 546, Westport, WA 98595; (800) 562-0157 or (206) 268-9120. Coho Charters, P.O. Box 1087, Westport, WA 98595; (800) 572-0177 or (206) 268-0111. Catchalot Charters, P.O. Box 348, Westport, WA 98595; (206) 268-0323. Sea Horse Charters, P.O. Box 327, Westport, WA 98595; (800) 562-0171 or (206) 268-9100.

Also Bran Lee Charters, c/o Holiday Motel, P.O. Box 525, Westport, WA 98595; (800) 562-0163 or (206) 268-9356. Neptune Charters, P.O. Box 426, Westport, WA 98595; (800) 422-0425 or (206) 268-0124. Ocean Charters, P.O. Box 548, Westport, WA 98595; (800) 562-0105 or (206) 268-9144. Deep Sea Charters, Float 6, Westport, WA 98595; (206) 268-9300. Westport Whale Watch, P.O. Box 548, Westport, WA 98595; (800) 562-0105 or (206) 268-9144. Whales Ahoy, P.O. Box 454, Westport, WA 98595; (800) 562-0145 or (206) 268-9150.

*Scenic cruises* ● Bran Lee Charters, P.O. Box 525, Westport, WA 98595; (800) 562-0163 or (206) 268-9356. Neptune Charters, P.O. Box 426, Westport, WA 98595; (800) 422-0425 or (206) 268-0124.

## ANNUAL EVENTS

For details on these and other functions, contact the Westport-Grayland Chamber of Commerce at (800) 345-6223 or (206) 268-9422.

**Driftwood Show,** late March in Grayland.

**Blessing of the Fleet,** May at the port of Westport.

**Cranberry Blossom Festival,** June in Grayland.

**Westport Kite Meet,** early June in Westport; (206) 268-0877.

**Saltwater Festival,** late June through the Fourth of July, Westport.

## WHERE TO DINE

*The Islander* ● △△ $$

◻ *Westhaven at Neddie Rose Dr., in the Islander Motel; (206) 268-9166. American, mostly seafood; full bar service. Breakfast, lunch and dinner daily. Major credit cards.* ◻ This typical motel dining room, done in a kind of nautical-Tahitian style, offers picture-window views of the harbor. The menu features glazed shrimp Tahitian, breaded razor clams, fried chicken and the usual seafood entrèes.

☺ *Pelican Point Restaurant* ● △△△ $$ ∅

◻ *2681 Westhaven at Cove; (206) 268-1333. American-continental; wine and beer. Sunday-Thursday 11 to 9, Friday-Saturday 11 to 10, Sunday brunch 11 to 3. MC/VISA.* ◻ This small dining room serves the best food around town. Try tasty preparations such as chicken Seville with sour cream and chablis, chicken Oscar topped with crab and hollandaise, scampi Provencale, or a captain's plate of sautèed salmon, broiled halibut, deep fried shrimp and grilled oysters. The look is cozy and prim, with angular wood paneling and tulip light fixtures.

### ☺ *Sourdough Lil's* ● △△ *$$*

□ *301 Dock Street at Nyhaus; (206) 268-9700. American, mostly seafood; full bar service. Daily 11 to 9, shorter hours in the off-season. MC/VISA, AMEX.* □ King Neptune meets Wyatt Earp? This lively restaurant has an aquatic-Victorian-Western look with print wallpaper, ships wheels, maple captain's chairs and portraits of Westport pioneers. The barroom ceiling is decorated with hundreds of dollar and foreign bills—souvenirs of past diners. The menu is mostly deep fried and grilled: oysters, clams, scallops and halibut.

## WHERE TO SLEEP

### *Alaskan Motel* ● △ *$$* Ø

□ *P.O. Box 314 (708 N. First St.), Westport, WA 98595-0314; (206) 268-9133. Couples and singles $40, kitchenettes $45.* □ Simple 11-unit motel with room phones, refrigerators and microwaves; barbecue area.

### *Albatross Motel* ● △ *$$*

□ *P.O. Box 1546 (200 E. Dock St.), Westport, WA 98595; (206) 268-9233. Couples and singles $46 to $56, kitchenettes from $52. MC/VISA.* □ A 13-unit motel with TV, phones; some refrigerators. Near marina; courtyard and fish-cleaning area.

### *The Islander Motel* ● △△ *$$$*

□ *P.O. Box 488 (Westhaven and Neddie Rose Drive), Westport, WA 98595; (800) 322-1740 (summers only) or (206) 268-9166. Couples $69.50 to $79.50, singles $65 to $79, kitchenettes and suites $82.50 to $125.50. Major credit cards.* □ 31-unit motel at the waterfront with TV and room phones; some water-view rooms; pool and gift shop. **Islander Restaurant** listed above.

### *Windjammer Motel* ● △ *$$* Ø

□ *P.O. Box 655 (461 E. Pacific), Westport, WA 98595; (206) 268-9351. Couples and kitchenettes $45 to $50, singles $40 to $45, suites $60 to $75. MC/VISA.* □ A 12-unit motel with TV, room refrigerators; barbecue area.

## WHERE TO CAMP

**Grayland Beach State Park** ● *c/o Twin Harbors State Park, Westport, WA 98595-9801; (206) 268-9717. RV and tent sites, $14. Reservations may be made in summer by requesting a form from the park. No credit cards.* □ Sites near the beach with hookups, barbecues and picnic tables; showers. Fishing, beachcombing and kite flying. South of Westport, between Grayland and North Cove.

**Kila Han Camperland** ● *931 S. Forrest St., Westport, WA 98595; (206) 268-9528. Full hookups $15, water and electric $13, tents $10. Reservations accepted; no credit cards.* □ RV park on the beach with showers, picnic tables, TV hookups, coin-laundry and rec hall.

**Twin Harbors State Park** ● *Westport, WA 98595-9801; (206) 268-9717. RV and tent sites, $14 and $10. No reservations or credit cards.* □ Large campground with full hookups, showers, barbecues and picnic tables. Minimart, fishing, nature trails, playground. Just south of Westport on a Grays Harbor inlet.

# TRIP PLANNER

**WHEN TO GO** ● The northern reaches and high elevations dictate that this is mostly a summer to early fall region. Unless you're a skier, of course. Most of the state's ski resorts are in the north and central Cascades. For fair-weather travelers, only I-90 over Snoqualmie Pass and Highway 2 over Stevens Pass are kept open in winter. They can be closed temporarily by storms.

**WHAT TO SEE** ● Old downtown Issaquah; Carnation Farms and Snoqualmie Falls near Snoqualmie; the quasi-Bavarian village of Leavenworth; Chelan County Historical Museum in Cashmere; the old mining town of Index; North Cascades National Park and particularly the Liberty Bell monolith; Western-style Winthrop and its Shafer Historical Museum; the awesome views from Harts Pass above Winthrop, and from Artist Point in the Mount Baker area.

**WHAT TO DO** ● Have an intriguing herbal tour and lunch at the Herbfarm near Fall City; look for *Northern Exposure* scenes in Easton and Roslyn; load up on Bavarian food in Leavenworth (our favorite is the Edelweiss); take the "Aplets and Cotlets" tour in Cashmere; hike the Deception Falls trail at Stevens Pass and the Rainy Falls Trail to Rainy Lake in North Cascades National Park; dine organically at the Mountain Song Restaurant in Marblemount; take the Artist Ridge Trail at Mount Baker's Artist Point.

## Useful contacts

**Cashmere Chamber of Commerce,** 99 N. Division St., Cashmere, WA 98815; (509) 782-1511.

**Cle Elum Chamber of Commerce,** P.O. Box 43 (211 E. First St.), Cle Elum, WA 98922; (509) 674-5958.

**Darrington Chamber of Commerce,** P.O. Box 351, Darrington, WA 98241; (206) 436-1177.

**Issaquah Chamber of Commerce**, 155 NW Gilman Blvd., Issaquah, WA 98027; (206) 392-7024.

**Leavenworth Chamber of Commerce,** P.O. Box 327, Leavenworth, WA 98826; (509) 548-5807.

**Mount Baker Ranger District,** 2105 Highway 20, Sedro Woolley, WA 98284; (206) 856-5700.

**North Bend Chamber of Commerce,** P.O. Box 357, North Bend, WA 98045; (206) 888-1678.

**North Cascades National Park,** 2105 Highway 20, Sedro Woolley, WA 98284; (206) 856-5700.

**Snohomish Chamber of Commerce,** P.O. Box 135, Snohomish, WA 98290; (206) 568-2526.

**Snoqualmie Falls Chamber of Commerce,** P.O. Box 356, Snoqualmie, WA 98065; (206) 888-4440.

**Snoqualmie Pass Visitor Center,** P.O. Box 17, Snoqualmie Pass, WA 98068; (206) 434-6111.

**Winthrop Chamber of Commerce,** P.O. Box 39, Winthrop, WA 98862; (509) 996-2125.

## Cascades area radio stations

Most of the Seattle stations beam into these heights (Chapter 4). Once you cross to the east, check our list in Chapter eight. In the North Cascades area, several stations from British Columbia will reach your antenna.

CKZZ, 95.3-FM, Vancouver, B.C.—hard rock
CJJR, 93.7-FM, Vancouver, B.C.—country
KAFE, 104.3-FM, Bellingham—soft rock
KVLR, 106.3-FM, Twisp—old and new top 40
KOMW, 92.7-FM, Omak—country

### Chapter seven

# CASCADE COUNTRY

### Snoqualmie, Skykomish and North Cascades corridors

---

***WITH THE OBVIOUS EXCEPTION*** of a few volcanic peaks, the Cascades are relatively low as Western mountain ranges go. While the main ridge lines of the Sierra Nevada and the Rockies often dance over 10,000 feet, the Cascades hover around 5,000 to 7,000.

Further, its major passes are no great automotive challenge. Snoqualmie Pass on Interstate 90 is but 3,022 feet high and Stevens Pass takes U.S. Highway 2 just over 4,000 feet. This is fortunate, of course, since Washington's northern location and wet winter climate would make these passes impassable if they were much higher. With icy highways and occasional snow closures, winter passage is still no picnic, but it is possible.

Although the Cascades are rather low, these are not weary, worn-down mountains like the Appalachians. Their rugged profiles rival the ramparts of the Rockies and the Sierra Nevada. The North Cascades are particularly awesome, piercing the ice-blue sky as they march into Canada.

The range extends about 500 miles from northern California into southern British Columbia. It divides the state into two distinctive climate zones, forming a rain barrier that keeps persistent Pacific storms bottled up on the western side. Inland Washington is warmer and drier in summer, colder and drier in winter. Named for its abundance of waterfalls, the Cascade Range has been forming during the past 40 million years, the result of upward rumpling as oceanic plates collided. Normally, a mountain range this age would be somewhat smoothed by wind and weather, but constant glacial action has kept its features ruggedly handsome.

The scouring ice machines continue their work to this day. Washington is second only to Alaska in its glacier count. In fact, North Cascades National Park contains 318 glaciers—half the total number in the lower Forty-eight. Several volcanoes rise above the rough-cut Cascade ridge lines like snowy exclamation marks. Mounts Baker, Rainier, St. Helens and Adams are new kids along this faulted block—a mere million or so years old.

The Cascade range is a favored playground of Washington's residents and visitors. In summer and fall, folks hurry from the western side to get out from under pervasive clouds, and they come from the east to escape the heat. Many change places, driving over scenery-ridden mountain passes to explore one another's back yards.

We've already visited the lower Cascades with voyages to Mount St. Helens and Rainier, and a brief side trip to the Mount Adams Wilderness. In this chapter, we'll prowl the upper half in a series of corridors: Snoqualmie along Interstate 90, Skykomish over U.S. 2 and the spectacular North Cascades corridor on State Highway 20. Finally, we'll suggest a side trip to what may be the most spectacular area of all—Mount Baker, far to the north.

The first two corridors can be done in a loop trip that offers an interesting mix of alpine scenery, thematic towns and some hamlets made famous by television.

# THE SNOQUALMIE CORRIDOR

Interstate 90 cleaves a wide swath through the spreading sprawl east of Seattle, allowing quick escape from both urbia and suburbia. Within minutes, you'll cross the concrete-pontoon **Lake Washington Floating Bridge** to Mercer Island and beyond to Issaquah. It's an old coal-mining town that has earned some historic immunity from suburban outreach.

First, you may want to pause at **Lake Sammamish State Park** by taking freeway exit 15 north. This large reservoir offers the usual water sports and several picnic areas, but no camping. For a pleasant diversion, drive around the wooded lakeshore on East and/or West Lake Sammamish Parkway. From the freeway turnoff, you can follow signs to the small **Washington Zoological Park** at 19525 SE 54th; (206) 391-5508. Its exhibits focus on endangered species, featuring close encounters with the critters. The park is open in summer Wednesday-Saturday 10 to 5 and Sunday 11 to 5; shorter hours the rest of the year; adults $4, seniors $3.50 and kids $3.

## Issaquah

**Population: 7,800**　　　　　　　　　　　　　　　　**Elevation: 98 feet**

☺ This old fashioned community began life as Gilman in the late 1880s when the Seattle Pacific and Lakeshore Railroad was extended to the Squak Mountain coal mines. The name was changed to the local Indian word "Issaquah" in 1899. It's now surrounded by *suburbia moderne,* although the downtown core has kept most of its historic appearance.

For a peek at yesterday surrounded by today, take exit 17 and go south, following Front Street several blocks to the historic district. First, you may want to pause at the Issaquah Chamber of Commerce **visitor center.** It's in an early American house at 155 NW Gilman Boulevard, two blocks west of Front Street; open weekdays 9 to 5 and weekends 10 to 4. Gilman is the first stoplight you hit on Front, although a center divider keeps you from turning left to the visitor center. To reach it, go a block past Gilman and turn right

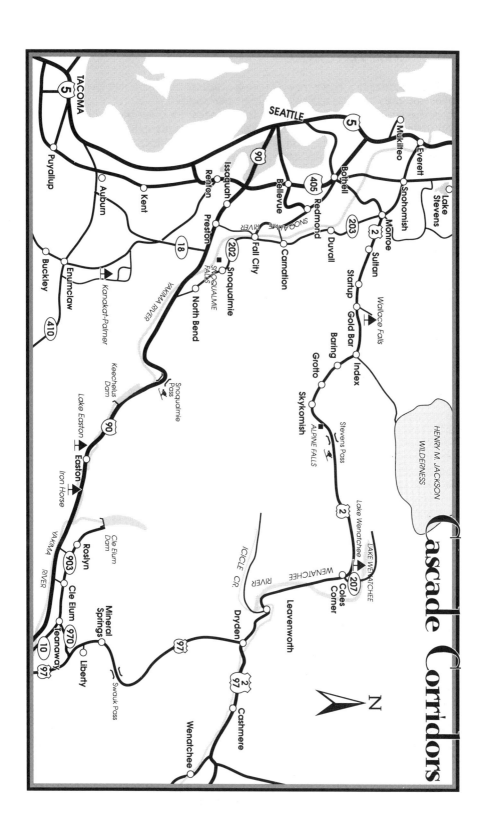

# Cascade Corridors

onto Holly Street (between a Chevron Station and SeaFirst Bank), which takes you into the side of the chamber's parking lot.

Although Issaquah isn't a major tourist area, its boutiques, antique shops and galleries attract shoppers and browsers. A goodly collection of them are in **Gilman Village,** at Rainier Boulevard and Gilman, just west of the chamber. Developers have dragged old homes and barns to this site and shaped them into a theme shopping complex.

☺ If you're a chocoholic, go east from Gilman Village to sample the hand-dipped goodies at **Boehm's Chocolates,** 255 NE Gilman; (206) 392-6652. It's housed in an appealing Swiss style structure, with a replica of a 12th century chapel nearby. The nationally-known chocolate firm, founded by a Swiss-Austrian immigrant, moved here in 1956.

To reach Issaquah's historic district, take Front Street south past a large yellow Darigold creamery facility and across a slanting railroad track. Most of the false front, brick and masonry structures are gathered along Front and Sunset Way. Nearby is the cute little gray and blue wood frame former Gilman Town Hall, now a museum. To reach it, drive a block past Sunset on Front and turn left onto Andrews.

**Issaquah Historical Society Museum** • *165 SW Andrews; (206) 392-3500. Saturday noon to 4 and Monday 10:30 to 2:30. Free; donations appreciated.* ☐ The small museum displays the "tools, toys and treasures" of local pioneer families. Exhibits focus on the mining, railroading and farming that led to the settlement of historic Gilman. Among displays are a turn-of-the-century grocery counter, period costumes, old kitchen appliances and—out back—a 1914 cement jail.

If you continue south on Front Street and turn right onto Sunset, you'll encounter the **Issaquah State Salmon Hatchery,** with the usual rearing ponds and fish ladder. Although not unusual as hatcheries go, it's one of the few in the country located within a town.

When you've finished with Issaquah, return to I-90, drive five miles east and take exit 22 to Preston/Fall City. This route will deliver you to an interesting herb farm, and beyond to the home of contented cows. As you exit, cross over the freeway to a stop sign and turn right to **Preston,** a tiny former lumbering town. Continue three and a half miles through thick woods to an "Herbfarm" sign. It directs you left across a green steel girder bridge, and around to your right, about a mile to Issaquah-Fall City Road. Turn right and you've found the farm, immediately on the left:

☺ **The Herbfarm** • *32804 Issaquah-Fall City Road, Fall City; (206) 784-2222. Daily 9 to 6; guided tours Saturday and Sunday at 1. Country store accepts MC/VISA.* ☐ Lola Zimmerman's herbal hobby of a few years back has grown into one of the Northwest's largest herb farms. It's also an outstanding restaurant (listed below), where a meal is a leisurely lesson in herbal dining. Visitors can browse among 400 herbs and hundreds of succulents and other specialized plants in 17 gardens and greenhouses. The country store offers such essentials as herbal flea collars, medicine, cosmetics and books on the role of herbs in cooking.

Beyond the Herbfarm, the road winds through a residential area (while changing its name to 332nd Avenue SE) and hits a stop sign at SE Redmond-Fall City Road. A right turn takes you into **Fall City**. Note the park and picnic area along the bank of the Snoqualmie River as you enter town. Drive through the small, neat business district, go left across the river and then left again onto State Highway 203, following signs to **Carnation**, six miles north. The settlement, established by Scandinavian farmers in 1865, preceded the famous dairy of the same name. Carnation Company founder E.H. Stuart introduced high-producing Holstein milk cows to the area in 1909 and established a large dairy nearby, so town adopted the company name. It's a prime little community, surrounded by lush green pasturelands and all those contented Holsteins. To reach its namesake dairy, continue north through town for about a mile, and watch for a small red and white Carnation sign. Turn left and drive about a mile and a half through a very appealing diary valley.

☺ **Carnation Farms** ● *Carnation Farms Road, Carnation; (206) 788-1511. Self-guiding tours Monday-Saturday 10 to 3, closed Sundays and holidays.* ☐ Visitors can pick up a guide at a small gift shop, then follow a yellow line through this modern, red-roofed dairy complex. The tour begins at a milk barn museum, then continues to a maternity ward, calf barn and modern milking shed. Here, one handler can turn 360 cows a day. (A far cry from my teen years on a small Idaho dairy farm, when a strong grip was the only machinery required.) Stuart founded his dairy in Kent, south of Seattle, in 1899. He later came to this valley and established his main breeding farm and an animal nutrition center. Carnation is now owned by Nestles, and Carnation-label products are no longer produced here. The milk flows to a different company in Seattle.

Retrace your route through Carnation and Fall City, then head east on State route 203 into the green and bucolic Snoqualmie Valley. A particularly rugged escarpment rises before you, and a small town of one-time TV fame basks in its shadow. Before you hit Snoqualmie, you'll encounter the waterfalls that gave it its name:

☺ **Snoqualmie Falls** ● *Gift shop and Salish Express Cafè open daily 9 to 6; Salish Lodge adjacent (listed below). Call (206) 454-6363 for Puget Power and (206) 888-2556 for the lodge. Major credit cards accepted at the lodge and gift shop/cafè.* ☐ Twin cataracts plunge 270 feet into a narrow gorge of the Snoqualmie River, gouging a pool 65 feet deep at its base. The falls have been under harness since 1898, when engineer Charles Baker drilled into the rock to install a power plant. It was the world's first underground power plant and the Northwest's first hydroelectric facility. Although water is diverted to this and a later power plant, there's usually a sizable flow over the falls.

Puget Power, the operating company, has installed an attractive park, scenic viewpoint and trail down to a second overlook near the base of the falls. The trail isn't exceptional, since you don't see the falls most of the way down. However, the one-mile round-trip is a good workout. The imposing **Salish Lodge** stands on a ledge above the falls, offering luxury accommodations and fine views.

## Snoqualmie/North Bend

**Snoqualmie population: 1,500**          **Elevation: 423 feet**

Just down the highway from the falls, Snoqualmie is a disarmingly cute rural enclave with a small false-front business district and flower baskets adorning its lampposts. Monolithic, 4,167-foot **Mount Si** rises just beyond the village, dominating its surrounding Cascade neighbors. The town and its mountain backdrop will be familiar to devotees of the former *Twin Peaks* TV series. A few businesses still cherish the town's fifteen minutes of fame, offering Twin Peaks T-shirts and other curios.

You'll pass a large collection of old steam engines and rail cars as you approach. Just beyond, a former railyard has been converted into a park, with lush lawns and some old rolling stock on display, adding more appeal to the small town. Note the massive chunk of a 400-year-old Douglas fir on a log carrier in the park's **Snoqualmie Historic Log Pavilion.** Just beyond is the town's cute little red and white depot with a witch's hat tower:

**Snoqualmie Depot** • *Railroad Avenue. Museum open Thursday, Friday and Sunday 11 to 3. Train rides $6 for adults, $5 for seniors and $4 for kids; call (206) 746-4025 for schedule.* ☐ Snoqualmie's depot is now a museum and ticket office for seven-mile round trip steam train rides to nearby North Bend. The museum is essentially a restoration of the old waiting room with period furnishings, including a pot bellied stove and ticket wicket.

Snoqualmie's Railroad Avenue will deliver you to North Bend, another town featured in *Twin Peaks*. First, you may want to take a short detour to a winery with a spectacular view. Drive less than a mile from Snoqualmie and turn right at a stop light, in front of a place called the Milk Barn. Go uphill about half a mile up hill to SE North Bend Way and turn right, following a Seattle/I-90 sign. Don't go on the freeway, but turn left to cross under it and climb a brief hill:

☺ **Snoqualmie Winery** • *1000 Winery Rd., Snoqualmie, WA 98065; (206) 888-4000. Daily 10 to 4:30.* ☐ There's not a vineyard in sight, but the winery's high perch with a stirring view of Mount Si is sufficient to give pause. Sip Washington wines in the attractive tasting room and stare out the picture windows. You may want to buy a bottle and adjourn to a grassy lawn or picnic table for lunch with a view.

From the winery, return to SE North Bend Way and head east. (There's no eastbound freeway on ramp here.) **North Bend,** a once-ordinary little farming town, has dressed itself in Bavarian garb. It, too, was featured in some of the *Twin Peaks* location shooting. As a thematic town, North Bend hasn't caught tourist fever like Leavenworth and Winthrop, which we visit later in this chapter. Thus, shopping and dining are limited, except for the huge **Great Northwest Factory Stores** outlet near the freeway exit.

After dragging the Bavarian main street, go uphill on North Bend Boulevard to return to the freeway. You'll pass the town's small **Snoqualmie Valley Historical Museum,** an informal place with the usual pioneer artifacts. It's open weekends 1 to 5 from May through November; closed the rest of the year; (206) 888-0062.

☺ A favorite hike in this area is a tough but non-technical four-mile grunt to the top of Mount Si, with a 3,100-foot elevation gain. Once you've accomplished it, the views are awesome. To reach the trailhead, take Mount Si Road from North Bend, cross the Snoqualmie River, turn right, then drive 2.5 miles to a parking area.

*RV advisory:* If you like a gentle climb over the Cascades, Snoqualmie Pass is your route. It's quite moderate with wide, sweeping turns; it's the lowest passage through the Cascades, except for the Columbia River Gorge.

The route follows an easy path carved by the south fork of the Snoqualmie River, through low hills that are punctuated occasionally by rugged outcroppings. Exit roads will invite you to explore the lakes and forests of the surrounding **Mount Baker-Snoqualmie National Forest.**

As you crest the pass, exit 54 will take you to a **Visitor Information Center,** operated by the U.S. Forest Service. It's open daily in summer 8:30 to 8 and Thursday through Sunday the rest of the year. The Snoqualmie Pass ridge line divides Mount Baker-Snoqualmie and Wenatchee national forests; the center offers material on both. You'll also find information on nearby communities, skiing, whitewater rafting and other outdoor lures. Incidentally, the state's area codes switch at the Cascade ridge line; it's (206) from Snoqualmie Pass west and (509) east to the Idaho border.

A small community atop the pass has a decidedly alpine look, inspired by the presence of four ski resorts. This is the state's largest ski area, with the most facilities and greatest selection of novice through advanced runs. See "Activities" below for details.

Like the west-flowing Snoqualmie River, the eastbound Yakima has carved a gentle valley down the far side of the Cascades. The stream soon fattens into **Keechelus Lake,** formed by Keechelus Dam. **Lake Easton State Park** here offers a boat dock, swimming, hiking and camping (listed below, under "Where to camp").

## TELEVISION EXPOSURE

If you've gotten off at Lake Easton, continue east on the frontage road instead of returning to the freeway. It will shortly deliver you to scruffy little **Easton,** one of two area towns that—like Snoqualmie and North Bend—found TV's spotlight. Fans of *Northern Exposure* will recognize Easton's century-old "Little White Church." It appears as the town hall in the show's fictitious town of Cicely, Alaska.

☺ The show's major location site is **Roslyn,** a few miles farther east. In the eyes and actions of local tourist enthusiasts, Roslyn *is* Cicely. Even if it hadn't found fresh fame, this weathered former coal mining town—dating from 1855—is worth a stop. To reach it, hop back on the freeway at Benson, drive nine miles to exit 80, head uphill a short distance to State Highway 903, turn left and follow it into town.

With its wooden false front buildings tucked among the trees, Roslyn could easily pass for an Alaska frontier community. As you enter town, note the combined city hall and library in a curious pitched-roofed clapboard building, topped by a fire bell tower. The small business district is just beyond, focused at First and Pennsylvania. The **Roslyn Museum,** recently spruced up through contributions from the *Northern Exposure* crew, features a pleasant disarray of pioneer regalia. It's open daily in the summer and by appointment in the off-season; admission $1. Phone (509) 649-2776 or (509) 649-3185.

Serious *Northern Exposure* aficionados will want to head for the Northwestern Improvement Company building at First and Pennsylvania. Once the company store for the coal mines, it now houses the show's fictitious radio station KBHR, visible through a front window. **Memory Makers** souvenir shop in the building offers an alarming variety of *Northern Exposure* T-shirts and other curios. Across First Street is **Ruthanne's General Store**, also a serious purveyor of souvenirs. You might see areas marked with yellow and black "hot set" tapes, set up for a future shoot.

The sturdy 1889 **Brick Tavern** at One Pennsylvania Avenue claims to be the oldest operating saloon in the state. You may or may not want to test its running water spittoon. A block away, at 33 Pennsylvania, **Roslyn**

**Brewing Company** offers micro-brews in its small stand-up bar. Tours are conducted on weekends from noon to 5; (509) 649-2232.

After your exposure to Roslyn, head east on State Highway 903 about six miles a mountain hamlet with a rather curious name.

# Cle Elum

**Population: 1,800**                    **Elevation: about 1,500 feet**

This town tucked into the Cascade foothills takes its name from the Native American "swift water," appropriate to the adjacent Yakima River. Gold brought the first visitors here in 1883. The discovery of a coal vein during railroad construction a year later spurred more growth. Coal mining continued until 1963. The town is modestly active as a jumping off point for folks exploring the surrounding mountain recreation areas. The river, with both gentle and lively stretches, is popular for float trips and whitewater rafting.

You'll note a transition from woodsy to Western as you prowl this community, which marks an invisible border between the Cascades and cattle and farming country to the east. "We don't have espresso" declares a sign on the Longhorn Tavern.

Coming from Roslyn, you'll roll into town on Second Street, a block north and parallel to First, Cle Elum's main drag. To visit the first of two museums, turn left up Billings (at the brick St. John the Baptist Catholic Church) and drive a block to a mansion recently turned museum:

**Carpenter House Museum** ● *Billings and Third streets; (509) 674-5702. Open Memorial Day through Labor Day, weekends only from noon to 4. Donations appreciated.* ☐ This 1914 plantation-style home was built in 1914 by Frank Carpenter, owner of a local bank. A granddaughter donated it to the Cle Elum Historical Society in 1989, and it's being refurbished as a museum. Some of the original furnishings are on display, including Tiffany lamps, a French version of the Victrola and an Empire style sleigh bed.

From the Carpenter House, drop down to First Street and turn left. The **visitor information center** of the Cle Elum Chamber of Commerce comes up shortly, at First and Wright streets. Hours are Tuesday-Thursday 9 to 4 and Friday-Monday noon to 4. This old red brick building also houses the town's other small museum:

**Cle Elum Historical Telephone Museum** ● *221 E. First St.; (509) 674-5702. Open Memorial Day to Labor Day, Tuesday-Friday 9 to 4, Saturday-Monday noon to 4. Admission $1.* ☐ An early Cle Elum switchboard, telephones and other primordial communications gear are displayed in this building, which was Pacific Northwest Bell's telephone office. Other exhibits include coal mining tools, post office fixtures and assorted pioneer artifacts.

You can stock up on hiking, camping and other outdoor recreational information at the **Cle Elum Ranger Station** at 803 W. Second St., open weekdays 8 to 5.

The **Cle Elum Bakery** at 501 E. First is something of a local legend. Since 1906, it has been turning out piping hot French bread, cinnamon rolls, *torchetti* and other savories from an ancient brick oven. It's open daily except Sunday; (509) 674-2233. For locally-crafted sausages and beef jerky, try **Glondo's Sausage Company** at 216 East First; (509) 674-5755.

An old railroad bed has been converted into a hiking trail at **Iron Horse State Park** at the foot of Fourth Street in the south end of town. It's part of the **John Wayne Pioneer Trail** that extends for several miles from Easton through Cle Elum's woodlands into the prairies of the Yakima Valley below. The path becomes a fine cross-country ski trail in winter. Eventually, it will reach west to east across the state, forming an "X" with the north-south Pacific Crest Trail that crosses near Snoqualmie Pass.

## ACTIVITIES
### Snoqualmie-Cle Elum area

**Biking** • Mountain bike rentals, shuttles and instructions are available through Ski Acres Mountain Bike and Hiking Center, Snoqualmie Pass; (206) 434-6646.

**Pack trips** • High Country Outfitters, 3020 Issaquah Pine Lake Road, Δ544, Issaquah, WA 98027-7255; (206) 392-0111. Three Queens Guide Service, HC 61, Box 3040, Cle Elum, WA 98922; (509) 674-5647.

**Raft rentals** • River Raft Rentals, Inc., Route 4, Box 275, Ellensburg, WA 98926; (509) 964-2145.

**Summer ski lift** • Aerial rides are available at Ski Acres; (206) 434-6646.

**Whitewater rafting** • River Excursion Company offers four-hour raft trips on the Yakima; P.O. Box 543, Ellensburg, WA 98926; (509) 925-9117. Allrivers Adventures, P.O. Box 12, Cashmere, WA 98815; (800) 74-FLOAT or (509) 782-2254.

### Winter sports

**Cross-country skiing** • Ski Acres at (206) 434-6400; and Pacific West Mountain Resort, (206) 633-2460. Both are near Snoqualmie Summit, and each offers miles of groomed trails. **Snowmobile tours** • Sasse Mountain Outdoor Experiences, Cle Elum, (509) 649-2794/(509) 925-3334.

**Downhill skiing** • Washington's most popular ski area, Snoqualmie Pass has four resorts. Three of them—Snoqualmie Summit, Ski Acres and Alpental—operate together, with one lift ticket good for all. Snoqualmie Summit is best for beginners, with novice and intermediate runs; Ski Acres has intermediate and advance runs and Alpental is the most challenging; call (206) 434-6400 for details. The forth Snoqualmie-area facility is Pacific West Mountain Resort, offering novice through advance runs, restaurants and lounges; (206) 633-2460. All four have equipment rentals, instruction and snack bars. Ski Acres and Pacific West have groomed cross-country trails. The Snoqualmie Pass snow report number is (206) 236-1600.

## ANNUAL EVENTS

**Brick Tavern Running Water Spittoon Race,** mid-March in Roslyn; (509) 649-2643.

**Pioneer Spirit Wagon Train** traveling from Vantage to Puyallup in late June; (509) 962-8889.

**Pioneer Days,** July 4th weekend in Cle Elum; (509) 674-5958.

**Roslyn Wing Ding,** Labor Day weekend; (509) 649-2756.

## WHERE TO DINE
### Issaquah to Cle Elum, in order of appearance

☺ *Mandarin Garden* • ΔΔ $ ∅

⊓ *40 E. Sunset Way, Issaquah; (206) 392-95678. Chinese; wine and beer. Sunday and Tuesday-Thursday 11:30 to 9:30, Friday-Saturday 11:30 to 10, closed Monday. MC/VISA.* ⊓ Basic Chinese mom 'n' pop Formica café with a large and versatile menu, ranging from Mandarin to Szechuan. This locally popular place has won a couple of regional dining awards. Among its better offerings are *kung pao* shrimp, *mushu* pork and spicy steamed fish.

### ☺ Herbfarm • ∆∆∆∆ $$$ Ø

◻ *32804 Issaquah-Fall City Rd., Fall City; (206) 784-2222. American; wine only. Lunch Friday-Sunday, late April through Christmas holidays. Reservations required, far in advance. MC/VISA.* ◻ Diners must plan ahead for this distinctive two-hour luncheon that's both a gourmet experience and an education in the use of herbs. The outing begins with an educational tour of the herb gardens. A sumptuous, creative meal follows, during which more herbs are discussed and sampled. The menu is *nouveau*-whole earth, using ingredients such as wild nettles, tulip petals and oil of chives. Entrèes can range from lamb to wild game and local fish.

### Holstein Diner • ∆∆ $$ Ø

◻ *Main Street, Carnation; (206) 333-6000. American; full bar service. Sunday-Thursday 6:30 a.m. to 8 p.m., Friday-Saturday 6:30 to 9. MC/VISA, DISC.* ◻ It's hard to miss this black-and-white painted building in the land of contented cows. The simple rural interior is decorated with folk crafts. The menu is simple and rural, as well: pork chops with applesauce, chicken fried steak, meatloaf, plus the usual steaks and fried seafood. All non-smoking.

### Salish Lodge Restaurant • ∆∆∆ $$$$ Ø

◻ *Snoqualmie Falls; (206) 888-2556. Continental-Northwest; full bar service. Daily 7 a.m. to 11 p.m. Major credit cards.* ◻ The product of extensive and expensive refurbishment, the Salish dining room offers an elegant 1930s look, and nice views of Snoqualmie Falls. The menu focuses on Northwest seafood and wild game, such as broiled venison and fricassee sea scallops with Oregon shrimp, plus a few continental dishes. The restaurant also is noted for elaborate brunches. The upstairs Attic Lounge features even better views than the dining room. The lodge is listed below.

### Timber Bar & Grill • ∆ $$

◻ *202 Railroad Ave., Snoqualmie; (206) 888-2230. American; full bar service. Weekdays 5 a.m. to 2 p.m., weekends 5 to 9. MC/VISA.* ◻ Simple family diner opposite Snoqualmie's railroad depot, with knotty pine trim and paisley print oilcloth. The menu is preoccupied with baby back ribs, prime rib, steaks, chicken and chops. With Twin Peaks pie for dessert, of course.

### Family Pancake House • ∆∆ $$

◻ *In Best Western Summit Lodge, Snoqualmie Pass; (800) 528-1234 or (206) 434-6300. American; wine and beer. Sunday-Thursday 6:30 a.m. to 9:30 p.m., Friday-Saturday 6:30 to 11. Major credit cards.* ◻ Attractive light knotty pine dining room with brass hurricane lamps. The fare is typically American, not innovative but tasty: grilled pork chops, steak, chicken and seafood.

### Webb's Bar & Grill • ∆∆ $$

◻ *Snoqualmie Pass; (206) 434-6343. American; full bar service. Monday-Thursday 11 to 9, Friday-Sunday 8 to 10. Major credit cards.* ◻ The dècor is modern alpine, although the exterior view is better. Large picture windows address Guy Peak and other Snoqualmie Pass terrain. The menu is basic steak, seafood, pasta and a rather good fish and chips. Outdoor dining deck.

### ☺ Roslyn Café • ΔΔ $$

⌸ *28 Pennsylvania Ave. (at Second); (509) 649-2763. American; wine and beer. Breakfast lunch and dinner weekends, lunch and dinner Tuesday-Sunday; hours vary with the seasons. MC/VISA, AMEX.* ⌸ This funky old place looks right at home in Roslyn, with high pressed tin ceilings, cut-stone walls, a 1950s jukebox with 78's, a long counter and a few wooden tables. However, the menu obviously was inspired by its new image as a campy tourist café. Try the Chinese stir fry pepper steak strips, tenderloin tips and a spicy chicken sauté. It also turns out good, honest hamburgers for lunch. The café's brick-wall mural is familiar to every *Northern Exposure* fan.

### Pioneer Restaurant and Bar • ΔΔ $$$

⌸ *Three Pennsylvania Ave. (at First); (509) 649-3032. American; full bar service. Monday-Thursday 11:30 to 8, Friday 11:30 to 10, Saturday 11 to 10, Sunday 11 to 8. MC/VISA.* ⌸ The Pioneer also occupies a weathered old building, with pressed tin ceilings from which dangle the requisite fans. However, it's fancier and more attractive, and therefore lacks the *kinche* of Roslyn's. It certainly is handsome, with high backed wooden booths, maple chairs and drop lamps. The menu, like that at the Roslyn, is rural *nouveau*—chicken sauté, champagne chicken breast, several pasta dishes and steaks. The place offers a good selection of Washington wines. A properly smoky knotty pine bar with an oversized TV screen occupies the cellar.

### Cavanilli's Restaurant and Lounge • ΔΔ $$ ∅

⌸ *302 W. First St., Cle Elum; (509) 674-2151. Italian-American; wine and beer. Sunday-Thursday 7:30 a.m. to 9 p.m., Friday-Saturday 7:30 to midnight, Sunday brunch 10 to 2.* ⌸ Cute little place with warm wood paneling, booths and hanging ferns. To call the menu eclectic is understated: offerings range from pasta to chops and steaks to a few Chinese dishes.

### ☺ MaMa Vallone's • ΔΔΔ $$

⌸ *302 W. First St., Cle Elum; (509) 674-5174. American-continental; full bar service. Tuesday-Saturday 5 to 9:30, Sunday 4 to 9:30, closed Monday. Early-bird dinners under $10 from 4:30 to 6:30. Major credit cards.* ⌸ Bright and cheery dining room decorated with lace curtains and artwork, in an old shingle-sided house. The menu focuses on house-made pastas and other Italian dishes, plus American steaks and chops. A specialty is steaks with Italian touches, such as spicy Sicilian sliced steak over fettuccine.

## WHERE TO SLEEP

### Issaquah to Cle Elum, in order of appearance

### Holiday Inn-Issaquah • ⌂⌂⌂ $$$$ ∅

⌸ *1801 NW 12th Ave. (I-90 exit 15), Issaquah WA 98027; (800) HOLIDAY or (206) 392-6421. Couples $72 to $75, single $64 to $67. Major credit cards.* ⌸ A 100-unit inn with TV movies, room phones; pool and coin laundry. **Annie's Garden Restaurant** serves regional American fare; 6 a.m. to 2 p.m. and 5 to 10; dinners $11 to $17; full bar service.

### Idyl Inn on the River • ⌂⌂⌂ $$$$ ∅

⌸ *4548 Tolt River Rd., Carnation, WA 98014; (206) 868-2000. Couples $75 to $225, singles $65 to $225. Five rooms, all with private baths; full breakfast. MC/VISA.* ⌸ Country inn beside the Tolt River with a swimming pool, garden, private beach, sauna and steam room. Large suites feature "European country" décor while smaller rooms have a Northwest look.

### Salish Lodge ● △△△△ $$$$$ Ø

❑ *P.O. Box 1199 (Snoqualmie Falls), Snoqualmie, WA 98065; (800) 826-6124 or (206) 888-2556. Couples and singles $170 to $220, suites $275 to $500. Major credit cards.* ❑ Luxuriously restored historic lodge, with a look of 1930s elegance—flagstone tile floors, beamed ceiling, brass light fixtures and polished wooden wall sculptures. All rooms have spa tubs, fireplaces and honor bars. Health club, outdoor spa, sport court and library. **Restaurant** and lounge listed above.

### Old Honey Farm Bed & Breakfast ● △△△ $$$$ Ø

❑ *8910 SE 384th Ave., Snoqualmie, WA 98065; (206) 888-9399. Couples $75 to $125, singles $65. Ten rooms with private baths; full breakfast. MC/VISA.* ❑ Modern New England-style inn with a mix of antique and modern furnishings. View of the Cascades and Mount Si from several rooms, and from a sitting room and outside deck. One suite with spa and fireplace.

### Edgewick Inn ● △△ $$$ Ø

❑ *14600 SE 468th Ave. (east end), North Bend, WA 98045; (206) 888-9000. Couples $53 to $59, singles $45 to $48, spa unit $97.38. MC/VISA, AMEX.* ❑ A 44-unit motel with TV, room phones; coin laundry, microwave and free coffee in the lobby.

### Best Western Summit Inn ● △△△ $$$

❑ *P.O. Box 163, Snoqualmie Pass, WA 98068; (800) 528-1234 or (206) 434-6300. Couples and singles $68 to $78, suites from $130. Major credit cards.* ❑ Alpine-style inn; 81 units with TV, rental VCRs, room phones; fireplaces and kitchens in suites. Coin laundry, spa, sauna, playground. Rental snowmobiles, tobogganing, trail riding; ski areas adjacent. **Family Pancake House** listed above.

### Coal Country Inn ● △△ $$$ Ø

❑ *405 N. Second St. (P.O. Box 860). Roslyn, WA 98941; (800) 543-2566 or (509) 649-3222. Couples $62, singles $57. Three units; full breakfast. MC/VISA.* ❑ Cozy country-style inn near downtown Roslyn, built in the early 1900s as a school teachers' boarding house. Restaurant at the inn serves Italian dinners. Rental cross-country ski gear, snowmobiles and bike.

### The Roslyn Inns ● △△ $$$ to $$$$$ Ø

❑ *P.O. Box 386, Roslyn, WA 98941; (509) 649-2936. Couples and larger groups, from $48 to $260. No credit cards.* ❑ Three houses refurbished as country inns. No TV or phones, but all have fully-equipped kitchens. Little Roslyn Inn has five double rooms; the Inn Between has ten bedrooms and a loft; the Roslyn Inn has seven bedrooms.

## WHERE TO CAMP

In addition to these listings, several forest service campgrounds are in the surrounding Mount Baker-Snoqualmie and Wenatchee national forests. Most are on the east side, around Easton-Cle Elum. For details contact: Snoqualmie Pass Visitor Center, P.O. Box 17, Snoqualmie Pass, WA 98068; (206) 434-6111.

**Blue Sky RV Park** ● *9002 SE 302nd, Issaquah, WA 98027; (206) 222-7910. RV sites; $20. Reservations accepted; no credit cards.* ❑ Terraced sites above the village of Preston; some shaded; some pull-throughs. Showers, cable TV. To reach it, take I-90 freeway exit 22 (82nd Street), go south (uphill) and then east.

**Issaquah Village RV Park** • *6509 NE First Ave., Issaquah, WA 98027; (206) 392-9233. RV sites only; $15 to $24. Reservations accepted; MC/VISA.* ⊡ Some pull-throughs; showers, coin laundry, playground, rec field.

**Lake Easton State Park** • *Off I-90, Easton, WA 98925; (206) 656-2230. RV and tent sites, $14 with hookups, $10 without. No reservations or credit cards.* ⊡ Attractive wooded sites with barbecues and picnic tables; some lakeside spots. Flush potties and showers; boat launch, hiking, swimming.

**RV Town** • *P.O. Box 12 (I-90 exit 70), Easton, WA 98925; (509) 656-2360. RV sites $15. Reservations accepted; MC/VISA, AMEX.* ⊡ Near Lake Easton; well-spaced, shaded sites; some pull-throughs. Showers, picnic tables, coin laundry, mini-mart and service station; rec room and playground.

## THE SKYKOMISH CORRIDOR

Instead of returning to I-90, continue east on Cle Elum's First Street, following signs to Highway 97/Wenatchee. It becomes State Highway 970. The rainshadow has done its work on this side of the Cascades, of course. As you continue east, the forest thins out, like an old man losing his hair. You're in the foothills, with attractive farms and ranches tucked into shallow valleys.

The route merges into U.S. 97, and a long, moderately steep upgrade takes you into Wenatchee National Forest, with the usual campgrounds and trailheads along the highway. Off to your right is **Liberty,** a tiny old mining hamlet consisting mostly of the Liberty Gift Shop and Grocery store. Gold panning is popular here, and the folks at the store can suggest some nearby areas. An historic plaque and small museum tell of the town's mini-gold rush a century ago. Call the store at (509) 857-2330 for museum hours.

**RV advisory:** As you approach **Swauk Pass** at 4,102 feet, you're back in thick forest. The highway offers a few twists and turns, although large RVs and trailers can handle it. This route often is closed in winter.

Spiraling downward from Swauk Pass, you'll reach its junction with U.S. Highway 2. Head east about five miles to **Peshastin Pinnacles State Park,** which embraces a dramatic cluster of sandstone formations. Trails wind along the base and if you glance upward, you're likely to see rock-climbers engaged in their dizzying avocation. Nearby is a one-industry town, and how sweet it is!

## Cashmere

**Population: 2,500**                                    **Elevation: 795 feet**

Early in this century, Armenian immigrants planted apples in this attractive valley, in a transition zone between the high Cascades and the Wenatchee agricultural valley. The community was named for the legendary "Vale of Kashmir" of southern Asia.

In 1918, two men in the community used apple bits to create a Washington version of the popular mideastern gelatin confection locum (*lo-KOOM*, which is Turkish for "easy to swallow.") They started marketing them as "Aplets" in 1920, followed by "Cotlets (with apricots) in 1932. From this has emerged a major industry, which dominates the town, both physically and economically. The plant employs about one out of ten Cashmere residents, and produces 15,000 to 25,000 pounds of confection a day.

To tour the plant and sample its products, turn right onto Division Street at the "Welcome to the home of Aplets and Cotlets" sign. Drive past the old fashioned arcaded business district and turn left onto Mission Street:

☺ **Aplets and Cotlets tour** • *Liberty Orchards, 117 Mission St.; (509) 782-2191. May through December: 8 to 5:30 weekdays, 9 to 5 weekends and holidays; January through April: weekdays only, 8 to 11 and 1 to 5; free. Gift shop takes MC/VISA.* ☐ Tours, departing every 20 minutes, take you through the sweet-smelling kitchens where confections are cooked, poured into sheets, chopped, dusted with powdered sugar and boxed by hand. (A nimble-fingered packer can do 5,000 pieces an hour!) Before or after the tour, you can sample Aplets, Cotlets and other fruitlets and buy some to take home, along with apple-focused souvenirs, cookbooks, gift packs, and such. It's best to visit on a weekday, since the plant rarely operates on weekends.

A block north, on Cottage Avenue (parallel to Mission), you can stroll the roofed-over early American style business district and poke into assorted shops and boutiques. If you continue east on Cottage Avenue, you'll encounter—on your right—one of the state's better pioneer village exhibits:

☺ **Chelan County Historical Society Museum** • *600 Cottage Ave.; (509) 782-3230. Open April through October, Monday-Saturday 10 to 4:30, Sunday 1 to 4:30. Adults $3, kids $1, family groups $5.* ☐ Nearly 20 old Chelan County buildings, most squared-log and all pre-20th century, have been assembled here and furnished to their respective periods. Peer into a blacksmith shop, saloon, general store, doctor's office, assay office and several pioneer homes. The museum building, a modest cinderblock structure, houses a major collection of Native American artifacts.

## WHERE TO DINE AND RECLINE

**The Pewter Pot** • △△△ $$$ Ø

☐ *124 Cottage Ave.; (509) 782-2036. American-continental; wine and beer. Tuesday-Saturday 11 to 8; English afternoon tea, 2:30 to 4:30; closed Sunday and Monday. MC/VISA.* ☐ The look is English tearoom, with floral print tablecloths, lace curtains and decorative pewter. The small, versatile menu ranges from American turkey dinner or applejack chicken sauced with apple cider and brandy, to British beef Wellington and beef pot pie. Everything, including breads and deep-dish pies, is made from scratch and the results usually are excellent. Smoke-free dining room.

**Cashmere Country Inn** • ⌂⌂⌂ $$$$ Ø

☐ *5801 Pioneer Ave. (near Division), Cashmere, WA 98815; (509) 782-4212. Couples and singles $75 to $85. Four units with private baths; full breakfast. MC/VISA, AMEX.* ☐ Early American style inn fashioned from an old farm house, with four cozy rooms and a large sitting and dining room. The inn's breakfasts are particularly elaborate and creative. Home-cooked dinners available on request.

**Village Inn Motel** • ⌂⌂ $$$ Ø

☐ *229 Cottage Ave., Cashmere, WA 98815; (509) 782-3522. Couples $30 to $62, singles $25 to $55.* ☐ Well-maintained 21-unit motel with TV, room phones, some room refrigerators. Quiet off-highway area, near downtown.

If you were to continue east on Highway 2/97 from Cashmere, you'd wind up in Wenatchee and central Washington's major agricultural, wine and cattle country. We've saved all that for Chapter 8. To consummate your loop through the Cascades, reverse your route from Cashmere and stay on westbound U.S. 2. Just ahead is a town transplanted intact from Bavaria, complete with the Alps.

# Leavenworth

**Population: 1,700**                                    **Elevation: 1,164 feet**

Well, dang my *leiderhosen*! As you approach Leavenworth, you'd swear that you just left the *autobahn* and not U.S. Highway 97. Cross-timbered architecture, hanging flower baskets and Hansel and Gretel gift shops provide a convincing picture of a Bavarian-Tyrolean village. Sheltering mountains and Wenatchee River glittering through town complete an idyllic setting.

You'll be reminded of Solvang, if you've visited that Danish-theme village in southern California. And you may be tempted to assume that, like Solvang, this Bavarianized village was born of ethnic roots. Not so. Leavenworth's look was born of a desire to save a dying lumber town. The Bavarian theme was one of several that were considered, including Old West and American-Victorian.

Settlement began here around 1890 when a lumber camp called Icicle was established. When a post office was assigned in 1893, the name was changed to Leavenworth. It thrived as a rowdy lumber camp and switching center for the Great Northern Railway's route over Stevens Pass.

Then the lumber mills closed and the rail line was rerouted in the 1920s. By the 1960s, more than half the storefronts along the main street were shut. Rejuvenation began in 1972 when the Vesta Junior Women's Club started a campaign called Project LIFE (Leavenworth Improvement For Everyone). A Bavarian theme was selected and, aided by advice from some Solvang visitors and by a Seattle-area designer who had fled East Germany, the conversion began. Redevelopers didn't rest until virtually every building, from Safeway to Exxon to the bank, was Bavarianized.

With no true ethnic roots, Leavenworth is mostly appealing as a place to photograph and to shop for European imports. And of course, you can feast on *wienerschnitzel, rindsrouladen* and *weisswurst* at every turn.

**RV advisory:** Daytime RV parking is available on a lot near Lions Club Park. It's on the north side of Highway 2, a couple of blocks past the Innsbrucker Building.

This small village is a park and walk place. Start with the **Leavenworth Chamber of Commerce** in the Innsbrucker Building (with the clock tower) at Highway 2 and Ninth Street in the heart of town; it's open daily 9 to 5. The best concentration of shops and cafés is along Front Street, a block below and parallel to the highway. Locals like to call it their Bavarian Village. After you park and begin walking, check out these attractions:

• A nicely-done mural of cows being herded from mountain pastures on the SeaFirst Bank building at 715 Front Street.

• Dancing figurines that emerge onto a balcony to announce the time on a green and yellow commercial building at the west end of Front Street.

• Brightly-trimmed Obertal Mall at Ninth and Commercial, with murals, turrets, towers and decorative windows real and painted.

• The Gingerbread Factory at 828 Commercial Street, where you can nibble still-warm gingerbread and/or have a light lunch.

• Leavenworth Brewery at 636 Front Street, a micro-brewery offering tours daily at 2 p.m., plus a pub, international restaurant, gift shop and chocolate factory.

• Riverfront Park near Eighth and Commercial Street, touched by the Wenatchee River, with inspiring views of Icicle Canyon.

*More Bavarian than Bavaria, the former lumber town of Leavenworth draws hundreds of thousands of visitors each year.* — **Betty Woo Martin**

## ACTIVITIES

Little Leavenworth offers a surprising array of activities and recreational lures, and the surrounding Wenatchee National Forest provides the usual outdoor stuff. Wenatchee is one of America's largest national forests, sprawled over 1.6 million acres, from Mount Rainier to the North Cascades. The Icicle and Wenatchee Rivers that merge near town lure seekers of trout and steelhead. The **U.S. Forest Service** visitor center is on the right as you enter town from the east; open weekdays 9 to 5.

**Biking** ● Downhill bike cruises offered by Cruise the Canyon, Box 285, Leavenworth, WA 98826, (800) 288-6491 or (509) 548-7171; and Gator's Gravity Tours, Highway 2 at Icicle Road, Leavenworth; (509) 548-5102.

**Bike rentals** ● Der Sportsmann, 837 Front St., Leavenworth, (509) 548-5623. Gator's Gravity Tours, Highway 2 & Icicle Road, Leavenworth; (509) 548-5102. Leavenworth Outfitters, 21312 Highway 207, Leavenworth, WA 98826; (800) 347-7934 or (509) 763-3733. Leavenworth Ski & Sports Center, Highway 2 at Icicle Road; (509) 548-7864.

**Hay and sleigh rides** ● Eagle Creek Ranch, P.O. Box 719, Leavenworth, WA 98826; (509) 548-7798. Red-Tail Canyon Farm, 11780 Freund Canyon Rd., Leavenworth, WA 98826; (509) 548-4512.

**Helicopter tours** ● Cascade Helicopters, Peshastin Sawmill Flats (five miles east of Leavenworth on Highway 2); (509) 548-4759.

**Horsepacking** ● Eagle Creek Ranch, P.O. Box 719, Leavenworth, WA 98826; (509) 548-7798. Icicle Outfitters and Guides, P.O. Box 322, Leavenworth, WA 98826; (800) 497-3912, (509) 784-1145 or (509) 763-3647.

**River running** ● Alpine Whitewater, Box 253, Leavenworth, WA 98826; (800) 926-RAFT or (509) 548-4159. Osprey Rafting Company, P.O. Box 668, Leavenworth, WA 98826; (509) 548-6800. Leavenworth Outfitters, 21312 Highway 207, Leavenworth, WA 98826; (800) 347-7934 or (509) 763-3733. Wenatchee Whitewater & Company; (800) 743-5628 or (509) 782-2254.

**Rock climbing** • Leavenworth Alpine Guides, P.O. Box 699, Leavenworth, WA 98826; (509) 548-4729.

## Winter sports

One small downhill facility and several groomed cross-country ski areas are within minutes of Leavenworth. For a brochure on downhill and cross-country skiing in the area, contact: Leavenworth Winter Sports Club, P.O. Box 573, Leavenworth, WA 98826; (509) 548-5115.

**Cross-country skiing** • Nordic skiers can schuss across the Leavenworth Golf Course, with eight miles of groomed trails. Or hit groomed trails at Ski Hill, en route to the downhill area; or the Icicle River Trail, south of town on Icicle Road.

**Dog sledding** • Enchanted Mountain Tours, 18555 Hazel Lane, Leavenworth, WA 98826; (509) 763-2975.

**Downhill skiing** • The small Leavenworth Snow Bowl at the north end of Ski Hill Drive has two rope tows and a few downhill runs; (509) 548-5115.

**Snowmobile tours** • Cascade Snowmobile Safaris, Leavenworth; (509) 548-5162 or 548-4337.

**Winter sports equipment rentals** • Der Sportsmann, Inc., 837 Front Street, Leavenworth; (509) 548-5623. Gustav's Cross-Country Ski Rental, Highway 2 at Front Street; (509) 548-4509. Leavenworth Nordic Ski Center, Highway 2 at Icicle Road, Leavenworth; (509) 548-7864.

## ANNUAL EVENTS

For details on these and other events, contact the Leavenworth Chamber of Commerce at (509) 548-7914.

**Great Bavarian Ice Fest** in mid-January, with snowman building contest, cross-country ski races and such.

**Maifest** over Mother's Day weekend, a traditional Bavarian festival with May Pole winding and a *volksmarch*.

**Art in the Park** weekends from May through September, in Leavenworth City Park.

**Washington State Autumn Leaf Festival** in late September.

**Christmas Lighting Festival** during the holiday season; lights go on at dusk the first Saturday in December.

## WHERE TO DINE

Although Leavenworth began as a lumberjack town, several German restaurateurs have been lured by its Bavarianization, so you'll find a goodly selection of ethnic foods.

**Andrea's Kellar** • ΔΔ $$

☐ 829 Front St.; (509) 548-6000. *German; wine and beer. Lunch daily 11 to 4:30, dinner from 4:30. MC/VISA.* ☐ A convincing-looking *rathskeller* which is, in fact, in a proper basement. The menu is classic Bavarian, with the usual red cabbages, pork hocks, potato salads, *schnitzels* and such. A specialty is spit-roasted Oktberfest chicken.

**Casa Mia Restaurant** • ΔΔ $

☐ 703 Highway 2, at the Innsbrucker Inn; (509) 548-5401. *Mexican, full bar service. Breakfast, lunch and dinner daily. Major credit cards.* ☐ What? Tyrolean tacos? This Latino café wrapped in a Bavarian-style motel features the usual Mexican fare, with most entrées under $10. Specialties include *camarones al mojo de ajo* (shrimp in butter garlic and spices) and *polo con molė* (sautėed chicken in spice molė sauce).

### ☺ *Edelweiss* ● ∆∆∆ $$ Ø

☐ *In the Edelweiss Hotel at 843 Front St.; (509) 548-7015. Bavarian-American; full bar service. Monday-Thursday 8 a.m. to 9:30 p.m., Friday 8 to 10, Saturday 7 to 10 and Sunday 7 to 9. MC/VISA.* ☐ This is our favorite Leavenworth restaurant, with typical stucco and dark-timbered interior, soft Bavarian music and a separate smoke-free dining room. Portions are huge and include the classic German dishes. Try the *cordon bleu, wienerschnitzel, schweinebraten* or specials such as pan fried trout and scallops brochette. Start with tasty beef-barley soup and end with a bit of cheesecake.

### *Hoelgaard's Danish Bakery* ● ∆ $

☐ *731 Front Street. Danish-Bavarian-American; no alcohol. Daily 8 a.m. to 6 p.m. No credit cards.* ☐ Leavenworth is curiously short of European bakeries, although Hoelgaard's fills that near void very nicely. A specialty is Bavarian waffle pastry, with buttercream and strawberry preserves between a crisp, flaky crust. Load up on the usual Danish cookies, Bavarian black forest breads, or pause for a light lunch with espresso.

### ☺ *Reiner's Gasthaus* ● ∆∆ $$

☐ *829 Front St.; (509) 548-5111. Bavarian-Hungarian; wine and beer. Daily 11 to 9:30. MC/VISA.* ☐ Very charming upstairs cafė with beamed ceiling, wainscotting and Bavarian murals. This chef-owned restaurant focuses on rural fare of middle Europe, including homemade *spaetzel*, sausages and sauerkraut, liver and egg dumplings, paprika *schnitzel* and—if you can pronounce it—*ungarisches gulya* (Hungarian beef goulash). Tasty food in ample portions is served at long, family-style tables.

### *Tumwater Inn Restaurant* ● ∆∆ $$

☐ *Ninth at Commercial; (509) 548-4232. American-Bavarian; full bar service. Sunday 8 a.m. to 9 p.m., Monday-Thursday 10 to 9, Friday 10 to 10, Saturday 8 to 10. Major credit cards.* ☐ You say you can't abide *bratwurst* but your wife's in a snit for some *schnitzel*? This attractively modern restaurant, done in burgundy and paisley, offers the variety you need. Choose assorted steaks, seafood or prime rib from the menu's American side, or try several Bavarian specialties. Our favorite here is honey-broiled chicken with mustard sauce.

## WHERE TO SLEEP

Like real European villages, Leavenworth offers a few pensions, in addition to several motels and bed & breakfast inns. Unlike Europe, however, Leavenworth's pensions aren't particularly inexpensive. For lodging reservations, from motels and B&Bs to cabins and vacation homes, you can contact Bedfinders at 305 Eight St., Leavenworth, WA 98826; (800) 323-2920 or (509) 548-4410.

### *Best Western Icicle Inn* ● ⌂⌂⌂ $$$$ Ø

☐ *505 Highway 2 (Icicle Road), Leavenworth, WA 98826; (800) 528-1234. Couples $90 to $95, singles $80 to $85, suites from $135; rates include continental breakfast. Major credit cards.* ☐ Very attractively furnished rooms in a new 66-unit motel with TV, room phones, some refrigerators; pool, spa and exercise room.

### Blackbird Lodge ● ⌂ $$$ Ø

⌂ 305 Eighth St., Leavenworth, WA 98826; (800) 446-0240 (in Washington and Canada only) or (509) 548-5800. Couples $59 to $95, singles $49 to $75; rates include continental breakfast. Major credit cards. ⌂ A 15-unit lodge with TV, room phones, refrigerators and microwaves; spa.

### Canyons Inn ● ⌂ $$$ Ø

⌂ 185 U.S. Highway 2, Leavenworth, WA 98826; (800) 537-9382 or (509) 548-7992. Couples and singles $56 to $120. Major credit cards. ⌂ A 32-unit motel with TV; pool and spa.

### Der Ritterhof ● ⌂⌂ $$$ Ø

⌂ 190 Highway 2, Leavenworth, WA 98826; (800) 255-5845 or (509) 548-5845. Couples and singles from $64, kitchenettes from $70. MC/VISA, AMEX. ⌂ A 54-room Bavarian-style inn with TV, room phones; pool and spa, barbecue area, volleyball court; mountain views.

### Edelweiss Hotel ● ⌂ $$

⌂ 834 Front St., Leavenworth, WA 98826; (509) 548-7015. Couples $25 to $54, singles $18 to $19; some private and some share baths. MC/VISA. ⌂ Fourteen simple, clean and comfortable rooms with TV, above the Edelweiss restaurant (listed below), in the heart of the Bavarian Village.

### Enzian Motor Inn ● ⌂⌂ $$$$ Ø

⌂ 590 Highway 2 (near Ski Hill Drive), Leavenworth, WA 98826; (800) 223-8511 or (509) 548-5269. Couples $86 to $165, singles $76 to $165; rates include buffet breakfast. Major credit cards. ⌂ Attractive 104-unit lodge with TV, room phones; indoor and outdoor pool and hot tub, racquetball court, ping pong, exercise equipment. Cross-country ski gear loaned free to guests.

### Leavenworth Village Inn ● ⌂⌂ $$$$ Ø

⌂ 1016 Commercial St. (two blocks off highway), Leavenworth, WA 98826; (800) 343-8198 or (509) 548-6620. Couples and singles from $70, suites $130 to $175; rates include continental breakfast. MC/VISA, AMEX. ⌂ Attractive Bavarian style inn; 18 units with TV, room phones. Suites have spa tubs, fireplaces, microwaves and refrigerators. All non-smoking.

### Linderhof Motor Inn ● ⌂⌂ $$$ Ø

⌂ 690 U.S. Highway 2 (near downtown), Leavenworth, WA 98826; (800) 828-5680 or (509) 548-5283. Couples and singles from $65, kitchenettes from $95, suites from $105; rates include continental breakfast. Major credit cards. ⌂ Attractive Bavarian-style lodge with hand-crafted furnishings, TV, room phones; some refrigerators. Some townhouse units. Swimming pool, spa.

### ☺ Mrs. Anderson's Lodging House ● ⌂ $$$ Ø

⌂ 917 Commercial Street (near Ninth), Leavenworth, WA 98826; (800) 253-673 or (509) 548-6137. Couples and singles $44 to $63, suite $63 to $70; rates include continental breakfast. MC/VISA. ⌂ Appealing ten-unit lodge with antique furnishings, tapestry throw rugs; sitting parlors with books and games. Downtown, with off-street parking.

### Wedge Mountain Inn ● ⌂⌂ $$$ Ø

⌂ 7335 Highway 2 (between Leavenworth and Cashmere), Cashmere, WA 98815; (800) 666-9664 or (509) 548-6694. Couples from $62, singles from $58. ⌂ Attractive 28-unit lodge with TV, room phones, private decks; laundry. **Big Y Café** adjacent; 7 a.m. to 9 p.m.; dinners $8 to $10; no alcohol.

## B&Bs and pensions

**All Seasons River Inn** ● ⌂⌂⌂ **$$$$$** Ø

⊡ *8751 Icicle River Rd., Leavenworth, WA 98826; (800) 254-0555 or (509) 548-1425. Couples $95 to $125, singles $85 to $115. Five units with full baths; full breakfast. MC/VISA.* ⊡ Northwest style cedar home, furnished with a blend of American and Victorian antiques. All rooms have decks or patios with river and mountain views; some have spa tubs or fireplaces. Common area facilities TV, VCRs, fireplace, refrigerators and games.

☺ **Abendblume Pension** ● ⌂⌂⌂⌂ **$$$$** Ø

⊡ *12570 Ranger Rd. (off Ski Hill Drive), Leavenworth, WA 98826; (800) 669-7634 or (509) 548-4059. Five rooms with TV and private baths; full breakfast. MC/VISA.* ⊡ Striking new European-style country inn with a limestone foyer, archways, window seats and hand-forged iron trim. All rooms have fireplaces, spa tubs, oversized German style showers and TVs with VCRs. Pantry with refrigerator available for guests; Austrian-style breakfast.

**Autumn Pond Bed & Breakfast** ● ⌂⌂⌂ **$$$** Ø

⊡ *10388 Titus Rd. (Pine), Leavenworth, WA 98826; (800) 222-9661 or (509) 548-4482. Couples $59 to $65, singles $49 to $55. Five units with private baths; full breakfast. MC/VISA.* ⊡ New ranch-style bed & breakfast on five acres with a duck pond and spa, half a mile from downtown. Antique and modern furnishings in units; Southwest ranch décor in the great room.

**Bosch Gärten** ● ⌂⌂⌂ **$$$$** Ø

⊡ *9846 Dye Rd., Leavenworth, WA 98826; (509) 548-6900. Couples from $80, singles from $70. Three units with private baths; full breakfast. MC/VISA.* ⊡ Attractive new cross-timbered Bavarian-style inn with gardens, covered deck, hot tub, fireplace in a large common room and a library. Rooms feature classical European furnishings; all three have TV and mountain views.

**Edel Haus Inn Pension** ● ⌂⌂⌂ **$$$** Ø

⊡ *320 Ninth St. (near Main), Leavenworth, WA 98826; (509) 548-4412. Couples and singles $60 to $90. Four units with TV and room phones; some private and some share baths; breakfast not included but lunch or dinner discounted 50 percent. MC/VISA.* ⊡ Comfortable rooms furnished with American antiques, in an old European-style home overlooking the Wenatchee River; outdoor hot tub; hiking and ski trails adjacent. **Dining room** serves lunch and dinner daily; changing menu with an emphasis on nutrition.

**Haus Rohrbauch Pension** ● ⌂⌂⌂ **$$$** Ø

⊡ *12882 Ranger Rd. (half mile up Ski Hill Road), Leavenworth, WA 98826; (509) 548-7024. Couples $65 to $160, singles $55 to $150. Twelve rooms, eight with private baths; full breakfast. Major credit cards.* ⊡ Handsome Austrian-style pension with outdoor pool, hot tub, gardens and a large common room. Units furnished in European country style; three are suites with hot tubs and fireplaces.

**Leirvangen Bed & Breakfast** ● ⌂⌂⌂ **$$$** Ø

⊡ *7586 Icicle Rd., Leavenworth, WA 98826; (509) 548-5165. Couples $60 to $80, singles $55 to $75. Three units with TV, private baths; full Norwegian breakfast. MC/VISA.* ⊡ A Norwegian mountain lodge on five acres of lawn and pasturelands, with Cascade views. Outdoor deck with spa and wood stove; some rooms have spas.

☺ *Pine River Ranch* • ⌂⌂⌂ *$$$$ Ø*

☐ *19668 Highway 207, Leavenworth, WA 98826; (509) 763-3959. Couples $74 to $125, singles $64 to $125. Six units with TV and private baths; full breakfast. MC/VISA.* ☐ Restored 1940s two-story farmhouse in Lake Wenatchee Recreational Area, surrounded by forest with hiking, fishing and cross-country skiing. Rooms furnished with brass beds, country antiques and folk art. A separate cottage has two suites with cathedral ceilings, skylights, fireplaces and kitchenettes. The facility was built as a dairy, with many of the original outbuildings still intact.

*Run of the River* • ⌂⌂⌂ *$$$$ Ø*

☐ *9308 E. Leavenworth Rd. (half mile west), Leavenworth, WA 98826; (800) 288-6491 or (509) 548-7171. Couples $90 to $140, singles $80 to $130. Six units with TV in rooms and private baths; full breakfast. Major credit cards.* ☐ Handsome hand-hewn log inn with matching log furniture created by a local craftsman; some units with spas and wood stoves. Picture windows with views of the Icicle River and Cascades. Deck with spa and wood stove; mountain bikes available.

## WHERE TO CAMP

In addition to these commercial RV parks, several National Forest campgrounds are in the area. Some may be closed in winter, so call ahead.

*Blu-Shastin RV Park* • *3300 Highway 97, Leavenworth, WA 98826; (509) 548-4184. RV and tent sites, $13 to $17. Reservations accepted; MC/VISA.* ☐ Mostly shaded sites, some pull-throughs; showers, coin laundry, mini-mart. Fishing in adjacent river, horse shoes, rec hall and rec field. Seven miles southeast of town.

*Chalet RV Park* • *9825 Duncan Road (at Highway 2), Leavenworth, WA 98826; (800) 477-2697 or (509) 548-4578. RV and tent sites, $12 to $18. Reservations accepted.* ☐ Some shaded sites and pull-throughs; showers, coin laundry, spa. Walking distance to Bavarian Village.

*Icicle River RV Park & Campground* • *7307 Icicle Rd., Leavenworth, WA 98826; (509) 548-5420. RV and tent sites, $15.50 to $22.50. MC/VISA.* ☐ Some shaded and pull-through sites. On the river, with picnic tables, showers, TV hookups, coin laundry, mini-mart, fishing in adjacent Icicle River, rec hall and rec field, horseshoes, spa. Three miles southwest of town.

*Pine Village KOA* • *11401 River Bend Dr., Leavenworth, WA 98826; (509) 548-7709. RV and tent sites, $13.95 to $17.95, "Kamping Kabins" $29 to $35. Reservations accepted; MC/VISA, AMEX.* ☐ Some shaded sites and pull-throughs; showers, coin laundry, mini-mart, fishing, rec room, playground, pool, wading pool and spa. Summer shuttle service to the Bavarian Village, a mile away.

☺ Immediately west of Leavenworth, you enter ruggedly radiant, steep-walled **Tumwater Canyon,** dressed in cascades of the Wenatchee River. With thick green forests and snowcapped peaks in the background, this area is so pretty that one enthusiastic tourist promoter described it as a "drive through a Christmas card." The river's shoreline hardwoods offer a spectacular color display in autumn. A right turn onto State Highway 207, sixteen miles west of Leavenworth, delivers you to a pair of woodsy camping areas: the forest service's **Nathan Creek Campground** and **Lake Wenatchee State Park.** Sites are $7 at the first, with flush potties, barbecues and picnic areas; and $10 at the second, with coin showers. Bordering on Lake Wenatchee reservoir, the state park also offers a lakeside picnic area, boat launch, swimming from a sandy beach, mini-mart and nature trails.

Back on Highway 2, the Christmas card drive continues for another 15 miles of river and canyon. **Stevens Pass,** at 4,061 feet, is relatively commercial-free, unlike Snoqualmie Pass. It's mostly a hikers' and backpackers' area, with trails reaching into the surrounding heights. **Stevens Pass Ski Area** is one of the state's larger winter sports venues, with ten lifts, novice through advanced runs and the usual ski shop, cafeteria and lounges. Call (206) 973-2441 for the ski area and (206) 634-1645 for snow conditions.

*RV advisory:* The climb up to Stevens Pass and down the other side is rather gentle; the highway becomes four-lane as you approach the crest. The west side drops rather quickly, although turns aren't too sharp.

☺ Just below the pass, take a break at the **Deception Falls Turnout,** with a hiking trail through an old-growth forest and interesting displays concerning the building of the Great Northern Railway. A half-mile nature walk passes the tumbled cataracts of lower Deception Falls and the imposing 60-foot drop of the upper falls. There are picnic tables and potties at the turnout. America's northern most transcontinental railroad came through here in early 1893. Said no-nonsense railroad builder James J. Hill: "It makes no difference whether the last spike is driven by President Harrison or a laborer. Just tell the shippers we are ready to haul their goods."

Hill stretched his steel rails from St. Paul to Seattle through 1,860 miles of prairie, north woods and mountain passes. Plans are afoot to build an interpretive trail along the old switchback grade that climbs Stevens Pass.

The highway tumbles gracefully and quickly down from the pass, following the cascading course of the south fork Skykomish River. It sheds three thousand feet in about ten miles before brushing the rustic mountain hamlet of **Skykomish,** in the upper reaches of the Skykomish Valley. Once a key stop on the Great Northern route, it is today a sleepy gathering of false front stores, offering gasoline, provisions and an empty railroad station. It's popular as a staging area for the Henry M. Jackson Wilderness Area and Mount Index Scenic Area of Snoqualmie National Forest. For a lunch or dinner stop, try the town's historic survivor of an inn:

*Skykomish Hotel* ● △ $$

□ *102 Railroad Avenue, Skykomish; (206) 677-2477. American; full bar service. Sunday-Thursday 6 a.m. to 10 p.m., Friday-Saturday 6 to 11. MC/VISA.* □ The place is pleasantly scruffy, with wainscoting, hurricane lamps, and old railroading photos on the walls. It serves basic American steaks and chops, with a proper Western style saloon adjacent.

Continuing westward, you'll pass some rather spectacularly rugged Cascade terrain. **Baring Mountain** on your right and **Mount Index** on the left raise their craggy brows high above the surrounding forest. Just below tiny **Baring,** take a short side trip north to one of the region's more appealing old hamlets.

# Index

### Population: approximately 250

☺ This former mining camp sits beneath the monolithic mass of Baring Mountain, alongside the sparkling current of the north fork Skykomish

River. With an infectious weathered charm, Index is the kind of place that tempts even the hurried traveler to linger.

The town emerged from this wilderness in 1891, when Amos Gunn opened a way station. He laid out the town two years later, then the railroad arrived in 1893. Index began booming toward the turn of the century with the discovery of gold in the area. By 1900, it boasted a water works, lumber mill, scores of stores, a newspaper, dance hall and even a hospital.

Progress has since gone elsewhere, although the town has weathered the lean years well. It offers an appealing collection of prim red and white buildings, such as the oldstyle **City Hall** with a slender totem out front. Step into the **Mount Index Tavern and Beer Garden** for a game of darts, and maybe a snack and beer on a deck over the river. The **Index General Store,** staffed by exceptionally friendly folks, functions as the local visitors bureau. It also shelters a great little bakery; try some of the huge molasses cookies that once were popular in lumber camps. Ask for an historic walking tour brochure and stroll the town's quiet streets. Or pick up picnic fare and have lunch at **Doolittle Pioneer Park.**

Fisherpersons like to wet their flies in the next-door river, and hikers can get a trail map from the store. If you're tempted to linger longer, lodgings and a restaurant were reopened in late 1993 in a century-old roadhouse:

☺ **Bush House** ● ⌂⌂⌂ **$$** Ø

▢ *Index Avenue at Fifth Street, Index, WA 98256; (206) 793-2312. Couples and singles $70 to $80. Rates include $10 breakfast credit. MC/VISA.* ▢ Newly restored inn set dramatically against a mountain wall, with an attractive garden out front. The interior is done in dark wood wainscotting, with a fieldstone fireplace, historic photos and pastel paintings. Rooms are furnished with white wicker and down comforters; most have balconies, where guests can sit and admire the mountains. **Restaurant** serves American fare in an attractive turn-of-the-century dining room, and at outdoor tables.

A few miles west on Highway 2, you'll encounter the small community of **Gold Bar,** with basic provisions and fuel. It offers neither the setting nor the charm of Index. However, it's the gateway to a state park campground and one of our favorite hikes in the Cascades. To reach it, turn right onto First Street and follow signs about two miles.

**Wallace Falls State Park** ● *P.O. Box 105, Gold Bar, WA 98251; (206) 793-0420. Tent sites only, $10.* ▢ Shaded sites with barbecues and picnic tables, flush potties; nature trails.

☺ **Wallace Falls** gushes 265 feet over a sheer cliff face about three miles from the parking area. Hikers have two choices: a trail that passes through a mossy forest and then follows a canyon above the Wallace River; or an old railroad grade. The first is more scenic; the rail grade (with the rails removed) is longer but more gentle. Maps available at the park explain these options. A couple of vista points at the base of the falls provide impressive vistas. You can continue to the top—a tough half-mile grunt, although the view of the falls isn't any better up there.

Just below Gold Bar is **Skykomish State Salmon Hatchery,** open 8 to 5. It's one of the few that permits visitors into the hatchery room, where stacked incubator trays are filled with millions of future game fish. However, the trays are covered, so it isn't terribly exciting. Graphics and a series of pickled specimens show visitors what's happening.

Beyond the hatchery, the terrain begins to flatten. The forest yields to pasturelands and the first hints of spreading Puget Sound suburbia. **Sultan,** with a strung-out business district, marks the end of the Highway 2 scenic route. You shortly pass through equally uninteresting **Monroe**, then the highway crosses Interstate 5 and terminates in **Everett** (see Chapter 5).

Before reaching the freeway, take a brief peek at the old fashioned downtown of **Snohomish,** less than a mile south of Highway 2. To reach it, take a half left onto Glenn Avenue, which blends onto First Street, with five or six blocks of 19th century buildings. Note particularly the Colonial style brick **Snohomish City Hall** at Glenn and Union. Incidentally, the area brims with antique stores, and the **Star Center Mall** at 829 Second Street has 165 dealers under one roof; (206) 568-2131.

# THE NORTH CASCADES CORRIDOR

If you intend to blend directly into the next corridor—as we did to research this chapter—you can shun the freeway by heading north from Snohomish on State Highway 9. Three different approaches will deliver you to North Cascades National Park—Highway 92 through Silverton and Darrington, Highway 530 from Arlington through Darrington, and Highway 20 from Sedro Woolley. We've chosen the longer, more scenic Highway 92 approach, with a return on Route 20.

*RV and general driving advisory:* The highway to Darrington and on to North Cascades National Park is gently curved and only moderately steep. There is a 13-mile gravel section, reasonably smooth but with a few bumps and steep turns, although it's navigable. It starts a few miles beyond Silverton and ends nine miles before Darrington. Make sure your fuel tank is topped; services are scarce between Granite Falls and Darrington. Also, there's no fuel along the 69-mile route through North Cascades National Park, from Marblemount to Mazama. Highway 92 to Darrington and Highway 20 through North Cascades are closed in winter, generally from November through April.

Your route begins with a few miles of stop lights in a wooded commercial and residential area north of Snohomish. After five miles, turn east on Route 92 toward **Granite Falls.** Beyond that small town, you shed civilization in favor of timbered foothills. Some patches have been clear-cut, giving the look of mountains with mange.

The setting soon improves. Just east of tiny **Verlot,** you'll enter Mount Baker-Snoqualmie National Forest, and the highway becomes a national forest scenic route. You can pick up maps and such at a Forest Service **visitor information center** just beyond Verlot; it's open weekdays 8 to 5.

Called the Mountain Loop Highway, this route carries you through a little-visited wilderness of thickly wooded hills and narrow river canyons. The craggy Cascades accent the far horizon. The highway often brushes the shoreline of the small Stillaguamish River, and you may be tempted to pause and dampen a dry fly. This corridor is a virtual rain trap, soaked by 80 to 140 inches a year. Thus, the woodlands are as lush as a tropic jungle. Campgrounds and picnic areas line the route, and trailheads beckon hikers into the **Boulder River Wilderness** to the north and **Henry M. Jackson Wilderness** in the south. **Silverton,** several miles from Verlot, is a rustically cute collection of 18th century houses, with no business district.

☺ A few miles beyond Silverton, watch on your right for a turnoff to the

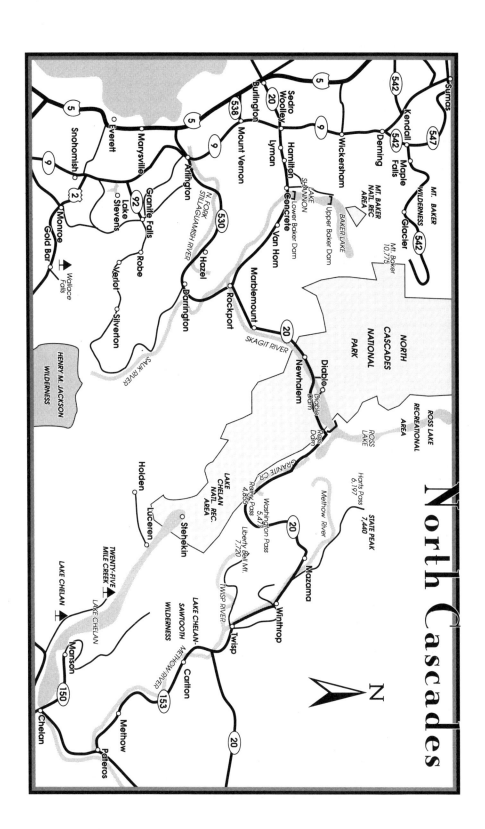

# North Cascades

**Sunrise Mine trailhead** and vista point, on Sunrise Mine Road. It's marked by a viewpoint sign with a camera icon. The dirt and gravel road take you about two miles to a spectacular river canyon. Morning Star Peak, a great wedge of tilted strata, dominates the horizon. Trails from here reach into the surrounding wilderness.

**RV advisory:** The Sunrise Mine Road is steep, winding and narrow in places. Turn-around space at the trailhead is limited for large RVs or trailer rigs. Small to mid-sized RVs should have no problem.

Back on the main highway, you'll hit gravel two miles beyond the Sunrise Mine Road turnoff. After following the twisting course of the Sauk River for 13 miles, you'll pick up pavement again and shortly enter a town that seems more remote than it is.

**Darrington** is a rather drab and ordinary little village in a spectacular mountain setting. It's a major staging area for hikers, campers, backpackers and rock climbers, since it's easily reached via all-paved Highway 530 from Arlington. We took the convoluted scenic route and came in the back door. Folks hereabouts apparently do more drinking than eating, for we found two taverns but only one active cafe. (Two were closed and for sale.) Visitors can get light bites in the bars, and the town offers a motel (see below).

Heading north from Darrington on State Highway 530, you'll pass the **visitor information center** of the Darrington Ranger District; open weekdays 8 to 5. The highway, now wide and level, follows the **Sauk River Valley** 19 miles through a mix of conifers and hardwoods that offer streamside brilliance in the fall. **Rockport,** at the junction of highways 530 and 20, consists mostly of a service station, a country store and a silly gimmick.

"You'd be surprised how many tourists do it," the store clerk grinned.

Do what?

Kick themselves.

Say what?

In front of the store is a "self-kicking machine"—four boots mounted on spokes, turned by a hand-crank. The gimmick is to have a companion take your picture, properly bent over, beneath a sign reading: "I have joined the self-kicking club."

From Rockport, kick your vehicle to the east on Highway 20 and head for a most imposing slice of Washington's Cascade Range. As you travel along the delta-like agricultural valley of the Skagit (*SKA-jit*) River, you begin catching your first glimpses of those craggy "American Alps," as locals like to call the North Cascades.

Facilities within North Cascades National Park are limited, so it's best to stock up and fuel up in **Marblemount.** Tiny, cute and woodsy, it sits near the park's western border. Also, you can load up on park information at the **Marblemount Ranger Station,** open daily from 8 to 6. Turn left at the western edge of town and drive about half a mile up Ranger Station Road.

## WHERE TO RECLINE AND DINE
### Darrington and Marblemount

**Stagecoach Inn ● ◠◠ $$**

◻ *1100 Seeman St. (P.O. Box 400), Darrington, WA 98241; (800) 428-1776 or (206) 436-1776. Couples $47, singles $44, kitchenettes $47. MC/VISA.* ◻ Twenty-four comfortable rooms in Western-style lodge with cable TV, continental breakfast; five kitchen units.

### The Shop • Δ $

☐ *Highway 530, north edge of Darrington. American; no alcohol. Week-days 4 a.m. to 7 p.m., weekends 7 to 7.* ☐ Very basic café with basic prices, serving pork chops, ham steaks, chicken and such. All entrèes are under $6.

### ☺ Mountain Song Restaurant • ΔΔ $$ Ø

☐ *5860 North Cascades Highway, Marblemount; (206) 873-2461. Ethnic-Northwest regional; wine and beer. Monday, Tuesday and Thursday 8 to 8; Wednesday 11 to 5, Friday-Sunday 8 to 9. MC/VISA.* ☐ Attractive, rustic café with a pole beam ceiling, hanging Boston ferns and a whole earth attitude. The health-conscious menu ranges from Bavarian sausages to baked local trout to turkey oat pie to organic Cascade salad.

### Log House Inn Restaurant • ΔΔ

☐ *North Cascades Highway, Marblemount; (206) 873-4311. Rural Ameri-can; full bar service. Daily 7 a.m. to 9 p.m. MC/VISA.* ☐ Typical down home food served in a simple, pleasing Victorian atmosphere, with hurricane lamps, bentwood chairs and red velvet wallpaper. Load up on generous serv-ings of chicken fried steak, fried prawns, breaded veal cutlets and such.

# NORTH CASCADES NATIONAL PARK

Although it covers half a million acres, North Cascades is not a national park busy with activities. It's primarily a hikers' and backpackers' venue. Hundreds of miles of trails lead into an awesome wilderness accented by some of the Cascades' most rugged peaks, and laced with more than 300 glaciers. Only tantalizing edges of these wilds are visible from highways.

They are, however, tantalizing enough to make the North Cascades Highway one of the most popular scenic routes in northwestern America. Expect this corridor to be busy with traffic in summer. Technically, this stretch of State Highway 20 doesn't enter the park. Rather, it travels through the narrow corridor of Ross Lake National Recreation Area, which slices the park into north and south sections. Ross Lake began taking shape in 1937 when Seattle City Light built Ross Dam on the Skagit River.

"Nowhere do the mountain masses and peaks present such strange, fan-tastic, dauntless and startling outlines as here," wrote explorer Henry Custer in 1859. On reconnaissance for the International Boundary Commission, he was one of the first outsiders to see this remote section of the Cascade Range. A bit of prospecting and homesteading followed, mostly from the late 19th and into the early 20th century, but the area was too remote and rugged for much settlement. Names still on maps speak of the frustration of early explorers: Forbidden Peak, Mount Despair, Mount Torment and Mount Challenger.

A wagon road was hacked into the area late in the last century, and the first segment of the North Cascades Scenic Highway followed this route in 1893. Road builders wanted to penetrate these formidable mountains, but washouts and landslides stopped the project after a year. The new road did-n't go much beyond Newhalem. Seattle City Light came along in the 1920s to begin harnessing the Skagit, which is Washington's second largest river after the Columbia.

North Cascades National Park wasn't created until 1968. Ross Lake, al-ready developed as a reservoir, was declared a national recreation area, along with the upper five mile-length of nearby Lake Chelan (which we visit in Chapter 8). The three units are jointly administered. Four years after this trio was established, the North Cascades Highway finally was completed. It was the culmination of a 12-year effort to carve a path over 5,477-foot Washington Pass.

## The essentials

**Visitor facilities and information:** A new visitor center at Newhalem was completed in 1994. To reach it, drive south through the Newhalem Creek Campground. It's open daily in summer, with an interpretive museum, information desk and a slide program. A Wilderness Office in Marblemount can provide backcountry information and backpacking permits, and a small information kiosk operates in summers at Colonial Creek Campground on Diablo Lake. The *Challenger* newspaper jointly produced by the national park and forest service, is available free throughout the park, offering details on facilities, programs and other pertinent information.

**Hiking:** Trails stretch into the park from the Ross Lake corridor, and into adjacent wilderness areas. Permits aren't needed for day hikes. They are required for overnighting and may be picked up free at any ranger station or visitor center, although it's best to get them at the Wilderness Office since the staff there has more detailed information on trail difficulties and such.

**Boating:** Boat launches are available at Colonial Creek Campground on Diablo Lake, Goodell Creek on the Skagit River at the lower end of the corridor, and at Hozomeen on the north end of Ross Lake (reached via British Columbia). Boat rentals are available at the Ross Lake Resort.

**Ranger activities:** Guided hikes, talks and campfire chats at the Newhalem Campground amphitheater are conducted in summer. Pick up a schedule at any visitor facility.

**Skagit Tour:** Seattle City Light conducts tours of its dam facilities Thursday through Monday from mid-June through Labor Day weekend, starting from the Skagit Tour Center in Diablo. The tour includes a slide show, a ride on an old incline railway to Sourdough Mountain, a cruise across Diablo Lake and a hefty lunch or dinner. Reservations are essential, and should be made weeks early. Prices are $25 for adults, $22 for seniors and $10 for kids. Shorter tours with no meals or boat ride also are available from July 1 through Labor Day, for $5 per person. Make reservations at the Skagit Tour Center or contact: Seattle City Light, 1015 Third Ave., Seattle, WA 98104; (206) 684-3030.

**Food and lodging:** One lodge operates within the complex, reached only by water taxi or private boat. Early reservation are recommended: Ross Lake Resort, c/o Rockport, WA 98283, (206) 386-4437. Other accommodations are available in Marblemount and in the Winthrop-Twisp area to the west (see below).

**Camping:** Newhalem Creek, Colonial Creek and Goodell Creek Campground are along State Highway 20, within Ross Lake National Recreation Area. They have tent and RV spaces with flush potties, no hookups or showers; rates are $10 at Newhalem Creek and $7 at the others. Sites are on a first come, first served basis, and space is generally available, even in midsummer. Several campgrounds are in the surrounding national forest and commercial RV parks and campgrounds are in Marblemount and the Winthrop-Twisp area (which see).

**When to go:** This is a summer-fall place. Because of high elevations and heavy snows, much of the park is inaccessible in winter. The North Cascades Scenic Highway is closed, generally from November to April 1.

*RV Advisory:* Highway 20 is wide and nicely graded through most of the Ross Lake corridor. Expect some switchbacks and hairpin turns over Washington Pass, particularly on the eastern descent. Any large RV or trailer rig can handle it, however. Pull-outs are available so slower-moving RVs can let other traffic pass.

## Driving the North Cascades Highway

Particularly useful for your drive through this corridor is the *North Cascades Scenic Highway* brochure and *Challenger* newspaper, produced by the national park and forest service, and available at all visitor centers. The brochure is essentially a milepost guide to the region, starting back at Sedro Woolley.

Highway 20 from Marblemount follows the Skagit River into Ross Lake National Recreation Area. The **North Cascades Visitor Center** at Newhalem will provide insight into this park-recreation area complex, and the **Skagit Project Information Center** a couple of miles beyond will flagellate you with facts about the Seattle City Light project.

Behind **Gorge Dam,** the Skagit is no longer a river, but a chain of lakes reaching dozens of miles back into this narrow, Cascade-rimmed canyon. Pause at the **Gorge Creek** overlook to watch a small side stream cascading from a narrow slot of a canyon. Just beyond, a short side road takes you to **Diablo,** a 1920s style company town with its cookie-cutter employee housing. The Skagit tour gathers in Diablo, stopping at a small museum and then catching the incline railroad, which originally carried construction materials. Back on Highway 20, you soon reach **Diablo Dam** and above it, a **Diablo Lake** overlook.

The canyon closes in as you continue past **Ross Dam.** It forms long, fjord-like **Ross Lake,** which extends more than 20 miles north into British Columbia. Half a mile east of Ross Dam, handicapped-accessible **Happy Creek Forest Walk** loops through an old growth forest, with interpretive signs along the route. Beyond Happy Creek, you'll shortly leave Ross Lake NRA behind and follow rugged, shallow Granite Creek canyon up to **Rainy Pass.** A one-mile paved trail leads to the little emerald of **Rainy Lake,** with access to the high country on the Pacific Crest Scenic Trail. The stroll to Rainy Lake and hike up Heather Pass on the Pacific Crest is one of the area's better day outings.

Until now, you've not seen the kind rugged beauty that was so visible from the highway in Mount Rainier National Park and the Snoqualmie and Skykomish corridors. That's all about to change.

☺ You begin a steep climb toward a near-vertical sawtooth wall. Granite spires thrust above their tree lines, seeming bent on piercing the sky. Dominate over all is the broken granite profile of the 7,808-foot **Liberty Bell,** one of the most photographed peaks in Washington. **Washington Pass overlook,** reached by a short drive just west of the pass, offers a fantastic view of Liberty Bell and the surrounding serrated peaks. A looping trail connects upper and lower viewpoints.

A glance downward may give you cause to pause if you're a timid driver. The highway literally corkscrews downhill, dropping from mile-high Washington Pass to the 1,700-foot Methow (*MEE-tau*) Valley. Since the highway is relatively new, the 17-mile downhill run is untouched by civilization, except for an occasional Forest Service campground. The **Early Winters Visitor Center** of the Forest Service is on your left as the route bottoms out in the Methow Valley. A few miles beyond is the ranching hamlet of **Mazama**.

☺ If you have a sturdy vehicle, you can backtrack into the Cascades on a 23-mile-long dirt and gravel road from Mazama through **Ballard Campground** to **Harts Pass** and remnants of the gold camp of **Chancellor.** The route to Ballard isn't too rough, but the road beyond is narrow and steep. It is definitely not recommended for large RVs, and trailers are prohibited. The road crosses the Pacific Crest Trail at Harts Pass, and two campgrounds are in the area. At 6,197 feet, this is the highest road pass in Washington. It's also the most northern road access to the Pacific Crest Trail. Cascadian views from the pass and from nearby Slate Peak lookout are spectacular.

As you continue eastward on Highway 20, the mountains begin shedding their evergreen fir, giving way to the brushy and brown Methow Valley. Thirteen miles down the valley from Mazama is a town that looks too darned Western to be real. Can this be a movie set?

# Winthrop

**Population: 400**                                **Elevation: 1,765 feet**

Like the people of Leavenworth, the folks in Winthrop decided a few years ago that their town needed a theme. With the North Cascades Highway opening and all those people passing through, why not snag a few?

Winthrop's roots are more authentic than Leavenworth's, since it began as a Western town, established in 1891 as a trading center for ranchers and miners. It was founded by Guy Waring from Boston and named for Theodore Winthrop, a Yale scholar who toured the northwest in 1853. Waring had been a classmate of Owen Wister, and the author apparently spent some time here to capture color for his first Western novel, *The Virginian*.

As Winthrop struggled into this century, it lost most of its business and all of its character. "Before we decided to go Western, the town had become a dump," said the nice lady at the visitor center.

The "new" Winthrop is tourist Western, of course. Three-Finger Jack's Saloon is a family restaurant, the blacksmith shop sells wrought iron decorator pieces, and various cowboy cafès serve teriyaki stir fry and key lime pie. Boutiques, curio shops and espresso parlors are popular. Old concrete sidewalks have been cleverly covered by properly weathered boardwalks. A few of the buildings are original and restored, although several new false front structures have been added. The gimmick is working. This place is mobbed most summer weekends, and finding a place to sleep without a reservation is well nigh impossible.

Start your Winthrop stroll with a stop at the **Information Bureau,** at the intersection of Bridge Street (Highway 20) and Riverside Avenue (the main drag). It's open daily in summer from 9 to 5, then only on holiday weekends the rest of the year. Ask the folks there to point you to the town's fine museum:

☺ *Shafer Historical Museum* ● *Castle Avenue near Bridge Street; (509) 996-2712. Daily in summer 10 to 5, shorter hours the rest of the year. Free; donations appreciated.* ☐ Several historic structures and old wagons, mining equipment and farm implements have been gathered at this large museum complex. Its focal point is a reconstruction of town founder Guy Waring's cabin, with period furniture and pioneer artifacts. Other structures include a general store with turn-of-the-century goods, the original Mazama post office and a stamp mill with old mining equipment.

Also worth a pause—perhaps a brief one:

**North American Wildlife Exhibit** • *Just south of town on Highway 20; (509) 996-2330. Open Friday-Sunday in summer from 10 to 6. Adults $2.50, kids $1.* ❏ This small exhibit features stuffed North American mammals, skulls, antlers and a small gift shop.

Winthrop is smaller than Leavenworth and folks can poke through most of its shops within a few hours. Of course, the adjacent alpine recreational area can dictate a much longer stay, and this is a handy staging area for westbound visitors to North Cascades National Park.

Ten miles south on Highway 20 is **Twisp,** which is as ordinary as Winthrop is cleverly contrived. It does offer several inexpensive motels to catch the Winthrop overflow, and at least one good restaurant (listed below). The town was platted at the merger of the Twisp and Methow rivers in 1899 by one Henry C. Glover. He named it Gloversville, but another Glover existed in the county, so a postal official convinced him to change it to Twisp, a Native American word for yellowjacket.

## ACTIVITIES

Like Leavenworth, Winthrop and Twisp are gathering spots for outdoor activities in the surrounding area. A good source is Methow Valley Central Reservations, an information and booking service: P.O. Box 505, Winthrop, WA 98862; (800) 422-3048 or (509) 996-2148.

**Air charters, scenic flights** • Winthrop Flight Service; (509) 997-6962.

**Climbing** • American Alpine Institute offers rock-climbing and technical mountain climbing outings in the North Cascades above Winthrop. The address is 1212 24th St., Bellingham, WA 98225; (206) 671-1505.

**Horseback riding** • Chewack River Ranch Riding Stables; 996-2497.

**Horsepacking trips** • Claude Miller Pack Trips, P.O. Box 250, Winthrop, WA 98862; (509) 996-2350. Early Winters Outfitters, Star Route Box 28, Winthrop, WA 98862; (509) 996-2659. North Cascade Outfitters, P.O. Box 397, Brewster, WA 98812; (509) 689-2813 or (509) 689-3131. Rendezvous Outfitters; (800) 422-3025 or (509) 996-3299. RockingHorse Ranch, Star Route Box 35, Winthrop, WA 98862; (509) 996-3263.

**Hiking, driving tours** • Nature Expressions; (509) 436-1771 or (509) 436-1500.

**Whitewater rafting** • Osprey River Adventures in Twisp, 997-4116.

## Winter sports

**Downhill skiing** • Methow Valley will become a major ski area when and if the long-planned and oft-delayed Early Winters downhill resort is built. You can still go downhill, if rather expensively, via helicopter skiing with Liberty Bell Alpine Tours, (509) 996-2250.

**Cross-country skiing** • Meanwhile, this is a popular Nordic area. The Methow Valley Sport Trails Association helps promote and maintain an extensive network of Nordic trails. For a brochure, contact them at P.O. Box 327, Winthrop, WA 98862 or call Central Reservations at (800) 422-3048 or

(509) 996-2148. Also call Central for details on hut-to-hut skiing in the nearby Rendezvous Hills.

## ANNUAL EVENTS

For details on these events, contact the chamber at 996-2125.

**Cross-country ski races** in January.

**Fortyniner Days** community celebration, second weekend in May.

**Winthrop Rodeo** over Memorial Day weekend.

**River Rat Days**, Winthrop to Twisp river race, Fourth of July weekend.

**Labor Day Rodeo** over Labor Day weekend.

**Mountain Bike Festival** in October.

## WHERE TO DINE
### Winthrop and Twisp

☺ *Duck Brand Inn* ● ∆∆ $$

⛾ *248 Riverside Ave., Winthrop; (509) 996-2192. American-Mexican; wine and beer. Breakfast, lunch and dinner daily. MC/VISA, AMEX.* ⛾ The Duck Brand is a recently constructed but made-to-look-funky combination café, bakery and hotel. It's decorated with old advertising signs and other early-day doo-dads. The busy menu leaps from chicken with cranberry sauce to fettuccine to assorted Mexican dishes. Some of the best offerings are muffins and pies emerging from the bakery. Indoor and outdoor dining.

*Giovanni's West* ● ∆ $

⛾ *173 Riverside Ave., Winthrop; (509) 996-2210. Italian-American; wine only. Daily 8 a.m. to 8 p.m. MC/VISA.* ⛾ Small, trim café in the General Merchandise Building, serving fettuccine, spaghetti, ravioli, pizzas, burgers and other light fare. Indoor seating and outdoor tables with a river view.

☺ *Riverside Rib Company* ● ∆∆ $$

⛾ *207 Main St. (Riverside), Winthrop; (509) 996-2001. American-Mexican; wine and beer. Lunch and dinner daily. No credit cards.* ⛾ The aroma of ribs smoking in the adjacent garden will draw you into this neat, funky Western style restaurant. Try the applewood smoked pork and beef combination with beans and Mexican rice, or the grilled chicken or smoked sausage dinner. Indoor and outdoor dining.

*Roadhouse Diner* ● ∆∆ $$

⛾ *Highway 20 in Twisp; (509) 977-4015. American; full bar service. Sunday-Thursday 8 a.m. to 9:30 p.m., Friday-Saturday 8 to 10.* ⛾ Attractively rustic café and lounge with log beam ceilings, decorated with turn-of-the-century food tins and other artifacts. A versatile menu lists Cornish game hens, razorback pork ribs and assorted steaks. On busy weekends, the Roadhouse is a nice alternative to the more crowded Winthrop restaurants.

*Three-Fingered Jack's* ● ∆∆ $$

⛾ *Riverside Avenue at Bridge Street, Winthrop; (509) 996-2411. American; full bar service. Daily 7 a.m. to 10 p.m. MC/VISA.* ⛾ One of the few original Winthrop businesses, this Western-style place claims to have been the state's first legal saloon. The menu is typical Gringo—steaks, prawns, coho salmon, chicken and some pasta dishes.

*Winthrop Palace* ● ∆∆ $$

⛾ *149 Riverside Ave. (near Bridge), Winthrop; (509) 996-2245. Eclectic menu; full bar service. Sunday-Thursday 7 a.m. to 9 p.m., Friday-Satuday 7 to*

10. MC/VISA. ☐ The look is more Victorian than Western, with lace curtains and ceiling fans. The menu has something of an identity crisis, wandering from Oriental stir fry to rainbow trout to steaks.

# WHERE TO SLEEP

### Best Western Marigot ● △△ $$$$ ∅
☐ 960 Highway 20 (P.O. Box 813), Winthrop, WA 98862; (800) 468-6754 or (509) 996-3100. Couples $48 to $75, singles $45 to $67; rates include continental breakfast. Major credit cards. ☐ New mountain-style inn with TV, room phones; coin laundry, spa, basketball and volleyball court.

### ☺ Early Winters Cabins ● △ $$$
☐ Mazama, WA 98833; (509) 996-2355 or (509) 996-2843. Couples and singles $55 to $80. No credit cards. ☐ Six rustic and cozy cabins tucked into the timber, opposite the Early Winters Forest Service visitor center. Fully equipped cabins with kitchens and utensils, private baths and fireplaces. Some are on Early Winters Creek; fishing, hiking and cross-country skiing are right on the grounds.

### Idle-a-While Motel ● △△ $$ ∅
☐ 505 N. Highway 20 (P.O. Box 575), Twisp, WA 98856; (509) 997-3222. Couples $41 to $46, singles $37 to $42, kitchenettes $46 to $57. MC/VISA, DISC. ☐ Well-kept 25-unit motel with TV, rental VCRs, room phones, some refrigerators. Tennis court, sauna and spa; winter ski trails.

### Hotel Rio Vista ● △△ $$$$ ∅
☐ P.O. Box 815 (downtown area), Winthrop, WA 98862; (509) 996-3535. Couples and singles $75 to $90. MC/VISA. ☐ New 16-unit western-style lodge within walking distance of shops and cafés. All units have private decks over the river, and all are non-smoking; TV and room phones.

### Sportsman Motel ● △ $$ ∅
☐ State Highway 20 at Burton, Twisp, WA 98856; (509) 997-2911. Couples $37 to $40, singles $29 to $40, kitchenettes $50 to $90. MC/VISA, AMEX. ☐ A nine-unit motel with TV and room refrigerators; barbecue area.

### ☺ Sun Mountain Lodge ● △△△ $$$$$ ∅
☐ P.O. Box 1000, Winthrop, WA 98862; (800) 572-0493 or (509) 996-2211. Couples and singles $115 to $160, kitchenettes $120 to $135, suites $200 to $230. Major credit cards. ☐ Rustically elegant, dramatically-situated mountain resort nine miles south of Winthrop, with a sweeping valley view. Emerging from a $20 million renovation, it's one of the finest hideaways in the Northwest. Rooms and public areas are dressed in warm woods, wrought iron, handcrafted furniture and hand-painted spreads. Amenities include a pool, miles of hiking and cross-country ski trails, horseback riding programs, tennis, mountain biking, water sports, golf, and rafting in nearby streams. The **Restaurant,** open for breakfast, lunch and dinner, features Northwest and continental cuisine; full bar service.

### Trail's End Motel ● △△ $$$ ∅
☐ P.O. Box 189 (130 Riverside Avenue), Winthrop. WA 98862; (509) 996-2303. Couples and singles $48 to $68. MC/VISA, AMEX. ☐ Appealing little Western-style inn with TV, VCRs and room phones. Small **Trail's End Way Station** serves soups, salads, sandwiches and other light fare, 7 a.m. to 10 p.m.; no alcohol.

*Craggy Mount Shuksan adds visual drama to the alpine view from Artist Point in the Mount Baker National Recreation Area.* — **Betty Woo Martin**

### Virginian Resort ● △△ $$$ Ø
◻ *P.O. Box 237 (808 N. Cascades Hwy.), Winthrop, WA 98862; (800) 854-2834 or (509) 996-2535. Couples and singles $52 to $75, kitchenettes $75 to $95, suites $125 to $200. Major credit cards.* ◻ An eight-unit complex with TV and room refrigerators. Pool, hot tub, volleyball court. **Virginian Restaurant** serves continental fare, 7:30 a.m. to 9 p.m.; full bar.

### Winthrop Inn ● △△ $$$ Ø
◻ *P.O. Box 265 (Highway 20), Winthrop, WA 98862; (800) 444-1972 or (509) 996-2217. Couples $56 to $60, singles $49 to $53. MC/VISA, AMEX.* ◻ A 30-unit motel with TV; barbecue area, pool and spa. Continental breakfast served in the off-season.

## WHERE TO CAMP

In addition to the facilities listed below, several Forest Service campgrounds are in the area.

**Derry's Resort on Pearrygin Lake** ● *Route 1, Box 307, Winthrop, WA 98862; (509) 996-2322. RV and tent sites; $8.50 to $12. Reservations accepted.* ◻ Lakeside camping resort with showers, laundry, mini-mart and RV supplies; swimming, boating and fishing, boat and tackle rental, horseshoes, playground and kiddie farm.

**Pearrygin Lake State Park** ● *Route 1, Box 300, Winthrop, WA 98862-9710; (509) 996-2370. RV and tent sites; $11 to $15. Reservations may be made in summer; contact the park for a form. No credit cards.* ◻ Shaded sites, some with water and electric, flush potties and showers. Boat ramp, swimming and boating, nature trails. Snowmobiling and cross-country skiing in winter.

**Methow River KOA** ● *Highway 20, a mile east (P.O. Box 305), Winthrop, WA 98862; (509) 996-2258. RV and tent sites, $15; "Kamping Kabins" $29.*

*Reservations accepted; MC/VISA.* ☐ On the Methow River; some pull-throughs; showers, coin laundry, mini-mart, swimming pool, playground and rec room, rental bikes, fishing.

**Riverbend RV Park** ● *Route 2, Box 30 (on Highway 20), Twisp, WA 98856 (509) 997-3500. RV and tent sites, $10 to $14. Reservations accepted; MC/VISA.* ☐ Grassy sites on the Methow River; showers, coin laundry, rec hall and rec field, play area, swimming and fishing; tackle available. Rental RV units available.

# SIDE TRIP: MOUNT BAKER

The northernmost volcano in the Cascade Range, Mount Baker is an attraction unto itself. Like Rainier, St. Helens and Adams, it is the photogenic focal point of a vast recreation area. Hundreds of miles of trails wind through its flanks, a scenic highway climbs to its heights, and a downhill resort offers the state's longest ski season.

Down in the valleys, ordinary cities like Bellingham are made attractive by having Mount Baker as a backdrop.

Like its volcanic sisters, 10,775-foot Baker is asleep but not dormant. An ash eruption in 1843 started a huge forest fire. Well over a century later, in 1975, a sudden hiss of volcanic steam melted glacial ice to form a new lake in the crater. The peak was named for Captain George Vancouver's first mate, Joseph Baker, who spotted the promontory as their ship sailed past in 1792. Indians had a more interesting name for it: *Koma Kulshan* or "Broken One," referring to an ancient eruption that shattered part of the summit.

Visiting Mount Baker from the North Cascades area requires a 180-mile round trip, and it is easily worth it. When you have finally achieved the end of the road at Artist Point, you will reach for your camera as quickly as we writers reach for our adjectives. This ranks among the great alpine viewpoints in America, and definitely the best vista point in Washington.

**RV and general driving advisory:** Pavement and patience will get you there. Most of the approach is gently hilly and it's all asphalt. However, the last few miles become a steep corkscrew climb, with an eight-foot width limit. Carefully driven, larger RVs and trailers can make it. There's an over-length parking area and turnaround at the end of the road. Incidentally, because of the ski area, the road is kept open throughout the year, although the final climb from the ski area to Artist Point is closed by winter snow.

If you've been following us through North Cascades National Park, you'll have to retrace your route on Highway 20 to visit Mount Baker. An option is to take an extremely long and obviously interesting detour, up Highway 97 into British Columbia, west on Highway 3 and Trans-Canada 1, then back across the border at Abbotsford.

Otherwise, pass again through the park, down through **Rockport** and westward to **Concrete,** named for a huge cement plant that provided most of its employment. This small town marks the end of your alpine descent and the start of 60 miles of Highway 20 pasturelands and rural homes.

☺ Hundreds of **bald eagles** take a winter salmon-fishing break in this Skagit River Valley, en route from Alaska and Canada. Watch the skies and the riverside trees carefully. Several area river-runners offer special eagle-watching float trips. Contact Downstream River Runners, 12112 NE 195th St., Bothell, WA 98011, (800) 732-RAFT within Washington or (206) 483-0335; Pacific Northwest Float Trips, P.O. Box 736, Sedro Woolley, WA

98284, (206) 855-0539; or Rivers Incorporated, P.O. Box 2092, Kirkland, WA 98083, (206) 822-5296.

As you drive westward through the Skagit Valley, other foothill hamlets approach and then disappear, offering little reason to hesitate, except for fuel and provisions: **Hamilton, Lyman** and **Sedro Woolley.**

The latter calls itself the gateway to the North Cascades, and we suppose it is if one is eastbound. It's also the major commercial center for the lower Skagit farming valley. The curious name comes from the merger of two earlier settlements. Actually, it started with an even curiouser name. In 1879, Mortimer Cook opened a general store and—as a gag—called his settlement Bug. Later, it was changed to Cedro, convoluted Spanish for the cedars that grew thick in the area. Meanwhile, P.A. Woolley built a sawmill nearby and the two communities grew toward one another. In 1898, citizens of the twin towns agreed to merge.

If you're driving an RV and want to make Sedro Woolley your gateway to Mount Baker, you can camp for $10 at **Riverfront Park.** Turn south on Township Street and follow it about 1.3 miles to the Skagit River. This community park has grassy sites with water and electric hookups, picnic facilities and a boat launch.

From Sedro Woolley, turn north onto State Highway 9. After driving through a surprisingly long stretch of residential area, you'll enter an attractive region of lush pasturelands and prosperous farms with contented Holsteins and fat silos. Rounded and thickly wooded hills complete this pleasingly bucolic picture.

Twenty-two miles north of Sedro Woolley, fork right onto State Highway 542. On most days, you'll emerge from pervasive Puget Sound cloud cover somewhere around here. Mount Baker may or may not present itself in the distance. Thirteen miles farther, at **Kendall** (marked on the map but not on the highway), go right again, staying with Route 542. (If you miss this turn, you'll be at the Canadian border at **Sumas,** just eleven miles away.) A sign advises that this is the last chance for gas in the 64-mile round trip to Mount Baker. A nearby Texaco station, standing in obedience to the sign, apparently comprises the entire Kendall business district.

You're now on the Mount Baker Highway, which later becomes—no surprise—a national forest scenic route. Pressing inland, you'll gradually shed verdant farmlands in favor of thickly wooded foothills. You're heading upstream alongside the chalky glacial flow of the north fork Nooksak River. On a good day, Mount Baker and neighbors will make occasional and dramatic appearances between foreground hills.

# Glacier

The only town you'll encounter on this route, Glacier doesn't have one. The name comes from nearby Glacier Creek. It does offer the last businesses (but no fuel) along this highway—a general store, some surprisingly good restaurants and a couple of places to sleep.

## WHERE TO DINE AND RECLINE

### Chandelier Restaurant and Lounge ● ΔΔ $$

☐ *Mount Baker Highway, east of Glacier; (206) 599-2233. Eclectic menu; full bar service. Daily from 6:30 a.m., dinner until ten Friday-Saturday, closes earlier other nights. MC/VISA, AMEX.* ☐ Fetching little Nordic style dining room with an outside deck providing a forest view. The busy menu offers teriyaki steak, prime rib, lasagna, prawns and the usual chops and chickens.

### ☺ Innisfree Restaurant ● ∆∆ $$

◻ *9393 Mount Baker Highway, 1.5 miles west of Glacier; (206) 599-2373. Northwest cuisine; wine and beer. Monday, Tuesday and Thursday 4 to 9 p.m., Friday 4 to 10, Saturday 3 to 10, Sunday 2 to 9, closed Wednesday; shorter hours in winter. MC/VISA.* ◻ Think of this attractive place as alpine whole earth. The chef owned restaurant features fresh Northwest seafood, trout and salmon, plus braised lamb, several chicken dishes and some vegetarian entrées. The menu changes nightly, depending on what's available. The focus is on natural and organic foods, with a choice of about four exceptionally creative entrées each day.

### ☺ Milano's Pasta Fresca ● ∆∆ $

◻ *9990 Mount Baker Highway; (206) 599-2863. Italian-American; wine and beer. Monday-Thursday 10 to 8, Friday 10 to 8:30, Saturday 7 to 9, Sunday 7 to 8:30. MC/VISA.* ◻ Fetching little place with black and white tile floors, white bentwood chairs, and a very creative kitchen. Several fresh pasta dinners are under $10, including some of the best ravioli in the state. From the Northwest side of the menu, try the halibut pizziola, baked in onions, capers and Greek olives. All this, plus an outside dining patio with a mountain view.

### Glacier Creek Motel ● △ $$

◻ *Mount Baker Highway (P.O. Box A), Glacier, WA 98244; (206) 599-2991. Motel units from $42, kitchen cabins from $60. MC/VISA.* ◻ Simple, clean motel units, and cabins with kitchens, on landscaped grounds. Barbecues and picnic tables; hot tub; coffee bar with espresso and warm pastries.

### Snowline Inn ● △△ $$$

◻ *10433 Mount Baker Highway (P.O. Box 5051), Glacier, WA 98244-5051; (800) 228-0119 or (206) 599-2788 and (206) 599-2772. Doubles from $55, singles from $40. MC/VISA.* ◻ Well-kept chalet-style inn with TV, room phones and balconies with forest views. Some kitchen units. Adjacent to the **Chandelier Restaurant,** listed above.

On the east side of town, the Forest Service's **Glacier Public Service Center** offers a few interpretive displays and lots of books and maps on the Mount Baker area. It's open weekends only from January to mid-May, Thursday-Monday until mid-June, daily in summer, then back to Thursday-Monday from mid-September to January. Call (206) 599-2714 for specific hours.

Just beyond the visitor center, you'll enter Mount Baker-Snoqualmie National Forest. The mountain itself remains an elusive target as you press eastward, playing tag-and-hide with the foreground hills. Those foothills begin to draw in, capturing the Nooksack River in a narrow valley. A dozen miles above Glacier, the gentle road suddenly tilts upward, offering a final twisting challenge before delivering you to the ski area and—just above it—Artist Point. You enter a sub-alpine zone, where the forest yields to shrubs and lichen clinging to naked granite.

**Mount Baker Ski Area,** tucked into a basin below Artists Point, has six chair lifts and a good mix of runs from novice to advanced, and some fine powder bowls. A few miles of cross-country trails are groomed. Among its facilities are the usual ski gear rentals and school, restaurant and bar, plus child care and/or kiddie ski lessons. Call (206) 734-6771 for ski activities and (206) 671-0211 for a snow report.

☺ A couple of twisted miles above the ski facility, you emerge onto a broad parking area at **Artist Point,** atop a lofty ridge. The high Cascades emerge suddenly from hiding and surround you with their jagged sawtooth ridges and snow-smothered peaks. Waves of granite sweep away in every direction. You're parked in the middle of a petrified, storm-tossed sea. Step out of your panting vehicle and gaze about in awe. Mount Baker is a massive presence, standing across a deep glacial-carved valley from the ridge.

Opposite Baker and even more imposing is 9,127-foot **Mount Shuksan,** an incredibly ragged ridge of granite. Serrated and wrinkled Shuksan is a faulted upthrust ten million years old, weathered by wind and glaciers. Baker is a new volcano, dating back a million years and barely showing her age. Also heavy snow accumulations, even in summer, tend to soften her lines. (The thought comes to mind that Shuksan is ruggedly handsome and Baker is softly feminine.)

Trails beg you to explore these heights further. For a relatively easy walk, take the **Artist Ridge Trail** in a one-mile loop toward Mount Shuksan. Interpretive signs explain the area's geology. A favorite masochists hike is up **Table Mountain Trail.** It switchbacks more than a thousand feet up an old lava flow that has eroded into a butte. Plan a couple of hours for this two-hour pant; views from the top are worth the effort. More trails reach from Artist Point into the inviting Mount Baker Wilderness.

Oddly, Mount Baker and its wilds are not part of North Cascades National Park, although Mount Shuksan is within its boundaries. But never mind boundaries. It will occur to you that these northernmost reaches of the Cascades—in or out of the park—are the wildest and thus the most glorious of the entire mountain range.

## Chapter eight
# *THE BIG MIDDLE*
## East of the Cascades: apples and wine

**IF AN APPLE A DAY** keeps the doctor away, and if moderate wine consumption enhances longevity, health enthusiasts should beat a path to central Washington.

The Evergreen State isn't very green east of the Cascades, since the mountains block most of the rainfall. Annual Yakima-Columbia Valley precipitation averages only eight inches. However, central Washington's highly mineralized volcanic soil, long sunny days and chilly nights are ideal for apples and grapes. The meandering Columbia River provides plenty of irrigation water. Washington is America's leading producer of apples, and it is second only to California in wine production.

These conditions also nurture apricots, cherries, peaches and pears. Tourist promoters like to call central Washington "America's fruit basket." Among all of America's counties, Yakima ranks first in total fruit trees, and first in the production of apples, winter pears, hops and mint.

Wine production is relatively new to Washington, going back only a few decades, compared with California's century and a half of grape concern. However, the Evergreen state's wines—particularly whites—are making quick strides, winning national and international awards. The Columbia Valley and the smaller Yakima and Walla Walla valleys have been designated as Approved Viticultural Areas (AVA) by the federal government. (This is the American equivalent of France's *Appellation d'Origine Contrôlèe*.)

Although Washington's wines are fine, the state doesn't have highly con-

# TRIP PLANNER

**WHEN TO GO** ● Autumn is the best window on central Washington, since the apples are ripening, wine grapes are being crushed and the days are crisp and clear. Spring and summer also offer plenty of sunshine in this east-of-the-Cascades land. Winter can be cold and unpleasant, with occasional snow-storms and icy roads to make travel difficult. Also, many of the museums and some of the wineries take a winter holiday, or they reduce their hours.

**WHAT TO SEE** ● Yakima Electric Railway Museum and Yakima Valley Museum; Yakima Nation Cultural Center and the many murals of Toppenish; Teapot Dome service station east of Zillah; Clymer Museum and Gallery in El-lensburg; Ginkgo Petrified Forest State Park near Vantage; North Central Washington Museum in Wenatchee; museum galleries of Rocky Reach Dam; Chief Joseph Dam at Bridgeport.

**WHAT TO DO** ● Walk or bike the Yakima River Greenway; tour the wineries around Zillah; walk the paths of Ohme Gardens in Wenatchee; ride the *Lady of the Lake* up Lake Chelan to Stehekin; take the "atomic tour" of nuclear facilities in Richland-Hanford.

## Useful contacts

**Ellensburg Chamber of Commerce,** 436 N. Sprague St., Ellensburg, WA 98926; (509) 925-3137.

**Lake Chelan Chamber of Commerce,** P.O. Box 216 (102 E. Johnson Ave.), Chelan, WA 98816; (800) 4-CHELAN or (509) 682-2022.

**Lake Chelan Ranger District,** P.O. Box 189 (428 W. Woodin), Chelan, WA 98816; (509) 682-2576. (For information on Lake Chelan National Recrea-tion Area and Stehekin.

**Moses Lake Area Chamber of Commerce,** 324 S. Pioneer Way, Moses Lake, WA 98837-1737; (800) 992-6234 in Washington only, or (509) 765-7888.

**Toppenish Chamber of Commerce,** P.O. Box 28 (219 S. Toppenish Ave.), Toppenish, WA 98948; (509) 865-3262.

**Tri-Cities Visitor and Convention Bureau** (Kennewick-Richland-Pasco), P.O. Box 2241, Tri-Cities, WA 99302; (800) 666-1929 or (509) 735-8486.

**Greater Yakima Chamber of Commerce,** P.O. Box 1490 (10 N. Ninth St.), Yakima, WA 98907; (509) 248-2021.

**Washington Wine Commission,** P.O. Box 6127, Seattle, WA 98121; (206) 728-2252. Send $2 for a guide to central Washington's wine country.

**Wenatchee Area Visitor & Convention Bureau,** Two S. Chelan Ave., Wenatchee, WA 98801; (800) 57-APPLE or (509) 662-4774.

**Yakima Valley Visitors & Convention Bureau,** 10 N. Eighth St., Yakima, WA 98901; (509) 575-1300.

**Zillah Chamber of Commerce,** P.O. Box 1294 (503 N. First Avenue), Zil-lah, WA 98953; (509) 829-5055.

## Central Washington radio stations

KAFE, 90.3-FM, Richland—National Public Radio
KYYT, 102.3-FM, Goldendale—old and new top 40
KATS, 94.5-FM, Yakima—news and old and new rock
KXDD, 104 and 106.3-FM, Yakima-Ellensburg—country
KWWW, 100.9 and 103.9, Wenatchee—top 40, mostly rock
KKRV, 104.9-FM, Wenatchee—soft rock and new wave
KONA, 105.9-FM, Tri-Cities—top 40; soft hits
KOZI, 93.5, 100.9 and 103.1, Chelan—rock and top 40
KPQ, 560-AM, Wenatchee—news and talk
KMWX, 1460-AM, Yakima—rock and roll oldies
KOZI, 1230-AM, Chelan—rock and top 40

centrated touring areas such as California's tightly-focused Napa Valley. Vineyards are more widespread, and often interspersed with orchards, pasturelands and hop yards. However, you'll find a fair concentration of vines and tasting rooms in the Yakima Valley, just east of Yakima. We'll tour them a bit later.

Yakima is easy to reach, sitting astride Interstate 82, which branches from I-90 at Ellensburg, 30 miles northwest. Another approach is north on U.S. 97 from the Columbia River Gorge, with a pause at Goldendale, Maryhill Museum and Stonehenge. (See the end of Chapter two.)

## Yakima

**Population: 56,000**                      **Elevation: 1,065 feet**

A stylish old town in an unlovely setting is a good way to describe central Washington's largest city. With a scant eight inches of rainfall a year, the surrounding low hills are barren and brown. Vineyards and orchards add swatches of green, particularly east of the city, and springtime blooms turn the Yakima Valley into a pink and white delight.

Downtown Yakima has saved the best of its old, while building anew, creating a nicely balanced and thriving business core. Fed by the valley's agricultural largess, it's obviously a prosperous community. A recent "livability poll" picked it as the 25th most desirable city in the country.

The town had a typical beginning, except for the fact that it was re-located from its original site. Ranchers came to the area in the mid-1800s and began crowding Native Americans off ancestral lands. This exploded into a brief war that ended with the signing of one of the first Indian treaties in the West. In 1855, Yakima tribes reluctantly settled on a reservation south of the city. Although extensive by today's measure, with 1.4 million acres, the Yakima Reservation represents only a tenth of their original lands.

The region was too dry for farming until settlers built irrigation ditches to divert water from the Yakima River. John W. Beck planted the area's first apple and peach trees in 1870, to launch Yakima Valley's lucrative fruit industry. Initially, settlers gathered around a narrow gap where the Yakima River slips between low hills. Yakima City was platted in 1869 and incorporated in 1883. When the Northern Pacific Railroad came through, residents refused to sell enough land for a station and switch yard. So the railroad company platted a new town four miles north and offered to donate land and pay moving expenses for anyone willing to re-locate. Many folks did, putting their buildings on log rollers and hitching them to teams. The new town was called Yakima, and the original became Union Gap, which is now a Yakima suburb.

### Driving Yakima

Before starting a driving tour of Yakima, you may want to visit two attractions to the southeast, just off I-82. **Yakima Sportsman State Park,** a recreation area on the Yakima River, occupies the point of a triangle between Yakima and Union Gap. It offers water sports, picnicking and camping (see below), nature trails, and bird watching along the river bank and at several ponds. Kids under 15 can fish the stocked ponds and anyone with a proper license can angle along the river bank. To reach it, take exit 33 from I-82, go east to Keys Road and follow signs. From the same freeway exit, botanical enthusiasts can visit the **Yakima Area Arboretum.** Open during

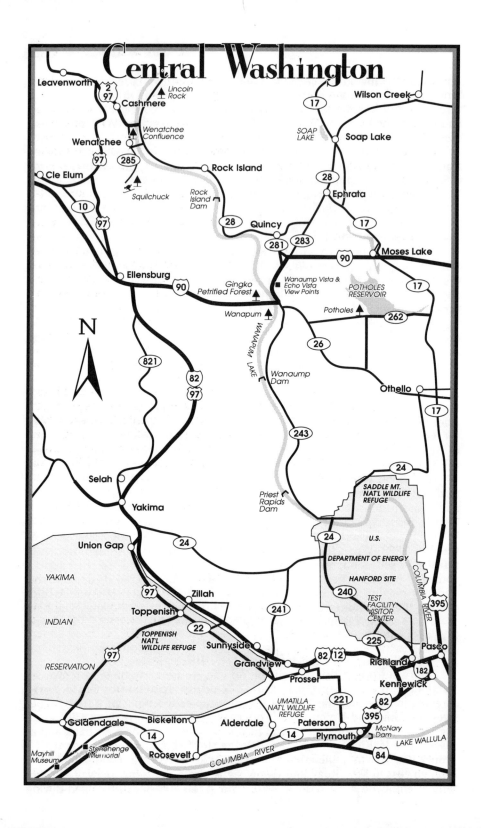

daylight hours, it has a Japanese garden, wetlands bird refuge, native plant exhibits, a gift shop and horticultural library; (509) 248-7337.

To explore Yakima proper—whether you approach from the west via I-82 or from the south on U.S. 97/I-82—take downtown exit 33 west onto West Yakima Avenue. You'll see, almost immediately, not just one but two visitor information centers; both are on your right. They even have similar addresses to add further confusion. Either can load you up on maps, brochures and wine country guides.

The **Yakima Chamber of Commerce** is just off Yakima Avenue at 10 Ninth Street, open weekdays 8:30 to 5. A block away, in the Cavanaugh Inn complex at 10 Eighth Street, is the **Yakima Valley Convention and Visitors Bureau,** open daily 8:30 to 5.

Continue west on Yakima Avenue, passing through the prosperous downtown area. Some of the old buildings have been preserved, and sidewalks have been extended and landscaped to create an appealing appearance. As you approach the railroad tracks, you enter the **Front Street historic district**, with shops and restaurants in restored old brick. Pause for suds at the British style **Grants Brewery Pub** at Front and B streets in the old Yakima train station. It offers hearty beers of the Yakima Brewing and Malting Company, founded in 1982 as the Northwest's first micro-brewery; (509) 575-2922. Nearby, at 27 N. Front, is the tasting room of the **Thurston Wolfe Winery,** offering sips and sales; (509) 452-0335.

Just across the tracks are two theme shopping complexes, **Track 29** and **Yesterday's Village.** The former offers a mix of shops and cafès in old boxcars and sleek aluminum passenger cars, while Yesterday's Village is primarily a large antique mall. **The Wine Cellar** in the village offers samples at $1 per sip, plus a good selection of area wines, regional food products and gift items; (509) 248-3590. Also in the complex is the **World Famous Fantastic Museum,** which is neither; see below. Continue out Yakima Avenue, and then turn left onto Third Avenue (not to be confused with Third Street downtown). Follow it a few blocks to the **Yakima Electric Railway Museum** in a big red brick car barn at Pine and Third. Turn right (west) onto Pine and follow it about three blocks until it blends onto Tieton Drive, and stay on this for about ten more blocks to Franklin Park and the **Yakima Valley Museum.**

From the museum, take 22nd Avenue south five long blocks to Nob Hill Boulevard and turn left (east). This cuts through a mile or so of Yakima residential areas, crosses the train tracks and shortly hits South First Street. Turn right and follow it into **Union Gap.** Yakima's predecessor offers a mix of old and ordinarily contemporary buildings. The route becomes Union Gap's Main Street, which takes you through town and eventually (watch for signs) to the **Central Washington Agricultural Museum.**

After examining a startling array of rusting farm equipment, return to the museum's road entrance and turn right onto Highway 97. This expressway takes you southeast to the Yakima Indian Reservation, with its fine cultural museum, and to Toppenish, noted for its downtown murals.

## ATTRACTIONS

***World Famous Fantastic Museum*** ● *In Yesterday's Village at 15 W. Yakima Ave.; (509) 575-0100. Adults $3.75, kids $2. Daily 10 to 6 in summer; Friday-Sunday 10 to 5 in the off-season.* ☐ This small, busily cluttered archive houses an abundance of collectibles, some personality cars, movie artifacts, a gauge from the Hindenburg and several antique pedal cars.

☺ **Yakima Electric Railway Museum** ● *306 W. Pine St. (at Third); (509) 575-1700. Museum open 10 to 5 from May to mid-October (longer in July and August); closed in winter. Free admission. Vintage trolley rides between Yakima and Selah from early May through mid-October; adults $5, kids and seniors $2.50, family ticket $14.* ⎕ Yakima's electric trolley system was started in 1907, and a non-profit group is keeping its memories and some of its cars alive. Visitors can wander about the cavernous car barn or catch a trolley for the hour and 40 minute round trip to the small hamlet of Selah.

☺ **Yakima Valley Museum** ● *2105 Tieton Drive; (509) 248-0747. Tuesday-Friday 10 to 5, Saturday-Sunday noon to 5, closed Monday. Adults $2.50, seniors and kids $1.25.* ⎕ This excellent museum is housed in a modern structure in Franklin Park. Highlights include an extensive carriage exhibit, a mock-up general store (complete with creaky wooden floors) and an apple packing shed display. The museum has duplicated the office of William O. Douglas, longest-seated member of the Supreme Court (36 years). He came to Yakima at age 6 and went through schools here. In a hands-on history room, kids can card wool, write on a slateboard and ring up pretend sales on an old cash register.

**Central Washington Agricultural Museum** ● *In Fulbright Park at 4508 Main St., Union Gap; (509) 457-8735. Museum open daily 9 to 5; grounds open 9 to 9; shorter hours in winter. Free; donations appreciated.* ⎕ Offering one of America's largest collections of farm equipment, this place will flood you with nostalgia if you grew up toiling the soil. Not well-kept but interesting, it displays scores of rusting tractors, weathered surreys, a sheep herder's wagon, heaps of harnesses and a collection of 6,000 hand tools. Since most of the stuff is displayed in open sheds, there's plenty to see even if the small museum building is closed.

## WHERE TO DINE

☺ **Birchfield Manor** ● △△△△ **$$$** ∅

⎕ *2018 Birchfield Rd. (I-82 exit 34); (509) 452-1960. Northwest and continental; wine and beer. One-seating dinners 7 p.m. Thursday-Friday and 6 and 8:45 p.m. Saturday; reservations essential. Major credit cards.* ⎕ This handsome French country style dining room occupies a country inn (listed below). Décor in this former mansion is opulent Victorian, if a bit tenebrous. The European trained chef draws from fresh local ingredients and classic continental recipes to create imaginative cuisine. Diners generally have four entrèes from which to choose, usually representing a fish, fowl and a meat dish or two, supported by an extensive Washington wine list. You must drive two miles into the country for dinner, and it's worth the trip. Ask for directions when you make reservations, which are essential.

☺ **Deli de Pasta** ● △△ **$$** ∅

⎕ *Seven N. Front St.; (509) 453-0571. Italian; wine and beer. Monday-Saturday 11 to 9. MC/VISA, AMEX.* ⎕ Much more appealing than its name, this disarmingly charming bistro serves fine home-made pastas and other Italian fare. One entrèe, smoked salmon ravioli in basil-cream sauce, recently was featured in *Gourmet* magazine. The cozy place is dressed in lattice, hanging plants, red nappery and the heady aroma of garlic-laced pasta.

### Greystone Restaurant • △△△ $$$

❑ *Five N. Front St. (at Yakima Avenue); (509) 248-9801. American; full bar service. Dinner Tuesday-Saturday 6 to 10. MC/VISA, AMEX.* ❑ The look is old San Francisco *nouveau* yuppie, with raw brick walls, pressed tin ceiling and hanging plants, and the menu is tantalizingly varied. Try the champagne fillet of salmon; baked breast of chicken with prosciutto, broccoli and Swiss cheese; or pork tenderloin in green peppercorn and port sauce. It's one of the town's more attractive restaurants, with a lively piano bar.

### Jade Tree • △△ $$

❑ *204 E. Yakima Ave. (downtown); (509) 248-0664. Chinese-American; wine and beer. Monday-Thursday 11:30 to 10, Friday 11:30 to 11, Saturday 4 to 11, Sunday noon to 9:30. MC/VISA.* ❑ An attractive place with brass *bas relief* Oriental wall trim, high-backed booths and paneled ceilings. The menu is mostly mild Cantonese. You'll also find a few spicier Mandarin items, along with some American steaks and chops.

### Olive Garden • △△ $$

❑ *222 E. Yakima Ave. (at Third); (509) 457-0485. Italian; wine and beer. Sunday-Thursday 11 to 10, Friday-Saturday 11 to 11. Major credit cards.* ❑ A versatile Italian menu features both classic and innovative *nouveau* dishes, such as chicken and artichoke, and a combination dinner of salmon filet, Venetian grilled chicken and fettuccine. The look is *Italian moderne*, with muted colors accented by tasteful tile work.

### Mustard Seed • △△ $$ ∅

❑ *402 E. Yakima Ave. (in Chinook Tower); (509) 576-8013. Eclectic Oriental; full bar service. Monday-Thursday 11 to 9, Friday-Saturday 11 to 10, Sunday noon to 9. MC/VISA.* ❑ It's one of several attractive Mustard Seeds scattered about the state, with a kind of Asian art deco look. The menu is primarily Japanese and Chinese, although it reaches beyond to include such fare as Maui chicken and cod Ceylon in a curry sauce.

### ☺ Sports Center Restaurant • △ $

❑ *Yakima Avenue between Third and Fourth; (509) 453-3300. American; full bar service. Daily 6:30 a.m. to 9:30 p.m. No credit cards.* ❑ Try this smoky old place for yesterday atmosphere and prices to match: full steak, halibut or Pacific oyster dinner for under $10. It's right out of the '30s, with a ribbed aluminum façade and a duck hunter on a rotating marquee. The waitress with the doily apron is probably named Mabel. Perch on a stool at a long counter or adjourn to a Formica table in the rear dining room.

### Tequila's • △△ $$

❑ *Track 29, off Yakima Avenue; (509) 457-3296. Mexican; full bar service. Breakfast, lunch and dinner daily. Major credit cards.* ❑ One of several Tequila's in the state, this place was undergoing remodeling when we passed, reopening in 1994. We've eaten at other branches and found the food to be consistently good, with innovative spices such as cilantro creating fresh new flavors.

## WHERE TO SLEEP

### Holiday Inn • ⌂⌂⌂ $$$$ ∅

❑ *Nine N. Ninth St. (at Yakima Avenue), Yakima, WA 98901; (800) HOLIDAY or (509) 452-6511. Couples $71 to $91, singles $61 to $81, kitchen-*

ettes $71 to $81, suites $110 to $195. Major credit cards. □ Attractive down-town hotel with TV movies, room phones; pool, hot tub and coin laundry. **Owl's Nest** serves American fare 6:30 a.m. to 10 p.m.; dinners $7 to $17; full bar service; poolside dining in summer.

### Huntley Inn ● ⌂⌂ $$$ Ø

□ 12 Valley Mall Blvd., Yakima, WA 98903; (800) 448-5544 or (509) 248-6924. Couples $48 to $52, singles $43 to $46. Rates include continental breakfast. Major credit cards. □ An 86-unit motel with TV, VCR rentals and room refrigerators. Swimming pool, barbecue area and coin laundry.

### Palomino Motel ● ⌂ $$ Ø

□ 1223 N. First St., Yakima, WA 98901; (509) 452-6551. Couples $34 to $45, singles $30 to $40, kitchenettes $45 to $50. MC/VISA, DISC. □ A 69-unit motel with TV, room phones; swimming pool.

### Red Apple Motel ● ⌂⌂ $$ Ø

□ 416 N. First St., Yakima, WA 98901; (509) 248-7150. Couples $40 to $50, singles $30 to $40, suites $60 to $86. Major credit cards. □ A 60-unit motel with TV, room phones; pool and coin laundry.

## Bed & breakfast inns

### Birchfield Manor ● ⌂⌂⌂ $$$$ Ø

□ 2018 Birchfield Rd. (I-82 exit 34), Yakima, WA 98901; (509) 452-1960. Couples $70 to $100, singles $60 to $90. Five units with private baths; full breakfast. Major credit cards. □ Large, former sheep ranch residence converted to a stylish bed & breakfast inn, furnished with Victorian and turn-of-the-century American antiques. Landscaped grounds with year-around spa and seasonal pool. **Restaurant** listed above.

### Irish House Bed & Breakfast ● ⌂⌂ $$$ Ø

□ 210 S. 28th Ave., Yakima, WA 98901; (509) 453-5474. Couples $55 to $60, singles $50 to $55. Three rooms with share baths; continental breakfast. AMEX. □ Turn-of-the-century Victorian with modern furnishings, accented by a few antiques. The home, listed on the national register of historic places, features polished woodwork, plate rails and a large front porch. It's within walking distance of the Yakima Valley Museum and Franklin Park.

### Meadowbrook B&B ● ⌂⌂ $$$ Ø

□ 1010 Meadowbrook Rd., Yakima, WA 98901; (509) 248-2387. Couples $59 to $69, singles $59 to $62. Four units; one with private bath; full break-fast. MC/VISA. □ Modern Dutch colonial style home in a secluded country setting, with views of Mount Rainier and the Yakima Valley. Modern décor in the large rooms; fireplace in the living room.

## WHERE TO CAMP

**Trailer Inns** ● 1610 N. First St. (I-82 exit 31), Yakima, WA 98901; (509) 452-9561. RV sites only; $15.50 to $19.50. Reservations accepted; MC/VISA. □ Paved sites, some pull-throughs; showers, coin laundry, mini-mart; in-door pool, spa, sauna, playground and rec room.

**Yakima KOA** ● 1500 Keys Rd. (I-82 exit 34), Yakima, WA 98901; (509) 248-5882. RV and tent sites; $15 to $19. Reservations accepted; MC/VISA. □ Grassy and gravel sites with picnic tables, some shaded; showers, coin laun-dry, mini-mart, swimming pool, game room. Rental bicycles, canoes and paddleboats; water sports.

*Yakima Nation RV Park* ● See below.
*Yakima Sportsman State Park* ● *904 Keys Rd. (I-82 exit 34), Yakima, WA 98901; (509) 575-2774. RV and tent sites; $14 with hookups, $10 without. No reservations or credit cards.* ☐ Well-spaced, shaded sites with picnic tables and barbecues; flush and pit potties; showers. Nature trails, boating, fishing, playground, bird-watching (see above).

# Yakima Reservation-Toppenish-Wine loop

East of Yakima, Highway 97 skirts the northeastern edge of the Yakima Indian Reservation. Within its borders are a fine Native American cultural center, a state park housing a former military post, and the handsome old town of Toppenish. Just to the northeast is the heart of the Yakima Valley wine country.

About ten miles southeast of Union Gap on Route 97, you'll encounter the large **Yakima Nation Cultural Heritage Center,** with a museum, restaurant, gift shop and RV park. It's difficult to miss, since the main building soars skyward as a modernistic version of a tule lodge. This complex serves as the administrative headquarters for the tribe.

☺ *Yakima Nation Cultural Center Museum* ● *280 Buster Rd. (at Highway 97), Toppenish; (509) 865-2000. Monday-Friday 9 to 6, Sunday 9 to 5. Adults $4, tens and seniors $2, kids $1.* ☐ Spilyay was a legendary trickster who placed difficult challenges before the Yakima people. Yet his intent was good, for he taught them how to survive and live in harmony with nature. This is the theme of this excellent museum, which ranks with the Makah in Neah Bay (chapter 6) as one of the best Native American archives in the West. It uses life-sized dioramas, wall displays and other exhibits to portray their past and present lives. Displays focus on hunting, social activities, conflict with the whites and contemporary tribal life. A series of mannequins portray famous American Indian leaders.

*Heritage Inn Restaurant* ● ΔΔ $$ Ø
☐ *280 Buster Rd.; (509) 865-2551. American and Native American; no alcohol. Monday-Tuesday 6:30 a.m. to 4 p.m., Wednesday-Saturday 6:30 a.m. to 9 p.m., Sunday brunch 8 to 2 and dinner 6:30 to 8. MC/VISA.* ☐ A few traditional Indian dishes such as buffalo steak share the menu with salmon, sweet mustard pork and other typical American fare. The restaurant is visually appealing, with light woods, high back booths and Native American designs. It's all smoke-free.

*Yakima Nation Resort RV Park* ● *P.O. Box 151 (280 Buster Rd.), Toppenish, WA 98948; (800) 874-3087 or (509) 865-2000. RV sites $16 to $18.50, tent sites $10, teepees $30. Reservations accepted; MC/VISA.* ☐ Nicely-maintained RV resort with some pull-throughs; showers, coin laundry, lounge and game room, picnic shelter, swimming pool and spa, one-mile jogging track and playground. Tepees take up to five people; bring your own sleeping gear or rent it for $2.50.

Just beyond the cultural center, turn right onto Highway 220 and follow it 26 miles to a former army fort. Ironically, it became the first headquarters for the Yakima reservation.

*Fort Simcoe State Park* ● *5150 Fort Simcoe Rd., White Swan, WA 98952; (509) 874-2372. Interpretive center open April 1 through September, daily 8 to 5; by appointment the rest of the year. Park grounds open April 1 through September, daily 6:30 a.m. to dusk; weekends and holidays the rest of the year from 8 to dusk.* ◻ Built to protect white settlers who were intruding on Yakima lands, Fort Simcoe lasted only three years, from 1856 until 1859. It then became the Indian agency headquarters for the reservation. Two original buildings survive and three have been reconstructed and furnished to the period. Two log blockhouses, the commanding officer's house and captains' quarters can be toured when the interpretive center is open.

# Toppenish

**Population: 7,400**                                        **Elevation: 757 feet**

☺ Returning from Fort Simcoe, cross Highway 97 and follow signs into Toppenish, a cute old Western style town famous for historic murals. Western muralist Fred Oldfield grew up here; his works and those of others have turned the town into an outdoor art gallery. More than two dozen murals grace sturdy old brick and masonry buildings, and more are on the way. Several artists join to create a new painting during the "Mural in a Day" celebration the first Saturday in June. The mural is painted in Pioneer Park, where bleachers are set up for spectators. When completed, it's moved to a building wall.

The Toppenish Mural Society was formed in the mid-1980s to coordinate this event and promote muralism in general; (509) 865-2619. With several paintings in the works, Toppenish seems likely to become to mural capital of the country. It has won the state's "Georgie" award for fostering tourism and the Governor's Art Award for promoting public art.

Stop by the **Tourist Information Office** at Toppenish Avenue and Division Street, for a mural map and other area information; it's open weekdays 9 to 5. An Indian arts and craft shop, candy store and Amish shop share the building with the chamber.

Across the way, local folks are refurbishing the old brick Toppenish Railroad depot to create the **Yakima Valley Rail and Steam Museum,** open Thursday-Saturday 10 to 5 and Sunday 1 to 5; (509) 865-1911. The ticket and telegraphers office and waiting room had been completed, and the place brims with railroad memorabilia; work on the project continues.

The **Toppenish Historical Museum** at One South Elm Street features a turn-of-the-century kitchen, work shed, Native American beadwork and basketry, and assorted pioneer relics. It's open Tuesday-Sunday 2 to 5 in summer and Tuesday-Saturday 2 to 5 the rest of the year; (509) 865-4510.

# WHERE TO SLEEP

### Toppenish Inn Motel ● ⌂⌂ $$ ∅

◻ *515 E. Elm St. (Highways 97 and 22), Toppenish, WA 98948; (509) 865-7444. Couples and singles $46 to $69. Rates include continental breakfast. Major credit cards.* ◻ A 41-unit motel with TV movies, room phones, refrigerators and microwaves; pool, spa and coin laundry.

## Yakima Valley wine country tour

A short drive northeast from Toppenish will put you in the pleasant little town of **Zillah,** which is surrounded by vineyards. Although wineries are strung out from here to Benton City, 55 miles east, we'll focus our tour around Zillah. Before starting your vineyard tripping and sipping, pause to examine this appealing village of about 2,000 residents, with its weathered masonry and wooden false front buildings. It was established as a farming center and rail stop in 1892 and was named for the daughter of the Northern Pacific Railroad's president.

Stop by the **Chamber of Commerce** at 503 First Avenue (corner of Fifth) to pick up a *Yakima Valley Wine Tour* map and a *Fruit Loop* guide that directs you to wineries and orchards. The chamber, open weekdays 9 to 5, shares quarters with the Zillah School District office. A mural map on the building pinpoints the valley's wineries. Before starting out, you might want to take a lunch break:

### ☺ *El Ranchito* ● ∆∆ **$**

◻ *1319 E. First Ave.; (509) 829-5880. Mexican; no alcohol. Summer 8 to 7 and winter 8 to 6. No credit cards.* ◻ El Ranchito is a delightful Mexican culinary carnival, all under one roof. You can load up on inexpensive food at a busy take-out and dine indoors or on a landscaped patio. If you're starved, order a combination plate that's big enough to sink your boat, with chicken, beans, rice salad and tortillas, for under $5. A bakery offers Mexican and American sweets. Fresh corn, flour and whole wheat tortillas emerge from an adjacent tortilla factory. This versatile market also sells Mexican specialty food, pinatas and other Latino arts and crafts.

### *Squeeze Inn* ● ∆∆ **$$**

◻ *611 First Ave.; (509) 829-6226. American; full bar service. Monday 8 a.m. to 9 p.m., Tuesday-Saturday 8 to 10, closed Sunday. MC/VISA.* ◻ More appealing than its silly name, the inn has a pleasing 1930s look, with tasseled drop lamps and wainscotting. It's been here since 1932 and the menu reflects this longevity, with standbys like chicken fried steak and breaded veal cutlets. It also ranges into more contemporary culinary waters, listing breast of chicken Chardonnay and some fresh seafood combinations.

To begin your winery tour, drive northwest through town along First Avenue and turn right onto Vintage Valley Parkway, just short of the downtown freeway on-ramp. This frontage road with the fancy name delivers you within seconds to **Zillah Oaks Winery,** in a modern wooden structure with picnic tables out front. The tasting room and gift shop are open Monday-Saturday 11 to 4:30 and Sunday noon to 4:30; (509) 829-6990.

From here, backtrack through town on First Avenue and turn left onto Cheyne Road (at the Cherry Patch). You'll cross Yakima Valley Road after about a mile. Another mile takes you to Highland Drive; turn right and follow signs to **Portteus Vineyards,** tucked into a corner of the grapelands at the end of a dirt road. (There are a few turns involved, but signs will keep you on track.) Housed in an oversized cottage, the tasting room is open daily noon to 5, February through November, and by appointment in December and January; (509) 829-6970.

☺ Backtrack on Highland Road a mile or less to Vintage Lane, turn right and follow it to **Covey Run.** It's our favorite Yakima Valley winery, crowning a hill with views of the patchwork of vineyards and orchards below. A lawn and picnic tables invite visitors to linger. From its paneled tasting room, windows look down into the recessed wine cellar. It's open Monday-Saturday 10 to 5 and Sunday noon to 5, with slightly shorter hours in winter; (509) 829-6235.

Return to Highland, go right about a mile to Roza Drive and turn left (west) onto Gilbert Road. This takes you to **Hyatt Winery** in a Dutch style

*The wonderfully silly Teapot Dome service station, just outside Zillah, was built in 1922.*
— **Betty Woo Martin**

barn, with a windmill and picnic area out front, and a valley view. The small tasting room occupies a corner of the winery, open daily 9 to 5 in summer and 9 to 4:30 the rest of the year (closed in January); (509) 829-6333.

Continue west briefly on Gilbert Road, turn left onto Bonair Road and follow it south across Highland to **Bonair Winery.** It has an appealing cross-timbered Scandinavian look. The tasting room/gift shop is open daily 10 to 5 in summer and weekends only 10 to 4:30 the rest of the year (or by appointment or chance, if you catch someone there); (509) 829-6027.

If you head briefly east on Highland Drive and turn south (right) onto Cheyne Road, you'll wind up back in Zillah. En route, you cross Yakima Valley Highway. It parallels I-82 and will take you east through the rest of the valley's wine country. The *Yakima Valley Wineries* map will guide you to tasting rooms along the way; most are just off the highway.

☺ Even if your winery appetite is sated, drive about a mile east of Zillah on Yakima Valley Highway to the ridiculously cute **Teapot Dome** service station. Built in 1922 in the shape of a teapot, this shingle-sided red and white structure is still in business, pumping gas and selling basic provisions from its tiny mini-mart inside the teapot. It was built as a joke to parody Wyoming's Teapot Dome oil lease scandal, and it has earned a niche on the National Register of Historic Places.

If you continue east on the highway, you'll pass through the nondescript towns of **Granger, Sunnyside** and **Grandview.** The state's leading wine company, **Chateau Ste. Michelle,** has a tasting room/gift shop and large winery in Grandview's industrial area. A right turn at a stoplight, down Avenue B to Fifth Street, will take you there. Daily 10 to 4:30; (509) 882-3928.

Beyond Grandview, the route changes its name to Wine Country Road, although you see little of the wine country from it. You eventually wind up in **Prosser,** much more appealing than the other towns, with an oldstyle main street. The **Benton County Historical Museum** at Seventh Street (the main drag) and Patterson Avenue has an extensive yet neatly arrayed collection of things that do and do not relate to Prosser and the Yakima Valley. It more resembles a well-stocked antique and memorabilia store than a museum. Hours are Tuesday-Saturday 10 to 4 and Sunday 1 to 5; 786-3842.

## Bickleton: Birds, carousels and cars

Lovers of bluebirds and old carousels may want to take a 30-mile detour southwest from Grandview to tiny **Bickleton.** During the 1960s, a local couple began building nesting sites to attract bluebirds, and by the time they'd finished, 1,500 birdhouses were scattered over a 150-mile area. About seven hundred survive, maintained by volunteers. With hundreds of the chirpers in residence, the town properly calls itself the Bluebird Capital of the World. Spring through early summer is the best time for bluebird-watching, since they start heading south for Mexican vacations in October.

Between bird sightings, pause at Cleveland Park for a look at a rare track-mounted **Herschel-Spillman carousel.** A merchant brought it here in 1928, and townsfolk maintain it. Another curiosity, midway between Bickleton and Roosevelt to the south, is the **Whoop-n-Holler Museum.** A busy collection of classic and antique cars and other odds and ends have been gathered by ranchers Lawrence and Ada Whitmore. It's open from April through September, daily from 10 to 4; adults $3; (509) 896-2344.

## ACTIVITIES
### Yakima and the Yakima Valley

☺ *Biking and walking* • The Yakima Greenway follows the river for seven miles, from Union Gap through Yakima to Selah Gap. Pick it up at Century Landing on the southern edge of Union Gap, Harlan Landing at Selah Gap, or anywhere in between. It's great for biking, strolling, bird-watching and pausing to fish. Both Harlan and Century landings offer boat ramps, parking, picnic sites and other recreational facilities.

*Farm product tours* • Pick up a copy of the *Yakima Valley Farm Products* tour map at the chamber or visitor bureau. Or send a stamped, self-address envelope to Farm Products Map, 1731 Beam Rd., Granger, WA 98932. It lists farms and wineries offering direct sales to the public.

*Lumber mill tour* • Boise Cascade at 805 N. Seventh, Yakima, offers free tours of its lumber and plywood mill, by two-day advance reservation; (509) 453-3131, extension 267.

*Mural tours* • Tours of the historic murals of Toppenish are conducted by two local firms. Conestoga Mural Tours uses covered wagons and stage coaches; call (509) 865-2898. Toppenish Mural Tours employs a horse-drawn trolley; (509) 697-3385, 697-8995 or 865-4515. Both firms also offer their rigs for special occasions.

*RV plant tour* • Alpenlite travel trailer and fifth-wheel manufacturer offers tours of its plant at 3401 W. Washington Avenue, west of Yakima Municipal Airport, weekdays at 10 a.m. and 2:45 p.m.; (509) 457-4133.

*Train rides* • The Yakima Valley Rail and Steam Museum in Toppenish offers three-hour passenger steam train rides between Harrah and Toppenish during the summer; (509) 865-1911. Also, the Yakima Electric Railway Museum at 306 W. Pine Street in Yakima features trolley rides between

Yakima and Selah from May through mid-October; details under railway museum listing above; (509) 575-1700.

## Annual events
### Yakima and the Yakima Valley

**Spring barrel tasting,** April at Yakima Valley wineries; 575-1300.

**Yakima Air Fair** in May at the Yakima Municipal Airport; 575-1300.

**Yakima Nation Cultural Pow Wow,** June at the cultural center between Yakima and Toppenish; (509) 865-2000.

**Mural in a Day,** mural painting in Pioneer Park, first Saturday in June in Toppenish; (509) 575-1700.

**Pow Wow Rodeo and Pioneer Fair,** Fourth of July weekend in Toppenish; (509) 865-5313.

**Yakima Valley Folklife Festival,** mid-July at the Yakima Valley Museum, Yakima; (509) 248-0747

**Prosser Food and Wine Show,** in mid-August; (509) 786-3177.

**Northwest Territorial Art Show,** late August at the Yakima Indian Nation Cultural Center; (509) 925-6770.

**Great Prosser Balloon Rally,** early September; (509) 786-1298.

**Central Washington State Fair,** September in Yakima; 575-1300.

**Holiday Wine and Food Festival,** November in Yakima; 575-1300.

**Thanksgiving in the Wine Country** in November, with special displays and activities at the Yakima Valley wineries; (509) 575-1300.

# YAKIMA TO ELLENSBURG

Although Yakima and neighboring Ellensburg are major apple growing areas, the region between is starkly barren. The Umtanem Ridge separates the Yakima and Kittitas valleys, pushing its sagebrush hills more than 2,500 feet skyward. It's actually a series of ridges and shallow valleys, like loaves of bread melting and running together. Taking advantage of this uninhabited jurisdiction, the government spreads its **Yakima Training Range** through the sagebrush hills, thus assuring that it will *remain* unusable.

Interstate 82 easily breaches these roller-coaster heights, traveling along the edge of the gunnery range. Its passage is aided by the longest single-arch concrete bridge in America. Dual spans of the **Fred Redmond Memorial Bridge** leap 1,336 feet across a 330-foot-high canyon. A rest stop at the south end offers imposing views of the surrounding countryside. Mounts Adams and Rainier will present themselves on a clear day.

The **Manastash Ridge vista point,** just beyond the final climb, offers a imposing view of the Kittitas Valley. Take pause to admire the valley's plaid patterns of orchards, sage, vineyards and pasturelands, and its communities tucked alongside the weaving Yakima River.

As an alternate to I-82, you can choose the twisting and winding State Highway 281. It follows the course of a wagon road along the basaltic cliffs of Yakima River Canyon. This stretch, designated as a state scenic highway, is protected by the Yakima River Conservancy, and its gentle waters are popular for floating. Rafters will find several put-ins along the route and pit potties at Roza Dam. You can pick up the road out of Selah, at I-82 exit 26.

*RV Advisory:* Highway 281 is twisty, with a couple of tough climbs. Although it offers some dramatic bits of scenery, folks with large motorhomes and trailers might prefer the easy-to-negotiate I-82 route.

# Ellensburg

**Population: 12,400**                              **Elevation: 1,577 feet**

Apples outnumber cows in the Kittitas Valley, yet Ellensburg is noted mostly for its Labor Day weekend rodeo. It's one of the largest and oldest in the Northwest, dating from 1923. Ellensburg certainly has the look of a sturdy Western town, with one of the state's most attractive collections of brick and false front stores. However, the presence of Central Washington University has softened its hell-for-leather image. You'll as likely see art galleries as tack shops. One of America's best-known artists, the late John Clymer, grew up here, and a fine museum marks his career.

Its rodeo reputation is appropriate to its beginning, since cattlemen first settled in this area. Farmers soon followed, diverting water from the Yakima River. The area's first business was a store built by Ben Burch and Jack Splawn in 1870 and called Robber's Roost. (A reference to their prices?) John Shoudy bought them out and began laying out a town, naming it for his wife Ellen. When the Northern Pacific Railroad was pushed through in the 1880s, Ellensburg thrived, and it was a serious contender for the state capital. A fire flattened the business district in 1889, and it was rebuilt of fireproof brick. Most of those sturdy buildings still stand.

Although it occupies an important junction on interstates 90 and 82, the town remains smaller than neighbors Yakima and Wenatchee. We suspect that most of its history-conscious citizens prefer it that way.

As you approach on I-82, merge onto I-90 and immediately exit onto Canyon Road. It becomes business loop 90 and takes you a mile and a half to the downtown area, merging onto Main Street. To get oriented, turn right from Main onto Fourth Avenue, drive four blocks to Sprague Street and turn left. The **Ellensburg Chamber of Commerce** occupies a storefront in a small shopping complex on Sprague, between Fourth and Fifth. Among its offerings is a walking guide to the region's 30 or more historic buildings. The chamber shares an office with the U.S. Forest Service, and both are open weekdays 8 to 5.

From the chamber, drive or stroll a block down Sprague to Third Avenue, turn right and go two blocks to the **Kittitas County Historical Museum** in the brick 1889 Cadwell building at Third and Pine. Note the unusual horseshoe-shaped windows. If you'd like to see a mild architectural curiosity, travel about six blocks east on Third. The **"castle"** at Third and Chestnut supposedly was built in 1888 as a potential governor's mansion. Painted an ugly green, this somewhat ornate three-story stucco structure is now an apartment building.

☺ Retrace your route on Third, turn right onto Pearl Street and go two blocks to the **Clymer Museum and Gallery** at 426 N. Pearl, near Fifth Avenue. Some of Ellensburg's more appealing old buildings are in this area. Note the **Davidson building** at Fourth and Pearl, with arched windows and a tower. The adjacent 1889 **Stewart Building** at 408 N. Pearl is home to the **Ellensburg Community Art Gallery,** exhibiting works of regional artists; (509) 963-2665. The **Liberty Theater** at Fifth and Pine displays a classic art deco marquee.

A couple of curiosities to look for while strolling downtown: **Dick and Jane's spot,** a conglomerated "artwork" in the front walk of a home at 101 N. Pearl Street; and the skeletal **cowboy sculpture** at Fifth and Pearl.

Old Ellensburg is serious antique country and a brochure available from the chamber can steer you to an assortment of shops. Largest is the **Showplace Antique Mall** at Third near Pearl. If you prefer something with more luster, shop for Ellensburg blue agates, distinctive gemstones found in the nearby hills. Local jewelers specialize in these stones, which range from light blue to a near royal purple. You'll find the best selection—either loose or set in jewelry—at **Kim's Gemstone Cutting,** 109 W. Third; (509) 925-4900. Owner Kim Leang does his own work and can stylize rings, earrings, pendants and other jewelry, using Ellensburg blues or other gemstones.

If you'd like to see more early-day architecture, head for **Central Washington University** campus northeast of downtown. Go north on Main (which becomes A Street) and curve to the right onto 14th Avenue. Dating from 1891, it has the look of an Ivy League school, with a carefully-tended campus of old brick, lawns and mature trees. Visitors can arrange for campus tours by calling (509) 963-3001.

Drive out to the fairgrounds at 512 N. Poplar, for a look at a **Frontier Village,** open summer weekends. Old homes and farm buildings have been moved to this site and furnished. During the rodeo and Kittitas County Fair over Labor Day Weekend, it becomes the scene of living history demonstrations of country cooking, weaving, rope making and such; (509) 962-7639.

## ATTRACTIONS

**Kittitas County Historical Museum** ● *Third Avenue near Pine Street; (509) 925-3778. Tuesday-Saturday 10 to 3. Free; donations appreciated.* ⊓ A nicely done amateur effort, the museum features several room groupings, plus a large mineral and petrified wood exhibits, and the usual Native American basketry. A nice touch is a pioneer kitchen scene with baking powder biscuits and an open Bible on the dining table.

☺ **Clymer Museum and Gallery** ● *416 N. Pearl (near Fifth); (509) 962-6416. Weekdays 10 to 5, weekends noon to 5. Adults $2, kids and seniors $1.* ⊓ This attractive new museum focuses on native son John Clymer, who did sketches for his high school yearbook and went on to become one of America's leading commercial and Western artists. A detailed retrospective covers his career from those yearbook sketches, through a Marine Corps stint when he captured the corps' history in paint, through dozens of *Saturday Evening Post* covers, and to his final years as a distinguished painter of Americana. He died in Teton Village, Wyoming, in 1989, then family and friends opened this museum two years later. In addition to his paintings and drawings, it exhibits works of other American artists, with emphasis on the West.

## ACTIVITIES

**Live theater** ● Laughing Horse Summer Theater is presented in July and August at Central Washington University; (509) 963-3400 or 963-1487.

**River running** ● The nearby Yakima River is popular for float trips downstream, and whitewater rafting upstream. Several local operators conduct trips and/or rent gear. Among them are: River Raft Rentals, Route 4, Box 275, Ellensburg, WA 98926, (509) 964-2145; River Excursion Company, P.O. Box 543, Ellensburg, WA 98926; (509) 925-9117; and Tent-N-Tube Outdoor Programs, Central Washington University campus, (509) 963-3537.

**Stagecoach trips** ● Ellensburg Equine Trolley runs coach trips between Ellensburg and Cle Elum; (509) 962-1889.

## ANNUAL EVENTS

**Western Art Show and Auction** in mid-May; (509) 962-2924.

**Central Washington Quarterhorse Show** and roping contest, late May at the Kittitas County Fairgrounds; (509) 697-8905.

**Gem Show Round-up,** mid-July at the fairgrounds; (509) 925-5381.

**Ellensburg Rodeo** and Kittitas County Fair, at the county fairgrounds over Labor Day weekend; (509) 925-5381.

**Old Time Threshing Bee,** mid-September at Olmstead State Park east of Ellensburg; (509) 925-3137. (See below.)

## WHERE TO DINE

### ☺ *Giovanni's on Pearl* • △△△ $$

☐ *402 Pearl St.; (509) 962-2260. Italian-American; full bar service. Tuesday-Thursday 11 to 9, Friday-Saturday 11 to 10, closed Sunday. Major credit cards.* ☐ Housed in the 1889 Davidson building, Giovanni's is an appealing blend of *Italo-moderne* and early American, with raw brick, ceiling fans, floral prints and sleek curved-backed chairs. The large menu wanders from typical pastas, American poached salmon and Ellensburg lamb to *nouveau* experiments like vegetarian *bucatini* with sun-dried tomatoes, mushrooms, spinach, garlic and Parmesan cheese.

### *Palace Restaurant* • △△ $$ Ø

☐ *232 N. Main St. (at Fourth); (509) 925-2327. American; full bar service. Sunday-Thursday 6 a.m. to 9 p.m., Friday-Saturday 6 to 10. MC/VISA.* ☐ The Palace dates back to 1892 and an old painted sign can still be seen on the original building on Third Street. This newer version is comfortable and attractive, with natural woods, brick and upholstered booths. The menu lists steaks, chickens and chops. Separate non-smoking dining room available.

### ☺ *The Valley Café* • △△ $$

☐ *105 W. Third St.; (509) 925-3050. American-Italian; wine and beer. Lunch and dinner daily from 11, plus breakfast Friday through Sunday. Major credit cards.* ☐ You step back to the 30s when you step into this art deco cafè with its wooden booths and ornate bar. The menu is more contemporary at this locally popular hangout, ranging from breakfast crèpes to Italian pastas to fresh seafood. It offers a good Northwest wine list.

## WHERE TO SLEEP

### *Best Western Ellensburg Inn* • △△ $$ Ø

☐ *1700 Canyon Rd., Ellensburg, WA 98926; (800) 528-1234 or (509) 925-9801. Couples $45 to $55, singles $40 to $55. Major credit cards.* ☐ Attractive 105-unit motel with TV movies, room phones, some refrigerators. Indoor pool, wading pool, spas, exercise room and playground.

### *Harolds Motel* • △ $$ Ø

☐ *601 N. Water St., Ellensburg, WA 98926; (509) 925-4141. Couples $35 to $46, singles $29 to $36. Major credit cards.* ☐ A 40-unit motel with TV movies, phones; some two-bedroom units and kitchenettes. Pool, laundry.

### *Rainbow Motel* • △△ $$ Ø

☐ *1200 S. Ruby St., Ellensburg, WA 98926; (509) 925-3544. Couples $33 to $48, singles $29. MC/VISA.* A 13-unit motel on landscaped grounds with TV, phones; some kitchen units. Coin laundry and playground.

## Bed & breakfast inns

**Surrey House Guest Rooms** ● ⌂ **$$$** ∅

☐ *715 E. Capitol, Ellensburg, WA 98926; (509) 962-9853. Couples $52 to $62, singles $47.50 to $62.50 AMEX. Rates include continental breakfast.* ☐ Five units with half-baths; simply furnished rooms in a turn-of-the century home. TV in living room, two kitchens available; large yard and picnic area.

**Murphy's Country Bed & Breakfast** ● ⌂ **$$$** ∅

☐ *Route 1, Box 400, Ellensburg, WA 98926; (509) 925-7986. Couples $60, singles $55. Two units with shared bath; full breakfast. MC/VISA, AMEX.* ☐ Comfortable rooms in a 1915 Craftsman farm bungalow, furnished with turn-of-the-century antiques. Large front porch and spacious lawns, shaded by maples and pines. Take I-90 exit 106 and drive 1.8 miles west.

## WHERE TO CAMP

**Ellensburg KOA** ● *Route 1, Box 252 (I-90 exit 106), Ellensburg, WA 98926; (509) 925-9319. RV and tent sites; $15 to $16. Reservations accepted; MC/VISA.* ☐ Attractive grassy sites along the Yakima River; showers, coin laundry, mini-mart, rec room, wading and swimming pools; fishing and water sports in the river.

**Kittitas County Fairgrounds** ● *P.O. Box 1045 (512 N. Poplar St.), Ellensburg, WA 98926; (509) 925-6144.* ☐ Campsites are available between major events at the fairgrounds, with water, electric and showers.

# TO WENATCHEE AND LAKE CHELAN

The most direct and certainly the most scenic route from Ellensburg to Wenatchee is along the foothills of the Cascades via U.S. Highway 97. However, if you were following our driving routes in Chapter seven, you already did that, as you migrated from Cle Elum to Leavenworth. Presumably, you stopped at Cashmere to pig out on free samples of Aplets and Cotlets. (If you haven't done all that, refer to page 258 in that chapter.)

An alternate route, staying more to central Washington, is east on I-90 and then north and northwest on state highways 281 and 28. The run eastward and then north to Quincy is rather drab, although there are some attractions along the way, and the drive along the Columbia River is quite pleasing. (This is the preferred route in winter, since snow may close Highway 97's Swauk Pass.) The first point of interest appears four miles east of Ellensburg; follow signs north to Squaw Creek Trail Road:

**Olmstead Place State Park** ● *Squaw Creek Trail Road; (509) 925-1943 or 856-2700. Open Thursday-Monday in summer 8 to 5; by appointment the rest of the year.* ☐ The original cottonwood log cabin and several outbuildings of the 1875 Olmstead cattle ranch have been restored and furnished to the period. Pause for a peek into a wagon shed, granary, dairy barn and other buildings. Nearby is the Seaton cabin schoolhouse, reached by a trail.

As you drive eastward, there's little else to see as I-90 passes through the barren Frenchman Hills. The picture brightens when you hit tiny **Vantage** on the Columbia River. Two state parks offer diversion, and one of them offers camping.

☺ **Ginkgo Petrified Forest State Park** ● *Vantage, WA 98950; (509) 856-2700. Park open daily 8 until dusk; interpretive center open daily May 1 through Labor Day from 10 to 6; by appointment the rest of the year.* ☐ The only trees that can survive in this desert climate, at least away from the riverbank, are petrified ones. Ginkgo State Park houses a fine collection, with than 200 species represented, including the world's only petrified ginkgo trees. The interpretive center has specimens of cut and polished woods and graphics describing the petrification process. Nearby, a quarter-mile interpretive trail winds through a fallen stone forest, and a longer trail reaches into the surrounding sage country.

## WHERE TO CAMP

**Wanapum State Recreation Area** ● *Four miles south of Ginkgo Petrified Forest; (509) 856-2700. RV and tent sites; $14. No reservations or credit cards.* ☐ Well-spaced sites near Wanapum Lake (the Columbia River) with picnic tables and barbecues; flush potties and showers. Boat dock, fishing, swimming and nature trails.

**Vantage KOA** ● *P.O. Box 135 (I-90 exit 135), Vantage, WA 98950; (509) 856-2230. RV and tent sites, $13.50 to $14.50, "Kamping Kabins" $23. Reservations accepted; MC/VISA.* ☐ Grassy sites above the Columbia, with showers, coin laundry, mini-mart; indoor pool, sauna, rec room, playground and nature trails. To reach the campground, drive half a mile north from exit 135; it's near Ginkgo State Park.

If you drive a few miles below Wanapum recreation area, you'll reach **Wanapum Dam.** Visitors can take self-guiding tours to the fish ladder and powerhouse. Its Heritage Center is open April through November, daily from 9 to 5, with irregular hours the rest of the year. Exhibits trace the history of the Wanapum Indians who once occupied this area, and the development of hydroelectric power. A fish-viewing room is adjacent. Guided powerhouse tours are available on request; (509) 754-3541.

Continuing northeast from Vantage on I-90, watch for a turnout, offering views of the beige river basin from which you just climbed. The freeway swings away from the Columbia, and then you swing away from the freeway in **George.** From here, State Highway 281 makes an arrow-straight shot due north to **Quincy.** You'll pick up State Route 28 and head west, rejoining the shallow canyon of the Columbia after a few miles. Along the way, you'll pass small **Rock Island Dam,** with no visitor facilities to speak of. 'Round a bend in the river, and Washington's apple capital lies before you.

# Wenatchee

**Population: 21,800**                    **Elevation: 651 feet**

Although not a pretty town, Wenatchee occupies an attractive setting, arrayed along and above the Columbia. Acres of orchards bring springtime pink and summer green to the otherwise tan landscape. There's a hint of the Rhine Valley here, although it's apples and not vineyards that are terraced above the river.

This all started when pioneer settler Phillip Miller planted a few apple seeds in 1872. Twenty years later, by the time the Northern Pacific Railroad had arrived, he was ready to ship apples to Seattle and elsewhere in the West. Irrigation projects spurred further plantings, and now apples roll around the world. Wenatchee is the largest center of the largest apple-growing state in the nation. You can learn all about it at the Washington Apple Commission's visitor center, off Highway 97, northeast of town. But first:

Approaching the Columbia River through East Wenatchee, cross the stream and take the first turn to your right, onto Wenatchee Avenue. It carries you through a long stretch of business district in this comfortably prosperous blue-collar town. To see its remarkably large museum, and to visit its visitor bureau, you need to hop off that thoroughfare as you enter the business district. That requires wrapping around a block with right-hand turns, since a left off Wenatchee Avenue isn't permitted.

Get to Mission Street, a block uphill and parallel to Wenatchee Avenue, and follow its one-way course to the **North Central Washington Museum.** It occupies the former post office near Yakima Street. Travel two more blocks on Mission, then go uphill on Palouse to the **Wenatchee Visitor and Convention Bureau** at Palouse and Chelan. It's housed in old brick that once contained the museum; open weekdays 9 to 5. Take Palouse back down to Wenatchee Avenue and continue your run through town. Many of its old buildings have been carefully preserved, now housing modern shops and businesses. Signs tell of their past uses. You can pick up downtown walking tour maps and shopping guides at the visitor's bureau.

If you'd like to explore the waterfront and perhaps have a picnic with a view, drop down Fifth Street to **Riverfront Park.** Or turn right from Wenatchee Avenue onto Ninth Street and then left onto Walla Walla Street and follow it to **Walla Walla Point Park.** A bit farther along is **Wenatchee Confluence State Park**, with picnicking, boat launch, swimming and camping (listed below). It marks the merger of the Wenatchee and Columbia Rivers.

Back on Wenatchee Avenue, you'll cross the Wenatchee River and enter a freeway section of northbound Highway 2/97. Fork to the right, following Highway 97 signs for Entiat/Chelan. You'll soon pass through a stop light at Easy Street; continue north on Highway 97 and take the next right down to the **Washington Apple Center.**

Highway 97 splits in Wenatchee, and follows both sides of the Columbia. We recommend staying on the west bank. It takes you to the elaborate **Ohme Botanical Gardens,** on a steep slope to your left, just north of the apple center, and then on to **Rocky Reach Dam,** with nicely landscaped grounds and an exceptional museum complex.

The Columbia River is a long and skinny lake through here, cradled between low but remarkably steep cliffs. Turnouts on this route between Wenatchee and Chelan invite you to pause and admire the thoroughly harnessed the Old Man River of the West. Scruffy little **Entiat,** about midway between Wenatchee and Chelan, offers basic services and a small park with picnicking, camping, swimming and a boat launch. A road from here leads six miles to the **Entiat National Fish Hatchery.** The route continues about 20 miles into the Cascades to trailheads for the **Glacier Peak Recreation Area.**

## ATTRACTIONS

☺ *North Central Washington Museum* ● *127 S. Mission St. (near Yakima Street); (509) 664-5989. Weekdays 10 to 4, weekends 1 to 4. Adults $2, kids $1, family groups $5.* ❏ This is one of the state's better community museums—a huge complex occupying several floors of the old post office. Features include a detailed mock-up of an 1871 trading post, complete turn-of-the-century room groupings, and a well-stocked general store. Another room contains extensive fossil exhibits, including Clovis points found at a site in East Wenatchee. Nearby, in an extensive bear exhibit, you'll learn that a grizzly eats the equivalent of 66 Big Macs a day. (No wonder they're cranky.) Of course, you'll expect to encounter an elaborate early day apple sorting and packing shed mock-up, plus an apple label exhibit and a video on the local industry. You'll come away with the knowledge that the apple worm is the larvae of the coddling moth.

**Washington Apple Center** ● *2900 Euclid Ave.; (509) 663-9600. May through December: weekdays 8 to 5, Saturdays 9 to 5, Sundays and holidays 11 to 5; January through April: weekdays only, 8 to 5. Free.* ⌑ The North Central Washington Museum is a hard act to follow, and the apple center doesn't quite manage. Although the museum's apple packing exhibit and videos are more interesting, the apple center is certainly worth a stop. There are curiously few apples here, although you can get free sips of cider and sample Aplets and Cotlets. The gift shop sells various apple-theme gift items and specialty foods. An 18-minute video informs you that a billion bees are turned loose in this valley each spring to pollinate the apple crop. (Given a choice, we'll take the coddling moth worms.)

☺ **Ohme Gardens County Park** ● *3327 Ohme Road (three miles north, off Highway 97-A); (509) 662-5785. Daily 9 to 7 in summer and 9 to 6 the rest of the year. Adults $5, kids $3.* ⌑ Starting in 1929, the Ohme family spent more than 60 years creating one of the most impressive botanical gardens in America, steeply terraced above the Columbia River. A dusty sagebrush hill was transformed into an alpine wonderland of forests, meadows, rocky enclaves, ponds and waterfalls. As you climb its terraces and walk its paths, you can divide your visual attentions between the gardens and the Columbia River far below.

☺ **Rocky Reach Dam** ● *c/o Chelan County Public Utilities District; (509) 663-8121. Visitor center and museums open daily 8 to 5.* ⌑ As you approach, Rocky Reach appears to be just another low-rise dam on the Columbia. Walk from the art deco style visitor center out to the dam, and you'll encounter two remarkably extensive and interesting museum exhibits. They occupy long galleries above the dam's giant generator room. The Gallery of the Columbia traces the mighty river's geological and human history, with fine exhibits on the Columbia Plateau tribes and the coming of the whites with their riverboats, railroads and agriculture. A geological clock puts our presence on earth in a compelling time frame: If the earth were 24 hours old, *homo sapiens* would have arrived at 11:59 p.m. and recorded history began a quarter of a second before midnight. The Gallery of Electricity offers one of the most comprehensive studies of the subject that you'll find anywhere. Exhibits trace the flow of electrons from early experiments by Faraday, Franklin, Edison and Marconi to the Space Age. The display is rich with old prints, artifacts and working models. You can even make your own lightning—without running the risks that Ben Franklin faced.

Something to add to your storehouse of worthless information: the word "electricity" comes from the Greek word for amber, *eaektpon,* indicating the effect of capturing and reflecting light.

## ACTIVITIES

**Ice skating** ● Wenatchee Riverfront Park; two rinks with public skating, hockey, lessons and skate rentals. Contact the concessionaires at (509) 664-5994 or the Wenatchee Parks Department at (509) 664-5980.

*River running* ● Wenatchee Whitewater of nearby Cashmere offers trips on area rivers; (800) 74-FLOAT or (509) 782-2254.

*Skiing* ● Mission Ridge, 13 miles southwest of Wenatchee off Squilchuck Road, has several lifts and 33 runs, mostly intermediate, plus a ski school, rentals and cafeteria. It also offers several miles of groomed cross-country trails. Call (509) 663-7631 for ski information and snow conditions. Nearby Squilchuck State Park has more cross-country trails, plus a modest downhill area with two rope tows, a ski school and snack bar.

## ANNUAL EVENTS

For details on these and other events, call the Visitor and Convention Bureau at (509) 662-4774.

**Apple Blossom Festival,** major community celebration, late April through early May.

**Wenatchee Youth Circus** opens here in July, then tours the rest of the Northwest.

**Wenatchee Valley Arts Festival,** sidewalk exhibits downtown in late September; (509) 662-1213.

## WHERE TO DINE

### *The Restaurant and Bake Shop* ● ΔΔ $ Ø

◻ *Eight N. Wenatchee Ave.; (509) 663-2811. American; full bar service. Monday-Saturday 5 a.m. to 10 p.m. MC/VISA, AMEX.* ◻ The prices match the age of this old, well-kept family-style restaurant with brick walls and hanging plants. Wrap your chops around some great dinner bargains, such as liver and onions, catfish fillet or veal Parmesan with spaghetti and salad, all for well under $10. A bakery case offers an array of diet-killing goodies, and there's a smoky lounge in back.

### *Siraco's Restaurant* ● ΔΔ $$

◻ *17 S. Mission St.; (509) 663-7985. American-Greek; wine and beer. Daily 7 a.m. to 9 p.m. No credit cards.* ◻ Bright and cheerful little café with red Naugahyde booths and floral print wallpaper. The American menu of halibut, steaks and chops has some interesting Greek accents, such as chicken *reganati* done with garlic and oregano.

### ☺ *Steven's at Mission Square* ● ΔΔΔ $$

◻ *218 Mission Street (at Second); (509) 663-6573. Regional American; full bar service. Lunch weekdays from 11, dinner nightly from 5. MC/VISA, AMEX.* ◻ It's Wenatchee's classiest diner, with mirrored walls, brick and brass and potted plants. The menu skips from Northwest salmon and halibut to properly done fresh pastas to chicken over a spinach base with sweet basil, pecans and Bermuda onions. (Not Walla Walla onions?)

### *Tequila's* ● ΔΔ $

◻ *800 N. Wenatchee Ave.; (509) 662-7239. Mexican; full bar service. Monday-Thursday 11 a.m. to 10 p.m., Friday-Saturday 11 to 11. MC/VISA.* ◻ We've started seeking out these cheery, well run places, which are found in several Washington cities. The large menu goes well beyond smashed beans and rice to offer tasties such as steak or chicken fajitas, picadillo (sliced steak cooked in broth with cubed potatoes, onions and tomatoes) and charcoal broiled prawns. The look is proper: brick, wrought iron, high-backed booths and requisite sombreros on the walls.

☺ **Visconti's Italian Restaurant** • △△ $$ Ø

☐ *1737 Wenatchee Ave.; (509) 662-5013. Italian; wine and beer. Lunch Monday-Friday 11 to 2, dinner nightly from 5. Major credit cards.* ☐ This pleasantly casual chef-owned *bistro* serves ample portions of properly cooked, artfully seasoned pastas. Popular with locals, it's a busy place most nights, alive with the good smells of garlic and olive oil. It offers a large selections of wines by the glass; the homemade desserts are excellent. Visconti's is divided into several cozy smoke-free dining rooms.

## WHERE TO SLEEP

**Avenue Motel** • △△ $$ Ø

☐ *720 N. Wenatchee Ave., Wenatchee, WA 98801; (800) 733-8981 or (509) 663-7161. Couples $42 to $55, singles $40 to $55, kitchenettes $5 extra. Major credit cards.* ☐ Well-kept 12-unit motel with TV movies, movie rentals and room phones; some refrigerators. Pool, spa, landscaped grounds; restaurant adjacent.

**Four Seasons Inn** • △△△ $$$ Ø

☐ *11 W. Grant Rd., East Wenatchee, WA 98802; (509) 884-6611. Couples $52 to $62, singles $44 to $52. Major credit cards.* ☐ Attractive river-side inn with TV movies, room phones; many rooms with balconies and rivr views. Pool, sauna, spa. **Barny's Eatery** has river-view tables; lunch and dinner daily; dinners $10 to $15; full bar service. **Coffee shop** open 24 hours.

**Lyles Motel** • △△ $$ Ø

☐ *924 N. Wenatchee Ave., Wenatchee, WA 98801; (509) 663-5155. Couples $39 to $48, singles $28 to $32.* ☐ A 22-unit motel with TV movies, phones; some efficiency units. Pool, spa.

**Scotty's Motel** • △△ $$$ Ø

☐ *1004 N. Wenatchee Ave., Wenatchee, WA 98801; (800) 235-8165 or (509) 662-8165. Couples $49 to $58, singles $35 to $43, kitchenettes $35 to $58. Rates include continental breakfast. Major credit cards.* ☐ A 34-unit motel near riverfront park; TV, room phones; some refrigerators and microwaves; coin laundry, pool, spa and sauna.

**WestCoast Wenatchee Center Hotel** • △△△ $$$$ Ø

☐ *201 N. Wenatchee Ave., Wenatchee, WA 98801; (800) 426-0670 or (509) 662-1234. Couples $78, singles $68. Major credit cards.* Very appealing 146-room hotel with TV, phones, some refrigerators. Indoor-outdoor pool, spa, exercise room. **Dining room** serves 6:30 a.m. to 10 p.m.; dinners $8 to $17; full bar service. Pedestrian way to adjacent convention center.

## WHERE TO CAMP

**Wenatchee Confluence State Park** • *Off Wenatchee Avenue; (509) 664-6373. RV and tent sites; $14. No reservations or credit cards.* ☐ Well-spaced sites in a meadow area adjacent to the Wenatchee and Columbia rivers. Barbecues and picnic tables, flush potties and showers. River-view picnic areas, boat launch, fishing and swimming.

**Wenatchee River County Park** • *Six miles west on Highway 2; (509) 662-2525. RV and tent sites $8 to $11. No reservations or credit cards.* ☐ Some shaded and grassy sites; showers, picnic areas and playground. Fishing, swimming and boating on the Wenatchee River. Closed from November through March.

# Lake Chelan

**Chelan town population: 3,000**          **Elevation: 1,238 feet**

Ice Age glaciers shaped much of north central Washington, and one of their most dramatic remnants is Lake Chelan (*chee-LAN*). Although this slender water finger bears some resemblance to Columbia River reservoirs, it's a natural lake. There is a dam at the lower end, put in place in 1927 to produce electricity.

Chelan was scoured by glaciers about 17,000 years ago, like the slender lakes of southern Switzerland. Stretching 55 miles northwest from the town of Chelan, it's one of the world's longest and skinniest lakes. Those glaciers did a rather thorough carving job. Although it's less than a mile wide in most areas, Chelan is the third deepest lake in America. It dips to 1,486 feet, compared with Oregon's Crater Lake at 1,932 and Lake Tahoe in California/Nevada at 1,645. Parts of Chelan's bottom are nearly 400 feet below sea level when the lake is at "full pool" during peak runoff in early summer. The water level doesn't dip too much from month to month, since Chelan is fed by 59 streams and 27 glaciers.

Unlike Columbia reservoirs, most of Lake Chelan has thickly wooded shorelines, since it extends into the mountains. It reaches toward North Cascades National Park, whose primeval glaciers did the carving. Not surprisingly, the lake is a popular boating, swimming and fishing area. It is thus highly commercialized, except for the upper five miles, which comprise Lake Chelan National Recreation Area.

Thus, the lake has two distinctively different faces. At the lower end, the cute little town of Chelan is busy with restaurants, boutiques and lodgings. The shoreline is lined with cabins, summer cottages and resorts. Surrounding hills are terraced with orchards. Upstream, shoreline homes thin out considerably, since upper lake can be reached only by boat. Once you enter the national recreation area, much of the shore is wild and free, offering hidden coves, cross-country hiking and a marked trails.

Tiny Stehekin is a rustically charming wilderness outpost within the recreation area. The *Lady of the Lake,* which sails the 55 miles from Chelan, is Stehekin's link to the outside world. For the thousands of tourists who crowd aboard, the *Lady* is a pleasing novelty. To Stehekin residents, she's a necessity, bringing not only all those moneyed tourists, but mail and cargo.

## Driving Chelan

Geography and man provide a curious transition as you travel north from Wenatchee to Chelan on U.S. 97-A. After following the Columbia's Lake Entiat reservoir most of the way, it swings from the water, climbs some low hills and soon delivers you to the shores of Lake Chelan. Since this end is below the evergreen belt, it could be taken for just another Columbia reservoir. Look upstream, however, and you'll see the gathering forests.

Before you reach the town of Chelan, turn left onto State Highway 971 for a pleasant lakeside drive. The shore is cluttered with homes initially, then they thin out as you approach **Lake Chelan State Park.** Press on into deepening lakeside forests and you reach **Twenty-five-mile Creek State Park.** This is as far as you can get upstream by road. Both parks offer water sports, hiking and nature trails, picnic sites and campgrounds (listed below).

*RV advisory:* The road is narrow and winding in some areas, with a few cliff side passes, but large RVs and trailers can handle it.

Returning to Highway 97, you'll shortly passes the office and dock for the *Lady of the Lake* cruise boat. Just beyond, fork to the left at the city center sign, which takes you on Woodin Avenue through the heart of this fetching little community. The look is a blend of Western false front and mid-America village. Downtown does not border the lake, although there is a marina nearby.

Pause at the **Chelan Ranger District office** at 428 W. Woodin to gather information on Lake Chelan National Recreation Area, Stehekin and Wenatchee National Forest. It's open weekdays 8 to 5; hours may be extended in summer. To load up on material concerning the lake and its activities continue downtown and turn left at the Texaco station onto Columbia Street to the **Lake Chelan Chamber of Commerce.** It's at Columbia and Johnson streets, open daily in summer and weekdays in the off-season. If you continue out Columbia, it becomes the Manson Highway (State Route 150), taking you eight miles along the northern lakeshore to the resort gathering of **Manson.** You'll catch a few lake views along the way. The **Manson Scenic Loop,** a popular driving and biking route, starts at Old Mill Park at Manson Highway and Wapato Lake Road, and winds through orchard lands, past several lakes and up to an imposing valley view from Slide Ridge.

Back in Chelan, you can browse through its few gift shops and pay a visit to the small **Lake Chelan Historical Society Museum** at Woodin and Emerson. It's open summers only, Monday-Saturday 10 to 4, with exhibits on archeology, Native Americans and pioneers; (509) 682-5644. If you have kids in tow, you might check out **Slidewaters,** a water park just off the highway at 102 Waterslide Drive; (509) 682-5751. Or haul them to **Lake Shore Bumper Boats** in Don Morse Memorial Park, open in summers.

## Stehekin/Lake Chelan National Recreation Area

Tiny Stehekin's charm lies in its isolation. This forest-shrouded village at the edge of the lake has no traffic and no TV (except for those who cheat and put up satellite dishes). It's also the focal point of Lake Chelan National Recreation Area, with a ranger station and trails leading into the into the Cascades wilds.

One can see all of the small settlement and have lunch in about an hour and a half. That's how much time the boat tours allow, for those who want to make this a one-day visit. Others can check into one of the small resorts or—with proper equipment and a wilderness permit—hike into the wilds toward North Cascades National Park.

The *Lady of the Lake II* takes about four hours to reach Stehekin, with a few shoreline stops along the way. (The original wooden-hulled *Lady,* which was built in 1940, is in semi-retirement.) Newest member of the fleet is the *Lady Express,* a turbo-charged boat that cuts the cruise time in half.

## ACTIVITIES

**Boat tours** ● Lake Chelan Boat Company launches the *Lady of the Lake* and/or *Lady Express* daily from May through mid-October, with departures at 8:30 a.m. The *Express* also runs in the off-season on Monday, Wednesday and Friday, generally leaving at 10. Prices are $14 one way and $21 round trip on the *Lady.* They're $24.50 and $39 on the *Express* from mid-May through September and $14 and $21 in the off-season. In summer, one can get a combo ticket for $38.50, taking one boat up and another back, which allows more time at Stehekin. Reservations aren't needed for the *Lady*, but they're recommended for the faster boat, particularly in summer. If all this sounds confusing, it is. Get a current schedule by contacting: Lake Chelan Boat Company, Box 186, Chelan, WA 98816; (509) 682-2224 or 682-4584.

Smaller firms also offer lake cruises; for a list, contact the Chamber of Commerce at P.O. Box 216, Chelan, WA 98816; (800) 4-CHELAN.

**Bicycle rentals** • Lake Chelan Boat Company, P.O. Box 186, Chelan, WA 98816; (509) 682-2224 or (509) 682-4584.

**Boat and/or jet ski rentals** • Chelan Boat Rentals, 1210 W. Woodin Ave., Chelan, WA 98816; (509) 682-4444. Ship-N-Shore Boat Rental, 1230 W. Woodin Ave., Chelan, WA 98816; (509) 682-5125. RSI Sports, P.O. Box 475, Entiat, WA 98822; (800) 786-2637 or (509) 784-2399.

**Charter boat cruises** • Lake Chelan and North Cascade Tours, P.O. Box 1119, Chelan, WA 98816; (509) 682-8287.

**Fishing** • Lake Chelan yields chinook, kokanee, cutthroat, rainbow and makinaws, as well as burbot, a type of cod. Surrounding streams are popular with fly fishermen. For fishy specifics, contact Lake Chelan Ranger District, Box 189 (428 W. Woodin Ave.), Chelan, WA 98816; (509) 682-2576.

**Fishing guides** • Rush's Fishing Guide Service, P.O. Box 1481, Chelan, WA 98816; (509) 682-2802.

**Horseback riding** • Stehekin Valley Ranch, P.O. Box 36, Stehekin, WA 98815; (509) 682-4677.

**River rafting** • Stehekin Valley Ranch, P.O. Box 36, Stehekin, WA 98815; (509) 682-4677.

**Scenic flights and air charters** • Chelan Airways, P.O. Box W (1328 Woodin Ave.), Chelan, WA 98816; (509) 682-5555. Sound Flight, P.O. Box 812, Renton, WA 98057; (509) 682-8287 or (206) 255-6500. Ads Up Aviation, Lake Chelan Airport; (509) 682-8618 or (509) 687-3180; vintage biplane rides in summer.

**Sightseeing tours** • Lake Chelan and North Cascade Tours, Box 1119, Chelan, WA 98816; (509) 682-8287. Destinations Unlimited, Box 1779 (311 E. Woodin Ave.), Chelan, WA 98816; (800) 447-2651 or (509) 682-4571. Guided bus tours and self-guiding bike tours offered by Lake Chelan Boat Company, Box 186, Chelan, WA 98816; (509) 682-2224 or (509) 682-4584.

## Winter sports

**Downhill** • Echo Valley, North shore Lake Chelan, (509) 687-3167; one poma and three rope tows, rentals and instructions.

**Cross country** • Bear Mountain Ranch, Route 1, Box 63-B, Chelan, WA 98816, (509) 682-5444; 50 miles of groomed trails, skating and telemark. Lake Chelan National Recreation Area, c/o Lake Chelan Ranger District, (509) 682-2576; three miles of trails around Stehekin, plus lots of open forest. Lake Chelan Municipal Golf Course, 1501 Golf Course Dr., c/o Lake Chelan Winter Ski Club, P.O. Box 99, Chelan, WA 98816; five miles of groomed trails.

**Snowmobiling** • Echo Valley, plus three Wenatchee National Forest snow parks; contact Lake Chelan Ski Club, P.O. Box 99, Chelan, WA 98816; or Lake Chelan Ranger District, (509) 682-2576.

**Snowmobile rentals and tours** • Guided Snowmobiles, 682-5125.

## ANNUAL EVENTS

**Fire & Ice Winterfest,** late January in Chelan; (509) 682-2381.
**Apple Blossom Celebration,** mid-May in Manson; (509) 687-3378.
**Chelan Street Fair,** mid-June in downtown Chelan; (509) 682-3501.
**Arts and Crafts Show,** early July in Chelan; (509) 687-3958.
**Bach Feste** of classical music, mid-July in Chelan; (509) 662-7536.
**Lake Chelan Rustlers' Rodeo,** mid-July at Rustlers' Rodeo Grounds in Union Valley; (509) 682-5526.
**Campbell Cup Crew Races,** late October; (800) 4-CHELAN.

## WHERE TO DINE

### *Apple Cup Café* • △△ $$

☐ *804 E. Woodin Ave.; (509) 682-5997. American; full bar service. Daily 6 a.m. to 11 p.m. MC/VISA.* ☐ Very inviting place with a bright and airy early American look; blonde woods, upholstered booths, simulated Tiffany and ceiling fans. The kitchen isn't innovative, but offerings are generally good. Choose from the usual chicken, steaks and chops and several pastas and other Italian dishes.

### ☺ *Emerson Street Café* • △△ $

☐ *113 S. Emerson; (509) 682-2750. American; no alcohol. Monday-Saturday 6:30 a.m. to 3:30 p.m., Sunday 8 to 3:30. No credit cards.* ☐ This cute little upstairs place is an appealing lunch stop. The look is early American, with blue and white table dressing, maple chairs and lace curtains. From the kitchen emerges beef stroganoff, beef stew, fettuccine and serious chili.

### ☺ *Campbell's House Restaurant* • △△△ $$$

☐ *104 W. Woodin Ave.; (509) 682-4250. American-continental; full bar service. Breakfast, lunch and dinner daily from 6:45. Major credit cards.* ☐ This handsome lakeside restaurant, housed in the venerable Campbell's Resort, is the area's most reliable dining venue. The menu, which changes frequently, is an interesting blend of American standbys with *nouveau* twists, and European classics. Try the Campbell country chicken with apples, shallots, mushrooms, sherry and cream; or the basic liver and onions.

### ☺ *Goochie's* • △△ $$

☐ *104 E. Woodin Ave.; (509) 682-2436. American; full bar service. Daily 11 to 10. Major credit cards.* ☐ It's the liveliest spot in town, a blend of Victorian and trendy San Francisco sports bar, housed in an historic hotel. Sidle up to the elegant cherrywood bar and choose from one of 30 beers on tap, or settle at a table and select from a busy menu, maybe with oyster shooters for starters. Offerings wander from prime rib to assorted steaks to Maui ribs to seafood and several pasta choices.

## WHERE TO SLEEP

Many resorts, summer homes and condos are at lakeside or tucked into the woods. Contact the chamber at (800) 4-CHELAN for a more detailed list.

### *Cabana Motel* • △△ $$$$ Ø

☐ *P.O. Box 596 (420 Manson Rd.), Chelan, WA 98816; (509) 682-2233. Couples and singles $63 to $78, kitchenettes $86 to $98, kitchenette suites $112. MC/VISA.* ☐ A twelve-unit motel with TV; most with refrigerators and lake views; swimming pool and barbecue area.

### Campbell's Resort ● ⌂⌂ $$$$$ ∅

◻ *P.O. Box 278 (104 W. Woodin Ave.), Chelan, WA 98816; (800) 553-8225 or (509) 682-2561. Couples $98 to $162, singles $98 to $156, kitchenettes $138 to $196, suites $156 to $276. Major credit cards.* ◻ Handsome 150-unit lakefront resort with two pools and spas and a barbecue area. Rooms have TV and phones; some have refrigerators, microwaves and in-room coffee; all are on the lake. **Restaurant** listed above.

### Darnell's Motel Resort ● ⌂⌂ $$$$$ ∅

◻ *P.O. Box 506 (901 Spader Bay Rd.), Chelan, WA 98816; (509) 682-2015. Couples $135 to $165 (including kitchenettes and suites), singles $75 to $165. Major credit cards.* ◻ Lakeside resort within walking distance of town; 38 units with TV, phones and refrigerators. Pool, spa, sauna, tennis courts, barbecue area, bicycles, kids play area, badminton and volleyball courts; extensive water sports program with rowboats, paddleboats and canoes, boat launching and moorage.

### Midtowner Motel ● ⌂ $$$ ∅

◻ *P.O. Box 1722, Chelan, WA 98816; (509) 682-4051. Couples $55 to $65, singles $50, kitchenettes $65 to $75. Major credit cards.* ◻ A 45-unit motel with TV, phones, refrigerators and microwaves. Pool, spa, coin laundry.

### Whistlin' Pine Resort ● ⌂ $$

◻ *P.O. Box 284, Pateros, WA 98846; (509) 923-2548. Cabins $30 for two, tent cabins $40 for four, also RV hookups (see below). Advance reservations required; no credit cards.* ◻ Rustic resort on Alta Lake, five miles southwest of Pateros. Guided horseback rides and fishing.

## Bed & breakfast inns

### Brick House Inn ● ⌂⌂ $$$$ ∅

◻ *P.O. Box 1976 (304 Wapata at Sanders), Chelan, WA 98816; (509) 682-4791. Couples $65 to $80, singles $40 to $55. Four units with share baths; full or continental breakfast. Major credit cards.* ◻ Turn-of-the-century brick Victorian with a wrap-around porch, modernized with country décor. TV lounge, community kitchen, hot tub and barbecue facilities.

### Holden Village Bed & Breakfast ● ⌂ $$ ∅

◻ *Route 1, Box 147-B, Chelan, WA 98816; (509) 687-9695. Doubles $35, singles $25, family rooms $45, dormitory $15. Rates include full breakfast. No credit cards.* ◻ Simple accommodations at a Lutheran church retreat center, 20 miles from Chelan near Twenty-five-mile Creek State Park. Quiet setting among the trees, with trails and lake activities adjacent. Country-style décor with handmade quilts, pottery, weavings and dinnerware.

### Hubbard House ● ⌂⌂ $$$$ ∅

◻ *P.O. Box 348 (Manson Boulevard and Wapato Way), Manson, WA 98831; (509) 687-3058. Couples and singles $80. Three units; one private and two shared baths; continental or full breakfast. MC/VISA.* ◻ Lakeview rooms in an attractive 1920s French Normandy style home, surrounded by elaborate gardens. Furnished with Victorian antiques. Private lake access.

### ☺ Mary Kay's Whaley Mansion ● ⌂⌂⌂ $$$$$ ∅

◻ *Route 1, Box 693 (415 Third St.), Chelan, WA 98816; (800) 729-2408 or (509) 682-5385. Couples and singles $105 to $125. Six rooms, all with TV and private baths; full breakfast. MC/VISA.* ◻ Beautifully restored early 20th century Edwardian "catalog house" furnished with heirloom antiques. Opulently decorated, with Victorian light fixtures, upholstered walls, white bamboo bird cages and garlands of artificial flowers.

**Proctor House Inn** ● △△△ **$$$$ Ø**

⊔ *495 Lloyd Rd., Manson, WA 98831; (509) 687-6361. Couples $85 to $125, singles $75 to $105. Five units with private baths; full breakfast. MC/VISA, AMEX.* ⊔ Four-level farmhouse on a knoll above Lake Chelan with impressive views. Rooms have a mix of antique and modern furnishings, accented with contemporary artworks

## Stehekin accommodations

**North Cascades Lodge** ● △ **$$ to $$$$**

⊔ *At Stehekin Landing; mailing address: P.O. Box 1779, Chelan, WA 98816; (509) 682-4711. Couples and singles $46 to $65, family units and apartments $75 to $82. MC/VISA.* ⊔ Rustic tree-shrouded lodge on the edge of the lake at Stehekin Landing. Apartments have kitchen facilities.

☺ **Silver Bay Lodging** ● △△ **$$$$ Ø**

⊔ *P.O. Box 43, Stehekin, WA 98852; (509) 682-2212. Couples and singles $85 to $130. Four units with private baths; continental breakfast. No credit cards.* ⊔ Modern rustic retreat in a distinctive "solar envelope" home in the Stehekin wilds. Two B&B units and two fully furnished cabins; furnished with mixed antiques and Native American art.

☺ **Stehekin Valley Ranch** ● △ **$$$**

⊔ *P.O. Box 36, Stehekin, WA 98852; (509) 682-4677. Rates $55 per person (less for children), including lodging, all meals and boat dock pickup. MC/VISA.* ⊔ Sample the rustic life at this old ranch nine miles up Stehekin Valley Road, sleeping in a wood-frame cabin tent, eating hearty meals, hiking and fishing. Small additional fees for horseback rides, white-water rafting and mountain bike rentals.

## WHERE TO CAMP

**Lake Chelan State Park** ● *Route 1, Box 90, Chelan, WA 98816-9755; (509) 687-3710. RV and tent sites; $14 and $10. Reservations accepted in summer; request a form from the park. No credit cards.* ⊔ Well-spaced, shaded sites near the lake, with barbecues and picnic tables. Showers, nature trails, swimming, boating and other water sports.

**Lakeshore RV Park** ● *619 W. Manson Hwy., Chelan, WA 98816; (509) 682-5031. RV and tent sites, $10 to $20. Reservations accepted by mail, with deposit. No credit cards.* ⊔ City of Chelan park with grassy sites near the lake; some pull-throughs. Coin showers, cable TV, picnic tables. Marina with boat launch, fishing, swimming, shuffleboard, horseshoes, playground. Open mid-February to mid-November.

**Twenty-five-mile Creek State Park** ● *Twenty miles east, south shore; (509) 687-3710. RV and tent sites; $14 and $10. No reservations or credit cards.* ⊔ Well-spaced, shaded sites near creek and lake, with barbecues and picnic tables. Showers, nature trails, swimming boating and fishing.

**Whistlin' Pine Resort** ● *P.O. Box 284, Pateros, WA 98846; (509) 923-2548. RV and tent sites; water and electric $18, tent sites $13. Also cabins, listed above. Advance reservations required; no credit cards.* ⊔ Rustic resort with picnic tables and showers. Fishing and conducted horseback rides.

# HIGHWAY 17 CORRIDOR

If you like being alone together, you may enjoy the meandering course of State Highway 17 that picks its way through central Washington. Other than the northeast corner, which we visit in the next chapter, this is the least populated part of the state. It doesn't offer a lot of visitor lures, other than Chief Joseph Dam and a couple of reservoir recreation areas near Moses Lake. At the lower end of this route, the Tri-Cities area *is* populated. That's not really tourist country, but you may want to visit the world's first atomic energy facility at Hanford. (Grand Coulee Dam and its lures are just west of Chief Joseph Dam, and we cover them in the next chapter.)

Getting to Highway 17 from Lake Chelan requires a pleasant drive northeast on U.S. 97, along more of the Columbia's shallow, steep-walled canyon. Orchards are terraced above, and again, visions of the Rhine Valley come to mind. This is one of the more pleasant moments along the becalmed river.

**Wells Dam,** about ten miles above Chelan, has a small visitor center with exhibits on hydroelectrics (daily 8 to 6). At a vista point, note the map of the elaborate 250,000 square mile, seven-state basin that the Columbia drains. A public boat launch, fishing area and salmon hatchery are nearby.

The hamlets of **Pateros** and **Brewster** are basically packing centers for the area's booming apple industry. Just beyond Brewster, you'll pick up Highway 17 at the confluence of the Okanogan and Columbia rivers. **Fort Okanogan State Park** here marks the site of a fur trading post, built in 1811 by John Jacob Aster's Pacific Fur Company. Facilities include a picnic area and interpretive center with graphics and exhibits concerning the fur trade. It's open Wednesday-Sunday 9 to 6; closed in winter; (509) 923-2473.

☺ A few miles south is **Chief Joseph Dam,** named for the great Nez Percè Indian leader. One of the largest dams on the Columbia, this concrete mass is more than a mile long. How can that be, since the river here is only 980 feet wide? The dam is L-shaped and set parallel to the river, providing room for 27 generators, housed in the world's longest straight-line power house. Their output of 2,457,300 kilowatts is second only to the mighty Grand Coulee, which generates 6,494,000 kilowatts of juice. These statistics and more are designed to dazzle you as you visit the visitor center, which is built into dam's powerhouse; (509) 686-5501. Visitors can drive across the dam face for views up and down the Columbia.

**Bridgeport State Park**, adjacent to the dam, offers camping (hookups $14, tents $10), fishing, swimming, picnicking and even a nine-hole golf course; (509) 686-7231. Just beyond the dam and park is the scattered and somewhat scruffy hamlet of **Bridgeport,** offering basic provisions and fuel. If you want to make this an overnight stop (there isn't much immediately south), the **Y Motel** at 2138 Columbia has rooms for from $35 a night and RV hookups from $12; (509) 686-3333.

There's little to see and less to do as you travel south on Route 17 from Bridgeport. The highway leaves the river's comforting presence and enters a vast, rolling sagebrush prairie. You'll see little sign of civilization until you hit U.S. Highway 2, just west of **Coulee City**.

***Driving advisory:*** There are no services between Bridgeport and Coulee City, a distance of 40 miles.

South of Coulee City, you encounter a primeval spur of the Columbia. The stream originally flowed through this area, then its course was shifted to the north about 100,000 years ago. Great floods swept through here as Ice Age glaciers upstream broke to free the dammed river. The old river bed now contains a chain of lakes. Since this is an extension of the large Coulee Dam complex, we explore this area in detail in the next chapter, during a side trip from the dam to Soap Lake; see page 346.

Highway 17 skims the edge of the Sun Lakes, Lake Lenore and Soap Lake. It then enters a beige landscape of grasslands and wheat as it heads south to **Moses Lake** on Interstate 90. This homely town of nearly 12,000 is rimmed by farmlands, a large U.S. Air Force base and two reservoirs. While passing through town, you might want to pause at the small **Adam East Museum and Art Center,** in the Civic Center at 122 West Third Avenue. It displays pioneer relics, fossils and Native American artifacts. Hours are Tuesday-Saturday noon to 5; free; (509) 766-9395. To reach it, turn right from Highway 17 onto Stratford Road and head south. Just after crossing the Parker arm of Moses Lake, turn right onto Broadway, drive two blocks to Ash and turn left. The Museum is at Third and Ash.

Moses Lake reservoir is backed up behind the dam of that name, and its various arms wrap around the town. Potholes Reservoir—about as attractive as its name—was formed by runoff from upstream irrigation. The two reservoirs lure boaters and fishing folks, and both have state parks at their shorelines. Water skiers dance over their surface in summer, and fisherpersons pull perch, walleye, trout, catfish and crappie from their waters.

**Moses Lake State Park** is a day use area with swimming bays, a shaded picnic area (a welcome refuge on hot summer days!), a snack bar and boat launches; (509) 765-5852. The 18-mile-long lake is one of Washington's largest (not counting those extended Columbia River reservoirs). You can reach it by taking Broadway Avenue southwest from downtown onto I-90, and then driving briefly west across an arm of the lake.

**Potholes State Park** has similar facilities, plus a campground on Potholes Reservoir (765-7271), which is held in place by O'Sullivan Dam. This 5.5-mile-long structure, actually a series of retaining walls between low basaltic ridges, is one of the longest earth and rock fill dams in America. **Columbia National Wildlife Refuge** occupies the southern edge of the shoreline, and it encompasses smaller potholes, where water gathers in basaltic depressions. You can pick up bird-watching information at kiosks. The refuge also has a free primitive campground at Soda Lake. To reach Potholes, turn right from Highway 17 onto State Route 262, about eleven miles south of Moses Lake. The highway crosses the long face of the dam.

Below Potholes Reservoir, Route 17 takes you past more monotonous miles of beige wheat and prairie grass to the farm hamlet of **Othello,** across State Highway 26 and on to **Mesa.** Here, you'll again see the contours of the wide and shallow Columbia River basin, as the route winds downhill toward the Tri-Cities area. Eight miles after Route 17 dissolves into U.S. 395, watch on your left for a sign to **Preston Wine Cellars.** The large tasting room/gift shop sits atop the winery for a pleasant countryside view. There are self-guiding tours; open daily 10 to 5:30; (509) 545-1990.

## Tri-City tour: going fission?

Although the Tri-Cities of Pasco, Kennewick and Richland aren't tourist areas, they offer some interesting lures, including enough nuclear energy visitor facilities for an atomic vacation.

This is primarily a prosperous agricultural area focused around the confluence of the Columbia and Snake rivers. We've fashioned a driving route that will direct you to the regions's few highlights. Several wineries are in the area, although they're more widespread than those in the Yakima Valley. For a winery driving tour, contact any of the three chambers of commerce or the Tri-Cities Visitor and Convention Bureau; see "Trip planner." To begin your quickie Tri-Cities tour, continue south on U.S. 395 to I-182 in **Pasco**. Turn west, then exit shortly onto Fourth Avenue, wrap under the freeway and go south for about eighteen blocks. Notice the unusual beehive-domed **Franklin County Courthouse** at the corner of Fourth and Market. Four blocks beyond, you'll hit the first of two small community museums:

**Franklin County Historical Museum** • *304 N. Fourth Ave., Pasco; (509) 547-3714. May 1 through Labor Day: Wednesday-Friday 1 to 6, Saturday 10 to 6 and Sunday 1 to 6; the rest of the year, Wednesday-Sunday 1 to 5. Free; donations appreciated.* ⊡ This nicely done little museum preserves the county's rural memories in uncluttered display cases. Photos and room groupings of antique furniture complete the picture. Equally interesting is the building, a stucco California mission-style former Carnegie library.

From the museum, continue along Fourth for two blocks, through the modest, low-rise business district, and turn right onto Lewis Street. Go left onto Tenth Avenue (State Route 397), and cross the Columbia River into **Kennewick**, on an unusual steel tower and spider-web cable bridge. As you clear the river, veer to the right onto East Columbia Drive. Go less than a mile, then turn left at a stoplight onto Washington Street. After about half a mile, as you cross a small canal, turn right onto Sixth (just short of a Baptist church), then take an immediate right onto Auburn and a quick left onto Keewaydin. Sitting before you is Keewaydin Park and the other archive:

**East Benton County Historical Museum** • *205 Keewaydin Dr., Kennewick; (509) 582-7704. Memorial Day to Labor Day: daily noon to 4; the rest of the year: Tuesday-Sunday noon to 4. Free; donations appreciated.* ⊡ Turn-of-the-century room groupings are the focal point of this archive. Other exhibits include a printing press, cream separator, 1920s dentist's office that looks painful, and a rather scattered collection of pioneer artifacts.

Return to Washington Street, retrace your route to Columbia Drive, turn left and stay with it until it blends onto Highway 240. Follow this freeway along the waterfront for a couple of miles, keeping to the south side of the Columbia River. (You will cross the smaller Yakima River as it enters the Columbia.) As you approach Freeway 182, stay to the left and follow a city center sign straight ahead, onto George Washington Way. After a bit over a mile, turn left onto Lee Boulevard (opposite a Red Lion Inn), and then right onto Jadwin Avenue. Before you is a post office and beyond that, a government building that houses the Hanford Science Center. This is your first stop on an atomic tour of Richland. (Behind you, should you need a map or other Tri-City information, is the **Richland Chamber of Commerce** at 515 Lee; open weekdays 8 to 5.)

**Atomic vacation advisory:** The U.S. Department of Energy's huge Hanford facility is about eleven miles north of Richland, out in the desert. If you're running late, you may want to go there first, then come back here. Visitor centers at its **Washington Public Power Plant** and the **Fast Flux Test Facility** (excuse me?) close at 4 on weekdays, while the science center here in Richland is open until 5.

☺ **Hanford Science Center** ● *825 Jadwin, Richland; (509) 376-6374. Weekdays 8 to 5, Saturday 9 to 5, closed Sunday. Free.* ☐ We aren't big fans of nuclear power and we took this center's many messages with grains of salt. However, it is a fine science museum, capable of teaching you more than you ever wanted to know about the atom. Videos, inter-active computers, cut-away models and graphics will keep you busy. You can calculate your daily dose of radiation from TV and other sources (too much exposure to *Northern Exposure?*), try to manipulate objects through one of those rubber-glove boxes and play computer games.

From the center, continue out Jadwin Avenue, which blends onto Stevens Drive. After several miles, you leave the city and enter a barren wasteland that attracted the atomic scientists in 1943. (The desert, with cooling water from the nearby Columbia and electricity from Grand Coulee Dam made this a great place to play with the atom.) No gate heralds your entry into the "Hanford Works"; the rest of civilization simply falls behind. After about ten miles of desert, turn right at a blinking signal and follow signs to your next atomic stop:

**Washington Public Power Plant Two** ● *Stevens Drive; (509) 372-5860. Thursday-Friday 11 to 4, Saturday-Sunday noon to 5.* ☐ Great billows of steam mark your target as you approach this nuclear generating plant. En route, you pass Power Plant One, which was never completed, apparently because of bonding problems. The visitor facility here is in a portable classroom outside that ominous looking containment dome. It, too, brims with nuclear information, and it's geared more to younger minds, with graphics showing the ABC's of nuclear energy. Hands-on exhibits allow you to generate electricity with sweaty palms and check radiation emitted from seemingly innocent materials such as potassium chloride (salt substitute).

Return to that blinking light and continue northward briefly, then follow signs to the left to your last radiation stop:

☺ **Fast Flux Test Facility** ● *Stevens Drive; (509) 376-3026 or (509) 376-6374.* ☐ Known affectionately in the fission trade as the "FFTF," this is an elaborate sodium-cooled nuclear reactor used to test fuels and materials for future nuclear fusion and other fast-breeder reactors. It also can produce radioactive isotopes for use in nuclear medicine. However, the facility was defunded in 1992 after failed attempts to find sufficient international markets for its output. At this writing, it was on hold. A video in the visitor center takes one on an illusory tour of the facility. FFTF itself is 69 feet below the ground, with a gleaming white containment dome above. It looks like an observatory without a telescope. Well-done graphics and a cut-away model of the facility will teach you all about fast fluxing.

The rest of the Hanford site is behind closed gates. Out there somewhere is B Reactor, the world's first, which made the stuff for the Hiroshima and Nagasaki bombs. It and eight more reactors were in operation at one time, brewing what the government chose to call "defense materials" for its Cold War arsenal. The eight original reactors were shut down by order of President Lyndon Johnson in the 1960s. They will be "decommissioned" (government jargon for cleaned up). The ninth, N-Reactor, is on cold standby.

"Security procedures and environmental radiation monitoring programs ensure interim protection of public health and safety until decommissioning begins," reads a DOE brochure.

Interim?

# TRIP PLANNER

**WHEN TO GO** ● The northeast corner isn't crowded even in peak season. Go during the summer when you can catch the fascinating laser show at Grand Coulee Dam (Memorial Day through September), and when the small-town museums are open. Also, the water is warmer on Lake Roosevelt and other liquid recreation areas. Midsummer days can get hot, but not oppressively so, and nights are cool in these northern climes. Some of the wooded areas present a nice color show in the fall, particularly along Highway 20. This corner of the state can get bitterly cold in winter; storms, although infrequent, are sometimes. Highways generally are snow-free between storms.

**WHAT TO SEE** ● Okanogan County Historical Museum in Okanogan; the semi-ghost town of Molson; Keller Heritage Center and Museum in Colville; the many lures of Riverfront Park, Cheney Cowles Memorial Museum and Crosby Room at Gonzaga University, all in Spokane; Fort Spokane north of Davenport; Grand Coulee Dam and its laser light show; coulee canyons along Banks Lake, south of the dam.

**WHAT TO DO** ● Dig for fossils with the Stonerose Interpretive Center in Republic; tour those dams—Box Canyon and Boundary in Pend Oreille County and of course Grand Coulee; drive to the top of Mount Spokane State Park; have a meal or at least a drink at Patsy Clark's Restaurant in Spokane; hike among the rocks of Steamboat Rock State Park; find a boat or houseboat and play on Lake Roosevelt.

## Useful contacts

**Colville Chamber of Commerce,** P.O. Box 267, Colville, WA 99114; (509) 684-5973.

**Coulee Dam National Recreation Area**, 1008 Crest Dr. (P.O. Box 37), Coulee Dam, WA 99116; (509) 633-9441.

**Grand Coulee Dam Area Chamber of Commerce,** P.O. Box 760, Grand Coulee, WA 99133-0760; (509) 633-3074.

**Kettle Falls Chamber of Commerce,** P.O. Box 119, Kettle Falls, WA 99141; (509) 738-2300.

**Newport Chamber of Commerce,** 108 S. Washington Ave., Newport, WA 99156; (800) 333-5812 or (509) 447-5812.

**Omak Chamber of Commerce,** Route 2, Box 5200, Omak, WA 98841; (800) 225-6625, (509) 826-1880 or (509) 826-4218.

**Spokane Convention and Visitors Bureau,** 926 W. Sprague, Suite 180, Spokane, WA 99204; (509) 747-3230 or (509) 624-1341.

## Northeastern Washington radio stations

KVLR, 106.3-FM, Twisp—old and new top 40
KOMW, 92.7-FM, Omak—country
KZZU, 93-FM, Spokane—rock
KISC, 98-FM, Spokane—70s to 90s rock and top 40
KKZX, 98.9-FM, Spokane—classic rock
K103, 103-FM, Coeur D'Alene—classic and contemporary country
KDRK, 94-FM, Spokane—country
KPBX, 91-FM, Spokane—National Public Radio
KXLY, 100 and 103.9-FM, Spokane—to 40 and news
KXLY, 920-AM, Spokane —news radio
KSBY, 1515-AM, Spokane—classic
KGA, 1510-AM, Spokane—country
KAQQ, 590-AM, Spokane—hits of the 40s through 60s
CJOR, 1490-AM, Oliver, Canada—rock and news

## Chapter nine
# *THE NORTHEAST*
## Okanogan country, Spokane and that grand dam

---

***IT'S CALLED THE INLAND EMPIRE***, a vast and slightly lumpy land of thin forests, low mountain ranges and contoured wheat fields radiating out from Spokane. In this corner, the explorer will encounter many Washington extremes, including its second largest city, its least populated areas and its largest reservoir behind its largest dam.

Overall, northeastern Washington is not a heavily visited area. Of course, busy Spokane, Grand Coulee Dam and its 150-mile-long Lake Roosevelt are important draws. Beyond these lures, visitor rewards are—to use the cliché—few and far between, but there *are* rewards. The fact that most travelers miss most of them make these discoveries at least a little bit special.

Of course, the area's three national forests—Okanogan, Colville and Kaniksu—dictate that outdoor recreation is plentiful. Folks come here to hike, backpack, fish, camp and just get away from the crowds. For those living here, tourism is a distant second to the area's primary economy. Outside of Spokane, logging earns about 65 percent of the region's income. In his unsuccessful bid for re-election, former President George Bush chose Colville as a place to give a speech about timber as a renewable resource. "Renewable" is the word. You'll find almost no old growth forests in this region.

Stitching northeastern Washington together is a little-traveled network of highways best suited to casual exploration. Beyond the freeway-wrapped Spokane, these are truly roads less traveled. It's interesting that this region's second largest city, Colville, is *forty times smaller* than its largest. Spokane, in fact, is the biggest inland city in the greater American Northwest, from the Cascade range to Minnesota. It's the commercial hub for most of eastern Washington and all of northern Idaho.

Our northeast trek will guide you along Highway 20 through the low mountains of Okanogan and Colville national forests, with curiosity side trips north toward Canada. The route next heads south to Spokane, then it travels back across the north central Washington prairie, through the wheat fields and small-town clotheslines to the Grand Coulee area.

# OKANOGAN COUNTRY: TWISP TO COLVILLE

We left some of you in the Winthrop-Twisp area (Chapter 7), after a drive on State Highway 20 through North Cascades National Park. As you head east from Twisp, you'll note that civilization—already light—shrinks even more.

The highway ahead takes you through a mix of sagebrush valleys and low woodlands of the Okanagan Mountains, which northeastern Washington shares with southeastern British Columbia. Few towns have established toe-holds in this remote and pleasantly attractive area. Highway 20 picks its leisurely way through shallow valleys, along stream beds and over low mountain passes.

*RV advisory:* There is nothing particularly challenging along this route. The up-and-down highways are mostly gently graded, with only a few significant curves.

Much of north central Washington lies within the Colville Indian Reservation. It's occupied by eleven different bands, including descendants of the Nez Percé tribe of Chief Joseph, one of the most famous and certainly the noblest of 19th century Native Americans. He is buried on the reservation, and we will visit his grave later, on a side-trip from Grand Coulee Dam.

East of Twisp, Highway 20 climbs easily from the Methow Valley into Okanogan National Forest, topping Loup Loup Pass at 4,020 feet. It spirals gently down into the **Okanogan Valley,** a sagebrush basin turned green in areas by Okanogan River irrigation. The dry, crisp climate—with warm summers and cold winters—is ideal for pasturelands and apples. Orchards line the highway as you swing north to approach the twin towns of large Okanogan County.

## Okanogan and Omak

**Okanogan: 2,300; Omak: 4,100**                    **Elevation: 837 feet**

This valley was settled by lumbermen and stockmen late in the last century, and a road sign on the highway south of Okanogan tells you that a classic cattle and sheep war was fought here in 1903.

Okanogan was the first of the valley's cities, established in 1888. It went through three name changes, from Alma to Pogue and finally in 1907, to the Native American word, Okanogan. Omak was established in 1910, just four miles north. Although Okanogan is the county seat, Omak is nearly twice as large, and it's the commercial center for the spread-out county. The Colville Reservation borders both communities, directly to the east.

During mid-August, the communities and adjacent reservation unite to present the Omak Stampede, Suicide Race and Indian encampment. The stampede is the largest rodeo in northeastern Washington and the suicide race is a wild gallop down a steep embankment and across the Okanogan

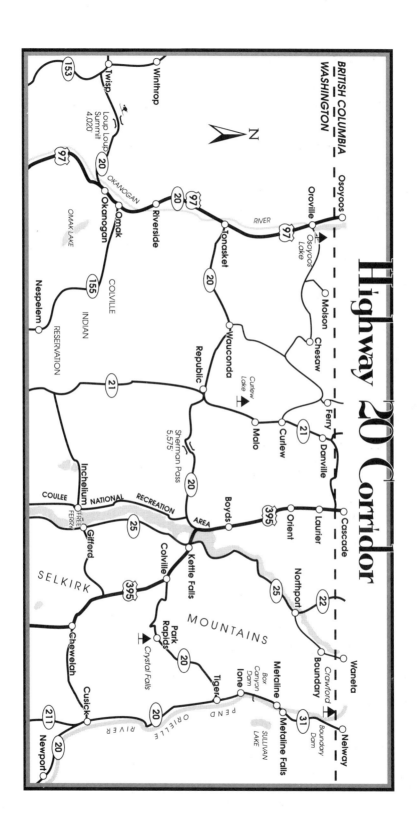

River. It has gained both fame and notoriety. The race has been featured in movies and on TV (most recently ESPN's 1992 *Amazing Games*). And it has drawn broadsides from animal rights groups, since horses often are injured in the downhill plunge.

As you approach Okanogan, you'll see a **Okanogan National Forest visitor center** on your right; open weekdays 8 to 5. Despite some old brick buildings, downtown is a rather lusterless place. It does boast a fine little museum, on the north end:

☺ **Okanogan County Historical Museum** ● *1410 Second., Okanogan; (509) 422-4272. Daily 10 to 4; donations appreciated.* ◻ Nicely done by an amateur staff, the museum traces the valley's development from its geology to the present. Pioneer artifacts are attractively displayed on a barnboard wall. Note the scale model of Fort Okanogan; this Canadian-based North West Company outpost was established nearby in 1812. Outside the museum building are storefronts of a typical turn-of-the-century town and a sod-roofed log cabin in need of a haircut.

Omak has a 1930s downtown and newer commercial development on its fringes. Here, Highway 20 intersects with U.S. 97, which will carry you north toward Canada. Before doing that, however, take State Route 155 south into the Colville Indian Reservation for another historic stop:

**St. Mary's Mission** ● *Four miles east, then 1.5 miles south of Omak; (509) 826-2097. Grounds and mission church open 24 hours; donations appreciated.* ◻ This mission complex, one of the few in the country still serving Native Americans, was started in 1896 by Father Steven Etienne DeRougè. The simple church dates from 1910. Nearby is the Paschal Sherman Indian School, the only Native American boarding school in the state.

North of Omak, highways 97/20 stay joined for 23 miles before separating at **Tonasket.** It's drab little town amidst apple orchards and grazing lands. (Curiously, despite the strings of orchards along the highway, we saw no fruit stands.)

If you follow Highway 97 north along the Okanogan River toward Canada, you'll encounter **Oroville,** still another ordinary rural community dominated by the apple culture. The town's **visitor information center** and a Washington state information center are in Oroville City Park at the north end of town. **Osoyoos Lake State Park**, just beyond Oroville, offers camping (listed below), boating, fishing and swimming. It occupies the point where the Okanogan River enters Osoyoos Reservoir. The border is a few miles farther north.

## WHERE TO DINE
### Okanogan to Oroville, in order of appearance
**Breadline Café** ● ∆∆ $

◻ *102 S. Ash St., Omak; (509) 826-5836. American; wine and beer. Breakfast and lunch Monday-Saturday, dinner Tuesday-Saturday, closed Sunday. MC/VISA, AMEX.* ◻ This cluttered cafè offers some culinary surprises for a tough little cowtown. Several whole earth entrèes are featured on a menu that ranges from thick steaks to health-conscious salads. With multigrain breads and that good salad selection, it's best as a lunch stop.

### Tequila's Restaurant ● ∆∆ $

◻ *635 Okoma Dr. (Highway 20), Omak; (509) 826-5417. Mexican; full bar service. Daily 11 a.m. to 10 p.m. MC/VISA.* ◻ Curiously cute cafè with bright Mexican trimmings tucked inside an old peaked-roof 1950s drive-in. Carved wooden booths, hanging flower baskets and bright curtains accent the interior. Entrées, while not innovative, are huge and well-prepared: the usual Mexican beef, chicken and pork dishes and *combinacions* thereof.

### ☺ *Whistlestop Restaurant* • △△ $$ ∅

☐ *1918 N. Main St., Oroville; (509) 476-2415. American; wine and beer. Daily 6 a.m. to 9 p.m. No credit cards.* ☐ The menu is basic Gringo—hearty servings of the usual steaks, chickens and chops. It's the décor that makes this place special. Both dining rooms (one non-smoking) are busy with artfully carved wooden train models. Check out the large model of the *C.P. Huntington,* a key player in the golden spike ceremony for the transcontinental railroad. Wicker drop lamps and rough beam ceilings accent the early American interior.

## WHERE TO SLEEP

### Omak to Oroville, in order of appearance

### *Cedars Inn* • △△ $$$ ∅

☐ *One Appleway (Highways 97 and 20), Okanogan, WA 98840; (509) 422-6431. Couples and singles $51 to $56. Major credit cards.* ☐ Well-kept 78-unit inn with TV, room phones; pool and coin laundry. **Restaurant** serves American fare, 7 a.m. to 10 p.m.; dinners $6 to $15; full bar service.

### *Motel Nicholas* • △△ $$

☐ *527 E. Grape St. (Route 3, Box 353), Omak, WA 98841; (509) 826-4611. Couples $42 to $48, singles $34 to $36. Major credit cards.* ☐ A 21-unit motel with TV, room phones, refrigerators, free in-room coffee.

### *Orchard Country Inn B&B* • △△ $$$ ∅

☐ *P.O. Box 634 (First at Antwine), Tonasket, WA 98855; (509) 486-1923. Couples from $50, singles from $36. Seven units with private baths; full breakfast.* ☐ Oldstyle inn fashioned from a 1920s orchard house. Rooms feature country décor, with Victorian and American antiques. Large yard and picnic area; within walking distance of downtown.

## WHERE TO CAMP

**Eastside Trailer Park** • *State Highway 155 (near U.S. 97), P.O. Box 72, Omak, WA 98841; (509) 826-1170. RV and tent sites; $5 to $10. No reservations or credit cards.* ☐ Municipal campground with showers, coin laundry. Adjacent park has swimming pool, tennis courts and playground. Fishing, boating and swimming on the Okanogan River.

**Spectacle Lake Resort** • *On Spectacle Lake at 10 McCammon Rd., Tonasket, WA 98855; (509) 223-3433. RV sites only; $13. Reservations accepted; MC/VISA.* ☐ Shoreside sites with showers, mini-mart, swimming pool, horseshoes, playground and rec field. Boat dock and rentals, lake swimming and fishing. To reach it, go north from Tonasket on Highway 97, then take the Loomis Highway eight miles to Holmes Road and follow signs.

**Osoyoos Veterans Memorial State Park** • *Osoyoos Lake, Oroville; (509) 476-3321. RV and tent sites, $10; hiker-biker $5. No reservations or credit cards.* ☐ Sites near the water, with picnic tables and barbecues, showers; no hookups. Boat launch, swimming, fishing and nature trails.

A 15-mile side trip from Oroville takes you into the Okanogan Highlands to one of the state's most interesting semi-ghost towns. To get there from downtown Oroville, turn right onto Central Avenue (by a Chevron station). The trip—through apple orchards and then sagebrush prairie—involves two left turns that aren't well marked, so stay alert. The town occupies a windy patch of prairie just a few miles south of Canada.

☺ **Molson** was established as a commercial center for nearby mines in 1900 by a family from Montreal. A homesteader complained that the town was on his land, so the founding family started New Molson a mile north. New and Old Molson later got together to build Central Molson School between them. Today's Molson is an almost ghost town, with a few contemporary homes tucked among its weathered buildings. Old Molson offers a large collection of farming and mining machinery, an assay office, bank and a few other buildings; some still contain yesterday relics. The **Molson Historical Museum** occupies the schoolhouse, with a classroom restored to the period, pioneer artifacts and post office fixtures. It's open daily 10 to 5 from Memorial Day through Labor Day.

To avoid repeating the Highway 97/20 route back to Tonasket, you can head east on Molson Summit Road. You'll wind up in tiny **Chesaw,** from where you can follow Lost Lake Road south through a patch of Okanogan National Forest. The route takes you past **Lost Lake** and **Bonaparte Lake**, both offering woodsy campgrounds. You'll pick up Highway 20 just west of Wauconda.

*RV advisory:* This route is all paved, although you will find some twists and turns and narrow areas, particularly climbing Molson Summit.

Back on Route 20, you'll pass through tiny **Wauconda** in a blink; it offers only a combination store, café and two gas pumps. Just beyond, a gradual climb will take you over **Wauconda Summit,** at 4,310 feet. You then slide gradually downhill to a jewel of a town.

# Republic

**Population: 900**          **Elevation: approximately 2,500 feet**

☺ After a succession of drab hamlets, **Republic** is a refreshing break. It's an appealing turn-of-the-century gold mining town, terraced into the flanks of a narrow canyon in the Kettle River Range. The Western style main street may not be as deliberately rustic as that of Winthrop, although it is certainly more authentic. Further, it's home to a distinctive museum, on the western edge:

☺ *Stonerose Interpretive Center* • *15 N. Kean St. (P.O. Box 987), Republic, WA 99166; (509) 775-2295. Open May through October, Tuesday-Saturday 10 to 5; fossil hunting tours 10 a.m. and 2 p.m.* ▢ This fine facility displays some of the thousands of insect, fish and plant fossils from the Eocene period that have been found nearby. In fact, they're still being found, and visitors can take part in fossil-hunting expeditions. They can even take a couple of fossils home, providing that it isn't a rarity. (It sure beats a souvenir T-shirt.) The center will even rent the proper tools. "Stonerose," incidentally, derives its name from one of the fossils found in the area, thought to be the earliest known ancestor to the rose.

An 1896 log cabin with period furnishings sits just behind the interpretive center, and the small Republic city park is next door. A huge simulated square nugget in the park tells you that gold is still being mined hereabouts. The town was founded in 1900 and this once was the state's most produc-

*The weather-weary buildings of Molson, an almost-ghost town near the Canadian border, house a lot of yesterday relics and memories.* — **Betty Woo Martin**

tive gold mining center. The Helca Mining Company removed two million ounces from this area from 1941 through 1989, and mining continues.

Beyond the museum and park, Highway 20 hits a T-intersection at Clark Avenue. The town's old fashioned business district stretches for a couple of blocks in either direction. If you've ever wanted to push through some bat-wing saloon doors, the **San Poil** affords the opportunity. Across the street is a good place for a lunch break:

### ☺ *Wild Rose Café* ● ∆∆ $$

⌑ *1899 Clark Ave.; (509) 775-2096. American; wine and beer. Monday-Friday 6 a.m. to 8 p.m., Saturday 7 to 8, Sunday 8 to 3. MC/VISA.* ⌑ Don't expect culinary surprises from the menu of chicken, chops, steaks and thawed seafood, although this café is as cute as a bug. It fits right into the theme of old Republic with Tiffany style lamps, wainscotting, café curtains and historic photos on wallpapered walls.

Three miles east of Republic, State Highway 21 leads to a Canadian border crossing at Danville. The drive up the shallow, wooded Sanpoil River Valley is pleasant, and the old hamlets of Malo and Curlew offer a couple of lures. Before reaching them, you'll reach a place to camp and play in a lake:

**Curlew Lake State Park** ● *On Curlew Lake; (509) 775-3592. RV and tent sites, $14 for water and electric, $10 without. No reservations or credit cards.* ⌑ Campsites clustered around an attractive lawn area, with barbecues, picnic tables, flush potties and showers. Swimming, boating and fishing in the lake; nature trails and lakeside picnic area.

Tiny **Malow**, a few miles beyond the lake, is home to **Back Country Burro Treks,** offering tours into the surrounding wilderness. You don't ride the burros (although your small kids can). They pack all your gear, leaving you free to stroll at their leisurely pace. Contact the folks at P.O. Box 151, Malow, WA 99150; (509) 779-4421.

**Curlew** has a few turn-of-the-century buildings, including the attractive wood-sided 1903 **Ansorge Hotel,** with a few museum exhibits. It's open weekends 1 to 5; (509) 779-4955. Also in the neighborhood is the **Antique Car & Truck Museum,** a bit weathered but interesting, with about 30 old vehicles on display. It includes some interesting vintage Fords and a 1926 "Yellow Night" sedan, one of three left in the world. The museum is free, open noon to 6 in summer and 2 to 6 in the off-season.

Pressing eastward on Highway 20 from Republic, you'll enter Colville National Forest, although it's looking a bit singed these days. A 20,000-acre fire swept through here in 1988, blackening eight miles of roadside. Graphics along the way discuss fire fighting techniques, reforestation and timber salvage. Beyond the burn, Route 20 ascends 5,575-foot **Sherman Pass.** The climb is so gradual, you'll be surprised to learn that this is the highest paved highway pass in Washington.

Half a mile below the summit, a short side-road leads to **Sherman Pass Campground** and a scenic viewpoint, where nearby peaks are identified. These are wooded, rounded peaks, lacking the drama of the Cascade crags. The campground has no facilities except pit potties and therefore no fees. The sites, suitable for tents or parked RVS, are shaded and well-spaced.

At the bottom of the pass, a sign points to **Canyon Creek Campground** (also no fee) and **Bangs Mountain Scenic Drive** on Canyon Creek Road. It's not a great drive, just a pleasantly bumpy dirt road through glacial carved Donaldson Draw. Beyond the draw, about ten miles from the highway, it loops into an overlook, with Roosevelt Lake views, far and away through the trees. (RVs and trailer rigs can make it, if carefully handled.)

Back on asphalt, Highway 20 meanders lazily down to the former Columbia River—now Lake Roosevelt—and a small shoreline community.

# Kettle Falls

**Population: 1,321**                    **Elevation: 1,237 feet**

The tree-shaded town comes in two pieces—a small business junction on the west bank, at the merger of highways 20 and 395; and a larger commercial section on the east side. Between them are Kettle Falls' two major economic elements: a large lumber mill and Kettle Falls Generating Station.

"Kettle Falls, 1,320 friendly people and one grouch," says the city limits sign. Apparently, the community has had trouble finding a grouch, so they elect one each year. Citizens cast votes for 25 cents each, with the money going to local charities.

Two highways lead from here to Canada, although neither offers much appeal. State Route 25, heading northeast to the Boundary/Waneta crossing, will take you to the upper reaches of Lake Roosevelt, if that's of any interest. What *is* interesting is that Grand Coulee Dam, which forms this reservoir, is more than 150 miles away.

☺ Because of this reach, **Coulee Dam National Recreation Area** passes through here. A Kettle Falls NRA facility, three miles west of town off Highway 395, has a campground (listed below), boat dock and launch and picnic area. From here, a serious boater can cruise to Canada, or halfway back down the state. In surface square miles, long and skinny Roosevelt is the largest lake in the state. For information on the upper Lake Roosevelt area, contact: North District Office, Coulee Dam National Recreation Area, 1230 Boise Rd., Kettle Falls, WA 99141; (509) 738-6266.

Just across the bridge, a dirt road leads to the left to **St. Paul's Mission,** marked by a reconstructed log building. A sign advises that Father Anthony Rivalli built a rough pole and brush chapel here in 1845, followed by a hand-hewn log church in 1847. It was restored in 1939.

The town of Kettle falls grew up around the turn of the century as the heart of a lumbering an orchard area. The original town is now submerged, drowned in the 1930s by the rising waters of Grand Coulee Dam. The residents and their businesses were relocated to Meyers Falls, four miles away, and the newly combined community took the Kettle Falls name.

## Where to dine and recline

### Barney's Junction Café ● ∆∆ $$
◻ *Highway 395 and 25; (509) 738-6546. American; full bar service. Daily 6 a.m. to 9 p.m. MC/VISA. Attractive Western style café with log beam ceilings, maple furniture and wagon wheel chandeliers. The predictable menu features prime rib, salmon, pork chops and ham steak.*

### Barney's Motel ● ◻ $
◻ *Highway 395 and 25, Kettle Falls, WA 99141; (509) 738-6546. Couples and singles from $25. MC/VISA.* ◻ Basic motel with clean, comfortable rooms; TV. Mini-mart and **café** adjacent (listed above).

### Grandview Inn & RV Park ● ◻ $
◻ *978 Highway 395 (at Highway 25), Kettle Falls, WA 99141; (509) 738-6733. Couples from $34, singles from $32, kitchenettes $37 to $40. Major credit cards.* ◻ Basic, well-kept 13-unit motel with TV, room phones, microwaves; coin laundry, barbecue area. (Also RV parking; see below.)

## WHERE TO CAMP

**Grandview Inn & RV Park** ● *978 N. Highway 395 (at Highway 25), Kettle Falls, WA 99141; (509) 738-6733. RV sites, $8 to $14. Major credit cards.* ◻ Grassy sites adjacent to motel; showers, horsesnoes, playground, rec hall, mini-mart, coin laundry.

**Kettle Falls Campground** ● *c/o Coulee Dam National Recreation Area, Kettle Falls, WA 99141; (509) 738-3711. RV and tent sites, $8. No reservations or credit cards.* ◻ Three miles west of Kettle Falls, off Highway 395 on Lake Roosevelt. Flush potties, barbecues and picnic areas; boat dock and launch, swimming, fishing, playground.

**Whispering Pines RV Park** ● *Near Highway 395/20 junction (P.O. Box 778), Kettle Falls, WA 99141; (509) 738-2593. RV and tent sites, $6 to $11.* ◻ Mostly shaded sites; some pull-throughs. Showers, coin laundry, horseshoes, game room and playground.

# Colville

**Population: 4,400**                                   **Elevation: 1,917 feet**

Colville, ten miles southeast of Kettle Falls on Highways 395/20, isn't a tourist center, although it offers a couple of good excuses to pause. A fine museum complex traces the area's history and the town's beautifully landscaped civic center is worth a brief detour.

Northeast Washington's second largest city is mostly a lumbering town, although predecessor Fort Colville was the heart of an important mining district after gold was discovered in 1855. The fort's roots reach back even further; it was established in 1825 as a Hudson's Bay Company trading post. A monument on Highway 20 east of town marks its existence.

As you enter Colville from the west, turn left at a museum/heritage center sign and drive three blocks uphill (past a "dead end" sign) to:

☺ **Keller Heritage Center and Museum** ● *700 N. Wynne St.; (509) 684-5968. Open daily 1 to 4 during May, then 10 to 4 June through September. Free; donations appreciated.* ☐ You'll first notice the elegant Victorian Keller mansion, so impeccably restored that you might assume it's still occupied. Tours through the beautiful interior can be arranged at the museum, which is in an adjacent cinderblock building. Among the museum's exhibits are a turn-of-the-century pharmacy, general store, mannequins in period dress and a Regina music box, which a docent will play on request. Just down the hill are several old buildings moved to the site—a blacksmith shop, log school, carriage house and sawmill. Just up the hill is a forest lookout, offering nice views of this farm-patched, mountain-rimmed valley.

☺ To reach the attractive **civic center complex,** follow the highway (Main Street) into the business district. Go a block past a flagpole traffic separator, turn left onto Birch Street, then left again on Oak. The handsome yellow brick **Stevens County Courthouse** at Oak and Astor streets is splendidly landscaped with flower gardens beneath huge evergreens and hardwoods. Across the way, the **city hall** and **library** are dressed in the same yellow brick. The **tourist information center** of the Colville Chamber of Commerce is between the city hall and Main Street on Astor; it's open weekdays except Tuesday, 10 to noon and 1 to 4.

## WHERE TO DINE

A couple of places downtown may induce you to stay for lunch:

☺ **Cookie's Café** ● ΔΔ $$ Ø

☐ *Second and Oak streets; (509) 684-8660. American; no alcohol. Daily 6 a.m. to 4 p.m. MC/VISA.* ☐ This cleverly cute place is a virtual dining museum, with early American memorabilia and collectibles lining plate rails and tucked into assorted nooks and crannies. The lunch menu lists an assortment of soups and sandwiches; the fare, while not innovative, is quite tasty. One of the two dining rooms is smoke-free.

**The Red Apple** ● Δ $

☐ *Main and First streets; (509) 684-3694. American, no alcohol. Weekdays 6 a.m. to 5 p.m. No credit cards.* ☐ Essentially a bakery-deli, it's a handy place for a quick and inexpensive lunch. Assorted soups, sandwiches and salads are offered, all under $5, plus the usual baked goods.

# PEND OREILLE COUNTRY

Folks hereabouts are quite proud of the fact that they live in one of Washington's most remote and least populated counties. It's a skinny wedge, squeezed between the boundaries of Stevens County, Idaho and British Columbia. A river runs through it, the Pend Oreille, providing water recreation. More than 50 lakes dot the surrounding Colville and Kaniksu national forests. Pend Oreille County obviously is a magnet for outdoor types.

The area has only one incorporated town. The county seat of Newport, population 1,700, is way down in the southeast corner. Another 5,300 folks are scattered through the rest of this thickly wooded county. A scenic drive toward Canada, a pair of interesting hydroelectric projects along the way, and a nice museum in Newport provide reasons for non-outdoor types to explore this final corner of northeastern Washington.

Take Highway 20 east from Colville, on a gentle climb toward Tiger Pass. About ten miles out, **Crystal Falls State Park** offers a view of cataracts on the Little Pend Oreille River, plus hiking trails and a picnic area. A few miles farther, you'll encounter a rustically woodsy resort that may tempt you to spend an extra day or few in Pend Oreille County.

### ☺ *Beaver Lodge Resort* ● ◠◠ *$$*

⌑ *2430 E. Highway 20, c/o Colville, WA 99114; (509) 684-5657. Cabins $35, RV sites $12 with water and electric, $8 for no hookups. MC/VISA.* ⌑ This cozy resort on Little Pend Oreille Lakes offers all the essentials for a mountain getaway—boating and fishing on the lakes, boat rentals, swimming, mini-mart, fuel and plenty of quietude. Rough-hewn cabins are tucked beneath sheltering evergreens. A **café** serves 7 a.m. to 9 p.m. in summer, 7 to 7 in winter. Specialties include fried chicken and Beaverburgers (which hopefully aren't).

Just beyond Beaver lodge, you'll top **Tiger Pass** and begin a gentle spiral down the other side, with a few modest switchbacks. The tiny hamlet of **Tiger** at the junction of state highways 20 and 31 consists of a general store and post office. From here, State Route 31 follows the Pend Oreille River 27 miles to Canada. Even if you aren't B.C.-bound, you may enjoy the drive along the river to a pair of hydroelectric operations and a couple of interesting villages.

**Ione,** just up from Tiger, is a sleepily cute town with historic murals on one of a weathered building. Take a left at the Ione city center sign, travel the town's three-block length and you'll encounter a small park and former rail switchyard with some old rolling stock. A Swiss-style depot (empty when we visited) and some vintage passenger cars of the Great Northern Railway are worth a gander.

Back on the highway, stop at **Box Canyon Viewpoint** for a look at a small concrete dam, wedged into a steep-walled gorge. In case you think the dam's backward, the Pend Oreille is a northward-flowing river, merging with the Columbia just over the Canadian border. Continue on to the dam, where can request an informal tour, given with a grin by whoever's handy when you show up.

### Box Canyon Hydroelectric Project ● *Pend Oreille Public Utility District; (509) 447-3137. Tours are available Monday-Tuesday 7 to 3:30 and Wednesday-Sunday 9 to 5:30 in summer and weekdays 7 to 3:30 the rest of the year.* ⌑ On the tour, you'll get a close-up view of the facility's four generators and learn more about hydroelectric power than you probably ever wanted to know. The facility also has a small visitor center with exhibits and photos of the dam's construction, and some picnic tables outside. The dam was built during the 1950s and provides virtually all of the Pend Oreille County's power.

North of the dam, the route stays with the meandering course of the Pend Oreille which, like the Columbia, is mostly lake. It's backed up by Boundary Dam, way up next to the Canadian border.

The twin towns of **Metaline** and **Metaline Falls** face one another across the reservoir a few miles above Box Canyon Dam. Metaline Falls is rather interesting, with prim green lawns and a turn-of-the-century downtown. Note particularly the red brick 1912 Metaline Falls High School. The village was founded in 1909 by gold prospectors and later became a company town for the now-closed LaFarge Corporation cement plant. Metaline Falls' **visitor center** (although there isn't much to visit) occupies a railroad car at the far end of town. It's open weekdays in summer, 9 to 5.

Cross back to Metaline and follow a paved road eleven miles to Washington's two northeastern most attractions. The route parallels Highway 20 on the west side of the river.

☺ **Boundary Hydroelectric Project** • *C/o Seattle City Light; (509) 446-3073. Open for tours Memorial Day through Labor Day, Thursday-Monday 10 to 5:30. Free; no reservations needed.* ☐ This isn't mighty large as dams go, but Boundary Dam is mighty interesting. It's a mini-Hoover Dam, wedged between sheer cliffs, and the entire powerhouse and visitor center are underground. Visitors follow a hacked-out tunnel to a balcony overlooking the huge generator room of the subterranean powerhouse. The whole thing smacks of a set for one of those James Bond 007 movies. You'll be flagellated with the usual facts during the tour: 3.5 million gallons of water per minute turn each of the six generators, which spin out 3.8 billion kilowatt hours of electricity a year, and so on. Even if you arrive during non-tour times, you can still walk down the tunnel to the glassed in overlook and study graphics of a cut-away model of the operation. Above the dam are a picnic area, boat launch and restored homesteader's cabin.

**Crawford State Park and Gardner Cave** • *c/o Metaline, WA 99153; (509) 446-4065 or (509) 456-4169. Cave tours on the hour from May 1 to mid-September, Wednesday-Sunday 9 to 5; closed the rest of the year. Free.* ☐ More than a thousand feet of limestone passageways reach into a hillside at Crawford State Park, with the usual stalactites and stalagmites. It's not an awesome cave, but worth the 1.5 mile side trip from the dam. The park has about a dozen primitive campsites, available at no charge.

The road to Boundary Dam doesn't cross the river, so you must duplicate your route back to Metaline and then south to Tiger on Highway 31. However, some local school students have provided something to help the miles pass. They've erected roadside signs showing the comparative size and distances of the sun and planets in our solar system. The sun starts in Metaline, then Mercury, Venus, the Earth and Mars are just a few hundred yards apart. They begin to space out relatively, with old Pluto about ten miles down the road near Ione.

At Tiger, pick up Highway 20 and follow the skinny Pend Oreille River reservoir south toward the Idaho border. There's little of along interest here: second-growth timber, that now-monotonous reservoir and a scattering of waterside homes. Not even planets to keep you company.

# Newport

**Population: 1,800**                    **Elevation: about 1,500 feet**

One could easily bypass the seat of Pend Oreille County by taking the State Highway 211 cutoff and hurrying south to Spokane. One shouldn't be tempted, however, because Newport is a pleasant, old fashioned town with a sturdy brick business district and a couple of antique railroad stations.

Just across the river is the Idaho community of Old Town, and therein lies a story. Newport was founded on the Idaho side by homesteaders in the 1860s. It earned its rather aquatic name from the fact that river steamers could reach this point from Spokane. Then the Great Northern Railroad was routed on the Washington bank of the Pend Oreille, and the entire town— even the post office—changed states. Idaho's Newport became Old Town.

Highway 20, which originates in the islands of the Puget Sound, finally ends at a stop sign in Newport. A left turn takes you eastward on U.S. Highway 2 into Idaho; a right delivers you to Newport's oldstyle business district. At the far end is **Centennial Plaza Park** with a gazebo, visitor information center (weekdays in summer 9 to 5), a stationary steam engine which powered a sawmill, and two railroad stations.

The Great Northern Depot, built in 1910, now houses the offices of PlumCreek Lumber Company. The 1908 Idaho Washington Northern Depot, later taken over by the Milwaukee Road, houses the area historical museum:

**Pend Oreille County Historical Museum** • *Highway 2 in Centennial Plaza Park; (509) 447-5388. Daily 10 to 4, mid-May through September. Free; donations appreciated.* ⊔ The most interesting thing here is the Nordic-style passenger depot. The museum itself is rather a disorganized clutter of pioneer relics that do little to interpret the history of the area. Some of the stuff is interesting, although the facility looks more like an antique shop than an archive.

Highway 2 heads west and then south from Newport, taking travelers rather quickly out of those low, wooded mountains and into a lumpy prairie. This tawny countryside will dominate the scene for the 50-mile drive south to Spokane and well beyond. Much of the region is in a transition zone of grasslands (now mostly wheat fields) and pine tree plains, with thicker forests on surrounding hills.

Before entering Spokane, turn east onto State Highway 206 just below the hamlet of **Colbert** for a winding visit to one of Washington's oldest and most interesting state parks.

☺ **Mount Spokane State Park** • *26107 Mount Spokane Park Dr., Mead, WA 99021; (509) 456-4169. Visitor Center near park entrance open daily in summer 8 to 5; park hours 6:30 a.m. to dusk May to mid-November (except campers) and 8 a.m. to dusk the rest of the year. Campsites $10, primitive sites with flush potties; closed in winter.* **Downhill ski area** *has five lifts (some going to the summit) and a 2,000-foot vertical drop. Night skiing; ski school, equipment rentals, restaurant and bar, lodging at Snowblaze Condominiums; (509) 238-4543.* **Cross-country skiing** *on groomed trails adjacent.* **Kirk's Lodge and Restaurant** *near the park gate has private and dorm rooms, starting at $35 a night, campground ($10 for water and electric, $5 for none) and a restaurant serving "American homestyle fare," open 9 a.m. to 6 p.m.; full bar service, MC/VISA, AMEX. The address is 24817 N. Mount Spokane State Park Dr., Mead, WA 99021; (509) 238-9114.*

All that being said in italics, Mount Spokane State Park obviously is a major recreation area. It covers more than 13,000 acres, with the 5,881-foot peak as its centerpiece. This is the oldest Washington park east of the Cascades, transferred from private ownership in 1927. Those who make the winding 12-mile drive to the summit will be rewarded with awesome views of three states (Washington, Idaho and across to Montana), British Columbia, two major mountain ranges (Selkirks in Canada, Bitterroot Rockies in

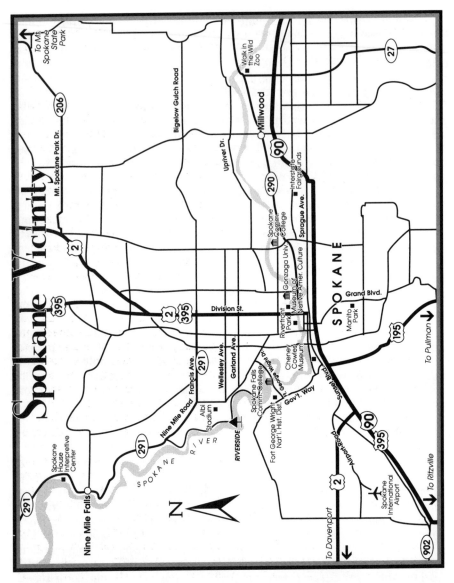

Idaho-Montana) and eight lakes. Hope for a sparking clear day, so you can count all these up.

En route to the top, you'll pass from a semi-arid prairie to a conifer zone, with turnouts, trailheads, picnic areas and a campground along the way. At the summit is a stone vista house, built by former owner Francis Cook, who carved the twisting road to the top.

**RV and general driving advisory:** Large RVs and trailer rigs can make the 4.5-mile climb from the park entrance to the campground, although the remaining 7.5 miles to the top is very steep and twisting. Weather can close the summit at any time. We ran into fog, rain and then snow and a closed gate in mid-September.

Below the state park, Highway 2 merges with U.S. 395 about six miles north of Spokane. The city's spreading suburbs reach you even before that. Expect several miles of stoplights, service stations and Safeways. The highway, incidentally, becomes Division Street.

# Spokane

**Population: 177,200**                       **Elevation: 1,898 feet**

Alive with old West spirit and yet surprisingly cultural, Spokane is the logical hub for an eastern Washington-western Idaho vacation. Within the city limits are enough parks, attractions and shopping facilities to occupy visitors for several days. Then, after hiking surrounding hills, playing in rivers, lakes or reservoirs, one can return to luxurious hotel suites or well-located inexpensive motels. Visitors can choose from a remarkable array of interesting restaurants. You can even get decent bagels in this town!

By stretching an historical point, Spokane can claim to be the oldest settlement in the Northwest. In 1810, David Thompson of England's Northwest Fur Company established a small trading post on the Little Spokane River. It was about ten miles northwest of the present city. His Spokane House thrived until 1826. The next settlers Elkanah Walker and Cushing Eels, who ran a Protestant mission in the area from 1838 until 1847.

For the next several decades, eastern Washington was ignored while settlement was focused between Portland and Seattle. In 1859, land that was considered surplus was lumped into Spokane County, which stretched from the Columbia River to the Rockies. Folks finally put down permanent roots in 1871, near a series of falls on the Spokane River. Here, they started cutting trees and planting wheat. Growth, slow at first, was spurred by the arrival of the Northern Pacific Railroad in 1881. Then, gold was discovered around the turn of the century in nearby regions of Washington and Idaho.

Spokane lost its county seat the hard way in 1880. Citizens of rival Cheney, suspecting graft in the balloting, stole the ballot and even kidnapped the election official. The fast-growing city won the seat back in 1886. Three years later, a 30-block downtown area was burned back to the dirt. Wooden buildings were replaced by sturdy bricks, which are still the city's architectural trademark. By century's end, Spokane had more than 20,000 residents, a number still not approached by any other northeastern Washington town.

Never known for modesty, Spokane earned world attention in 1974 when it became the smallest city ever to stage an international exposition. Its Expo '74 was the first such affair with an environmental theme. Appropriately, a rundown, polluted industrial area on Havermale Island near Spokane Falls was cleaned up to become the fair's center stage. It is today Riverfront Park, an ongoing cultural and entertainment center and amusement park within steps of downtown Spokane. The city also is noted for a resident who left to croon his way to stardom. Bing Crosby attended Gonzaga University and his tenure is enshrined in the Crosby Room on campus.

## Approaching Spokane

It seems appropriate to first inspect Spokane's roots—however tenuous—before exploring the city itself. As you work through that long stretch of suburbs along Highway 2/395 (Division Street), watch for a right turn onto State Highway 291. A sign will indicate Nine Mile Falls and Riverside State Park.

*The kids sliding down the wagon tongue are normal size; it's the wagon that's huge! The play area is part of Spokane's Riverfront Park.* — **Betty Woo Martin**

After the appropriate nine miles, you'll hit **Nine Mile Falls,** where a small powerhouse has obscured a small cataract on the Spokane River. You can turn left onto Charles Street for a better look at the spillway. A mile beyond the falls on Highway 291, a short side road takes you to the site of the Northwest's first settlement.

☺ *Spokane House* ● *Interpretive center open Wednesday-Sunday in summer, 10 to 6; free. Many be closed in the off-season; grounds open all year.* ◻ Graphics, photos and artifacts tell the story of Spokane House, established in 1810 by the Northwest Fur Company. American John Jacob Astor built a rival post nearby in 1812. Both operations were taken over by the Northwest Company in 1813, and ultimately by the powerful Hudson's Bay company in 1821. The visitor center sits in a weedy field rimmed by pines, between the Spokane and Little Spokane rivers. Nothing remains of the fort except painted steel posts outlining perimeters of the original complex.

Head back toward Spokane and then, just beyond Seven Mile Road, turn right onto Parkway Road. This takes you down to Aubrey L. White Parkway, which follows the high, curving banks of the river. Fancy, pine-shaded home line the stream until you enter long, skinny **Riverside State Park.** It shelters the river bank for several miles, with streamside hiking and equestrian trails. After a couple of miles of these shoreline parklands, you'll enter a park gate and campground (listed below). Pause for a look at the "Bowl and Pitcher" formation of rounded stones and columns in a narrow gorge of the river. Go back out the gate and take an immediate right at a sign indicating Spokane. After a couple of miles, turn right onto Fort George Wright Drive and follow it past Spokane Falls College.

☺ Turn right again onto Randolph Road, into the beautifully landscaped campus of **Mukogawa Fort Wright Institute Center.** Originally an army fort, it now houses the institute and Spokane Lutheran School. The **Fort Wright Museum** near the cemetery traces the fort's history from its establishment in 1899; unfortunately, hours are limited to weekend afternoons. However, visitors can drive about and admire the immaculately kept grounds and the colonial style red brick buildings with front porch columns.

Return to Fort Wright Drive and drive a short distance to a T-intersection at Government Way. Follow it along the high banks of the Spokane River, past a well-kept cemetery and into the city. At the first stop light, go left onto Sunset Boulevard; it becomes Business Route 90 and Third Avenue.

Note the multi-steepled sandstone **First Presbyterian Church** on your right, between Walnut and Cedar streets. Turn left from Third onto Lincoln Street (at the International House of Pancakes), pass under a railroad bridge and, when you cross Sprague, look for a place to park. (This isn't difficult in the city center, and most of the parking meters have been decapitated.)

### Walking Spokane

Items marked with a ☻ are listed with more detail below, under "Attractions."

Downtown Spokane is a sturdy mix of old brick and new masonry. It's a likable city, laid back yet thriving, old and yet modern. Skywalks link several department stores, allowing shopping until dropping while staying warm and dry in winter. Before you become too engrossed, stop at the **Visitors Information Center** at 926 W. Sprague (between Lincoln and Monroe); open weekdays 8:30 to 5. It's in the old beige brick **Spokane Chronicle building** which itself is an attraction. Although the newspaper is defunct, a two-story Goss printing press sits behind glass off the lobby. It's still used print flyers and periodicals, so you may see it functioning.

While looking properly metropolitan, downtown Spokane is small enough to cover on foot; folks at the visitor center can provide a handy map of highlights. Note particularly the elaborate façade of the recently restored **Davenport Hotel** at Sprague and Post, and the twin-spired **Our Lady of Lourdes Cathedral** on Sprague between Jefferson and Madison.

End your exploration with a walk through ☻ **Riverfront Park.** It borders downtown along Spokane Falls Boulevard and spreads onto Havermale Island. You can cross into the park at several points. A popular pedestrian access is at the end of Howard Street, past the glittering **Looff carousel.** Note the giant Radio Flyer red wagon and other king-sized toys in a nearby kids' play area. **Spokane Falls** on the park's west side can best be seen from Bridge Avenue, an extension of downtown Post Street. Or catch an aerial view by catching the park's sky bucket.

If you're a serious walker, you can hike northwest through the park and cross the river to the ☻ **Flour Mill,** a themed shopping complex off Mallon Avenue. From here, walk west on Mallon to Lincoln, turn left, drop down a block, turn right and go another three blocks.

☺ Before you is the wonderfully elaborate **Spokane County Courthouse.** Completed in 1895 at a cost of $340,000, it looks more like a castle than a courthouse, complete with towers and turrets. Your eyes will then be drawn to a nearby building that is as ugly as the courthouse is handsome— the excessively modern **Spokane County Public Health Center.** With puffy towers at four corners, it looks like a silo complex.

## Driving Spokane

Items marked with a ● are listed with more detail under "Attractions," below.

The city's street patterns are complicated in areas, so fetch a map before attempting to follow this driving tour. The route will seem erratic, although it's the simplest way to see Spokane's urban highlights. And when you've finished, it takes you easily onto the I-90 freeway. (A series of arrowhead-shaped signs will conduct you on a city drive, although it's even more complicated than ours.)

Take one-way Second Avenue west from downtown into **Brown's Addition**, following Cowles Museum and city drive signs. It's a grand old neighborhood of elaborate homes—many impeccably restored—along streets shaded by century old trees.

☺ You'll shortly see, on your right at the corner of Hemlock, the stunning **Patsy Clark's Restaurant,** housed in a baronial mansion (listed below, under "Where to dine"). Opposite is a thickly-shaded park with a Byzantine style gazebo.

Three blocks from Patsy Clark's, turn right onto Popular Street, and follow it a few blocks as it curves around to the right onto First Avenue. Just ahead, at 2616 First is the ● **Cheney Cowles Museum,** the finest Washington archive east of the Cascades. The next-door is the ● **Campbell House,** a beautiful English Tudor mansion, is part of the museum complex. After visiting the museum, you may want to wander through this fashionable neighborhood to admire its homes.

After you've had your fill of palace envy, head back downtown on First Avenue—being careful to survive the minor confusion of a traffic circle between Maple and Walnut. About nine blocks beyond, turn right (uphill) onto one-way Stevens Street, pass under the freeway and fork to the right onto Grand Boulevard. You'll see the imposing Gothic towers of the ● **Episcopal Cathedral of St. John the Evangelist** on your left. Catch it on the way back down, since a traffic separator prevents a left turn here.

☺ Just beyond, turn right into **Manito Park,** following one of those arrowhead city drive signs. Spread over the crest of a hill above the city, this large park offers several formal gardens and fine views. For the best of them, follow signs from a duck-busy lagoon uphill to **Duncan Gardens Conservatory** and **Rose Hill.** The conservatory, rose gardens and Japanese garden will keep plant lovers occupied for hours. Head back downhill from Manito Park and stop at the cathedral at 12th and Grandview. Then cross Grandview on 13th Avenue and follow it west to **Cliff Park.** Occupying the nub of an old volcanic core, it provides a fine 360-degree view of the Spokane sprawl. Follow Ben Garnett Way downhill from Cliff Park and blend onto Washington Street, which will take you back downtown.

Turn right onto one-way Main Street, follow it for several long blocks, then go left onto Division Street (Highway 2/395). Cross the river and take the first left onto Cataldo Avenue and follow it a block to the ● **Museum of Native American Cultures,** on your right. From here, take Ruby Street three blocks north (paralleling Division) to Sharp Avenue and turn right. ● **Gonzaga University** is just ahead on your right, marked by the imposing twin spires of St. Aloysius Church. To find the ● **Bing Crosby exhibit**, turn into the campus, park in a lot opposite the administration center and ask directions to Crosby Student Center. You can get a campus map in the administration building. Even if you aren't a fan of the crooner, you may enjoy this impressive old European style campus, with its Gothic architecture and lawns shaded by ancient trees.

You've now completed an erratic circle around and through Spokane. Return to Division Street and follow it back downtown, where signs will direct you to I-90 and Highway 2. Head west a couple of miles on the freeway, then take the Highway 2 exit toward the airport. This puts you on course for Grand Coulee Dam, about 80 miles and several hundred wheat fields away.

## ATTRACTIONS
### In order of appearance

☺ *Riverfront Park* • *507 N. Howard St., Spokane, WA 99201; (800) 336-PARK or (509) 625-6600; park hours and prices (509) 456-4FUN; special events (509) 625-6685; IMAX information, 625-6687. One-day pass $10.95 for adults, $9.95 for seniors and kids; individual prices for various rides and attractions.* ⬜ An amazing assortment of lures occupies small Havemale Island and its shorelines. They include an IMAX wide-screen theater, sky ride over Spokane Falls, genuine Looff carousel, ferris wheel, train ride, petting zoo, public market and pavilion with live entertainment. Should all this prove to be too much, you can stroll landscaped paths or sit and admire the falls, have a picnic and perhaps share it with resident squirrels and ducks.

*Flour Mill* • *621 W. Mallon; (509) 838-7970. Most shops open 10 to 6 Monday-Thursday and Saturday, 10 to 9 Friday and noon to 5 Sunday; restaurants open longer.* ⬜ Built in 1890 to grind flour from the surrounding wheat fields, this five-story brick structure is now an attractive themed shopping center. Within are 22 boutiques, specialty shops and restaurants.

☺ *Cheney Cowles Memorial Museum* and *Campbell House* • *2316 First Ave.; (509) 456-3931. Tuesday-Saturday 10 to 5, Sunday 1 to 5, closed Monday. Adults $3, seniors and kids $2, family groups $7.50; Wednesday is half-price day.* ⬜ This excellent museum presents an historic and sociological portrait of the Inland Empire. You've got your geology, your stuffed critters, your Indian reed shelter, your Lewis and Clark, your trappers, missionaries and lumbermen, and your 20th century memorabilia, from a glossy black Rauch and Lang electric automobile to early television. You learn that Bing Crosby wasn't the only famous Spokane personage. The Chad Mitchell Trio came from here, and so did John Bruce Dodd. Who? He convinced Washington legislators in 1910 to set aside a day to honor fathers, and the idea caught on nationwide.

The next-door Campbell House, built in 1898 by mining millionaire Amasa B. Campbell, is being restored to its original opulence. Rooms are opened for touring as they're completed. A Campbell house visit, as the docent points out, provides an opportunity to view turn-of-the-century Spokane through the household of one of its wealthiest families.

☺ *Episcopal Cathedral of St. John the Evangelist* • *12th and Grand; (509) 838-4277. Guided tours in summer, Monday, Thursday and Saturday noon to 3 and Sunday following the morning service; less frequently the rest of the year. Cathedral open daily 8:30 to 4:30.* ⬜ St. John's is one of the most impressive cathedrals in the Northwest, a classic example of Gothic architecture, with soaring vaulted arch ceilings. Plan a visit at noon, when the 49-bell carillon clangs out in concert.

☺ **Museum of Native American Cultures** • *200 E. Cataldo Ave.; (509) 326-4550. Tuesday-Sunday 9 to 5. Adults $3, kids $2, family groups $7.* ⬚ The teepee-style architecture is a bit much, although the museum contains fine exhibits of historic and contemporary Native American lore. The collection of traditional weapons, beadwork, basketry, pottery and contemporary paintings and other art is one of the largest in the Northwest.

☺ **Gonzaga University and the Crosby Room** • *502 E. Boone Ave. Call (509) 328-4220, extension 6133 for information concerning campus tours.* ⬚ Non-Crosby fans can explore this handsome old world campus on their own or with student-led tours. The rest of us can check out the gold records, Oscar for *Going My Way* and other memorabilia in the Crosby Room, in the red brick Crosby Student Center. Out front is a bronze of *Der Bingle*, clutching pipe and golf clubs. Bing attended classes here in the 1920s but left three months short of graduation to pursue his showbiz career. He was given an honorary doctoral degree in 1937.

## ACTIVITIES

**Art hotline** • Call (509) 747-ARTS for a rundown on cultural activities 24 hours a day. The service is sponsored by the Spokane Arts Commission.

**Bus tours** • Sightseeing is offered by Grayline, (509) 624-4116; and Karivan Tours, (509) 489-TOUR.

**Horseback rides** • Last Chance Stables offers rides from Indian Canyon Park; (509) 624-4646.

**Professional sports** • Spokane Indians play Class A baseball at the Interstate Fairgrounds; (509) 535-2922. Horse racing is held at the Playfair Race Course from May through October; (509) 534-0505. Spokane Chiefs is a Tier One (NHL minor league) hockey club; (509) 328-0450.

**Symphony** • The Spokane symphony offers a year-around season of classic and popular music at the Spokane Opera House; it also presents concerts in Riverfront Park; (509) 624-1200.

**Theatre** • Two theater groups keep the footlights busy, presenting dramas, comedies and musicals throughout the year: Spokane Civic Theater, (509) 325-2507; and Spokane Interplayers, (509) 455-PLAY.

**Winery tours** • Four wineries are within a short drive of Spokane. Pick up a map/brochure at the visitor center for the Livingstone (328-5069), Arbor Crest (927-9894), Worden (455-7835) and Latah Creek (926-0164).

## Transportation

**Airlines** • Alaska, Continental, Delta, Horizon Air, Morris Air, Northwest and United Airlines and Express offer service from Spokane International Airport; (509) 624-3218. **Amtrak** • The *Empire Builder* stops at the Amtrak station at 221 W. First St., on daily runs between Seattle and Chicago/Minneapolis. Call locally (509) 624-5144 or (509) 800 USA-RAIL. **Bus** • Greyhound provides service from the terminal at 1125 Sprague; (509) 624-5251. Spokane Transit serves the downtown area and surroundings; 328-7433.

## ANNUAL EVENTS

Call the Spokane Visitors and Convention Bureau at (509) 747-3230 for details on these and other events.

**Diamond Spur Rodeo,** March at the Spokane Coliseum; 328-6761.

**Arts and Crafts** show and sale, in March at the Convention Center.

**Lilac Festival** in mid-March, downtown and elsewhere.

**Rodeo Days,** mid-July in nearby Cheney; (509) 235-4848.

**Spokane Interstate Fair,** mid-September; one of the largest in the Northwest; (509) 535-1766.

**Nutcracker Ballet** in early December, presented by the Spokane Symphony; (509) 624-1200.

## WHERE TO DINE

### Akeny's ● ΔΔΔ $$$

☐ *In the WestCoast Ridpath Hotel at 515 W. Sprague; (509) 838-2711. Continental; full bar service. Monday-Thursday 11:30 to 10, Friday-Saturday 11:30 to 11, Sunday 10 to 2. Major credit cards.* ☐ This is where tourists and expense account businessmen go, and why not? The kitchen's not bad (if expensive) and the view from the top floor of the downtown Ridpath Hotel is impressive. Prime rib's a specialty, and the menu offers a mix of American steaks and fresh seafoods and some typical continental entrèes.

### ☺ Clinkerdagger Restaurant ● ΔΔΔ $$$

☐ *In the Flour Mill at 621 W. Mallon; (509) 328-5965. American-continental; full bar service. Lunch Monday-Saturday 11:30 to 2, dinner Monday-Thursday 5 to 9, Friday-Saturday 5 to 10, Sunday 4 to 9. MC/VISA.* ☐ Handsomely overdone English style restaurant with a decèr bordering on Arthurian: wrought iron crown chandeliers, cross timbers and lots of brick and brass. Some tables have river views. A specialty is English-style prime rib, then the menu shifts mostly to American; try the pork chops with garlic plum sauce or herb lamb.

### El Toreador ● ΔΔ $

☐ *336 W. Riverside; (509) 455-8826. Mexican; wine and beer. Monday-Thursday 11 to 9, Friday 11 to 10, Saturday 4 to 10, closed Sunday. MC/VISA.* ☐ Highly regarded cantina serving well-prepared fare; all entrèes are under $10. Go for the enchiladas Monterey with shrimp and melted jack cheese or the crab *melaque* (enchiladas with snow crab, sautèed in wine, butter, garlic and guacamole), or the hearty smashed beans and rice dishes. The interior is cozy and cheerful, with typical Latino doo-dads.

### Fort Spokane Brewery ● ΔΔ $

☐ *401 W. Spokane Falls Blvd. (at Washington); (509) 838-3809. Pub grub; wine and beer. Monday-Wednesday noon to midnight, Thursday-Saturday 11 to 1:30 a.m., Sunday noon to 10. MC/VISA.* ☐ Simply-decorated high ceiling cafè with a scattering of tables and chairs beside a working microbrewery. The fare is appropriate to the hearty brews served: beer-simmered bratwurst, flank steak, spicy chicken and French bread pizza.

### Great Harvest Bread Company ● Δ $

☐ *816 W. Sprague; (509) 624-9570. Whole earth bakery; no alcohol. Weekdays 6:30 a.m. to 3:30 p.m. No credit cards.* ☐ This is where you go for decent bagels and whole-grain baked goods. Try the creation bagel, with anything from jalapeno cheese to shrimp to cranberry sauce. It's an attractive little bakery-cafè, with raw brick, wooden floors and bentwood chairs.

### Luigi's ● ΔΔ $$

☐ *113 N. Bernard (near Main); (509) 624-5226. Italian; full bar service. Lunch Monday-Friday 11 to 4 and Saturday 11 to 3, dinner Sunday-Thursday 4 to 10 and Friday Saturday 4 to 11. MC/VISA.* ☐ Locally popular bistro serving hearty and well-prepared fare, with a focus on fresh pasta. The *gnocchi* Parmesan and *tortellini michelli* with black olives and tomatoes in cream sauce are particularly tasty. Late-hour service available, featuring simple pasta dishes and sandwiches. Typical Italiano interior; sidewalk tables.

### ☺ Milford's Fish House and Oyster Bar • △△△ $$

◻ 719 N. Monroe (at Broadway); (509) 326-7251. American, mostly seafood; full bar service. Dinner nightly. MC/VISA. ◻ The look is simple—raw brick, potted plants and a bit of brass—and the fare is excellent and inexpensive. One of Spokane's oldest restaurants, it focuses on fresh fish, from the ubiquitous salmon and fresh halibut to an extensive raw bar.

### Mustard Seed • △△ $$

◻ 245 Spokane Falls Blvd. (between Bernard and Browne); (509) 747-2689. Asian mix; wine and beer. Lunch Monday-Friday 11:15 to 2:30 and Saturday 11:30 to 4, dinner Monday-Friday 5 to 10 and Saturday-Sunday 4 to 10; lounge open to midnight Monday-Thursday and 1 a.m. Friday Saturday, with light food service. MC/VISA. ◻ The look is Japanese, with light woods and bamboo, although the menu steps considerably beyond to include several Southeast Asian cuisines. It skips from Maui chicken to assorted teriyakis to Szechuan shrimp and chicken to cod Ceylon in a curry sauce.

### Niko's Greek Café • △△ $

◻ 725 Riverside Ave. (at Post); (509) 624-7444. Greek; wine and beer. Monday-Thursday 11 to 8, Friday 11 to 9, Saturday 4 to 9. Major credit cards. ◻ Appealing and inexpensive tavern in a handsome old downtown storefront. The Greek décor is limited to a few framed pictures. However, the menu is definitely ethnic: Athenian chicken with tomato, basil and feta; shrimp Byzantine in olive oil, lemon, garlic and white wine; chicken curry over seasoned rice; and assorted lamb dishes.

### ☺ O'Doherty's Irish Grill • △△△ $$

◻ 525 W. Spokane Falls Blvd. (near Riverfront Park); (509) 747-0322. Irish-American; full bar service. Daily 11:30 to 11. MC/VISA. ◻ Lovable Irish café with dark woods, raw brick, brass and print wallpaper. The place has an infectious attitude, a properly noisy bar and an Irish-American menu. From my side of the family, try the Guinness beef and dingle pie (seasoned lamb with vegetables in a pastry); from the other side, steak, crab cakes and salmon. For a quick snack, order the pub fries with malt vinegar or Deegan fries with cheddar cheese melted over.

### ☺ Patsy Clark's • △△△△ $$$$ Ø

◻ 2208 W. Second Ave. (at Hemlock); (509) 838-8300. American-continental; full bar service. Lunch weekdays, dinner nightly. Major credit cards. ◻ Patsy was no lady, but he was a man of expensive taste. Anaconda copper billionaire Patrick F. Clark built this astonishingly elegant mansion at the turn of the century. He spared no expense for its Italian marble, 4,000-piece Tiffany stained glass window and other trimmings. It's now a restaurant or more accurately, a Victorian museum that serves food. Dining here is an event and—not surprisingly—an expensive one. The menu ranges from steamed clams and sautéed prawns to prime rib. The food has gotten mixed reviews, but at least go for a drink (served on a second story veranda) and enjoy the luxury. Several dining rooms are individually decorated, ranging from floral Italianate to dark, clubby American-Victorian.

### ☺ *Riverview Thai Restaurant* ● ∆∆∆ *$$*

⊓ *In the Flour Mill at 621 W. Mallon; (509) 325-8370. Southeast Asian; wine and beer. Monday-Friday 11:30 to 9, Saturday noon to 9, Sunday 5 to 8:30. Major credit cards.* ⊓ Exceptionally pretty restaurant with Thai carvings and filigree, drop lamps, lots of plants and white nappery accented by red brick. All this and an imposing river view. The menu is mostly Thai, with other Asian fare such as Vietnamese barbecued shrimp paste on sugar cane; scallops in white wine sauce; and spicy steamed fish, squid and clams mixed with chili paste, coconut milk and shredded cabbage.

### *Tandoor* ● ∆∆ *$$*

⊓ *Spokane Falls Boulevard at Washington; (509) 456-8131. Indian; wine and beer. Tuesday-Sunday 11 to 10, closed Monday. MC/VISA.* ⊓ Small, rather inexpensive cafè decorated mostly with a few classic East Indian paintings. You can get a full *tandoori* dinner for about $17, or chose from a variety of spicy dishes under $10. Try the chicken coconut curry or *saag* lamb with spinach and Indian spices. A lunch buffet is a good buy.

## WHERE TO SLEEP

### *Apple Tree Inn Motel* ● ◠◠ *$$* Ø

⊓ *9508 N. Division St., Spokane, WA 99218; (800) 323-5796 or (509) 466-3020. Couples $44 to $49, singles $42 to $46, kitchenettes $49 to $79, suites $52 to $79. Major credit cards.* ⊓ A 71-unit motel with TV, room phones, refrigerators and microwaves. Pool, coin laundry, barbecue area and game room.

### *Best Western Trade Winds* ● ◠◠ *$$$* Ø

⊓ *907 W. Third Ave. (at Line), Spokane, WA 99204; 528-1234 or (509) 838-2091. Couples $42 to $66, singles $36 to $56. Rates include continental breakfast. Major credit cards.* ⊓ Attractive 59-unit motel with TV movies, phones, in-room coffee. Pool, sauna, spa, weight room, pool table, laundry.

### *Best Western Thunderbird Inn* ● ◠◠◠ *$$$* Ø

⊓ *120 W. Third Ave. (McClellan), Spokane, WA 99204; (800) 57-TBIRD or (509) 747-2011. Couples $60 to $79, singles $45 to $50. Rates include continental breakfast. Major credit cards.* ⊓ A 90-unit inn with TV movies, room phones; some refrigerators. Pool, spa and exercise room. **Rancho Chico** serves Mexican fare from 11 a.m. to 10 p.m.; dinners $5 to $10; full bar.

### ☺ *Cavanaugh's Inn at the Park* ● ◠◠◠◠ *$$$$* Ø

⊓ *303 W. North River Dr. (Division and Washington streets), Spokane, WA 99201; (800) THE-INNS or (509) 326-8000. Couples $95 to $137, singles $85 to $132, suites $175 to $800. Major credit cards.* ⊓ Very stylish 402-unit hotel near Riverfront Park, with TV, room phones, refrigerators and microwaves. Opulent rooms and suites; fitness center, indoor and outdoor pools and other resort amenities. **Windows** and **Atrium Deli Cafè** serve from 6 a.m. to 11 p.m.; American and Northwest fare; dinners $10.50 to $40; full bar service. Windows restaurant overlook the Spokane River.

### *Cedar Village Motel* ● ◠◠ *$$* Ø

⊓ *5415 W. Sunset Highway (Lewis), Spokane, WA 99204; (800) 700-8558 or (509) 838-8558. Couples $34 to $45, singles $28 to $40, kitchenettes $47 to $60. Major credit cards.* ⊓ A 28-unit motel with TV movies, room phones and refrigerators. Microwaves and coffee available; barbecue area.

### Courtyard by Marriott ● ⌂⌂⌂ $$$$ Ø

◻ *401 N. Riverpoint Blvd. (Division and Trent), Spokane, WA 99202; (800) 321-2211 or (509) 456-7600. Couples and singles $69 to $75, suites $91 to $101. Major credit cards.* ◻ Attractive 149-unit hotel with TV movies, work desks, room phones; refrigerators in suites. Indoor pool, spa, coin laundry and mini-gym. **Courtyard Cafè** serves breakfast from 6:30 to 10:30; $5 to $8; cocktail lounge adjacent.

### Nendels Valu Inn ● ⌂⌂ $$ Ø

◻ *1420 W. Second Ave. (exit 280 from I-90), Spokane, WA 99204; (800) 24-MOTEL or (509) 838-2026. Couples $38 to $46, singles $35 to $39, kitchenettes $38 to $46, suites $42 to $55. Major credit cards.* ◻ A 54-unit inn with TV movies, VCRs, room phones, refrigerators and microwaves; pool. **Denny's Restaurant** is adjacent, serving American fare 24 hours; dinners $8 to $10; wine and beer.

### Sheraton Spokane ● ⌂⌂⌂ $$$$$ Ø

◻ *322 N. Spokane Falls Court (near Division), Spokane, WA 99201; (800) 848-9600 or (509) 455-9600. Couples $118 to $128, singles $108 to $118, suites $120 to $450. Major credit cards.* ◻ A luxury 370-room hotel with TV movies, phones, refrigerators on request. Facilities include a pool and sauna, gift shop, fitness room and beauty salon. Two restaurants, **Lobby Grill** and **1881 Dining Room** serve from 6:30 a.m. to 9:30 p.m.; varied menus; dinners $5 to $20; full bar service.

## Bed & breakfast inns

For a list of inns, in and about Spokane, contact the Bed & Breakfast of Spokane Association at 627 E. 25th, Spokane, WA 99203; (509) 624-3776.

### Fotheringham House ● ⌂⌂⌂ $$$ Ø

◻ *2128 W. Second Ave. (in Browne's Addition), Spokane, WA 99204; (509) 838-1891. Couples and singles $65 to $70. Three units; one private and two share baths; full breakfast. MC/VISA.* ◻ An 1891 Victorian, home of Spokane's first mayor, furnished with American and French antiques. Comfortable parlor with FAX and phone available to guests.

### Marianna Stoltz House ● ⌂⌂⌂ $$$ Ø

◻ *427 E. Indiana (near Gonzaga University), Spokane, WA 99207; (509) 483-4316. Couples $60 to $70, singles $50 to $60. Four units with in-room TV, some private and some share baths; full breakfast. Major credit cards.* ◻ Early American "foursquare" style home, with dark woods, Oriental carpeting, quilts and antique furniture. Built in 1908, the home features a wraparound veranda and landscaped yard; shaded by mature trees.

### Waverly Place ● ⌂⌂⌂ $$$

◻ *709 W. Waverly Place (opposite Corbin Park), Spokane, WA 99205; (509) 328-1856. Couples $60 to $75, singles $55 to $70. Four units; one private and three share baths; full breakfast. Major credit cards.* ◻ Handsome 1902 Victorian home in the Corbin Park District, with wood floors, original carpets and polished wood trim. American and French antiques.

## WHERE TO CAMP

**Alpine RV & Tent Park** ● *18815 E. Cataldo (P.O. Box 363), Greenacres, WA 99016; (509) 928-2700. RV and tent sites; $18 to $21. Reservations accepted; MC/VISA.* ◻ Showers, some picnic tables and barbecues; coin laundry, mini-mart, pool and playground. Ten miles east of Spokane on I-90; take exit 293.

**Peaceful Pines Campground** • *1231 W. First St., Cheney, WA 99004; (509) 235-4966. RV and tent sites; $11 to $13. Reservations accepted; no credit cards.* ☐ Small campground with showers, picnic tables, barbecues.

**Riverside State Park** • *Off Aubrey L. White Parkway; (509) 456-3964. RV and tent sites; $10. No reservations or credit cards.* ☐ Sites near the river, some shaded; barbecues and picnic tables, flush potties and coin showers; no hookups. Hiking, biking and equestrian trails, boat launch, swimming. Near Cheney Park, off Cheney Highway (Route 904).

**Park Washington/Ponderosa Hill** • *7520 S. Thomas Mallen Rd., Spokane, WA 99204; (800) 494-7275 or (509) 747-9415. RV sites $22, tent sites $14. Reservations accepted; MC/VISA.* ☐ Shaded spots, some pull-throughs; showers, TV hookups, coin laundry and playground. RV car wash and Fairways Gold Course nearby. Eight miles west on I-90; take exit 272, go a mile east on Hallet Road, then half a mile south on Thomas Mallen.

**Spokane KOA** • *3025 N. Barker Rd., Otis Orchards, WA 99027; (509) 924-4722. RV and tent sites, $16; "Kamping Kabins" $29. Reservations accepted; MC/VISA.* ☐ Showers, coin laundry, mini-mart, swimming pool, playground. About 25 miles east; take I-90 exit 293, and go south 1.5 miles on Barker Road.

**Williams Lake Resort** • *18617 W. Williams Lake Rd., Cheney, WA 99004; (800) 274-1540 or (509) 235-2391. RV and tent sites, $12 to $15. Reservations accepted; MC/VISA.* ☐ Lakeside RV resort with boat rentals, boating, waterskiing, fishing, swimming, water slide and playground. Showers, picnic tables, barbecues; mini-mart, rec hall and full service restaurant. To reach it drive south from Cheney on Cheney-Plaza Road to Williams Lake Road and turn right.

## SPOKANE TO GRAND COULEE DAM

Think of the terrain between Spokane and Grand Coulee Dam as a lumpy Kansas. Or think of that Garth Brooks song about the youth losing his innocence in the wheat fields, "a thousand miles from nowhere."

After passing through a stretch of Spokane suburbs, State Highway 2 heads west into this vast prairie of wheat fields and plowed ground. Silky, beige feminine curves reach to every horizon. Towns are infrequent little clusters of old red brick, green trees and huge silos.

**Reardon** has some of those silos, a pleasantly scruffy old brick downtown and not much else. **Davenport** is somewhat more substantial. It's the seat of Lincoln County (Washington's second biggest wheat producer), and it's home to the county's historical museum. To reach it, follow the highway into the well-kept old business district and turn left at the museum sign:

☺ **Lincoln County Historical Museum** • *Seventh and Park streets; (509) 725-7631. Open 9 to 5, daily from Memorial Day to through Labor Day, then closed Sundays in May and September; by appointment the rest of the year. Free; donations appreciated.* ☐ This nicely done archive lacks a chronology, although its exhibits are neatly arrayed, with some room groupings. One display that brought back memories (unfortunately) was an early 20th century kitchen with flour sacks made into dish towels. Farm equipment, carriages and such are housed in outside buildings.

For an interesting side trip, backtrack through Davenport's business district and turn north onto State Highway 25. Drive 24 miles to an historic fort overlooking Lake Roosevelt:

☺ **Fort Spokane** ● *C/o Coulee Dam National Recreation Area; (509) 725-2715. Visitor center open 9:30 to 5:30, daily in summer, weekends only from mid-March through June and September to mid-November, closed the rest of the year. Grounds always open. Campsites are $8; flush potties, no hookups.* ⊓ Sitting at the confluence of the Columbia and Spokane rivers, Fort Spokane was established in 1880 to keep area settlers and Indians from attacking one another. It must have worked, for no hostilities were recorded in this area. Four buildings survive today. One, a brick guardhouse, serves as the visitor center, where interpretive programs are conducted in summer by rangers of the Coulee Dam National Recreation Area. Trails lead about the weedy, neatly mowed parade ground, where signs mark the sites of other buildings. Life at the fort was boring for the enlisted people, whose only casualties resulted from bad whisky and barroom brawls. The brass had it better, according to an interpretive sign: "A few officers and ladies gathered at our noble commanding officer's to pass the evening in dancing, and all went as merry as a marriage bell."

The campground is a quarter mile below the fort. Just north on Highway 25 are a swimming area, grassy picnic site overlooking the river and a boat launch. A bridge crosses the Spokane arm of Lake Roosevelt, with fuel and convenience markets on either side.

To avoid duplicating the drive back to Davenport, backtrack briefly from Fort Spokane and turn right, following signs to **Seven Bays Marina.** You soon shed grassy prairie in favor of trees, with some nice views down at the reservoir. The marina offers a boat launch, convenience store and small café. On a hill overlooking the reservoir is an RV park with hookups for $12, water only for $8; coin showers. These are Coulee Dam NRA concessions.

From Seven Bays, the road—somewhat winding but paved—takes you back to Highway 2. At the townlet of **Wilbur,** head north on State Highway 174 to that grandaddy of dams.

## COULEE DAM NATIONAL RECREATION AREA

We've touched pieces of this spidery complex before, since Grand Coulee Dam's Lake Roosevelt backs up more than 150 miles, wriggling across northeastern Washington and stopping just short of Canada. Obviously, the massive concrete dam is the area's star attraction.

One of President Franklin D. Roosevelt's pet Depression-era projects, Grand Coulee the largest thing ever built when it was completed in 1941. It's the kingpin of the Columbia Basin Project, which irrigates hundreds of thousands of acres in the Northwest and produces more total electricity than any other hydroelectric project in the world—an incredible 40 percent of America's total output. One is tempted at this point to spout superlatives, but we'll offer a few; you can collect the rest when you get there. The dam is more than a mile long, twice the height of Niagara and it is still the world's largest producer of hydroelectric power.

Normally, such giant dams are built in narrow-walled canyons. However, prehistoric floods provided perfect conditions for damming the low-level Columbia. Eons ago, massive sheets of basaltic lava called *coulees* oozed over the plains of eastern Washington and parts of Montana, Idaho and Oregon. In some areas, the deposits are as much as a mile deep. Many have eroded

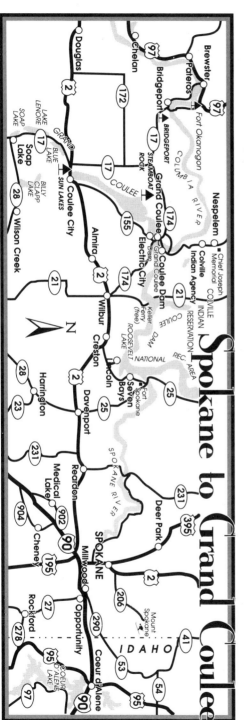

into bluffs, mesas and buttes. A primordial Columbia River picked its way through these basaltic plains, slowly carving corridors for 25 million years. Then, within the last 100,000 years, Ice Age glaciers in present-day Montana alternately dammed and then released the Columbia's headwaters. When the ice suddenly broke, great torrents of these "Missoula Floods" roared through the basaltic plains, scouring the deep and wide coulee canyons that still rim the river. Since the banks are so high, an ideal channel was available for the snakelike Roosevelt Lake.

The term "coulee" often is applied to the river canyons and narrow washes that have eroded into this great mass of basalt. If you're in a mood for redundancy, "coulee wash" or "coulee canyon" is appropriate.

## The essentials

**Tour facilities:** Approaching the area on Highway 174, you'll pass through the community of **Grand Coulee**, and then swing north to the dam itself. A right turn will take you across this giant concrete wedge. Or you can continue on to the **Visitors Arrival Center** for orientation. It's open daily 8:30 a.m. to 10 p.m. in summer and 9 to 5 the rest of the year; (509) 633-9265. The center features exhibits on the dam's construction, the geology and history of the area and two films: *The Columbia: A Fountain of Life,* and *Of Time and a River.* **For information:** Coulee Dam National Recreation Area, 1008 Crest Dr. (Box 37), Coulee Dam, WA 99116; 633-9441.

**Guided tours** are conducted frequently, taking visitors down an incline glass elevator into the dam's innards. Tour guides love to point out that Grand Coulee generates four times as much power as the Colorado River's Hoover dam. Get directions to the tour starting point at the visitor center. One also can follow signs on self-guiding tours.

**Laser shows** (see below) are presented nightly against the face of the dam's powerhouse and spillway, from Memorial Day weekend through September. Hours vary with the changing sunset. Although the laser show draws surprisingly large crowds, plenty of seating is available on long concrete risers.

**Camping:** Several national recreation area campgrounds are along the shores of Roosevelt Lake, with RV and tent sites for $8 a night; flush potties, picnic tables and barbecues; no hookups. The nearest to the dam is **Spring Canyon,** a few miles east, off Highway 174. There also are several boat-in campgrounds.

**Houseboat and other boat rentals:** Roosevelt Recreational Enterprises, c/o Colville Confederated Tribes, P.O. Box 587, Grand Coulee, WA 99133-0587; (800) 648-LAKE within Washington or (509) 633-0201.

**Boating and fishing:** The closest boat launch in the dam area is **Spring Canyon;** others are scattered throughout the NRA. Anglers fish for white sturgeon, rainbow trout, perch, bass, landlocked kokanee salmon and pike in these stretched-out waters.

**When to go:** Try to visit the dam between Memorial Day weekend and the end of September, so you can catch the laser show.

## Doing the Grand: a dam fine show?

It's easy to build a late afternoon and evening around this man-made wonder. Arrive in time to take one of the guided tours and see the films at the visitor center. *The Columbia: A Fountain of Life* is particularly intriguing, not just for its content (about the development of the Columbia hydroelectric project), but for its sound track. Woodie Guthrie was hired at $14 a song to write and sing the praises of FDR's make-work projects. A couple of the songs are sung in this 1950s film by his son Arlo, and by Judy Collins.

After the tours and films, adjourn for dinner, then return for the laser show. (The **Melody Restaurant** below the Coulee House Motel in Grand Coulee has an outdoor deck and some tables with a dam view. The closest motel to the laser show is the **Ponderosa,** just across the street from the visitor center.) The 36-minute laser program, started in 1989 to replace an earlier colored light show, plays across the mile-wide width of the dam and powerhouse. The show's best moment comes at the beginning, when a two-inch sheet of water is released over the spillway (with an appropriate roar) to form a glossy white screen for the dancing laser beams. On this giant liquid palate, colored lasers paint a history of the area and its mighty dam. It is, of course, pro hydropower and gushily patriotic. Limbaugh would love it.

## A pilgrimage to a great chief

Chief Joseph, the legendary leader of northeastern Oregon's Wallowa Band of the Nez Percè, rests in a simple grave in Nespelem, on the Colville Indian Reservation north of Grand Coulee Dam.

The 2,300-square-mile reservation, larger than Rhode Island, was established in 1872 to confine the broken remnants of several Northwest tribes. It includes descendants of survivors of the heroic Nez Percè flight toward Canada. The eleven small bands have since merged as the Colville Confederate Tribes. About 7,500 live on the gently hilly, semi-arid reservation.

As you head north toward the reservation, stop in the attractive town of **Coulee Dam** for a visit to the tribes' fine little museum. It's just to the right, off the main highway; a sign points the way.

☺ *Colville Confederated Tribes Museum* • *516 Birch Street, Coulee Dam; (509) 633-0751. Museum admission $1; entry to gift shop free.* ☐ This attractive little archive features dioramas of tribal life, a fine collection of Native American basketry and beadwork, a teepee, the usual projectile points and assorted artifacts dating back 8,000 years. The adjacent gift shop sells modern Native American jewelry, beadwork and other crafts.

Continue north from Coulee Dam about 25 miles to **Chief Joseph's grave.** It's in a small cemetery just northeast of the general store and Chevron station in tiny **Nespelem**. To reach it, go east from the highway a block to Tenth Street, then follow it north a short distance as it curves up to the right at the base of a low hill. Although modest, the slender grave marker is the largest in the cemetery, so it's easy to find. Around its base are a few modest offerings, from small change to an apple to a Snoopy key fob.

All who feel sympathy for what was done to our Native Americans will be touched by a visit to this site. Particularly so after reading this inscription at the base of the monument, written on a board with a black marker pencil by students of the Colville Reservation's Class of 2001:

*Your spirit is strong and it will always remain with your people.*

For an interesting loop trip back to the dam, head east from Nespelem over a thickly wooded mountain pass, then down the far slope to State Highway 21. Go south about ten miles to the hamlet of **Keller,** on the rarely-visited Sanpoil Arm of Lake Roosevelt. Follow it south along the reservoir bank until the road dead-ends. But don't panic. You cross Lake Roosevelt on a free ferry, which runs every fifteen minutes from 6 a.m. until 11:30 p.m. A national recreation area campground is on the south shore. From there, State Route 21 continues south to U.S. Highway 2 at **Wilbur.**

**RV advisory:** The steep climb out of Nespelem, although paved, is very twisting and switch-backed. A cautiously driven RV or trailer can make it. But, it may not be worth the effort to wrestle a large rig over the grade; this is a pleasant—but not awesome—side trip.

## WHERE TO DINE IN THE COULEE AREA

### Melody Restaurant • △△ $$

☐ *512 River Dr. (at Coulee House Motel), Coulee Dam; (509) 633-1151. American; full bar service. Daily 6 a.m. to 10 p.m. MC/VISA.* ☐ Naugahyde diner, appealing for its view of the dam and laser show. Ask for a seat on the outside deck. The menu includes pork chops, breaded veal cutlets, chicken fried steak, liver and onions and other rural fare.

### R&A Café • △ $

☐ *514 Birch St. (beside the Confederated Tribes museum), Coulee Dam; (509) 633-2233. American; wine and beer. Breakfast, lunch and dinner daily. MC/VISA.* ☐ Simple, prim little family diner with wainscotting, café curtains and chrome tables. It serves the usual chicken, chops and steaks.

### Siam Palace • △ $

☐ *213 Main St., Grand Coulee; (509) 633-2921. Southeast Asian; wine and beer. Lunch Tuesday-Friday 11 to 2, dinner Tuesday-Saturday 4 to 10 and Sunday noon to 9. MC/VISA.* ☐ Fundamental little café with wooden booths, cheered by a floral planter. The food is a peppery mix of Thai and Chinese.

**Wild Life Restaurant • ∆∆ $$**

⌂ 113 Midway (Highway 174/155), Grand Coulee; (509) 633-1160. American; full bar service. Daily 7 a.m. to 9 p.m. MC/VISA. ⌂ The "Wild Life" refers to a game animal theme in the adjoining lounge; the dining room is decorated mostly with old movie posters. The menu is decorated with American chicken, chops, steaks and fish, served in generous portions. Several budget dinner platters are listed for under $10.

## WHERE TO SLEEP

**Coulee House Motel • ⌂ $$$ Ø**

⌂ 110 Roosevelt Way., Coulee Dam, WA 99116; (509) 633-1101. Couples $44 to $58, singles $44 to $52. Major credit cards. ⌂ A 61-unit motel with views of the dam; TV movies, room phones; some balconies and refrigerators. Pool, sauna, spa and coin laundry. **Melody Restaurant** listed above.

**Ponderosa Motel • ⌂ $$$ Ø**

⌂ 10 Lincoln St., Coulee Dam, WA 99116; (509) 633-2100. Couples and singles $45 to $65. Major credit cards. ⌂ Clean, well-kept motel within walking distance of the visitor center and laser show. TV, room phones and refrigerators; pool and private spa rooms.

## WHERE TO CAMP

**Coulee Playland Resort •** Highway 155 (P.O. Box 457), Electric City, WA 99123; (509) 633-2671. RV and tent sites, $9 to $13. Reservations accepted; MC/VISA. ⌂ On the shores of Banks Lake; some shaded sites and pull-throughs. Barbecues, showers, coin laundry, mini-mart, fishing gear, game room, horseshoes. Swimming, boating and fishing on Banks Lake; tackle and boat rentals.

**Grand Coulee RV Park •** Highway 174 (a mile northwest), Grand Coulee, WA 99133; (509) 633-0750. RV sites, $8 to $12. ⌂ Small, basic park with full hookups, showers; some pull-throughs.

**Spring Canyon •** Just off State Highway 174, Grand Coulee, WA 99133; (509) 633-9441. RV and tent sites, $8. No reservations or credit cards. ⌂ Shoreside sites on Lake Roosevelt, picnic tables and barbecues, flush potties. No hookups. Boat launch, swimming and other water recreation.

**Steamboat Rock State Park •** P.O. Box 370, Electric City, WA 99123-0370; (509) 633-1304. RV and tent sites, $10 to $14. Reservations available in summer; contact the park for a form. ⌂ Ten miles south of the dam on Highway 155, with beautifully situated campground among eroded coulee cliffs; grassy campsites surrounded by poplars. Picnic tables and barbecues; water electric; flush potties and showers. Swimming area, boat launch, fishing, hiking trails.

## South of Grand Coulee Dam

To see some dramatically eroded coulee deposits, head south from the dam on State Highway 155, following an ancient stream bed of the Columbia. It's now occupied by Banks Lake, backed up behind Dry Falls Dam in Coulee City. Some of the rough cliff faces are more than 300 feet high through here, with chocolate brown alluvial aprons spreading from their bases.

Along the way, you'll find a scatter of national recreation area and commercial campsites and picnic areas. After passing through small, scruffy

**Electric City,** the route takes you into a wide, steep walled canyon, carved out by one of the Missoula Floods. This is brown basalt and gray sage country, accented by the blue of the reservoir and—in late summer and fall—yellow flashes of blooming rabbit brush.

☺ **Steamboat Rock State Park** (listed above) captures some of the canyon's most dramatic shapes, particularly its massive namesake butte. Hiking trails will tempt you to explore this rugged terrain. Approaching **Coulee City,** you pass through a swatch of irrigated desert. The town is a small collection of stores and grain elevators; there's little to entice visitors, although several RV resorts are in the area. Below Coulee City, cross small **Dry Falls Dam** and pick up State Route 17. It wanders southwesterly past a string of small lakes that were left behind when the floods washed through this area.

☺ **Dry Falls turnout** takes you to a viewpoint above a deep and rugged coulee canyon. Stand on the brink and stare down into the remains of what was once one of the world's largest waterfalls, 400 feet high and three miles wide. Through the eons, this prehistoric cataract eroded into a deep canyon with quiet pools at the bottom. You can learn more about this moonlike landscape and the primeval floods that carved it at an interpretive center, open in summers, Wednesday-Sunday 10 to 6.

The vista point is part of **Sun Lakes State Park,** with camping and extensive recreational facilities (listed below). Sun Lakes and other ponds in this area are large sumps left over from the floods. With no outlet, some—like Soap Lake—have become highly mineralized. Those not quite so salty are popular fishing holes, and they're all good for swimming (great for folks with negative buoyancy). Several RV resorts have grown up on several of these lake shores; some are listed below.

Continuing south, you shortly encounter a sign to the **Lake Lenore Cave Shelters,** just up a gravel side road. Waters from the receding ice age undermined basaltic walls, leaving natural shelters. Primitive man found temporary housing here during hunting and gathering trips. A short, steep trail leads up to the base of a cliff, and you can hike in either direction to find some of these depressions. They're not particularly interesting, although the hike is a good workout. The 500-mile-long Cariboo Cattle Trail crossed through this area to provide meat on the hoof and other food for the Cariboo and Thompson mines in British Columbia. Starting in the Pasco-Richland-Kennewick area, it was in use from 1859 until 1868.

Just below the shelters is **Soap Lake,** a name applied to a small reservoir and a smaller town. That name comes from the soapy feel of the water because of it's high mineral content. It even acquires a surface froth on windy days. Local Native Americans claimed these were healing waters, and they took their tribal name from that translation: *Skokiam.* Early settlers apparently felt the same way; mineral resorts were active here from the turn of the century until the Depression.

As you approach the lake and community, you'll see the city-operated **Skokiam Campground** on your right, a lakeside picnic area just beyond and the Soap Lake Chamber of Commerce **visitor center** between them. If you want to dip a toe or other parts into the lake's mineralized water, you can do so at the campground, picnic area or at **Notaras Lodge** (listed below). The town, wrapped around the lower end of the lake, has a few stores, cafès and motels. It was incorporated in 1919. The only significance here is that Soap Lake is the first town you've encountered south of Grand Coulee that wasn't born as a direct result of the dam's construction.

## WHERE TO CAMP AND SLEEP
### Coulee City to Soap Lake

**Coulee Lodge Resort** • *33017 Park Lake Road NE, Coulee City, WA 99115; (509) 632-5565. RV and tent sites, $13.50 with hookups, $10 without. Also cabins and mobile homes, $39 to $49 with bath, $29 without, small travel trailer (no bedding furnished) $25. Reservations accepted; MC/VISA.* ☐ RV resort on Blue Lake with some pull-throughs; showers, picnic tables and barbecues; coin laundry, mini-mart and fuel. Beach with rental boats, marina, launch, water-skiing, swimming and fishing. Eight miles south of Coulee City on State Highway 17.

**Laurent's Sun Village** • *33575 NE Park Lake Rd., Coulee City, WA 99115; (509) 632-5664. RV and tent sites; $12 to $15. Reservations accepted; MC/VISA.* ☐ Showers, coin laundry, mini-mart. Sandy swimming beach, marina and boat launch, rental fishing tackle and boats, canoes and paddleboats; fishing and water skiing. Eight miles south on State Highway 17, then just east on Park Lake Road.

**Sun Lakes State Park** • *Highway 17, seven miles south of Coulee City; (509) 632-5583. RV and tent sites, $10 and $14. No reservations or credit cards.* ☐ Well-spaced sites with water and electric hookups, flush and pit potties and showers. Restaurant and mini-mart adjacent. Visitor center, boat ramp, rentals, fishing, recreational program, nature trails; golf course and riding stables adjacent.

**Smokiam Campground** • *On Soap Lake. RV sites; $10.* ☐ Small city-operated campground over the lake, with flush potties and showers; picnic area adjacent.

☺ *The Notaras Lodge* • ◠◠ *$$*

☐ *242 Main St., Soap Lake, WA 98851; (509) 246-0462. Couples $$, singles $$; MC/VISA.* ☐ Attractively rustic log inn with Western dècor in its "upscale bunkhouse" rooms. Some are named for Western personalities with dècor to match, such as the Bonnie Guitar Suite; she's a Western singer who grew up in this area. The lodge features a mineral bath house with a spa, sauna and massage. Nearby **Don's Steakhouse** serves rural American fare, with full bar service.

This flight south from Grand Coulee has taken you into southeastern Washington, and thus into the final chapter of this trek through the Evergreen state.

## ANNUAL EVENTS
### Coulee Dam to Soap Lake

**Colorama Festival and Rodeo** in mid-May in the Coulee Dam area; (509) 633-3074.

**Greek Festival** on Memorial Day weekend, Soap Lake; 246-1821.

**Memorial Day Festival** (including the start of the laser light show), Coulee Dam; (509) 633-9441.

**Smokiam Days** on Fourth of July weekend, Soap Lake; 246-1821.

**American Indian Pow Wow,** Fourth of July weekend in Coulee Dam and on the Colville reservation; (509) 634-8212.

**Great Canoe Race** between Sun Lake and Soap Lake; (509) 246-1821.

## Chapter 10
# THE SOUTHEAST
### Wheat, Hells Canyon and higher education

*TOTO COULD BE FOOLED* by Washington's southeast corner. If Dorothy's tornado-tossed house had landed in Palouse Country instead of Oz, she and her dog would have thought they'd never left Kansas.

Over most of this land, tawny wheat fields stretch to every horizon. A wedge of northeastern Oregon's Blue Mountains reaches into the region's bottom corner, and the last few miles of Hells Canyon of the Snake River form the Washington-Idaho border near Clarkston. But for the most part, this is a land of soft, low hills.

These contours were formed as wind-blown deposits of fine-grain loam called *loess*. This fertile soil, as much as 200 feet deep, supported great stretches of grasslands, most of which have been converted to dry-farm wheat. French trappers, who apparently passed through during a wet spring, saw the rolling green prairie and described it as *pelouse* or lawn. (Most of the year, the area was and still is beige.) Anglicized to palouse, the name was applied to local Native Americans, their spotted ponies (Appaloosas) and to the region itself.

An area that's mostly wheat doesn't offer a lot of visitor lures. However, Clarkston, the historical twin to Idaho's Lewiston, is a gateway to Hells Canyon National Recreation Area in Oregon and Idaho. Campus-crawlers may want to pause at the handsome hillside expanse of Washington State University in Pullman. And one just might get teary-eyed over Walla Walla, home to famous onions.

# TRIP PLANNER

**WHEN TO GO** ● This is primarily a summer to fall region. Like northeastern Washington, the southeastern corner isn't crowded even in peak season. The high Palouse plateau doesn't get beastly hot in mid-summer and even lower areas such as Walla Walla have very few 100-plus days. The southeast is particularly nice in September and October, with crystal clear days and crisp nights. Winter storms, although infrequent, can get nasty.

**WHAT TO SEE** ● Connor Museum of Zoology and the Fine Arts Center on the University of Washington campus in Pullman; Asotin County Historical Museum in Asotin; Chief Timothy State Park west of Clarkston; oldstyle Dayton and its depot museum; Fort Walla Walla Park and Museum and Kirkham House Museum in Walla Walla; Whitman Mission National Historic Site.

**WHAT TO DO** ● Drive to the top of Steptoe Butte and hike to the top of Kamiak Butte; run the Snake River in a jetboat or go downriver on a dory or whitewater raft; drive south into Hells Canyon National Recreation Area.

## Useful contacts

**Asotin Chamber of Commerce,** P.O. Box 574, Asotin, WA 99402; (509) 243-4659.

**Clarkston Chamber of Commerce,** 502 Bridge St., Clarkston, WA 99403; (800) 933-2128 or (509) 758-7712.

**Hells Canyon National Recreation Area,** 2535 Riverside Drive (P.O. Box 699), Clarkston, WA 99403; (509) 758-0616.

**Pullman Chamber of Commerce,** 415 N. Grande Ave., Pullman, WA 99163; (800) 365-6948.

**Ritzville Chamber of Commerce,** P.O. Box 122, Ritzville, WA 99169; (800) 873-8648 or (509) 659-1936.

**Southeast Washington Tourism Association,** P.O. Box 490, Clarkston, WA 99403; (800) 879-9104 or (509) 758-1618.

**Walla Walla Area Chamber of Commerce,** P.O. Box 644 (29 E. Sumach St.), Walla Walla, WA 99362; (800) 743-9562 or (509) 525-0850.

## Southeastern Washington radio stations

The big Spokane broadcasters beam their sounds into the southeast corner (see previous chapter), and you can pick up these local stations. They dig down-home music down here.

KWIQ, 100.2-FM, Moses Lake—country
KHTR, 104-FM, Pullman-Moscow—rock
KONA, 105.9 FM, Tri-Cities—top 40; soft hits
KNSN, 97-FM, Walla Walla—country
KHSS, 101-FM, Walla Walla—soft hits
KLKY, 98-FM, Walla Walla—adult contemporary
KVJ, 1420-AM, Walla Walla—oldies
KWIQ, 1020-AM, Moses Lake—country
KCLK, 1430-AM, Pullman—country

If you've been prowling about northeastern Washington in the previous chapter, you can drop down to the southeast from Spokane or angle across from the Grand Coulee area. If you're coming from the west, a long, wide interstate will get you there in a hurry.

## I-90 TO PULLMAN

By our unofficial measure, Interstate 90 forms the northern border to southeastern Washington. It's a straight, fast and monotonous route to eastern Washington, passing through a pedestrian panorama of wheatfields and prairie. **Moses Lake,** which we routed you through in Chapter eight, is a handy stop for provisions and fuel, and the only town of size in this stretch. Another 50 miles of I-90 wheat fields will get you to **Ritzville,** a small farm community founded in 1881. It's worth hopping off to explore its lazy old brickfront business district and turn-of-the-century brown brick Northern Pacific railroad station. Also note the neat 1907 **Carnegie Library** at 302 West Main Street.

The depot, at Railroad Avenue and Washington Street, houses the area's **visitor information center** and a small museum. Here, you can pick up a tour map of the town's other oldstyle buildings. The museum is open daily in summer 9 to 6; (509) 659-1936. It's little more than a clutter of non-related objects, the most interesting of which is a glossy black 1890 horse-drawn hearse. For a better archive experience, adjourn to the **Burroughs Wheatland Museum** at 408 West Main Street; open daily in summer 1 to 7, or by appointment; (509) 659-1656. Built in 1890 as the home of a prominent physician, this two-story double-balcony structure contains period furnishings and old medical equipment.

After 23 more wheat field miles, take freeway exit 245 to tiny **Sprague,** then head southeast on State Highway 23. The monotony of wheat fields is broken briefly by small, scattered basaltic mesas and prairie grass. Then, it's back to amber waves of grain. You'll whisk through the dusty farming town of **St. John** and then, after 22 miles, hit U.S. Highway 195 at **Steptoe.**

Look to the northeast and you'll see Steptoe Butte, a 3,612-foot mount standing boldly above the rolling countryside. To reach it, continue across Highway 195, swerve to the right past a red brick school house and drive out into the countryside. (No sign instructs you to do this, but it works.) After a couple of miles, turn left at a directional sign and keep driving until the road coils into a spiral that winds to the top.

☺ **Steptoe Butte State Park** shelters a cone-shaped hunk of igneous rock that managed to keep its head above lava flows ten to thirty million years ago. The view from the top is impressive. Spread before you are hundreds of square miles of Palouse Country—a great, slightly rumpled patchwork quilt in varying shades of brown. On a clear day, you can see much of southeast Washington and even the Bitterroot Mountains of Idaho. Other than the view, the only park offering is a picnic area at the base, where you can get free dessert in the fall—apples from an abandoned orchard.

The butte was named for Lieutenant Colonel Edward J. Steptoe, whose command was routed from this area in a humiliating defeat by Native Americans in 1858. Geologists now call these old volcanic cores that rise above newer deposits "steptoes."

Return to the town of that name and motor south on U.S. 195. You'll shortly drop down out of the Palouse highlands and pass through **Colfax,** a

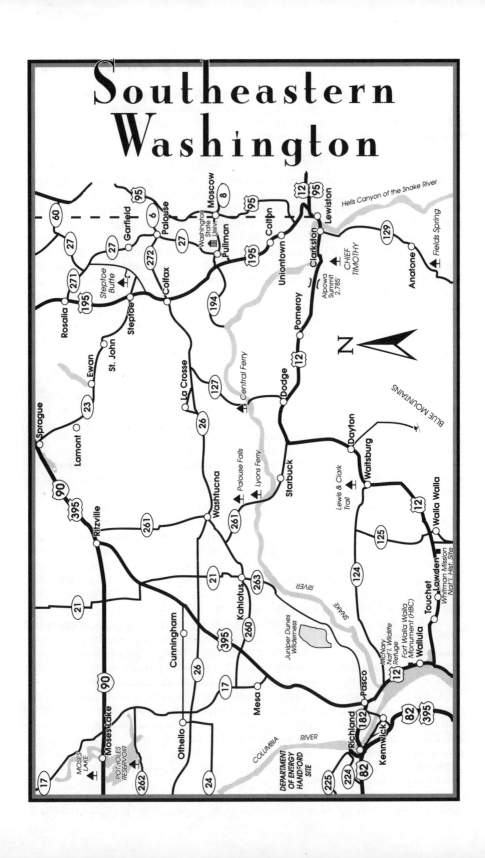

# Southeastern Washington

hardy brickfront town of 2,700. It occupies a niche in a shallow canyon.

☺ **Kamiak Butte,** about seventeen miles east of Colfax, provides a Palouse Country view as impressive as that from Steptoe Butte. To reach it, head northeast from Colfax on State Highway 272, then, after a few miles, fork to the right at the Kamiak Butte County Park sign. You'll have to hike the last mile to the forested crest of this 3,360-foot butte to achieve the promised view. Picnic facilities and a campground are on the lower reaches.

Fourteen miles south of Colfax is a community with only one serious claim to fame. If you're a Pac Ten football fan, that may be enough.

# Pullman

**Population: 23,500**                                    **Elevation: 2,500 feet**

Founded in 1876 as a farming community, Pullman got its name from an obvious source, for a rather thin reason. Chicago millionaire George Pullman sent $50 for a community Independence Day celebration, so folks named their town in his honor. Since it sat in the middle of farm country, this seemed to be a logical place for an ag school, so the Washington Agricultural College opened here in 1892 with about two dozen students. That enrollment has swelled to 17,000, and the name has been changed.

The smallest school in the Pac Ten, Washington State University fields some remarkably gifted football teams that occasionally rate among the top 25 nationally. NFL quarterback Drew Bledsoe is proof of the school's success as a gridiron factory. Of course, WSU excels scholastically as well. In fact, higher education is a major industry in this area. Just seven miles away, across the state line, is the University of Idaho in Moscow.

At first glimpse, Pullman doesn't resemble a college town, even though the student population almost equals the number of permanent residents. It *is* an attractive community, an island of scrubbed-clean brick and green trees surrounded by beige countryside. The small, neatly-tended business district isn't busy with collegiate book stores, coffee galleries and whole earth bakeries. Glance uphill, however, and you'll see the red brick campus literally towering over the town. This scene could be an Ivy League postcard.

To reach those halls of learning, cross the Palouse River, turn east onto Main Street (State Highway 270), then follow it through the downtown area and uphill. A left turn onto Stadium Way will carry you into the campus.

☺ ***Washington State University*** • *General information, (509) 335-3564; WSU Cougar sports events, (509) 335-9626; Beasley Performing Arts Coliseum events and tickets, (509) 335-1515.* ◻ Drive about half a mile into the campus, then turn left and uphill onto Wilson Road opposite **Martin Stadium.** Go about a block to the **campus visitor center** in the Safety Building, where you can pick up a parking pass (one day for $1.08) and a campus map that will direct you to these areas of interest:

**Connor Museum of Zoology** • *In the Science Building, a short walk west of the Safety Building. Weekdays 7 to 10, Saturdays 10 to 10 and Sundays 10 to 6.* ◻ The museum consists of several rooms of stuffed critters. The focus is more on identification than interpretation. You won't learn much about their habits and habitats but you can get a good close-up of an aardvark. The museum is in the building's south end. Note the elaborate greenhouse of the botany department, which occupies the structure's roof.

**Museum of Anthropology** • *Weekdays 8 to 5.* ◻ This archive, with interesting exhibits on the prehistory of the Northwest and the world in general, is located in College Hall. It's a short walk west of the Safety Building (en route to the Science Building).

**Fine Arts Center** • *Corner of Stadium Way and Wilson Road. Hours similar to those at the Science Building, although individual gallery hours may vary; (509) 335-1910.* ◻ This large facility has several galleries with rotating exhibits, mostly by contemporary artists and by students. It also houses a select gathering of works by noted American painters, and two fine collections by American photographers. In the student galleries, you'll see delightful mixed-media curiosities such as reed wall hangings and multi-hued geometric paintings. (Lovers of landscapes, Rembrandt masters and classic Grecian urns need not apply.)

**Compton Union Building** • *(509) 335-9444.* ◻ To feel the pulse of campus life, hang out at this new student center, immediately northwest of the Safety Building. It has the usual whole earth bagels and other sociologically correct fare at the student cafeteria, plus a Cougars logo shop, and even a billiards room and bowling alley.

If you'd like to see the **University of Idaho** campus, or if you're a horse person, continue east from the WSU campus on Highway 270. It becomes State Route 8 in Idaho, taking you past the **Appaloosa Museum and Heritage Center,** a small gallery devoted to the Appaloosa horse. It's open Monday-Saturday 8 to 5; (208) 882-5578. Beyond the horsey museum, the route—which becomes Pullman Road—takes you to the U of I campus. There's an information center on your right at Line Street.

## WHERE TO DINE

### ☺ *Rathhouse Pizza and Ale Shoppe* • ΔΔ $

◻ *630 E. Main St. (just below the campus turnoff); (509) 334-5400. American; wine and beer. Sunday-Wednesday 11 to 10, Thursday 11 to 11, Friday-Saturday 11 to midnight. MC/VISA.* ◻ Well of course it's a student hangout, because it offers 50-cent beer. This scholastic gathering place, draped with Cougar regalia and funky artifacts, serves interesting pizzas, plenty of beer and college spirit. If you're gastronomically prepared, try the WSU Special: pepperoni, sausage, Canadian bacon, salami, ground beef, green peppers, onions, olives and mushrooms. Hold the anchovies, please.

### *Seasons* • ΔΔΔ $$ Ø

◻ *215 SE Paradise St. (off Grand); (509) 334-1410. American regional; wine and beer. Dinner nightly 5 to 9. Major credit cards.* ◻ Elegant dining salon in a restored turn-of-the-century house with a hill top vista. The frequently changing menu features innovative treatments of chicken, fresh seafood, chops and pastas. In-house breads and desserts are fine and the wine list features Washington products. The dining room is smoke-free.

### ☺ *Swilly's Café* • ΔΔΔ $$

◻ *200 NE Kamiaken (at Olsen Street); (509) 334-3395. Eclectic menu; wine and beer. Monday-Saturday 8 a.m. to 9:30 p.m. MC/VISA, AMEX.* ◻ Built into an old train depot, this is an exceptionally attractive café with a casual-modern look: old brick, natural woods, ceiling fans and hardwood floors. Works of local artists adorn the walls. The kitchen focuses on fresh, wholesome ingredients and the results generally are tasty: Cajun chicken, lime prawns, interestingly spiced pastas and a wide selection of calzone. There's an oudoor patio near the Palouse River.

## WHERE TO SLEEP

### American Travel Inn ● △△ $$ Ø

❑ *515 S. Grand, Pullman, WA 99163; (509) 334-3500. Couples $37 to $75, singles $33 to $60, suites $55 to $78. Major credit cards.* ❑ A 34-unit motel with TV, room phones and pool. **Old European Restaurant** serves breakfast and lunch from 6 a.m. to 2 p.m.

### Hilltop Motel ● △△ $$$ Ø

❑ *928 Olsen St., Pullman, WA 99163; (509) 334-2555. Couples $49 to $57, singles from $41, suites $89 to $146. Major credit cards.* ❑ A 17-unit motel with TV movies, room phones and refrigerator; barbecue area. **Hilltop Restaurant** serves lunch weekdays, dinner nightly and Sunday brunch; dinners $10 to $15; full bar service; view tables.

### Quality Inn Paradise Creek Motor ● △△ $$$ Ø

❑ *SE 1050 Bishop Blvd., Pullman, WA 99163; (509) 332-0500. Couples and singles $52 to $57.50, suites 71.50 to $87. Major credit cards.* ❑ Very attractive 66-unit inn with TV movies, phones; some refrigerators; suites with spa tubs. Pool, sauna, spa; free evening cookies and milk. **Sea Galley** serves 11 a.m. to 10 p.m.; dinners $7 to $25; full bar service.

## WHERE TO CAMP

### Pullman RV Park ● *South and River View; (509) 334-4555, extension 227. RV and tent sites, $8.50. No credit cards.* ❑ Small facility adjacent to the city's playing field, with hookups, cable TV, flush potties and barbecues. Open April through November. To reach it, go east a mile on Paradise Road from Highway 195, then north for half a mile on Spring Street.

# PULLMAN TO CLARKSTON

Heading south toward Clarkston on Highway 195, you'll encounter two small farming towns. **Colton** will arrive suddenly as you top a rise, as if it sprouted along with the wheat. This brief scattering disappears just as quickly. A few miles beyond, **Uniontown** is more substantial, with some nice old brick shaded by the ubiquitous grain elevators. The highway dips across the border, hitting Idaho's Lewiston before Washington's Clarkston. In doing so, it tops a rise for a rather dramatic entry.

☺ **Lewiston Hill** is a 2,000-foot drop into the Snake River Valley. A new highway, very steep yet with graceful, well-engineered turns, saves motorists the anxiety of spiraling down the original corkscrew. At the crest, before beginning your ascent, fork to the right and follow a short section of the old highway to a scenic overlook at the **Vista House.** The view is imposing: Lewiston and Clarkston far below, snuggled against the curving Snake River, with the deep V-canyon rimmed by gentle palouse hills. Signs review the history of Lewiston, which began as a steamboat landing in 1861, during a gold rush in nearby Pierce. This upriver port served briefly as Idaho's territorial capital.

Near the viewpoint, the Vista House sells souvenirs and light snacks. You have choices for the drop into Lewiston/Clarkston. Turn left just below the viewpoint to return to the new highway. Or, if you want to test your nerves, driving skill and brakes, stay with the original highway, with its paper clip turns and ten-mile drop.

***RV advisory:*** If you're in a big RV or trailer rig, you'd best turn left.

At the base of the hill, fork to the right onto U.S. Highway 12, following signs toward Lewiston and Clarkston. Lewiston's chamber of commerce **visitor center** is on your right, just before you cross the Clearwater River.

Highway 12 skirts the edge of Lewiston's attractive old fashioned downtown area. To pass through it, drop a block or so south. Signs will merge you back onto Highway 12 at the west end, just before you cross the Snake River. You might like to pause at the **Luna House Museum** at Third and C streets, on the site of Lewiston's first hotel. Exhibits include material on Chief Joseph, pioneer regalia and artifacts from the original inn. It's open Thursday-Saturday 9 to 5; (208) 743-2535. You can pick up a walking tour map of historic downtown Lewiston here.

# Clarkston

**Population: 6,800**                                     **Elevation: 740 feet**

Lewiston and Clarkston obviously were named for leaders of the Corps of Discovery, which camped nearby, at the confluence of the Snake and Clearwater rivers. Both towns began as upriver shipping, cattle and farming communities. However, Lewiston got the railroad and grew much faster.

Today, it's still four times the size of its Washington counterpart, the largest community in northern Idaho. With most of the area's commercial activity across the river, Clarkston has a small business district, strung out along the highway.

As you cross the Snake River and re-enter Washington, you'll see an attractive little streamside park and picnic area, on your right. Just beyond, also on the right, is the Clarkston Chamber of Commerce **visitor information center.** It's open June through August weekdays from 9 to 7 and Saturday 9 to 5, then weekdays 9 to 5 the rest of the year.

Clarkston is the portal to the ☺ **Hells Canyon National Recreation Area,** although the facility itself is along the Oregon-Idaho border, formed by the Snake River. The most direct road access is south from Clarkston on State Route 129 (Riverside Drive.) You'll encounter the NRA's main office and visitor center after three miles, at **Swallows Nest State Park**. The route becomes Highway 3 in Oregon, leading to the isolated little community of **Joseph,** in the beautiful Wallowa Valley. It was named for the great Indian leader who led his people on an epic flight toward Canada (see Chapter 9). From Joseph, a road winds around the crest of the Wallowa Mountains and into the national recreation area. (Our *Oregon Discovery Guide* has all the details.)

The quickest route into Hells Canyon, of course, is by water. More that a dozen outfitters in Lewiston and elsewhere offer river trips. Jet boats churn noisily upstream from here, although they're not permitted to go into deep canyon areas farther upriver. Along the route, operators pause to point out petroglyphs, canyon features, wildlife and historic sites. Many reach the point where Chief Joseph led his band across the turbulent stream. Trips range from a few hours to several days.

We prefer the serenity of dories or whitewater rafts to jet boats for canyon exploration. They go downstream only, of course, so most operators put in below Hells Canyon Dam on the Oregon-Idaho border. They churn through wild rapids and float serenely in the calm stretches, moving to the call of canyon wrens. They go ashore frequently for day hikes, and they camp at river's edge. Most trips take out near Lewiston, so that's home base for some of the operators. The *ultimate* Hells Canyon trip is in dories operated by **Oars.** Based in California, this outfit runs Hells Canyon and the Snake rivers, either in dories or inflatable rafts. Fashioned after small flat-bottom, double-prowed New England fishing boats, the nimble dories offer a much livelier ride than conventional inflatable rafts. (Dory riders, with amicable scorn, refer to the rafts as "baloney boats.")

For a worthwhile side trip from Clarkston, take a six-mile detour south on Highway 129 to the village of Asotin (*Ah-SO-tin*):

☺ **Asotin County Historical Museum** ● *Third and Fillmore streets. Tuesday-Saturday 1 to 5. Free; donations appreciated; (509) 243-4659.* ⊡ Located in a former funeral parlor two blocks west of the highway, the nice little museum features a large collection of early day artifacts. Several old buildings have been moved next door to form a pioneer village. Among them are a sheepherder cabin, one-room school, blacksmith shop, and a log barn with a large carriage and branding iron collection.

## CLARKSTON AREA ACTIVITIES

Most of these outings are in Hells Canyon National Recreation Area or the adjacent Wallowa Mountains in Oregon and Seven Devils range on the Idaho side. For a more complete list of operators, including those based outside the Lewiston/Clarkston area, write: Hells Canyon National Recreation Area, 2535 Riverside Drive (Box 699), Clarkston, WA 99403; 758-0616.

**Horsepacking** ● Wally Beamer, P.O. Box 1223, Lewiston, ID 83501; (509) 743-4800.

**Jetboat outfits** ● Cougar Country Lodge, P.O. Box 448, Asotin, WA 99402; (800) 727-6190 or (509) 243-4866. Beamer's Landing Jet Boat Tours, P.O. Box 1223, Lewiston, ID 83501; (208) 743-4800. Snake River Adventures, 717 Third St., Lewiston, ID 83501; (800) 262-8874 or (208) 746-6276. Snake Dancer Excursions, 614 Lapwai Rd., Lewiston, ID 83501; (800) 234-1941 or (208) 743-0890. Myrna B. Resorts, P.O. Box 1223, Lewiston, ID 83501; (208) 743-4800.

**Whitewater outfits** ● Oars, P.O. Box 67, Angels Camp, CA 95222; (800) 346-6277 or (209) 736-4677. River Odysseys West, P.O. Box 579, Coeur d'Alene, ID 83814; (800) 451-6034 or (208)765-0841. Adventures Afloat, 717 Third St., Lewiston, ID 83501; (800) 262-8874 or (208) 746-6276.

**Watercraft rentals** ● Mac's Cycle, 700 Bridge St., Clarkston, WA 99403; (509) 758-5343.

## DINING AND RECLINING

Lewiston has most of the area's restaurants, hotels and motels and you can get a list by contacting: Lewiston Chamber of Commerce, 2207 E. Main St., Lewiston, ID 83501; (800) 473-3543 or (208) 743-3531. However, should you choose to remain on the Washington side—

### Dining

**El Sombrero** ● △△ $

⊡ *2315 Appleside Blvd.; (509) 758-2416. Mexican; wine and beer. Lunch weekdays 11 to 3, dinner nightly. MC/VISA.* ⊡ Cheerful Latino café with an extensive menu that goes well beyond the usual smashed beans and rice. Try prawns and mushrooms sautéed in butter, garlic and spices; Mexican steak topped with grilled tomatoes, onions and bell peppers; or chicken ranchero, grilled with salsa, guacamole and sour cream. All dinners under $10.

### Henry's ● △ $$

◻ *200 Bridge St. (Highway 12); (509) 758-9613. American; wine and beer. Lunch and dinner daily. MC/VISA.* ◻ Family style diner serving substantial Gringo fare, ranging from thick steaks to chops, chicken and seafood. It's a good sandwich stop for lunch.

### Phoenix Mountain Restaurant ● △△ $$

◻ *701 Sixth St.; (509) 758-9618. Chinese and American; full bar service. Weekdays 11 to midnight, Saturday 4 to midnight, Sunday noon to 10. MC/VISA.* ◻ Nicely decorated Chinese cafè with a versatile menu, featuring a range of spicy Mandarin dishes and milder Cantonese fare.

## Reclining

### Hacienda Lodge ● △△ $$ Ø

◻ *812 Bridge St. (Ninth), Clarkston, WA 99403; (800) 600-5583 or (509) 758-5583. Couples $36 to $46, singles $30 to $36. Major credit cards.* ◻ A 30-unit motel with TV, room phones, refrigerators and in-room coffee.

### Best Western RiverTree Inn ● △△△ $$$ Ø

◻ *1257 Bridge St., Clarkston, WA 99403; (800) 597-3621 or (509) 758-9551. Couples $55 to $95, singles $50 to $60, kitchenettes from $63. Major credit cards.* ◻ Attractive 47-unit motel with TV movies and room refrigerators; swimming pool, spa, sauna and barbecue area.

## WHERE TO CAMP

**Chief Timothy State Park** ● *Highway 12, eight miles west; (509) 758-9580. RV and tent sites; $14 with hookups, $10 without. No reservations or credit cards.* ◻ Well-spaced, shaded sites on the Snake River; flush potties, showers, picnic tables and barbecues. Boat dock and ramp, fishing and swimming, water skiing; nature trails; summer programs at Alpowai Interpretive Center (listed below).

**Hells Gate State Park** ● *On the Idaho side, three miles south of Lewiston on Snake River Avenue; (208) 743-2363. RV and tent sites; $9 with hookups, $7 without. No reservations or credit cards.* ◻ Well-spaced shaded sites on the Snake River; flush potties, showers, picnic tables and barbecues. Boat dock and ramp, rental boats, swimming, fishing, water skiing; visitor center with summer programs; playground; hiking, bike trails; mini-mart.

## WEST TO WALLA WALLA

The trip west from Clarkston takes you into the Lewis and Clark Valley, through steep-walled Snake River Canyon, now mostly filled by Granite Lake. The reservoir curves northwest from Highway 12 to meet its maker, Lower Granite Dam. For a scenic and twisting side trip, take State Highway 193 north from Clarkston and follow the canyon's curving course for about 25 miles.

Pressing west on U.S. 12 through the dry, rocky canyon, you'll shortly encounter a state park which marks the classic clash of cultures in the white occupation of the West.

☺ **Chief Timothy State Park** ● *Highway 12, Clarkston, WA 99403; (509) 758-9580. Alpowai Interpretive Center open in summers, daily 1 to 5; by appointment the rest of the year. Camping details above.* ◻ Chief Timothy of the Nez Percè tried to adjust to white man's ways insterad of fighting, but even that didn't work. Limited to a reservation, he and his people gave up their nomadic ways and tried farming. Then, their farmlands disappeared as white officials shrunk their reservation to establish the town of Silcot. The Alpowai Interpretive Center at this state park named in his honor, focuses on the chief and his people, and on the Lewis and Clark expedition. The Corps of Discovery made camp in the area, although the campsite, Chief Timothy's reservation and remnants of Silcot are now under water.

A steep and gently curving climb out of the Snake River Canyon carries you over 2,785-foot **Alpowa Summit** and back into wheat country. **Pomeroy** is the first of the wheat towns through here, with basic services, requisite grain elevators and some fine examples of turn-of-the-century architecture. Note the quasi-Victorian style **Garfield County Courthouse** at Eighth Street, on your right. A block beyond, turn left down Seventh Street to call on the small **Garfield County Historical Museum** at Seventh and Columbia. Displaying a loose gathering of the usual pioneer artifacts, it's open on summer weekdays 1 to 5, and Fridays only the rest of the year; (509) 243-4659. About 40 miles beyond Pomeroy is another community with fine examples of turn-of-the-century architecture.

☺ **Dayton** is a prosperous farming town of 2,500, with a carefully-tended old business district surrounded by fine homes on tree-lined streets. Downtown's historic star is the **Dayton Depot** on Main Street, where you can pick up walking tour maps of other historic buildings. The depot was built in 1881 by the Oregon Railroad and Navigation Company, and it remained in use for 93 years. It now houses a museum with railroad gear, period furnishings, historic photos and assorted pioneer artifacts. It's open Tuesday-Saturday 11 to 6; (509) 382-2026. Old Dayton also has an exceptional restaurant:

☺ *Patit Creek Restaurant* • △△△ **$$** Ø

⊡ *725 E. Dayton Ave. (northeast end); (509) 382-2625. American regional; wine and beer. Lunch Tuesday-Friday, dinner Tuesday-Saturday. MC/VISA.* ⊡ Exceptionally tasty fare emerges from the chef-owned kitchen of this ordinary looking rural café. Steaks, chops, poultry and fresh seafood emerge in creative sauces, and the in-house desserts are excellent. Start with innovative appetizers such as broiled stuffed dates wrapped in bacon, or smoked salmon cheesecake. Many of the wines come from the Walla Walla area, as do most of this small country restaurant's clientele.

# Walla Walla

**Population: 26,500**                    **Elevation: 949 feet**

Never mind the gags about this town's funny name. Walla Walla, WA, is an attractive mini-city, a refreshing sea of green in this dusty brown countryside. With a fine old brick downtown and tree-lined residential streets, it more resembles a New England community than a rural Washington farm town. The town's curious name came from the Native American band inhabiting the valley; it means "swift-running small stream" or "many waters."

This is not a tourist center, although it's obviously a nice place to live. It has a good selection of restaurants, live theater and art galleries and the cultural influence of Whitman College and Walla Walla College. The Blue Mountains, just to the southwest, draw outdoor types. **Ski Bluewood**, 52 miles from Walla Walla, offers 1,125 vertical feet of novice through expert runs, two chair lifts, and a sled and platter pull. Phone (509) 545-6651.

Agriculture is Walla Walla's economic mainstay and it isn't just wheat. This region, including Oregon's Milton-Freewater to the south, offers a mix of grain, livestock, dairy barns and row crops—particularly the Walla Walla onion, said to rival the Maui onion for its firm sweetness. It's known in the trade as the "Walla Walla Sweet." Several wineries are just to the west, in the Walla Walla Valley viticultural district. We covered this area in our wine-focused Chapter 8.

Dr. Marcus Whitman and his wife Narcissa were the first outsiders to put down roots in this area. In 1836, they built an Indian mission and the first pioneer settlement in the Pacific Northwest. They became victims of an infamous massacre, resulting not from maltreatment of the local Cayouse Indians, but from a tragic misunderstanding. A missionary and a doctor, Whitman ministered to the Indians both medically and spiritually—although they showed little interest in his religion. More settlers came to the area and, after eleven years of peaceful co-existence, a measles epidemic ravaged the Cayouse tribe. Blaming Whitman's religion for failing to protect them, they attacked the mission in 1847, killing every member of the family and several others. Whitman Mission National Historic Site is seven miles west of Walla Walla, off Highway 12 (see below).

That violent act curbed further settlement until 1856, when Lieutenant Colonel Steptoe, of Steptoe Butte fame, built an army barracks. The village of Steptoeville developed around it, later changed to Walla Walla. Thus the town name went from silly to curious. The farming community prospered, giving Washington its first bank, its first college (Whitman), and the Northwest's first railroad.

As you approach Walla Walla from Highway 12, which becomes a freeway, take the Second Avenue/city center exit to the handsome downtown area. Rising above it is the ten-story brick 1928 **Marcus Whitman Hotel** at Second and Rose. For a locator map to other historic buildings here and in the neighborhoods, stop at the **Walla Walla Chamber of Commerce.** It's at the end of Sumach Street, a block northeast of the Whitman. Just east of downtown, south off Isaac Street, is **Whitman College,** whose tree-shaded brick campus further enforces Walla Walla's New England look. It's the oldest college in the Northwest, chartered in 1859. Also near downtown is the city's historical museum:

**Kirkham House Museum** ● *214 N. Colville St. (near Main); (509) 529-4373. Open Thursdays only, 10 to 5, or by appointment.* ◻ Listed on the National Register of Historic Places, this opulent mansion was built in 1880 by a wealthy businessman. Docents steer visitors through its attractive rooms, furnished with period antiques.

After prowling downtown, follow Rose Street a couple of miles through an industrial area, past a shopping mall, and then left on Myra Road to:

☺ **Fort Walla Walla Park and Museum** ● *Myra Road near Dalles Military Road; (509) 525-7703. Museum open daily except Monday, April through October from 10 to 5, weekends only the rest of the year. Adults $2.50, kids $1.* ◻ More than a dozen buildings, original or recreated, have been moved to this site, including an 1880 railroad station, 1859 settler's cabin and several old stores. Western America's largest collection of "horse-era" farm equipment is housed in five barn-like structures, and a reconstruction of Fort Walla Walla is nearby. This extensive facility also includes picnic areas, playgrounds, a playing field, horse barn and campsites (listed below).

Retrace your route up Myra, turn right on Rose and, after a few blocks, go left (north) onto South 13th Avenue and follow signs to Highway 12. A few miles west on the highway is the Whitman monument.

☺ **Whitman Mission National Historic Site** ● *Seven miles west; (509) 522-6360. Daily 8 to 6 in summer, 8 to 4:30 in the off-season. Adults $1, seniors and kids free.* ☐ The Whitman home and mission were burned during the attack and nothing has been rebuilt. However, a visitor center contains a fine museum focusing on the ill-fated family and on the settlement of the West. Living history demonstrations of candle-making, butter churning, Indian cornhusk weaving and tule mat construction are presented on summer weekends. A self-guiding trail leads through the former settlement, where signs mark sites of the mission buildings. The Whitman Memorial Shaft and mass grave of the massacre victims is nearby.

Since Walla Walla is a hub city, this is a good place to pick a direction for further exploration. If you head south, our *Oregon Discovery Guide* can take it from here.

## WHERE TO DINE

### Homestead Restaurant ● △△△ $$ Ø

☐ *1528 Isaacs; (509) 522-0345. American; full bar service. Lunch Monday-Saturday 11:30 to 2:30, dinner Sunday-Thursday 5 to 9 and Friday-Saturday 5 to 10, Sunday hours noon to 8. Major credit cards.* ☐ As the name implies, this is an American country style restaurant, yet with some elegant Victorian touches. The versatile menu features a variety of steak, chicken, chop and seafood dishes.

### ☺ Ice-Burg Drive-In ● △△ $

☐ *616 W. Birch St. (at Ninth); (509) 529-1793. American; no alcohol. Lunch and dinner daily 11 to 10. No credit cards.* ☐ It's back to the Fifties tonight (or today) when you motor up to this nostalgic drive-in—actually, a drive-up. The menu fits the mood, with excellent hamburgers and fries and rich milkshakes. No cherry phosphates, though.

### Merchants Ltd. ● △ $ Ø

☐ *21 E. Main St.; (509) 525-0900. Deli; wine and beer. Daily Monday-Friday 6 to 6 (until 8 Wednesday), 6 tp 4:47 Saturday. MC/VISA.* ☐ This is a Manhattan delicatessen that somehow found its way to Walla Walla. It features an impressive array of salads, pastries and breads, plus breakfasts, sandwiches, house-made soups and such.

### Modern Restaurant ● △△ $

☐ *2200 Melrose (in Eastgate Plaza); (509) 525-8662. Chinese; full bar service. Sunday and Tuesday-Thursday 11 to 10, Friday-Saturday 11 to 11, closed Sunday. MC/VISA.* ☐ Attractive Asian dècor accents this family-owned place. The menu focuses on spicy Szechuan and Mandarin cuisine, with a few milder Cantonese dishes.

## WHERE TO SLEEP

### Best Western Pony Soldier Inn ● ⌂⌂⌂ $$$ Ø

☐ *325 E. Main St., Walla Walla, WA 99362; (800) 528-1234 or (509) 529-4360. Doubles $61.50 to $70.50, singles $59.50 to $66.50, kitchenette suites with spa tubs from $95; rates include continental breakfast. Major credit cards.* ☐ Attractive 85-unit inn near Whitman College; TV movies, rental

VCRs, room phones, refrigerators; some rooms with patios or balconies. Spa, sauna, workout room, coin laundry.

**City Center Motel ● ⌂ $$ Ø**

☐ *627 W. Main St. (Ninth), Walla Walla, WA 99362; (800) 453-3160 or (509) 529-2660. Couples $36.50 to $46.50, singles $32.50 to $38.50. Major credit cards.* ☐ A 17-unit motel with TV movies, room phones, refrigerators and microwaves; pool.

**Green Gables Inn ● ⌂⌂⌂ $$$$ Ø**

☐ *922 Bonsella (Estrella), Walla Walla, WA 99362; (509) 525-5501. Couples $75 to $100, singles $65 to $90. A five-unit bed & breakfast with TV and private baths; full breakfast. Major credit cards.* ☐ Beautifully restored 1909 early American home with large guest rooms with antique and modern amenities. Master suite has a fireplace and spa tub; all rooms have TV and mini-refrigerators. Large wrap-around porch overlooks extensive gardens.

**Nendels Whitman Inn ● ⌂⌂ $$$ Ø**

☐ *107 N. Second Ave., Walla Walla, WA 99362; (509) 525-2200. Couples $49 to $52, singles $45. Major credit cards.* ☐ Nicely restored Marcus Whitman Hotel, with period décor in the public areas. Rooms are modern and simply furnished, with TV movies and phones; heated pool. **Dining room**, with an attractive 19th century look, serves 6:30 a.m. to 9 p.m.; dinners $6 to $15; full bar service.

**Super 8 Motel ● ⌂⌂ $$ Ø**

☐ *2315 N. Eastgate (Wilber Avenue), Walla Walla, WA 99362; (800) 800-8000 or (509) 525-8800. Couples from $44.88, singles from $40.88. Major credit cards.* ☐ A 61-unit motel with TV, room phones; pool and spa.

## WHERE TO CAMP

**Fort Walla Walla Campground ●** *Myra Road at Dalles Military Road; (509) 527-3770. RV and tent sites; $8.50 to $11. No reservations or credit cards.* ☐ Adjacent to pioneer village and other park facilities (listed above). Water and electric hookups, some pull-throughs; flush potties and showers.

## SOUTHEASTERN WASHINGTON EVENTS

**Asotin County Fair,** late April in Asotin; (509) 243-4659.

**Seaport River Run,** late April in Clarkston; (800) 933-2128.

**Walla Walla Balloon Stampede,** early May; (800) 743-9562.

**Antique and Classic Car Show,** May in Ritzville; (800) 873-8648.

**Tumbleweed Festival,** mid-June in Pomeroy; (509) 843-1104.

**Walla Walla Air Show,** late June; (800) 743-9562.

**Northwest Heritage Air Show,** June in Clarkston; (800) 933-2128.

**Mountain Men Rendezvous and Indian Salmon Bake,** mid-July in Walla Walla; (800) 743-9562.

**Walla Walla Sweet Onion Fest,** mid-July; (800) 743-9562.

**Walla Walla County Fair and Frontier Days,** Labor Day weekend; (800) 743-9562.

**Wheatland Communities Fair,** Sept. in Ritzville; (509) 873-8648.

**Thunder on the Snake** boat races, early September in Clarkston; (800) 933-2128.

**National Lentil Festival,** September in Pullman; (800) 365-6948.

**Holiday Crafts Show,** early November in Pullman; (800) 365-6948.

## Chapter eleven
# *AFTERTHOUGHTS*
## The very best of Washington

*AFTER SPENDING* the previous chapters exploring Washington's diverse lures, we'll indulge in some harmless fun and select the very best of the Evergreen State. We've picked our favorites in each category, followed by the other nine in alphabetical order. We thus have no losers in the *Washington Discovery Guide*, only winners and runners up.

## THE TEN BEST ATTRACTIONS
1. **Mount Rainier National Park,** chapter 2, page 54
2. Deception Pass State Park, chapter 5, page 174
3. Fort Vancouver National Historic Park, chapter 2, page 38
4. Grand Coulee Dam, chapter 9, page 342
5. Mount Baker National Recreation Area, chapter 7, page 281
6. Mount St. Helens National Volcanic Monument, chapter 2, page 43
7. North Cascades National Park, chapter 7, page 271
8. Olympic National Park, chapter 6, page 212
9. Pike Place Market, Seattle, chapter 5, page 136
10. Fort Canby State Park, chapter 2, page 77

## THE TEN BEST MUSEUMS
1. **The Museum of Flight,** Seattle, chapter 4, page 144
2. Cheney Cowles Memorial Museum, Spokane, chapter 9, page 335
3. Cowlitz County Historical Museum, Kelso, chapter 2, page 86
4. Maryhill Museum of Art near Goldendale, chapter 2, page 93

## THE TEN BEST ACTIVITIES

## THE TEN BEST VISTA POINTS

## THE TEN MOST INTERESTING TOWNS OR CITIES

These are nice places to visit, and we might want to live there— In selecting our favorite cities and towns, we looked for places with a balance of scenic, historic and cultural attractions. Certainly, some of these would be fine places to live and work, although we didn't consider employment or other economic factors.

8. Spokane, chapter 9, page 331
9. Steilacoom, chapter 3, page 105
10. Vancouver, chapter 2, page 35

## THE TEN BEST RESTAURANTS

1. **Fullers,** Seattle Sheraton, chapter 4, page 153
2. The Ark, Nahcotta on the Long Beach Peninsula, chapter 2, page 78
3. Birchfield Manor, Yakima, chapter 8, page 288
4. Christina's, Eastsound, Orcas Island, chapter 5, page 191
5. The Herbfarm, Fall City, chapter 7, page 254
6. Pacific Rim, Tacoma, chapter 3, page 114
7. The Painted Table, Alexis Hotel, Seattle, chapter 4, page 154
8. Patsy Clark's, Spokane, chapter 7, page 338
9. Salish Lodge, Snoqualmie Falls, chapter 7, page 254
10. The Shoalwater, Seaview, chapter 2, page 79

## THE TEN BEST HOTELS

1. **Four Seasons Olympic Hotel**, Seattle, chapter 4, page 161
2. The Alexis, Seattle, chapter 4, page 160
3. Best Western Harbor Plaza, Oak Harbor, chapter 5, page 177
4. Cavanaugh's Inn at the Park, Spokane, chapter 9, page 339
5. Inn at the Market, Seattle, chapter 4, page 161
6. Majestic Hotel, Anacortes, chapter 5, page 183
7. Mayflower Park Hotel, Seattle, chapter 4, page 161
8. Sheraton Seattle Hotel and Towers, chapter 4, page 162
9. Stouffer Madison Hotel, Seattle, chapter 4, page 162
10. Westin Hotel, Seattle, chapter 4, page 162

## THE TEN BEST RESORTS AND INNS

1. **Sun Mountain Lodge,** Winthrop, chapter 7, page 277
2. Campbell's Resort, Chelan, chapter 8 , page 310
3. Captain Whidbey Inn, Coupeville, chapter 5, page 177
4. Darnell's Motel Resort, Chelan, chapter 8, page 309
5. The Inn at Langley, Langley, chapter 5, page 176
6. Lake Quinault Lodge, Lake Quinault, chapter 6, page 239
7. Rosario Resort and Spa, Orcas Island, chapter 5, page 192
8. Salish Lodge, Snoqualmie Falls, chapter 7, page 256
9. Skamania Lodge, Stevenson, chapter 2, page 91
10. Whistlin' Jack Lodge, Natches, chapter 2, page 59

## THE TEN BEST BED & BREAKFAST INNS

1. **Mary Kay's Whaley Mansion,** Chelan, chapter 8, page 310
2. Abendblume Pension, Leavenworth, chapter 7, page 264
3. Albatross Bed & Breakfast, Anacortes, chapter 5, page 184
4. All Seasons River Inn, Leavenworth, chapter 7, page 264
5. Ann Starrett Mansion, Port Townsend, chapter 6, page 221
6. Eagles Nest Inn, Langley, chapter 5, page 178
7. James House, Port Townsend, chapter 6, page 222
8. Run of the River Inn, Leavenworth, chapter 7, page 265
9. Sweetbriar Bed & Breakfast, Vashon Island, chapter 3, page 122
10. Turtleback Farm Inn, Eastsound, Orcas Island, chapter 5, page 192

# OTHER USEFUL BOOKS
## Travel, dining and lodging

**Bed and Breakfast Washington** by Lewis Green; New Horizons Publishers, Seattle.

**Best Places to Stay in the Pacific Northwest** by Marilyn McFarlane; Harvard Common Press, Boston, Mass.

**Exploring Puget Sound by Car** by Janice Krenmayr; The Writing Works, Seattle.

**Exploring Washington's Smaller Cities** by Clifford Burke; Quartzite Books, Seattle.

**The Ferryboat Islands: A Practical Guide to Washington State's San Juan Islands** by Gordon Keith.

**Northwest Best Places,** edited by Stephanie Irving and David Brewster; Sasquatch Books, Seattle.

**Northwest Wines and Wineries** by Chuck Hill; Ballard, Bratsberg, Inc., Seattle.

**Places to Go With Children Around Puget Sound** by Elton Welke; Chronicle Books, San Francisco.

**Seattle Best Places,** by Stephanie Irving; Sasquatch Books, Seattle.

**The Seattle Guidebook** by Archie Satterfield; The Globe Pequot Press, Old Saybrook, Conn.

## History and background

**The American Northwest: A History of Oregon and Washington** by Gordon B. Dodds; The Forum Press, Inc., Arlington Heights, Ill.

**The Pacific Northwest: Past, Present and Future** by Dale A. Lambert; Directed Media, Inc., Wenatchee, Wash.

**Washington State** by Charles P. LaWarne; University of Washington Press, Seattle.

**Washingtonians: A Biographical Portrait of the State** by David Brewster and David M. Buerge, Sasquatch Books, Seattle.

## Outdoors, boating, hiking

**Bicycling the Backroads** by Bill and Erin Woods; The Mountaineers, Seattle.

**Fifty Hikes in Mount Rainier National Park, 100 Hikes in the North Cascades** and **100 Hikes in the South Cascades and Olympics,** by Ira Spring and Harvey Manning; The Mountaineers; Seattle.

**The Hiker's Guide to Washington** by Ron Adkison; Falcon Press, Helena, Mont.

**Kayak Trips in Puget Sound and the San Juan Islands** by Randel Washburne; Pacific Search Press, Seattle.

**North Puget Sound: Afoot & Afloat** and **The San Juan Islands: Afoot and Afloat** by Marge and Ted Mueller; The Mountaineers, Seattle.

**Pacific Northwest Camping** by Tom Stienstra; Foghorn Press, San Francisco.

**Walks and Hikes Around Puget Sound** by Rich Landers and Ida Rowe Dolphin; the Mountaineers, Seattle.

**Water Trails of Washington** by Werner Furrer, a kayaking and canoeing guide; Signpost Books, Edmonds, Wash.

# *INDEX:* Primary listings indicated by *bold face italics*

# REMARKABLY USEFUL GUIDEBOOKS
## by Don and Betty Martin

Critics praise the "jaunty prose" and "beautiful editing" of Don and Betty Martin's guides. They're available at book stores, or you can order directly; see below.

### THE BEST OF ARIZONA — $12.95

This comprehensive guide covers Arizona's attractions, dining, lodgings and campgrounds. It also features maps, hikes and scenic drives. A special "Snowbird Directory" helps retirees plan their winters under the Southwestern sun. **336 pages**

### THE BEST OF THE GOLD COUNTRY — $11.95

It's a remarkably useful guide to California's Sierra foothills gold rush area and old Sacramento, covering attractions, historic sites, dining and lodging. **240 pages**

### THE BEST OF NEVADA — $12.95

It covers all of Nevada's attractions, with particular focus on the gaming centers of Las Vegas, Reno-Tahoe and fast-growing Laughlin. A special section advises readers how to "Beat the odds," with tips on gambling in the state's casinos. **352 pages**

### COMING TO ARIZONA — $12.95

This is an all-purpose relocation guide for job-seekers, retirees and winter "Snowbirds" planning a move to Arizona. Dozens of cities are featured, with data on climate, recreation, schools, job markets, housing and other essentials. **232 pages**

### INSIDE SAN FRANCISCO — $8.95

It's the ideal pocket guide to everybody's favorite city, covering attractions, activities, shopping, nightlife, restaurants and lodging; with maps and photos. **248 pages**

### NORTHERN CALIFORNIA DISCOVERY GUIDE — $12.95

This guide focuses on driving vacations for motorists and RVers, helping them discover the very best of Northern California. It features both popular attractions and little-known jewels, along with places to eat, shop, play and sleep. **356 pages**

### OREGON DISCOVERY GUIDE — $12.95

From the wilderness coast to the Cascades to urban Portland, it takes motorists and RVers over Oregon's byways and through its cities. It features popular attractions and hidden jewels, along with places to eat, shop, play and sleep. **352 pages**

### SAN FRANCISCO'S ULTIMATE DINING GUIDE — $9.95

The Martins surveyed the *real* dining experts to compile this upbeat guide to 300 restaurants: chefs, hotel concierges, cafe critics and community leaders. **224 pages**

### THE ULTIMATE WINE BOOK — $8.95

It's the complete guide for wine enthusiasts, covering the subject in three major areas: wine and health, wine appreciation and wine with food. With a foreword by noted vintner and wine aficionado Robert Mondavi. **176 pages**

### WASHINGTON DISCOVERY GUIDE — $13.95

This handy book takes motorists and RVers from one corner of the Evergreen State to the other, from the Olympic Peninsula and Seattle to the heights of the Cascades and to Eastern Washington's wine country and great rivers. **372 pages**

*If you can't find your selection in a book store, ask a clerk to order it. Or you can order directly from the publisher. Include $1.05 postage and handling for each book; California residents add proper sales tax. Please give us a complete mailing address and a phone number, in case there's a question about your order.*

**Send your order to: *Pine Cone Press***
P.O. Box 1494, Columbia, CA 95310